Generali in History

Tales from the Archive | Twentieth Century

GENERALI | Marsilio

Assicurazioni Generali's Historical Archive contains the documentation that was created and received by the Trieste Central Head Office as part of the company's day to day activities. The minutes of the governing bodies; the documents of the senior management; the technical documentation of the divisions and departments (such as life, transport and space, human resources, central secretariat, special accounts, and real estate just to name a few); the collection of financial reports and charters; or the small scale communication materials, for example, all recount how the company evolved over time, how it changed and how it interacted, not only with the social and financial fabric of the city, but also nationally and internationally.
It is from this perspective that the book narrates the contents of the Archive; based on the many referenced twentieth-century sources, collating fragments of unique events, and turning them into stories. In so doing, the company's history is enhanced. The reader is led through the various plots of history, which are nothing more than logical links or the "archival bond" connecting the various kinds of documents that are as diverse as the people who put them there; even though they are all part of one single entity: Assicurazioni Generali. Therefore, it is not a single document but rather the entirety of the documentation that conveys the individual story of each protagonist who embodies the national and international spirit of the company.
A company that has weathered two world wars; developing and restructuring itself; adapting to new geopolitical challenges; and altering its image according to the area of expertise. The rise of the new national States from the Hapsburg Empire's ashes, demanded a complete review of the territories reporting to the Trieste Head Office once the city had become part of Italy. After World War II there was a review of all businesses in Central and Eastern Europe, and in the countries under Russia's influence, all areas where Assicurazioni Generali's interests had been significant. For the company, those were years of intense diplomatic negotiations, which saw a great number of staff resume their activities in the very foreign countries where the permission to operate had been withdrawn. Great effort was devoted to a return to normality and to mend the ties in a Group that over the years had succeeded in all five continents by sheer tenacity and hard work.
Small and major stories testify to the way in which the company was able to overcome political obstacles and position itself as an international player. Thanks to its representatives, it was always first to shape, anticipate and adapt to the shifting market trends. Assicurazioni Generali was also quick to embrace technological advancement by investing in the development sector and playing a key role in fostering scientific research of global importance.
A pioneering spirit and the ability to adapt to political and financial challenges, are the Group's trademark, which is appropriately described in the opening speech of the future chairman, Enrico Randone, at the first conference on space insurance in 1979, in Trieste. Randone emphasized that: "Generali's interest in space insurance is not fleeting nor inspired by marketing concerns, but responds to clear operational goals, consistent with the philosophy of a company that wants to be of its time."

The Historical Archive of Assicurazioni Generali

Monographs by Pietro Egidi, Marco Marizza, Anna Millo,
Diego Redivo, Roberto Rosasco, Roberta Spada e Silvia Stener.

'In Brief' timelines by Roberto Rosasco and Raffaella Zanola.

Corporate representation tables by Marco Marizza
and Andrea Mazzetti.

Photographs: Duccio Zennaro for the documents from the Historical Archive of Assicurazioni Generali (except p. 13 fig. 3, p. 38 fig. 5, p. 75 fig. 4, p. 77 fig. 1, p. 81 fig. 1, p. 122 fig. 2, p. 149 fig. 1, p. 151 fig. 2, p. 161 fig. 1, p. 181 fig. 3, p. 211 fig. 1, p. 212 fig. 2, p. 223 fig. 1, p. 224 fig. 2, p. 235 fig. 1, p. 241 fig. 3, p. 247 fig. 1, p. 265 fig. 1, p. 266 fig. 2, p. 267 fig. 3, p. 297 fig. 1, p. 298 fig. 2, p. 300 fig. 3, by the Historical Archive) and Massimo Goina for the works in the Collezione Assicurazioni Generali.

List of abbreviations

ACS	Archivio Centrale dello Stato, Rome
AFG	Archivio fotografico Genagricola
ASAG	Historical Archive of Assicurazioni Generali, Trieste
ASBI	Archivio storico Banca Intesa, Milan
ASCET	Archivio storico della Comunità ebraica di Trieste
AS INA	Archivio storico INA Assitalia, Rome
ASMAE	Archivio storico del Ministero degli affari esteri, Rome
AST	Archivio di Stato di Trieste, Trieste
BCAG	Biblioteca centrale Assicurazioni Generali, Trieste
CGG	Collezione Gruppo Generali
IRSML	Archivio dell'Istituto regionale per la storia del movimento di Liberazione nel Friuli-Venezia Giulia

b., bb.	box, boxes
cart., cartt.	folder, folders
class.	classification
fasc., fascc.	file, files
vol., voll.	volume, volumes

CONTENTS

Generali in History

Tales from the Archive | Twentieth Century

ASSICURAZIONI GENERALI
VENEZIA
GL. SORMANI
ANNO
DI FONDAZIONE
1831
ASSICURAZIONI
VITA INCENDI
TRASPORTI E
FURTI
STAB. GRAFICO
M. NORSA
VENEZIA
ASSICURAZIONI GENERALI
VENEZIA
CAPITALE SOCIALE L.13.230.000
DI CUI VERSATI I 4 DECIMI
FONDI DI GARANZIA L.358 MIL.
DANNI PAGATI DALLA FONDAZIONE
1 MILIARDO E 26 MILIONI
CAPIT. ASSICURATI SULLA VITA IN VIGORE
1 MILIARDO E 85 MILIONI

GENERALI DURING THE "SHORT CENTURY"

The History of the Company from the Early Twentieth Century to the Celebration of its 150th Anniversary

ROBERTO ROSASCO

The twentieth century got off to an excellent start: the world economy was at the height of what would go down in history as the Belle Époque, a long period of peace and prosperity that benefited all countries and that only came to an end with outbreak of the Great War, while science and technology continued to stun the world with major inventions, including that of the airplane.

Generali, which celebrated its 75th anniversary in 1906, was also at the apex of a period of lively development: in the preceding twenty-five years, the overall volume of premiums in the non-life divisions had more than doubled (from 13.5 to 31 million crowns), while the income in the life division literally exploded (from 5 to 39 million). And the amount of guarantee funds progressed at an even more lively pace, increasing during the same period from 56 to 293 million. In Italy, the company confirmed its place at the very top of the life division—which was also experiencing a boom on the peninsula—and of the fire division, while the two subsidiary companies held, respectively, first place in the hail division and second in the accident division. Generali's fame was also increased by its advertising posters [*fig.* 1], which starting in 1910 began to be produced alongside the wall calendars that it had been publishing since the end of the nineteenth century.

The strengthening of assets gave further stimulus to the vast program of property investment launched by Marco Besso (appointed chairman in 1909), the goal of which was to give the company premises in the center of the most important cities and, at the same time, visual expression of the financial power it had achieved. Between 1900 and 1910, a number of prestigious buildings were therefore constructed that enrich the company's assets still today, like the ones in Piazza Venezia in Rome and Piazza Solferino in Turin. Abroad, between the end of the nineteenth century and the beginning of the twentieth, the company embarked on building projects in such cities as Belgrade, Budapest, Constantinople, Cairo, Lemberg [Lviv], Ljubljana, Paris, Prague, Tunis, Vienna, and Zagreb.

The Group's international expansion continued in the early twentieth century, not only with property investments but also with the constitution or acquisition of companies in various countries. In particular, in Paris in 1905 it founded La Concorde, which was specialized in accident and theft insurance, and is today part of Generali France.

The Climate Turns Stormy

But the times were changing. In 1907, a major economic depression spread from the United States (where a failed attempt to corner the market spread panic among depositors, who rushed to withdraw their savings from the banks) throughout all of Europe, followed shortly after by the violent reignition of the Balkan question. The precarious organization of the area defined by the Congress of Berlin in 1878 entered into crisis in 1908 when the Ottoman Empire was weakened by the rebellion of the "Young Turks" against the sultan and Austria seized the opportunity to annex Bosnia and Herzegovina, which had been until that point governed by a provisional administration. This move embittered relations between the Hapsburg Empire and Serbia and Russia, which further deteriorated after the two Balkan Wars in 1912 and 1913. The anti-Turkish coalition, comprising Serbia, Montenegro, Greece, and Bulgaria, defeated the Ottoman Empire, which lost the greater part of its European possessions, but the peace treaties established—at the instigation of Austria and its allies—the independence of Albania, taking the sea access from Serbia that it had only just acquired and nourishing its nationalist drive and ambition to unite all of the Slavic populations under its own crown.

As we read in the company reports, Generali was heavily affected by the block of insurance activity in the countries engaged in conflict, the fall of government debt securities and fixed-interest securities, and the uncertainty that was spreading in international relations.

1.
Venice was the most frequent subject of the company's early posters, like this one designed by Gian Luciano Sormani
[CGG, poster, 1910]

2.
The first policy of the Istituto Nazionale delle Assicurazioni, issued on January 10, 1913 and underwritten by the minister Francesco Saverio Nitti [Archivio storico INA, *Fondo del Cinquantenario*, Series 9, Subseries I, file 3]

ISTITVTO NAZIONALE
DELLE
ASSICVRAZIONI
TARIFFA
N° 3
LEGGE IV APRILE MCMXII · N: CCCV
LE POLIZZE DI ASSICVRAZIONE EMESSE DALL' ISTITVTO NAZIONALE SONO GARANTITE DALLO STATO
ARTICOLO I DELLA LEGGE
I CAPITALI E LE RENDITE ASSICVRATE PRESSO L' ISTITVTO NAZIONALE SONO INSEQVESTRABILI
ARTICOLO XIX DELLA LEGGE
POLIZZA
AD EFFETTI MULTIPLI
N° 1
POLIZZA DI ASSICVRAZIONE
EMESSA IN BASE ALLE DICHIARAZIONI CONTENVTE NELLA RELATIVA PROPOSTA IN DATA 5 Gennaio 1913 PER LA SOMMA DI LIRE ITAL. Ventimila
E PER VNA RENDITA ANNVA VITALIZIA DI LIRE ITAL. Millenovantotto
SVLLA VITA di S. E. Francesco Saverio Nitti
L'ISTITVTO NAZIONALE ASSVME L'OBBLIGO DI PAGARE LA SOMMA DI L. 20.000
E LA RENDITA DI L. 1098 ALLE CONDIZIONI TVTTE SPECIALI E GENERALI INDICATE NELLA PRESENTE POLIZZA.
ROMA, LI 10 Gennaio 1913
IL DIRETTORE GENERALE
IL PRESIDENTE DEL CONSIGLIO D'AMMINISTRAZIONE

In this tempestuous atmosphere, which anticipated the outbreak of the Great War, a new obstacle to Generali's development came in the form of the introduction in Italy of a life insurance monopoly, driven by the desire to limit the domination enjoyed by foreign companies (which included those based in Trieste) over the industry. While the response of many was to abandon the market and hand over their portfolios to the new Istituto Nazionale delle Assicurazioni (INA) [*fig.* 2], Generali decided to continue its activity within the terms permitted by law.
In spite of the difficulties that had been weighing on its activity in recent years, the company's financial statements continued to produce satisfying results, to the point that even the 1914 annual report, right in the midst of World War I, closed with profits of more than seven million crowns and payment of a dividend of 500 gold francs. At the same time, work was completed in Venice on the renovation of the historical Palazzo delle Procuratie Vecchie—attributed to Jacopo Sansovino, the most important architect in Venice in the sixteenth century—a project begun in 1909 when Generali purchased a large part of the building, in a major economic effort oriented towards gaining control over almost all of the industry.

A Priceless Certificate of Nationality

Italy's entry into the war, on May 24, 1915, heavily conditioned relations between the Trieste and Venice Head Offices, and exposed the company to operational limitations on both fronts. The Austrian government viewed the initiatives of the Central Head Office and the behavior of the men who worked there with diffidence, considering the latter to be sympathizers of the irredentist movement, and even threatening to sequester its assets to prevent flight abroad. In the report of the Austrian command, *Die italienische Irredenta,* Generali figures among the suspected institutions, with a long list of directors and employees sheltered in Italy at the outbreak of hostilities.

The uncertainty of the circumstances led to the transfer of some of the Central Head Office's operations to Vienna, while a special office was opened in Rome for the transport division, assigned to the Romanian Mihail Schwefelberg, who later obtained Italian citizenship and changed his named to Michele Sulfina. The company's situation was made even more complicated by the pressure exerted in Italy by its competitors, which aimed to bar the company, as had already happened in France and England, from carrying out its activity. The arrival in 1916 of the certificate of Italian nationality (issued by the government to Assicurazioni Generali, following a request presented by the chairman Marco Besso, the director Nicolò Papadopoli Aldobrandini, and Giuseppe Luzzatto, secretary director in Venice) was therefore heaven sent.

After the Caporetto debacle in 1917, while the Ca' Corniani estate was being flooded to stop the enemy's advance, fear of Austrian reprisals in Venice led the company to move the administrative offices still operational in that city temporarily to Rome, while Vienna carried on operations for Central Europe.

Evidence of how Generali's sterling reputation remained intact in all of the countries where it operated, even at the height of the war, includes the policy taken out in 1918 by Emperor Karl I of Austria [*fig.* 3]. The war ended on November 11 that same year, and the company—which suffered terrible human losses (dozens of its employees died in battle on various fronts)—found itself operating in a profoundly changed world. The issued capital was converted to liras and on November 4, 1919, the company was able, for the first time, to hold its General Shareholders' Meeting in Italian Trieste. In 1920, Edgardo Morpurgo was elected company chairman, after the sudden death of Marco Besso, and thus it fell to Morpurgo to lead the reorganization of the Group, adapting it to the structure of the new political situation in Europe, where profound territorial changes followed the dissolution of the Central Empires.

K.K.PRIV.

ASSICURAZIONI GENERALI

TRIEST

ERRICHTET IM JAHRE 1831.

Volleingezahltes Aktienkapital: K 12,600.000 – Gewährleistungsfonds: K 456,949.184.97.

VERSICHERUNGSURKUNDE

Tabelle: 17 A. Spez. — No. 517901 — Alter und Dauer: 31/18

über folgenden auf Grund des Antrages d. d. 15. Juli 1918 und der sonstigen schriftlichen Erklärungen des Versicherungsnehmers und des Versicherten abgeschlossenen Versicherungsvertrag auf das Leben

SEINER KAISERLICHEN UND KÖNIGLICH APOSTOLISCHEN MAJESTÄT

KAISER UND KÖNIG KARL I.

KAISER VON ÖSTERREICH, KÖNIG VON BÖHMEN usw. UND APOSTOLISCHER KÖNIG VON UNGARN DIESES NAMENS DER VIERTE, geboren laut Dokument in Persenbeug am 17. August 1887.

Die k. k. priv. Assicurazioni Generali verpflichtet sich, unter den in dieser Urkunde enthaltenen allgemeinen und besonderen Versicherungsbedingungen die Summe von

K 500.000.– ⟨fünfhunderttausend Kronen⟩ österr.-ung. Währ.

am 31. Mai 1936 ⟨eintausendneunhundertdreißigsechs⟩ auszuzahlen, und zwar an den VERSICHERTEN SELBST, wenn er diesen Tag erlebt, oder im Falle Allerhöchstseines vorherigen Ablebens an IHRE MAJESTÄT KAISERIN UND KÖNIGIN ZITA und wenn auch IHRE MAJESTÄT alsdann nicht am Leben wäre, an SEINE KAISERLICHE UND KÖNIGLICHE HOHEIT ERZHERZOG FELIX und im Falle des vorherigen Ablebens auch SEINER KAISERLICHEN UND KÖNIGLICHEN HOHEIT DES ERZHERZOGS FELIX an Höchstdessen GESETZLICHE ERBEN.

Für diese Versicherung ist eine ganzjährliche Prämie von K 20.363.– ⟨zwanzigtausenddreihundertsechzigdrei Kronen⟩ nebst der gesetzlichen Stempelgebühr zu leisten, zahlbar am 31. Mai eines jeden Jahres, solange der Versicherte lebt, längstens jedoch 18 Jahre hindurch. Vom 31. Mai 1921 an nehmen die Jahresprämien nach Maßgabe des umstehenden Nachtrages ab.

Die Versicherung beginnt, unbeschadet der Bestimmung des § 2 der Allgemeinen Versicherungs-Bedingungen, am 31. Mai 1918, mittags 12 Uhr.

Als Versicherungsnehmer wird SEINE KAISERLICHE UND KÖNIGLICH APOSTOLISCHE MAJESTÄT KAISER UND KÖNIG KARL I. von der Gesellschaft anerkannt.

Prämie bis 31. Mai 1919	K 20.363.–
Stempelgebühr	„ 407.26
Zusammen bar bezahlt	„ 20.770.26

TRIEST, am 24. Juli 1918.

K. K. PRIV. ASSICURAZIONI GENERALI.

DIMITRI BARON ECONOMO. EMANUEL EHRENTHEIL.

3.
In 1918, the company could boast Emperor Karl I of Austria as one of its policyholders
[ASAG, *Versamenti*]

The Change in European Geography

With the fall of the Hapsburg Empire, a politically united State was replaced by a plurality of national States, each with its own economic, monetary, and judicial framework and independent regulation of insurance activity. It was therefore necessary to create new organizational structures that could manage, in a decentralized way, operations in the various nations: with this in mind, the main Generali agencies in the capitals of the new States (Vienna, Prague, Budapest, and Warsaw) were transformed into territorial offices with superintendency over the agency networks in their respective countries as well as considerable autonomy.

Monetary problems presented particular difficulties, being connected to the heavy depreciation (if not zeroing) of many of the old currencies. In addition to needing to redefine, whether in compliance with peace treaties or with a series of agreements between States, the relationships of previous debt and credit, the company found itself shouldering substantial burdens due to the radical devaluation of its reserves, which were in great measure invested in State securities.

The development of the regulation of life insurance in Italy was, on the other hand, taking a positive turn, with Generali's ideas being heard by the government: the plan for the absolute monopoly to take effect in April 1923 was revoked and the company could therefore resume its normal operations, even if with the obligation to hand over a quota of premiums to INA. The improved climate favored Generali's participation in various initiatives and investments that were being launched in Italy both in the field of insurance and in support of the country's economic recovery.

In 1924, its international activity, as one deduces from the information presented at the meeting held the following year, developed in the form of eight foreign offices (France, Belgium, Spain, Great Britain, Austria, Yugoslavia, Hungary, and Czechoslovakia), around sixty branches and agencies spread among thirty countries, including some outside of Europe (Palestine, Syria, Sudan, Egypt, China, India, Indochina, the Philippines, Mexico, and Brazil), and sixteen subsidiary or associated companies, all located in Europe.

In support of company growth, new, more incisive decisions were also being made on the advertising front, in particular through the involvement of a figure of unquestionable prestige: Marcello Dudovich, one of Trieste's great artists and a leading figure in Italian poster art for more than half a century, from the end of the nineteenth century on. Dudovich's collaboration with Generali began in the second half of the 1920s and continued over the course of more than ten years, until 1937–1938. His most common theme was the picturesque "Venetian scene"—the fluttering shawl of a female figure turned facing the lagoon [*fig.* 4], the statues of *Todaro* (Saint Theodore) and of the winged lion in Saint Mark's Square, the prayer before the shrine, and other classic city views—but there were also images of farmers, used to advertise insurance for sheaves of grain catching fire [*fig.* 5] and, later, references to the Fascist colonial endeavors.

At the end of the 1920s, which would later be remembered as the Roaring Twenties in emphasis of the sparkling economic and cultural climate of the time, Europe and the world seemed ready to overcome the trauma and wounds of World War I. In the midst of apparent stability and widespread prosperity, however, the unexpected and catastrophic crisis of 1929 exploded, giving rise to the Great Depression in the years to follow. At the end of October, the value of securities listed on Wall Street suddenly plunged, after a long period of uncontainable speculative euphoria, which in reality rested on fragile foundations. The first to suffer its effects were the wealthy, but the drastic reduction of their purchasing and investment power had an effect on the American economy overall, leading to a consequentially high unemployment rate, and the recession quickly spread all over the

4.
This splendid work by Marcello Dudovich is known to poster art enthusiasts as *La veneziana*
[CGG, poster, 1928]

5.
Other works designed by Dudovich for Generali were on the theme of farm life
[CGG, poster, 1938]

6.
The company's centennial was celebrated in Rome
[ASAG, *Versamenti*, file 28265]

7.
Italy's conquests in East Africa provided inspiration for original advertising initiatives, like the pamphlet *I risparmi di Faccetta nera* [ASAG, *Direzione Veneta, Circolari*, vol. 1936-1938]

world. Its negative impact was particularly felt by the European countries, such as Germany, that had been granted American loans to improve their financial situation after the war.

Celebrating 100 Years

In 1932, Generali reached one hundred years of activity and celebrated this achievement with due prominence that May. The head of the Italian government, Benito Mussolini, participated in the official event held by the company in Rome [*fig.* 6]. Whereas in Trieste, Duke Amedeo d'Aosta congratulated the company on behalf of the royal house at the Shareholders' Meeting. For the official event, the company had a commemorative coin minted, designed by Gigi Supino, and published a volume on its history, edited by Giuseppe Stefani with the collaboration of Oscar de Incontrera.

In the 1930s, Generali was in excellent health, with an international presence and financial solidity that could boast few rivals, after having survived a world war and financial crises that, from the Panic of 1873 to the Great Depression that began in 1929, had upended the world economy. It owned guarantee funds totaling nearly one and a half billion liras and property and agricultural investments totaling nearly 300 million. Its issued capital rose from 13 million right after the war to 60 million, and a few years later it gratuitously doubled. And the dividend payment continued without interruption, even during the most critical moments.

New companies were added to the Group in those years—in Italy, Germany, Spain, the Netherlands, Hungary, and Poland—bringing the total number of subsidiaries to thirty-six in 1935: twenty-nine in Europe, four in the Americas, two in Africa, and one in Asia. And property investments received major stimulus, such that by the end of the decade the value of the company's property exceed 700 million. The importance given to the sector was effectively summarized in the "city of Generali," a representation

of an ideal landscape comprising the outlines of the company's most prestigious buildings, and used in various calendars and printed advertising.
The company's activity in the agriculture sector was also intense, and between 1933 and 1936 it added five new farms, extending over nearly 5,000 hectares, to the property acquired in the middle of the nineteenth century.

Informatics Enters the Scene

The fast, continuous growth of the company's interests, organization, and assets required the parallel development of its administrative and management structures, as well as use of the most modern equipment that technology could provide. Herman Hollerith's first punch card machines were introduced in 1932 for calculating actuarial reserves. The success of this experiment led, on the instigation of the great mathematician Bruno de Finetti (world-famous for his revitalization of the theory of probability, and also a Generali employee and, later, consultant) to the creation in 1937 of an electric accounting center operating as an independent department, which primarily served the accounting needs of the life division, but also the technical needs of the other divisions. The new Hollerith calculators were able to handle both alphabetical and numerical data.
During this decade, the company's advertising activity also intensified: in addition to the already mentioned posters by Marcello Dudovich, wall calendars by Pollione Sigon, and works by other artists, there were the company's participation in numerous trade fairs in Italy and abroad and what were defined as "small ads," but that often met with massive success. Such was the case, for example, with the *Agendina del calcio*, dreamed up by the international referee (and Generali agent) Rinaldo Barlassina, which still lives on in the memories of fans, and the brochure called *I risparmi di Faccetta nera*, with texts by the famed writer and journalist Orio Vergani [*fig.* 7].
To officially celebrate the twenty-year anniversary of the World War I, the head of government, Benito Mussolini, made a trip in 1938 to the Tre Venezie, visiting sites of combat and war memorials. During this trip, he gave a speech on September 18 in Trieste, in Piazza dell'Unità d'Italia, in which he announced the imminent introduction of the pernicious racial laws, which came into effect that November. Generali felt the force of this measure, with more than sixty of its employees forced to leave the company, but its solidarity with respect to its own remained strong, as noted by various historians, including Tito Favaretto in "Assicurare 150 anni di Unità d'Italia" and Anna Millo in her talk on the study day *Le leggi razziali e l'economia italiana* (Università Bocconi, 2008). In particular, referring to Generali's response to the persecution of Jewish staff in countries occupied by the Germans during World War II, Millo wrote: "[...] insofar as possible and sparing no means, employees and managers forced to leave their posts for racial reasons were helped to find new posts in the company's other offices or to move abroad."
Another victim of the storm that struck those with Jewish origins was Edgardo Morpurgo: a few days before the new laws were publicly announced, he stepped down as Generali chairman and managing director, moving to Argentina. The company's new chairman was Count Giuseppe Volpi di Misurata, a successful entrepreneur, former governor of Tripolitania and Finance Minister of the Kingdom of Italy, and chairman of Confindustria and the Venice Biennale [*fig.* 8]. Among the high-ranking executives who left Generali in 1938 and sought refuge abroad, we also find Ottocaro Weiss, who went on to handle the company's affairs in the United States after the war.
In 1939, Generali was at the height of its success in terms of assets and business expansion: the Italian sales network counted more than 3,000 agencies and sub-agencies, while there were offices and agencies connected to the Head Office in forty countries and the Group comprised sixty companies. But World War II was by then on the horizon.

8.
Giuseppe Volpi di Misurata opened the 1942 Venice Biennale in the presence of King Victor Emmanuel III, the Italian Minister of Education Bottai, and other prestigious figures

9.
Fulvio Balisti, a Generali agent in Brescia, dedicated himself to literature after the war, writing memoirs and composing poetry in dialect

10.
Oskar Helmer, a collaborator of Erste Allgemeine and then the Interior Minister of the Austrian government

The Turmoil of War

Right from the beginning, it was clear that World War II would be catastrophic for Generali, with ruinous consequences for its business. Contact was immediately lost with the company's offices in enemy territory and even relations with many non-hostile countries were plagued by increasing obstacles. When the United States entered the war, the company suffered the sequestration of two and a half million dollars in assets that it had not been able to transfer.

When the war arrived in Italian territory, in 1943, relations within the vast national network also become difficult: while it was to some degree possible to maintain contact with the agencies in the north, the others passed under the jurisdiction of the Rome agency, which became a Special Head Office and took over the work of the Venice Head Office in Central and Southern Italy that it was no longer able to do. In the meantime, abroad, the Head Office maintained contact with Austria and Germany alone.

Even the company's top leadership got caught up in the turmoil of war: on September 23, 1943, Volpi di Misurata was arrested by the Germans in Rome. "Volpi, chairman of Wagons Lits and Assicurazioni Generali, friend of French, Belgian, and American financiers, must have seemed particularly suspect to Berlin," wrote the journalist and writer Sergio Romano, who published a document-supported biography of the count. "The *Völkischer Beobachter* of October 15, 1943," he continued, citing the official daily of the national socialist party, "accused Volpi of having purchased land in Rome for Assicurazioni Generali, thus permitting the 'Synagogue to come to the traitor king's aid.' On November 14, one read in the same journal that Generali was a Jewish center that circulated the worst news about Germany and its internal and military situation." After having passed nearly two months in the Regina Coeli prison, Volpi was transferred to a clinic, due to his poor health, where he remained under surveillance until February 24 the following year, 1944. On November 4, 1943, he wrote to the general manager Gino Baroncini, resigning from his chairmanship. Antonio Cosulich was appointed to the post a few weeks later.

The war affected the fate of many of the Group's collaborators—starting of course with those deployed to the front, as discussed in detail in this volume in "Employees at War"—as well as the Jews who were forced to leave Generali at the end of the 1930s due to the racial laws. The contrasting fates of two brothers from Trieste, Alfredo and Bice Morpurgo, are representative. Bice, who had obtained a disability pension in 1938, was hired back in Rome in 1944, three months after the city came under the control of the American troops, continuing to work for the company for another four years. Whereas Alfredo, after having lost his job in 1939 (despite having been an irredentist and a volunteer in the Great War, and in spite of the general manager Gino Baroncini having supported his request to transfer abroad to Tunisia), was sent into forced confinement in Urbisaglia, where the Interior Ministry had set up an internment camp for Italian Jews suspected of anti-fascism, from June 23, 1940 to February 19, 1942. The provision was overturned, but Alfredo, who had become gravely ill, died shortly after.

There were also notable men who worked for the company among those on the losing side of the war, an example being Fulvio Balisti: a volunteer during the Great War and a Fiume legionnaire under Gabriele D'Annunzio in his youth, Balisti then dedicated himself to the insurance business, and rose to become manager of the main Generali agency in Brescia. During World War II, he commanded the 1st Battalion of the Young Fascists and was gravely injured during the Battle of Bir el Gobi, Libya, losing his left arm. He then joined the RSI and in January 1944 was nominated to become the new secretary of the Republican Fascist party instead of Alessandro Pavolini, but the Germans' support for Pavolini meant that the nomination faded in the space of a couple of days. Balisti was arrested in 1945, but was soon freed without judicial consequenc-

es. His incorruptible character also emerges through the judgment of history: for Renzo De Felice, he was "perhaps the most morally pure figure among the entire Republican leadership," while Francesco Paolo Calvaruso described him as "an officer and a gentlemen, the stuff of times gone by."
Even the employees of the agency in Brescia where Balisti was an agent mobilized themselves in his defense, writing to the Venice Head Office, "driven by the strong desire, which is shared—we are certain—by a large proportion of the most important clients, to whom he attended with all of his wisdom and technical expertise, as well as the entirety of the Agency's peripheral collaborators, who have always had his unstinting superior assistance and understanding, to not be deprived of his presence at this Agency" (this letter is published in its entirety in Lodovico Galli's volume *Pagine libere sulla Repubblica Sociale Italiana. Brescia 1943–1945*). Balisti eventually retired to his estate on the Mincio River, dedicating himself primarily to poetry and writing [*fig.* 9], leaving his residence, the "Piccola Caprera," to his soldiers in his will, "so that you might have a place to gather and honor our Fatherland."
Another important figure in the history of postwar Europe was Oskar Helmer [*fig.* 10], who collaborated with Erste Allgemeine, the company that the Generali Group had founded at the end of the nineteenth century, as well a prominent member of the socialist party. In 1945, Helmer was appointed Interior Minister of the new Austrian Republic, a post that he held until 1959.

The Uncertainties of the Postwar Period

Returning to company matters true and proper, Generali, despite the irreparable deterioration of the situation, still managed to close on time and hold Shareholders' Meetings until 1944. The regular fulfillment of institutional requirements resumed immediately after the war, with a Meeting in February 1946 during which the 1944 financial statement was approved. The company also needed to reckon with the judicial investigations and purging that were launched after the war in Italy, as much in the public sector as in the private, against the old ruling class, which was believed to have colluded with the Fascists. In 1945, both the managing director Gino Baroncini and the general manager Michele Sulfina left the company, returning in the years to follow, once absolved of all accusations. The investigations also involved the ex-chairman, Volpi, but in early 1947 the Court of Assizes in Rome decided not to order him to stand trial. The count, whose health was rapidly declining, died in November of that year.
During the postwar period, the future of Trieste seemed uncertain: the city management was subject to the Allied Military Government and its territory was divided into two areas of military occupation, one controlled by the British and Americans and the other by the Yugoslavians. The company therefore decided to move its registered office to Rome in 1947, to formalize its position as an Italian company, while the Central Head Office remained in Trieste, even though its building had been partially requisitioned for use by the British command [*fig.* 11].
Also in 1947, it was decided to incorporate Anonima Grandine and Anonima Infortuni [*fig.* 12] into Assicurazioni Generali in order to reduce management expenses; the merger was completed by the end of the year.
During the second half of the 1940s, Generali needed to come to terms with the loss of a considerable proportion of the Group's business and international organization. All of the assets and interests it had held in Central-Eastern Europe—especially in Hungary, Czechoslovakia, Poland, and Romania, but also Bulgaria, Yugoslavia, Albania, and East Germany—were in fact irreparably lost: a vast network of branch offices and agencies, fourteen insurance companies, often at the top of their respective markets, property totaling 186 buildings and every other asset controlled by Generali were confiscated in recompense

11.
The building that houses the Central Head Office, in the period during which it was partially requisitioned and used as the headquarters for the British command. Above the door, one reads H.Q. Betfor (British Element Trieste Force)

12.
In 1947, the company decided to incorporate Anonima Grandine and Anonima Infortuni into Assicurazioni Generali; in the photo, Anonima Infortuni shares, advertising material, and a stock or security register (nineteenth-twentieth century)
[ASAG, *Versamenti*, OGG001131772 and OGG001062035]

ASSICURAZIONI GENERALI

V Serie - Anno V - N. 10-11 BOLLETTINO Ottobre-Novembre 1954

TRIESTE NOSTRA

Trieste è ritornata all' Italia, l' Italia è ritornata a Trieste. La città che or sono centoventitre anni creò questa nostra operosa Compagnia, accomunando le speranze, il lavoro e il destino con l'antica Dominante, madre a tutti i Veneti dell'Adriatico, ha veduto dopo un decennio di sofferenze, di umiliazioni e di delusioni la fine del suo lungo calvario. I fatti hanno resa giustizia al diritto e han dato a Trieste il premio, che ben meritavano il coraggio impavido e la fede intemerata dei cittadini : sul suo Municipio e sul suo colle romano è ritornato a garrire al vento della libertà, ardentemente invocato, il tricolore d' Italia.

Da tutti i nostri collaboratori sparsi nel mondo, da ogni angolo della Penisola, come dai più lontani paesi stranieri, dove le "Generali" hanno portato l' onorato nome e la secolare insegna, è giunta alla Direzione Centrale l'eco di quei sentimenti, che in quest'ora solenne accomunano gli italiani tutti in un palpito solo d'amore, in una sola commossa esultanza, anche se velata dal cocente rimpianto per le terre dell'Istria sventuratamente perdute. Questo plebiscito ci ha offerto una nuova prova di quella solidarietà di pensieri e di opere, che fa della nostra Compagnia veramente una sola grande famiglia e ne ha costituito attraverso tanti anni e tanto mutevoli vicende il privilegio e l'usbergo.

Siamo riconoscenti a ciascuno ed a tutti per i messaggi, vibranti di patriottici sensi, che hanno voluto inviarci in così fausta occasione ed accompagniamo i nostri ringraziamenti con qualche immagine delle due storiche giornate triestine : quella del 5 ottobre, che vide risalire sui pili della piazza Unità la nostra bandiera, e quella del 26 ottobre, che ricondusse l' esercito d' Italia a Trieste per la seconda volta redenta.

I

13.
In 1954, even the *Bollettino* joined in the celebration of the return of the company's birth city to Italy, publishing a moving article [BCAG, *Bollettino delle Assicurazioni Generali*, 10-11 (1954), p. 1]

for damage suffered during the war or nationalized. In the other areas, the work of reconstruction, arduous though it was, began without delay, and in 1948—when the company chairmanship was entrusted to Mario Abbiate—activity had already resumed in a good part of Western Europe, where assets had been completely blocked, whereas it would take a few more years to reestablish normalcy in the Middle East and across the ocean.

New Momentum after the Storm

Generali, in search of new business directions, looked to Latin America, opening a branch office and acquiring Providencia in 1948 in Argentina, rounding out an already substantial presence that covered Brazil, Guatemala, Venezuela, Ecuador, and Colombia, and to North America, taking over Buffalo, a company with headquarters in New York State, in 1950. The chairmanship of the latter was entrusted to one of the company's own from Trieste, who had left the country before the war due to the racial laws: Ottocaro Weiss.

1950 was also the year in which, in the interest of providing a "sign of serene faith in the company's future," Generali resumed publication of the *Bollettino*, "a flower from the company's past," wrote Chairman Abbiate, "its stem bent back by the maelstrom of war." Thanks to the intense reconstruction work carried out over the previous five years, Generali arrived at the threshold of the 1950s having returned to normalcy.

Leaving out its losses in Eastern Europe, in some territories in areas under British influence (India, Burma) and in China, after the proclamation of the People's Republic, the company's international network was practically restored to its pre-war state. At the same time, its attention was turned to new and more dynamic markets: in addition to Latin America, Australia, and the biggest global market, the United States, where—after the acquisition of Buffalo—it reopened the New York Branch in 1952. In the middle of the decade, the Group was present in around sixty countries on five continents, a territorial breadth that it had never achieved in the past, and firmly established with prominent positions in the key European markets (France, Spain, Austria, and Germany), where Generali had been by then operating for decades.

The expansion of business was of course helped by the international and internal economic upswing: the recovery was strong and smooth across the board, thanks above all to the massive reconstruction effort launched by the countries hit most heavily by the war. In Italy, one of the most important reconstruction initiatives was Piano INA Casa: a wide-ranging building and social program through which 350,000 residences for workers were built between 1949 and 1963.

In 1951, the company reconstituted the General Council, a body that had already been in operation between the two world wars, assigning it the functions of an advisory body with the aim of affirming Generali's international character and activity, streamlining the Board of Director's activity and composition, and dealing with problems of an insurance and financial nature. At a meeting held on June 13, 1953, unanimous approval was given to a plan to adopt, nationally and in Europe, "every measure oriented towards traffic safety and recompense for damage caused by road circulation," demonstrating itself to be ahead of its times, since the law on obligatory insurance covering the civil liability of car drivers in Italy did not come into effect until eighteen years later. At that meeting, Mario Abbiate expressed "the hope that this Council will be the seed of a future international council on free insurance in order to achieve, gradually and with a sense of responsibility, a lofty aim of human solidarity." This speech, which met with enthusiastic applause, was in substance the final act of his chairmanship: a few days later, at the expiry of his mandate at the end of June, Abbiate asked not to be re-elected, for health reasons; he was replaced in senior management by Count Mario Tripcovich.

Joy at the Return of Trieste to Italy

On October 26, 1954, at the end of its long ordeal, Trieste returned to Italy. A touching editorial by the director Giuseppe Stefani in the Generali *Bollettino* made even the company periodical a mouthpiece of "the sentiments that at this solemn time unite all Italians in a single surge of love, a commonly felt joy" [*fig.* 13]. The poet Biagio Marin, who was the Generali librarian from 1942 to 1954, would later write of Stefani's fervent patriotism, and how his support for the company library allowed it to become the organizational center of the nascent Circolo della Cultura e delle Arti di Trieste, which had been founded during the Anglo-American occupation in support of the city's Italian identity.

The Italian economy, in addition to being a part of the climate of general expansion, found its calling in exports, which were the real driver of its development, thanks to a high balance of payments surplus: in the 1950s, the volume of goods sold abroad increased four times over, and that of currency reserves eight times. In an early phase, exports were above all led by products from the agricultural industry, which still employed 40% of the working population. In the second part of the decade, Italy's nascent industry, in the fields of textiles and metal, began to gain ground internationally, laying the foundations for the boom of the 1960s.

In this positive context, Generali paid special attention to reorganizing its own structures in accordance with criteria for more rational management, coordination, and administrative economy. In particular, in 1955 it founded the Milan Head Office, which was to operate on the Italian market in the civil liability, accident, and illness divisions. Two years earlier, productivity competitions in the life and non-life divisions were introduced to stimulate sales activity.

Another important event for the company during that period was its 125th anniversary: the celebrations culminated in two major events, one on May 20, 1956 in Trieste, and the other the next day in Venice, gathering together more than 8,000 Group collaborators coming from thirty-one countries. Camillo Giussani was appointed chairman that same year.

On March 25, 1957, the treaty instituting the European Economic Community and the European Atomic Energy Community was signed in Rome, the first step of a process that would lead to the foundation of the Economic and Monetary Union. Generali, which had always been European by vocation, was already prepared to handle the looming challenges of the new scenario.

1960 began on a sad note for Generali, with the sudden death of Chairman Giussani. He was succeeded in the company's highest post by Gino Baroncini, who led it towards renewed success for eight years. Twenty years after the resignation of Edgardo Morpurgo, there was once again a man who had dedicated his entire career to the Group at the top of the company.

The Italian Economic Miracle

After the devastation wrought by war and then the recovery of the 1950s, the new decade promised to be a period of widespread prosperity and economic stability. For Italy, these were the years of the "economic miracle." The national income was on the constant increase in real terms, industrial production continued without interruption, and the balance of payments showed a solid profit, even though there were also a few basic imbalances, including the emergence of strong shortfalls in the national budget and that of local organizations. The strong development of traffic and exchange between the various economic areas and the spread of mass motorization further contributed to an overall situation that was favorable to expansion in the insurance sector.

In Europe, premium income was increasing at an annual rate of 15% and the dynamic of new, rapidly expanding markets, specifically Japan, Australia, and Latin America, was even livelier. There were, however, also elements of unrest, above all in connection to the predominance of supply over demand. The field of motor vehicle liability was immediately thrust into the spotlight, in all of the markets, due to the negative impact of the explosive, disorganized growth of circulation in the context of a deficient road network, a backward regulatory framework, and lack of effort applied to prevention.

At the same time, the international insurance scene was facing the issue of big risks, a direct consequence of the gigantification of transportation means and the spaces used for production and trade activity: those were the years of the jumbo jet and supertankers and the multiplication of big warehouses and mega-industrial systems. Requests for increasingly large-scale coverage tested the capabilities not only of individual companies but, sometimes, even of the entire international insurance industry. The effect was to push the concentration of a single national market among companies, with the primary aim of creating an entity with greater underwriting power, while agreements for collaboration spread among companies from different countries, especially for the expansion of service for international clients.

In the context of this economic scenario, the Generali Group promoted a range of important projects, including the founding in 1963 of Europ Assistance, the first professional organization for quickly assisting customers finding themselves in difficulty while far from home, on the initiative of Pierre Desnos and with the help of Concorde, a French affiliate led at the time by André Rosa. That same year, aware of the importance of having a strong presence on a key market for underwriting international risks, Generali opened the United Kingdom Branch in London, thus strengthening its relationships with the British market, which had been broken off during the war. It was also during this period that the coverage for space risk debuted, a sector that the company got involved with right from the start, guaranteeing the San Marco project, launched by the Centro Ricerche Aeronautiche in Rome in collaboration with NASA. Finally, in 1966, it signed an important cooperation agreement with Aetna Life & Casualty, the biggest multi-division insurance group in the United States. Generali's increasing attention to the international insurance market included awareness of a growing protectionist trend that was cropping up in numerous emerging countries: nationalist interventions in the banking and insurance spheres and restrictive measures against foreign companies were spreading in the very markets towards which Generali had turned its attention right after the war, forcing the company to abandon such countries as Syria, Egypt, Iraq, Pakistan, Algeria, and Congo, and reduce its presence in Latin America.

The Turn of 1968

1968, the year of a mass protest that seemed to lead to the radical transformation of social and political imbalances in many countries, was also a turning point for the company. It was presided over by Cesare Merzagora, a tough man, driven by an invincible critical spirit, and known as an uncompromising keeper of public morals. Senate chairman from 1953 to 1967, he resigned from the post after denouncing the ills of Italy and partitocratic degeneration in a speech addressed to the Knights of Labor, "accusing the government—as another senate chairman, Nicola Mancino, recalled many years later in a commemorative volume published in honor of the hundredth anniversary of Merzagora's birth—of coming apart in the face of the Country's emergencies: corruption and favoritism, irresponsible management of financial resources, and threats to the freedom of the press." Although lacking explicit experience in the insurance sector, the new chairman led the company with great authority and visionary intuition, which translated over the subsequent decade into a profound modernization of company strategy. He was supported by a first-class executive team—as he himself affirmed on many occasions—which in the first half of the 1970s included, among others, managing directors Franco

Mannozzi and Fabio Padoa and general managers Eugenio Coppola di Canzano, Emilio Dusi, Carlo Polacco, Enrico Randone, and Giorgio Zanardi.

The former senate chairman accelerated the interventions to strengthen the company assets begun at the end of the 1960s, thus completing a plan for massive property [*fig.* 14] and agricultural investment [*fig.* 15] that led, in the space of three years, to the doubling of the value of the company's real estate.

At the same time, a project was launched in the most important markets to rationalize structures and bundle services with the dual aim of increasing productivity and reducing administrative duties.

In Italy, starting in 1971, all of the accounting and administrative operations were concentrated in the new data processing center in Mestre, whereas in the middle of the decade a single commercial office was created for the divisions handled by the Venice and Milan Head Offices, to give unity and greater incisiveness to the sales policy and territorial presence. Another important innovation that emerged during this period was the constitution, in 1974, of Genagricola, a specialized company that launched its activity with the purchase of numerous estates and that, starting in 1980, took over all of the Group's farms.

The modernization of the company also extended to its image: the aim was to standardize the abbreviated name "Generali," which is easy to pronounce in all languages, pairing it with a more up-to-date graphic representation of the winged lion. The new logo was launched in 1971, supported by a press campaign that revolved around the slogan, "From now on, call us Generali." Consistent with the overall goals, the logo and name of the parent company were adopted by the new companies founded in the subsequent years as part of the reorganization carried out in France, Belgium, Brazil, and Austria.

A Group logo was also introduced for the first time, testifying to the increasingly felt need for coordination and support to benefit the companies in the various markets, with the aim of accentuating the unified nature of the strategies employed, while still respecting the traditional operational independence. In this spirit, consulting activity and technical assistance for the Group's companies were increased in the areas of underwriting more specialized risks, reinsurance relationships, and financial, property, and agricultural management.

At the same time, central structures were created for underwriting new, sophisticated risks, like coverage for artificial satellites, and managing international affairs. The latter sector could boast particularly profitable collaborations with prime insurance groups—like Mitsui, Taisho, and Tokio (all based in Japan) and General Accident (Great Britain)—which complemented the agreement stipulated at the end of the 1960s with Aetna.

An Award-Winning Financial Report

The increasing attention to the market that permeated the company's policies in the 1970s was also expressed in a series of initiatives primarily addressed to shareholders and the wider public, with the aim of broadening information about the company's activity. Of special note were the creation of a consolidated Group financial statement, held to be the most suitable tool for representing the complexity of the various interests controlled by Generali, and the circulation of the chairman's statement on the company's performance during the first semester: these were cutting edge initiatives at the time, and won the company official recognition, including the Tagliacedole d'Oro, awarded by the Associazione Nazionale dei Procuratori degli Agenti di Cambio, and the Oscar di Bilancio (the prize for best financial statement), awarded by the Federazione Relazioni Pubbliche Italiana.

In the early 1970s, the breakneck development that had characterized the Italian economy for the previous two decades, like that of the world overall, began to show signs of collapse: demands for wage increases and inflationary pressure combined with the politi-

14.
Standing out among Generali's property investments in 1970s, the massive Segrate building, which was designed by the Brazilian architect Oscar Niemeyer as the new Mondadori headquarters
[CGG, photo Massimo Crivellari]

15.
Poggiobello, in the eastern hills of Friuli, is one of the farms that was acquired following the constitution of the holding Genagricola
[AFG]

Roberto Rosasco

cal tensions and strain over ideals already anticipated during May 1968 in France.
The whole world was shaken by a violent crisis in growth that first took shape on the monetary front (with the termination of the convertibility of the dollar into gold in August 1971) and then in the energy sphere (with the explosive increase in the price of oil imposed by the producer countries in 1973). In Italy, these global phenomena were joined by an industrial crisis, the corollaries of which were heated conflict and the loss of Italian products' competitive edge.
The insurance industry was directly affected by the difficult situation overall: inflation, which quickly became "runaway," combined with recession, resulting in stagflation, had negative effects on savings and production, penalizing premium income in all branches. In turn, currency fluctuation added a new exchange risk to the usual technical gambles. The area of motor vehicle liability gave rise to major worry, particularly in Italy, when it was made compulsory in 1971: the government's "political" determination of the rates, rather than based on technical requirements, created market imbalances that quickly led to the liquidation of many companies.
Convinced of the usefulness of initiating a dialog with its counterparts, with the goal of finding solutions to the most important problems of common interest, Generali collaborated with Confindustria to create an opportunity for periodical discussion: "industry and insurance" meetings held twice annually at the Villa Manin at Passariano, the residence of the last doge of Venice. The first meeting was held on May 13, 1978, and was presided over by the managing director Enrico Randone, who was called to the chairmanship of the company the following year, replacing Cesare Merzagora.
Merzagora, having turned eighty (the age that he himself had designated as that at which his mandate would end), declined reappointment and was acclaimed honorary chairman.

Company Goals and Corporate Solidarity

December 1981 marked Generali's achievement of a century and a half of activity. This anniversary found the company in a period of great prosperity: it was firmly positioned at the top of the Italian market and controlled a group of thirty-five insurance companies and sixty-seven other companies, in top positions in Europe; its financial statements reported constantly growing profits and assets of unequaled soundness; and the Generali share led the Italian Stock Exchange, a position strengthened by a 46.5% appreciation of its price in 1981.
The anniversary, also commemorated with a medal by Emilio Greco and a special stamp cancellation, was officially celebrated in June the following year, to coincide with the Shareholders' Meeting held to approve the 150th financial statement. For this occasion, the annual Shareholders' Meeting was held at a larger, more prestigious venue, the Giuseppe Verdi opera house in Trieste, while the gala evening was hosted in the picturesque castle of San Giusto [*fig.* 16]. In the context of the anniversary celebrations, the company also launched two major social initiatives: the founding of the Fondazione Generali, dedicated to contributing to scientific progress, and participation in the expansion of the children's hospital of Trieste.

16.
The company celebrated its 150th anniversary with numerous events, including a gala evening at the castle of San Giusto on the hill by the same name, overlooking Trieste
[BCAG, *Bollettino delle Assicurazioni Generali*, 54-55 (1982), cover]

Der Anker
ALLGEMEINE VERSICHERUNGS-AKTIENGESELLSCHAFT
WIEN
LEBENSVERSICHERUNGS-GESELLSCHAFT
PHÖNIX
WIEN-I-RIEMERGASSE 2
VERSICHERUNGS-URKUNDE No
A EQUITATIVA
ESTADOS UNIDOS DO BRAZIL
LA FENICE
COMPAGNIA DI ASSICURAZIONE SULLA VITA DELL' UOMO
Polizza di Assicurazione INFORTUNI N. 405043
ASSICURAZIONI GENERALI
REPUBBLICA ITALIANA
PASSAPORTO PER L'ESTERO

ARCHIVE TO COMMUNICATE
Preserving and Promoting the Generali Archives

ROBERTA SPADA and SILVIA STENER

Protect to Preserve: The Archive as Cultural Property
Standards for archives kept for political and administrative reasons go back to the origins of archives themselves, while interest in documents emerged with humanistic historiography. In the middle of the sixteenth century, various Italian States promulgated statutory regulations for keeping the archives of public offices and, the idea having become popular during the French Revolution that archives should be public, the first public archives were opened in the nineteenth century. In the years following the unification of Italy, a need arose to protect and preserve the archives of the pre-unification States as well as those of the central and peripheral bodies of the new State. The first laws regulating this material date back to the *Decreto per l'ordinamento generale degli Archivi di Stato* of 1875, which was subsequently replaced in 1902 and in 1911 by decrees that gave considerable autonomy to the management of non-state archives. The issue was not dealt with in a legislatively methodical fashion until 1939, with Law no. 2006, *Nuovo regolamento degli archivi del Regno*, which also regulated preservation and vigilance. This law was later renewed by the Decree of the President of the Republic September 30, 1963, no. 1409, *Norme relative all'ordinamento ed al personale degli Archivi di Stato*. Archive management was entrusted to the Interior Ministry, privileging the juridical and political aspect of the documentation. As for non-state archives, and so including private ones, responsibility for preservation was assigned to the documents creator, while the State carried out supervisory duties through the Soprintendenze Archivistiche.

In the 1960s, a new regulatory process began following the rise of the concept of "cultural heritage," coined in 1950 at the Fifth Session of the General Conference of the United Nations Organization for Education, Science and Culture (UNESCO), and clarified in 1964 by the Franceschini Commission, which was set up to review the laws regulating the promotion and preservation of things of cultural interest, as "everything that constitutes material evidence having cultural value." The definition proposed by the Commission encompassed "all expressions of human activity," and so included archives as evidence of human activity in the practical/juridical sphere, the work of archivists and historians then being to translate them into "cultural fact" [*fig.* 1]. As cultural property, archives were already protected and regulated by the Decree of the President of the Republic September 30, 1963, no. 1409, but it was not until the institution of the Ministero per i Beni Culturali e Ambientali in 1974, today the Ministero dei Beni e delle Attività Culturali e del Turismo (MIBACT), that the definitive recognition of archives as cultural property was ratified, assigning archival administration to the new ministry. Methodical preservation regulations for all cultural property were instituted by the *Testo unico delle disposizioni legislative in materia di beni culturali e ambientali*, which implemented the greater part of the previous directive and was approved in 1999. It was replaced by the current *Codice dei beni culturali e del paesaggio* in 2004. With regard to the *Codice*, it is important to point out the weight it gives to the concept of preservation, which also includes provisions for the physical preservation of documents, and to that of promotion, which has the aim of promoting knowledge of the material and ensuring that it can be used.

Responsibility for preservation and promotion is referred by law to the documents creator, and, in the case of private archives declared to be of "cultural interest," under the supervision of the competent Soprintendenza Archivistica. The declaration, which was communicated to Generali in 1983, attributes particular obligations to the archive owner, possessor, or holder: to preserve, organize, and catalog the historical archive and make it available for consultation recognizing its dignity as "cultural heritage" and fully respecting privacy protection regulations.

On the global level, the first major reports on national archival administration in the science sphere were prepared in the middle of the twentieth century. In 1950,

1.
Policies of various companies associated with the Generali Group (twentieth century)
[ASAG, *Versamenti*, scheda 62440]

The Historical Archive preserves a small collection of nineteenth- and twentieth-century policies relative to the company's various divisions that were issued by the parent company, for agencies and companies outside the Group

2.
Policies (twentieth century)
[ASAG, *Direzione centrale, Ufficio delegato, Corrispondenza*, OGG001125161]

Note the theft and fire policies registered in the name of, respectively, Enrico De Nicola (Naples, August 6, 1935) and Edgardo Morpurgo (Rome, May 14, 1927)

UNESCO supported the foundation of the International Council on Archives (ICA), an international organization that connects individual national bodies and the mission of which is to preserve, make use of, and promote the world's archival heritage. In 1976, the ICA officially recognized a committee for business archives that had been established in London in 1974. The 1980s saw the emergence of openness to the problems of industry historiography: historians, archivists, individual entrepreneurs, trade associations, Chambers of Commerce, foundations, and other organizations began discussing management and preservation problems, fueling interest in and the debate on corporate archives, finding fertile ground for comparison in industry literature and periodicals, and on the thematic portals of associations and institutions. In particular, as concerns insurance archives, in 2001 the Associazione Nazionale fra le Imprese Assicuratrici (ANIA) promoted a fundamental initiative to carry out a census of the historical archives of member companies, the aim of which was to raise their awareness of their own documentary heritage and discover the potential for using this material for cultural ends as well as for internal and external communication. It was an awareness-raising project addressed to all staff, focused on the documents that they produced daily while carrying out their work, since the archive was for everyone and, accordingly, practicable for all.
In fact, the proper management of the current archive ensures the methodical formation of bodies of archival material slotted for permanent preservation and, consequentially, for the clear memory of the company's history. The archive not only has legal and, if declared as such, cultural property value, but it is also a source of information, and it is the archivist's responsibility to develop its potential with the aim of promoting and strengthening the company image as well as maintaining ties with the region.
In the case of Generali, a company that provides a service and that consequentially uses and has used communication as a means of reaching clients, the Historical Archive makes preservation, its primary responsibility, the fundamental condition for promoting the memory of "what has happened and been done," in order to be able to communicate it to the public, in memory of its history and as a guarantee of its own brand. From this point of view, it should be remembered that the Generali Group preserves the documentary heritage of three historical companies: Assicurazioni Generali, Istituto Nazionale delle Assicurazioni (INA) Assitalia, and Toro, all of which have been declared to be of noteworthy historical interest. The Historical Archive of Assicurazioni Generali preserves not only the papers produced by the Central Head Office in Trieste [*fig.* 2], but also a portion of the documentation of the Venice and Milan Head Offices, Anonima Grandine and Anonima Infortuni, the general agency in Trieste, the agency in Asmara, and other subsidiary companies.

The Generali Archives in Times of War and Peace

Over the years, the company issued internal instructions for keeping the current archives and for preserving the less recent documentation; sparse, but useful information about the management of the latter was discovered during the census.
The company's internal bylaws of 1832 provided for a keeper of the archives, Angelo de Rosmini, who was in charge of correspondence. The archives are mentioned again, this time in terms of securing them against fire risk, in a few directors' minutes from the year 1875, which also cite the use of a "storeroom" (no less clearly identified today, but probably in the old company premises on Via della Procureria) for keeping the account books and where a hoist was set up for moving them. One copy of the keys was given to the secretary-general, Masino Levi (in 1837, he was also responsible for preservation and for recording the minutes of the Management, Board of Directors, and General Meetings) and one to the recorder, Davide Cusin. When planning the Central Head Office in Palazzo Geiringer, a special room was included, the "cell," for preserving General and Board of directors' meeting minutes and the company's securities,

GENERALI
Bavlna-látky
DEKORACE
AUTO-MOTO-SERVICE
oil silk
SERVICE

which in accordance with the accounting records had to be deposited in the cell in Trieste, rather than in banks or other institutes. The cell is also mentioned in a note dated 1927 and addressed to the company chairman, Edgardo Morpurgo, that refers to the machine transcription of all of the executive meeting minutes kept in the cell.

The first useful information on the preservation of the technical documentation of the divisions and departments dates to World War I, when Generali found itself needing to reorganize its offices and secure its documentation. The first precautionary measures were implemented in August 1914, when the company took steps to send its security deposits in Vienna, as a branch of the Trieste Head Office, in order to ensure continued contact with the agencies in the Empire, should the city find itself isolated. Two years later, the Management also ordered the transfer of the accounting and administrative documentation as well as that of the life division, as a preventative measure in response to the fear that the Italians would occupy Trieste, the permanence of the Central Head Office in the city being, however, understood (in fact, the documentation of the non-life divisions remained on site, awaiting appropriate action). In January 1919, the company's securities, staff, and books returned to Trieste, as well as all of the material in general no longer needed in Vienna. We learn from the executive meeting minutes that precise instructions were given on this occasion regarding the organization of the securities and the precautions to be adopted in order to secure the cell. Provision was also made for organizing all of the documentation produced by the life division during the war, a project carried out by the archivist Angelo Giacomello with the assistance of another (future) archivist, Giuseppe Porro, who was afterward absorbed in the everyday work of handling and reorganizing the division's documentation. Information relative to the archives of the Venice Head Office is scarce and sporadic. From the recorded organizational measures and circulars sent to agents on the change in the documentation's location, we may gather that following the decision to transfer all of the Venice offices to Rome after the Caporetto debacle, the archives followed the same road to the Italian capital. In this regard, a circular from March 1919 complained of the enormous effort exerted for the return to Venice, involving moving both people and things, and especially the archives, including those of the fire division, contained in around 8,000 cases. The move was not carried out all at once: in order to concentrate the administration of all of the foreign work in the Central Head Office, it was decided in 1926 to move only the foreign portion of the administration of the transport division to Trieste, along with, presumably, the relative documentation (in 1931, the entire division was moved to the Central Head Office). For that occasion, the administration of the real estate in the various provinces of the Kingdom of Italy was moved from Venice to Trieste, in order to centralize the management of all of the company's buildings [*fig.* 3]. A certain degree of interest in the company archives is found in the *Bollettino* of 1932, which illustrated the grand deposits of the Venice Head Office's fire division, where around one million policies were kept in fourteen rooms. The article "Norme per la tenuta degli archivi" was published that same year (and then proposed again in 1950), and served as a simple guide to the documentation to be preserved at each agency, based on the regulations in force at the time.

During World War II, Generali again found itself needing to think about the reorganization of work both in Italy and abroad. The Trieste administration was to remain untouched, out of loyalty to the "precise, unanimous intention to maintain Trieste—premises included—as the organizational and moral base that has been the company's honor for a century and which must also always remain in place as a declaration of patriotism" (Management Committee minutes of June 21, 1943). However, it was also recognized as an opportunity to move a few of the offices, with their relative archives, to places better suited to handling the incessant increase of business, during a

3.
Assicurazioni Generali's building, Prague (1937)
[ASAG, *Versamenti*, scheda 29805]

period in which communication was becoming increasingly difficult. The archive in Stra, in the province of Venice, was confirmed as the deposit for the documentation of all of the Venice divisions (the transfer of the life division archive had already been arranged in 1941) and it was also decided to move the Central Head Office's most important archives (first, the current life division archive and then all of the other departments and divisions) to the Chiozza farm in Scodovacca, near Cervignano del Friuli. At an earlier stage, as a precautionary measure, the company's securities were transferred for safekeeping to specially appointed spaces in various banks and to the cell at the Rome office. The agencies were also instructed to do everything necessary to protect their archives and other critical accounting and administrative documentation from possible air attacks. In fall 1944, the archives of the various offices were moved back to their original deposits, against the substantial expense of the daily transfer of the documents needed by the offices to carry out their work and the off-site employment of the archive staff, including Ugo Avian, Marcello Baracchini, Giordano Fuga, and Giuseppe Porro, who worked in the life division. Upon the archives' return, the spaces needed for their reorganization and for discarding the documentation that had exceeded the legally required period of preservation were immediately prepared, as we read in a few notes discovered among the documents of the central secretariat regarding its own documentation.

Periodic inspections of the archives were carried out by order of the individual divisions and departments (particularly the more complex ones, like the life division and the secretariat office, with the aim of distinguishing the composition and functions of the various structures) as well as analysis of the archival systems currently in place, followed by suggestions for facilitating access to documents and creating space for new material. What emerged from this were suggestions concerning archival and filing systems, periods of preservation, and repacking, transfers, and discards (accompanied by topographical maps of the archival spaces and discard lists). These instructions became increasingly detailed starting in the 1960s, when the work became mechanized, and especially from the 1970s forward, consequent to the review of the company's administrative organization. Notes have also been preserved concerning to the flow of information, or procedural systems, for some of the technical divisions with respect to data conversion by the data processing center (CED). This is valuable information that allows us to reconstruct the way in which the offices were organized, the original order of the documents, and, consequentially, that of the archives, in both conceptual and physical terms. Also of interest are the opinions expressed on how long documents needed to be preserved, which the legal consultant provided on a case by case basis on request by the offices involved in "clearing out" the archives. From what has emerged, we may infer that due to the various moves and transfers, the material was subjected to a physical and periodic selection process, which could be defined as having been born of necessity, creating gaps in the executive and technical documentation from after the war up to the 1960s.

In the twentieth century, document management was entrusted to division staff and the archivists. The company agreement reached by the Venice Head Office in 1946, which was adopted by the Central Head Office the following year, established a new job category, that of the "archivists." There were two types of archivists at the company: employees dedicated exclusively to archival work, who were required to exercise a certain degree of autonomy in their management of the documents, and the archive assistants, who dealt with the manual archival tasks, including retrieving and replacing the individual files requested by the various offices. There were two collection types, if they can be thus described, at the Trieste Head Office, categorized according to the complexity involved in the organization of the department or division: one that was more specialized

4.
Advertising brochure for Tel Aviv fair
(1932)
[ASAG, *Versamenti*, scheda 9062]

5.
Carlo Ulcigrai (Trieste, July 9, 1959)
Ulcigrai (third from left, wearing glasses) at the ceremony for the completion of the training course for new hires at Generali. Also present, Dieter Strasser, former senior advisor for the Generali Group in Frankfurt, and Gianfranco Gutty, company chairman in 2001-2002 (in the second row, third and fourth from the right)

6.
Sticker for the company posters "Generali: un libro aperto" (1984) [ASAG, *Direzione centrale, Segreteria centrale, Relazioni pubbliche e pubblicità, Corrispondenza*, U2GE047960]

(such as legal consulting, the foreign business office, staff services, and, especially, the life division), which was kept by the office staff, and one that was simpler, merely requiring the assistants to keep the insurance files in order (for example, the transport division). Over the years, document preservation, particularly in the case of "dead" archives, was transferred to external companies, which carried out the virtual reorganization of the documentation into collections and series based on the producing or transferring offices, broadly following the classification system dictated by the discretion of the individual offices.

The Venice archives were also reorganized over the years, especially in terms of logistics, but a scarcity of sources prevents us from outlining an exhaustive programmatic framework for the types of intervention undertaken. An analysis of the general archives was prepared in the second half of the 1970s, due to the need to move the dead archive and for a deposit on the mainland, the aim being to free-up buildings, scattered throughout Venice, of considerable art-historical value that were unsuited for use as archives, as well as to clear out spaces that would be useful for receiving new deposits, due to the lack of planned discards. This reorganization became even more critical with the introduction of the single national numeration of policies in the non-life divisions. In 1991, after the institution of a single Head Office for activity in Italy, all of the archives were moved to appropriate premises in the new headquarters in Mogliano Veneto.

Communicate to Promote: Generali "Communication" (1930–1992)

From the institutional perspective, the first mention of a company press and advertising office dates to 1930, and that continued to be the name of the office until 1960. It was headed by Giuseppe Stefani, a cultured publicist and the former editor and head of *Il Piccolo* in Trieste and the *Corriere della Sera*, who was hired in April 1930 to "handle publicity, advertising, and press" (Executive Committee minutes of May 15, 1930). He was the first journalist to be placed expressly in charge of this area at Generali (local press had been handled previously by the deputy general manager Angelo Ara), and the appointment came at a critical time, due to the rise of mass communication and the spread of new communication means, like cinema, radio, and television. In fact, his hiring coincided with the modernization and return of the *Bollettino*: the company periodical was then led by Stefani until the end of the 1960s, during which time he also held other important positions within the company. As co-manager, from 1938, and then as central manager from 1948, Stefani oversaw all of the activity of the Trieste central secretariat, which was in charge of not only general areas that would long remain the concern of this department (like press, library, shareholders, cash, supplies, etc.), but also many of the relevant functions that over the years developed into separate, independent service departments, like the foreign business office and staff services.

Concerning advertising material produced by Generali during the twentieth century, numerous pocket diaries, brochures, and posters are preserved in the Historical Archive and the Central Library, and are also widely illustrated in the issues of the *Bollettino* from the same period. Atlases and maps were another exceptional advertising medium used by Generali. In 1920, for example, the company had a geographic map printed with the new Italian borders, decorated with vignettes featuring the company's prestigious properties and highlighting the names of the city's where it had agencies. The map was to be displayed not only in the agencies, but also "for a long period of time in the most popular gathering places and establishments visited by the public" (*Bollettino* of 1920). In the following years, it had pocket atlases produced, which indicated the company's properties and agencies.

For the period between the 1930s and 1960s, however, and even for the previous years, it is not easy to find documentation that systematically addresses the issue of communication or allows us to reconstruct the decision-making process behind the various commissions for posters and promotional advertising, which were, however, entrusted to well known designers and poster artists.

Considering this, a written exchange between the administration of the life division and Giuseppe Stefani in 1937 is of special value. On February 17, Ettore Gentilli wrote to Stefani, complaining that the publicity slotted for Italy and abroad was "scanty and insufficient," and ten days later Stefani replied with a sweeping letter, citing almost all of the company's promotional advertising from the period, highlighting general criteria, and indicating a few communication problems between different internal services. Stefani noted a few of the company's well known initiatives, which were repeatedly reprinted over the years due to their popularity, like the *Agendina del Calcio* (1932), the *Atlantino geografico* (1932), *Il mio bambino* (1934), the *Atlantino etiopico* (1935), *Faccetta Nera* (1936), and *Roi Soldat*, which met the company's requirement to avoid using "direct advertising on the usefulness of Insurance," preferring to attract interest in the Generali name through "indirect forms of advertising." Stefani also added the special brochures printed for the fairs in Tel Aviv [*fig.* 4] and Lviv and for the buildings of Beirut, Jerusalem, and Rio de Janeiro, in addition to those for particular types of life insurance (*La previdenza per il clero*, from 1935, and the *Orologio del risparmio*, from 1934, as well as those for the surgery benefit), the *Memorie illustrate* attached to the 1934 and 1935 financial statements—which became a custom that continued until the 1970s—and, finally, the traditional publications on real estate.

It is not yet possible to reconstruct the precise names of these initiatives. Stefani doubtless played an important role: he was certainly behind the ambitious official history of the company, the weighty *Centenario delle Assicurazioni Generali*, which was printed in multiple languages—and capable of resisting the appetites of even Filippo Tommaso Marinetti, who had introduced Chairman Volpi in 1941 to an inspector from Allsecures who wanted to write a "history of Generali di Trieste e di Venezia" (letter from Volpi di Misurata to Stefani dated Rome, January 6, 1941)—as well as various official publications on the company, its farms, and its real estate, and the printing of the annual financial statements.

However, Stefani did not monopolize all of the activity in this area within the company, sharing with the Venice Head Office all of the promotional initiatives for the Italian agencies and, with the various technical offices in Trieste, those for the foreign agencies.

To take an example, the choice of theme was at the discretion of the manager of the life division in Trieste. In his above-cited letter to Gentilli, Stefani wrote that in his view one could still do much more, particularly abroad, towards effective advertising, which in his opinion needed to be focused on pushing specific insurance products. It was his hope, therefore, that the various divisions would offer technical recommendations that could serve as inspiration, maintaining that with "better communication between the Division Administrations and this office, we could easily fill in the gaps that this esteemed Administration had found in the development of the company's advertising."

The Venice Head Office was instead directly in charge of advertising posters, pocket diaries, calendars, and brochures for the Italian agencies. The circulars issued by the Venice Head Office, which include precise instructions for posting the material and concerning the various forms the agencies had to use when requesting advertising material, provide us with specific dates for the various campaigns. The campaigns mentioned by Stefani from the 1930s were probably promoted by Marco Ara, who was the general manager in Venice. We know that in November 1933, Ara had appointed an "inspector for development and advertising," Romolo Volpini, who was working on the booklet *Il mio bambino*, to be published by the end of the year.

The dialectical relationship between the two Offices was also in play for the company periodical, with both the

Trieste and the Venice Head Offices having been actively involved in the *Bollettino* since 1930, it, too, the subject of special circulars, which warmly recommended its perusal and distributing it among agents. A written exchange between Stefani and Gino Baroncini provides valuable insight into the terms of the relationship. Baroncini, who was a central figure at the company for decades, had a relationship of absolute trust with Stefani, who long served as secretary of the Board of Directors (from 1938 to 1965), the Management Committee (1938–1944), the Executive Committee (1944–1965), and, finally, the General Council (1951–1965). Replying to a note from Baroncini concerning the most recent issue of the company periodical, Stefani wrote on July 26, 1941 that to resolve what had become the vexed question of the *Bollettino*, it would be necessary to move the editorial office from Venice to Trieste, "in part to avoid a situation where everyone is involved in the *Bollettino* but no one is truly in charge of it."

Major changes needed to be made starting around the years 1938 and 1939. When the Jewish staff members left in 1938, and in particular, with respect to the present discussion, Marco Ara, the company's internal balances needed to be reconfigured, perhaps strengthening Stefani's role in the area of advertising. In any case, when Italy entered the war, in June 1940, the climate and perspectives changed radically. The circulars no longer reported new advertising campaigns. Moreover, in 1942, as per instructions from the industry association, all insurance companies suspended the distribution of "advertising materials of every kind," for the entire duration of the war, "including gift books and anything else distributed by the companies, agencies, and producers for advertising purposes" (circular issued by the Venice Head Office, April 15, 1942). In 1943, publication of the company periodical was also suspended, and was not resumed until 1950, when the Office was transferred to Trieste.

During the period after World War II, the variety of the advertising campaigns, noted above, was undiminished. More generally, in 1950 the first collective insurance campaign was launched, the fruit of an agreement between ANIA and INA with the aim of spreading the concept of insurance without making reference to any specific insurance company.

After Stefani, Carlo Ulcigrai [*fig.* 5] became the head of the press office and the *Bollettino*, in 1965. He had joined the Central Head Office in 1960, after two years as a stock market operator, and enjoyed a long career at the company, until 1992, spent entirely in the area of press, advertising, and public relations. He was greatly appreciated by all who worked with him. One of his first contributions to the *Bollettino* was a review of the insurance films that the company sponsored in 1960 (these films, which included animated films and documentaries, resulted from the careful selection of material from insurance companies and industry organizations in various countries). This initiative is significant in that it attests to Generali's promotional use of film in the insurance field, at a time when its practical use was not yet on the horizon.

Ulcigrai's years at the company coincided with a period of great change for both Generali and its industry policy. In 1970, it was decided to use the name "Generali" all over the world (the motto of the campaign was "Da oggi chiamateci Generali") and to regulate the use of the crest emblazoned with the lion through the publication of a manual (the "red book") for the company's offices and agencies, both decisions that highlight the importance of entrusting itself to an image that would be clearly recognized nationally and internationally. The subsequent years were marked by gradual steps made towards the strong coordination of the company's promotional activity, which could be seen in the chosen communicative approach and was reflected in the organization of the offices in charge of promotion. In 1975, a publicity office (later the public relations and publicity office) was set up at the Central Head Office, with responsibilities that gradually came to include the entire Group in Italy and abroad, in order to protect "the image of the Company in all of its geographical areas of operation and

7.
Armando Zimolo (1990s)
[CGG]

the institutional aspect of its communications" (internal memorandum no. 189 of May 23, 1984). In 1984, the office of public relations and publicity had a new office under its charge, an inter-supervisory publicity office for Italy, set up in Milan that year in order to concentrate the publicity activities of the Venice and Milan Head Offices in one place and manage all of the programs for the Italian market. 1984 was also the year in which the first systematic advertising campaign was launched ("Generali: un libro aperto" [*fig.* 6]), while 1990 saw the first international campaign, in eight European countries ("Generali, l'assicuratore senza frontiere", also translated in English, "Generali, The Insurer without Frontiers") and the parallel presentation of the new single Group logo. Finally, in 1992, "out of the need to give systematic structure to and strengthen the communicative activity addressed to shareholders, clients, institutions, the general public, and the company and Group's collaborators" (internal memorandum no. 286 of June 27), the Board of Directors decided to found a new company unit, the communication department, which emerged from the fusion of public relations, institutional relations, publicity, internal press, and media relations. It was directed by Armando Zimolo [*fig.* 7], a prominent figure in the company, who had long served as head of the research office and, later, that of the representative office, a post that he held simultaneous to that of head of the new department. Under Zimolo, the company's promotional initiatives, along with its advertising activity, took a multitude of forms, from support for exhibitions and the publication of numerous volumes on the company (including through its own publishing house, Editoriale Generali) to the organization of economic and insurances research conferences and the production of videos, created by the audio-visual production center in Mogliano Veneto.

The Company Periodical

Closely tied to the institutional history of the company's communication activity, the company periodical, the *Bollettino*, is one of the oldest and most long-lived in Italy, in print since 1893, but it was not the only periodical produced by Generali. It is important to note, in fact, that the history of the company's internal periodicals fully mirrors the double-headed structure of its administration. Based on the *Mitteilungen* filled with instructions for agents that Wilhelm Lazarus, head of the general agency in Hamburg, had published since 1860, the Trieste Head Office published, between 1880 and 1914 (1880–1897; 1901; 1911–1914), with some interruptions, the *Mitteilungen der k.k. Allgemeinen Assekuranz in Trieste*, for internal, confidential use ("vertraulich," was the term used in the presentation of the first issue) and addressed to German-speaking areas. *Mitteilungen* was instead the name of the Vienna periodical, published beginning in 1933. The history of the company periodicals of Generali's foreign branches is also rich. The double series of periodicals, the Central Head Office's *Notiziario*, for the foreign agencies, and the Venice Head Office's *Bollettino*, for the Italian agencies, continued even after World War I, when Trieste passed to Italy, even though from that point both were of course published in Italian. The *Bollettino* (which was the *Bollettino delle Assicurazioni Generali di Venezia* until 1920) was printed monthly from March 1893 until August/September 1912, from which point the issues were published irregularly (seven between August 1914 and March/April 1915, twelve in 1920, plus a special issue in 1919). It comprised just a few, simply laid out pages and its news were divided by technical division. Its aim was to inform executives and agents about the company's performance and internal appointments, as well as the most important news from the insurance world. The pages of the Central Head Office's *Mitteilungen* were just as simple; starting in 1911, it was also published in Italian, under the title *Notiziario*.

In 1930, publication resumed of both the *Bollettino* (in July) and the *Notiziario* (in March), and both were now more substantial under the editorship, in Trieste, of Giuseppe Stefani, although the editorial committee of the *Bollettino* was Venetian. The new *Notiziario* was published periodically, rather than monthly, and its aim was to gather together "the scattered voices of all of the members of the big Generali family, especially from abroad" (from the presentation of the first installment). The *Bollettino* was instead published monthly, and was addressed to executives and buyers all over Italy, providing news "about everything that could be useful to them, in the way of incentive, advice, and help, in their everyday work." The two periodicals were different in terms of size, graphic design, and regular features. The last issue of the *Notiziario* was published in June 1937, but some of its distinctive characteristics, such as its more dynamic use of photography and its news on the company's illustrious policies, acquisitions, and building projects, were immediately transferred to the *Bollettino*, although the true fusion of the two periodicals took place in 1940. In that year, the larger format and use of color of the *Notiziario* were picked up by the new version of the *Bollettino*, the cover of which featured the lion with the world in the background that was used by the periodical until 1970. Printing of the magazine stopped in 1943, but resumed with a fifth series in 1950, its administration and committee now in Trieste, and over the years it developed a solid, well defined character, with features dedicated to the company's gallery of policy holders, blue inserts for the insurance-themed "Letture nel cassetto," drawn from famous literary works, and pink ones for the Italian agencies' performance competitions. The sixth series was inaugurated by Ulcigrai in 1971, and its cover featured the image of the crest with the lion, which the company had decided, right at that time, to use as the Group's logo in Italy and abroad. Publication was temporarily interrupted in 1986, but resumed at the end of 1988 with a new series, coordinated by Giuliano Pavesi (research office). When Ulcigrai died in 1992, the editorship of the periodical was passed to Armando Zimolo. In the 1990s, the layout became more modern, enlivened with scores of color photographs.

3050 costo da Coen £ 1087.50
carta bianca Nodari + 133 90
1221 40
al Pittore Montalti 500
1721. 40
Per I
Nostri Bambini
VENEZIA
Stab. Tip.° Lit.° C. Coen & F.
1883

LA
SOCIETÀ ANONIMA DI ASSICURAZIONI
A PREMIO FISSO
contro la Grandine
con sede in Milano
VIA BASSANO PORRONE, 8
CAPITALE SOCIALE L. 4.000.000.00
CAPITALE VERSATO L. 1.200.000.00
ALLA
ESPOSIZIONE GENERALE ITALIANA
DEL 1898
IN TORINO
PER IL 50° ANNIVERSARIO
DELLA PROMULGAZIONE DELLO STATUTO
DA S. M. IL RE CARLO ALBERTO
MEMORIA.

SMALL-SCALE CORPORATE COMMUNICATION

Brochures, Small Volumes, and Leaflets from the Historical Archive (1883–1973)

PIETRO EGIDI

The monumental work of cataloging and filing that the staff of the Generali Historical Archive has already been carrying out for years has made it possible to rearrange and use a considerable proportion of the documents relative to the company's history. The company Archive constitutes a valuable resource, one that goes well beyond strictly corporate and insurance sphere interests, ample evidence of which has been provided in the first volume of this series, which is dedicated to the people and events of Generali during the nineteenth century.

The numerous collections and files that have been recently analyzed and censused by the Archive staff also include a fair number of brochures, leaflets, and small volumes of various kind—promotional materials often called "small-scale business communication" or "small-scale advertising", due to their small size—that illustrate insurance products and the activity of Generali, its affiliate companies, and agencies, between the end of the nineteenth century and the first half of the twentieth.

For the most part, these are forgotten materials, which therefore enrich our knowledge of this category of "document"—small in size but extremely effective for advertising purposes—and of the company and Group's advertising activity.

The development and gradual spread of these means of business promotion date to the end of the nineteenth century and the beginning of the twentieth century, basically to the birth of modern advertising, the origins of which are commonly considered to have coincided with the appearance of that formidable and innovative commercial communication tool, the chromolithographic poster.

For insurance companies and financial institutions, the use of brochures and leaflets has been and continues to be—given the nature of the products they offer, which require not only images but also descriptions and detailed explanations—especially important, not just for external communication, but also for informing and training staff, as evidenced by one of the volumes presented here.

Assicurazioni Generali, its affiliated or acquired companies, and its Italian and foreign offices and agencies made broad use of these tools, pairing them, beginning in the last decades of the nineteenth century, with the numerous other forms of communication and advertising that were in use at the time.

Two of the oldest documents that have been "unearthed" and made usable by the patient work of the staff of the Historical Archive in fact date to that period.

The first, from 1883, is a small volume containing a children's story written by Napoleone Panerai [*fig.* 1]. Embellished with an elegant neo-Gothic/Renaissance-style cover and text, this little book—which must have been part of a series of complimentary volumes offered by the company—remains the oldest example of this type of advertising material used by Generali over the years.

The second of the two nineteenth-century documents dates to 1898, and was published strictly for use within the company [*fig.* 2]. Specifically, it is a "memento" of the Società Anonima di Assicurazione contro la Grandine, known as Anonima Grandine, founded by Generali in Milan in 1890 and incorporated in 1948.

The pamphlet, which was published for the Turin Esposizione Generale Italiana celebrating the fiftieth anniversary of the Albertine Statute, traces back over the activity of the company, which was awarded a gold medal at the exhibition. The decoration, gracing the front and back covers and on the theme of rural life, is in the nineteenth century academic/neo-classicizing style, and features a reassuring female figure symbolizing, with a threatening sky in the background and assisted by a cupid, insurance coverage for hail damage: imagery that seems to have been drawn from a study by the sculptor Vincenzo Cadorin and that was also used by Anonima for posters and other promotional material during the late nineteenth and early twentieth century.

The elegant, sinuous Art Nouveau style was instead

1.
Brochure advertising life insurance (Venice, 1883)
[ASAG, *Versamenti*, scheda 6962]

2.
Esposizione Generale Italiana del 1898 in Torino. Memoria, ed. Anonima Grandine (Milan, 1898), cover
[ASAG, *Miscellanea*, scheda 6808]

3.
Life insurance rate book
(Trieste, 1907)
[ASAG, *Versamenti*, scheda 7890]

4.
Life insurance rate books from
the Venice Head Office (Adria, 1912)
and the France and Algeria Branch
(twentieth century)
[ASAG, *Versamenti*, scheda 7890]

5.
Brochure advertising the surgery
benefit (Venice, 1928), cover
[ASAG, *Miscellanea*, scheda 6809]

6.
Brochure advertising life insurance
with photos of Pope Pius X and his
policy (Trieste, 1928), inner pages
[ASAG, *Versamenti*, OGG001114940]

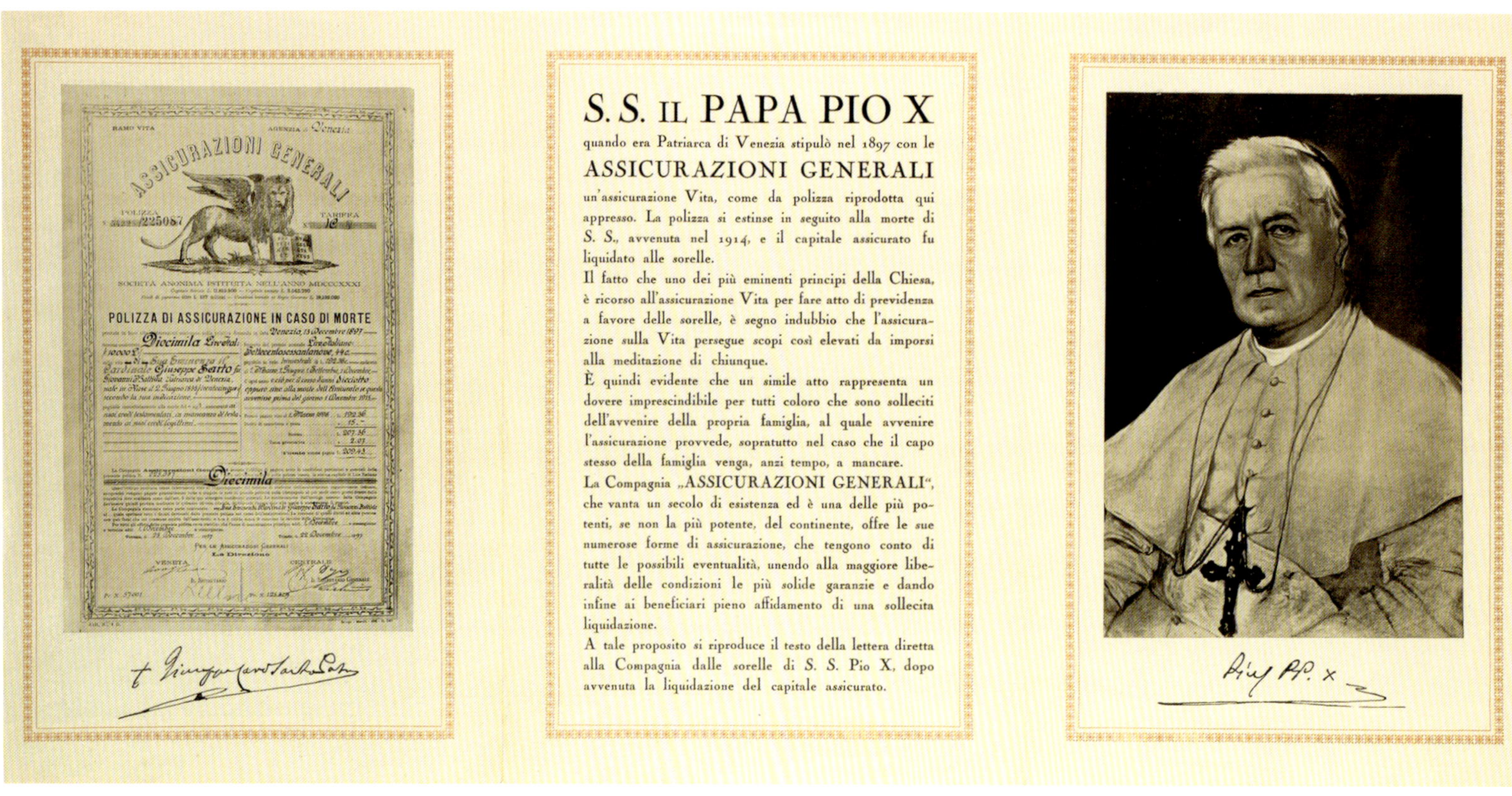

S. S. IL PAPA PIO X

quando era Patriarca di Venezia stipulò nel 1897 con le

ASSICURAZIONI GENERALI

un'assicurazione Vita, come da polizza riprodotta qui appresso. La polizza si estinse in seguito alla morte di S. S., avvenuta nel 1914, e il capitale assicurato fu liquidato alle sorelle.

Il fatto che uno dei più eminenti principi della Chiesa, è ricorso all'assicurazione Vita per fare atto di previdenza a favore delle sorelle, è segno indubbio che l'assicurazione sulla Vita persegue scopi così elevati da imporsi alla meditazione di chiunque.

È quindi evidente che un simile atto rappresenta un dovere imprescindibile per tutti coloro che sono solleciti dell'avvenire della propria famiglia, al quale avvenire l'assicurazione provvede, sopratutto nel caso che il capo stesso della famiglia venga, anzi tempo, a mancare.

La Compagnia „ASSICURAZIONI GENERALI", che vanta un secolo di esistenza ed è una delle più potenti, se non la più potente, del continente, offre le sue numerose forme di assicurazione, che tengono conto di tutte le possibili eventualità, unendo alla maggiore liberalità delle condizioni le più solide garanzie e dando infine ai beneficiari pieno affidamento di una sollecita liquidazione.

A tale proposito si riproduce il testo della lettera diretta alla Compagnia dalle sorelle di S. S. Pio X, dopo avvenuta la liquidazione del capitale assicurato.

7a.
Exposición de Barcelona 1929,
ed. Assicurazioni Generali di Trieste e Venezia (Milan, [1929]), cover
[ASAG, *Versamenti*, scheda 9062]

7b.
Exposición de Barcelona 1929,
ed. Assicurazioni Generali di Trieste e Venezia (Milan, [1929]), inner page
[ASAG, *Versamenti*, scheda 9062]

8a.
Advertising brochure *Il mio bambino* (Trieste, 1935), cover
[ASAG, *Versamenti*, scheda 9062]

8b.
Advertising brochure *Il mio bambino* (Trieste, 1935), inner page
[ASAG, *Versamenti*, scheda 9062]

9.
Anonima Infortuni brochure advertising a policy covering travel and stays in Africa Orientale Italiana [Milano, 1936], *recto*
[ASAG, *Miscellanea*, scheda 6808]

10.
Anonima Infortuni brochure advertising accident and civil liability insurance for cyclists [1936]
[ASAG, *Miscellanea*, scheda 6808]

chosen for a small volume published by Generali in 1907. This publication, the cover of which features the representation in relief of a statue made for the company in 1888 by the sculptor Ivan Rendić, is a rate book for the life division, a sector of the company's activity since its very first years in operation [*fig.* 3]. Two other life division rate books were also recently discovered in the Archives: one, dated 1912, is from Generali's Venice Head Office, while the other, datable to between 1919 and 1923 on the basis of the indicated issued capital, was published for France and Algeria [*fig.* 4].

A significant proportion of this type of promotional material in the Historical Archive dates to the 1920s and 1930s, decades during which the tools for advertising and business communication in general were becoming increasingly refined, and heading toward becoming a science, with a proliferation of agencies, firms, and publicity offices, including in Italy.

During that period, Generali launched various kinds of insurance coverage, including, in 1928, the "BOC policy" (Beneficio operazioni chirurgiche, or surgery benefit), which provided for the reimbursement of expenses sustained for surgery and the relative hospital stay. The company promptly provided information about this new type of coverage in a brochure with texts by a certain Scampoletti—very likely a pseudonym—and illustrations by Gorgone Tanozzi [*fig.* 5], who, as we shall see, also worked on other projects for the company.

A Generali life division leaflet from the same year emphasizes the company's reliability by exploiting the fame and importance of one of its policyholders: Pope Pius X (born Giuseppe Sarto) [*fig.* 6].

The leaflet features a photo of the pope and the title page of the life insurance policy he took out in 1897, when he was Patriarch of Venice, and also cites the letter that his sisters, the beneficiaries of the insured sum, sent in November 1914 to Generali, just after the pope's death, emphasizing "all of the diligence and care that you have dedicated to the prompt liquidation of the insurance policy."

11.
German version of an advertising brochure for the France Branch (Paris, [1937]), inner pages
[ASAG, *Versamenti*, scheda 6854]

12.
Le Aziende Agricole delle Assicurazioni Generali, ed. Assicurazioni Generali di Trieste e Venezia (Milan, [1939])
[ASAG, *Versamenti*, scheda 7605]

13.
Advertising brochure for the 110th anniversary of the Ljubljana agency (Trieste, 1941), cover
[ASAG, *Miscellanea*, scheda 6808]

14a.
Advertising brochure for the 120th anniversary of Assicurazioni Generali (Bergamo, 1951), first page
[ASAG, *Miscellanea*, scheda 6808]

14b.
Advertising brochure for the 120th anniversary of Assicurazioni Generali (Bergamo, 1951), inner pages
[ASAG, *Miscellanea*, scheda 6808]

15.
Note per l'agricoltore. Cerealicoltura e Notizie tributarie, ed. Assicurazioni Generali (Venice, 1951)
[ASAG, *Versamenti*, scheda 7890]

16.
Note per l'agricoltore. Viticoltura, Enologia, Canapicultura e Notizie tributarie, ed. Assicurazioni Generali (Venice, 1952)
[ASAG, *Versamenti*, scheda 9062]

17.
Brochure advertising insurance savings, contest for students (1967), first page
[ASAG, *Miscellanea*, scheda 6808]

18.
Informational brochure for new hires (Trieste, 1957)
[ASAG, *Miscellanea*, scheda 6808]

The exquisite cover of the brochure printed by the company for the Barcelona International Exhibition in 1929 was designed by Rosmann [*figs.* 7a, 7b]. This Spanish-language brochure contains data and charts on Generali's assets and activity as well as an image of the highly original "graphic," presented at the exhibition, tracing the development of the life division: a series of elegant Lenci figurines, arranged in ascending order, each dressed in the style of the period of reference.
Various promotional materials date to the 1930s, beginning with the brochure *Il mio bambino*, which was published by the company in 1935 [*figs.* 8a, 8b]. In line with fascist social policies—in 1933, the Fascist regime had instituted the Day of the Mother and Child, one of initiatives conceived in support of the "demographic battle"—this publication, illustrated by Tanozzi, is a rich compendium of advice for young mothers interspersed with short reminders about the usefulness of savings and insurance. It was so successful that it was reprinted, in various languages, until at least the 1950s, with slight modifications to the text and illustrations by other artists.
Linked to the Fascist regime's colonial campaign, one of the 1936 brochures for Anonima Infortuni—founded by Generali in Milan in 1896 and incorporated in 1948—illustrates the "Ethiopia policy," which provided coverage for travel and stays in Africa Orientale Italiana [*fig.* 9].
This policy, which provided a broad range of guarantees that were also extended to the colonies of other countries in the same area, was instituted just a few weeks after Mussolini's proclamation of the empire on May 9, 1936.
Another Anonima Infortuni brochure from 1936 was for the "cyclist policy," which provided various forms of insurance coverage, for just a few cents per day, at a time when millions of people, especially workers and people from the lower classes, were using bicycles [*fig.* 10].
The authority and broad popularity enjoyed by Generali during those years are emphasized in a pamphlet from 1937 that was published by the France Branch and is seen here in the version for German speakers.

19.
La Concorde brochure advertising the motor vehicle liability insurance policy [second half of the twentieth century], first page
[ASAG, *Miscellanea*, scheda 6809]

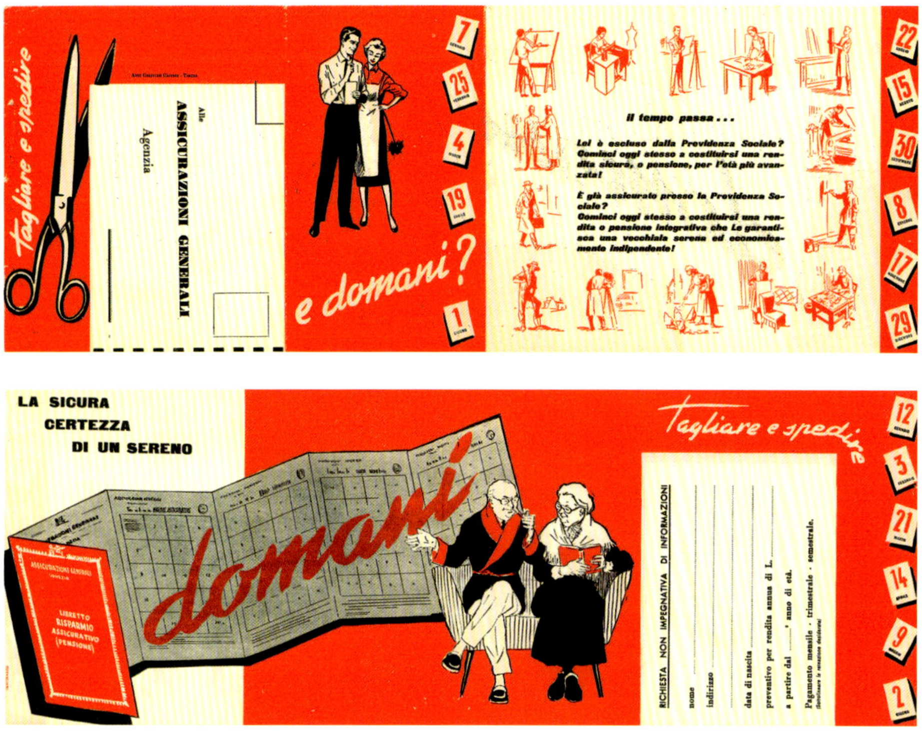

20a-b.
Brochure advertising life annuity policies and supplementary pensions (Turin, [second half of the twentieth century]), *recto, verso*
[ASAG, *Miscellanea*, scheda 6808]

The message about the company's prestige and solidity is communicated through a collage of images of the impressive buildings housing the company's headquarters in Italy and abroad [*fig.* 11].

In 1939, a small volume was published that was entirely dedicated to the company's farms, an important field of investment for Generali. The volume [*fig.* 12], the cover of which features an illustration of work in the fields in the style of Resentera, Dudovich's son-in-law, takes a detailed look at the company's various farms, starting with its first, the "historical" Veneto estate, Ca' Corniani, which was taken over by Generali in 1851 and up and running in 1879, following major reclamation work.

In 1941, a lavish brochure was published in Italian and Slovene, celebrating the 110-year anniversary of the company's office in Ljubljana [*fig.* 13]. The brochure, which dates to just after the Italian Fascist regime's occupation of Slovenia in April of that year, also presents an overview of the company's farms, buildings, and headquarters.

Many of the brochures and leaflets in the company Archives date to the 1950s and 1960s.

In 1951, a leaflet was published in English for the company's 120th anniversary—*1831–1951 From one century to the next*—which presents the progression, in twenty-year periods, of the number of policies taken out and of the premiums collected in the life division. The numerical figures and text are accompanied by lively vignettes that trace the evolution of transportation during the period [*figs.* 14a, 14b].

Also from 1951, the small agricultural volume *Cerealicoltura e Notizie tributarie*, from the series "Note per l'Agricoltore" [*fig.* 15], was followed the subsequent year by one dedicated to wine and hemp growing, *Viticoltura, Enologia, Canapicoltura e Notizie tributarie* [*fig.* 16]. The two volumes, which have cover illustrations created by Achille Beltrame in the 1920s for Anonima Grandine, are serious little manuals filled with information and practical advice for farmers.

The "Insurance savings campaign," launched by Ge-

nerali in 1954 and based on participation in a contest, was instead addressed to primary school students. The initiative, which was a success and continued for nearly fifteen years, was promoted with a leaflet that remained substantially unchanged over the years, with drawings and graphic design by Mario Missaglia [*fig.* 17].
In 1957, a small, lavishly illustrated volume was published for training new hires, *Benvenuto alle Generali* [*fig.* 18], which summarized the company's history, goals, and structure. In the preface, new staff members read that "Generali is more than a company: it is a tradition, a custom, and a world." Similar volumes, either with the same title or that of *Buon lavoro alle Generali*, were published by the company for decades. Two leaflets, one for La Concorde—a company founded by Generali in 1905 and then merged in 1997, together with La France, acquired in 1995, to form Generali France Assurances—and one for Generali, also seem to date to the 1950s.
The La Concorde leaflet, *Pour rouler tranquille,* advertised car and passenger insurance, and its message about the importance of this kind of coverage was communicated through a blunt image of a car crash on the last page, which was a quite unusual solution for insurance advertising at the time [*fig.* 19].
The company leaflet *e domani?* was of an entirely different nature, inviting its readers to start, or supplement, their retirement fund [*figs.* 20a, 20b].
Three Generali leaflets date to the subsequent decade, two of which can be securely dated. The first, from 1965, was addressed to parents, urging them to provide for their daughters' dowries without delay, using the various forms of pension accumulation offered by the company [*fig.* 21a, 21b]. Illustrated exclusively with photographic images, this leaflet is indicative of the continued importance in those years of the "institution" of the dowry—banned in Italy in 1975, with the reform of family rights, because "felt to be a legacy of the past"—and of the progressive and increasingly popular use of photography in advertising, from the 1950s and 1960s forward.

21a.
Brochure advertising the dowry policy (Vicenza, [1965]), first page
[ASAG, *Miscellanea*, scheda 6808]

21b.
Brochure advertising the dowry policy (Vicenza, [1965]), inner pages
[ASAG, *Miscellanea*, scheda 6808]

22.
Brochure advertising the employee Group life insurance policy (Venice, 1967), first page
[ASAG, *Versamenti*, scheda 8233]

Le Generali per voi, from 1967, was instead addressed to company heads, and advertised an entirely new type of policy, designed to ensure employees and their families, should the employee predecease, a long-service allowance, available upon reaching retirement [*fig.* 22].
The third leaflet, which is not dated but seems to be from the same period, illustrates the "comprehensive residential buildings insurance" policy, an innovative product for the time offering twelve kinds of insurance in a single contract [*fig.* 23].
Finally, the little volume titled *Le aziende agricole delle "Generali"* [*fig.* 24] brings us to the 1970s. Produced in 1973, it provided current information about the Generali farms, an important area of investment for the company, which handed over their management to Genagricola, a specially created corporation, in 1974. The small volume, which has a painting by Arturo Tosi on the cover (*La messe*), provides detailed descriptions of the company's historical and newly acquired estates as well as business developments and special crops produced at the time at its various farms, the majority of which have been among the top brands in the agricultural and food industry for decades.

23.
Brochure advertising the buildings policy [second half of the twentieth century]
[ASAG, *Versamenti*, scheda 6817]

24.
Le Aziende Agricole delle "Generali," ed. Assicurazioni Generali (Trieste, 1973)
[ASAG, *Versamenti*, OGG001130090]

The Age of Imperialism: The World Heading toward Ruin

Territories and Populations Were the Stakes Wagered by Opposing Powers on a Planet that Had Become a Slave to the Economy

1901 1913

Although posterity has insisted on including the first years of the twentieth century in the Belle Époque, which was a period of peace and global development, a clear-eyed examination of the characteristics germinating at the time shows that all of it foretold the imminent future catastrophe. It was a historical period during which everything—scientific discoveries (medicine, chemistry, and physics were progressing unabated), technological inventions (the airplane and the radio being two that radically changed human life), seemingly unstoppable economic progress, and cultural, political, and philosophical theories—was oriented towards a vision of domination, competition, power, and, further on, violence. Everything presupposed the unlimited development of the individual and communities with the view, considered inevitable and desirable, that the strongest and most capable would succeed. Not even the world of art and culture was immune. In every area, change and innovation were adopted as stimulus for new beginnings and new points of view. Intervention was, during this period, focused as never before on serving as a tool for revolution. Among the various avant-gardes (Pablo Picasso and Cubism in the field of art; Arnold Schönberg and atonal music), one in particular was marked by its disruptive, challenging approach: Futurism. Founded by Filippo Tommaso Marinetti, who adopted many of the ideas promoted by the Catalan intellectual Gabriel Alomar in *El futurisme* (1904), the movement became widely known when the *Manifesto of Futurism* was published in French in the newspaper *Le Figaro*, on February 20, 1909 (although the text was first published fifteen days earlier in the *Gazzetta dell'Emilia*).

Futurism was the first organized, mass avant-garde movement, and was made possible in part by Marinetti's considerable wealth. It championed the religion of speed, the machine, dynamism, movement, everything that the real world, in its state of constant transformation, was proposing to (or imposing on) humankind at the time. It fought, using hawkish tones, for the destruction of the old world ("war, the world's only hygiene"), so that a new one could emerge every ten years, considering war necessary for continuous, radical renewal [*fig.* 1]. Through the struggle against "pastism"—breaking the "genetic chain of the past" and of tradition, murdering "moonlight" but also Venice and Rome as well as the museums and academies—Futurism proposed total revolution: the Futurist reconstruction of the universe ("we hurl our challenge to the stars") using all of the languages and forms of art suggested by the incessant scientific and technological progress that was unfolding before the eyes of humankind.

Discoveries and inventions were immediately enlisted in service of economic development, generating devastating phenomena tied to the politics of power, such as colonialism (which was not, however, new on the world stage) and imperialism, wielded not only by the primary great powers, but by any European State, even the smallest, such was the mania for greatness and expansion.

This dynamic led to a reorganization of the planet in which territories and populations were no more than the stakes wagered by opposing hungers. Business and finance seemed to be life's only purpose, for both individuals and States. There were 1.2 billion people on the earth, one-quarter of which were Americans and Europeans, who were, however, in possession in 1913 of nine-tenths of industrial production. The divvying up of colonial territories was only an advantage for the "old continent," which completed the colonization of almost all of Africa, most of Asia, and all of Oceania.

What had been, especially at the beginning, a personal ambition of explorers, scientists, and profiteers increasingly became a tool for conquest wielded by States, which were by that point keenly aware of the wealth of labor, raw materials, and natural resources in those areas. Europe proclaimed itself the model of civilization, and capable of, sooner or later, unifying the world with its economic and social superstruc-

1.
The *Plastic Synthesis of the Idea of War* is the title of a work made in 1914 by the Futurist painter Gino Severini, a detail of which is reproduced here

2.
Lord Curzon, Viceroy of India, during the lavish procession for the opening of the Delhi Durbar in 1903, the ceremony celebrating the coronation of Edward VII as emperor of the country

3.
Emigrants leaving Italy around 1900

4.
Ford's first assembly line, launched in 1913 in Michigan: the workers are assembling the flywheel for the Model T

tures and principles of culture and democracy. It was an epoch-making strategy that constituted, in the words of Rudyard Kipling, "the white man's burden," which is to say that the duty of the "superior," modern civilization was to "redeem" those that were considered "primitive" [*fig.* 2]. The colonized countries were therefore placed under guardianship, and the figures of the missionary, the teacher, and the doctor came to play an especially important role: with their charitable and educational training, they became the tools of the new global proselytism, rendering Europe cultural dominant and omnipresent through the spread of languages like French and English as well as the education of local élites.

There were sporadic revolts in some of the colonized countries, such as the Second Boer War (1899–1902) in the Transvaal, or, at the turn of the century, the Boxer Rebellion in China, which, however, did not prevent the break-up of the country. In any case, these uprisings ended up having very little influence overall.

Contrary to what one might think, a real paradox was at play: at the turn of the century, it would seem that rich, powerful Europe would have been sending well-heeled emigrants of a certain social status all over the world, but instead, demographic expansion, which created significant overpopulation, sent millions of the poor out in search of a better life, especially to the United States [*fig.* 3]. In fact, between the end of the nineteenth century and the outbreak of World War I, the European population rose from 250 to 450 million. This demographic explosion was caused by reduced mortality, which was in turn the result of improved hygiene, better, more balanced nutrition, and constant medical progress. There were no more major epidemics, although tuberculosis and smallpox continued to be a problem, and the European mortality rate was far lower than the birth rate. On top of which, with Europe overpopulated, the modernization and rationalization of industry and agriculture gave rise to unemployment, which led to a dramatic increase in emigration, particularly among Italians, Greeks, Poles, Hungarians, Slovakians, the English and the Irish: millions and millions of young, poor, illiterate farmers without land, unemployed artisans, and Jews fleeing the pogroms in Eastern Europe. However, although this mass migration was made up of people from humble origins and with little education, it contributed to the spread of European lifestyles and habits.

In terms of politics, Europe seemed to be divided between absolutism and democracy. In European society, which had been changed by a fresh industrial revolution that created a massive urban proletariat, collective problems began to spread like the struggle for universal male suffrage, the need to establish secular, obligatory schools, and a pressing need for provisions for social assistance. It was the birth of mass society, and on the political front movements sprang up (for the most part socialist) that were increasingly focused on organizing the masses, towards the gradual extension of political and social rights.

In a period marked by what could be termed the second technological revolution, capitalism needed efficient structures, organized and rationalized labor, and available manpower. During the last twenty years of the nineteenth century, Frederick W. Taylor theorized a distinction between manual and intellectual labor, which was used to rigidly separate and clarify roles in the productive system, and in 1913 Henry Ford debuted the assembly line [*fig.* 4] and mass production: both men were pursuing the goal of maximized production.

Germany was the first to adopt Taylor's system, rationalizing and training highly efficient middle-upper management that allowed it to flood the world with its German-made products and industrial giants (Siemens, Bayer, etc.) and to beat Great Britain in the four most cutting-edge industries at the time (iron and steel, chemistry, electronics, and mechanics).

The German *Weltpolitik*, adopted in the last decade of the nineteenth century, thus emerged from the capitalistic need to look towards the still unconquered lands across the sea and towards the sick man of Europe, the Ottoman Empire. While until 1904 the most intense rivalry was between France and Great Britain (which almost came to a head with the Fashoda incident in Africa), this was succeeded by competition between Great Britain and Germany, in particular when Admiral Alfred von Tirpitz rearmed the German Navy, challenging British domination of the seas. Germany needed supplies and outlets in order to continue its economic and industrial development, but in reality, the *Weltpolitik* reinforced cooperation between the other great powers against the German colossus. Particularly, France, for colonial reasons (the Morocco crises of 1905 and 1911), and Great Britain (later joined by Italy and Russia), for the Berlin-Baghdad railroad, for which Germany obtained definitive permission in 1903.

The result was that in 1906, at the Algeciras Conference, the world united against the feared German "monster," even if Europe appeared to be divided at the time, with its purportedly defensive alliances, between the Triple Entente in 1907 between Great Britain, France, and Russia, and the Triple Alliance between Germany, Austria-Hungary, and Italy, which was renewed periodically following the original agreement in 1882.

To sum up the political and economic situation in play at the time, London seems to have been the world's main economic market, with its banks and insurance companies, Great Britain and France were the planet's safes, with their hyper-protected currency, and, while the United States and Germany were the giants of industry, Russia, 80% agricultural and dependent on foreign capital, and Japan, which was starting to adopt foreign technology, were still, in this sense, dwarfs. Austria-Hungary, which was not in any sense an economic power, found itself needing to fight internal tensions caused by the multiple ethnicities within its borders, in a context in which social and national oppression often coincided, and Italy, under

Giovanni Giolitti's leadership (1903–1913), was beginning an industrial revolution that would soon make it one of the great world powers, albeit as a "clay vase among those of iron."

An alarm bell for Europe's supremacy, at least in military terms, came in the form of the Russo-Japanese War of 1904–1905 over control of Korea and Manchuria: repeated Russian defeats, in particular its naval defeat in the Battle of Tsushima (1905), put the undisputed belief in the wartime superiority of the European powers in doubt, also provoking an early Bolshevik revolution in the czarist empire, the suppression of which only postponed its triumph for a little more than a decade.

In an overall European climate in which, as Mario Isnenghi put it, "the returning war was greeted with passion," the signs of crisis were drawing closer with increasing speed to the Balkans, the true epicenter of the coming conflict. The German project for the Berlin-Baghdad railroad, the aim of which was a monopoly over the Balkans and Anatolia in order to reach the mining and oil riches of the East, which seemed to offer a guarantee of world economic domination, also involved Austria-Hungary, which, with the port of Trieste, was in a position to obtain a maritime monopoly over the Adriatic, steering all traffic on the north-south axis in favor of the German economy. No other power accepted this supremacy. What emerged was an interweaving of interest-based alliances, with Russia supporting the Slavs in the south in order to have a seaport on the Mediterranean and therefore entering into conflict with the Hapsburg Empire, which, in turn, with the annexation of Bosnia and Herzegovina (1908), fell out with Serbia, which became the center of the conflicts in the years to come. Italy, working with various other States, tried to launch projects that would shift railroad and maritime traffic west-east, therefore looked to the port of Trieste with new interest. Moreover, in this same geopolitical area, the death throes of the Ottoman Empire were wearing it away day after day, the Young Turk Revolution of 1908 (called the "Turkish French Revolution") updating its political structure in radically nationalistic terms, foreshadowing dark times for the components of the State that were not part of the Turkish community.

Stimulated by economic competition, protectionism, and the overall reorganization of the State system to correspond to the needs of the modern economy, old and new nationalist movements flourished across the entire continent, no longer evoking the "romantic" or revolutionary ideas of nation, instead aiming at defending and laying claim to the more or less "natural" frontiers essential to national military and economic development. The case of Italy is emblematic, with the emergence of the Associazione Nazionalista Italiana in December 1910 and a new political catch phrase that described the country as a "proletarian nation." This notion was developed by the Tuscan intellectual Enrico Corradini, who wanted to transport the class struggle to the plane of international conflict, since if it were to remain within the borders it would shatter national unity. In his view, with the world divided between dominant nations and proletarian nations, Italy—which was considered proletarian since it suffered foreign domination with the oppression of Italians in Austria-Hungary and the exploitation of workers who had emigrated from the Italian peninsula—needed to start a world revolution in order to conquer the territories, even beyond the natural limit, that would allow it to become a military and economic power.

From this perspective, the problem of Trieste gained new centrality ("our pretty little powder keg," as Marinetti called it) as did that of irredentism, which, distorted in its original principles, needed to cease being nourished by Risorgimento-style idealism, and instead make Trieste the operational base for the imperialistic expansion of Italy to the east.

On the emigration front, Giolitti, who was ordinarily removed from war adventurism, tried to resolve the problem by declaring war on Turkey in 1911, invading Libya [*fig.* 5], which, in a treaty signed in 1912 in Lausanne, became Italy's "fourth shore," with the intention of creating job prospects for the masses of Italian emigrants without scattering them all over the world. In a climate of national exhilaration, where even the socialist poet Giovanni Pascoli proudly noted that the "great proletariat got moving," this triggered a mechanism that revealed the fragility of the Ottoman Empire. This state of affairs pushed the Balkan League (Serbia, Montenegro, Bulgaria, and Greece) to start the Balkan Wars (1912–1913) in order to free itself from the dying Empire and resolve various territorial questions [*figs.* 6–7], which, however, led to conflicts between the members of the League and served as a prelude to World War I. (D.R.)

5.
Artillery troops in the desert during the Italo-Turkish War over Libya between 1911 and 1912

6–7.
Two prints illustrating episodes of the First Balkan War (1912–1913): the arrival of Ferdinand I of Bulgaria in the conquered territories and the flight of the Turkish peasants to Constantinople

In Brief

1901
January 22: Queen Victoria died at her favorite residence, Osborne House, on the Isle of Wight. She was succeeded by her son Edward VII, called the "Peacemaker" for his impressive diplomatic skills.

1901
December 12: Guglielmo Marconi, who later won the Nobel Prize, sent the first radio transmission across the Atlantic Ocean, from Cornwall to Newfoundland, ushering in the era of telecommunications.

1902
8 maggio: nell'isola di Martinica May 8: The volcano La Pelée erupted on the Island of Martinique, destroying the nearby city of Saint-Pierre and killing almost all of its residents, around 30,000 people.

1902
September 1: Georges Méliès' film *A Trip to the Moon*, was screened for the first time. It was the first science-fiction film and is today considered a milestone in the history of cinema.

1903
June 11: King Alexander I of Serbia and his wife were assassinated by soldiers who were opposed to his domestic and foreign policy. The coup d'état brought Peter I, of the Karađorđevic family, to power.

1903
July 1: The first Tour de France began. After six stages, completed by twenty-one cyclists, Maurice Garin from Val d'Aosta won. A two-time winner of the Paris-Roubaix as an Italian, he became French in 1901.

1903
October 10: Emmeline Pankhurst founded the women's suffrage movement in England. For years, the suffragists' demonstrations were suppressed by police charges and arrests.

1903
December 17: The Wright brothers got their propeller biplane off the ground: the first flight, covering 36 meters in 12 seconds, was completed by Orville, assisted by Wilbur on the ground.

1904
June 16: The day on which the events of James Joyce's novel *Ulysses* take place in Dublin; the anniversary (Bloomsday, after the name of the main character, Leopold Bloom) is celebrated every year in various cities.

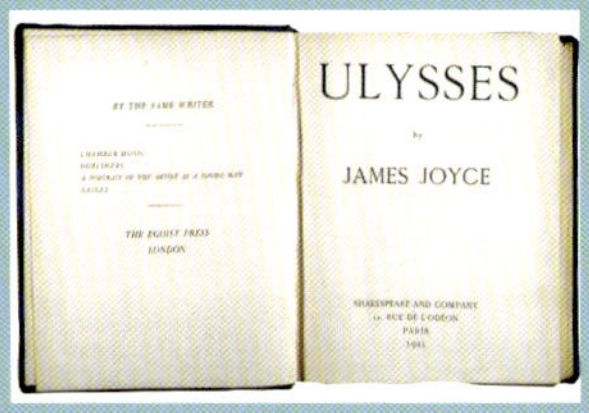

1905
May 28: The Japanese fleet destroyed the Russian navy in the Battle of Tsushima, which decided the Russo-Japanese War. This expanded the sphere of Japanese influence on the mainland and on the sea.

1905
June 30: Albert Einstein, who was still working at the Swiss patent office at the time, published the paper *On the Electrodynamics of Moving Bodies*, in which he laid out the theory of special relativity.

1906
July 21: After the condemnation in 1894 for espionage and treason, and the pardon in 1899, the innocence of the French Jewish Alfred Dreyfus was recognized, and he was reinstated and decorated.

1906
December 10: Baron de Bildt, the Swedish minister in Italy, presented the Nobel Prize in literature to Giosuè Carducci, who was gravely ill and near death, at the poet's house in Bologna.

1907
January 6: The educator Maria Montessori, founder of the teaching method that bears her name, which gives children more independence in the educational process, opened her first school in Rome.

1907
August 1: Organized by the British general Robert Baden-Powell, a hero in the Boer War, a group of twenty boys gathered on Brownsea Island, marking the start of the Boy Scouts

1908
July 24: Dorando Pietri collapsed, exhausted, just as he was about to win the marathon of the London Olympics. Two competition judges helped him to be the first to cross the finish line, for which he was, however, disqualified.

1909
April 6: The explorer Robert Peary reached the geographic North Pole, noting the event in his diary. Today, historians believe that in reality, due to calculation errors, he had actually arrived just shy of his goal.

1911
May 30: The first Indy 500 took place on the Indianapolis Motor Speedway, which had been built two years earlier: the winner was Ray Harroun, driving a Marmon Wasp.

1911
July 24: The American archaeologist Hiram Bingham discovered the ruins of Machu Picchu, the cradle of the Inca civilization, in the Urubamba jungle in the Peruvian Andes, putting the site in the world spotlight.

1911
December 14: The race to the South Pole was won by the Norwegian team of Roald Amundsen, which beat the British team of Robert Falcon Scott by one month; the members of the British team died on the return journey.

1912
February 14: In China, after the abdication of the last emperor, Pu Yi, and the revolutionary leader Sun Yat-sen's refusal to become president of the republic, the post went to Yuan Shikai.

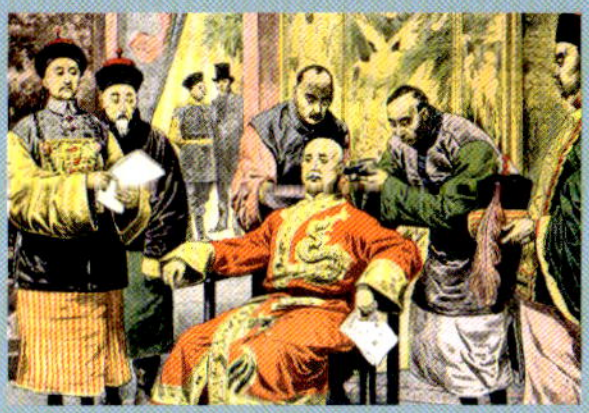

1912
April 15: The ocean liner *Titanic* sank after striking an iceberg. More than 2,200 people were on board, only 706 of whom were saved, finding space on the insufficient number of lifeboats.

1913
June 4: The suffragist Emily Davison was trampled by King George V's horse while attempting an activist stunt at the Epsom Derby. She died four days later from her injuries.

1913
October 10: President Wilson telegraphically triggered the spark that set off the explosion of the Gamboa dike, in order to complete the Panama Canal, which was opened to navigation the following year.

Celebrating Milestones
Anniversaries, Photo Albums, and Diplomas

1881
1913

The minutes of the Management meetings are peppered with references to gifts commissioned for important personnel and company anniversaries. Already in the nineteenth century, it was customary for the company to recognize internal anniversaries, awarding bonuses, presenting diplomas, parchments, books, and portraits, and founding charities in the name of the executives being honored.

For nearly a century, the rooms of the Central Head Office have preserved precious, often elaborately made, objects that were given to Assicurazioni Generali on its various anniversaries [*fig.* 1]. These gifts are naturally to be situated within the context of the various initiatives that the company, aware of the communicative value of celebrations, organized starting with its fiftieth anniversary in 1881. For this first major anniversary, the Management had at first planned to publish a special volume, involving Giuseppe Besso, the deputy secretary-general in Trieste, Vitale Laudi, the manager of the life division, Angelo Bargoni, the secretary in Venice, Wilhelm Lazarus, agent in Hamburg, and Leone Pincherle, agent in Paris, but when the latter two refused, the project was called off. Nevertheless, the company did publish that year a commemorative edition of the financial statement, enriched with tables and graphs, and it had the handwritten deed of partnership of 1831 rebound in a beautiful leather cover. The Historical Archive preserves a few tables with information relative to reserves, shares, and lists of staff members in 1881, which were very likely drawn up for those publications. Also in honor of the fiftieth anniversary, the staff in Trieste, Vienna, Budapest, and Prague and the Italian inspectors were given an extra month's pay, and Giovanni Battista Scrinzi, the sole surviving member of the original group of founders, was presented with a silver cup.

Celebrations were also organized for the company's 75th (1906), 100th (1931), and 125th (1956) anniversaries, for which special volumes were published (*Il funzionamento matematico delle Assicurazioni Generali in Trieste*, 1906; *Il centenario delle Assicurazioni Generali 1831–1931*, 1931; *Insurance in Venice from the origins to the end of the Serenissima*, 1958) as well as special issues of the company's internal periodical, the *Bollettino*; the company's employees again received bonuses.

In addition to the gifts received for its anniversaries, the company also has a small collection of photo albums and finely decorated diplomas, which it commissioned in honor of its executives upon their retirement or for major career anniversaries, especially the twenty-fifth year of service, which are also recorded in many directors' minutes. The oldest diploma preserved in the Archive, from 1880, is documented in a photostatic reproduction contemporary to the cover, presumably made of leather and metal, that enclosed the illustrated pages of the diploma and a large photograph in which the portrait of the man of honor, the general agent of Vienna, Ludwig Mekler, was surrounded by those of the Vienna staff.

Other albums, diplomas, and gifts from the company are of course kept in the personal archives of the recipients. Those of Marco Besso, to take an example, are preserved at the homonymous foundation that he himself instituted. Masino Levi instead bequeathed the company the silver stand given to him in 1872 in celebration of the fortieth financial statement, which is still displayed at the Central Head Office today.

The photographs in the albums preserved in the Archive, dating to the late nineteenth/early twentieth century, most of which are accompanied by signatures or captions identifying the people in the images, are important documents for reconstructing company life, as is also the case for the diplomas and certificates, many of which were followed by a list or the signatures of the office or agency staff.

Some of the honored executives are well known names in the history of the company. This is the case, for example, of Giuseppe Besso, Marco's brother, who long served as secretary-general and then director in Trieste, Edmondo Richetti, also secretary-general, the lawyer Ettore Richetti, who sat for decades on the Generali Board of Directors, and Arturo Kellner, secretary of the Venice Head Office. Others are

now perhaps a bit less known, like Antonio Kenda and Ermanno Gentilli, but their anniversary diplomas provide important testimony of them.
In 1892, Antonio Kenda left Generali to become a department head at the Frankfurter Transport-, Unfall- und Glas-Versicherungs-Gesellschaft, and for the occasion his colleagues in the transport division presented him with a beautiful photo album with a cover in gilded, punched leather decorated in oils with the images of a female figure and flowers [*fig.* 2]. Kenda returned to Assicurazioni Generali in 1904, to become the manager of the transport division. Interestingly, his replacement in 1892 was Edgardo Morpurgo.
From directors' minutes. no. 1904 of February 21, 1895, we learn that for the celebration in honor of Giuseppe Besso's appointment to the post of secretary-general in 1895, the Central Head Office commissioned a life-size photographic portrait of him for the conference room. The company's collection preserves an album filled with photographs and the signatures of the Trieste executives as well as a beautiful diploma, made by the Hoflithographie Haase in Prague, with an image of the Generali building on the Václavské nám and the signatures of the general agency in Prague, both of which were commissioned for that same occasion. The album and the diploma are both enclosed in luxurious leather covers decorated with crests and Besso's monogram.
For Arturo Kellner, who was the secretary of the Venice Head Office from 1892 to 1907, and later director, his twenty-fifth year of service (1899) was honored with a large-format album filled with photographs and the signatures of the proxy representatives, inspectors, and agents operating in Italian territory. His personnel file also preserves a printed dedication certificate decorated with colorful friezes, which might have accompanied the gift.
For Ermanno Gentilli, who became director of Erste Allgemeine Unfall-Versicherungs-Gesellschaft in Vienna in 1890, there are six certificates in honor of his twenty-fifth anniversary, in 1902, that were commissioned by

1.
Photograph taken in a room at the Central Head Office for an anniversary [Trieste, 1890s]
[ASAG, *Versamenti*, scheda 28264]

A handwritten caption identifies some of the people in the photograph, from right to left: Vitale Laudi (who became the manager of the life division in 1876, deputy secretary-general in 1895, and died in 1901), Vitale di San Segré (who became director in 1879 and died in 1900), Carlo Schütz (hired by the Central Head Office in 1879), Arturo Kellner (secretary of the general agency in Prague, and later secretary of the Venice Head Office), and Ermanno Gentilli (head of the general agency in Trieste, and later director of Erste Allgemeine)

2.
Photo album commissioned by the transport division for Antonio Kenda (Trieste, April 27, 1892)
[ASAG, *Versamenti*, scheda 28112]

Generala in Bucharest, Ungarische Sparcassa, the Trieste, Vienna, and Budapest offices, Erste Allgemeine, the agents from Erste in southern Germany and the East department of Assicurazioni Generali (which was under the Trieste agency), all of which were companies or offices where Gentilli was well known. The Archive also preserves Gentilli's officer of the order of Franz Joseph certificate, issued in 1903. Gentilli's anniversary diplomas are vastly different from one another: some are made of paper and decorated to varying degree, while those presented to him by Erste Allgemeine and Generala are far more elaborate. The former is kept in a leather cover embellished with precious stones and enamel plaques depicting views of Vienna and Trieste (by the goldsmith August Klein of Vienna [*fig.* 3]), while the latter, enclosed in a leather, Art Nouveau cover, has an intriguing tree on its interior made up of the photographs of the company's directors and Board members. The diplomas were painted by artists and calligraphers, some of whom also signed their work. Pietro Antonio Sencig, the artist who made the beautiful parchment for the brothers Ettore and Edmondo Richetti, trained at the Fine Arts Academy of Vienna and made a considerable mark on local painting as a poster designer, portraitist, and fresco painter in Trieste and Udine. For Ettore Richetti, in 1914, he painted an illustrated diploma commissioned by the Public Charity Office in Trieste in honor of the twenty-five years of free legal assistance that Richetti had provided to the organization [*fig.* 4]. Ettore Richetti, a lawyer and prominent industrialist, as well as a member of the company's Board of Directors, was a leading figure of the Trieste national-liberal party and deputy chairman of the City Council. For Edmondo Richetti, Sencig was commissioned by the company to decorate a small booklet with eight parchment pages comprising a title page and the transcription of the speech made in his honor on March 26, 1913 by Abramo Sabato Besso, the manager for the East department, followed by a list of the names of the staff of the Trieste and Venice Head Offices and numerous agencies, serving today as a valuable source for the company history. (R.S.)

3.
Diploma commissioned by Erste Allgemeine for Ermanno Gentilli in honor of his twenty-fifth anniversary with the company; detail of the leather and metal cover with views of Vienna and Trieste (Vienna, 1902) [ASAG, *Versamenti*, scheda 62407]

4.
Diploma for Ettore Richetti, calligrapher Pietro Antonio Sencig (Trieste, 1914) [ASAG, *Versamenti*, scheda 9062]

Long Live the Secretaries
Edmondo Richetti, the Pacifist

1895
1914

One of the most prominent Jewish families in Trieste, the Richettis held important posts not only in city life but also in the Assicurazioni Generali administration, for at least three generations. Eugenio Richetti, who dedicated a long career to the insurance industry, was a Generali agent during the first half of the nineteenth century in Lemberg [Lviv], Galicia, where one of his three sons, Egidio, was born in 1855. Egidio also worked for the company, first in the Fiume [Rijeka] agency, until 1895, and then in Prague, until his retirement in 1921. Eugenio's other sons, Ettore and Edmondo, held primary positions at the Central Head Office: Ettore, a lawyer, was a member of the Board of Directors from 1896 to 1915, the year in which he became director, while Edmondo served as secretary for nearly two decades [*fig.* 1]. Edmondo's son Francesco, and Egidio's son, who was named Edmondo after his uncle, also worked for the company.

Edmondo Richetti was an exponent of the Trieste economic aristocracy defined by the scholar Anna Millo as the "power élite" (*L'élite del potere a Trieste. Una biografia collettiva 1891–1938* [Milano: Franco Angeli, 1989]): he was the head of the Jewish Community, immediately after his brother Ettore, and was one of the few members of the middle class to be made a knight (in 1904, he became Richetti de Terralba). An independent entrepreneur (he was, among other things, the founder of Alba, the first car manufacturer in Trieste), he was the chairman of the local Chamber of Commerce, where he represented the company. His biography seems to perfectly embody, and therefore express, the complexity of Trieste during the Hapsburg period.

There are numerous sources for him in the Historical Archive, which are useful for reconstructing his career at the company while at the same time shedding light on many lesser-known aspects. His personnel file and, especially, the directors' minutes mark out his history at Assicurazioni Generali, where he arrived in 1883 when he was twenty-seven years old, after having worked at Foncière in Budapest. His first posts at Generali were linked to Carlo Levi: Richetti was a department head at Erste Österreichische Allgemeine Unfall-Versicherungs-Gesellschaft in Vienna (a daughter company specialized in the accident division and the first subsidiary founded by Generali), when Levi was its director. In 1884, when Levi stepped down, Richetti took his place, as also happened in 1890, when Levi left the post of deputy secretary at the Central Head Office (Richetti's letter announcing his candidacy is preserved in his personnel file). Richetti thus began to assist secretary-general Giuseppe Besso, receiving a further delegation of powers at the end of 1893, and becoming secretary-general in 1895, upon Besso's promotion to the post of director. The secretary-general was a critical figure for the company, representing the link between management and administration, since a member of the Management, the Board of Directors and the head of a secretariat with a vast range of functions, which was then called the general secretariat and handled relations with non-Italian agencies and the subsidiaries, managed relations with the banks, and supervised the staff. The secretary-general also represented the company at some of the subsidiaries operating both inside and outside the Empire and at the industry organizations (Comité des Assureurs Maritimes de Paris) [*fig.* 2], advanced proposals, and presented research and reports, combining unquestionable technical expertise with the necessary skill for mediating within the Board. Richetti was secretary-general until 1909 and director-in-charge—when the statutory reforms reinstated the post of chairman the name of this function was changed—until 1913, just before his retirement and death, in August 1914. When he presented his resignation during his final months at the company, the Board decided to promote him to the post of director.

The most direct evidence of Richetti's activity is found in the directors' minutes and the volumes of the secretary-general's correspondence. It can be dif-

1.
Photograph of Edmondo Richetti when he was thirty-nine years old, in the album given to Giuseppe Besso by the Central Head Office when he was appointed director (Trieste, January 14, 1895)
[ASAG, *Versamenti*, scheda 28112]

ficult to perceive the presence of different visions for the industry in minutes, due to their neutral tone, but we know from Anna Millo's reconstructions that there were heated disagreements between Marco Besso and the Trieste side of the Board over Besso's idea to concentrate Generali's Italian portfolio in a specially created company. The idea for the new company was proposed in 1906, 1911, and 1914 ("Il capitalismo triestino e l'impero," in *Storia economica e sociale di Trieste*, vol. II, eds. Roberto Finzi, Loredana Panariti and Giovanni Panjek [Trieste: Lint, 2003]). Richetti played a key role in this matter, sitting on the committees to study the technical aspects of the proposal in both 1906 and 1911. The minutes reveal that he took a conservative position with respect to the project and was not in favor of it, although as secretary he "did his best to reconcile the ideas of his colleagues in Trieste with those of Besso" (directors' minutes no. 2264 of September 4, 1906), participating in drafting the plan, while, however, also recommending that it be unofficially submitted to the Austrian government before presenting it to the Board of Directors. The directors' minutes of September 4 reports the debate over the plan, with those against it including the directors Camillo Bozza, Fortunato Vivante, Emanuele Romanin-Jacur, and Giuseppe Da Zara, the deputy director Giacomo Fano, and Richetti, who in the end decided to vote against it because he shared the concern that a new Italian company would compromise Generali's international status. The Management decided "that it is sufficient to take steps when the need to do so is unavoidable," and at the subsequent session, Besso formally withdrew the project, presenting it anew in 1911, immediately prior to the approval of the State monopoly of life insurance law. At the meeting on October 12, 1911, taking note of Giolitti's offensive position on insurance companies, Besso proposed setting up a seven-member committee to study the legal, accounting, and financial aspects of creating an Italian company. Besides Besso, Bozza, Gioberti Luzzati, Edgardo Morpurgo, Romanin-Jacur, Vivante, Giuseppe Luzzatto,

COMITÉ DES ASSUREURS MARITIMES

DE PARIS

DIPLÔME D'AGENT

En vertu des pouvoirs dont ils sont investis, les soussignés, Directeurs des Compagnies d'Assurances maritimes, à Paris, attestent à tous ceux que cela peut intéresser qu'ils ont nommé Monsieur Edmond Richetti leur Agent à Trieste (Autriche) sous la condition expresse qu'il demeurera soumis aux instructions générales ci-après, instructions qu'il devra exhiber dans toutes les occasions où il interviendra afin que les assurés ou leurs représentants puissent apprécier avec exactitude l'étendue de ses pouvoirs.

Paris, le Quatre Mai mil neuf cent

2.
The diploma with which the Comité des Assureurs Maritimes elected Edmondo Richetti their agent in Trieste (Paris, May 4, 1900) [ASAG, *Versamenti*, scheda 8068]

and Richetti were asked to sit on the committee. The minutes make no further mention of this committee, however, until 1914, when Besso raised the issue once again. Richetti was no longer with them by that point, but the Trieste faction was still very strong and in the end prevailed over Besso's idea.

Richetti's activity is documented, as has been noted, in numerous volumes of the central secretariat. In addition to the more properly administrative correspondence exchanged with Assicurazioni Generali agencies, other companies, banks, businesses, and private individuals, there are also, solely in the case of Richetti, collections of correspondence with other important figures in the company, in particular Marco Besso and Arturo Kellner, who were, respectively, director and secretary of the Venice Head Office. In 1913, in honor of his work, the officers of the Central Head Office and of the foreign offices created a foundation in Richetti's name, to support employees' children attending university, in particular those studying business. The foundation was active after 1923 and at least until 1937. The parchment diploma celebrating his retirement commemorates the important social measures for employees implemented during his term of office, including Sunday rest, at the end of 1903, profit sharing, and adaptation to labor law with the first modern retirement plan [*fig.* 3].

One of the last documents in Richetti's personnel file is of special interest: a printed invitation to attend the founding meeting for the association Europäischer Staatenbund, which he promoted in Vienna in May 1914 [*fig.* 4]. On the eve of the outbreak of World War I, Richetti invited all of the citizens of Europe to join the Europäischer Staatenbund, on the premise that all of the European populations, regardless of class, gender, or religion, wanted peace and unity between the European States, to keep the specter of war at bay.

"Organisieren wir uns in eine grosse Vereinigung" ("Let's organize ourselves into a great association"), with members from every corner of Europe, was his battle cry. His appeal began with these incisive words: "All of the people of Europe, regardless of origin, want peace. All of them, regardless of class, would be filled with joy to see the European States united and joined together, to keep the horrors of war at bay. The people are urgently asking for social reform and improved economic relations." And: "We do not want war, we want peace. We do not want the monstrous expense of armies, which lead the people into poverty. We want economic recovery and well-being" (translation).

In the fifteen-page pamphlet, which was printed by the Buchdruckerei of the Mekhitarists (Armenian Christians) in Vienna, Richetti laid out a detailed explanation of the social and economic reasons that made the "Union" so urgently needed, and concluded with the articles of the association's statute. The association's four main goals were: disarmament, the institution of obligatory life insurance for all citizens, the introduction of single, direct taxation, and the free circulation of necessities. Richetti invited anyone who was interested to get in contact with him, providing the address for his home in Vienna, Wohllebengasse 15, near the Belvedere, to organize the first general members' meeting and elect the board of directors, once the statute received approval from the competent authorities.

The pamphlet was incredibly modern and almost prophetic, seeming to anticipate the spirit of the European Community by half a century, in its lofty aim to serve as an antidote to war. It was a European union that started from below, directly representing the citizens, not the States, and was designed as a means of compelling the European governments, peacefully, without danger of war or anarchy, to make a drastic change in the direction of their economic policies. It is a complex document, and many things all at once: it is full of idealism but also packed with statistics and numbers; it was published in Vienna, but the British Prime Minister at the time, H.H. Asquith, is mentioned more frequently than the emperor; it strives to

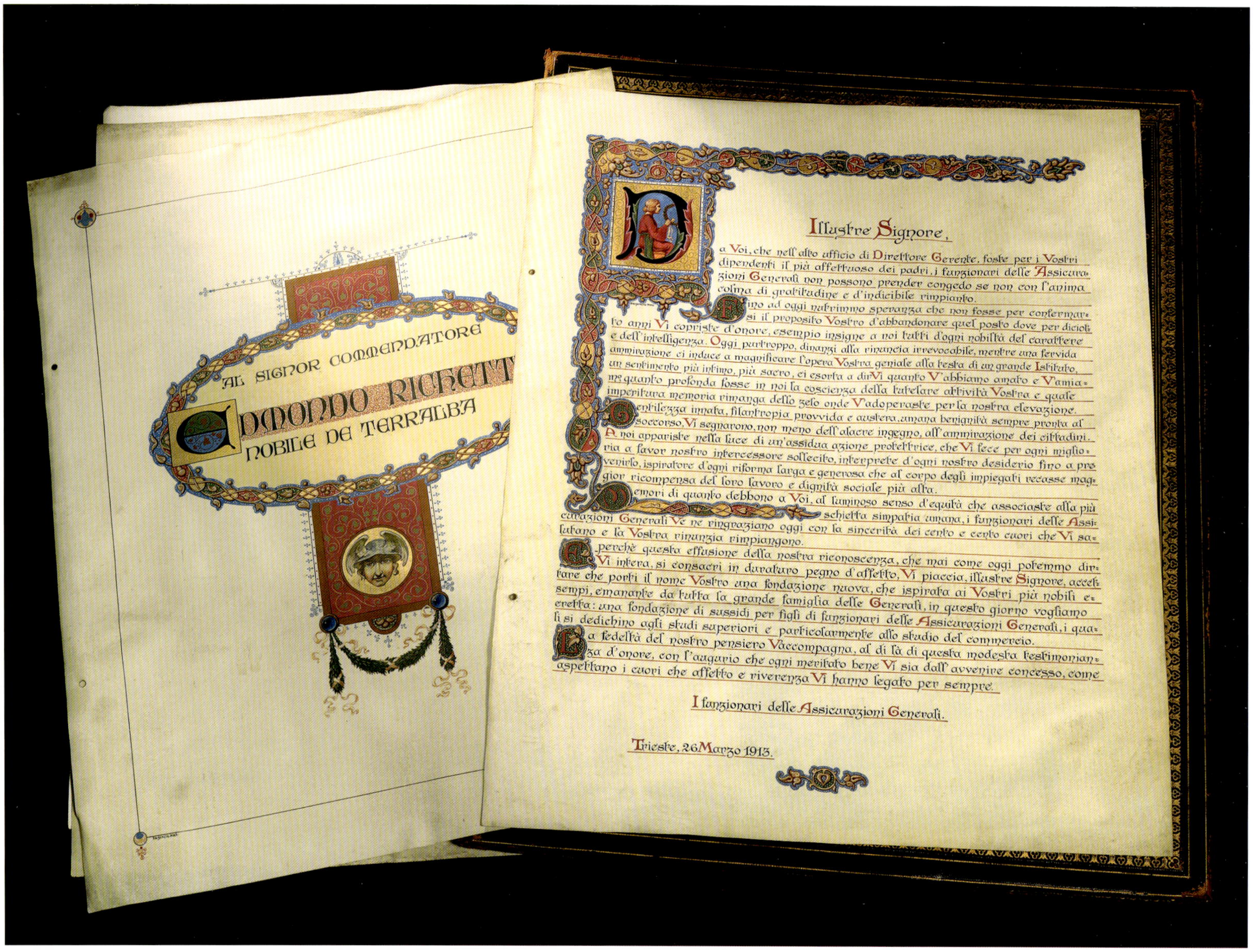

3.
Diploma in honor of Edmondo Richetti, commissioned from the calligrapher Pietro Antonio Sencig by the Central Head Office for Richetti's retirement (Trieste, 1913) [ASAG, *Versamenti*, scheda 9062]

situate disruptive socio-economic changes in a domain of peaceful, democratic normalcy; and it declares itself opposed to revolution and war, but in its pacifism was in fact revolutionary.

The Verein Europäischer Staatenbund promoted by Richetti doubtless developed outside Generali, and derived from his own personal beliefs, but it does have some connections with the company. Besides the fact that there are traces of it in the Generali Historical Archive, the proposal to make life insurance obligatory for all citizens, in order to guarantee collective welfare, is certainly linked to his experience as an insurer.

The idea for the Verein seems to have first emerged in 1903, it being very likely that it was Richetti who underlined an article in his office's copy of the March 25, 1903 edition of Vienna's *Neue Freie Presse*, "Zur Schaffung eines mitteleuropäischen Zollbündnisses" (For the creation of a middle-European customs union), which was inspired by the words of the Austro-Hungarian Foreign Minister in 1897: "[...] the European people must unite, to defend the premises at the basis of their vital force" (translation).

From an ideal perspective, the pamphlet certainly owes something to the pacific ideas circulating during that period. Many European countries were home at the time to peace movements and associations based on the model of the International Peace and Arbitration Association founded in London by Hodgson Pratt in order to resolve disputes between States at international arbitral courts, rather than through war. The figure that comes to mind is Bertha von Suttner, an Austrian writer and journalist, who is famous for the novel *Die Waffen nieder* (*Lay Down Your Arms!*), which was published in 1889 and then translated and published in numerous other countries. The winner of the Nobel Peace Prize in 1905 (briefly Alfred Nobel's secretary, and then his friend for many many years, she might have been the inspiration behind instituting the prize), Suttner worked for peace, promoting and coordinating peace organizations in numerous countries, from the 1880s until her death in June 1914, just before the assassination of Franz Ferdinand. Suttner, together with her husband, fought against anti-Semitism, she was the chairwoman of the Österreichische Gesellschaft der Friedensfreunden, which was founded in 1891, the co-founder, with the publicist Alfred H. Fried, of the German society for peace in 1892, and the vice-chairwoman of the central office of the Peace Society in Bern. Among other things, in a letter written to Nobel on April 11, 1894, Suttner mentioned that she had given a talk at the Schillerverein in Trieste and set up a section of the association immediately after in the same city. In 1896, Suttner set up an association for peace in Budapest, and one of the members of its management committee was the writer Mór Jókai, who was also on the Generali Board of Directors and doubtless knew Richetti (for all of the references to Alfred Nobel and Bertha von Suttner, see *Un'amicizia disvelata. Carteggio 1883–1896*, ed. Edelgard Biedermann [Bergamo: Moretti & Vitali editori, 2013]).

The affinity between the Europäischer Staatenbund and Suttner's work is particularly clear in the motion presented by Suttner, together with the pacifists Ernesto Teodoro Moneta (from Italy) and Samuel James Capper (from Great Britain) in 1892, at the Fourth Universal Peace Congress in Bern, titled "Europäischer Staatenbund". Richetti's association and the Suttner-Moneta-Capper motion shared both their premises and their goals, in particular the avant-garde idea to form an association of European States in order to keep the peace, much earlier than the founding of the United Nations and the European Union. For Suttner, peace among the European States was a first step, to be later extended all over the world, and she believed that it was a productive idea, even if it was often distorted, with the federation of European States with the model of the United States. In 1913, Suttner joyfully listed all of the pacifistic initiatives aiming at a "European Federation," particularly since at that time the danger of war was increasingly imminent (Brigitte Hamann, *Bertha von Suttner. Ein Leben für den Frieden* [Munich: Piper, 1991]).

Nevertheless, Suttner's name does not appear among the many references cited by Richetti in his pamphlet, nor does Richetti's name appear in the archives of the European peace movements, preserved in the United Nation's Library in Geneva. In his pamphlet, Richetti clearly expresses an aversion to war, but this, as with his distaste for revolutions and anarchy, was economically motivated: "[…] the achievement of this goal does not require 420 million Europeans to become incensed with their governments, nor does it require revolution or anarchy, but rather emphasis on a right shared by all Europeans […], the right to promote that which can be as useful to governments as it would be to citizens" (translation: 1).

Richetti's reflections on the stagnation created by decades of "armed peace," on the crystallization of the fronts of the two triple alliances (the "zwei Dreibünden"), and on the economic and human resources diverted in vain for a mad arms race were similar to the positions that had been taken by others, like the British essayist Norman Angell, who won the Nobel Peace Prize in 1933, and was in fact cited in Richetti's pamphlet: "Norman Angell observes, hitting the mark, that the costs, economic difficulties, and consequences of war have increased beyond measure with respect to the past" (translation: 8).

Or that of the American philanthropist Andrew Carnegie (who was also one of Suttner's patrons), who wrote the book *The Empire of Business*, which Richetti paraphrased: "Capital, product, and work are three parts of a whole, and together they work wonders, but separate they generate catastrophes. Can one maintain that the base of capital is tied to the other two, product and work […], if 22% of the entire sum of the needs of the European States is used for armies and the navy?" (translation: 9).

While the declared foundation for Richetti's ideas was drawn from writers, theoreticians, and scientists with various points of view, but in all cases far removed from Suttner's radical spirit, the destiny of the Europäischer Staatenbund brought Richetti and Suttner's experiences fatally close. Suttner died on June 21, 1914, before the events in Sarajevo, and with her death and the start of the war, her plan to organize a peace conference in September 1914 collapsed. The Vienna archives seem to preserve only a single trace of Richetti's association. In the Haus-, Hof- und Staatsarchiv of the Österreichisches Staatsarchiv in Vienna, there is a record of a letter written on June 22, 1914 by the Russian ambassador in Vienna to the Austrian Foreign Minister, which attests to Richetti's desire to "submit" the "pamphlet he had written" to the Russian Czar (HHStA MdÄ AR Fach 18, Karton 48, Einsendungen an fremde Souveräne Nr. 273/1914). In the letter, the embassy asked the Ministry for Information about Richetti and about the possibility of carrying out his request. We know that the paperwork arrived at the Ministerium des kaiserlichen und königlichen Hauses und Äußern on July 2, but not whether it came to anything; most probably it did not.

The name of Nicholas II was not fortuitous: although up until then he had not enjoyed fame as an illuminato, at the end of the nineteenth century, many pinned their hopes on him, Suttner included, when he supported an international conference on disarmament in 1898 (see Antonella Salomoni, "Lev. N. Tolstoj and Bertha von Suttner," in *Parlare di pace in tempo di guerra. Bertha von Suttner e altre voci del pacifismo europeo*, proceedings of the seminar, Rovereto, November 4, 2014, ed. Paola Maria Filippi [Rovereto: Accademia Roveretana degli Agiati, 2015: 129–143]). The conference was held in The Hague in 1899, and the representatives of numerous States participated, but no agreement on limiting arms was made. Many pacifists, including Tolstoy, harbored no great illusions about Nicholas II's plan, although Richetti seems to have considered the czar to have been at least an interesting interlocutor, even many years later.

Sarajevo also had an impact on Richetti's plan, since shortly after, World War I broke out, with Russia on the side opposite Austria and Germany. Richetti died on August 12, 1914, thus living to witness the criss-crossing declarations of war between the main European States. The file preserved in the Haus-, Hof- und Staatsarchiv concludes with the record, dated September 18, of Richetti's death on August 12, 1914, in Payerbach-Reichenau in Niederösterreich, near Vienna.

The Europäischer Staatenbund association left very few traces: besides the founding document, which is preserved in both the Generali Historical Archive and the Österreichische Nationalbibliothek in Vienna, the only other surviving evidence seems to be the file in the Haus, Hof- und Staatsarchiv.

A magazine with the same name, *Europäischer Staatenbund*, but without any documented connections to Richetti's project, published during the summer months of 1914 and also printed by the Mekhitarists, was presented as the mouthpiece for a homonymous association. The magazine's editors were "Fr. X. von Mayer und E. M. Vusio." Recent research has revealed that Eugenio Maria Vusio was a Hapsburg loyalist. Vusio was a former priest and an adventurer, who enjoyed a certain degree of support, prior to 1914, in Viennese military circles, thanks to which he was able to found a small monarchist association (La Società Monarchica) in Trieste (Almerigo Apollonio, *La "belle Époque" e il tramonto dell'Impero asburgico sulle rive dell'Adriatico (1902–1918)*, 1, *Gli anni prebellici (1902–1914)* [Trieste: Deputazione di storia patria per la Venezia Giulia, 2014: 289]). We lose all trace of Vusio in Trieste in 1914, but he resurfaces again in Vienna after the outbreak of World War I: the third issue of *Europäischer Staatenbund*, published in September 1914, included a poster with a call, in Italian, to take out Austrian government bonds. When war broke out, nationalism therefore seems to have gotten the upper hand over Richetti's pacifist, international vision, and the idea of being citizens of the world, as was also the case on the political front and in a few cases within the pacifist movements themselves. (R.S.)

4.
The Europäischer Staatenbund association pamphlet (Vienna, May 1914)
[ASAG, *Direzione centrale, Servizio del personale, Posizioni personali*, U2GE042621]

Gründung des Vereines

„Europäischer Staatenbund"

in Wien.

Einladung.

Die p. t. Herren, welche als Mitglieder dem neuen Vereine beizutreten wünschen, werden höflichst ersucht, dem Gefertigten ihren Beitritt anzumelden. Sobald die Satzungen von der kompetenten Behörde genehmigt sein werden, wird der Gefertigte alle Einsender verständigen, wo und wann die erste Generalversammlung stattfinden soll, in welcher die Wahl der Vereinsdirektion und des Schiedsgerichtes auf Grund der Mehrheit der abgegebenen Stimmen vorzunehmen ist.

Wien, im Mai 1914.

Edmond Richetti Edler von Terralba
Wien, IV. Wohllebengasse 15.

Aufruf.

Alle europäischen Völker, ohne Unterschied des Stammes, wünschen den Frieden. Alle Völker, ohne Klassenunterschied, würden mit Freuden die europäischen Staaten miteinander vereinigt und verbunden sehen, damit die Schrecken eines Krieges vermieden werden. Alle Völker verlangen dringend eine Sozialreform und eine Besserung der wirtschaftlichen Verhältnisse.

Die Milliarden von Schulden, welche die Staaten erdrücken, und die Milliarden von Kosten für die Erhaltung der Heere beängstigen 420 Millionen Europäer, welche, ganz verloren in der Finsternis einer vollständig unsicheren Zukunft, sich voll Schrecken fragen, was für eine entsetzliche Katastrophe zu erwarten ist, wenn ein europäischer Krieg oder eine Revolution ausbrechen sollte.

Angesichts dieses düsteren Horizonts, voll gewitterschweren Wolken, hat der gegenwärtige Premierminister Englands Lord Asquith den Europäern einen sicheren Weg gezeigt, als er erklärte, dass, um das zu erreichen, was ganz Europa herbeisehnt und will, die Völker selbst sich organisieren müssen, um die eigenen Regierungen zu zwingen, ihren Willen zu erfüllen.

Um nun diesen Zweck zu erreichen, ist wohl nicht nötig, dass 420 Millionen Europäer sich gegen ihre Regierungen empören; ist nicht nötig, die Revolution oder Anarchie auszurufen, sondern nur jenes Recht zur Geltung zu bringen, das alle Europäer besitzen; jenes Recht, das alle Staaten ihnen feierlich gewährt haben; das Recht, das zu fordern, was sowohl den Regierungen als auch den Staatsbürgern sich nützlich erweisen kann.

Man will nicht den Krieg, sondern den Frieden haben: man will nicht die ungeheuren Auslagen für die Heere, welche die Völker an den Bettelstab bringen, sondern den wirtschaftlichen Aufschwung und den Wohlstand der Völker. Nun denn, das, was man wünscht, das, was gefordert wird, das haben die 420 Millionen Europäer in ihren Händen; es ist ihr unumschränkter Besitz, den die Staaten und Regierungen weder unterdrücken, noch aufheben oder in Beschlag nehmen können.

Organisieren wir uns in eine grosse Vereinigung, welche ihre Teilnehmer in jeder noch so kleinen Ortschaft besitzt, die von Europäern bewohnt wird.

Organisieren wir uns, das ist unsere Schlachtordnung, die auch den Regierungen nicht unwillkommen sein wird.

Edmondo Richetti

1857
1914

Edmondo Richetti was born into a Jewish family on March 23, 1857 in Trieste—although his birth and that of his two brothers are recorded in Gorizia's registry. His father, Eugenio Richetti, was a native of Gorizia, but in those years lived in Lemberg [Lviv]. He later moved to Trieste, where in 1850, he had already married a local, Emilia Padoa. He was a businessman and an agent for Assicurazioni Generali in Lemberg. The years in Gorizia, however, constitute only a small part of the family history (the details of which are not yet fully clear based on the current research) between 1851 (the year of birth of the first child, Tommaso, said Ettore) and 1857, the year that the census shows the family moved to Trieste. Moreover, their presence there does not appear to have been uninterrupted given that the second son Egidio, who was also registered as born in Gorizia in 1855, was in fact born in Lemberg, as the personnel file of Assicurazioni Generali (where he would be employed in Fiume and in Prague, during the World War I) testifies.

The decision to transfer to Trieste on a permanent basis dates back to 1856, when Eugenio Richetti was offered a more promising role as the secretary-general for the Nuova Società Commerciale d'Assicurazioni. This was a small company, established in Trieste in 1835, and operating in the transport sector. Despite the challenging financial climate for the insurance business, around 1856, the company enlisted the support of Vienna's Creditanstalt to increase its share capital and expand into other sectors including that of life insurance. The ambitions of the Nuova Società Commerciale d'Assicurazioni went unrewarded and after controversial vicissitudes, in 1866 the company went into liquidation. Eugenio Richetti found employment as the representative in Trieste for the Pester Versicherungs-Anstalt, an established Hungarian company. At the turn of the 1880s he appears well connected to the city's financial circles, partaking in the conversations about overcoming the free port crisis (which was abolished in 1891), and alongside commerce, to undertake the road towards industrialization. The notable social and professional ascent of his children, specifically that of Edmondo and Ettore, was therefore due to the family's already well established social status.

Edmondo Richetti cuts his teeth in the insurance business in Pester's Budapest headquarters, where he is sent in 1873, at just sixteen years of age, soon after finishing his diploma at the Accademia di Commercio in Trieste; a well-established professional institution (built in 1817), which had updated its *curriculum* in response to the demands of economic growth, training managers and executives for the banking and insurance sectors.

Edmondo remained at Pester, which merged with Foncière in 1879, for ten years. In 1883, after consolidating his experience in a market considered as established as the Hungarian one, he joins Assicurazioni Generali; first in Venice, as the director of the Italian accidents sector, and shortly thereafter in Vienna where, in 1884, he becomes director of the Austrian affiliated company specializing in accidents, the Erste Österreichische Allgemeine Unfall-Versicherungs-Gesellschaft. In 1890 he takes on the role of deputy secretary-general in the Trieste Central Head Office and in 1895, he is appointed secretary-general. In 1909 he is the first to be appointed director-in-charge and in June 1913, having already retired, he is co-opted into the Central Head Office by the last wave of directors before the war [*fig.* 1].

His thirty-year career coincides with a period of immense international growth for the company; an expansion that lead to the development of a corporate structure, fostering new systems to effectively implement the Management and the Board's powers. Unlike most of the company's leaders, Edmondo Richetti did not emerge from within, but was sourced externally, bringing with him specialized skills and knowledge that were recognized as strategic for the development of the business, and which he deepened and refined over time while also attaining higher positions. The title of director-in-charge, the

1.
The Management in Palazzo Geiringer (Trieste, [1906–1910]) [ASAG, *Versamenti*]

First to the left is Giovanni Costi, behind him is Edgardo Morpurgo, first to the right is Edmondo Richetti and behind him is Carlo Schütz, second seated from the right is Giacomo Fano, third from the right is Gioberti Luzzatti, and Camillo Bozza is at the center

first in the company's history, was introduced to the charter in 1909 and can be considered a formal acknowledgement of what in practice had already happened, namely the transformation of Assicurazioni Generali into a modern company, the technical and administrative management of which were guided by senior staff members that were separated from the property. The latter entitled instead the strategy and the control. Richetti represents the advent of a new generation of managers, technicians employed as distinct from the property.

Richetti's responsibilities were operational and concerned fiduciary powers that included the representation of Assicurazioni Generali on several foreign affiliate councils and on the Boards that were of strategic importance to the city's economy. Such were the roles invested by him prior to the outbreak of World War I: director of the first section of Österreichischer Lloyd, president of Veritas, president of the Società fra i Proprietari di Stabili, president of the Stock Exchange delegation, and president of the Chamber of Commerce. Next to these roles, he also managed his private interests of entrepreneur, having inherited a series of investments set up by his father Eugenio in the industrial processing sector (husking rice, oil mills, pasta factories), which had developed alongside the harbor, and which in the years before the war were the cause of financial woes.

Therefore, one may say that with regard to Assicurazioni Generali's shareholders, who comprised the company's controlling bodies despite the diverse functions of each, Richetti was to all effects and purposes part of the same social circle and shared their financial and cultural interests, with a set of values and beliefs that governed his actions within the life of finance and society.

His successful business career and the loyalty he expressed towards the Hapsburg State were rewarded with public recognition. In 1896 the emperor awarded Richetti the "Order of the Iron Crown Third Class" for his advice to the government on the 1887 law for compulsory, State work-accident insurance. In 1904 he was elevated to the rank of nobility with the title "Edler von Terralba."

The impact of his participation in the city's social life also manifested in his leadership among the Jewish Community, in which his father Eugenio and his brother Ettore also had played significant roles, and on the governing bodies of which Edmondo was present from 1902. At that time, the incessant emergence of anti-Semitism caused unrest, anticipation and much concern among Trieste's Jewish Community, which in a testimony to its secular assimilation into the city, in 1912 inaugurated a new temple under the leadership of Edmondo Richetti.

Equally significant was the life path of his elder brother Ettore as one of Trieste's most eminent lawyers, who in 1901, was elected president of the local Chamber of Lawyers. In his capacity as lawyer he was a board member for Trieste's most significant companies; from the shipyards of the Stabilimento Tecnico Triestino and Cantiere San Rocco, to the Società di Navigazione Austro-Americana e Fratelli Cosulich, to the Società di Spedizioni Adriatica, and Assicurazioni Generali, whose Board he joined in 1896 before being appointed director in February 1915. As vice president of Trieste's City Council, he was a well-known member of the national-liberal party, and a supporter of the Italian bourgeoisie's nationality and language in Trieste. A few months after Italy entered the war, Ettore Richetti sought refuge in Milan. Being wanted by the Austrian police for being a "fanatical Irredentist," in 1916 he is struck from Trieste's register of lawyers.

Unlike his brother, Edmondo identified with the empire's multinational institutions and its conservative but liberal culture, which typified many exponents of the ruling class; a culture that did not embrace democratic values but was nonetheless imbued with humanitarian sentiments and ideals of peaceful coexistence for the sake of a common civilization. Considering himself both European and cosmopolitan, at the outbreak of World War I Edmondo Richetti was convinced that peace in Europe should be preserved at all costs. From Vienna, where he was based, in May 1914 he promoted a manifesto for the establishment of an organization called "Europäischer Staatenbund." The individual European peoples needed to mobilize from the ground up in order to urge their governments to keep peace and avert the catastrophe of war, which would interrupt the continent's path toward progress, leading to revolution and anarchy. Richetti did not live to see the fulfilment of the catastrophe of war, which he had predicted. He dies in Reichenau near Vienna on August 12, 1914.

Sources

ASAG. *Direzione Centrale, Servizio del personale, Posizioni personali.* U2GE042621, personnel file of Edmondo Richetti, 1886–1926; personnel file of Egidio Richetti, 1891–1948; U2GE042620, personnel file of Ettore Ricchetti, 1896–1915.

ASAG. *Versamenti*, scheda 6960, appointment of Eugenio Richetti for the Nuova Società Commerciale d'Assicurazioni, Trieste, 1856.

ASCET. *Registri delle nascite e dei matrimoni, ad nomina* Richetti e Padoa.

ASCET. *Registri delle nascite della comunità di Gorizia, ad nomina* Richetti.

AST. *Imperial Regia Luogotenenza del Litorale (1850–1918), Atti presidiali.* b. 187, anno 1896, categoria 1/24.1, *Onorificenze*, K.K. Polizei-Directions-Präsidium, Triest, 14. April 1896; b. 273, anno 1904, categoria 1/24.1, *Onorificenze*, K.K. Statthalterei Präsidium in Triest, Triest, 22. Februar 1904; b. 308, categoria 1-b/2, *Casa imperiale, distinzioni, medaglie d'onore, titoli di corte, restituzione di ordini*, K.K. Statthalterei Präsidium in Triest, Triest, 17. Mai 1907; ibid., *Atti presidiali riservati*, b. 6, fasc. 36, K.K. Finanzminister, Wien, am 10 Februar 1912.

ASMAE. *Rappresentanza italiana a Vienna (1862–1938)*, b. 245, Präsidium des k.k. Ministeriums des Innern, 12. Dezember 1916.

[Richetti, Eugenio]. *Studj sull'industria in Trieste*. Trieste: Herrmanstorfer, 1881.

Kohári, Gustav. *Erinnerungen eines alten ungarischen Assureurs*. Wien: Verlag der Oesterreichischen Revue, *sine anno* [1906]: 104–116.

"La morte del comm. Edmondo Richetti." *Il Piccolo* August 13, 1914.

Bibliography

Il centenario delle Assicurazioni Generali, 1831–1931, [edited by Giuseppe Stefani]. Trieste: Editrice la Compagnia, 1931: 187–188.

Altieri Biagi, Orietta *La comunità ebraica di Gorizia. Caratteristiche demografiche, economiche e sociali (1778–1900)*. Udine: Del Bianco, 1985: 225–228.

Millo, Anna. *L'élite del potere a Trieste. Una biografia collettiva, 1891–1938*. Milan: Franco Angeli, 1989.

Catalan, Tullia. *La Comunità ebraica di Trieste (1781–1914). Politica, società e cultura*. Trieste: Lint, 2000.

(A.M.)

Generali Italy
Marco Besso and the Plan for a Great Italian Company

1906
1915

In response to a proposal to form a transport business partnership with German insurers, Marco Besso categorically refused to work under the "German label." As he wrote in his *Autobiografia*, his strong Italian spirit and stance "might have been judged by some as detrimental to the interests of the Company [...]. But not only was it not detrimental, it would appear that I was in the right, as clearly demonstrated by the Government's protection of us throughout the entire Great War, as a consequence of my unchanging, perennial, and I can now say, visionary position. The tricks of those who, whether due to ignorance or bad faith, wanted to use our legal status in Austria to pass us off as an Austrian company, put us under a union and so on, were discredited when we, figuratively speaking, sailed into the port, the port of liberated Trieste, on November 6, 1918, more appreciated and respected than ever. But this position, which was also that of my predecessors in Venice, gratifying our personal sentiments, provided the company with legitimate defense for its appreciable interests."

In 1877, Besso was called to Trieste to take the post of secretary-general. After about ten years, he handed over the position to his brother, Giuseppe, who had been working with him for a few years. At the same time, he joined the company's administration [*fig.* 1], which also elected him to the post of technical consultant (1885). This gave him greater freedom of action, in turn allowing him to "do more for the Company and in a more methodical way, than I would have been able to do without that freedom."

On relations with the Austrian government, he continued: "in regard to my work as Generali Director, my demeanor towards the Government of Vienna, [...], was always appropriate, and nor did I ever have reason for complaint about its behavior towards me [...]. My sentiments were, however, known, since I of course defended Italian nationality, always on legal grounds but to the point that, particularly in the final years, when I needed to go to Vienna, [...] to the Interior Ministry, which, for political reasons, oversaw all Companies indiscriminately, the head of service said to me in Italian: 'And here is our unredeemed man!'" He also recalled experiencing the following "insignificant" episode during his period in Trieste. Called to court to give evidence in a dispute that was being debated within the monarchy, he refused to testify in German, declaring "in Trieste I cannot help but use our language." In the end, the president of the court yielded on condition that a translation would be made in German, "which the clerk wrote next to my original deposition [...], although, much to my amusement, in a couple of instances I had to correct the judge's shaky translation, suggesting a more precise one of my own." It was a relationship of reciprocal opportunism dictated by the unusual two-headed structure of the company, being overseen by both the Central Head Office in Trieste and the Head Office in Venice, cities that were controlled by different administrations until the early twentieth century.

His far-sightedness in anticipating potential future national political scenarios led him, in 1906, to propose a change that if implemented would have dissolved the company's dual representation. At a Management meeting on July 4, those present learned of the positive outcome of negotiations between the secretary-general, Edmondo Richetti, and the head of the insurance department at the Interior Ministry, Wolf, concerning increasing the company's issued capital by issuing 1,000 new shares and earmarking the resulting profits for the life reserve, instead of the accumulated profits as per law, or part to the non-life divisions and part to the life division, as provided for in the charter. A report was also presented at this meeting on the vicissitudes of Marco Besso's proposal [*fig.* 2].

Having secured the Ministry's support, Richetti went to Rome to request that of director and technical consultant Besso, who did approve the project, but only if subordinated to the simultaneous founding of an "Italian general insurance Company," his reasons being the "dangers to which the Company's activity in Italy

1.
Members of Venice Head Office
[1896–1907]
[ASAG, *Versamenti*]

Pictured in the photo, from left to right: Nicolò Papadopoli, deputy director; Carlo Ara, deputy secretary; Marco Besso, director; Arturo Kellner, secretary, and Giacomo Levi, deputy director

would be exposed if not continued under the national flag, given the current provisions of the law and those to come, and since, irrespective of said provisions, Italian economic development could give rise to other powerful Companies, which could then gather up that which is today ours. We therefore need to act in advance, and not wait for a law or an economic situation to impose the change."

The initial idea was to create a life company, followed by one for the fire sector, and to either assign the transport sector to a special company or transfer it to Anonima Infortuni in Milan. The envisioned starting capital would have been divided as follows: 40% to the parent company and 40% to an Italian group, with the remaining 20% offered to Generali shareholders. Assicurazioni Generali would have provided the new company financial support for its start up expenses, and handed over, with the transfer of shares, the proportional quota of the reserves.

Upon hearing the plan, his colleagues were unconvinced, maintaining that measures of such a kind should only be taken in case of real need, and that, should the Italian activity be transferred, the company would in any case need to hold all or at least the majority of the new company's shares. Later, the Management decided in favor of the project in modified form, and Richetti proposed officially submitting it to the government before making it a point of discussion for the Board of Directors and at the General Meeting, "maintaining that discussing and publicizing such an operation prior to being certain of government approval would be damaging to the interests of the Company."

The official plan envisioned the creation of the "Società di Assicurazioni Generali," with headquarters in Venice and Rome, with the aim of taking over the Assicurazioni Generali Italian life and fire portfolios, and continuing its activity with the benefit of the company organization, which would be transferred to it, and all of the officials working for the parent company. The new company, which would be founded with capital of 30 million liras (divided into 30,000 registered shares, 24,000 taken by Generali and 6,000 by the group of founders so that it would be issued entirely within the Kingdom of Italy), was to receive, corresponding to the transfer of the portfolio, the guarantee deposited with the royal government for the deposits that had already been made and those to come, the other Italian security papers in the parent company's portfolio, and its Italian real estate. It was to be managed by a Board of Directors, operating within which would be an appointed Executive Committee, with Generali guaranteed a "fitting" majority in both. Moreover, the two companies would have reciprocally pledged to avoid operating in their respective territories.

At the same meeting, it was also agreed to set up, within a short space of time, an Italian company for the transport division.

The Management approved the plan and instructed Besso and Richetti to continue negotiations with the government authorities, on condition that, should they reach a stalemate in October, the Board and General Meeting would immediately be convened to decide solely on the matter of issuing shares.

The matter was discussed again in September. The Management revised its position, declaring itself opposed to the plan, and Richetti agreed. The company's international character, organizational soundness, and reputation in Italy and abroad were deemed reason enough for trusting in Assicurazioni Generali's ability to face the danger posed by future laws and to regain the ground in the life division it had lost abroad.

Besso formally abandoned the plan, while still maintaining that it was necessary to found an Italian life and fire company. He was, however, given the go ahead to investigate founding an Italian transport company, without, therefore, giving up direct management of the division, since handled by Generali in all of the territories under the Central Head Office, emphasizing the usefulness of strengthening that office's position by creating companies that would be attractive to

Historical Sources: The Directors' Minutes

The directors' minutes are the primary source for reconstructing the company's history. They record the topics discussed, and the relative decisions made, during the weekly Management meetings.

The series begins with minutes no. 1 of February 21, 1832. The minutes report that on that date, the Provisional Administration, which marked the transition from Ausilio Generale di Sicurtà to Assicurazioni Generali, handed over to the Management all of the documents relative to its administration, which are still preserved to this day. The minutes, which are numbered progressively, were rebound by meeting and accompanied by various loose inserts (printed invitations to the meetings, special instructions, rates, bylaws, etc.), and finally mandatorily transcribed into volumes, beginning on November 1, 1832. They were written in Italian, as provided for in article 58 of the company bylaws of 1832, and handwritten until 1915.

The Historical Archive preserves the complete series, in nineteen recently restored and digitized volumes, from 1832 to 1922, the year in which the company made major changes to its internal organization after Trieste passed to the Kingdom of Italy, conforming itself to the current structure of joint stock companies: as a consequence, the Management's duties were inherited by the Executive Council. There are four volumes of minutes, covering the year of its institution until 1938, when this body was rescinded and its duties incorporated into the Board of Directors.

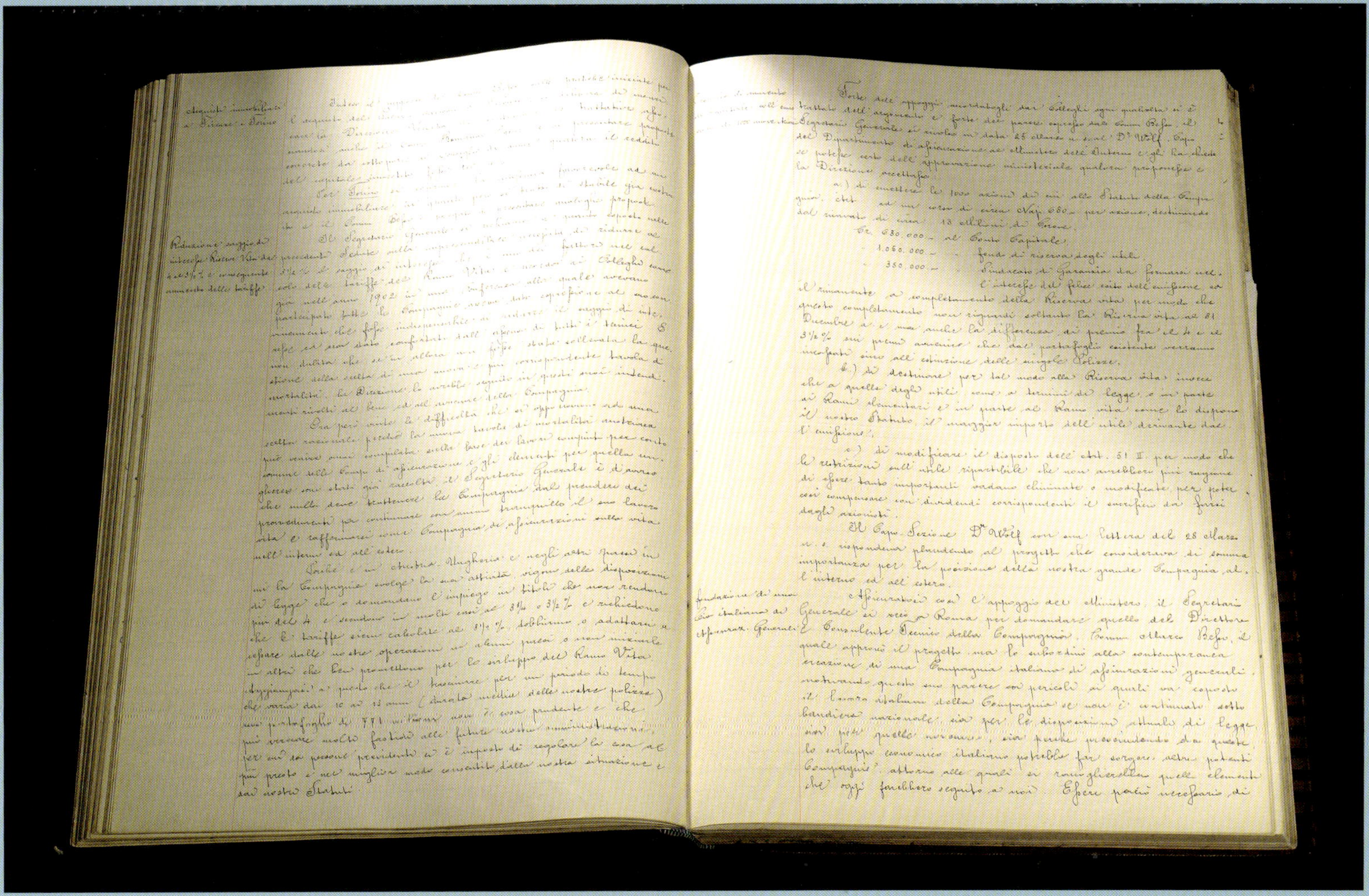

2.
Directors' minutes no. 2263 of July 4, 1906, with a report on the plan for the "Compagnia italiana di Assicurazioni Generali"
[ASAG, *Presidenza e organi sociali, Verbali, Direzione*, vol. 1295]

"new influential and prominent individuals" and that would stimulate the expansion of its business network. At the October meeting, the Board of Directors approved setting up a special oversight committee in the capital, in accordance with article 36 of the charter, with the Management in charge of selecting the committee members and set up procedures. This committee, made up of "prominent, influential individuals, who would provide our Company with both moral and material support," would not have interfered in any way in the management of the company.

At an Extraordinary General Meeting held on November 5, 1906, approval was given to issue new shares, to carry out the consequential modifications to the charter relative to profit distribution, and to expand the life division with the introduction of disability and old age pensions, in light of a new Austrian law concerning pensions for private sector employees, acknowledging that this kind of social security needed to be provided not only by the State organization but also by private companies.

The year 1907 also opened with a focus on the life division. Due to the volume of work and consequential increase in staff, the office needed to be divided into two sections: a technical section and an administrative section. Julius Graf was appointed director of the former, Massimiliano Engel of the latter.

The Venice Head Office also needed to be reorganized, in terms of both staff, since "it was not functioning as it should," and space. At a meeting on May 6, Richetti proposed a staff rotation for the post of secretary. The idea was for the current secretary, Arturo Kellner, to take the post of deputy director, appointing an executive from the Central Head Office to that of Venice secretary. The change was formalized at a meeting on November 20, with the appointment of Edgardo Morpurgo, who was director of Anonima Infortuni at the time, to the post.

Once work on the Rome office in Piazza Venezia was completed, various solutions were proposed for the unstable environmental situation of the Venice Head Office's work spaces. The deputy director, Giuseppe Da Zara, who was opposed to incurring substantial expenses and found it "neither necessary nor useful for the Italian Head Office to remain in Venice for all of eternity," proposed moving it to Rome or Milan. The solution adopted in the end was less radical, involving continuing the negotiations for the acquisition of the San Marco hotel (which has not been identified beyond this name, but was probably located in the back part of the Procuratie Vecchie, towards the Bacino Orseolo), as we read in the directors' minutes of October 3.

There was no further discussion of founding a life company, and the idea for an Italian transport company was definitively abandoned.

In 1909, Marco Besso was called to take the post of chairman, in honor of his professional record and especially his career at Generali. The decision to reinstate this post, vacant since 1835, was made in the interest of the administration, which, while leaving the Trieste and Venice Head Office unchanged, along with the number of their staff and their statutory powers and competences, would gain cohesion in the figure of chairman, and bring the company in line with current practice at joint-stock companies. At a Board meeting on March 15, Giuseppe Burgstaller de Bidischini proposed introducing the post of deputy chairman together with that of chairman. The relative motion was not taken into consideration, as we read in the minutes for a General Meeting held on March 18, when the director Emanuele Romanin-Jacur proposed reintroducing the post of chairman, communicating that "our colleagues would like to elect Director *Commendatore* Marco Besso to the post of Chairman. In a few months, Besso will be celebrating fifty years in the insurance industry, and his valuable contributions to the Institution and in particular the Company are well known to all."

At the same meeting, it was also decided to change the title of secretary general. The new name for the post was "director-in-charge," in conformity with the title used at other companies, and more reflective of the post's actual responsibilities, as an integral component of the Management. As a consequence, the title of secretary at the Venice Head Office was changed to "secretary director" [*fig.* 3]. Apart from Business Code regulations, the Head Offices could, in individual cases, delegate one of their members or a third party to carry out actions referred to them by the charter with a special proxy to be issued on a case by case basis: accordingly, the director-in-charge was delegated the technical and administrative management of the company for all activity overseen by the Central Head Office, while the secretary director was responsible for all activity subordinate to the Venice Head Office .

When Giolitti's bill for an Italian life insurance monopoly was approved, Besso revived his plan at a directors' meeting on July 21, 1911, the "unavoidable need" mentioned a few years earlier having become a reality, and underlined its advisability given the difficulties foreign companies would be encountering.

At a meeting on October 12, it was decided to set up a committee to investigate the implementation of the plan and then report its findings in December. The elected members of this committee were Besso, Morpurgo, Richetti, the directors Romanin-Jacur, Camillo Bozza, Gioberti Luzzati, and Fortunato Vivante, and the deputy director-in-charge Giuseppe Luzzatto.

The directors' minutes are silent on any developments that might have been made. While the committee's work was well underway, a bill emerged in 1912 with the regulations for life insurance activity (the complete monopoly was supposed to go into effect in April 1923, but it was afterward revoked), by the Istituto Nazionale delle Assicurazioni (INA). It was therefore deemed preferable to postpone change and wait until the project itself was translated into law and it could be seen which direction would best suit the company given the new state of affairs.

At a meeting held on January 4, 1913, it was announced that the company had received the minis-

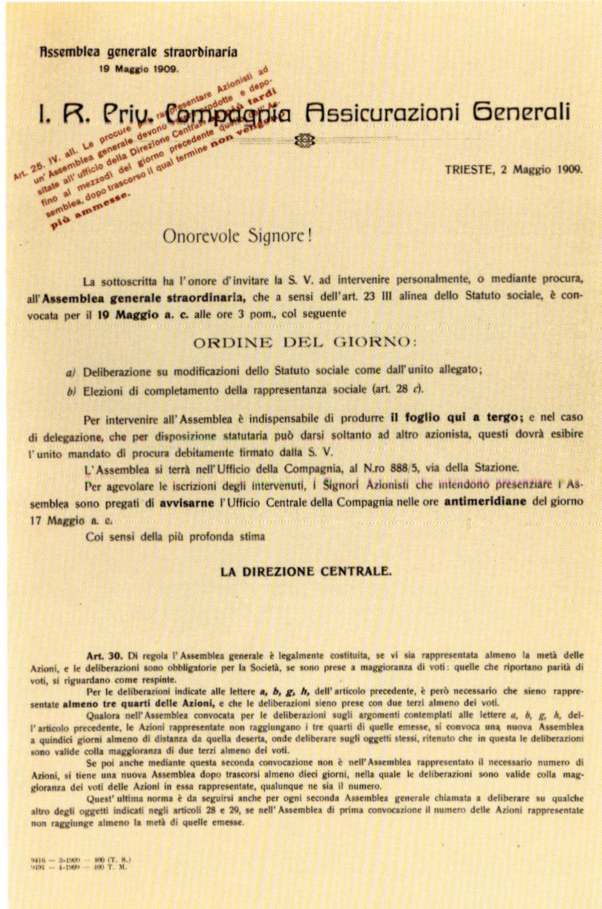

Assemblea generale straordinaria
19 Maggio 1909.

Art. 25. IV. all. Le procure per rappresentare Azionisti ad un' Assemblea generale devono essere prodotte e depositate all' ufficio della Direzione Centrale al più tardi fino al mezzodì del giorno precedente quello dell'Assemblea, dopo trascorso il qual termine **non vengono più ammesse.**

I. R. Priv. Compagnia Assicurazioni Generali

TRIESTE, 2 Maggio 1909.

Onorevole Signore!

La sottoscritta ha l'onore d'invitare la S. V. ad intervenire personalmente, o mediante procura, all'**Assemblea generale straordinaria,** che a sensi dell'art. 23 III alinea dello Statuto sociale, è convocata per il **19 Maggio a. c.** alle ore 3 pom., col seguente

ORDINE DEL GIORNO:

a) Deliberazione su modificazioni dello Statuto sociale come dall'unito allegato;
b) Elezioni di completamento della rappresentanza sociale (art. 28 *c*).

Per intervenire all'Assemblea è indispensabile di produrre **il foglio qui a tergo;** e nel caso di delegazione, che per disposizione statutaria può darsi soltanto ad altro azionista, questi dovrà esibire l'unito mandato di procura debitamente firmato dalla S. V.

L'Assemblea si terrà nell'Ufficio della Compagnia, al N.ro 888/5, via della Stazione.

Per agevolare le iscrizioni degli intervenuti, i Signori Azionisti che intendono presenziare l'Assemblea sono pregati di **avvisarne** l'Ufficio Centrale della Compagnia nelle ore **antimeridiane** del giorno 17 Maggio a. c.

Coi sensi della più profonda stima

LA DIREZIONE CENTRALE.

Art. 30. Di regola l'Assemblea generale è legalmente costituita, se vi sia rappresentata almeno la metà delle Azioni, e le deliberazioni sono obbligatorie per la Società, se sono prese a maggioranza di voti: quelle che riportano parità di voti, si riguardano come respinte.

Per le deliberazioni indicate alle lettere ***a, b, g, h,*** dell'articolo precedente, è però necessario che sieno rappresentate **almeno tre quarti delle Azioni,** e che le deliberazioni sieno prese con due terzi almeno dei voti.

Qualora nell'Assemblea convocata per le deliberazioni sugli argomenti contemplati alle lettere *a, b, g, h,* dell'articolo precedente, le Azioni rappresentate non raggiungano i tre quarti di quelle emesse, si convoca una nuova Assemblea a quindici giorni almeno di distanza da quella deserta, onde deliberare sugli oggetti stessi, ritenuto che in questa le deliberazioni sono valide colla maggioranza di due terzi almeno dei voti.

Se poi anche mediante questa seconda convocazione non è nell'Assemblea rappresentato il necessario numero di Azioni, si tiene una nuova Assemblea dopo trascorsi almeno dieci giorni, nella quale le deliberazioni sono valide colla maggioranza dei voti delle Azioni in essa rappresentate, qualunque ne sia il numero.

Quest'ultima norma è da seguirsi anche per ogni seconda Assemblea generale chiamata a deliberare su qualche altro degli oggetti indicati negli articoli 28 e 29, se nell'Assemblea di prima convocazione il numero delle Azioni rappresentate non raggiunge almeno la metà di quelle emesse.

9416 — 3-1909 — 400 (T. S.)
9491 — 4-1909 — 400 T. M.

3.
Letter convening an Extraordinary General Meeting on May 19, 1909 (Trieste, May 2, 1909) and the company charter (1909) [BCAG]

try's permission to continue its life insurance activity in Italy for the ten-year period allowed by law. This authorization was granted based on the policy rates and conditions enclosed with the application [*fig.* 4]. In the spring, the company posts were renewed, and they remained unchanged until the end of World War I. Besso was reappointed chairman and Richetti was co-opted to the Management following his resignation as director-in-charge, that post being in turn taken over by Morpurgo.
The life insurance monopoly law placed Generali in a position of uncertainty, paralyzing its activity in Italy and increasing the difficulties inherent in its reconstruction abroad. Besso was empowered to take the steps necessary to protect Generali's interests in Italy as a foreign company, trying to overcome the difficulties that were becoming increasingly problematic and compelling the company to quickly transform its Italian activity for all practical purposes into a national company.
After long, careful consideration, it was decided to carry out the previously presented plan to found a new sister company, which would only take over the activity of the non-life divisions, since the life division activity would continue to be carried out exclusively by Assicurazioni Generali, it being the license-holder for the duration of the life insurance law. It was further decided that once the joint Managements had weighed in and the intentions of the Austrian authorities were known, a committee would be appointed to draft the plan, including changes to be made to the structure and charter of the parent company (directors' meetings of October 22 and November 11, 1914).
There were probably objections to the plan, since the situation degenerated to the point that Besso resigned as chairman at a meeting on December 12, citing "various reasons, including of a personal nature," while, however, remaining a member of the Venice Head Office. Unswayed by attempts to convince him to withdraw his resignation, Besso presented the definitive plan to the Board of Directors at a meeting on February 11, 1915, aware of the need to adopt tactics that would ensure and improve the future of the company's Italian activity and of the urgent need, given the circumstances, to research and implement same.
Citing the company's long-held policy to "gradually decenter" its activity in its various regions of operation (for example, founding an accident company in Vienna in 1882 and another in Milan in 1896, and setting up two hail companies in 1890, one in Italy and one in Austria-Hungary) as the primary grounds, Besso proposed creating an independent Italian company in such a way that it would be possible to "give the new company the proper degree of autonomy while ensuring that the parent company receives all of the benefits to which it is entitled." Towards this end, it was decided that Assicurazioni Generali would take on a significant number of the new company's shares and that an equal number would be offered to its current shareholders, while the remaining shares would be made "available exclusively to the public with criteria intended to draw new contacts and new support to the new company, putting it in an increasingly better position to carry out its work." Moreover, for a long period, the parent company would be guaranteed an appropriate share of the new company's industrial profits.
The newly formulated plan was unofficially endorsed by the government authorities, but the Board vetoed the creation of the "Società italiana di Assicurazioni Generali" along with the simultaneous authorization to sell the company-to-be the Generali buildings located in Saint Mark's Square in Venice, Piazza Cordusio in Milan, and Piazza Venezia in Rome [*fig.* 5]. Just two weeks later, it was announced that the creation of the new Italian company needed to "be deferred" for the time being (directors' minutes no. 2456 of March 6, 1915). The issue was discussed no further and in December, given Marco Besso's resignation, the company proceeded with the suspension of the chairman's powers. (S.S.)

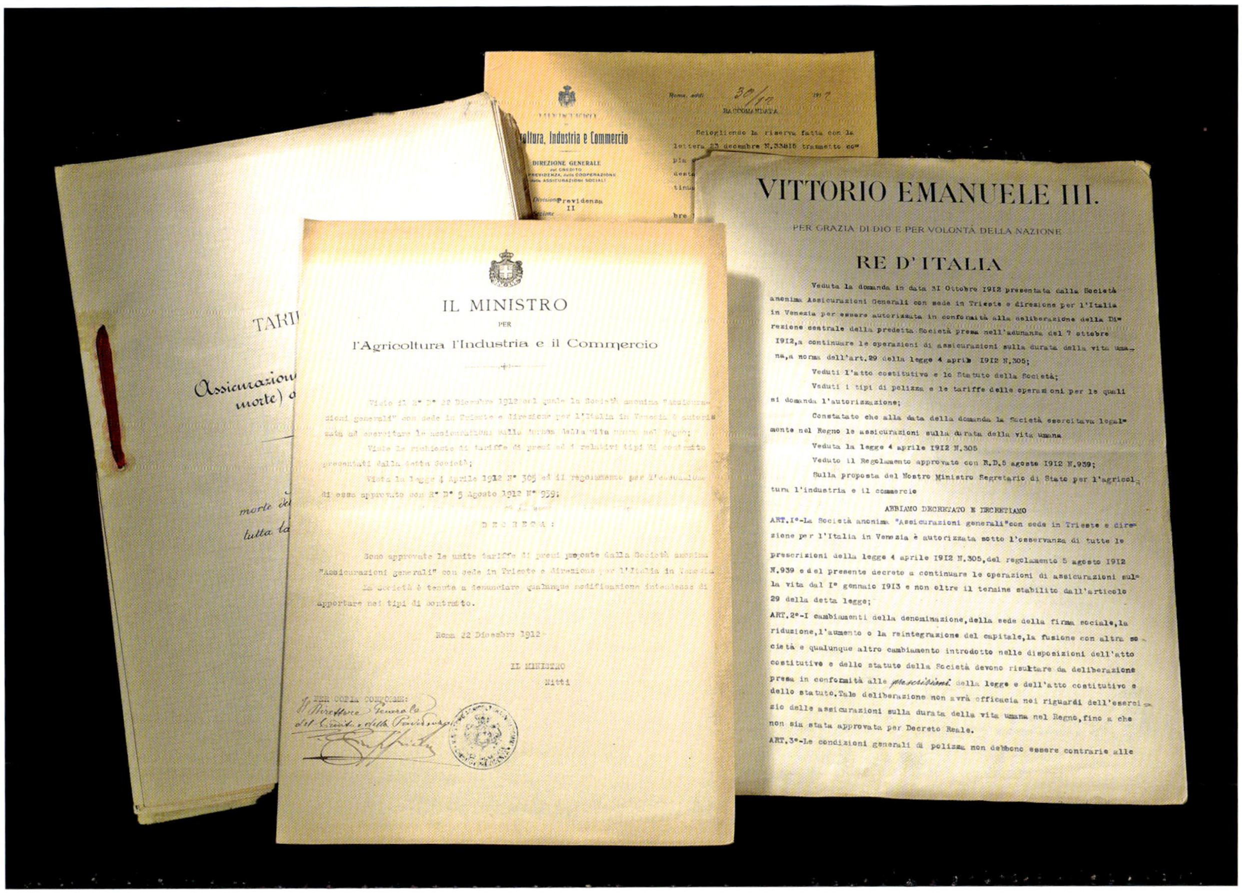

4.
Certified copy of the Royal Decree authorizing the company to continue its life insurance activity (Rome, December 22, 1912) and relative documentation
[ASAG, *Versamenti*, scheda 7911]

Law April 4, 1912, no. 305 (repealed by article no. 69 of the Royal Law Decree April 29, 1923, no. 966) established that Italian and foreign companies operating in the life insurance sector in the Kingdom could be authorized to continue their activity for no more than ten years from the effective date of same. This authorization, granted by Royal Decree, was subordinate to, among other things, transferring to INA 40% of every assumed risk; use of half of the collected premiums in State securities; and deposit of the applied premium rates at the Italian Ministry of Agriculture, Industry, and Trade for approval

5.
The Assicurazioni Generali's buildings in Piazza Cordusio, Milan, Saint Mark's Square, Venice and Piazza Venezia, Rome [twentieth century]
[ASAG, *Versamenti*, scheda 64703 and OGG001062047]

Franz Kafka at Generali
The Writer's Personnel File

1907
1908

As is well-known, Franz Kafka worked for a brief time at the company's general agency in Prague. He was hired on October 1, 1907 as an *Aus-hilfskraft*, or temporary employee, in the agency's life division, and he left for health reasons on July 4, 1908. The Central Head Office's archive of personnel files is very well preserved from the second half of the nineteenth century on, nearly completely so, and therefore also includes the famous writer's file.

His personnel file contains the usual office documentation: the letters sent by the Prague agency to the Head Office in Trieste to communicate that he had been hired and then that he had left the company; the carbon copies of the Head Office's letters of confirmation to Prague; the pre-printed forms used at the time for new Assicurazioni Generali employees (employment application with information about education and skills, and medical check-up questionnaire). Employees also filled out a *curriculum vitae* as part of their employment application, and Franz Kafka was no exception, and so Generali preserves his employment application together with his *curriculum vitae* and signature [*figs*. 1–2]. Kafka's signature also appears on the medical report, at the bottom of the page with questions for the employee.

Kafka's personnel file is well-known at the company, and has long been a source of pride [*fig*. 3]. Giuseppe Stefani, the editor of the *Bollettino*, used it as a source for various articles written in the 1950s, two of which were published in the company periodical ("Franz Kafka impiegato delle Generali" in 1952 and "Una lettera di Franz Kafka al suo capoufficio presso le Assicurazioni Generali" in 1954) and another in the literary magazine *La Nuova Antologia* ("Kafka e l'Italia" in 1957). That was the period during which the complete works by Kafka in German were published, as well as various texts by Max Brod, the writer's celebrated friend, who, after fleeing to Tel Aviv from Prague in 1939 with Kafka's manuscripts in hand, gradually began to publish them, rather than burning them as the writer had asked him to do in a letter. Stefani was in frequent contact with Brod while writing his articles, which naturally made use of the recent editions of Kafka. For example, he learned from Brod that Ernst Eisner—the cousin of Adolf Schreiber, a composer from Prague who was also friends with Brod, and so this was first-hand information—was the head of Kafka's office and also about a letter that reveals the intellectual affinity between Eisner and Kafka (who were nearly the same age), which Stefani translated and republished. Whereas it was thanks to Stefani's article of 1952, which was cited by Brod in *Über Franz Kafka: Franz Kafka, eine Biographie* and thus included in the writer's official biography, that Kafka's Assicurazioni Generali personnel file, and in particular his *curriculum vitae*, came to contribute to biographical research on Kafka. Documents relative to the writer's youth being scarce, the Generali file is of special importance, as emphasized by Klaus Wagenbach (*Franz Kafka. Biografia della giovinezza 1883–1912*, Italian edition [Turin: Einaudi, 1972]), who, after receiving a copy of the *Bollettino* from Stefani, carefully examined Kafka's file.

In order to support himself, Kafka worked in the insurance industry for almost all of his short life, first at Generali, then at the Arbeiter-Unfallversicherungs-Anstalt für das Königreich Böhmen, also in Prague, until 1922, when he retired due to poor health, dying two years later in 1924.

After graduating in law and spending an obligatory year working in the Prague courts, in 1907 Kafka was looking for a job that would provide him with a decent living and short work hours so that he could write. His uncle Alfred Löwy, the general manager of the Spanish railroad, contacted the United States vice consul in Prague, Arnold Weissberger, who was the father of the Generali representative in Madrid, José A. Weissberger, and secured him a position at the general agency of Prague, albeit "with more than a little difficulty" (letter from Kafka to Max Brod at the end of 1907; for all of the letters, Ernst Pawel, *The Nightmare of Reason: A Life of Franz Kafka* [London: Macmillan, 2011]). Weissberger is in fact indicated on the employment application as

1.
Franz Kafka's Assicurazioni Generali job application, inside section with *curriculum vitae* (Prague, October 2, 1907)
[ASAG, *Direzione centrale, Servizio del personale, Posizioni personali*, U2GE042904]

The *curriculum vitae* reads: "I was born in Prague on July 3, 1883.
I attended the Altstädter Volksschule through the fourth year. I then enrolled at the Altstädter deutsches Staatsgymnasium. When I was 18 I began studying at the Deutsche Karl-Ferdinands Universität in Prague. After taking the final state exam, on April 1, 1906, I began working as a trainee in the office of the lawyer Richard Löwy, on the Altstädter Ring. In June I took the "Rigorosum" [state exam] and was awarded my degree in law that same month.
As I immediately explained to the lawyer, I was working in his office with the sole aim of making use of my time, as it was never my intention to continue working as a lawyer.
I began practicing law on October 1, 1906, and stopped on October 1, 1907"

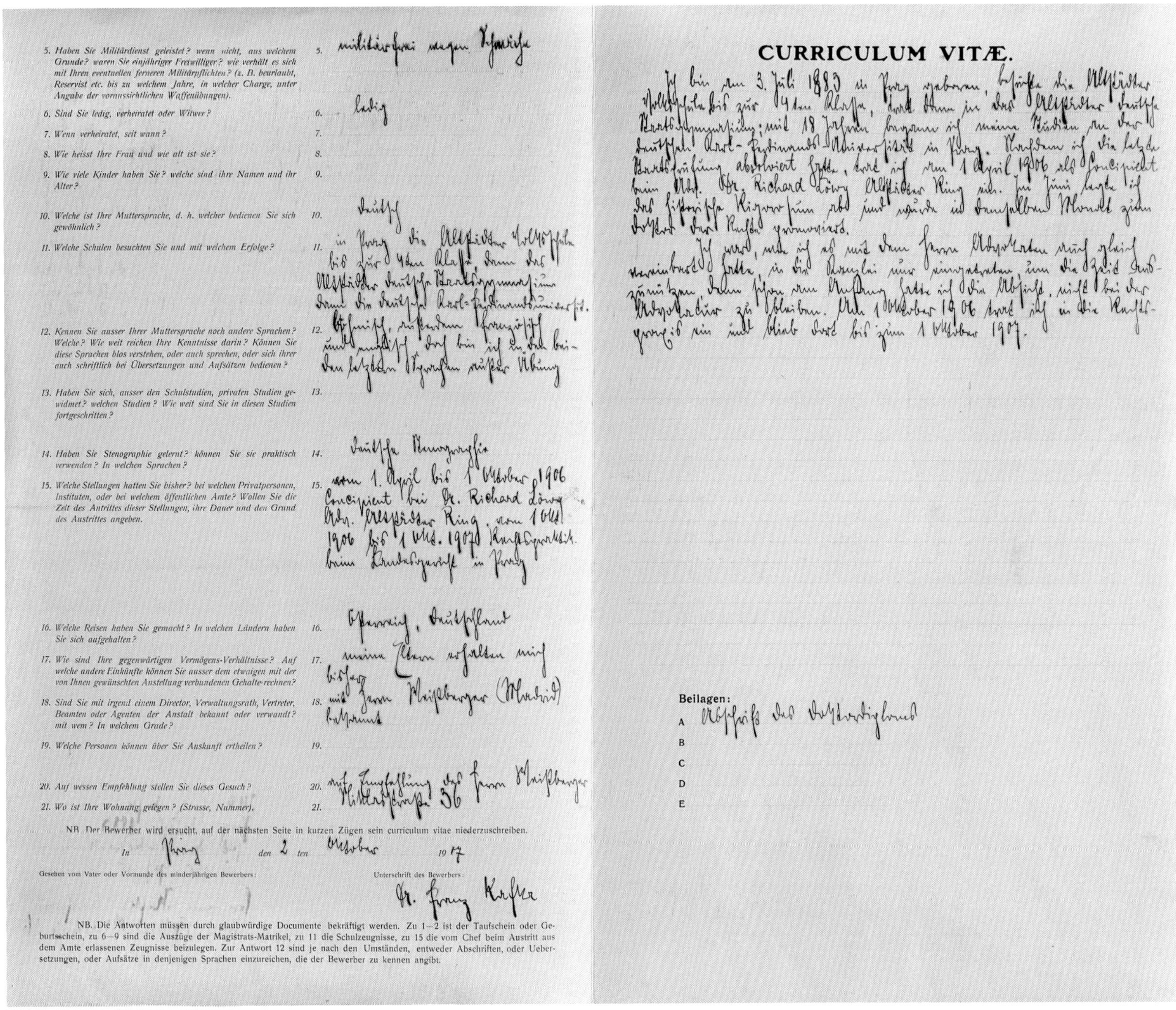

5. *Haben Sie Militärdienst geleistet? wenn nicht, aus welchem Grunde? waren Sie einjähriger Freiwilliger? wie verhält es sich mit Ihren eventuellen ferneren Militärpflichten? (z. B. beurlaubt, Reservist etc. bis zu welchem Jahre, in welcher Charge, unter Angabe der voraussichtlichen Waffenübungen).* 5.

6. *Sind Sie ledig, verheiratet oder Witwer?* 6.

7. *Wenn verheiratet, seit wann?* 7.

8. *Wie heisst Ihre Frau und wie alt ist sie?* 8.

9. *Wie viele Kinder haben Sie? welche sind ihre Namen und ihr Alter?* 9.

10. *Welche ist Ihre Muttersprache, d. h. welcher bedienen Sie sich gewöhnlich?* 10.

11. *Welche Schulen besuchten Sie und mit welchem Erfolge?* 11.

12. *Kennen Sie ausser Ihrer Muttersprache noch andere Sprachen? Welche? Wie weit reichen Ihre Kenntnisse darin? Können Sie diese Sprachen blos verstehen, oder auch sprechen, oder sich ihrer auch schriftlich bei Übersetzungen und Aufsätzen bedienen?* 12.

13. *Haben Sie sich, ausser den Schulstudien, privaten Studien gewidmet? welchen Studien? Wie weit sind Sie in diesen Studien fortgeschritten?* 13.

14. *Haben Sie Stenographie gelernt? können Sie sie praktisch verwenden? In welchen Sprachen?* 14.

15. *Welche Stellungen hatten Sie bisher? bei welchen Privatpersonen, Instituten, oder bei welchem öffentlichen Amte? Wollen Sie die Zeit des Antrittes dieser Stellungen, ihre Dauer und den Grund des Austrittes angeben.* 15.

16. *Welche Reisen haben Sie gemacht? In welchen Ländern haben Sie sich aufgehalten?* 16.

17. *Wie sind Ihre gegenwärtigen Vermögens-Verhältnisse? Auf welche andere Einkünfte können Sie ausser dem etwaigen mit der von Ihnen gewünschten Anstellung verbundenen Gehalte rechnen?* 17.

18. *Sind Sie mit irgend einem Director, Verwaltungsrath, Vertreter, Beamten oder Agenten der Anstalt bekannt oder verwandt? mit wem? In welchem Grade?* 18.

19. *Welche Personen können über Sie Auskunft ertheilen?* 19.

20. *Auf wessen Empfehlung stellen Sie dieses Gesuch?* 20.

21. *Wo ist Ihre Wohnung gelegen? (Strasse, Nummer).* 21.

NB. Der Bewerber wird ersucht, auf der nächsten Seite in kurzen Zügen sein curriculum vitae niederzuschreiben.

In   *den* 2 *ten*   19

Gesehen vom Vater oder Vormunde des minderjährigen Bewerbers:

Unterschrift des Bewerbers:

NB. Die Antworten müssen durch glaubwürdige Documente bekräftigt werden. Zu 1—2 ist der Taufschein oder Geburtsschein, zu 6—9 sind die Auszüge der Magistrats-Matrikel, zu 11 die Schulzeugnisse, zu 15 die vom Chef beim Austritt aus dem Amte erlassenen Zeugnisse beizulegen. Zur Antwort 12 sind je nach den Umständen, entweder Abschriften, oder Uebersetzungen, oder Aufsätze in denjenigen Sprachen einzureichen, die der Bewerber zu kennen angibt.

CURRICULUM VITÆ.

Beilagen:

A

B

C

D

E

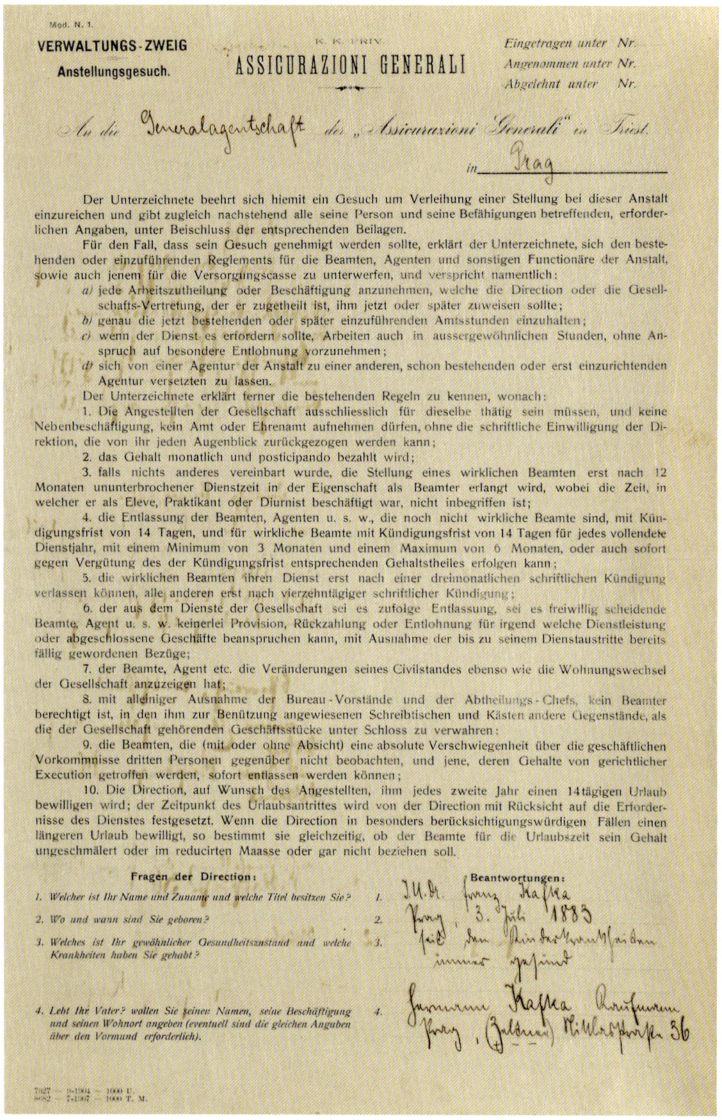

Mod. N. 1.

VERWALTUNGS-ZWEIG
Anstellungsgesuch.

K. K. PRIV.
ASSICURAZIONI GENERALI

Eingetragen unter Nr.
Angenommen unter Nr.
Abgelehnt unter Nr.

An die Generalagentschaft *der „Assicurazioni Generali" in Triest.*
in Prag

Der Unterzeichnete beehrt sich hiemit ein Gesuch um Verleihung einer Stellung bei dieser Anstalt einzureichen und gibt zugleich nachstehend alle seine Person und seine Befähigungen betreffenden, erforderlichen Angaben, unter Beischluss der entsprechenden Beilagen.

Für den Fall, dass sein Gesuch genehmigt werden sollte, erklärt der Unterzeichnete, sich den bestehenden oder einzuführenden Reglements für die Beamten, Agenten und sonstigen Functionäre der Anstalt, sowie auch jenem für die Versorgungscasse zu unterwerfen, und verspricht namentlich:

a) jede Arbeitszutheilung oder Beschäftigung anzunehmen, welche die Direction oder die Gesellschafts-Vertretung, der er zugetheilt ist, ihm jetzt oder später zuweisen sollte;
b) genau die jetzt bestehenden oder später einzuführenden Amtsstunden einzuhalten;
c) wenn der Dienst es erfordern sollte, Arbeiten auch in aussergewöhnlichen Stunden, ohne Anspruch auf besondere Entlohnung vorzunehmen;
d) sich von einer Agentur der Anstalt zu einer anderen, schon bestehenden oder erst einzurichtenden Agentur versetzten zu lassen.

Der Unterzeichnete erklärt ferner die bestehenden Regeln zu kennen, wonach:

1. Die Angestellten der Gesellschaft ausschliesslich für dieselbe thätig sein müssen, und keine Nebenbeschäftigung, kein Amt oder Ehrenamt aufnehmen dürfen, ohne die schriftliche Einwilligung der Direktion, die von ihr jeden Augenblick zurückgezogen werden kann;
2. das Gehalt monatlich und posticipando bezahlt wird;
3. falls nichts anderes vereinbart wurde, die Stellung eines wirklichen Beamten erst nach 12 Monaten ununterbrochener Dienstzeit in der Eigenschaft als Beamter erlangt wird, wobei die Zeit, in welcher er als Eleve, Praktikant oder Diurnist beschäftigt war, nicht inbegriffen ist;
4. die Entlassung der Beamten, Agenten u. s. w., die noch nicht wirkliche Beamte sind, mit Kündigungsfrist von 14 Tagen, und für wirkliche Beamte mit Kündigungsfrist von 14 Tagen für jedes vollendete Dienstjahr, mit einem Minimum von 3 Monaten und einem Maximum von 6 Monaten, oder auch sofort gegen Vergütung des der Kündigungsfrist entsprechenden Gehaltstheiles erfolgen kann;
5. die wirklichen Beamten ihren Dienst erst nach einer dreimonatlichen schriftlichen Kündigung verlassen können, alle anderen erst nach vierzehntägiger schriftlicher Kündigung;
6. der aus dem Dienste der Gesellschaft sei es zufolge Entlassung, sei es freiwillig scheidende Beamte, Agent u. s. w. keinerlei Provision, Rückzahlung oder Entlohnung für irgend welche Dienstleistung oder abgeschlossene Geschäfte beanspruchen kann, mit Ausnahme der bis zu seinem Dienstaustritte bereits fällig gewordenen Bezüge;
7. der Beamte, Agent etc. die Veränderungen seines Civilstandes ebenso wie die Wohnungswechsel der Gesellschaft anzuzeigen hat;
8. mit alleiniger Ausnahme der Bureau-Vorstände und der Abtheilungs-Chefs, kein Beamter berechtigt ist, in den ihm zur Benützung angewiesenen Schreibtischen und Kästen andere Gegenstände, als die der Gesellschaft gehörenden Geschäftsstücke unter Schloss zu verwahren:
9. die Beamten, die (mit oder ohne Absicht) eine absolute Verschwiegenheit über die geschäftlichen Vorkommnisse dritten Personen gegenüber nicht beobachten, und jene, deren Gehalte von gerichtlicher Execution getroffen werden, sofort entlassen werden können;
10. Die Direction, auf Wunsch des Angestellten, ihm jedes zweite Jahr einen 14tägigen Urlaub bewilligen wird; der Zeitpunkt des Urlaubsantrittes wird von der Direction mit Rücksicht auf die Erfordernisse des Dienstes festgesetzt. Wenn die Direction in besonders berücksichtigungswürdigen Fällen einen längeren Urlaub bewilligt, so bestimmt sie gleichzeitig, ob der Beamte für die Urlaubszeit sein Gehalt ungeschmälert oder im reducirten Maasse oder gar nicht beziehen soll.

Fragen der Direction:		**Beantwortungen:**
1. Welcher ist Ihr Name und Zuname und welche Titel besitzen Sie?	*1.*	JU.Dr. Franz Kafka
2. Wo und wann sind Sie geboren?	*2.*	Prag, 3. Juli 1883
3. Welches ist Ihr gewöhnlicher Gesundheitszustand und welche Krankheiten haben Sie gehabt?	*3.*	seit den Kinderkrankheiten immer gesund
4. Lebt Ihr Vater? wollen Sie seinen Namen, seine Beschäftigung und seinen Wohnort angeben (eventuell sind die gleichen Angaben über den Vormund erforderlich).	*4.*	Hermann Kafka Kaufmann Prag, (Zeltner) Niklasstrasse 36

2.
Franz Kafka's Assicurazioni Generali job application (Prague, October 2, 1907) [ASAG, *Direzione centrale, Servizio del personale, Posizioni personali,* U2GE042904]

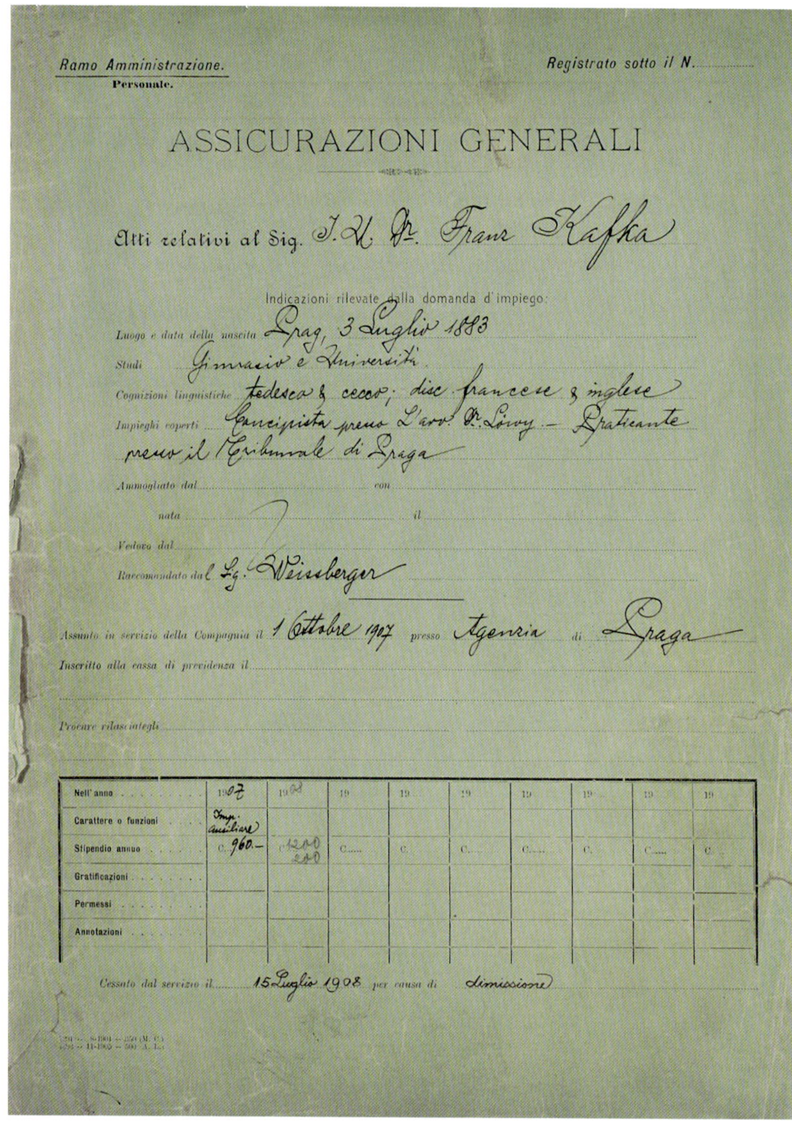

Ramo Amministrazione.
Personale.

Registrato sotto il N.

ASSICURAZIONI GENERALI

Atti relativi al Sig. J. U. Dr. Franz Kafka

Indicazioni rilevate dalla domanda d'impiego:

Luogo e data della nascita Prag, 3 Luglio 1883
Studi Ginnasio e Università
Cognizioni linguistiche tedesco & ceco; disc. francese & inglese
Impieghi coperti Concipista presso L'avv. Dr. Löwy – Praticante presso il Tribunale di Praga
Ammogliato dal … *con* …
nata … *il* …
Vedovo dal …
Raccomandato dal Sg. Weissberger

Assunto in servizio della Compagnia il 1 Ottobre 1907 *presso* Agenzia *di* Praga
Inscritto alla cassa di previdenza il …
Procure rilasciategli …

Nell'anno	1907	1908	19	19	19	19	19	19	19
Carattere o funzioni	Imp. ausiliare								
Stipendio annuo	C. 960.–	C. 1200 240	C.	C.	C.	C.	C.	C.	C.
Gratificazioni									
Permessi									
Annotazioni									

Cessato dal servizio il 15 Luglio 1908 *per causa di* dimissione

3.
Franz Kafka's personnel file (Trieste-Prague, 1907–1908) [ASAG, *Direzione centrale, Servizio del personale, Posizioni personali,* U2GE042904]

an acquaintance of Kafka and the contact person for the recommendation (points 18 and 20). The application is dated October 2, 1907, the day following the completion of his court traineeship. On the application, Kafka indicated knowledge of German, his native language (Czech), French, and English, although with regard to the latter two he specified that he was "out of practice." He also indicated knowing German shorthand, and, in answer to question number sixteen, which countries he had stayed in, he wrote Austria and Germany. Upon request, Kafka enclosed his degree certificate, which was returned to him when he left the company. On the same day, October 2, 1907, the company physician gave him a medical examination, finding him to be absolutely suited to the job ("he is delicate, but in good health"), and the general agency in Prague wrote to the Central Head Office to accept his application for employment, offering him a job as a temporary employee in the life division and a salary of 80 crowns. There is a note at the foot of the page from the Prague agency: "We intend to give Dr. Kafka special training in life insurance operations so as to use him later for assignments abroad. He came to us highly recommended by the US vice consul in Prague, Mr. Weissberger, father of our representative in Madrid. Dr. Kafka's family enjoys an excellent reputation."

Kafka was not very happy at Generali, as his short-lived career there suggests. His autobiographical writings and *Letter to My Father* include a few references to his work at the agency in Václavské náměstí ("my life is now totally disorganized. True, I have a position with a tiny salary of 80 crowns and an immense eight to nine hours of work, but I gobble up the hours outside the office like a wild beast," letter from Kafka to Hedwig Weiler, October 8, 1907). From the letters we learn that the writer was studying Italian at the time ("I am studying Italian, since I will probably be sent to Trieste," letter from Kafka to Hedwig Weiler, November 1907), and dreamed of being transferred abroad, to far-off, exotic countries ("Now as to the office. I am with Assicurazioni Generali, and there is at least hope of my someday gracing an armchair in some faraway country and gazing out of the office window upon sugarcane fields or Moslem cemeteries. The insurance business as such interests me very much, but my present work is dreary," letter from Kafka to Hedwig Weiler, October 8, 1907).

An opportunity to transfer did not come his way, and by the end of 1907 the writer had already begun looking for a new job, taking a course on accident insurance at the Prager Handels-Akademie from February to May 1908. The end of Kafka's connection with the company was made official in a letter from the Prague agency to the Central Head Office, dated July 14, 1908, communicating his resignation for health reasons. A note explained that "Dr. Kafka has been distressed recently and very much on edge and now he has produced a medical certificate from Dr. Hahn who attests that Dr. Kafka is suffering from neurasthenia as well as grave cardiac excitability, and urgently requests that he be released from his post."

Generali's view of the matter emerges in the reply from Trieste, which survives in a worn, infrequently cited carbon copy of the letter closing Kafka's file, which is preserved in the Historical Archive. On July 23, 1908, the deputy secretary Gioberti Luzzati wrote to acknowledge Kafka's resignation and communicate that his degree certificate would be sent to Prague, adding in a handwritten note: "We are astonished that the health of the above-mentioned, who, after having been carefully examined by our trusted physician last October, was recommended as absolutely fit, has become so bad in such a short time that he must immediately resign."

According to the scholar Michael Müller, Kafka believed that resignation for health reasons would be less damaging to his *curriculum vitae* than simply quitting. Immediately after leaving Generali, Kafka began working for the Arbeiter-Unfallversicherungs-Anstalt für das Königreich Böhmen, a semi-autonomous authority, with an only six-hour work day. The documents written by Kafka while working at this institute were recently published (*Amtliche Schriften*, edited by Klaus Hermsdorf und Benno Wagner, 1984; *Relazioni*, edited by Michael Müller, 1988; *The Office Writings*, by Stanley Corngold, Jack Greenberg and Benno Wagner, 2009). These volumes, together with the exhibition *Le Siècle de Kafka*, held in Paris at the Centre Pompidou in 1984, reveal Kafka's ambivalent and complex relationship with his work at the institute, and these observations might also be valid for his work at Generali. On the one hand, it crops up frequently in his writings that he was afraid that the office was stealing energy from his writing. On the other hand, his dedication to his work is demonstrated by his career at the institute (from auxiliary employee to upper secretary), his meticulous technical reports, and the goodwill that surrounded him at the workplace, even after the purge that struck German executives after the founding of the Czechoslovakian Republic. Kafka's reports were of course technical documents and as such adhered to rigid rules, and yet he was still able to infuse them with his own unique mark: he must have been proud of them, considering that he sent them to his friends. In any case, Kafka's relationship with his job went through different phases. On January 18, 1915, he wrote in his diary: "I think it is a special inability to work that I feel now, similar to what I felt when I was employed by the Generali. Immediate contact with the workaday world deprives me—though inwardly I am as detached as I can be—of the possibility of taking a broad view of matters, just as if I were at the bottom of a ravine, with my head bowed down in addition" (Müller: 26). However, according to Müller, at a certain point Kafka understood that "writing was not the only legitimizing factor of his existence, that office work also tied him to *life*."

In addition to the personnel file, the Historical Archive also preserves documents referring to Kafka from the collection relative to the management of the company's foreign agencies. Kafka is, for example, listed as having been present at a meeting held on April 8, 1908, attended by the administration, inspectors, and agency staff, the minutes for which have been preserved. The meeting agenda included reports on the state of business in the life division, the staff of which included the writer. There is also an accounting document that lists which employees worked internally (including Kafka) and which had contacts outside the company. And then there is the "Personal-Stand am 31. December 1907," an important document listing, in alphabetical order, all of the staff who were working at the agency in a given year, indicating each employee's place and date of birth, job title, hire date, and family status. The Prague Personal-Stände series, which is complete for the years 1893 through 1944 (1907 includes Franz Kafka), makes it possible to more precisely reconstruct the features of the general agency in Prague, which had hundreds of employees and was one of Generali's most important agencies at the time, with numerous regional agencies under it. Established in 1832, it opened up new directions on numerous fronts. In 1884, it was the first to hire female employees, which turned out to be a successful experiment, with the Head Office in Trieste following suit in 1892, and it was the first Generali agency to be located in a purpose-built modern building [*fig.* 4]. The Prague agency also underwent a major change in the organization of its activity, involving the replacement of traveling buyers with inspectors assigned to the various territories. (R.S.)

The Prague Building

In 1894, the company took advantage of a prime moment for property investment in Prague and purchased a few structures on the corner of "Wenzelplatz" and "Heinrichgasse" (directors' minutes no. 1862 of March 1, 1894), with the intention of building an edifice that would be part used for the offices of the local general agency and part rented out to private individuals. The new building in Prague was an architectural and economic success, and seems to have kindled the company's enthusiasm for acquiring and building other edifices in major Italian and European cities between the late nineteenth and early twentieth century.

The lot in Václavské náměstí had already been suggested in 1890 by Arturo Kellner, the head of the Prague agency at the time, although the purchase was not made until later, between April and May 1894. Planning and construction began almost immediately and were overseen by Eugenio Geiringer, who dealt with the planners, and Emanuel Horst, the new office head. The building was complete in 1896. When the idea to hire the Viennese architect Otto Thienemann was rejected, Geiringer modified a plan by Friedrich Ohmann, Josef Roslapil, and Stribral, assigning the development of the estimates and detailed plans to Ohmann, who was replaced as overseer by the architect Polioka in 1895. Construction was carried out by the company Starke and Gregor. The design for the four-story building included two elevators, central heating, and a modern lighting system.

4.
The Assicurazioni Generali building in Václavské nám stí in Prague, anastatic reproduction (Prague [early twentieth century])
[ASAG, *Versamenti*, scheda 28267]

Disaster Foretold

The Bloody Carnage of World War I and the Dissolution of the Empires

1914
1921

On that tragic June 28, 1914, almost no one seemed to think that war would be the response to the assassination of the Austrian archduke Franz Ferdinand and his wife Sophie, countess of Chotek [*fig.* 1]. Not even the radical nationalists of Young Bosnia who were responsible for the assassination and armed by the terrorist organization "Union or Death," better known as "Black Hand," under the Serbian secret service, seem to have thought of it. They had long thought of striking a symbol of tyranny, but, as one of their members, Vaso Čubrilović, put it, for them, "one person was worth as much as any other" and it was only by chance that they leveled their arsenal against the heir to the Hapsburg throne. They were, however, aware of the importance of the man killed by Gavrilo Princip. The archduke was, in fact, a champion of the *Reichspartei*, the Empire's party, which aimed to create a concept of a unified State among the various nations, based on total devotion to the dynasty and its religion, Catholicism, which meant that, favoring the Empire's Slavic populations and promising either trialism or federalism against the enemies of state unity (Magyars, Italians, and Serbs), he was undermining the foundation of the Yugoslav idea. As a consequence, with the assassination of Franz Ferdinand, the Bosnian Serb terrorists forced their Yugoslavist brothers to choose between nation and Empire.

After June 28, the entire political and diplomatic world adopted an attitude of prudence, waiting to see how Austria, which was eagerly hoping to find proof that the Serbian government was behind the assassination in Sarajevo, would react; if this could have been proved to be the case, it would have presented a long-hoped for opportunity to humiliate the Balkan State, long considered unavoidably necessary for reasserting its centuries-long authority over the Slavic world. The war began on July 28, with the Hapsburg Empire declaring war on Serbia. At that point, although there was not yet any real prospect of war, beyond reciprocal threats, all of the European powers came up with more or less plausible reasons to get involved. Among the Central Empires, Austria-Hungary was focused on regaining its position as a major power, while Germany held itself to be at the peak of a period of economic and military development that it could no longer contain within its own borders. Whereas the Allies used defensive reasoning, Russia entered the war in order to protect free passage through the Straits, which was essential for its economy. France got involved by virtue of its membership in the alliance, which in turn ensured it a role as a major continental and colonial power, and also for its interest in the Balkan region. And Great Britain fought to protect the independence of the sovereign States as well as to prevent German dominance on the continent.

In Italy, pro-war excitement in nationalist circles (and beyond) peaked. Italian intervention was considered necessary, although the country actually maintained a position of neutrality for nearly a year in order to negotiate its participation in the war with all of the powers involved.

At that juncture, not even the position of the Italians in Trieste seemed clear. Just as the Austro-Hungarian masses were gripped by enthusiasm for war and an unexpected patriotic zeal, during the first days of the war the people of Trieste were jubilant over what was interpreted as a showdown with the Slavs. Even the Italian newspaper correspondents felt caught off guard, reporting on the unusual situation the war had created in Trieste, where the population, after so many accusations and so much rabble rousing, was now in favor of the Hapsburg Dynasty. This position was, however, then justified by the conclusion that Italy could not participate in the war.

In 1914, Italy stuck to its position of neutrality, on the grounds that the Triple Alliance was exclusively defensive in nature and that negotiation over expected territorial gains would not have brought it any great advantage.

The deadlock created a clear division in the country between those who wanted neutrality to the bitter end and the interventionist front, which brought side by side, although not without plenty of heated disagreement, the champions of the democratic war, in the mold of irredentists and Risorgimento supporters, and those of the imperialist persuasion, the latter being tragically more in step with the times.

For more than nine months, the interventionists threw themselves into feverish propaganda activity, with the motto "now or never," which was coined by Cesare Battisti, who saw the European conflict as Italy's last chance to conquer irredentas and clinch its Balkan and Mediterranean interests. As a result, Italy signed the Treaty of London with the Allied Forces on April 26, 1915. This was a secret treaty that guaranteed significant territorial gains and required Italy to join the war within one month.

After what came to be known as "Radiant May", on May 24, 1915, Italy entered the war against Austria-Hungary [*fig.* 2], but not against Germany, leaving the Allies dumbfounded until August 27, 1916, when pressure from the Entente forced Italy to acquiesce.

And so Italy threw itself into the vortex of World War I, an epoch-making war that changed the course of humanity, triggering a series of events that made the twentieth century the "century of genocide". What happened in the subsequent decades was rooted in that devastating war, which, at first enthusiastically welcomed by European youth, who were evidently tired of the overly long period of peace that preceded it, quickly became an exhausting "war of attrition," bloody, incomprehensible slaughter for trifling advantages won through relentless assault of opposing trenches [*fig.* 3], involving everyone and everything in what is remembered as the first total war in history. Ernst Jünger described those battles as "storms of steel," in which technological power supplanted even the gloriously human traits and actions that, according to some zealous poets, emerge out of conventional war: courage, heroism, and individual and collective sacrifice. Which is not to say that these were

1.
The assassination of the archduke Franz Ferdinand in Sarajevo, illustrated by Achille Beltrame for the July 5, 1914, edition of *La Domenica del Corriere*

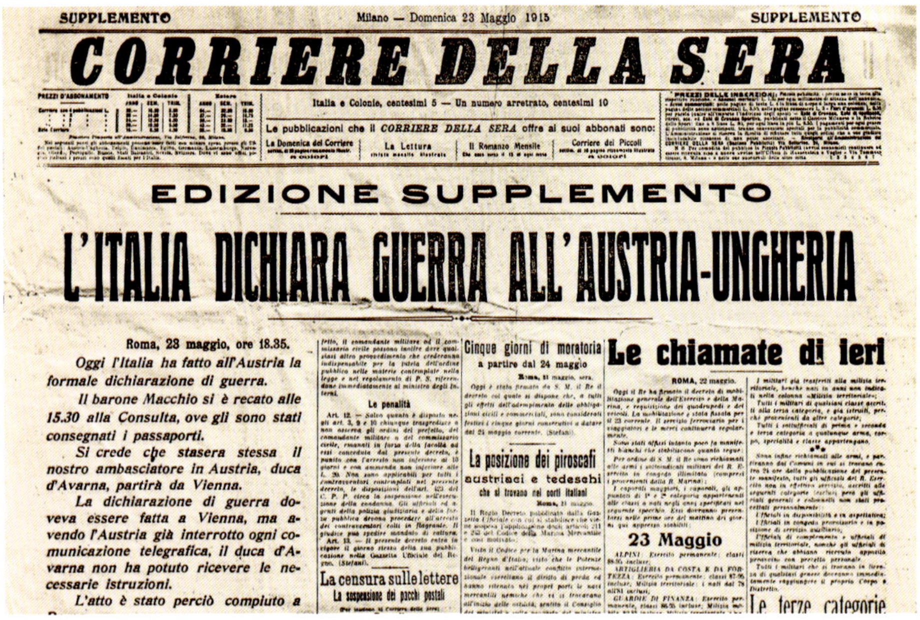

SUPPLEMENTO — Milano — Domenica 23 Maggio 1915 — SUPPLEMENTO

CORRIERE DELLA SERA

Italia e Colonie, centesimi 5 — Un numero arretrato, centesimi 10

Le pubblicazioni che il CORRIERE DELLA SERA offre ai suoi abbonati sono:

La Domenica del Corriere | La Lettura | Il Romanzo Mensile | Corriere dei Piccoli

EDIZIONE SUPPLEMENTO

L'ITALIA DICHIARA GUERRA ALL'AUSTRIA-UNGHERIA

Roma, 23 maggio, ore 18.35.

Oggi l'Italia ha fatto all'Austria la formale dichiarazione di guerra.

Il barone Macchio si è recato alle 15.30 alla Consulta, ove gli sono stati consegnati i passaporti.

Si crede che stasera stessa il nostro ambasciatore in Austria, duca d'Avarna, partirà da Vienna.

La dichiarazione di guerra doveva essere fatta a Vienna, ma avendo l'Austria già interrotto ogni comunicazione telegrafica, il duca d'Avarna non ha potuto ricevere le necessarie istruzioni.

L'atto è stato perciò compiuto a

Le penalità

La censura sulle lettere

Cinque giorni di moratoria a partire dal 24 maggio

La posizione dei piroscafi austriaci e tedeschi

Le chiamate di ieri

23 Maggio

Le terze categorie

2.
The supplement for the May 23, 1915, edition of the *Corriere della Sera* announcing the declaration of war against Austria. The hostilities began the next day

3.
Painting of the Battle of Podgora (July 19, 1915) by Vittorio Pisani

absent, quite the opposite, but rather that they were by then serving solely the increasingly lethal power of devastating machines, which offered no possibility of independent—or human—choice.

In addition to suffering, devastation, and death, World War I also brought long-lasting social and political changes, first and foremost, in 1917, the Russian Revolution [*fig.* 4] which, with the Bolsheviks consequentially in power after Lenin's return to the country, ushered in an altogether too long period of Communism, lasting around seventy years. This not only led to Russia's gradual detachment from the war—with dramatic consequences for the allies, firstly the Caporetto fiasco for Italy, and heralding, moreover, a dramatic, oppressive war in the countries that were forced to join the new Union of Soviet Socialist Republics (USSR)—but also launched a period of totalitarian regimes intent on (or aiming to) determining the future of the new "mass culture" that came to characterize the twentieth century.

In the same year, the United States entered the war against the Austrian-German alliance in order to protect its economic interests in Europe. This intervention, although carried out from a defiladed position, unveiled the United States as the decisive new leader of subsequent world history. On January 8, 1918, the proclamation of United States President Woodrow Wilson's "fourteen points" put Italy in particular in a difficult position. Wilson's speech foreshadowed the diplomatic guidelines that would need to be followed to end the war and, in the name of the self-determination of peoples, disclaimed the need to acquire "strategic borders," the very goal for which all of the European belligerents were fighting.

After the Austro-German defeat and the Armistice of Villa Giusti (in Padua) November 3, the Italian troops occupied the territories promised to them in the Treaty of London, including Trentino (but also Alto Adige) and Venezia Giulia, as well as a few other strategic points. The dissolution of the Hapsburg Empire and the creation, on December 1, in Belgrade, of the new kingdom of the Serbs, Croatians, and Slovenians (from 1929, Yugoslavia) started a dispute over the eastern border of Italy at the Paris Peace Conference [*fig.* 5]. This dispute was not satisfactorily resolved and the Italians were left feeling that they had won a "maimed victory." As a result, on September 12, 1919, Gabriele D'Annunzio and his men occupied Fiume [*fig.* 6], which was not included in the territories guaranteed by the Treaty of London, but which a plebiscite had determined was definitely Italian. The border problem was partially resolved by the Treaty of Rapallo on November 20, 1920, which declared Fiume a free State. This decision, however, forced the Royal Italian Army, in compliance with its international obligations, to drive D'Annunzio and his men out of the city one month later, a sorrowful event known as "Bloody Christmas." The dramatic postwar period saw the dissolution of the empires (Russian, Turkish, German, and Austro-Hungarian) and the start of intense unrest in many European countries, in particular Germany, which had been shelved by a punitive peace that served as the harbinger of the rise of Nazism.

In Italy, fear of the elitist restoration of the prewar liberal-bourgeois system or the rise of Socialism, the neutralism of which had in fact undermined the country's military commitment, propelled large groups of veterans to mobilize themselves with the goal of political recognition of their sacrifices in the trenches. The former socialist and maximalist Benito Mussolini took advantage of this climate, and was more successful than D'Annunzio at gathering around him the discontent of the former combatants, forming the "Fasci Italiani di Cobattimento" on March 23, 1919 in Milan, which became the Partito Nazionale Fascista in 1921. Italy—and the world—were about to enter a new age. (D.R.)

4.
Lenin haranguing the crowd (detail of a painting by Irakliy Toidze)

5.
The "Big Four" at the Paris Peace Conference of 1919. From left to right, seated: Vittorio Emanuele Orlando, David Lloyd George, Georges Clemenceau, and Thomas Woodrow Wilson

6.
Gabriele D'Annunzio addressing his men during the occupation of Fiume, which ended after sixteen months with Bloody Christmas in 1920

In Brief

1914
August 15: The American freighter *Ancon* was the first ship to cross the Panama Canal, which connects the Atlantic and Pacific oceans. The opening ceremony did not take place until 1920, after the war.

1914
December 25: A spontaneous Christmas truce spread across the western front, and enemies socialized with one another. Near Ploegsteert, in Flanders, British and German soldiers posed for a photo together.

1915
February 8: A preview of the controversial film *Birth of a Nation* was screened in Los Angeles. Directed by David Wark Griffith, it was filmed using innovative techniques that made it one of the first spectaculars.

1915
April 22: The Germans used asphyxiating gas against the French on a section of the front in the region of Ypres in Belgium, leaving 5,000 dead. It was the first act of modern chemical warfare.

1915
May 6: Babe Ruth, a young pitcher for the Red Sox, hit his first Major League home run. By the end of his career in 1935, he had racked up 714, a record that remained unbeaten for 39 years.

1916
February 5: The opening of the Cabaret Voltaire marked the beginning of the short-lived Dada movement, a form of paradoxical art that developed to protest the culture and values that gave rise to the war.

1916
February 21: The Germans launched a violent offensive against France in Verdun, which became one of the longest (ten months) and bloodiest battles of World War I.

1916
March 9: Pancho Villa led his soldiers in an attack on Columbus, a city in New Mexico defended by a United States garrison, and then escaped General Pershing's retributive expedition.

1916
November 12: After working for hours at his desk, in spite of his lung disease, the Hapsburg emperor Franz Joseph died at Schönbrunn Castle, where he had been born eight-six years earlier.

1917
October 15: The fascinating Dutch dancer known as Mata Hari, the stage name of Margaretha Geertruida Zelle, was shot for her activity as a spy for Germany; her code name was Agent H21.

1917
October 28: Signor Bonaventura, a character by Sergio Tofano often rewarded with a "one million" slip, debuted in the *Corriere dei Piccoli* (the first Italian weekly comic strip supplement, launched in 1908).

1918
April 21: The German flying ace Manfred, Baron von Richthofen, known as the Red Baron, died in Vaux-sur-Somme, shot down by enemy anti-aircraft during an air fight with Royal Air Force pilots.

1918
July 17: Czar Nicholas II, forced to abdicate and imprisoned by the Bolsheviks after the October Revolution, was killed in Yekaterinburg along with his wife, five children, and various attendants.

1918
October 24: The Italian army, which had driven back the Austrian offensive on the Piave River in June, launched a decisive attack against the enemy troops, who were forced into a disastrous retreat a few days later.

1919
January 21: The bloody Irish War of Independence broke out. In just three years, before the truce of 1921, more than 1,400 British soldiers, guerrillas, police officers, and civilians lost their lives.

1919
April 13: The Massacre of Amritsar, ordered by General Dyer, exasperated tensions in British India; Mohandas Karamchand Gandhi began a nonviolent campaign for Indian independence.

1920
January 16: The Prohibition began in the United States, after the Eighteenth Amendment of the Constitution, approved the previous year, banned the consumption and production of alcoholic beverages.

1920
January 28: The Spanish Legion *el Tercio* was formed to deal with Berbers during the Rif War, in Morocco. One of its founders was the future *caudillo*, Francisco Franco (to the right in the photo).

1920
April 20: The flag with five rings, designed by De Coubertin in 1914, was raised for the first time at the opening of the Olympics in Antwerp. The countries that were defeated in the war were excluded from the event.

1920
May 16: Pope Benedict XV canonized Joan of Arc, the French heroine of the Hundred Years' War who, captured, was condemned to death by burning at the stake by the English in 1431 for heresy.

1921
February 6: The successful debut of *The Kid* made Charlie Chaplin a star. Chaplin was the film's director as well as its star, playing the character of The Tramp, alongside Jackie Coogan.

1921
July 1: The founding Congress of the Chinese Communist Party was held in Shanghai. One of the young participants was the future leader Mao Zedong, who was born to a peasant family in Hunan.

1921
November 4: The body of the Unknown Solider, chosen from among eleven unidentifiable candidates by Maria Bergamas, the mother of a volunteer lost in battle, was buried in the Altare della Patria in Rome.

1921
December 6: The Anglo-Irish Treaty was signed, creating the Irish Free State and Northern Ireland. Michael Collins, the charismatic Irish leader who supported the accord, was killed eight months later.

Employees in Times of War

Stories of Generali Staff During the First and Second World Wars

1914
1945

The two world wars had a negative impact on Generali's economic activity. At the beginning of the Great War, the fact that the company found itself on both sides of the conflict had major repercussions on its relations with Italian institutions and those of its allies, on the one hand, and Hapsburg institutions on the other. During the Worls War II, it suffered from damage and destruction spread throughout all of Europe, and when Italy entered the war, the company's assets were sequestered by the enemy nations. But the lives of individual employees were also dramatically changed, with the war having a direct impact on both those who were called to arms and the everyday life of civilians. The documents preserved in the staff services collection, in particular those in individual files, but also administrative documents relative to single agencies, offer a detailed picture of life during those tragic years, with episodes that mirror, on a reduced scale, the whole range of situations that were shaking Europe and a good part of the world. Studying this documentation, one sometimes finds entire lives compressed between the brief lines of a *curriculum vitae* or in a note inserted into a file, bringing painful events and surprising personal experiences back to the surface.

At the beginning of World War I, during the summer of 1914, the Austro-Hungarian army began its call-ups, and with them came the first difficulties in the workplace. A letter dated July 27, 1914—the day before Austria declared war on Serbia—effectively describes the climate at the time: in the letter, the Zagreb agency informed the Central Head Office in Trieste that, given that the general mobilization had begun, even though none of its employees had been enlisted thus far, it had decided "as a precaution and in order to avoid hindering work, to suspend all of the previously granted authorizations," while one of its buyers, Gerson Mandić, a Serbian subject, had been arrested and held, along with his brother. Absences were heavily felt at the smaller agencies, like the one in Ljubljana: out of the eleven employees on the staff lists (*Personal-Stand*), five were already enlisted by the middle of 1915 [*fig.* 1], and they remained in service for almost the entire duration of the war. But nor were larger agencies exempt from the conscriptions. The correspondence from the period between February and April 1916 reveals staff changes at the general agency of Leipzig: at the beginning of the war, the agency had around twenty employees, ten of which were called up and replaced by trainees and young women, who turned out to be not fully suited to the job, while the four remaining men were elderly and in poor health. To remedy the situation, the number of female staff was temporarily increased, a phenomenon that touched all areas of civil and productive life and, as is well known, stimulated major social transformation throughout Europe. Adolescents were also used as replacements.

In terms of human life, the company paid a painfully heavy toll: no fewer than forty-five deaths on the Hapsburg side, and fourteen on the Italian. As we learn from the numerous sorrowful communications of "heroic death" (*Heldentod*) sent to Trieste and Vienna by its director, Jakob Poór, the Budapest Branch paid the heaviest price, with more than one-third of the company's total number of fallen and the first victim of the war on the Generali staff: Leo Fränkel. Born in 1892, he was killed by a large piece of shrapnel during a battle on the Russian front in early September 1914, as reported by one of his brothers-in-arms in a letter thick with war rhetoric: "He fought as only a good Hungarian can fight!" Most of the employees enlisted in the Austro-Hungarian army found themselves on the eastern front, against the Russians, and later against the Romanians as well, fighting in battles in Galicia, Bukovina, and Transylvania. Géza Goldberger, who worked in Trieste in the life division, died on May 10, 1915 in Kadlikow, Galicia. He was the first fallen soldier from the Central Head Office [*fig.* 2]. Emerich von Csernyák, who worked in the Budapest Branch, distinguished himself in October 1914 during the long Russian siege in Przemyśl (an important fortress city which at the time belonged to the Hapsburg Empire and is now in Poland at the Ukrainian border), by bringing an entire train loaded with gasoline into the surrounded city, receiving a commendation for what was described as a "impressive heroic feat." Franz Aigner, who began working in the fire division in Vienna in June 1910, died in battle in Galicia on May 1, 1915. The news of his death did not reach his family and the office until just over one year later, when his wife Berta Lippert received a death certificate compiled by a military chaplain and said that up until that moment she had received no news at all: her husband's personal effects had not been returned to her and his fellow soldiers maintained that he could not be dead since his company was not in a combat zone, and so until she received the certificate she had been hoping he had been instead taken prisoner. The documents concerning Aigner also report that he left three young children in addition to his wife, with no means of support whatsoever. Stories of lost hope also came from the theater of operations in Serbia, where other employees were involved, like Rudolf Rezniček. News of Rezniček dried up after November 1914, and then a newspaper reported that he had died in the Drina River, but this information was not confirmed by the lists of the fallen. Hope was kept alive and the search for news of him continued until September 1917, when he was definitively given up as missing and it was accepted that he was dead. Starting in 1915, there were also deaths on the Italian front, in the Battles of Isonzo, in the area of Tolmein, on Monte San Michele. We learn from a letter dated April 4, 1916, sent by the Budapest Branch to the Vienna Branch that Oskar Auszterweil, not yet twenty years old, died there on December 7, 1915. That same day, it also fell to Poór to communicate the death of another employee, Josef Szablics.

There were also those who experienced imprisonment. Some of the stories are dramatic, others less so, but they always reflect everyday life in the Russian

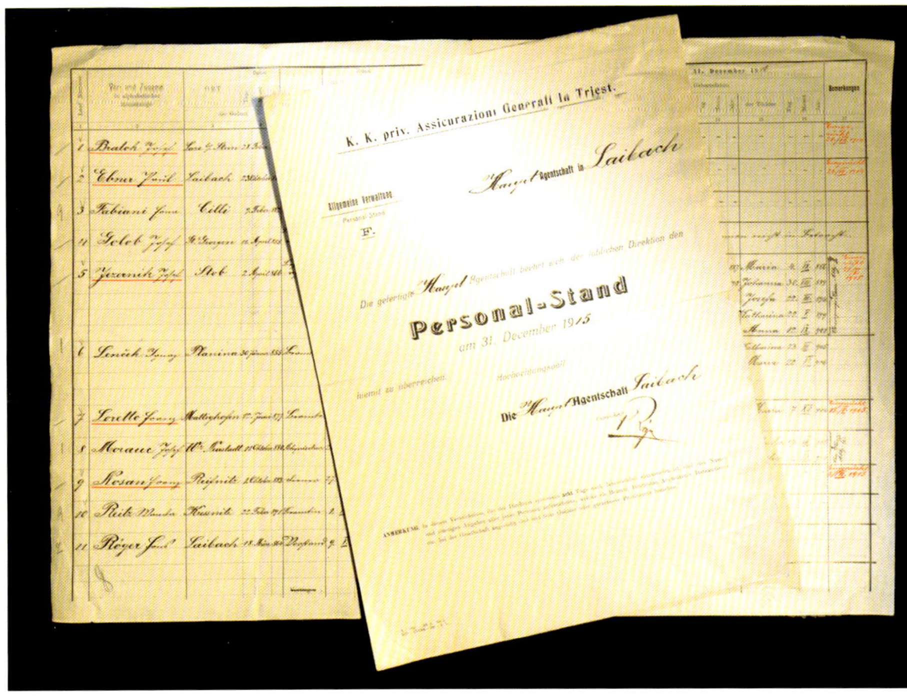

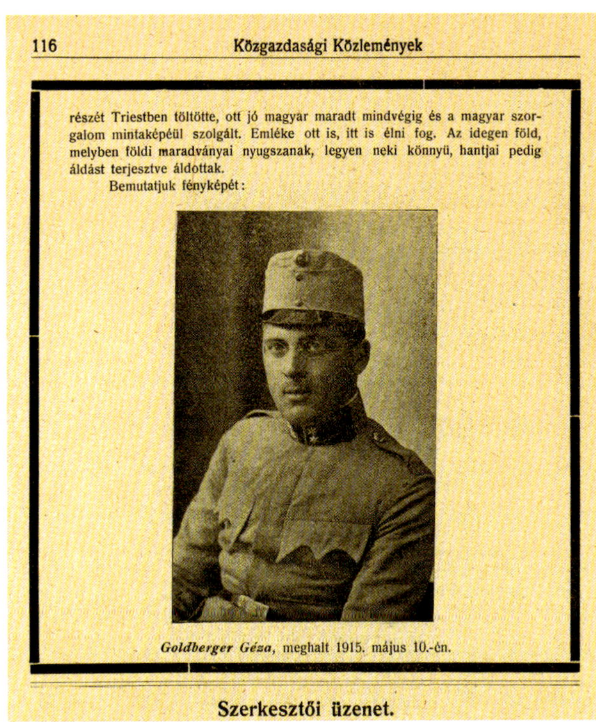

116 Közgazdasági Közlemények

részét Triestben töltötte, ott jó magyar maradt mindvégig és a magyar szorgalom mintaképéül szolgált. Emléke ott is, itt is élni fog. Az idegen föld, melyben földi maradványai nyugszanak, legyen neki könnyü, hantjai pedig áldást terjesztve áldottak.

Bemutatjuk fényképét:

Goldberger Géza, meghalt 1915. május 10.-én.

Szerkesztői üzenet.

1.
The Ljubljana agency's *Personal-Stand* for 1915 and 1916 [1916–1917]
[ASAG, *Direzione centrale, Servizio del personale*, U2GE014117]

2.
Commemorative announcement of the death of Géza Goldberger (Budapest, July 1, 1915)
[ASAG, *Direzione centrale, Servizio del personale, Posizioni personali*, U2GE042941]

3.
Documentation relative to the imprisonment and repatriation of Eugen Hetényi and Emerich Antscherl (1917–1921)
[ASAG, *Direzione centrale, Servizio del personale, Posizioni personali,* U2GE042887 and U2GE050083]

and Italian prison camps. We learn of the experience of Karl Novotný through the correspondence exchanged between Generala of Bucharest, the Vienna Branch, and the general agency of Prague. Captured by the Russians, in March 1916 an attempt was made to provide him with fifty rubles so that he could survive the prison camp, but the news arrived in June that he had by then died of tuberculosis. The return home from Russia became even more challenging after the revolution of 1917. The explosive local disorder and conflict throughout Central Europe when the war ended and the fall of the Hapsburg Empire led many veterans to ask to be reinstated in Trieste. The return home of Emerich Antscherl and Eugen Hetényi was a true odyssey, which literally took them around the world. Captured after the surrender of Przemyśl in spring 1915, they were transferred to one Russian camp after another, each time further east, from Tobol'sk in Western Siberia to Petropavlovsk in Kazakhstan, and then Nikol'sk Ussurijsk in the Far East. Thanks to contact with the Swedish and American Red Cross and help from the Italian Military Mission in Vladivostok, they were finally released in April 1920. In a letter dated October 10, 1919, Antscherl, who had in the meantime begun working at the English Military Mission in Vladivostok, asked the Central Head Office to work with the Italian military authorities to get him citizenship "and to ask this Mission to consider me one of the redeemed Italians and make it possible for me to return to Trieste. [...] I am taking the liberty of being insistent about my request as I see no other way of saving myself from this terrible situation." The two were, however, in for a great deal more travel. They boarded the Japanese ship *Yomei Maru*, which was transporting several hundred Russian children fleeing the war and saved by the Red Cross. They arrived in San Francisco and, from there, via the Panama Canal, New York. Then, having crossed over the Atlantic, they touched at Brest in France, Cuxhaven and Kiel in Germany, Copenhagen, and Tallinn, then making longer stops at various cities in Finland. They arrived in Hungary in January 1921 [*fig.* 3]. Similar, but more fortunate, stories played out in Italy. Generali repeatedly sent money to many of its employees in prison camps, such that we can now get an idea of the geographic distribution of the detention areas. Andor Ligeti returned home from Cefalù in 1920, after fifty months in prison. Moritz Stolz, an employee from the general agency in Lviv, also found himself in Sicily, first in Vittoria and then in Paternò. Stolz, writing that he just wanted to "return through Trieste and not through Lviv, since that city was immersed in chaos," promised that he would soon go home, but in the end asked for economic assistance throughout all of 1919, leading the Central Head Office to suspect that Stolz was "remaining there for particular personal reasons," and on March 12, 1920, it asked a local agency to look into the situation. Whether by coincidence or not, three days later Stolz left for Trieste, since, as he had already stated, he did not intend to go to his own country. A more curious story is that of Sergeant Leopold Malcsevsky, which sheds light on another sad situation that prisoners of war experienced to some degree throughout Europe. Captured in September 1917, he wrote from Cassino in December 1918 asking for 100 liras, a request that was promptly granted. Unfortunately, however, the money never reached him. When Malcsevsky returned to work in August 1919, the Central Head Office began to investigate the fate of the money. It turned out that it had been stolen by an Italian soldier by the name of Pelosi who had been working at the camp, but his present whereabouts could not be traced. The dispute, the outcome of which is unknown, continued until the first half of 1921, with the military authorities and the post offices that had handled the transaction each blaming the other.

In addition to those who died in battle, in prison, or in military hospitals from their wounds or disease, there were also civilian victims and those who paid much later for the physical and psychological wounds brought home from the front. Stefan von Beszedits, who was called up on August 1, 1914, and captured by the Russians in March 1915, was sent home from Taškent (today in Uzbekistan) only in 1922, after more than seven years in prison, but he died on the journey home of an epidemic disease he had contracted in Germany. There were also many instances of what is now called post-traumatic stress syndrome, caused by nervous breakdowns during combat. There were two suicides, and one employee from Prague died in March 1919: discharged in November 1914, according to the documentation he had suffered from hystero-epilepsy from that point on. Another case, which expresses the mentality and sense of personal pride of that period, is that of Nándor Steinfeld. Wounded on the Russian front, Steinfeld was taken to the hospital where he fell ill and suffered from such terrible neurosis that the doctor estimated it would take at least three or four years to cure. Given the circumstances, in December 1915 he wrote to the Head Office in Trieste to request permission to resign, since for health reasons he was unable to work and he preferred to find a new job that he could carry out with dignity in spite of his situation.

City life also became increasingly difficult as the war dragged on. In a note written in October 1916, we read that "the porter Ettore Maraspin [...] is beginning to suffer since he has no winter coat. And since he does not have the means to buy one, I would like to urge the Management to provide one [...]. I believe it should be mentioned that Maraspin's mother is a widow, to whom he gives his all of his wages, and he has a brother in the army. He also has a delicate constitution, and therefore suffers more than many others from the current devastating food situation."

Citizens of Italian origin in the Empire experienced a vast range of fates. Many of them from the area of Venezia Giulia were enlisted in the Austro-Hungarian army, and in particular the 97th Infantry Regiment. On May 23, 1918, this unit led a revolt in Radkersburg, Styria, as mentioned in a letter from the employee Giuseppe Huszak to the Central Head Office: "[...] due to the military proceedings, I was required to remain available, since I was accused along with all of the other petty officers of the 97th Regiment stationed in Radkersburg, under orders to not leave that location, because of the disorder on May 23." However, more than a few joined the irredentists. Even before the war, there was tension in Trieste between employees of Italian and German origin, to the point that one official, Graziadio Cusin, notified a superior that "for some time now, the Germans Schröker and Widmer have been stirring things up and snarling like rabid dogs at anyone they see as Italo-irredentist, and today there was a serious row that involved Chiassutti, Paggiaro, and lots of others from the backroom. [...] Be advised that Widmer [...] has already laid his hands on more than one person." And that was just on August 18, 1880. Later, during the war, some employees with irredentist involvement were investigated by the Austrian police and marked as having *radikal-italienisch* leanings. The delicate nature of the general political situation, and so also that of the company, emerges in the documentation concerning Giuseppe Liebermann. In October 1914, Liebermann left Trieste "to avoid the draft, going to Venice. For obvious reasons, they did not want him working at the Venice Head Office at that time, and he was forced for find work elsewhere." When the war broke out, he volunteered for the Regio Esercito under the name Giusti, while his father was interned for two years in Austria. In a letter dated 1917, Angelo Ara, the secretary of the Rome Head Office at the time, explained to Liebermann why he was not rehired by the company in 1914: the "Company was not in a position, in spite of itself and much to its sorrow, to employ You at the Venice Head Office. All of the normal considerations aside, it is enough to remember that because Your name was known and also because of the quantity of information proliferating in the city at that time, hiring You in Venice would have been impossible."

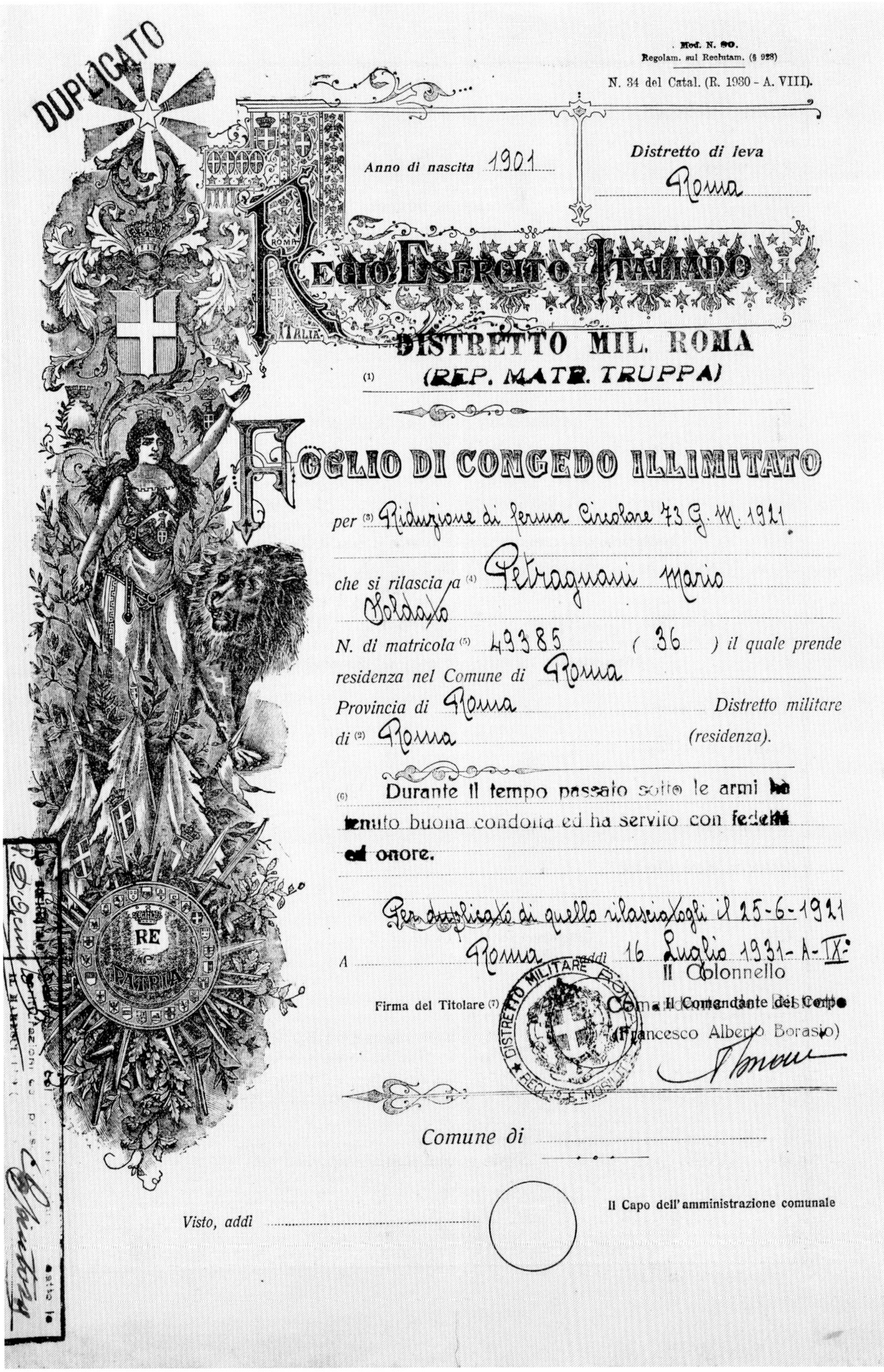

DUPLICATO

Mod. N. 80.
Regolam. sul Reclutam. (§ 928)

N. 34 del Catal. (R. 1930 - A. VIII).

Anno di nascita 1901

Distretto di leva Roma

REGIO ESERCITO ITALIANO

DISTRETTO MIL. ROMA
(1) (REP. MATR. TRUPPA)

FOGLIO DI CONGEDO ILLIMITATO

per (3) Riduzione di ferma Circolare 73 G. M. 1921

che si rilascia a (4) Petragnani Mario
Soldato

N. di matricola (5) 49385 (36) il quale prende residenza nel Comune di Roma
Provincia di Roma Distretto militare di (2) Roma (residenza).

(6) Durante il tempo passato sotto le armi ha tenuto buona condotta ed ha servito con fedeltà ed onore.

Per duplicato di quello rilasciatogli il 25-6-1921

A Roma addì 16 Luglio 1931- A-IX-

Firma del Titolare (7)

Il Colonnello
Comandante del Distretto
Il Comandante del Corpo
(Francesco Alberto Borasio)

DISTRETTO MILITARE ROMA

Comune di

Visto, addì

Il Capo dell'amministrazione comunale

4.
Mario Petragnani's certificate of discharge (Rome, July 16, 1931) [ASAG, *Direzione centrale, Servizio del personale, Posizioni personali*, U2GE042674]

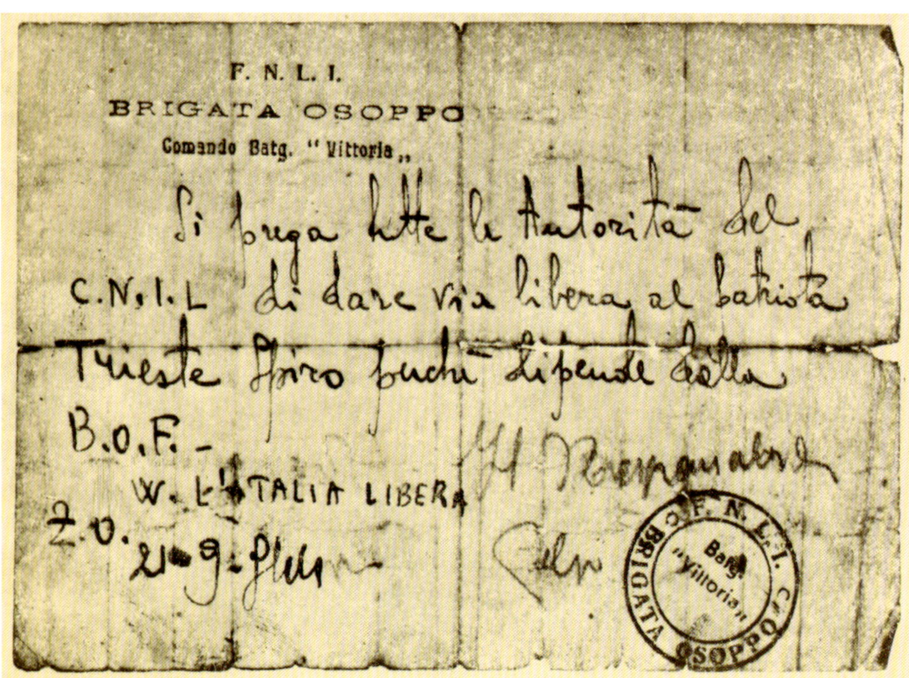

F. N. L. I.
BRIGATA OSOPPO
Comando Batg. "Vittoria"

Si prega tutte le Autorità del C.N.L.I. di dare via libera al patriota Trieste Spiro perchè dipende dalla B.O.F. -
W. L'ITALIA LIBERA
Z.O. 21-9-1944

F. N. L. I. BRIGATA OSOPPO Batg. "Vittoria"

5.
Postcards from the front sent by called-up employees to the Central Head Office (1941–1943)
[ASAG, *Presidenza e organi sociali, Presidenti e vicepresidenti, Gino Baroncini*, U2GE023978 and *Direzione centrale, Servizio del personale, Posizioni personali*, U2GE050104]

6.
Osoppo brigade pass for Spiridione Santon (September 21, 1944)
[ASAG, *Direzione centrale, Servizio del personale, Posizioni personali*, U2GE042600]

Others, arrived in Italy after having deserted or having been captured, some on the Serbian front, others on the Russian, like Giovanni Della Martina, who, once freed, enlisted in the Regio Esercito and was sent in 1918 to fight with the Italian contingent in France. Vittorio Fonda caused Generali considerable embarrassment. Called to join the Territorial Army, he found himself in Pula from July 1914. In early 1915, the company requested and received permission from the army for Fonda to return to the office temporarily. In a letter dated February 5 to the Central Head Office, we read that "since Mr. Vittorio Fonda has not been in the Office since the 27th, a staff member was sent to his home to inquire as to his health, where he learned that Mr. Fonda had not been at home since that date either. His relatives imagine that he has gone abroad. I am writing to you of this with deep regret, and I ask you to please send a suitable replacement straightaway." Three days later, Generali communicated to the authorities its "profound regret that one of our employees was able to commit such treachery." But that was not the end of it: in a "confidential" letter dated November 1916, addressed to Giuseppe Luzzatto, secretary director in Venice, we learn that Fonda was serving as a second lieutenant in the Regio Esercito and that after his discharge in 1919 he was assigned to the transport division in Rome, which had been a refuge during the war for those taking shelter in Italy, employing many Italian exiles and Empire deserters. Others were not so fortunate, like Antonio Sereni, a university student in Vienna. On May 7, 1915, he tried to cross the Italian border and join his brother, but he was recognized and arrested by the Austrian police. Condemned to one year of military prison in Graz, where he met many irredentists, he was also permanently banned "from all Austrian universities." In 1916 he was conscripted into the Hapsburg army and sent to Galicia and Bukovina, while the rest of his family was interned in Graz. He was able to return to Trieste in February 1919. Ettore Kers, whose last name was later changed to Chersi, experienced internment firsthand, since he had joined the "Mazzinian party" in 1907. Deported to the Wagna internment camp in Styria, in 1915 he wrote to director Carlo Schütz asking for director Ehrentheil to intercede in his favor with the Interior Ministry, and his detention was commuted such that he was able to go to Vienna, where he could resume work, although still under surveillance by the local police. Kers was not able to get to the Vienna Branch until May 3, 1917, and in December 1918, the war having ended only one month before, he committed an act of insubordination, returning to Trieste without permission from the Vienna Branch. In a letter dated January 10, 1919, he justified his action with his deep desire to return home, after long years in prison and internment, also describing the Austrian capital as a city "driven by hunger and ravaged by factions." Stories of other Italian soldiers are revealed in job applications and relative documentation sent to the company's various main Branches in the 1920s [*fig.* 4]. Among the many different stories, there is also one of a woman. Virginia Calzolaio, born in Rome in 1894, described her experience during World War I in her Generali job application, which she presented at the Rome Head Office in 1923: a housewife until 1915, in July of that year she volunteered for the Red Cross and, after having served in various hospitals in Rome, "in September 1916 she entered the operational zone, specifically Cormons, with an English unit, and then joined the Italian troops to enter Gorizia. In December 1916 she transferred to a small field hospital near Caporetto [...] She then withdrew with our troops in November 1917 [...]. She was decorated with the campaign ribbon and is awaiting the certificate for the Distinguished Service Cross."

As already noted, when the war ended, the fall of the Hapsburg Empire and the claims of the newly formed states had considerable political and social consequences of their own. Drafted into the Austro-Hungarian army on August 1, 1914, Leon Stanislaus Weizmann went over to the newly formed Polish army in December 1918, and found himself fighting with the Ukrainians and Soviet Russians at a time when the borders were extremely fluid. When the conflicts ended in 1921, Weizmann, who had in the meantime changed his name to Wieckowski, resumed his former job back at the general agency of Lviv. In Italy, the discontent following the peace treaty led to the occupation of Fiume. At least five Generali employees were involved, one of whom, a former petty officer in the Regia Marina, described his experience in the *curriculum vitae* he sent in 1923: "I was excited about the matter of Fiume and I decided along with a few of my fellow soldiers to go over to D'Annunzio. At the time I was in Lussimpiccolo with a tugboat and I teamed up with a lieutenant engineer. He took command of a financial police steamboat, I took the helm, and we went to Fiume. I then had to resign, for propriety's sake, otherwise the desertion could have damaged my career."

Another problem was the reinsertion of thousands of veterans, many of whom were disabled, into civil life and the workforce. The company received requests from veterans' associations and for assistance for those who had been disfigured or disabled during the war.

Many scenarios similar to those described thus far also arose during World War II. All of the company's Branches, both abroad and in Italy, experienced the same problems that had surfaced twenty-five years earlier: difficulties at work after employees had been called to arms, men working together at the same company finding themselves fighting on opposite sides (Italians, Germans, Hungarians, French, Belgians, etc.), and at least forty employees, military and civil, among the war dead; still others were wounded, imprisoned or interned, and, out of these, many Italians were deported to Germany after September 8, 1943.

There were, however, significant and dramatic differences between World War II and the Great War with respect to civilian life, especially after the Italian armistice and consequential German occupation. As is well-known, the situation for Jews in Germany had already become very difficult in the 1930s: on October 31, 1939, the London office wrote to the Central Head Office that the employee Karl Mayer had arrived in the English capital, after having first left the Berlin office in 1937 and now the one in Vienna, "due to the political situation." Generali employees were not spared from the unleashing of persecution during the war. When a decree was issued in December 1940 that made all foreign and Polish Jews equal, the director in charge of Poland, Viktor Wiener, who was Czechoslovakian, was arrested on the 30th of that very month and later transferred to the Warsaw ghetto. Included on a list of people to be exchanged with Germans held in America drawn up in June 1941, he was instead seen only one last time by an acquaintance, "going from Cracow to Oswięcim (Auschwitz), where the notorious death camp was located." Oscar Smolensky, an executive in the Brussels Branch and brother of the former manager of the life division, Pietro Smolensky, was initially interned on May 10, 1940 by the Belgian authorities, since he was an Austrian citizen, and later captured by the Germans and sent to a concentration camp, where he died. When Yugoslavia was occupied in 1941, four Jewish employees were deported: Artur David, from the Sarajevo office and Viktor Rainer, Ladislav Misner, and Rudolf Eisenstädter from the Zagreb Branch. The first two were sent to Germany, since they were prisoners of war, whereas Misner and Eisenstädter, "sent by the competent Authorities out of Zagreb," died in December of that year. As for Italy, when the racial laws were passed in 1938, employees of Jewish origin had to be dismissed en masse. The situation plummeted when the Germans occupied the country. In 1944, after the roundups in Venice, Aurelio Trevi was killed by the SS in the city jail, and Ignazio Luft was deported to Auschwitz. Mario Alhaique was luckily able to save himself: the SS came looking for him at his house in Trieste on November 12, 1943, but he had already fled to Florence in September.

Numerous aspects of the conditions of everyday and office life are revealed in the documentation. In a letter dated August 15, 1941, Gino Baroncini, who was the general manager at the time, wrote the following in regard to requests for promotions and salary increases: "It seemed and seems proper to avoid a situation where the employees who are still at home can improve their positions while so many other members of the staff are exposed to the discomforts and dangers of war." During the same period, the Generali Head Office in Trieste opened a soup kitchen on the ground floor of Via Trento 3, which could serve up to 1,500 meals per day to help the most needy. The problem of staff shortages due to enlistments worsened when further employees were "requis par le Service du Travail Obligatoire," as we read in a few documents from the Brussels and Paris Branches from 1943 and 1944. In November 1944, in Trieste, as had already happened in previous months, the German authorities asked Generali for a contingent of as many as fifty-four employees, needed for territorial defense work; this number was reduced to nineteen after a meeting with the Germans. In addition to all of this, there was a shortage of ordinary, everyday items. On March 22, 1944, the Venice Head Office issued a circular that asked all employees to save paper in any way possible, eliminating blank pages, writing smaller, simplifying the formulas of the policies: the situation was clearly becoming increasingly unsustainable.

The Generali employees who fought in the war found themselves on a range of fronts [*fig.* 5] and the list of those who lost their lives or went missing covers a broad territory: Africa (Roberto Dussi in El Alamein), the eastern front (Alfred Benn and Leone Lanza), the Balkans (Franco Chiais and Guglielmo Wieland), the Mediterranean (Benedetto Girardelli), and the sky (the pilot Fulvio Nonveiller and Bruno Depetroni, a member of the Alpine troops and student paratrooper, both of whom died in flight-related incidents). As for World War I, during World War II Generali mourned with its employees' families and offered them economic assistance. In the case of those who had gone missing or were interned, the company also did all it could to get information from the authorities about their whereabouts. The civil war that broke out in Italy after September 8 brought more death and created more factions. On September 23, 1943, Domenico Aita, staff sergeant in the Divisione Acqui, died fighting the Germans in Cephalonia. Bernardo Malberti, who had to be dismissed due to the racial laws and immigrated to the United States, enlisted in the American merchant marines and went on numerous war missions. In 1944, Karl Golücke and Giuseppe Tassara were killed fighting the partisans. While others fought in the Resistance [*fig.* 6]. Examples in France include Edouard Steiner and André Dutheil, both of whom worked in the Paris Branch. The former, an Italian citizen, was mentioned in two letters sent to the Central Head Office: on December 26, 1943 it was communicated that he had left work without explanation, and on July 2, 1945 that the *maquisard* Steiner had returned to work. In Italy, Livio Finzi, a veteran of the campaign in Eastern Africa, also left work, in March 1944, without explanation. Persecuted for reasons of race, sought by the Germans, and his father and sister having been deported to a concentration camp, he joined the partisans' Pellegrini brigade in the province of Venice, helping numerous former prisoners of war and allied spies and transmitting information about the movements and fortifications of the German troops via radio. Some justified their absence from work with "formal" doctor's certificates. Alfredo Polesi was one of these. Previously a member of Fascist University Groups (GUF) and an officer in the Sassari Brigade during the first part of the war, Polesi took a leave of absence on September 16, 1944. On December 9 of the same year, he informed the company that he could not return to work, as he was ill in Milan. The leave of absence was renewed three months later for three additional months, until spring 1945, but in May, Polesi, who had theoretically been on sick leave for quite some time, appeared on a list published by the newspaper *Avanti* of those who had lost their lives during the liberation of Milan. The Central Head Office, worried by this news and evidently unaware of the real situation, asked for information from the Milan general agency for the transport division. It thus learned that Polesi had made contact with the partisans in Milan in 1944 and had been working for the Comando Piazza maintaining contact with areas on the periphery. During the rebellion on April 25, he was actively involved in bringing orders to various points in the city to coordinate the action. On the morning of April 26, he was killed in a gunfight with the Germans on Corso Buenos Aires.

The postwar period was scarred by the deep wounds left by the conflict, and here again the company's employees had a range of different experiences: veterans, war widows without the means to feed their families, and refugees fleeing regions that were still in difficulty were hired, employees believed to be associated with fascism and in particular with the Repubblica Sociale Italiana were subjected to purges, and those who went missing during the Nazi persecutions and, in Trieste, during the weeks of Yugoslavian occupation, were desperately searched for. One of the many victims during the latter period was Umberto Fegitz, a Generali cashier. His job required him to have a gun permit. Because of this, he, along with other cashiers from a few of the city's banks, was arrested on May 4, 1945 by Tito's troops and incarcerated until the 29th of that month, the "day on which he was deported to an unknown destination," according to the ruling of presumed death issued by the Trieste court in 1953, after all of the attempts to obtain information about him from the Yugoslavian authorities had failed. (M.M.)

The World War I Memorial Relief

The Generali World War I memorial in honor of the employees fallen for Italy is found at the entrance to Palazzo Geiringer, in Piazza Duca degli Abruzzi, the historical seat of the Central Head Office. The work was created within the broader context of celebrations for the end of the war and the unification of the irredenta territories with Italy.
Angelo Ara, co-manager from 1922 and then deputy general manager, handled the project overall, from communication with the sculptor to collecting information about the fallen and the invitations to the ceremony. The engineer Giorgio Polli was also involved, seeing to the technical aspects of installing the monument by the grand staircase, below the large central sculpture group. The sculptor Gigi Supino was commissioned to do the work when he was just over thirty-three years old. Born in Genoa in 1893 to a mother from Trieste, he fought on the Karst plateau. He had already been commissioned to sculpt a bust of the chairman Marco Besso, and in a letter dated January 15, 1926, Angelo Ara asked him to formulate a few concepts for the memorial. The artist presented three ideas. The first features a woman on a pedestal holding a child in her arms and a cornucopia symbolizing peace, family, and the land, defended by two wounded fighters carrying shields. The second depicts the liberation of Trieste, with a female figure, symbolizing Italy, holding a winged Nike in her hand and stopping her horses just before the city, represented by another female figure, who stretches out her arms, having broken the chains that bound them. The third, which was the one chosen for the relief, is of Glory blessing the fighters and the fallen. The scene represents four figures: three warriors—an archer, a figure armed with a spear, and a dying figure, whose sword has been thrust into the ground to suggest a cross—and a Winged Victory who protects and glorifies the three. On the right margin are the names of the fourteen fallen in rubricated letters: in addition to the eleven from the Venice Head Office are three from the Central Head Office: Roberto Liebmann, Riccardo Magris, and Luigi Muran. At the top there was originally an inscription, sculpted into the marble, "Onore ai caduti nostri nella guerra di redenzione MCMXV – MCMXVIII" [In honor of those who fought and died in the War of Redemption] its letters also painted red.
The inauguration took place on December 20, 1926, on the anniversary of the death of Guglielmo Oberdan. The first date chosen was, however, November 4, the anniversary of the victory, but the sculpture was accidentally sent to Florence, and the celebration had to be postponed. Moreover, when it arrived, the spear was broken into three pieces, which Supino himself repaired. And so, at 12:30 pm on Monday, December 20, the chairman Edgardo Morpurgo read a speech remembering these men and the circumstances that led to their deaths. In addition to many civilian and military authorities, the families of the fallen, and all of the employees, Maria Bergamas was also invited: in 1921, Bergamas had represented all of the women who had lost their sons and husbands in the war, choosing the unknown soldier to be buried in Rome in the Altare della Patria from eleven nameless bodies.
Today, the main entry to the Palazzo Geiringer is much changed: the grand staircase was removed in 1966 and this whole area of the building was refurbished, but the sculpture remains at the main entrance, in memory of all of those who sacrificed their lives fighting for Italy.

7.
The Assicurazioni Generali World War I memorial relief dedicated to the employees fallen for Italy (1926) [ASAG, *Versamenti*, OGG001114928]

Trieste-Vienna, Venice-Rome
The Wartime Reorganization of the Company

1915
1931

The last Ordinary General Meeting was held on April 14, 1915. World War I was still in its early phase, with Italy joining the conflict five weeks later. A large proportion of the company's Management of Directors and Board members, and around one hundred employees from the Central Head Office, left Trieste for the Kingdom of Italy. The company looked after its refugee staff and their families, at first providing for their needs and then finding them suitable work. The first precautionary measures had already been taken in August 1914, when Generali safeguarded its security deposits by sending them to Vienna, in response to the worsening of the political situation following the breaking off of relations between Austria and France, and considering that all of the main banks had made the transfer by order of the Austrian government.

This move did not escape the attention of the main newspapers, which, supposing that the company was transferring its headquarters, seized the opportunity to throw the company's Italian identity into doubt. In response, Marco Besso wrote an open letter, dated February 23, 1915, in which he stressed the close ties that united the "sister" cities, Trieste and Venice, the locations of company's administrative offices from its founding, through the appointment to the Board of Directors of Alfonso Valerio and Filippo Grimani, respectively the podesta of Trieste and the mayor of Venice, and the firm commitment to keeping its headquarters where they were.

Considering the way in which events were unfolding, the Management was called upon to make a statement as to the measures that would need to be taken should the situation worsen, involving the departure of a large part of the staff of the Central Head Office. At a Management meeting held in May, it was announced that the director-in-charge, Edgardo Morpurgo [*fig.* 1], had decided, firstly, to move some of the offices in Venice to Rome, to ensure that the fire business in Italy and the East would be properly covered, and, secondly, to set up a temporary office in Vienna for handling business in Central Europe, while operations for the rest of the world would be handled in Italy, under Besso and the special director for Italy, Giuseppe Luzzatto. The Venice Head Office fearlessly remained active for more than two years, and all of its departments and divisions continued their activity in the city. The only exception was the transport division, which, due to its special nature, required easier and faster communications, and so it was transferred to Rome, where it was headed by Morpurgo. The possibility of opening a temporary office in Zurich was also considered. The purpose of this "mediator office" would have been to ensure communication with all of the agencies in countries that could not communicate with Trieste and to carry on the company's transport and fire activity, in light of the great difficulties expected in regard to reinsurance work in Spain, Greece, and Italy separated from that in the other territories, leaving the Head Office in charge of damage negotiations (handwritten note enclosed with the minutes for the Management meeting held on May 12, 1915). Morpurgo put himself in charge of the procedures relative to founding the office, taking steps to ensure that the issue would be settled as quickly as possible. The important mission to create and manage an administrative office in neutral territory that would connect all of the territories where the company was active during the war was entrusted to Nathan Rogers, who worked at the time in the East department, as we learn from a memo dated January 25, 1940, preserved in his personnel file.

There was also a precautionary plan to send, if necessary, one of the deputy directors-in-charge, either Emanuele Ehrentheil or Carlo Schütz, to Vienna with a few of the officers from the Central Head Office in order to maintain direct and constant contact with the agencies in the Hapsburg Empire, in case communications with Trieste became interrupted, even though steps had also been taken to keep the Central Head Office open for as long as possible. During the war, Schütz was alone in charge of the Head Office in Trieste, since all of the other executives were forced to leave the city, and Ehrentheil took the helm in Vienna. It was an extremely difficult situation, not

1.
Edgardo Morpurgo (Venice, October 14, 1913), postcard
[ASAG, *Versamenti*, scheda 28265]

TORINO
VENEZIA
NAPOLI

AGENZIA PRINCIPALE
DI ROMA

MDCCCXXXI

POLIZZA
N° 56867

MILANO
GENOVA

ASSICURAZIONI GENERALI
DI VENEZIA

SOCIETÀ ANONIMA ISTITUITA NEL 1831
CAPITALE SOCIALE INTIERAMENTE VERSATO L. 13.230.000

Incendi - Vita - Trasporti - Furti

POLIZZA DI ASSICURAZIONE
CONTRO I DANNI DELL' INCENDIO

FIRENZE
MILANO

. DITTA ASSICURATA .

SPETT. ASSICURAZIONI GENERALI DI VENEZIA
Direzione Speciale Ramo Trasporti
IN ROMA

VERONA
PALERMO

ARTI GRAF. V. POLACCO - ROMA

NAPOLI
ROMA
TORINO

PRINCIPALI PALAZZI DELLA COMPAGNIA

merely for the overall circumstances, but also because the Austrian authorities were aware of the considerable number of Italian volunteers who were on the company's staff.

This tension was intensified when the securities were transferred from Vienna to Trieste and Venice to cover the reserves in Italy. A dispute erupted with the competent authorities, who were concerned that Generali was planning to sell Austrian securities in order to buy Italian ones, perhaps in preparation for setting up an Italian company. This was denied by the company, which was instead transferring the securities because the reserves in Italy needed to be fully covered, a claim easily verified by reading through the accounting documents, which were kept in Trieste at the time, given the "temporary" nature of the Viennese transfer (letter from Ehrentheil to Schütz on May 25, 1915).

The double identity of Generali also caused problems on the Italian side. The ongoing defamation campaign against the company became even more vicious than it had been in previous months. The company's solvency was placed in question and its national identity was denied, since its headquarters were in the Empire, playing on the ambiguity "out of a desire to confuse the concept of ethnic nationality with that of legal nationality and since asserting that Trieste is not a nationally Italian city is the most Hapsburgian thing one can say" (circular no. 16/8 of July 1916). This denial was countered with the history of the company, its two-headed statutory structure (Trieste had been chosen as the headquarters due to more favorable conditions than would be found in Venice for the development of a company aimed towards expanding its sphere of activity beyond State boundaries), the distribution of shares, the formation of the Management, and the fact that the books and all of the documents were in Italian. The company denied that it was transferring its Head Office from Trieste to Vienna and emphasized the fact that company had an independent statutory office in the Kingdom of Italy, in Venice, and not just a representative office, as we read in various circulars addressed to the shareholder body and its agents in the Kingdom.

In early June, it being impossible to assemble the members of the Management the company decided that the director-in-charge and the secretary director and their respective deputies should operate independently (meetings were held alternately in Trieste and Vienna) until the end of the war and that the internal reorganization of the company should be completed through the redistribution of the duties concerning staff, work management, issues of a general nature, and, above all, ensuring the security of the building after the demonstrations that had erupted in Trieste.

Besso and Morpurgo labored for the recognition of the company's Italian identity, which was an indispensable condition for continuing activity in the Entente countries: Morpurgo consequently traveled frequently to France and England. The company's interactions with the various governments were fundamental for making the Italian identity of Generali undeniably clear, while its activity required a large base for developing its transport business, especially with the risk of war on the horizon, and so relations were established with the international market in London. The French government, which had sequestered the Paris headquarters when war broke out with Austria, recognized the company's complete freedom to resume its operations in France in the Decree of April 11, while the British government, following careful investigation, decided that the Venice Head Office was free to conduct its business in England. Of critical importance here was Morpurgo's work to strengthen the company's transport business, especially in the area of maritime insurance. In order to develop the division he set up a Special Office in Rome that was officially active starting on September 4, 1915 [*fig.* 2].

In February 1916, the Italian Ministry of Agriculture, Industry, and Trade proclaimed that all of the reserves pertaining to insurance policies taken out in Italy, regardless of the division, were covered by

2.
Fire policy from the Special Office for the Transport Division in Rome (Rome, December 10, 1919)
[ASAG, *Direzione centrale, Ufficio delegato, Corrispondenza,* OGG001125161]

businesses already set up within the Kingdom, which were bound in favor of the insured, in accordance with the King Deputy's Decree of July 29, 1915 no. 1167. The certificate issued by the Prime Minister's office on April 26 removed all doubt as to the company's legal status and national identity, leaving no room for objections.

At the end of August, the Management ordered the transfer of the accounting and administrative documentation as well as that of the life division, as a preventative measure in response to the fear that the Italians would occupy Trieste, the permanence of the Central Head Office in the city being, however, understood. The documentation of the non-life divisions was to remain on site, awaiting either the first government request or the emergence of a threat. As for the clerical staff, only a few were transferred, with the rest remaining in Trieste to cover the numerous vacancies created by the last call to arms (directors' minutes no. 31 of August 29, 1916).

When the threat to Venice worsened following Caporetto, and some of the government offices, the courts, banks, and commercial institutions abandoned the city, the Management decided to temporarily transfer its offices to Rome, having consulted the Board of Directors and upon recommendation by the authorities. The move took place on November 6, 1917, while the main agency remained in place, continuing its operations. It again fell to Morpurgo to organize the arrangement of the Venice offices in the Italian capital. In Rome, he set up a special office for foreign countries, which opened in November 1917 and had managerial functions for the more urgent measures, while Vienna continued to handle Central Europe.

In the meantime, in Trieste, the Head Office accepted the military authorities' request to temporarily occupy its left wing. The building, on Via di Torrebianca (formerly Contrada Carinzia), was almost empty, and according to the agreement the military would use it for a maximum of six weeks, for compensation to be decided, to aid soldiers (directors' minutes no. 45 of November 22, 1917).

At a meeting held in Trieste on January 20, 1919, with the entire Management present, the chairman, Marco Besso, filled with intense emotion, extended "a warm welcome to our colleagues who, after a long and forced interruption" had been brought together for the first time in liberated Trieste, at Generali's Central Head Office. The next day, arrangements were made to return the company's securities, which had been deposited at various Viennese banks when war broke out. At the same time, arrangements were also made for the return to Trieste of the staff, books, and all of the material in general no longer needed in Vienna.

On April 4, the Venice Head Office that had been transferred to Rome returned to Venice, even though there were major advantages to having a Head Office in the capital of the Kingdom for a company like Generali, branched out as it was over the entire peninsula. But "devotion to the City of St. Mark" and the company's "historical traditions" provided the motivation for going through the "serious inconvenience" of a new move, which involved not only the staff and their families but also the archives (circular no. 5/2 of March 20, 1919). Only the Special Office for the Transport Division remained in Rome.

Morpurgo dedicated himself to reorganizing the company in Italy and making business trips to restore the company's presence abroad, traveling in particular to Paris, as a member of the financial committee at the Paris Peace Conference.

Reporting that the transport division in Rome, which had proven to be extremely advantageous during the war, was continuing its remarkable growth, he outlined the advisability of subordinating the activity of the transport division of the general agency of Trieste to the Rome Office, setting up a general transport agency in Trieste. Duilio Romano and Vittorio Mussafia, who had been transport managers at the agency in Trieste, were entrusted with its management. The office was independent from the transport division administration

Generali-RAS: A New Italian "Holding"

As we read in the draft of the agreement, "in view of the affinity of their origins and company aims, and in light of the near concurrence of their activity in the same geographic regions," Generali and RAS "consider it opportune to adopt, in the upper management of their businesses, common guidelines, such as to operate in mutual, trusting union in all cases in which their material and moral interests require it." The aim was to establish a unified direction for their two Head Offices in Trieste, having first made the necessary changes to their charters, which would have constituted their corporate representation through the Board of Directors, the Council of Directors and the Executive Committee. For their respective Council of Directors, each company was to appoint individuals who were either members of the Council of Directors or general managers of the appointing company. Arnoldo Frigessi was to join Generali as general manager and managing director, maintaining the post of managing director of RAS in order to ensure administrative continuity and serve as a link between the two Executives Committees. His office would have been at Assicurazioni Generali in Trieste, and he would have been the company's top executive, without any executives above him or of the same rank, with Morpurgo remaining in an unquestionable position of preeminence, as chairman of the Council of Directors of each of the two companies and managing director of Generali. The Executive Committee of the two companies was to be made up of the same people, as it was to be for the chairman of the Council of Directors, with responsibility for providing general guidelines that were to be translated into practice by the Management. The two companies were to pledge to follow common guidelines in the geographic areas where they were active and for the companies that were part of their groups, limiting reciprocal competition, and providing mutual assistance with technical, administrative, and financial management. Moreover, they were to ensure that money was saved on the management of their respective affairs by sharing offices and executives and promoting joint projects and initiatives.

The agreement was to last for fifteen years. It would have gone into effect on January 1, 1922, and ended on December 31, 1936, with the possibility of extension.

According to the agreement, which was to be discussed within the respective Managements and presented to the General Meeting of both companies for final approval, the Head Office in Trieste would be directly in charge of the full management of the company's affairs, the only exception being that handled by the Venice Head Office and the Special Office for the Transport Division, maintaining, however, its authority over the two. The transport office in Rome would have been required to keep the Head Office in Trieste up to date on its affairs and the division's more salient issues, operating in agreement with that office and, as necessary, with Venice on organizational matters.

The correspondence between Morpurgo and Frigessi includes the drafts relative to the agreement, the terms of the covenant, and the organization of the corporate representation at both companies. No documentation has been found concerning the planned changes to the organization of the Venice Head Office or the special agreement for the management of the transport division, which was to have the same duration as the agreement between the two companies.

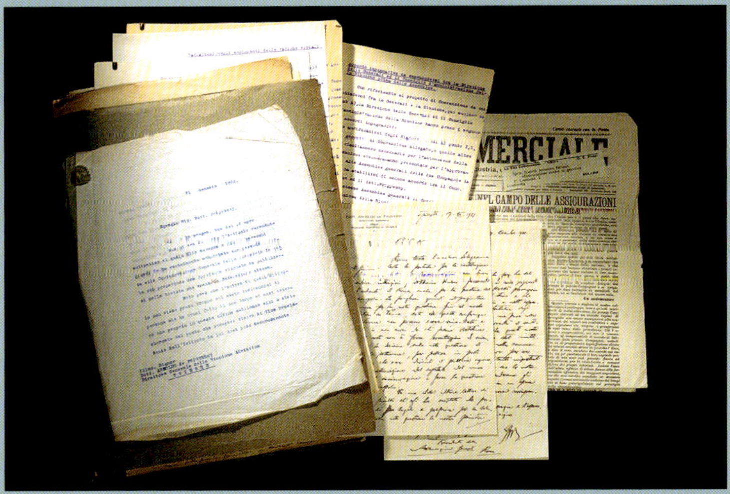

3.
Documentation relative to the agreement between Generali and RAS (1921-1922)
[ASAG, *Presidenza e organi sociali, Presidenti e vicepresidenti, Edgardo Morpurgo*, U2GE024230]

in Trieste, reporting directly to the one in Rome, as we read in the directors' minutes of January 16, 1920.
During a Management meeting on October 28, and after a few words in memory of the greatness of Marco Besso, who had recently died, the Management declared its support for electing Edgardo Morpurgo chairman, which would "not only duly recognize *Grand'Ufficiale* Morpurgo's distinguished gifts, but would also respect the wishes of the recently deceased *Commendatore* Marco Besso, who nominated *Commendatore* Morpurgo as the best-suited candidate for succeeding him in this important top post."
As for relaunching the company in national territory, it is fascinating to read the correspondence between the new chairman and Arnoldo Frigessi, general manager of Riunione Adriatica di Sicurtà (RAS) from the years 1921–1922, concerning creating a union between the companies' administrations and a partnership between their respective transport offices under a single Central Head Office. This project was not officially brought to the attention of the company leadership, and there is in fact no mention of it in the top management documentation and nor was it formalized at the Shareholders' Meeting, as had been proposed. The only evidence of the plan, which never got off the ground, or better, was "postponed until a better time," are the papers preserved among Morpurgo's private correspondence [*fig.* 3]. Within the élite Generali circle involved in the preliminary meetings for drafting the definitive plan to be presented to the respective administrations, doubts were voiced from the start, in particular with respect to the key role that Frigessi would have assumed at the Venice Head Office. After the débâcle in Central Europe, Italy was now the driver of the company's activity and so bringing the two companies together would have been to the advantage of RAS, the weaker of the two. The competition took a dim view of the partnership: there was a danger that the "quasi-merger" would be interpreted as a kind of monopoly over the life industry and, at a delicate moment for resolving the issue at a national level, it was better for the company to avoid exposing itself too much. The plan for profit-sharing remained undecided: there was no certainty that RAS would be able to keep pace with Generali, and danger of profits leveling out due to lack of healthy competition. There were even greater misgivings about the idea to unite the companies' leadership: RAS, organizationally weaker, would have enjoyed the greater advantage. There were also strong doubts about the neutrality of the interests involved. Sharing Council of Directors and Committees and the near-commonality of the administration would have been "almost embarrassing" in some ways, since the interests of the two companies were not, and could not have been, identical (letter from Giuseppe Luzzatto to Morpurgo on November 20, 1921).
In spite of the far-sightedness of Morpurgo's belief that the project would develop in Generali's favor, Frigessi's doubts postponed the negotiations to fall 1922, and in the end they never even took place. Worried about the difficult economic situation, he committed to "remaining in the post of chairman until he had resolved at least most of the problems that had emerged out of the abnormal situation we all still find ourselves in." The issue having been raised with the Committee, he decided to suspend discussion of the "the merits and terms" of the agreement with the Board (letter from Luzzatto to Morpurgo on December 9, 1921).
As chairman, Morpurgo dedicated himself in the years that followed to restructuring and reorganizing the vast network of companies in the Generali Group. He improved the situation for Assicurazioni Generali of Constantinople and the French La Concorde; in Bohemia, he set up the national company Moldavia-Generali and contributed to the creation of Securitas of Prague. In Yugoslavia, he founded Sava of Zagreb; in Austria he contributed to the founding of an Austro-German company, Heimat of Vienna; in Spain he acquired an important share in the Banco Vitalicio de España, one of the oldest institutions in Spain, and created a new fire

insurance company in Madrid. He restructured Generali of Bucharest, and in Great Britain he joined forces with Cornhill and set up a large office in London not only for generating business, but also to serve as a mirror for the global insurance industry, London being its center: this was a first step towards extending the company's activity throughout the rest of the United Kingdom.

In September 1926, Morpurgo informed the Council of Directors that, in the interest of concentrating the administration of all of the company's foreign activity at the Central Head Office, the administration of the foreign part of the transport division would be moved to Trieste. The unification of the administration of all of the divisions simplified and created greater coherence between the various services. The main ones were already functioning, when, after the war, the Trieste administration was restored to its earlier structure. The transport divisions for operations in the Kingdom of Italy instead remained in Rome. The management of real estate in the Kingdom's old provinces was also transferred from Venice to Trieste, in order to centralize administration of all of the company's buildings. These changes required many staff members to move to Trieste, including Michele Sulfina, most of the top management from the Rome Office, and about seventy employees. The move was complete at the end of November. Most of the apartments in the building on Via Trento, which was next to the Central Head Office, were vacated, making it possible to set up the offices "in a satisfactory way, such that right for the beginning there was a notable improvement in work," especially since, all direct and reinsurance activity now concentrated in Trieste, communication between the Head Office and the foreign agencies had become faster and more regular.

In 1930, in accordance with the regulations laid down in article 42 of the company charter, the Rome Head Office had, for the transport sector, powers relative to the technical management of the division, ordinary administration, and availability of the administration's accounts (minutes from the Executive Committee meeting on June 27, 1930). At a meeting on April 8, 1931, in the interest of fully unifying the organization of the transport sector and, consequentially, optimizing spending, the Council of Directors decided to concentrate the division's administration entirely in Trieste, transferring the remaining offices in Rome by the end of the month. While the Rome Head Office temporarily stopped its activity, directives relative to its executives followed. In this regard, we read that Leo Levi, secretary-general of the office, "will remain in Rome as the lead of the representative office that will be set up there and will be assigned the following duties, without the authority to involve the Company, except in the case of special powers of attorney for specific operations: a) the Chairman's secretariat; b) negotiation of cases assigned to it with public and private entities, insurance companies, similar entities, and businesses and individuals; c) operations relative to the securities service." These directives were communicated to Levi, as we read in a letter in his personnel file, when he joined the staff of the Central Head Office with the rank and title of deputy manager, without power of signature, remaining in Rome as the head of the office. The chairman's right-hand man, in the 1940s he became a social insurance consultant at the company as director of the Istituto Nazionale per l'Assicurazione contro gli Infortuni sul Lavoro (INAIL).

The final step towards restoring the original structure of the Central Head Office was complete. (S.S.)

Edgardo Morpurgo

1866
1948

Edgardo Morpurgo was born in Trieste on August 28, 1866, son of Angelo and Carolina Levi [*fig.* 1]. His parents' marriage renewed the allegiance that for almost a century had bound the business affairs of their respective families, and which was based on an agreement exemplified by the marriage between the founder of the company, Giuseppe Lazzaro Morpurgo, and Rachele Levi in 1786. The bankers Elio and Giuseppe de Morpurgo, whose contributions over more than fifty years were instrumental to the establishment and subsequent development of the company, were related to the family. Although their bank had to close its doors in 1891, their descendants (Emilio, Marco, and Pietro Luigi Morpurgo) were on the governing bodies of Assicurazioni Generali representing the Trieste shareholders. Edgardo Morpurgo, who was promoted to manager without being an investor, is an example of the family's close and persistent bonds, which nurtured relationships based on reciprocity, and of the environment of trust that was essential in ensuring cohesion between the organization's leaders and the owners-shareholders who controlled its assets. Edgardo Morpurgo's career, with its developing functions in accordance with the company's growth and organizational changes following World War I, embodies the continuum of a historical family, the presence of which was uninterrupted until the dramatic, racial persecutions at the end of the 1930s.

Edgardo's father, Angelo Morpurgo (1829–1903), was a prosecutor for Michele Levi & C., an established trader of colonial goods that was deeply affected by the crisis and the market's transformations into commercial transit taking place in Trieste during the mid-nineteenth century. Since this phenomenon had narrowed the opportunities for the family's sons to join the firms as a merchant, Angelo's three sons received an education to enable them to seek out new opportunities for professional success. The oldest, Giuseppe (born in 1860), and Benedetto (born in 1861), graduated in medicine in Vienna in 1882 and in Padua in 1884 respectively. Both became established scientists and professors; the first in Austria, the second in Italy, specifically in Pavia and Turin, where he would distinguish himself as an anatomical pathologist. Edgardo undertook technical studies at the Accademia di Commercio in Trieste, where in 1882, he graduated after training in accounting, calculation of probability, banking, and foreign languages, which was then considered adequate knowledge to undertake a career in banking and insurance [*fig.* 2].

In 1883 he was hired by Assicurazioni Generali, and a few years later, under the supervision of Marco Besso he was entrusted with a post abroad; a practical training during which he acquired technical expertise and experience, fostering useful relationships within the world of international insurance and refining his business acumen. In 1887 he was assigned to Budapest, two years later he was transferred to Greece. After a short interlude in Trieste, he took up a post in Argentina, a distant country with a large number of Italian emigrants where he promoted the company's work. Following a sojourn in Spain and one in France, in 1892 he returned to Trieste as the deputy manager of the transport division. In 1895 he became the manager of the general agency in Trieste while still involved in work abroad. He was then requested to collaborate on the establishment of the new Romanian subsidiary, the Generala, created in 1897. After this, he was sent to Germany to investigate theft insurance, and being assigned to the organization and technical management of this new division. In March 1901 he was entrusted with running Anonima Infortuni, the Italian subsidiary established in Milan in 1896. In November 1907 he was appointed secretary of the Venice Head Office, a title that in May 1909 was changed to secretary director in order to "give the distinguished official a well-deserved gratification" as the directors' minutes reported on that occasion, which suggests a deep level of trust and understanding between Morpurgo and Marco Besso. In 1913, following Edmondo Richetti's retirement, Morpurgo stepped in to replace him as director-in-charge in Trieste.

In 1902 Edgardo Morpurgo transferred to Milan where he became an Italian citizen, even after returning to Trieste under the Austrian sovereign. His patriotic sentiments are evident from his enrolment, in 1892, in the Ginnastica Triestina, a renowned Trieste gymnastics club with Irredentist leanings. Although in May 1915 Italy needed to repair, the conflict did not relent its international activities. While the company's European network was crossed and divided by the fighting, during intermittent meetings alongside Marco Besso in Zurich, Morpurgo maintained contact with the company's leaders in Vienna, where part of the Management in Trieste had transferred. Having obtained permission from the various governments concerned—including the Italian one—to continue operations in those companies situated within the allied nations, he left for London's world market, seeking reinsurance contracts, which had become absent on the continent.

On October 7, 1920 Chairman Marco Besso passed away and Edgardo Morpurgo, who was his closest executive, took over the reins on October 28. Based on his international expertise, technical savvy, first-hand knowledge of Italy's banking circles (the Banca Commerciale Italiana–COMIT), the understanding of the Venetian entrepreneurial milieu—which was expected to inject more capital to increase its corporate influence (the Volpi–Cini group)—Morpurgo was best equipped to fulfill the prerequisites and take on the challenging tasks of postwar renovation.

Morpurgo was the guarantor behind the company's new structure, its Italian governance's formal and definitive framework, and the ensuing corporate synergies. In 1919 the share capital was first stated in liras and increased to 13,230,000 liras; in 1923 in order to meet the new demands, it was boosted to 40 million liras; in 1925 to 60 million liras; all along however, without forgoing the distinctive structure of being divided among many shareholders, rather than controlled by a single group. The traditional, Austro-Hungarian shareholder from Trieste retained

1.
Edgardo Morpurgo (twentieth century)
[ASAG, *Versamenti*, scheda 28265]

2.
Handwritten *curriculum vitae* of Edgardo Morpurgo (January 20, 1901) [ASAG, *Presidenza e organi sociali, Presidenti e vicepresidenti, Edgardo Morpurgo*, U2GE024230]

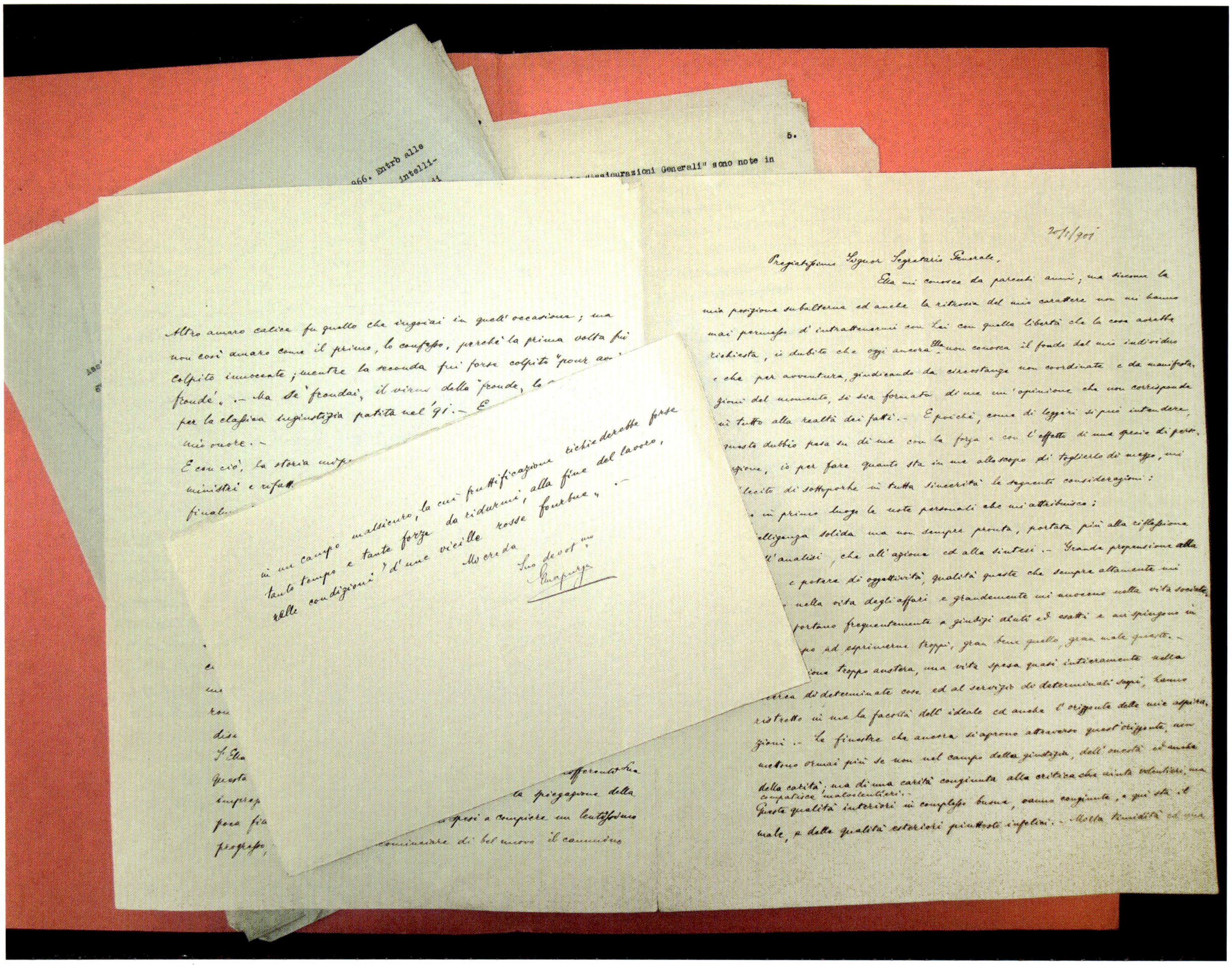

his coalition powers and therefore, the Council of Directors' majority, specifically within the new, small Executive Committee (in which Rodolfo Brunner, Giovanni Scaramangà, Demetrio Economo, Carlo Bois de Chesne, would participate on several occasions between 1922 and 1938). Having Edgardo Morpurgo won the trust of the local financial élite, it was not surprising that in 1923 he was nominated President of Trieste's Chamber of Commerce, a role which he refused due to his many commitments. This first-past-the-post system would prove robust enough to overcome the great crisis of the 1930s, while also making room for new Italian shareholders.

The first twenty years were devoted to the reconstruction in Italy and in Europe, which proved particularly problematic in the States that replaced the Hapsburg Empire; where new borders had been drawn, new protective restrictions were implemented, and new currencies were issued that were soon eroded by inflation. The recovery and transformation that the company was able to achieve, were discernible in the changes to its corporate and governing bodies.

From 1926 Edgardo Morpurgo embodies total corporate power as chairman, general manager and managing director. He shares the general administration with three other managers (Michele Sulfina, Gino Cavaglieri, and Marco Ara in Venice) who managed various areas (finance, the life and transport divisions; the fire and property divisions; personnel, secretariat and press respectively), and assisted by three deputy general managers (Angelo Ara, Giulio Cleva, Sante D'Alvise). At that time the company, which in addition to the Central Head Office in Trieste had a Head Office in Venice and also one in Rome, had developed into an extremely complex organization with a multi-divisional structure. The managers reporting to Morpurgo provided a continuous flow of information and assisted him with their expertise, while also delegating to the middle-management overseeing the various operational departments (co-managers, deputy managers, central managers and assistant managers). The strategic direction was entrusted to the Council of Directors resolutions and the Executive Committee emanating from it, which was tasked with evaluating the overall outcomes, and setting the long-term objectives. The Board of Directors' functions were mainly advisory and not surprisingly, membership from the Trieste contingent was under-represented (Taino Bonacossi, Emanuele Vittorio Parodi, Vittorio Cini, Antonio Revedin, Giuseppe Volpi).

In 1932, while celebrating its first centenary in Rome, the company activated its international activities across four continents by mobilizing ten regional offices (i.e. the constituencies comprising the former agencies, organized according to new European borders) and thirty subsidiaries, six of which in Italy and 24 abroad.

The extent of Assicurazioni Generali's assimilation into the Italian financial sphere is evident from Edgardo Morpurgo's presence on numerous boards of directors during the 1920s and 1930s, namely: the Banca Commerciale Italiana, which in the postwar period mediated the company's inclusion into the Italian banking sector and on whose Board Morpurgo sat since 1921; the state-controlled bodies for public works (Istituto di Credito per le Imprese di Pubblica Utilità–ICIPU, 1924, Credito Fondiario Sardo); the entities for the support of banks and other industries affected by the 1929 crisis (Istituto Mobiliare Italiano–IMI, 1931, and Consorzio Mobiliare Finanziario–COMOFIN, 1931); the Boards of publicly-funded companies (Italgas, Bastogi, Società Meridionale di Elettricità SME, Credito Navale di Venezia, and Finmare). During the recovery of the Italian industry and banking system, the focal point of which was the Istituto per la Ricostruzione Industriale (IRI), built in 1933, and in whose founding capital Assicurazioni Generali was called upon to participate, the company operated as an institutional investor, prudently guarding its activities' autonomy and uniqueness. More crucially, its role and its alliances with the various interested parties, including the private and public sectors, guaranteed influence. Equally significant was Morpurgo's contribution to the companies in the insurance consortium: in 1923 he became deputy chairman of the Unione Italiana di Riassicurazione (for which in 1929, he orchestrated a State bail out) and the Società Italiana di Riassicurazione Consorziale.

In 1934 the share capital was doubled from 60 to 120 million liras. New additions were the electricity magnate Vittorio Cini, who was nominated for the Council of Directors together with a number of political figures within the General Council such as the ex-Fascist action-squad member and newly-appointed senator, Dino Perrone Compagni, and Francesco Giunta, president of the Cantieri Riuniti dell'Adriatico, who demonstrate the political class's growing attraction for an IRI-supported economic system.

In 1934 Mussolini intended to appoint Edgardo Morpurgo to senator of the Kingdom. However, Morpurgo had already observed signs of a disquieting anti-Semitism, which were destined to become increasingly more aggressive within the regime. Morpurgo, whose origins felt distant and alien to him, had requested to be struck from Trieste's Jewish Community in 1921. His disillusion would be bitter. His appointment to senator fell through and, in April 1936—at the start of the racial persecutions in Germany—the Italian State became interested in obtaining detailed information on the company's managers' religious affiliations, through the local prefecture. The racial laws introduced from September through November 1938, were preceded by a violent press campaign, which was not unexpected for the insurers in Trieste who had close business contacts and friendships in Central Europe and had understood the Fascist regime's intent to follow the Nazis' endeavors. The result was an agreed change at the top of the two companies to remove the Hebraic management from Assicurazioni Generali and RAS. On September 12, 1938 Morpurgo resigned from all his charges within Assicurazioni Generali and was replaced by Chairman Giuseppe Volpi. Having been advised of a Law Decree coming into effect on 17 November, which excluded all Jews from filling any administrative positions in all Italian companies, on November 2, Alberto Beneduce from IRI and Ettore Conti from COMIT, requested Morpurgo's resignation as member of the Board of Directors of COMIT. Similarly, he had to leave all the companies and associations of which he was a part. In addition to those already mentioned namely: the Anonima Infortuni and Anonima Grandine (of which he was chairman and deputy chairman respectively); the Confederazione Fascista delle Aziende del Credito e delle Assicurazioni; and a cultural institution, the Istituto per gli Studi di Politica Internazionale (ISPI).

Although he was granted a partial exemption on the grounds of "exceptional merits" (a reinstatement of his denied civil rights), in March 1939 he requested to be issued with a passport and moved to Argentina with his family.

In 1947 he returned to Italy to negotiate his reinstatement in Assicurazioni Generali; a security measure that had been introduced by the Allied Military Government for Occupied Territories (AMG) for all victims of racial persecution and which was in force in Trieste.

Before a definite agreement could be finalized, Morpurgo died in Rome on April 22, 1948.

Sources

ACS. *Presidenza del Consiglio dei ministri (1928–1930)*, b. 1274, fasc. 6.4/9392, Unione Italiana di Riassicurazione.

ASAG. *Presidenza e organi sociali, Presidenti e vicepresidenti, Edgardo Morpurgo.* U2GE001055.

ASAG. *Presidenza e organi sociali, Presidenti e vicepresidenti, Edgardo Morpurgo.* U2GE024230.

ASBI. *Banca Commerciale Italiana, Consiglio di Amministrazione. Membri*, cart. 6, fasc. Morpurgo Edgardo.

AST. *Prefettura di Trieste. Gabinetto (1923–1954)*, b. 522, class. 0111 (M–N), *Corrispondenza riservatissima*, personal letter from the prefect of Trieste to His

Excellency the Head of Government, Trieste, March 12, 1934.
AST. *Prefettura di Trieste. Gabinetto (1923–1954),* b. 501, class. 0111 (A), *Corrispondenza riservatissima,* fasc. *Assicurazioni Generali in Trieste. Personale dirigente.*
In onore del cav. Edgardo Morpurgo, Milano, 22–23 novembre 1907. Milan: Tip. degli Operai, 1907.
Morpurgo, Edgardo. *La famiglia Morpurgo di Gradisca sull'Isonzo.* Padua: Premiata Società Cooperativa, 1909.
"Morpurgo, Edgardo." In *Biografia finanziaria italiana. Guida degli amministratori e dei sindaci delle società anonime per azioni*, edited by G. Casellato, Ezio Lodolini, Alessandro Welczowsky, 553–54. Rome: Ditta E. Armani, 1931. *Ibid.* 1935: 701.
Società Italiane per Azioni. *Notizie statistiche 1937.* Rome: Stabilimento Tipografico Castaldi, 1937.
A Edgardo Morpurgo. Trieste: Editoriale Libraria, December 1938.
Abbiate, Mario. *La vita e le carte di Edgardo Morpurgo.* Trieste: Assicurazioni Generali, 1948.
In memoria di Edgardo Morpurgo. Trieste: n.p., s.a. [1948].

Bibliography

Sapelli, Giulio. *Trieste italiana. Mito e destino economico.* Milan: Franco Angeli, 1991.
Baglioni, Roberto. "L'affermazione della società assicurative nel capitalismo italiano (1919–1940)." *Studi storici* 2 (1997): 431–468.
Fanfani, Tommaso. *Alleanza Assicurazioni: cento anni di storia.* Milan: Alleanza Assicurazioni, 1998: 155–170.
Bon, Silva. *Gli ebrei a Trieste. Identità, persecuzioni, risposte.* Gorizia: Libreria Editrice Goriziana, 2000.
Feldman, Gerald D. "Concorrenza e collaborazione tra le compagnie d'assicurazione dell'Asse: Munich Re, Generali e Ras (1933–1943)." *Imprese e storia* 24 (2001): 249–271.
Millo, Anna. *Trieste, le assicurazioni, l'Europa. Arnoldo Frigessi di Rattalma e la Ras.* Milan: Franco Angeli, 2004.
Favaretto, Tito. "Lo sviluppo dell'attività internazionale delle Assicurazioni Generali tra il XIX e il XX secolo." In *Assicurare 150 anni di Unità d'Italia. Il contributo delle assicurazioni allo sviluppo del Paese*, edited by Paolo Garonna, 93–151. Rome: ANIA, 2011.
(A.M.)

A Special Agency
The General Agency of Trieste

1918
1954

Trieste and environs had naturally always been an important insurance market for the company, even though the full-scale agency, responsible for managing and developing activity in the Litorale, Istria, and Dalmatia, was only founded in 1877, under the leadership of Arturo Kellner. From the start, the Trieste agency was distinct from the others, not only because it was entrusted with some of the Central Head Office's executive functions relative to agencies, but also because it oversaw a vast geographic area, the borders of which shifted frequently over the years, in part due to geopolitical changes.

The particular features of the agency should doubtless be considered in light of its proximity to the Central Head Office, which maintained tight control over its activity, determining, at least in the early years, insurance conditions and premiums on a case-by-case basis. This proximity was also physical, since the agency's premises were, with a few brief exceptions, always in the same building as the Central Head Office. From the list of the company's agencies in the printed financial statements from 1879 to 1942, it seems that the entrance to the agency was, at least from 1919, on the present Piazza Duca degli Abruzzi and later, from 1933, on Via Machiavelli.

The internal structure of the agency developed over the years. In 1881, it was active in the fire, transport, hail, glass, and life sectors (in 1880, it spun off its maritime division), and had its own fund; in 1900, it added the accident sector. Within just a few decades, each division had its own office space and staff, the latter growing rapidly.

Edgardo Morpurgo was also an important figure in the history of the Trieste agency, directing it as an executive from 1895 to 1902 and later envisioning its reform when he became company chairman. Morpurgo was assisted in the management of the agency by Carlo Liebman, who then became its head for more than twenty years. We learn from a circular that the office was reorganized in 1903, "in view of the development of operations in the territory of the General Agency of Trieste." That same year, Girolamo Terni and Liebman took up management of the agency. Then, from 1907 to 1919, Liebman's co-manager was Lorenzo Romeo Carmelich, and after Liebman's retirement, Carmelich's co-manager was Michele Pimpach.

The subsequent years were filled with change for the agency. The creation of new national States out of the ashes of the Hapsburg Empire after World War I necessitated the revision of the territory of all of the company's agencies that had been under the Empire, with direct consequences for the Trieste agency, which became Italian. In 1920, the administration assigned the agency the area of Alto Adige and the Italian portion of Carniola, which had been previously under the Ljubljana agency.

The political change also had an effect on the graphic design of the Trieste agency's policies, which are preserved in the Historical Archive, together with other Generali policies, from between 1833 and 1962, although most are from the first half of the twentieth century. Among them are six life policies (of different types: in case of life, in case of death, mixed, and annuity), issued by the agency between 1914 and 1924 and illustrative of the graphic design change after World War I and the partial reuse of prewar exemplars during the 1920s [*fig.* 1]. Before 1914, the policy, in bifold format with a lovely foliate border, featured two eagles with the crest of the Austrian Empire on the upper part of the first page. Before the war, another policy design was developed, it, too, featuring the Hapsburg crest and decorative border, but red, and distinctive for the more angular lettering used for the company name. Both types were still being used in the early 1920s, with the imperial crest duly covered (by either a silver stamp bearing the company's initials or a red stamp imitating a wax seal with the date of Generali's foundation), and the latter was officially adopted, after Trieste passed to Italy, for policies that had the city crest, with the spear of St. Sergius, on the front. Curiously, there is also a policy that reused the

1.
Life policies issued by the general agency of Trieste (Trieste, 1914–1924) [ASAG, *Versamenti*, scheda 62440]

model for the Kingdom of Hungary, which mirrored that of Austria but with two angels holding up the Hungarian crest. In the 1930s, a graphically simpler life policy design, which opened on the left side, became popular.

Immediately after the war, the agency's transport division broke off to become a transport agency, headed by Giuseppe Mussafia and Duilio Romano (the transport department heads at the general agency), which was in administrative and technical terms under the Special Office for the Transport Division in Rome. In 1931, after the transfer of duties and staff from Rome to Trieste, foreign and Italian transport activity was once again under the transport division of Trieste, and it is highly probable that this was also when the transport agency was reabsorbed by the general agency.

The documentation produced by the Trieste agency, preserved as an aggregate collection in the Historical Archive, makes it possible to indirectly reconstruct the boundaries of the territory it oversaw, using the lists of securities of the various dependent agencies. Already in the 1920s, the agency oversaw not only Alto Adige and Carniola [Krain], but also activity in Trento, Rovereto, Rhodes, Durazzo [Dürres], and other agencies in Istria and Dalmatia. In a study of the agency's "definitive structure" prepared by Arturo Coen, co-manager at the Central Head Office, for the chairman, Morpurgo, and the general manager, Baroncini, in November 1937, we read that there were around seventy agencies under Trieste. Coen pointed out that Trieste, Bolzano, Gorizia, Durazzo, and Rhodes nearly functioned as general agencies, given the extent of the zones they oversaw; Rhodes returned under Trieste after having referred for a few years to the Foreign Agencies secretariat. Two other city agencies were under Trieste: the B agency, under company management (located from 1928 to 1932 at the Volti di Chiozza and later on Via Carducci) and the C, or special, agency, under independent management, which was in operation in 1937/1938 and headed by Martelli, the administrative secretary of the Trieste Fascio.

The correspondence between the central secretariat (before the staff office broke off from the secretariat in 1960) and the Trieste agency, on the one hand, and the Venice Head Office, on the other, is valuable for shedding light on the 1940s and 50s, a period during which the agency gradually lost its special prerogatives. In 1939, Francesco Scolari was assigned the representation of the agency, with the title of general agent, Demetrio Nimira was named general co-agent, and Guido Salvi deputy general agent. The mandate, which probably reflected the structure of the agency desired by Morpurgo, stated: "The General Agency of Trieste is in charge of the technical, administrative, and disciplinary agency organization for all of the territory in the provinces of Trieste, Gorizia, Pola [Pula], Trento, Bolzano, Fiume [Rijeka], and Zara [Zadar], as well as the Italian possessions in the Aegean and in the Kingdom of Albania, with the power of maintaining or lowering the number of existing Agencies in said territory and of opening new ones, both company agencies and independent." Moreover, the agents themselves were assigned management of the Anonima Infortuni general agency of Trieste.

In 1940, Chairman Volpi di Misurata, instigated radical reform at the agency: the competencies "outside its natural territory" were transferred to the Venice Head Office, to put an "end to conditions that have become anachronistic" (minutes of the Board meeting held on October 15, 1940). The Venice Head Office thus came to oversee the following main agencies: Bolzano, Trento, Rovereto, Gorizia, Cervignano, Pola, Fiume, Villa del Nevoso [Illirska Bistrica], Zara, Durazzo, and Rhodes, which in turn oversaw all of the remaining main agencies, which became sub-agencies. The general agency in Trieste also formally passed to the Venice Head Office, although its staff continued to be managed by the Central Head Office, and it preserved some of its autonomy in its new function as the general agency for the province of Trieste and part of the province of Pola.

The reformation of the agency continued in 1943,

1946, and 1948, with detailed analyses of its operations, in part to apply the research carried out by Bruno de Finetti and Arturo Scabar, future general manager, towards the end of streamlining and lightening up the workload. From 1949, management of the agency's staff (which at the time had around one hundred employees, salesmen, and producers) was also entrusted to the Venice Head Office. During those years, the agency was run by Guido Salvi and Alessio Cargnelli [*fig.* 2].

In addition to the internal changes, the agency experienced problems connected to the war and, later, the unusual political and administrative structure of Trieste provided for in the Treaty of Paris.

The official state of war (a law of war instituted with Royal Decree no. 1415, July 8, 1938, and which entered into force with Royal Decree no. 566, June 10, 1940) created difficulties for insurance activity as well, and therefore for the Trieste agency, which oversaw, at least until 1940, operations in a great many territories outside Italy. The obligation to report financial debts to persons of enemy nationality (enemy subjects or persons resident in enemy territory) required the company to carry out a series of administrative procedures with the competent authorities, in order to liquidate the policies and settle the reinsurance. The procedures changed according to the nationality of the citizens considered enemies, in a markedly fluid political context. For the reinsurance balances, for example, until October 1943, Generali paid the equivalent in Italian liras to the Istituto Nazionale per i Cambi con l'Estero, "enemy assets fund," and later on the Finance Ministry would issue orders for the suspension of this obligation. As for the French insurance companies, the Italo-French agreements made in 1940 with the Vichy regime resulted in the release of seized assets and permission to handle insurance contracts with companies of enemy nationality in the normal way, provided that Italian companies would be treated in the same way. The documentation from the company's central accounting depart-

2.
An interior shot of the Trieste agency, probably the transport division, in the mezzanine of Palazzo Geiringer (Trieste, 1967), original photo by Foto Pozzar, Trieste
[ASAG, *Versamenti*, scheda 28267]

In May 1971, the general agency was moved to new offices in Piazza Unità d'Italia, where it is still located today

ment has made it possible to reconstruct the overall regulatory framework that governed the activity of the various departments of the Central Head Office and the Trieste agency. A circular published by the Federazione Nazionale Fascista delle Imprese Assicuratrici (the insurance association during that period), dated August 8, 1941, communicated that application of the wartime laws to the stateless persons of the USSR and Finnish, Estonian, Latvian, Lithuanian, and Romanian citizens was to be suspended, excluding, however, persons who "did not merit special treatment, having expressly declared their support for the Soviet regime or for other political reasons." In Arturo Scabar's copy, a Generali executive made a note in pencil next to the words "having expressly declared their support for the Soviet regime:" "and how could anyone know this?"

In a circular dated June 19, 1942, the Federazione reported that Italy was in a state of war with Great Britain (British possessions and colonies and mandated countries), Greece, Yugoslavia, the USSR, the USA, Guatemala, Cuba, Panama, El Salvador, Honduras, Haiti, the Dominican Republic, Costa Rica, Nicaragua, "China under Chiang Kai-shek," the Dutch Indies, and the Belgian Congo. The wartime law did not apply to natural persons who were living, on April 7, 1941, in territories that were then annexed to Italy, Germany, Hungary, Romania, Bulgaria, and Albania, as well as Montenegro and the new Kingdom of Croatia.

The state of war ended in 1946 (Law Decree no. 49, February 6, 1946), although the regulations governing the handling of enemy assets, which at the time concerned Germany and Japan, remained in force.

After World War II, all of the agencies that were not in either Italy or the Free Territory of Trieste (FTT) controlled by the Americans were gradually closed. In June 1945, the Rijeka agency was closed, and in 1947, the sub-agencies of Lokev, Dutovlje, Motovun, Buzet, Oprtalj, Postojna, Šempeter, Senožeče, and Sežana were all closed when their respective territories became a part of Yugoslavia. In 1948, the Trieste agency oversaw Monfalcone in Italy, Aurisina, and Servola in the FTT controlled by the Americans, and Koper, Novigrad, Izola, Piran, Umag, and Brtonigla in the FTT controlled by the Yugoslavians. In January 1954, around the time FTT Zone A passed under the Italian Civil Administration, Assicurazioni Generali closed its sole remaining sub-agency in FTT Zone B, that of Izola, which also included Piran. (R.S.)

During the Nineteenth Century

Arturo Kellner, a promising executive and future secretary of the Venice Head Office, was the first manager (and, at the same time, inspector general) of the general agency of Trieste, which began its activity in 1878, initially with an extremely small staff, just three employees from the agencies in Graz, Prague, and Budapest. But the staff grew quickly, along with the agency's areas of responsibility, which almost immediately came to include management of the numerous small agencies in Tyrol, the province of Ljubljana, and that of Postojna, buildings management for the agencies of Gorizia and Trieste, and responsibility for the agencies in the Levant (the latter possibly thanks to Ermanno Gentilli's appointment to the post of agency manager in 1884, since Gentilli had worked extensively with that area).

The agency shared the Central Office's building, which was at first in Piazza Piccola (as an interesting aside, in 1871 the mezzanine of the building was rented out to the Trieste's agency of the reinsurance company Salus), and then in the building designed for the company by Eugenio Geiringer, where the Head Office is still located today. In the years just before the Palazzo Geiringer was built, the agency was temporarily moved, along with the transport division, to the second floor of the Tergesteo, where its offices were "light, airy, and spacious," as described by Kellner in a thank you letter to the secretariat on July 29, 1883. In 1896, while work was under way to expand the main building, the adjacent "Sandrini building" was purchased and put in communication with the Central Head Office's building. It was used for the agency and the accounting department, and the renovation was overseen by Geiringer [*fig.* 3].

3.
Letter from the general agency of Trieste to the Central Head Office (Trieste, July 27, 1883) and volumes containing the correspondence between them
[ASAG, *Direzione centrale, Segreteria centrale, Corrispondenza*, U2GE007944, U2GE008154, U2GE008234, U2GE008252 and U2GE008264]

The Age of Totalitarianism

Mass Culture and its Revolutionary Reactions to the Catastrophe of World War I

1922
1938

After the war, the world found itself facing a true paradox. On the one hand, the defeat of the autocratic empires seemed to indicate the triumph of liberal parliamentary democracies. On the other hand, the revolutionary outcome of the new mass society, which fully emerged with the war, determined the rise of dictatorial and totalitarian systems that tried to impose themselves as the only option for handling the new overwhelming reality and forging a new world and a new humanity. Soon, Europe was nearly entirely conquered by these opposing totalitarianism systems (Communism and Fascism), which had the ambition of creating a "New Man," or in the case of Nazism, bringing back the ancient Teutonic Knight, corrupted by centuries of modernity. It was ideological madness, set into motion by the first catastrophic war, which presaged, during what Ernst Nolte defined as a twenty-year European civil war, the new conflict, which would lead the continent to its suicide. The incapacity of the winning ruling classes to handle the postwar period, bleeding Germany dry and abandoning it to constant attempts at revolution during the ungovernable Weimar Republic, opened the way for the gradual rise of Adolf Hitler. The future *Führer*, after various attempted *putsches* (1923), months in prison, and a political strategy presented in the pages of *Mein Kampf* (and underestimated by the self-important intellectuals and democratic politicians of the day), rose, in full legality, to the head of government in 1933. With widespread approval gained on the basis of revanchism, the racial myth, and his total opposition to Bolshevism, Hitler deliberately sought out a pretext for a conflict that could establish a new world order and German supremacy.

The unquestioned success of Hitler [*fig.* 1] was a classic case of the student surpassing the teacher, and his admiration for Benito Mussolini, who, with the March on Rome on October 28, 1922, had brought fascism to the Italian government [*fig.* 2] and whose teachings Hitler had thirstily absorbed, was in fact gradually waning. In his eyes, Mussolini, in spite of his "ultra-Fascist laws" and other dictatorial measures, was constantly faced with limits to his exercise of power due to the presence in Italy of the House of Savoy and the Church, especially after the signing of the Lateran Treaty of February 11, 1929 [*fig.* 3], which was necessary for resolving the "Roman Question," a dispute that had been ongoing since 1870. These interferences made Fascism, as historians describe it, an "imperfect totalitarian system." Further aggravating the situation was the fact that the Europeans managed to make the utopia of continental unity a miserable failure. The idea had emerged right after World War I and was the brainchild of Richard Nikolaus von Coudenhove-Kalergi, who founded the Paneuropean movement in 1923, whose initiatives were supported by the French Foreign Minister Aristide Briand and his German counterpart, Gustav Stresemann, both Nobel Peace Prize winners. The hope represented by this project was immediately scuttled in 1930, when the governments of the European Member States of the League of Nations rejected Briand's proposal to create a federal union founded on economic cooperation that would above all serve as a tool for coordination and dispute resolution.

The terrible decline of Europe was to the advantage of the United States, which benefited from the role that it played at the end of the war, positioning itself during the Roaring Twenties in the center of the global transformation on all fronts, and in particular dictating new trends in art, culture, and music, which were increasingly circulated by the film industry. The American Way of Life thus spread throughout the world, symbolizing ease and a new, affluent society. However, even the sunny American system soon came to an end, when on Black Tuesday, October 29, 1929, Wall Street crashed and the West found itself facing a new dramatic economic emergency, which reduced millions to poverty [*fig.* 4], forcing governments to radically change their concepts of State intervention.

While the United States managed to emerge from

1.
Adolf Hitler at a Brownshirts parade in 1927 in Nuremberg

2.
The March on Rome in 1922 was celebrated, ten years later, in a famous painting by Giacomo Balla that depicts Benito Mussolini and the quadrumvirate in the foreground

3.
The signing of the Lateran Treaty on February 11, 1929, by Achille Beltrame

4.
The unemployed waiting in line during the Great Depression: in order to create a network of support, the notorious gangster Al Capone ordered his restaurants and clothing stores to offer food and clothing to those in need

5.
The German director Leni Riefenstahl during the filming of *Olympia*, a documentary on the Berlin Games, considered to be her masterpiece and, although controversial, one of the world's best films dedicated to sports

6.
Marshal Badoglio entering Addis Ababa in 1936, at the head of the victorious Italian troops, in one of the celebrated illustrations by Achille Beltrame for *La Domenica del Corriere*

7.
The Francoist conquest of Madrid on March 28, 1939 (cover for *La Tribuna Illustrata* by Vittorio Pisani). In just a few days, the last strongholds of the republican army fell, ending the Spanish Civil War.

the economic disaster relatively quickly, thanks to US President Franklin Delano Roosevelt's "New Deal," launched in 1933, the new economic theories that developed out of it, proposed by John Maynard Keynes, led to the centralization of economic management and forms of protectionism and strengthened egotistical nationalism that intensified state authoritarianism. Under Stalin, who succeeded Lenin in 1924, the USSR, in the name of the class struggle, adopted an economic plan and policy of forced collectivization that caused unprecedented massacres in the 1930s, one example being the Golodomor in Ukraine. It is said that the famine that followed the extermination of the kulaks (landowners) caused six million deaths and the emergence of various forms of cannibalism within families, out of the sheer need to survive.

In Germany, the rise of Hitler brought the persecution of the Jews, along with the disabled, mentally ill, homosexuals, and gypsies, in short all of those who could be considered, in the name of the alleged purity and superiority of the Arian race, a threat to authentic German stock and potential originators of a fantastical global plot against the Germans, contemptuously described as the "Judeo-Masonic conspiracy." The Nazi racial policy was expressed in full in the Nuremberg Laws introduced in 1935. During the same period, the German production system was revived, and Germany quickly found itself back in the center of the world economy. The Berlin Olympics in 1936 were an extraordinary propagandistic showcase for Nazi ideology [*fig.* 5].

Italy was instead led by the myth of the Roman Empire, which inspired Mussolini to occupy Ethiopia [*fig.* 6], proclaiming the birth of the Italian Empire, and to intervene in the Spanish Civil War, a conflict that led to the rise of a new dictatorship, led by Generalissimo Franco [*fig.* 7], and in which Italians fought on both sides. For Il Duce, it was a period of massive popular support, reaching its height with the signing of the Munich Agreement on September 30, 1938, when the western democracies, facing the aggressivity of a Germany that had already annexed Austria (*Anschluss*) and that was targeting Czechoslovakian territories in the name of reclaiming its "vital space," had to settle for supporting Mussolini in the role of mediator and apparent peace maker. As noted by Galeazzo Ciano in his diary, this success surprised even Mussolini himself, who, on his return to Rome, where he received a triumphant welcome for having successfully created peace, on the other hand stigmatized the Italians' small appetite for war. This popular stance was in stark contrast with the warlike spirit with which he had announced, just days earlier in the Piazza dell'Unità in Trieste, the infamous Italian racial laws, which had been stipulated the previous month and are a permanent stain on Italian history. The approval of the Laws for the Defense of the Race revealed Italy's subservience to German policy, which had been sealed earlier by the Rome-Berlin Axis, a diplomatic agreement concerning future warfare that would in the years to follow lead Italy to defeat. (D.R.)

In Brief

1922
November 4: In the Valley of the Kings, in Egypt, the English archeologist Howard Carter discovered the entrance to the nearly pristine tomb of Tutankhamun (fourteenth century BC). His coffin is of solid gold.

1925
March 11: The musical *No, No, Nanette* debuted at the Palace Theatre in London; it went on to be performed 665 times. The song *Tea for Two*, with lyrics by Irving Caesar and music by Vincent Youmans, was a huge success.

1925
July 21: The "Monkey Trial," which triggered the debate between creationists and evolutionists, ended with John T. Scopes receiving a fine for having taught Darwin's theory at a school in Tennessee.

1926
January 21: After a preview in December for Soviet leaders, Sergej Ejzenštejn's film *Battleship Potëmkin*, celebrating the revolutionary mutiny of 1905, was released to the public.

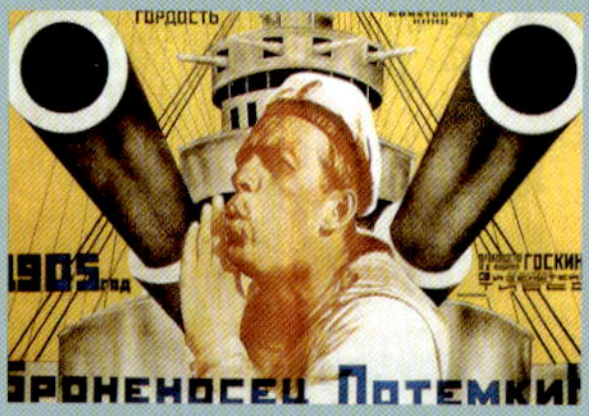

1927
May 20: Charles Lindbergh, flying the monoplane *Spirit of St. Louis*, left Paris to complete the first nonstop solo flight across the Atlantic Ocean. He arrived in New York thirty-three and a half hours later.

1927
August 28: In Boston, an emotional crowd attended the funeral of the anarchists Nicola Sacco and Bartolomeo Vanzetti, wrongfully condemned to death. The governor of Massachusetts cleared their names in 1977.

1928
September 3: In his laboratory at St Mary's Hospital in London, the Scottish bacteriologist Alexander Fleming discovered penicillin, observing a culture plate contaminated with a bactericidal fungus.

1928
October 10: Chiang Kai-shek, successor of Sun Yat-sen as leader of the Kuomintang, was appointed generalissimo of the Chinese forces and head of the Nationalist government, based in Nanking.

1928
November 18: In the short movie *Steamboat Willie* the character Mickey Mouse gives its debut; the humanized mouse created by Walt Disney immediately is a huge success with the audience.

1929
April 14: The Monaco Grand Prix was held for the first time on the Circuit de Monaco, and is still a traditional part of the Formula One World Championship today.

1930
April 1: *The Blue Angel* was the first German talkie to be a big success and made a star out of the actress Marlene Dietrich, who played a cabaret singer and the love interest of an austere teacher driven to insanity by his passion for her.

1931
August 1: The launch of the *Rex*, the largest Italian ocean liner at the time. In 1933, it won the Blue Riband crossing the Atlantic from Genoa to New York at a record speed of 28.92 knots.

1932
February 12: The Citroën caterpillared trucks of the "Yellow Cruise" arrived in Peking, completing a ten-month expedition across such challenging terrain as the Gobi Desert and the Himalayas.

1933
May 23: The police trapped and killed Bonnie Parker and Clyde Barrow in Louisiana. The outlaws had been on the run for two years, with Clyde wanted for a murder committed during a robbery.

1933
June 29: In New York, Primo Carnera, a boxer from Friuli, 1.97 meters tall and 118 kilograms, won the world heavyweight title, knocking out the reigning champion Jack Sharkey in the sixth round.

1934
January 1: Agatha Christie published one of her most surprising detective novels *Murder on the Orient Express*, in which the Belgian investigator Hercule Poirot solves the case during a trip on the famous train.

1934
June 10: The charismatic coach Vittorio Pozzo led the national team to winning the FIFA World Cup. His winning streak continued with the 1936 Olympics and another World Cup title in 1938.

1934
October 9: King Alexander I of Yugoslavia, previously King the Serbs, Croats, and Slovenes, was assassinated by a Macedonian separatist in Marseilles. A French minister also died during the attack.

1934
December 10: The writer Luigi Pirandello won the Nobel Prize for Literature in Stockholm. One year later, he donated his medal to the Fascist regime's "Gold for the Fatherland" campaign.

1935
October 22: The "Long March", the retreat of the Chinese communist army, with Kuomintang troops hot on their heels, ended in Yan'an, which became Mao Zedong's operational base for the Party.

1936
August 4: At the Berlin Olympics, where he won four golds, American athlete Jesse Owens won the long jump, beating the German Luz Long, who had helped him with technical advice out of good sportsmanship.

1937
May 6: The *Hindenburg*, a German airship, caught fire while preparing to land. Thirty-six people died and this disaster marked the end of the use of airships for transportation.

1938
October 30: The radio broadcast of H.G. Well's science fiction novel *The War of the Worlds*, narrated by Orson Welles, unleashed widespread panic, listeners believing that the Martian invasion was real.

1938
November 9: Using the murder of a German diplomat in Paris by a Jewish refugee from Poland as a pretext, Germany launched the anti-Semitic reprisal known as "The Night of Broken Glass" in response.

From Morpurgo to Volpi
The Story of a Change: The Company Becomes a "Group"

1920
1943

The arduous task of pulling Generali out of the vicissitudes of World War I fell to the company chairman, Edgardo Morpurgo. The chosen heir of his predecessor Marco Besso, thanks to his "distinguished technical expertise" and deep knowledge of the international insurance market, Morpurgo was unanimously elected on October 28, 1920, considered the most suitable candidate for reconfiguring the company structure into that of a global Group.
The fall of the Austro-Hungarian Empire shattered the politically unified State and opened the door to the emergence of new national States also creating complex economic, monetary, and legal problems for the insurance industry. The difficult task of relinking the vast network of companies belonging to Generali fell to Morpurgo, renewing the business relationships and friendships that he had learned how to build and nurture while carrying out important assignments abroad in his younger years, particularly in France, Spain, and Central Europe, the social and economic conditions of which he had studied with great acumen and were important for the company's expansion, so much so that between the wars the foreign portfolio enjoyed primacy over the domestic one.
Morpurgo took part, along with other companies, in the foundation of the Società di Riassicurazione Consorziale in Milan. This company, with Morpurgo as its most authoritative consultant, was founded to free Italy from the foreign reinsurance market, and in just a few years it had not only reduced the exportation of Italian reinsurance but was also importing foreign reinsurance.
From this point forward, Generali expanded through financial interest and stake in various insurance, financial, credit, and productive companies, particularly abroad, involving itself with ones that already existed as well as creating new ones. Due to the changed geopolitical situation, the company needed to reorganize its direct activity, through the transformation of the old general agencies, located in cities that had become the capitals of the new States, into branch offices in charge of all of the agencies that ended up within the borders of the respective States, and its indirect activity, through the foundation of national companies. The company needed to cope with the mass of new special laws and decrees that were branching off from the old legislative core, which were used by the new States to regulate the insurance business. In this regard, after World War I, a special department emerged, "special accounts," for the management of the accounts and pension funds of the former Austrian-Hungarian territories, which, together with other units, like the foreign operations department, which became operationally independent at the end of the 1930s, were set up especially for administering, or rather coordinating, and observing foreign markets from a Group perspective, in accordance with local requirements. In the early 1920s, for example, it joined with a company called Moldavia to create a new Czechoslovakian company, Moldavia-Generali, which had a crest that included both the Bohemian lion and the lion of Saint Mark, in recognition of the critical role played by the company in its foundation and administration, and also participated in the founding of a Yugoslavian company called Sava. Morpurgo and Emanuele Ehrentheil, deputy director-in-charge at the time, were appointed to the Board of Directors of both. It restructured Generali, a daughter company in Bucharest, and founded a company in Prague, Sekuritas, appointing Morpurgo as deputy chairman of its Board of Directors. Seizing the opportunity to have a national company in Bulgaria in addition to its Branch, it became the majority shareholder of a company called Europa, in Sofia. It then became the majority shareholder of Polonia, in Warsaw, and acquired the Italian portfolios of Erste Ungarische Allgemeine Assekuranz-Gesellschaft, Wiener Versicherungsgesellschaft, and the fire insurance company in Leipzig.
When Trieste was annexed to Italy, the company needed to change its technical organization: previously an Italian organization operating on Austrian soil, with its foreign activity carried out in Italy, the situa-

tion was now reversed. It thus found itself needing to operate in accordance with Italian law, necessitating first and foremost radical changes in its regulations. In March 1922, the new charter was approved, with the company name being translated for the first time into the languages of the various countries in which it operated. The Management was eliminated and replaced with an Council of Directors, and the Executive Committee and two new managerial figures were instituted: the managing director and general manager. The latter was a change in title for the already existing post of director-in-charge, previously "secretary," shifting from a single company head to between one and three general managers, i.e. area managers overseeing various divisions, departments, and offices. Morpurgo, Ehrentheil, Giuseppe Luzzatto, and Michele Sulfina were reconfirmed and Vittorio Besso replaced Adolfo Errera. The first managing director was not appointed until four years later. The company administration was therefore divided into three levels: the Board of Directors, with a consulting function fundamental for the definition of company strategy; the Council of Directors with administrative functions; and the Executive Committee, a select body elected annually by the Council of Directors to carry out the latter's faculties more efficiently, invested with decision-making functions for operational guidelines and general coordination.

Assicurazioni Generali found itself in a state of uncertainty due to the threat of a life insurance monopoly that was scheduled to enter into force in April 1923, as per the Giolitti law of 1912. It was instead revoked by Law no. 966, and replaced by the institution of mandatory transfers, obligating private companies to cede a quota of all risks assumed to the Istituto Nazionale delle Assicurazioni (INA). With the possibility for working in Italy guaranteed, Generali could more confidently focus on adapting its structure to the new political and financial landscape and profit from room for its full territorial development.

While for the first twenty years the company was represented in Italy by a network of more than three thousand agencies, branches and representative offices were set up, or reorganized, throughout Europe and overseas. To cope with the protectionist measures implemented by various countries in order to prohibit foreign competition, it also had a stake in around thirty insurance and reinsurance companies located in Europe, the United States, and Latin America. In Spain, where Generali was already represented not only by the parent company but also by Italiana Infortuni, it reorganized and acquired a dominant interest in the Banco Vitalicio de España, one of the oldest Spanish institutions, and in the Caja de Previsión y Soccorro in Barcelona. In 1924, it also set up a new fire insurance company in Madrid, Covadonga. With the acquisition of the fire insurance portfolio of Basilea, its presence on the transalpine market grew thanks to the French company Concorde, a daughter company founded in 1905, for which Morpurgo appointed an Italian manager, Mario Padoa, who was later replaced by Vittorio Besso, the former deputy general manager in Trieste, when he became the head of Anonima Infortuni in 1923.

In Great Britain, Morpurgo partnered with Cornhill and Guardian Eastern and set up a large office in London not only for generating business, but also to serve as a mirror for the global insurance industry, London being its center: this was a first step towards extending the company's activity throughout the rest of the United Kingdom. Working with Tokio, he founded a national company, Lombard, which was run by Generali staff in operating in Europe and the Levant, while Tokio oversaw the Far East. It bought a block of shares in National in Copenhagen and Deutscher Lloyd in Berlin. And it also participated in the creation of an Austrian/German company, Heimat of Vienna, acquired a share in Union Suisse of Zurich, which operated in the glass sector, and in Athinaiki of Athens, and set up a business in Eritrea.

On the suggestion of Morpurgo, in 1924 the company opened a representative office in the Philip-

1.
Documentation relative to the Philippines representative office (1924–1938)
[ASAG, *Versamenti*, scheda 8713]

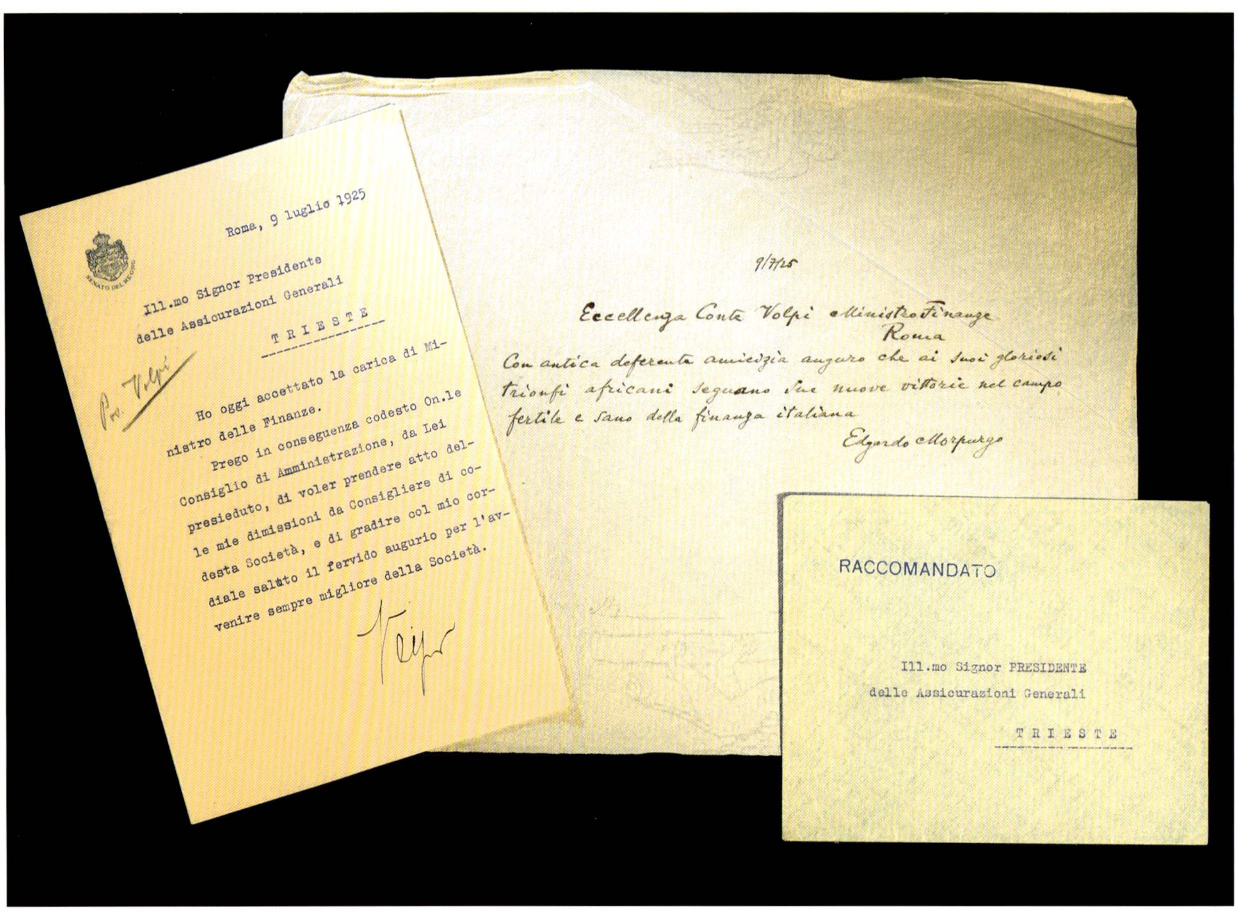

2.
Note congratulating Giuseppe Volpi on his appointment as Finance Minister ([Trieste], July 9, 1925) and Giuseppe Volpi's letter of resignation from the Board of Directors (Rome, July 9, 1925)
[ASAG, *Direzione centrale*, *Servizio del personale*, *Posizioni personali*, U2GE042522]

pines to operate in the fields of fire and transport insurance and reinsurance: the relative mandate was issued by the Compañía General de Tabacos de Filipinas in Manila [*fig.* 1].

In 1926, Morpurgo, formerly general manager and chairman, was elected the first managing director, with responsibility for presiding over the running of the company's branch offices. He strengthened the company's presence in the Americas, moving forward with the acquisition of a block of shares in a Mexican life insurance company called Latino-Americana, as well as interest in life reinsurance, and in an American company, Pilot, in New York. Meanwhile, work continued toward the organization of the agency network in Brazil, and feasibility studies were carried out to explore the extension of activity to Argentina and Peru. Work in China and Indochina continued slowly but steadily.

At the same time, business was falling off in almost every country, paired with major economic difficulties caused by inflation and sharp changes in the exchange rates.

It was during this period that currency exchange and exchange operations subject to control by authorized banks were regulated for the first time, while State intervention was entrusted to the Istituto Italiano dei Cambi, a supervisory body for the currency market. The Finance Minister at the time, Giuseppe Volpi [*fig.* 2], on the Generali Board of Directors since 1915, implemented a series of directives "in order to facilitate," as he explained in an official note, "the operations carried out for insurance companies by banks authorized to exchange currency, the companies themselves not being able, particularly due to the significant splitting of business, to produce the necessary documentation for transferring abroad the sums needed for reinsurance and for conducting their business in other countries," as reported by Anna Millo in *Trieste, le assicurazioni, l'Europa. Arnoldo Frigessi di Rattalma e la Ras*. Once again, Generali did not let itself be caught out: in 1930, it set up a special unit, the financial secretariat, for the management of financial investments, appointing Giuseppe Foà and Ottocaro Weiss as its deputy managers.

The American stock market crash of 1929 had powerful repercussions on the global market. The crisis quickly spread beyond the United States and the first to feel its effects were the countries that had close financial ties with that country, starting with those that had received economic assistance from America after World War I—Great Britain, Austria, and Germany—where the withdrawal of American loans derailed the system of war reparations, drawing France and Italy into the crisis as well. In spite of the fragile economic situation, the company strengthened its presence in non-European countries in the 1930s, reporting a positive trend, since, as we read in the financial statement for 1931, "Such is the most valuable fruit of one hundred years of mindful and honest activity, which has formed in the heart of all of our staff what we might call 'Generali citizenship.'" Research was carried out to investigate the possible development of operations in new territories, whether directly or through interest in national companies, like Segurança Industrial of Rio de Janeiro and Italia in Lima, as well as in Canada, the United States, Mexico, Venezuela, Colombia, Ecuador, Argentina, South Africa, and the Dutch Indies.

As a result of the insurance industry crisis in Germany and the consequential collapse of a few major insurance groups, Generali withdrew its request to extend its life division activity to the whole country, being unwilling to give up an old license that allowed the company to carry out life and non-life insurance activity in just a few specific German States, since mixed companies were not permitted, and opted for the creation of a Deutscher Lloyd "life" company and the contingent acquisition of a relative portfolio.

The North American economic and banking crisis, which emerged one year after the English monetary crisis, had an effect on the insurance business:

in some States, for example, insurance in foreign currency was prohibited by the authorities due to the loss in value of national currency, leading to a downturn in the insurance market. These difficulties were joined by those caused by the competition, "which lure policy holders away with basic monetary commitment clauses of all kinds and offers of single-premium insurance that verge on the incredible." In Italy, a measure aimed to fight the competition's "excesses" was adopted by the Comitato Tecnico della Previdenza, with the appointment of a three-delegate committee, representing Generali, INA, and the Ministry of Corporations, which had the task of "working out measures that would reduce production expenses, prohibit discounts, and render the misappropriation of business impossible" (minutes for the meeting of the Council of Directors no. 132 of March 1, 1932).

In 1932, the company prepared to celebrate its first century of activity as a global insurance Group in Piazza Venezia with Benito Mussolini in attendance [*fig.* 3]. It launched activity in India and Mexico, as a partner of Seguros America, and it acquired Alleanza & Unione Mediterranea, merging it with the subsidiary Securitas Esperia to create a new company, Alleanza Securitas Esperia (Allsecures). The company continued its projects for expansion abroad through representative offices and interest in local companies, for example in Portugal and the Netherlands, where it acquired almost all of the shares of the life insurance company De Nederlanden of Amsterdam. In Egypt, it founded Misr, with headquarters in Cairo. In the same year, 1934, it opted to close the independently managed general agency and found in its place an office under company management, called the Egyptian Branch to increase its prestige, and definitively acquired a share in the newly founded Palestinian insurance company, Migdal. In 1935, it opened a general agency in Teheran, Iran. Also in 1935, it founded a representative office in Vienna for the development of the Group in Central Europe. In the United States, it made plans to found a central office with operations at first limited to New York, Pennsylvania, New Jersey, and South Carolina, initially entrusting the management and technical responsibility for the fire, transport, and cotton business to local companies. In 1936, it founded a general office for the transport, fire, and machinery sectors in Philadelphia called the General Insurance Company Limited of Trieste and Venice [*fig.* 4]. The following year, in view of the nationalization of insurance activity, the chairman proposed requesting permission from the competent authorities to transform the representative office in Brazil into a Brazilian company called Assicurazioni Generali do Brasil. An agency was opened in Baghdad and work was begun in Ethiopia.

The Generali Group was thus becoming one of the most important, if not the most important, of its kind, and, at the end of the decade, it had a direct global profile comprising thousands of representative offices, more than sixty insurance companies operating in more than fifty different countries in Europe, Asia, Africa, and the Americas, and more than three thousand agencies all over the world.

At the same time, financial activity in Italy was also focused on supporting the government trend to bring back to private enterprise companies that had been taken on by parastatal bodies for incidental reasons, thus ensuring a larger stake in the national economy. The operations carried out following these criteria were primarily equity participation in the Cantieri Riuniti dell'Adriatico and the Strade Ferrate Meridionali. Among the new investments in movable assets, Assicurazioni Generali made a significant contribution to the issue of government-backed bonds by a few public interest companies, including the Società Finanziaria Marittima (Finmare), the Società Finanziaria Siderurgica (Finsider), and Prestito italiano.

In the meantime, the socio-political and economic situation was becoming increasingly tense, both within Italy and internationally. In spite of his good relations with the government at the time, not even Morpurgo was spared the consequences of the accord between Italy and Germany and submitted his resignation in September 1938, just before the promulgation of the racial laws. Generali's top management and structure were completely reformed. Forced to resign, the Venice managers, Marco Ara and Giorgio Vivante, were replaced by Luigi Baroffio, Francesco Ommassini, and Vittorio Brovedani. In Trieste, the new chairman, Giuseppe Volpi, was assisted by two deputy chairmen (as per a proposal by Morpurgo, who had also designated Volpi as his successor): Antonio Cosulich and Giorgio Pitacco, who were already part of the company's governing bodies. This was the start of a series of chairmen who were not appointed from within Generali, but rather sat on the Board of Directors or were part of the administration of Anomina Grandine or Anonima Infortuni, which were well known in the commercial, industrial, and financial sectors.

With the aim of updating the statutory bodies and thus coming into alignment with general practice for Italian joint stock companies, a new company charter was introduced at an Extraordinary General Meeting held on December 20, 1938. The company thus returned to a two-tier hierarchical administration type, comprising a Board of Directors and a Management Committee. The changes essentially consisted of the appointment of two deputy chairmen, the elimination of the General Council (the functions of which were almost exclusively advisory), the Council of Directors (which had properly administrative functions), and the Executive Committee, and their replacement by a Board of Directors and a Management Committee with precisely determined functions.

The General Council was founded in 1930, absorbing the advisory competencies of the eliminated Board of Directors. Its purpose was to draw notable individuals to the company in order to increase its prestige, but this aim could be "better assisted" by the "inclusion

3.
Edgardo Morpurgo and Benito Mussolini at the company's centennial celebrations (Rome, May 1, 1932) [ASAG, *Versamenti*, scheda 28265]

The celebrations were originally planned to take place during the Ordinary Shareholders' Meeting on May 8 at the Teatro Comunale in Trieste, but at Mussolini's request they were rescheduled for May 1 at the company's offices in Piazza Venezia. For the occasion, the company published the volume *Il centenario delle Assicurazioni Generali: 1831–1931* edited by Giuseppe Stefani in four languages (Italian, French, English, and German) and minted a commemorative medal designed by Gigi Supino. Generali celebrated this historic achievement with a series of initiatives, including donations to charitable institutions and bonuses for its employees

of such individuals in the normal Board of Directors, which was made up towards this end of a congruous number of members." The position of foreign Board members was "delicate, given the precise responsibilities that Italian law attributed to the members of the Boards of Directors of joint stock Companies." The chairman therefore proposed that Board members should henceforth be exclusively Italian, in part also because the practice followed up until then of appointing to the General Council representatives of a few of the foreign territories where the company operated had not produced the desired results (minutes of General Council no. 363 of November 30, 1938). In accordance with this decision, the General Council was eliminated and a Board of Directors instituted in its place, assigning it the functions of the Council of Directors. The company also instituted a Management Committee (formerly, the Executive Committee), to which the Board of Directors assigned specific powers, it being considered more in keeping with practice for the administration to be able to avail itself of a more restricted and more expeditious body.

One year after Volpi was elected chairman, World War II broke out. Faced with German interference, the chairman protected Generali's work and possibilities for growth, which were important for Italy's global expansion. In this area, Volpi deployed all of the skills he had gained from his long career in business and the prestige and authority that he had acquired through his political and administrative posts. He protected the company's interests in every single area of its activity, in particular in the foreign markets that were still open. Similarly, he did everything possible to ease the situation for the staff hit by the racial laws, even finding a way to keep some of the company's executives employed who had already been struck by the measures. It was thanks to Volpi's intervention that Sulfina was able to continue his work at the Central Head Office until the fall of Fascism, supported by Gino Baroncini, formerly a manager at Anonima Grandine and then appointed general manager in 1937, an important company organizer who, after the war, continued the company's process of internationalization. It fell to him to reorganize the company and improve exchange between the two Head Offices, considering the expediency of tighter coordination, the Italian activity being important for Generali, and of keeping the Venice Head Office constantly up to date on the activity of the Central Head Office abroad. Another aim of the reorganization was to eliminate duplicated functions and overlapping competences, leaving their respective duties, sanctioned in the charter, unchanged. The new regulations were explained and approved at a Board meeting held on March 7, 1939.

In 1939, the foreign organizational structure was adapted to the territorial and political changes in a few important areas of operation. The organization of the Group in Germany after its annexation of Austria (*Anschluss*), begun the previous year, continued based on a joint arrangement between Assicurazioni Generali and the Austrian affiliate, Erste Allgemeine. After the breakup of the Czechoslovakian Republic and the consequential constitution of the Protectorate of Bohemia and Moravia, two affiliates, Moldavia-Generali and Sekuritas, were merged into a single organization in order to, together with the Prague Branch, increase business in Bohemian/Moravian countries. A new representative office for Slovakia was set up in Bratislava. In the Netherlands, the reinsurance company Alhermij was founded. In Spain, while continuing to maintain interest in a few important national companies, it was decided to take on direct management of the life and transport sectors, opening a Branch in Madrid, and assigning management of the other sectors to companies within the Group. Committed to developing business in Argentina and expanding activity in other Latin American countries, the company, supported by an affiliate, Italia, participated in the foundation of La Nacional in Ecuador, with headquarters in Quito, and opened an agency in Colombia.

The company was finding it increasing difficult to

carry out its activity abroad, especially in France and England and in territories under their sway. Due to the state of war, all of the European countries, not just the ones at war, and many non-European countries were adopting financial and commercial measures. The chairman recognized that Generali stock was an anomaly, being the only one in Italy with such a high market price (due to the company's tradition of concentrating the issued capital in a limited number of hands), and determined that it would be necessary to open up the equity to a broader circle of savers, especially policy holders, dividing the value of 1,000-lira shares into five 200-lira shares. Moreover, he held it necessary to bring together the two Head Offices, and possibly also that of Anonima Infortuni, in Switzerland, as already prearranged by a few Italian organizations. In September, a representative office was set up in Bern, "to be used, in case of need, as a sorting point for our foreign agencies in belligerent States and in order to keep up with the international financial market" (note of September 4, 1939).

On May 10, 1940, Italy entered the war. When the hostilities broke out, the company immediately lost contact with its representative offices in enemy territory. Its direct interests were subjected to the law of war, while its indirect activity suffered a blow, with the cancellation of important reinsurance contracts. It was clearer than ever before that the reinsurance options offered by the Italian insurance industry were insufficient, not only in terms of meeting internal needs but also with respect to the preeminent position that Italy aimed to acquire abroad. Volpi considered the idea of creating a large organization, to be promoted in collaboration with INA and, possibly, other companies, "that would make it possible for the Italian industry to present itself, even in the reinsurance field, with means that would ensure sufficient economic independence for national reinsurance activity and solid penetration of the foreign markets, both through reinsurance agreements and

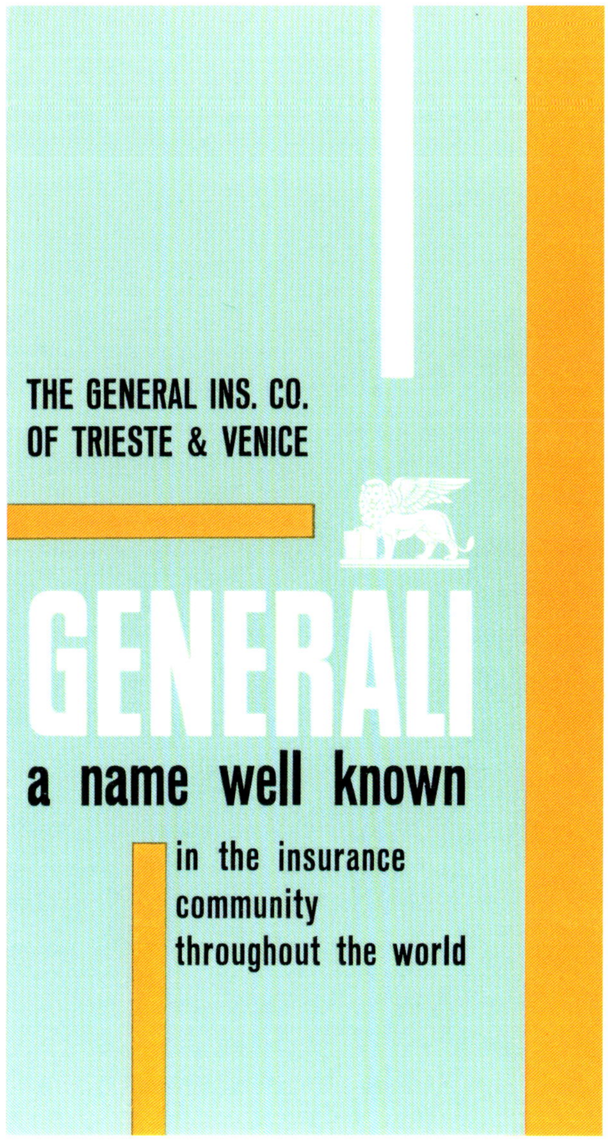

4.
Brochure for the General Insurance Company Limited of Trieste and Venice [1960–1968]
[ASAG, *Archivi aggregati, Agenzia di Asmara*, U2GE025888]

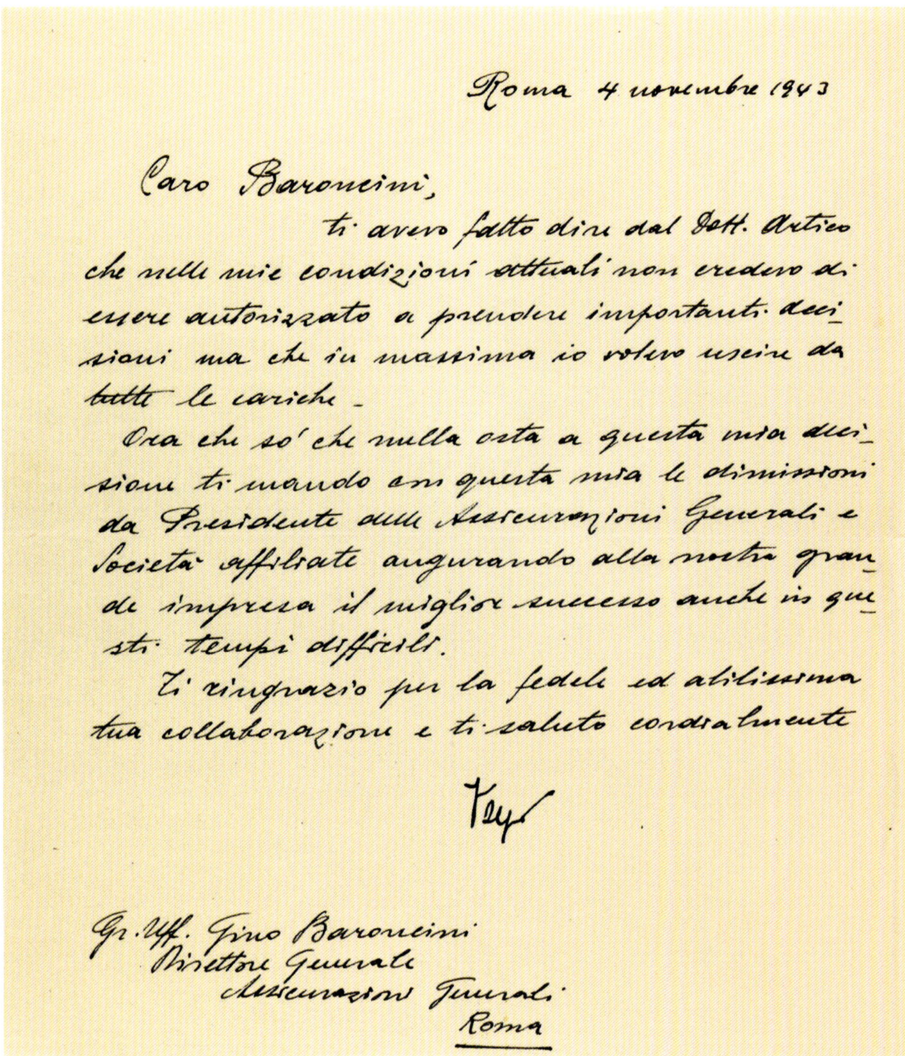

Roma 4 novembre 1943

Caro Baroncini,

ti avevo fatto dire dal Dott. Artico che nelle mie condizioni attuali non credevo di essere autorizzato a prendere importanti decisioni ma che in massima io volevo uscire da tutte le cariche.

Ora che so' che nulla osta a questa mia decisione ti mando con questa mia le dimissioni da Presidente delle Assicurazioni Generali e Società affiliate augurando alla nostra grande impresa il miglior successo anche in questi tempi difficili.

Ti ringrazio per la fedele ed abilissima tua collaborazione e ti saluto cordialmente

Gr. Uff. Gino Baroncini
Direttore Generale
Assicurazioni Generali
Roma

5.
Letter from Giuseppe Volpi to Gino Baroncini announcing his resignation (Rome, November 4, 1943)
[ASAG, *Direzione centrale*, *Servizio del personale*, *Posizioni personali*, U2GE042522]

through financial interest as much in insurance organizations as in reinsurance organizations" (minutes of the Management Committee meeting on July 20, 1940). The Compagnia di Roma was thus founded in October, under the joint leadership of co-managers Giuseppe Bufano and Giorgio Ugolini. The consequences of the war were critical for Generali, being an industrial and financial company present on four continents in the form of branches, representative offices and agencies as well as affiliate offices and associated companies, and with major interests represented by a complex organization. In countries like England, France, Egypt, the East Indies, and Indochina, its activity came to a complete stop, shattering the organization. In other countries, like Belgium, the Netherlands, Greece, Yugoslavia, and the United States, its operations suffered a major decline. The difficult circumstances drove governments to adopt increasingly restrictive measures in all sectors, like the nationalization of certain areas of activity. This phenomenon was especially common in the sector of war risk insurance, with State intervention increasing daily. In Brazil, Spain, Yugoslavia, Greece, and Turkey, initiatives and projects emerged for nationalizing fire insurance, instead of transport, through the obligatory transfer of reinsurance to public institutions, if not a complete State insurance monopoly. The problems encountered by Generali were different in every country, depending on local conditions and on the breadth of its interests and organization in each. The work of everyday reconstruction and adapting to the needs of the moment was carried out by the men at the helm of the company's management, in the center and in the periphery, like Sulfina and Baroncini, and by "the young staff," which, through their intelligence, training, and commitment to Generali, "proved themselves to be equal to the task" (minutes for the Board of Directors meeting on February 24, 1940).
When hostilities broke out with the United States, the entire organization, which had been the fruit of

major financial efforts and years of work, abruptly collapsed. This situation was aggravated by the start of hostilities with Brazil: at the declaration of war, the representative office in Rio de Janeiro was stormed and destroyed. In Europe, in the areas where military operations were gradually petering out, the company regained its former positions and intensified its interrupted activity.

In February 1943, when the Board member Vittorio Cini resigned due to his appointment as Communications Minister, Baroncini was coopted onto the Board of Directors and appointed managing director. The appointment was not only provided for by the charter, but was also of "practical utility for the management of the company, transforming an existing situation into a legal situation," with the duty of "overseeing the operations of the company's administrations, the powers inherent to his post as general manager being understood" (minutes for the Board of Directors meeting on February 26, 1943).

After September 8, the company lost contact with all of its foreign offices and a large part of Italy: the only work that it was able to continue was with the Repubblica Sociale Italiana, the regions of Trentino Alto Adige and Friuli Venezia Giulia, the province of Belluno, and Istria, which were annexed to the Third Reich after that date. As a precaution, the company's paper files and general archive were sent to Scodovacca, near Cervignano del Friuli, where all of the documents, policies, and correspondence of the life division were gathered. Central-south Italy, which was in effect cut out, passed under the jurisdiction of the Rome agency, which became a "Special Head Office." It was entrusted with the functions normally assigned by statutory provision to the Venice Head Office, for the period during which that office was prohibited from operating on national territory (peninsula and island), while the Central Head Office continued to handle the company's foreign activity and interests.

On September 15, Volpi resigned from the affiliates in Vienna and Prague, due to strong pressure from the government and public opinion. One month later, Sulfina also left the company, in effect being dismissed. In October, the Board elected Antonio Cosulich as the new chairman, while awaiting Volpi's formal resignation. He stalled, communicating this through Giuseppe Artico, who was the head of the representative office in Rome at the time, but in the end he decided that he could not resign since, in his present position, he did not feel "free" to make a decision that would not jeopardize the fate of the company, which was at risk of being placed under an external commissioner, if a compromise could not be agreed upon (meeting between Volpi and Artico on October 29, reported in a letter from the latter to Baroncini dated October 30).

In early November, Volpi announced his resignation in a letter to Baroncini [*fig.* 5], which was read at a Board meeting on November 8, opening the way for the appointment of Cosulich to the chairmanship. On November 22, 1943, Volpi formally resigned as chairman of Assicurazioni Generali and its affiliates. (S.S.)

Giuseppe Volpi di Misurata

1877
1947

Giuseppe Volpi di Misurata was born on November 19, 1877 into a bourgeois family in Venice [*fig.* 1]. In 1897 the sudden death of the father, who was a building engineer, led him to quit his legal studies and veer course into the area of business. Interestingly, the young Volpi who was a stranger to the business milieu he aspired to be a part of, began his activity by following an established pattern in the city by the lagoon. First, he became the agent in Veneto for L'Urbaine, a small French insurance company where in 1899 he was permitted to add the fire insurance to the existing life insurance. Also in 1899, he opened his own business, G. Volpi e C., which sold Hungarian and Serbian agricultural products, and which would soon be followed by a mining company to exploit the coal deposits in Carnia.

It would appear that at the root of Volpi's luck, though he was undoubtedly a most charismatic personality with a knack for networking, were some key connections that enabled him to secure bank credits and loans. The most pivotal encounter was probably that with Giuseppe Toeplitz, who at the time was a young agent for the Banca Commerciale Italiana (COMIT) in Naples and Venice and, together with Otto Joel, was in charge of the largest universal bank in Italy and who, for over thirty years, would back his projects. At the start of the century, Volpi's projects also attracted a number of influential figures among Venice's financial and political sphere such as Senator Nicolò Papadopoli Aldobrandini (deputy director of Assicurazioni Generali in Venice) and Count Piero Foscari, a local advocate of the industrialization program for the port of Venice. The scheme's purpose was to revitalize the city's Adriatic trade with the East, while also promoting the national, colonialist and imperialist expansion policies that would give Italy access to new markets in the Balkan and Mediterranean regions. In this context, the imminent demise of the Ottoman Empire and the ensuing new international alliances in 1903, induced Volpi and his partners to seek new opportunities in Montenegro. The small Balkan country, which was ruled by a dynasty related to the House of Savoy became the spearhead of a planned Italian penetration to develop commerce and railways. Other entrepreneurial schemes targeted Anatolia (Società Commerciale d'Oriente founded in 1907 with COMIT's support) and its mines. The latter's technical aspects being entrusted to Bernardino Nogara, a mining engineer whose personal friendship with Volpi would keep them connected beyond the Ottoman phase and who, a few decades later, would move on to deal with Vatican finances.

The enterprises in the Balkans and Anatolia were not conceived to reap financial rewards, but were initiated to build solid political and diplomatic relationships with Rome, aided by Volpi's connections to the government circles in Belgrade, Constantinople, and Antalya. Business and government in postwar Libya, gave life to a complex web of interests between Volpi and Nogara on one side, Joel and Toeplitz's COMIT on the other, and Giolitti and his Foreign Affairs Ministry San Giuliano on another. In June 1912, Giolitti commissioned Volpi to head a delegation of Turkish diplomats to Constantinople, and to mediate peace talks aimed at recognizing Italy's conquest of Tripolitania and Cyrenaica. Subsequently, Volpi would be part of the Italian delegation to sign the compromise in Ouchy. In April 1913 he took part in an international conference in Paris, to resolve economic issues arising from the defeat of the Ottoman Empire in the Balkans.

Alongside these diplomatic engagements, Volpi nurtured a second activity that was part of his core business, namely hydroelectric power. Early on he had understood its importance as the driving force of industrialization at a time of definite progress in Italy. In 1905, with the financial contribution from the COMIT, in addition to other investors such as Count Ruggero Revedin, Foscari and Papadopoli, Volpi established the Società Adriatica di Elettricità (SADE), the expansion policy of which was based on the acquisition of existing equipment, to reduce industrial

1.
Giuseppe Volpi di Misurata
[1930s–1940s]
[ASAG, *Versamenti*, scheda 28264]

and market risks, as well as to immediately widen its coverage across Veneto's territory. Thus, the foundations were in place for the construction of what would become in 1917, the industrial complex of Porto Marghera, which in the 1920s and 1930s would see the establishment of energy-intensive production activities.
In 1907 SADE merged with another electric company, Cellina (Società Italiana per l'Utilizzazione delle Forze Idrauliche del Veneto) by means of a significant contribution to the latter's capital. Cellina was founded in 1900 with a loan provided by COMIT; later the Milanese bank continued to provide ongoing support during its development. Its vice president was Marco Besso who in 1905, was also on the Board of another company supported by Volpi, Montenegro's Società di Antivari, also funded by COMIT. Therefore, the relationship between Besso, the man at the helm of Assicurazioni Generali, and Giuseppe Volpi the Venetian industrialist on his way to the top of Italy's financial and political spheres, had been consolidated for quite some time.
Around this time (in 1906, 1911, and 1914) a number of Venetian shareholders involved in Volpi's enterprises (Papadopoli, Giuseppe Da Zara) and supported by Besso, demanded that Assicurazioni Generali's Venice Head Office be made into an Italian company. Although the process of releasing the reserves and portfolios would have required considerable technical and financial resources, it also freed up a number of assets, the investment of which for financial and speculative purposes, would have been at the disposal of the new company's Italian management. The dogged opposition of the shareholders in Trieste (who bore greater power both as proprietors and administrative bodies) was eventually overcome in December 1914, when the war had already broken out in Europe; by then however, the project was put on hold due to Italy's imminent involvement in the conflict. Nonetheless, it would be difficult not to attribute the promotion of an entrepreneurial component characterized by the support for Italy's imperialist policies, to Giuseppe Volpi joining the company's Board in February 1915.
The postwar era constituted for Volpi a fundamental continuum with the past and the transition from Liberalism to Fascism (of which, in any case, he shared the fundamental principles) did not inhibit any connections to power for his interchanging private and public interests. In 1919 he resumed his diplomatic activities as the Italian representative for the Consiglio Superiore Economico at the Versailles Peace Conference (joined by other entrepreneurs such as Alberto Pirelli, Oscar Sinigaglia, Bernardino Nogara). In 1920 he took part in the Rapallo negotiations that ended the dispute over the Yugoslavian borders (he favored a compromise and did not support the more extreme views of the nationalists). In 1921 he was appointed governor of Tripolitania until July 1925, when he became Finance Minister and traveled to Washington to negotiate Italy's war debt with the United States, then to London to discuss the debt with Great Britain. In the world of finance from 1919, he was president of the Associazione tra le Società Italiane per Azioni (ASSONIME); in 1934 he took on Confindustria's presidency; from 1922 he was senator of the Kingdom, minister of State from 1923, plenipotentiary minister and, in 1929, he joined the Gran Consiglio del Fascismo (from which he would be excluded in May 1943). In 1930 he became president of the Ente Autonomo Biennale di Venezia and in this capacity promoted events of international appeal, including the film festival. In 1920 he was given the title of count, and in 1925 he was able to add the honorary "di Misurata".
With the exception of the time as Finance Minister from 1925 through 1928, these activities did not hinder his participation on Assicurazioni Generali's Board. The same is true for the Italian subsidiary Anonima Infortuni, which he'd joined in 1921. Though, during the 1920s and 1930s a more active role in the SADE, the Credito Industriale di Venezia

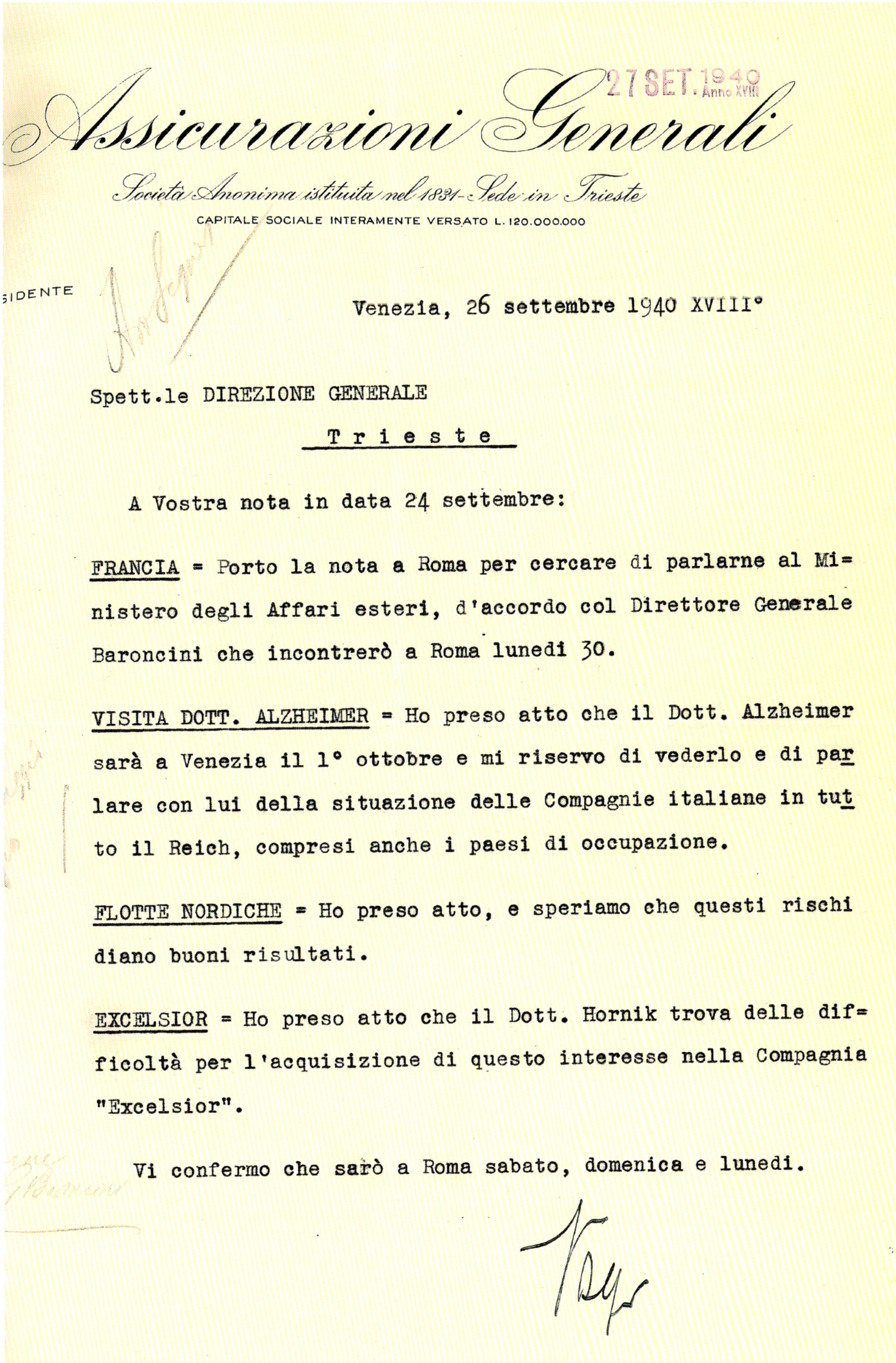

Assicurazioni Generali

Società Anonima istituita nel 1831 - Sede in Trieste

CAPITALE SOCIALE INTERAMENTE VERSATO L. 120.000.000

27 SET. 1940 Anno XVIII

[PRE]SIDENTE

Venezia, 26 settembre 1940 XVIII°

Spett.le DIREZIONE GENERALE

Trieste

A Vostra nota in data 24 settembre:

FRANCIA = Porto la nota a Roma per cercare di parlarne al Ministero degli Affari esteri, d'accordo col Direttore Generale Baroncini che incontrerò a Roma lunedì 30.

VISITA DOTT. ALZHEIMER = Ho preso atto che il Dott. Alzheimer sarà a Venezia il 1° ottobre e mi riservo di vederlo e di parlare con lui della situazione delle Compagnie italiane in tutto il Reich, compresi anche i paesi di occupazione.

FLOTTE NORDICHE = Ho preso atto, e speriamo che questi rischi diano buoni risultati.

EXCELSIOR = Ho preso atto che il Dott. Hornik trova delle difficoltà per l'acquisizione di questo interesse nella Compagnia "Excelsior".

Vi confermo che sarò a Roma sabato, domenica e lunedì.

2.
Letter from Giuseppe Volpi to the Central Head Office (Venice, September 26, 1940)
[ASAG, P*residenza e organi sociali, Presidenti e vicepresidenti, Giuseppe Volpi*, OGG001042025]

and the Adriatica Società di Navigazione was played by his partners Vittorio Cini and Antonio Revedin. In 1938, after the anti-Semitic laws depleted the company's leadership, Volpi was most likely Assicurazioni Generali's only spokesperson to be close to Mussolini and thus, was able to negotiate (with Fulvio Suvich of the Riunione Adriatica di Sicurtà–RAS and Felice Guarneri as mediator) a solution that was not just in response to an emergency, but also provided political protection from the regime's most extremist factions, and which secured the kind of local and international prestige that justified a new management structure. In September 1938 he, a Venetian, became Assicurazioni Generali's chairman and, beside him as deputy chairmen were two shareholders from Trieste, Antonio Nicolò Cosulich, descendant of an ancient family of ship owners, and Giorgio Pitacco, an eminent national-liberal politician, who after the war became the mayor and podesta of Trieste.

One of the most pressing issues was the aggressive attitude of the insurance companies of the Greater Germanic Reich. From Volpi's earliest reports to the Council of Directors it is clear how the fragile and constantly shifting balance between competition and collaboration in business moved toward collaborating with the stronger German competitors. In May 1939 the company restructured its activities around two cornerstones: Assicurazioni Generali's life and transport insurances, and Vienna's Erste Allgemeine for the non-life policies. The collaboration was tightened in 1941 with a mutual exchange of shares that saw the Münchener Rück. join the capital of the Erste Allgemeine with a minority shareholding, while Assicurazioni Generali acquired a similar participation in the Milanese La Pace, which was under the German company's control [*fig.* 2]. However, during the course of the war, Assicurazioni Generali's traditional market participants such as Poland and Bohemia-Moravia were gradually removed from the Italian operations, slightly offset by the development opportunities that the Netherlands and Denmark offered Assicurazioni Generali. Volpi's youthful aspirations for the Balkans lead him to seek business opportunities in a dismembered Yugoslavia, in Greece and Romania; alas with meager results as these economies had been impoverished by the war. Meanwhile, the United States' participation in the war, had made it impossible to carry on working with the two Americas. The company's financial statements during this initial phase of the conflict, 1940–1943, show a slight but constant contraction in operational income, and a progressive increase in guarantee funds, capital reserves and technical reserves. Although this may be attributed to the effects of inflation, it is true that the company tried to protect itself from a most unfavorable situation.

The events between July 25, and September 8, 1943 took place when Volpi was seriously ill in his home in Rome, by then distanced from any political influence. From the first days of the German occupation he and Assicurazioni Generali became the targets of anti-Semitic attacks by the most extremist factions of the restructured Fascist Party. Attacks that persisted in the months that followed and were echoed by the German press and radio. On September 15, he resigned the presidency of Vienna's Erste Allgemeine, and from Moldavia-Sekuritas in Prague; a decision that the Nazis must have taken as proof of his refusal to collaborate. On September 23, he was arrested by Herbert Kappler's SS and taken to the prison in Via Tasso while his house was ransacked. Following his arrest, he spent almost two months at Regina Coeli prison, after which he was hospitalized and finally released in February 1944. Concerned about leaving a power vacuum at the helm of the company, he did not resign from Assicurazioni Generali's chairmanship until November 1943, and only after yielding to the pressure coming from Trieste. In July 1944 he found refuge in Switzerland. At the end of the war his fortune was seized and he was remitted to the

Alta Corte di Giustizia per le Sanzioni contro il Fascismo. In January 1947 he was partly acquitted and partly amnestied from the allegations of having participated in the voiding of the constitutional guarantees, and for having contributed through "significant deeds" in the support of the regime.
He died in Rome on November 16, 1947.

Sources

"Una relazione di S. E. Volpi sull'attività delle Assicurazioni Generali." *Il Popolo d'Italia* November 11, 1938.
Assicurazioni Generali, Trieste. *Relazioni e bilanci per l'anno 1940 (109° esercizio)*. Trieste: 1941.
Assicurazioni Generali, Trieste. *Relazioni e bilanci per l'anno 1941 (110° esercizio)*. Trieste: 1942.
Assicurazioni Generali, Trieste. *Relazioni e bilanci per l'anno 1942 (111° esercizio)*. Trieste: 1943.
Assicurazioni Generali, Trieste. *Relazioni e bilanci per l'anno 1943 (112° esercizio*). Trieste: 1944.

Bibliography

Volpi di Misurata Giuseppe, www.senato.it.
Webster, Richard A. *L'imperialismo industriale italiano 1909–1915. Studio sul pre-fascismo*. Turin: Einaudi, 1974.
Romano, Sergio. *Giuseppe Volpi. Industria e finanza tra Giolitti e Mussolini*. Milan: Bompiani, 1979.
Feldman, Gerald D. "Concorrenza e collaborazione tra le compagnie d'assicurazione dell'Asse: Munich Re, Generali e Ras (1933–1943)." *Imprese e storia* 24 (2001): 249–71.
Reberschak, Maurizio. "Gli 'uomini capitali.' Il gruppo veneziano (Volpi, Cini e gli altri)." In *Storia di Venezia, L'Ottocento e il Novecento*, edited by Mario Isnenghi and Stuart J. Woolf, vol. II, 1255–1311. Rome: Istituto dell'Enciclopedia Italiana, 2002.
Millo, Anna. *Trieste, le assicurazioni, l'Europa. Arnoldo Frigessi di Rattalma e la Ras*. Milan: Franco Angeli, 2004.
Favaretto, Tito. "Lo sviluppo dell'attività internazionale delle Assicurazioni Generali tra il XIX e il XX secolo." In *Assicurare 150 anni di Unità d'Italia. Il contributo delle assicurazioni allo sviluppo del Paese*, edited by Paolo Garonna, 93–151. Rome: ANIA, 2011.
(A.M.)

"Circulating" Policies

Discovering Special Insurance Types through the Study of the Venice Head Office's Circulars

1921
1937

"The men of the Trieste venture had vision, grit, and faith, and approached their work with tenacity and perseverance. And the small Company, brilliantly conceived and firmly desired by this group, quickly surpassed its natural boundaries and exceeded its own plan, almost as if it having no, and rightly so, clearly defined targets." Thus Camillo Orlando-Castellano summarized the enterprising spirit that characterized Generali from its founding, in his essay "Il centenario delle Assicurazioni Generali" (in *Il Diritto Marittimo*, June/August 1932). This spirit was clearly expressed in the deed of partnership of 1831, which also explained the careful reasoning behind the company name, "Assicurazioni Generali Austro-Italiche," indicating the company's technical and geographic sphere of activity. The adjective "Generali" conveyed the company's aim to go beyond the traditional insurance fields (maritime and river transport), extending them to any and all other insurance branches permitted by law, arriving at the highly varied insurance activity of the present day, conducted either directly or through subsidiaries and associated companies. The name "Austro-Italiche" indicated both the territory where the company intended to develop its business and the composition of its shareholder body.

The story of Generali shows how inventiveness, in concert with solid scientific and technically sound foundations, driven by insurance criteria, selection and division of risk, and a balanced approach to mathematical calculations of probability and statistical aspects, was able to create new types of insurance: from agricultural risks, livestock mortality, hail and accidents, civil liability, theft, and glass to credit insurance and coverage for car and aeronautical risks, meeting all of the needs of civilized existence. As a result, the company was a constant presence in all areas of the insurance world, establishing rates, devising policies, and determining premiums. Alongside its own commercial organization, it created another, with a sophisticated technical, actuarial, and statistical bent.

The circulars of the Venice Head Office preserved in the Historical Archive testify to the company's industriousness [*fig.* 1]. Produced or adopted by the Head Office and addressed to its agents, executives, and shareholders, they offer a cross-section of company life, touching on organizational, administrative, and accounting matters. Reading through the various insurance proposals and instructions given to the agency network, we see how Italy changed over the years, both economically (for instance, consideration of industrial risks sheds light on the development of industry and transport) and socially. One example in this regard is "tourist" insurance, a sector set up at the beginning of the century when travel was becoming increasingly common. In substance, it was a guarantee offered through hoteliers to tenants, the effects of whom were insured against fire and theft, excluding personal effects with monetary or sentimental value. There were also supplementary clauses linked to fire policies, like "earthquake risk," which was introduced after the catastrophe in Sicily and Calabria in which all of the staff at the Messina agency lost their lives. Or "riot and looting risk," as a supplement to fire and theft insurance, since the damage caused by disorder and civil unrest was not covered by standard insurance policies. A supplementary clause offered exclusively to "regulars," it needed to be considered "solely with prudence and extremely careful selectiveness," following the numerous claims, some for sizable amounts, in the early 1920s after the Biennio Rosso ("two red years"). Daily strikes, factory fires, and the constant looting of farms and businesses induced the company to continue offering this type of insurance and develop it while taking the necessary precautions, making sure to have precise knowledge of the risk to be assumed and its characteristics. A special "riot" plaque was also developed, for affixing to insured buildings "in the hope that it would serve to protect the items insured against damage, destruction, fire, etc., communicating to and warning the rioters about the uselessness of attack, since the damage that they wanted to inflict on the insured person or entity would fall entirely on our company,

which would be obligated to settle the claim" (circular no. 1190 of November 20, 1922).
In the early 1920s, there was a sharp rise in fire claims: the reasons behind this gradual worsening were general in nature, and first and foremost inherent to the economic, trade, and industrial crisis and the state of unrest and unease pervading a large part of Italy. It was therefore necessary to try to restore balance by shrewdly grading risks and intensifying the search for "favored" business opportunities. Attention was thus paid not only to the standard, commonly cultivated insurance types, but also to the diffusion of the kinds more rarely proposed to clients. Emphasis was placed on the intense energy that "a few small foreign companies and some newly founded Italian ones" had been pouring for a decade already into forming business relationships with public and, especially, city and provincial administrations, as well as those of charities, banks, savings banks, consortia, and schools, offering them fire insurance for books, account books, documents, and everything else constituting their archives. The assumption of these risks was regulated by special policy wording according to which the company, in case of fire, would pay for the cost of the material and labor required for recreating the documents, except in the case of indirect damage or artistic value. This type of policy therefore offered the broadest guarantee for preserving everything that concerned the materiality of the insured entities, whereas, since it could not guarantee irreplaceable items or things that did not at least have sale value, it did not cover manuscripts or documents with historical or sentimental value. It instead applied to items that were indispensable to the running of the administration, the recreation of which would necessarily require spending and labor. These items included, for example, marriage certificates and vital records, registers, receipt books, copies of contacts and all similar documents, forms and office supplies, and statute books (circular no. 9/4 of July 26, 1921).
After the war, Assicurazioni Generali found itself

1.
The volumes containing the Venice Head Office's circulars (1916-1938) [ASAG, *Direzione veneta, Circolari*, voll. 1916-1920, 1921-1925, 1926-1930, 1931-1932, 1933-1935, 1936-1938]

The circulars were rebound at different times into thirty-four one-year volumes (1884-1888, 1894-1926) and sixteen multi-year volumes (1901–1945)

2.
Postcard celebrating the Giornata della madre e del fanciullo, enclosed with circular no. 9520 from the Venice Head Office (Venice, December 21, 1933) and the promotional handbook *Il mio bambino*, enclosed with circular no. 11/2 from the Venice Head Office (Venice, December 18, 1933) [ASAG, *Direzione veneta, Circolari*, vol. 1933–1935]

In compliance with the newborn policy promoted by the government for circulating standards and scientific methods of prenatal and infant hygiene in order to protect mothers and children, the handbook for young mothers offered useful advice about infant hygiene, the wake time and rest cycle, feeding, weaning and diet, growth parameters, etc.

needing to adapt to the changed political and economic requirements of the territories where it was traditionally active. At the fall of the Hapsburg Empire, new national States were formed, creating, among other things, complex economic, monetary, and legal problems for the insurance industry. First and foremost, the company's financial systems needed to be modified in adherence to the monetary division subsequent to the creation of so many new States. The insurance types were perfected, the production criteria streamlined, and the work of foreign expansion that gave Generali its global importance stepped up. While in Italy the company was represented in all cities, large and small, by a vast network of agencies, it also had many offices in Europe and, above all, a vast network of agencies, branches, and representative offices in the Levant, North Africa, Sudan, China, the Philippines, India, South America, and the United States. In addition to this direct activity, the company also substantially increased its creation of and merging with insurance companies in both Italy and abroad. In 1924, the Consorzio Italiano Assicurazione Aeronautica (Consaero) was founded in Rome at the Unione Italiana di Riassicurazione, in order to consolidate the field and coordinate the development of the aeronautical insurance industry. Generali was one of the first Italian insurance companies to join the Consorzio. It proposed offering a single policy that included fire, theft, transport, accident, and civil liability coverage. The aeronautical risks assumed were those concerning anything to do with commercial air traffic companies, flight schools, and facilities for construction, repairing, or assembling aircraft. To better regulate relations between the Central Head Office and agencies, a central head office for aeronautical insurance was set up at the Head Office in Rome, with a direct connection to the Consorzio and serving as a consultancy, as we read in circular no. 2/1 March 17, 1924. Air navigation was regulated with Royal Decree January 11, 1925, no. 356, and, in 1926, the rules regulating flight insurance were adopted in agreement with the Istituto Nazionale delle Assicurazioni (INA). This insurance type was a supplement to life policies held by all insured parties in the army, navy, and air force, covering them as passengers, and also covered all hang gliders and paragliders while in flight.

During the Fascist period, the government supported families with a series of legal measures providing for financial assistance to large families, birth and marriage bonuses for State employees, the extension of family allowances, disbursed by the Istituto Nazionale Fascista di Previdenza Sociale (INFPS) to employees of private companies, and the institution of marriage and birth loans. The population stimulus provided by the government measures induced the company to join the newly founded Comitato Italiano per lo Studio dei Problemi della Popolazione in 1928, agreeing to a five-yearly contribution. Various ideas for new types of insurance were also scrutinized, one example being "insurance for young women," which, even though it could be considered a form of dowry insurance, offered a special advantage to young women who married before turning twenty-five, winning approval from the Italian Economics Ministry for "its promotion of social order" and also for noting "the opportunity to introduce contracts of this type" (circular no. 5/4 of April 1, 1929). For the Giornata della Madre e del Fanciullo, proclaimed on December 24, 1933, Assicurazioni Generali introduced free birth insurance premiums in response to Mussolini's call for population increase [*fig.* 2]. For this initiative, the company gifted policies in the name of the newborns, free of premiums and all other charges, to all heads of family who had taken out a life insurance policy between December 24, 1933 and March 24, 1934, and who celebrated the birth of one or more children by the end of the year such that the total number of children in the family was brought to at least five. These policies were to be paid by the company when the children turned eighteen, "on the sole condition that at least five annual premiums had been paid on the policy taken out by the father" (circular no. 9520 of December 21, 1933).

Generali also actively promoted insurance for young couples, in brochures like *Il Poema della Famiglia* [*fig.* 3], which was distributed by priests after the wedding ceremony, or the *Almanacco degli Sposi*, published by the Istituto Editoriale Nazionale after a special prize-giving wedding competition. The competition, announced by the Istituto Editoriale Nazionale, awarded prizes to the twenty youngest couples who got married in Italy between January 1 and December 31, 1936. First prize was a life insurance policy offered by Generali (the policy was won by Giuseppe Cirillo, from the province of Salerno, whose age together with that of his wife totaled 32, circular no. 57970 of May 11, 1937).

In 1934, the Central Head Office received full permission from the Church authorities to develop special forms of life insurance for circulation in the religious sphere. One of them was "ordination and clerical benefice" insurance, offered to young men completing their priesthood studies, to help with any economic problems they might face due to their decision to become priests. The policy guaranteed the money needed for the clothing ceremony and the basis for building up a savings and benefit fund, the "benefice" or security needed in case the priest were invested with the selfsame benefice, as established "by the instructions given on June 30, 1929 no. 2076-29 by the Sacra Congregazione del Concilio" (circular no. 5/2 of July 2, 1934). This policy was also valid for young men who, when taking their vows, normally needed to bring a small contribution. The graphics were entrusted to the famous adman and painter from Trieste, Marcello Dudovich, who came up with a design inspired by the twisted columns of Bernini's baldachin in St. Peter's Basilica in the Vatican, holding up a portrait of Pope Pius XI framed by the four patriarchal basilicas in Rome: St. Peter's, St. John Lateran, St. Mary Major, and St. Paul Outside-the-Walls [*fig.* 4].

An especially curious form of life insurance was the "Bellini policy," promoted in 1935 in celebration of

3.
Life policy advertising brochure
(Rome, 1933)
[ASAG, *Versamenti*, scheda 7890]

the centenary of the famous composer Vincenzo Bellini, with the backing of the Ministry of Corporations, Ministry of Education, and distinguished musicians and designed for conservatory students [*fig.* 5]. The purpose was to provide freshly graduated young musicians with the initial funds for launching their music careers, providing the means for completing their training, even abroad. To promote this initiative, Generali proposed sending the "well known" orchestra conductor Alberto Consiglio to its agencies in regions where there was also a conservatory, to give promotional talks to the students (circular no. 4/3 of March 2, 1935).

The collection of circulars is an endless source of information for many different areas of inquiry: the development of language, human relations (through study of the use of civilities, for example), work organization, relations between agencies and the Head Office, and the evolution of the company logo. (S.S.)

Polizza
della
Ordinazione
e del
Beneficio Sacerdotale

Del Sig. ....
Figlio di ....
Nato a ....

Chierico

nel Seminario ....
di ....

Officine I.G.A.P. – Milano-Roma

POLIZZA BELLINIANA

CONDIZIONI PARTICOLARI

Nel caso di decesso del Contraente prima della scadenza della polizza, semprechè la stessa sia in pieno vigore, il contratto avrà ugualmente corso, senza ulteriore pagamento di premi.

Nel caso di decesso dello studente assicurato prima della scadenza della polizza, il Contraente, semprechè la polizza stessa sia in pieno vigore, avrà diritto, entro trenta giorni dalla scadenza della rata di premio successiva al decesso dello studente:

di volturare la polizza sulla vita di altro assicurato per le stesse somme, pagabili in conformità ai punti 1), 2), 3) della prima facciata della presente polizza.

oppure:

di chiedere la liquidazione della polizza incassando la somma assicurata al punto 1), della prima facciata della presente polizza ridotta in proporzione agli anni di assicurazione trascorsi dal principio dell'assicurazione stessa al momento del decesso dello studente assicurato in confronto dell'intera durata della polizza restando questa annullata e di nessun effetto.

La Compagnia procederà alla liquidazione della polizza in quest'ultimo modo qualora il Contraente non ne chieda la voltura entro il termine predetto.

Nel caso di decesso dello studente assicurato dopo la scadenza della polizza, gli eredi del medesimo avranno diritto alle rispettive scadenze, alle somme di cui ai punti 2) e 3) della prima facciata della presente polizza non ancora pagate dalla Compagnia.

Qualora dopo il decesso del Contraente avvenisse quello dello studente prima che sia avvenuta la scadenza della polizza, la Compagnia pagherà agli eredi legittimi del Contraente la somma assicurata al punto 1) della prima facciata della presente polizza ridotta in proporzione agli anni di assicurazione trascorsi dal principio della assicurazione stessa al momento del decesso dello studente assicurato in confronto dell'intera durata della polizza restando questa annullata e di nessun effetto.

RIDUZIONI E RISCATTI

Gli art. 6 (polizza ridotta), 8 e 9 (riscatto) delle Condizioni Generali di polizza vengono sostituiti dai seguenti:

POLIZZA RIDOTTA

Qualora il contraente sospenda il pagamento dei premi:

a) la somma assicurata al punto 1), della prima facciata della presente polizza verrà ridotta nella stessa proporzione in cui il numero dei premi pagati sta al numero complessivo dei premi stipulati;

b) nella stessa proporzione resteranno ridotte le somme di lire 1000 di cui ai punti 2) e 3) della prima facciata della polizza.

RISCATTO

Quando siano state pagate almeno tre annualità di premio, su domanda del contraente - semprechè sia in vita lo studente assicurato - la Compagnia effettua il riscatto della polizza:

a) procedendo al pagamento della somma ridotta di cui al punto *a*) del precedente articolo, scontata al 4,25 % all'anno per il periodo decorrente dal giorno del pagamento a quello della scadenza della polizza;

b) rilasciando una polizza franca da corresponsione di premi per le somme ridotte di cui alla lettera *b*) dell'articolo precedente, somme che saranno pagabili alle date prestabilite, semprechè lo studente assicurato sia in vita **nel giorno di scadenza della polizza.**

Venezia, li ....

La Direzione Veneta delle Assicurazioni Generali

4.
Ordination and benefice policy enclosed with circular no. 5/2 from the Venice Head Office (Venice, July 2, 1934)
[ASAG, *Direzione veneta, Circolari*, vol. 1933–1935]

5.
Bellini policy enclosed with circular no. 4/3 from the Venice Head Office (Venice, March 2, 1935)
[ASAG, *Direzione veneta, Circolari*, vol. 1933–1935]

Marco Ara

1883
1950

Born in Trieste on March 14, 1883, son of Davide Coen Ara and Rosina Levi, Marco Ara's paternal family had been associated with Assicurazioni Generali for generations and was united by strong patriotic feelings [*fig.* 1].
His grandfather, Angelo Coen Ara, was a businessman who between 1850 and 1859 had held important positions in the company's representative bodies, while his uncle, Carlo Coen Ara, was more closely related to the insurance profession. Hired in 1862 in Venice, his uncle's career path followed some significant stages inside Italy's major agencies, until he returned to Venice in 1896 with the title of deputy secretary, which he retained until 1907. In 1866, at the age of twenty, he joined Garibaldi's forces and fought against Austria, taking part in the battles of Bezzecca and Condino. Following a similar path, between a career within the company and a commitment to irredentism, were the three Ara brothers: Camillo (born in 1876), Angelo (born in 1877) and Marco. The eldest brother, Giuseppe, was a lecturer in Venice and Genoa; at first he followed the ideologies to Mazzini's later period after which he became a nationalist. The youngest sibling, Enrico, was an officer of Anonima Infortuni in Milan [*fig.* 2].
Of the three brothers who devoted their careers to Assicurazioni Generali, Marco achieved the highest position through internal promotions. Starting off in the Milanese subsidiary, Anonima Infortuni in 1902, in 1907 he moved to Naples in the capacity of branch inspector. Having returned to Trieste, from 1910 through 1914 he managed the accident insurance division in Trieste's general agency, a post that he would resume in 1919, after the interruption caused by the war. In 1921 he was transferred to the general agency in Rome, in 1922 he becomes a manager of the Venice Head Office, in 1926 he was promoted to general manager in Venice.
His brother Angelo's experience was more international. Having joined the company in 1896, in 1901 he was an authorised signatory for the maritime office in Brăila, Romania, in 1904 he was transferred to Anonima Infortuni in Barcelona in the capacity of director-in-charge. Called back in Trieste in 1911, he became later the head of the central secretariat. In 1915, shortly before Italy entered the war, he moved to the Venice Head Office and, in 1916, he was transferred to Rome where he managed the transport division. In 1922 he returned to Trieste in the capacity of co-manager and, in 1926, he was promoted to deputy general manager.
Unlike his brothers Marco and Angelo, Camillo Ara pursued a law degree in Vienna and worked as a lawyer in Trieste. From 1908, following the death of the political leader Felice Venezian, he became the leader of the national-liberal party, which represented the Italian bourgeoisie under the Hapsburg rule, and through the City Council's administration, promoted the Italian language and culture; not without the occasional expression of irredentist and separatist views. During the war, in the Ufficio Affari Civili del Comando Supremo, Camillo Ara prepared financial and legislative projects in view of the Italian provinces' annexation. At this time, thanks to the valuable contacts he'd nurtured within Italy's political and financial establishments, the postwar period saw him become conduit for Trieste's large network of industrial, commercial and banking enterprises, which, due to the loss of the traditional central European markets, and due to the competition over Italian assets in that difficult and uncertain climate, were forced to join the Kingdom's economy. In 1922 he was nominated for a position in Assicurazioni Generali's Council of Directors and the smaller Executive Committee, on which he would continue to serve until 1938. Additionally, he sat on the Boards of many other businesses of the Venezia Giulia region; a business world that would fail to withstand the crisis of 1929. At the time of the State's decisive intervention to repair the country's entire industry and banking sectors, Camillo Ara was recruited into the key roles of the financial bodies created for that

purpose: in 1932 he becomes the president of the Società Finanziaria Industriale Italiana (SOFINDT), and in 1934 vice president of the Istituto per la Ricostruzione Industriale (IRI).
His political commitments under the Austrian rule were supported by his brothers. In 1909 Marco was nominated as a member of the national-liberal party for Trieste's City Council. In March 1915 Marco and Angelo had both illegally crossed the border into Italy and consequently, became deserters and were wanted by the Austrian police in Trieste. Marco joined the Italian army, reaching the rank of infantry captain. After he was wounded on Mount Podgora, he was awarded a silver medal. Angelo was transferred to the Venice Head Office and in July 1915, he took advantage of his frequent business trips to Zurich to volunteer as an informant for the Italian police headquarters.
In 1926 Assicurazioni Generali's top management comprised among others, four people connected by kinship: the three brothers Ara and their cousin, Chairman Edgardo Morpurgo, whose mother Carolina Levi was Rosina's sister. This peculiar feature in the company's organizational chart, represents a particular time in its history between the nineteenth and the twentieth centuries, as there are other such connections between the Besso and the Morpurgo families. These interesting examples recall the specific social milieu that developed among the bourgeoisie in Trieste's marketplace. Through the covenant of marriage, business associates and members belonging to the same community gave rise to solid and homogeneous family structures, whose members were educated according to shared values and behavioral norms favoring personal honesty and duty. Such family ties proved ideal, within companies, for creating networks that were based on trust, not material values, and which were essential in navigating an era of profound transformations and change, as the one after the World War I was for Assicurazioni Generali. Managers such as Ara and Morpurgo, with their

1.
Marco Ara (Trieste, [1930s])
[ASAG, *Versamenti*, scheda 28264]

admirable irredentist pasts, valued the Italian component of the company at the very time in which it had legally become Italian.

Two other elements that demonstrate the homogeneity of values and education that define these members of management, are their religious affiliation and national identity.

At the start of the twentieth century, all three Ara brothers had formally cancelled their affiliation to the Jewish Community in Trieste. The first, in 1903, was Angelo at the age of twenty-six, followed in 1904 by Camillo who was twenty-eight and, in 1907, Marco at the age of twenty-four. These choices, which were expressed at a young age and at the start of their professional activities—choices that at that time were common among the Trieste Jews—typify the predominant cultural values of the time, i.e. a secular liberalism, at the center of which, were individual and personal fulfilment. Imbuing the individual with meaning and making him feel part of a collective destiny, was the national identity. The Ara brothers recognized themselves in the Italian identity, which they experienced more prominently compared to the Jewish tradition and therefore wished to be assimilated.

Given that similar events were taking place in many European countries, the Italian racial laws of 1938 did not catch the insurance environment by surprise. Nonetheless, the bewilderment among the ranks of the Italian Jewish community was complete; specifically, among those who had renounced the Jewish faith, and who saw themselves stigmatized, their civil rights eradicated based on biological concepts of race, whereas they based their identity on nationality and culture. In Trieste, during the war, many among them had volunteered to wear the uniform of the Italian Army. There were attempts to retaliate: the prefecture of Venice reports that, in September 1938, in the villa in Mirano: "The Israelite, Marco Ara, manager of Assicurazioni Generali in Venice" held a meeting with about thirty Jews to discuss measures to avert the anti-Semitic laws.

Although in 1939 they were granted a partial exemption (i.e. exoneration from anti-Jewish measures) on the grounds of "exceptional merits," in November 1938 Marco and Camillo were forced to step down. Marco Ara applied for early retirement, which the Council of Directors readily accepted.

Angelo would die in 1943, Camillo in 1944.

Of the three brothers, Marco Ara was the only one who was still alive in the postwar period; he was reinstated in the company and remained in service until his death, in Mirano, on May 13, 1950.

Sources

ACS. *Ministero dell'Interno*, *Direzione Generale della Pubblica Sicurezza*. A I, 1915, b. 4, fasc. Ara Angelo.

ASAG. *Direzione centrale*, *Servizio del personale*, *Posizioni personali*. U2GE050084–U2GE050085, personnel file of Marco Ara, 1914–1968; U2GE050083, personnel file of Angelo Ara, 1897–1943.

ASAG. *Versamenti*, scheda 6819, biographical notes on Carlo Ara, undated.

ASBI. *Banca Commerciale Italiana*, *Archivio di Arnoldo Frigessi di Rattalma*. Cart. 35, fasc. 3, family tree of Giuseppe Levi, 1928.

ASMAE. *Rappresentanza italiana a Vienna (1862–1938)*, b. 246, *Präsidium des k.k. Ministeriums des Innern*, Trieste, 1917.

"Una relazione di S. E. Volpi sull'attività delle Assicurazioni Generali." *Il Popolo d'Italia*, November 11, 1938.

"L'opera e la figura di Marco Ara." *Bollettino delle Assicurazioni Generali* I (1950): 9–10.

Bibliography

Il centenario delle Assicurazioni Generali, 1831–1931, [edited by Giuseppe Stefani]. Trieste: Editrice la Compagnia, 1931: 203–04.

Migliucci, Mario. "Ara, Camillo." In *Dizionario Biografico degli Italiani*, vol. III, 679–80. Rome: Isti-

tuto dell'Enciclopedia Italiana, 1961.
Franzina, Emilio and Magliaretta, Leopoldo. "La società." In Franzina, Emilio, *Venezia,* 314–15, Storia delle città italiane. Rome-Bari: Laterza, 1986.
Millo, Anna. *Trieste, le assicurazioni, l'Europa. Arnoldo Frigessi di Rattalma e la Ras*. Milan: Franco Angeli, 2004.
(A.M.)

2.
The Ara brothers, from the left: Marco, Giuseppe, Angelo and Camillo (Udine, 1915–1918)

Umberto Nobile's Arctic Expeditions
Successes and Tragedies Seen through Life Insurance Policies

1926
1928

Various attempts to reach the North and South Poles were made between the late nineteenth and early twentieth centuries. The Norwegian explorer Roald Amundsen, who had reached the South Pole in an expedition carried out between late 1911 and early 1912, had tried but not yet succeeded in arriving as far as the North Pole. He made another attempt in 1926, this time in collaboration with Italians. Umberto Nobile was in fact the one who convinced him that an airship would be a viable means of getting there. *N-1*, a semi-rigid airship designed by Nobile, was built in Ciampino between 1923 and 1924 and then sold by Italy to the Norwegians, the expedition's main supporters, who renamed it *Norge*.

The documentation from the life division preserves the preparatory phases for the stipulation of a policy to cover the Italians on the team in case of death or disability. Although these documents do not tell us whether or not the agreement was finalized (a definitive policy has not been found so far), they do make it possible to reconstruct a short detailed account of the endeavor from the insurance perspective. In a note stamped April 7, 1926, we read that the initial negotiations took place in Rome between April 2 and 3, the scheduled day of the team's departure from Ciampino, which was, however, postponed until April 10 due to poor weather. The policy was to be taken out by the Consorzio Aeronautico together with an English group, the name of which is never specified. The morning of Friday, April 2, a meeting was held at the Istituto Nazionale delle Assicurazioni (INA), with the representatives of the interested companies in attendance: Major Vetta from the Consorzio Aeronautico, the head actuary and deputy director of INA, Ambron, along with the actuary Sobrero and the engineer Castellini from Riunione Adriatica di Sicurtà (RAS). Assicurazioni Generali was represented by Francesco Berti from the general agency of Rome and the author of the report, whose name is not listed but was probably Pietro Smolensky, legal representative and head of the technical section of the life division and, later, division manager. This first meeting was focused on examining the nature of the risk involved, discussing the premium to be applied, and establishing the initial bases for the contract. That afternoon, a second meeting was held, this time at the "Aeronautica Headquarters," which lasted until Saturday, April 3 and was attended by representatives from the various insurance companies, Umberto Nobile, commander of the Italian team and a colonel at the time (he was promoted to general on his return to Italy), and Rolf Thommessen, chairman of Norsk Luftseiladsforening, the Norwegian aviation society that bought the airship from Italy. An initial letter of intent was drafted, dated Rome, April 3, 1926, and addressed to Thommessen [*fig.* 1]. In the letter, INA, Generali, and RAS committed to assuming the risk for the team's six Italians: Umberto Nobile, Natale Cecioni, Ettore Arduino, Dante Lippi, Attilio Caratti, and Vincenzo Pomella, who were all in the Italian Regia Aeronautica. The policy covered death and permanent disability and the amounts of coverage were expressed in pounds (6,000 for Nobile, 1,500 for Cecioni, and 900 for each of the other four). The coverage was to last for the entire period starting from arrival at the first "town," defined as an inhabited place with a doctor and a post office or telegraph office, until the return to Italy. A letter dated April 6 from the Central Head Office in Trieste to the Venice Head Office, which was to have more direct responsibility in the matter, communicated the outcome of these negotiations and reported that INA would assume fifty percent of the coverage and Generali and RAS would divide the remainder equally between them. Before long, however, a number of difficulties arose, as we read in a letter sent on April 8 by Giuseppe Massimo Sacerdoti in Rome to the Venice Head Office and Trieste on copy. Nobile had rejected the English group's limit on the duration of the expedition to a few months, while the English group refused to cover risk of freezing, which Nobile instead insisted

upon. The Consorzio Aeronautico was to therefore independently grant Nobile's request and support him in the subsequent negotiations with the English insurers, which were to take place when the Norge stopped over in London. The letter also reveals that the airship's departure, which had already been postponed once due to poor weather and rescheduled for that very day, was postponed a second time.
There was also correspondence between Smolensky and Eucardio Ottolenghi, deputy manager in Venice. On April 14, he wrote to Smolensky: "Dearest friend, a few days ago, Cavalier Berti forwarded me a letter in Rome that had been sent to him by the Venice Head Office, concerning the polar flight. He received this letter after the explorers had already begun their journey north, and for this reason alone it would not have been possible to have them sign the proposals. But even if they had not yet departed, I do not believe that we would have been able to ask them to complete and sign our proposals, busy as they were preparing for an expedition that is not only at the center of our own country's interest, but also of that of a large part of the world." Moreover, while a few days earlier it had emerged that the Venice Head Office preferred issuing a policy separate from the others and relative only to the Generali quota, Smolensky communicated a few thoughts that ended up reflected in the policy drawn up in 1928 for Nobile's second expedition: "I believe that this matter should not be handled in the standard way. In my view, the best solution would be to have INA handle it, issuing a single policy indicating the quotas taken on by each Company, the specific conditions, and, with regard to the general conditions, just the few fragments of articles that absolutely must be preserved: two or three items at most. It should all therefore be typed up on blank paper, and not on a policy form printed with the standard general terms and conditions. The proposal will be replaced by a letter of confirmation from Mr. Thommessen, which will contain the insured party's commitment." Evidently, the ne-

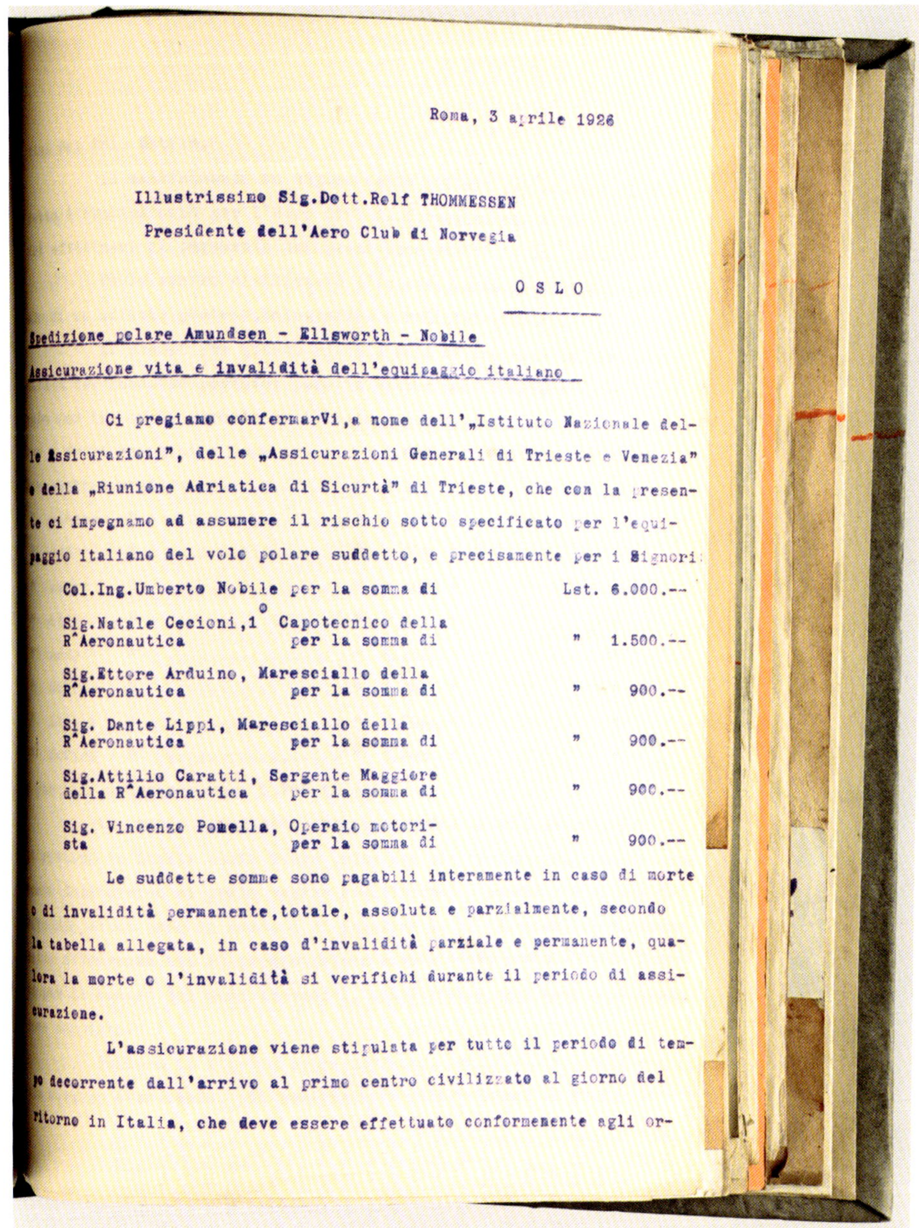
Roma, 3 aprile 1926

Illustrissimo Sig.Dott.Rolf THOMMESSEN
Presidente dell'Aero Club di Norvegia

OSLO

Spedizione polare Amundsen - Ellsworth - Nobile
Assicurazione vita e invalidità dell'equipaggio italiano

Ci pregiamo confermarVi, a nome dell'„Istituto Nazionale delle Assicurazioni", delle „Assicurazioni Generali di Trieste e Venezia" e della „Riunione Adriatica di Sicurtà" di Trieste, che con la presente ci impegnamo ad assumere il rischio sotto specificato per l'equipaggio italiano del volo polare suddetto, e precisamente per i Signori:

Col.Ing.Umberto Nobile	per la somma di	Lst. 6.000.--
Sig.Natale Cecioni, 1° Capotecnico della R^Aeronautica	per la somma di	" 1.500.--
Sig.Ettore Arduino, Maresciallo della R^Aeronautica	per la somma di	" 900.--
Sig. Dante Lippi, Maresciallo della R^Aeronautica	per la somma di	" 900.--
Sig.Attilio Caratti, Sergente Maggiore della R^Aeronautica	per la somma di	" 900.--
Sig. Vincenzo Pomella, Operaio motorista	per la somma di	" 900.--

Le suddette somme sono pagabili interamente in caso di morte o di invalidità permanente, totale, assoluta e parzialmente, secondo la tabella allegata, in caso d'invalidità parziale e permanente, qualora la morte o l'invalidità si verifichi durante il periodo di assicurazione.

L'assicurazione viene stipulata per tutto il periodo di tempo decorrente dall'arrivo al primo centro civilizzato al giorno del ritorno in Italia, che deve essere effettuato conformemente agli or-

1.
Letter of intent for the Amundsen-Ellsworth-Nobile polar expedition, addressed to Rolf Thommessen (Rome, April 3, 1926) [ASAG, *Direzione centrale, Ramo vita, Attuariato, Corrispondenza tecnica*, U2GE000555]

2.
Insurance policy for the team of the airship *Italia* (Rome, April 5, 1928) [ASAG, *Versamenti*, scheda 62411]

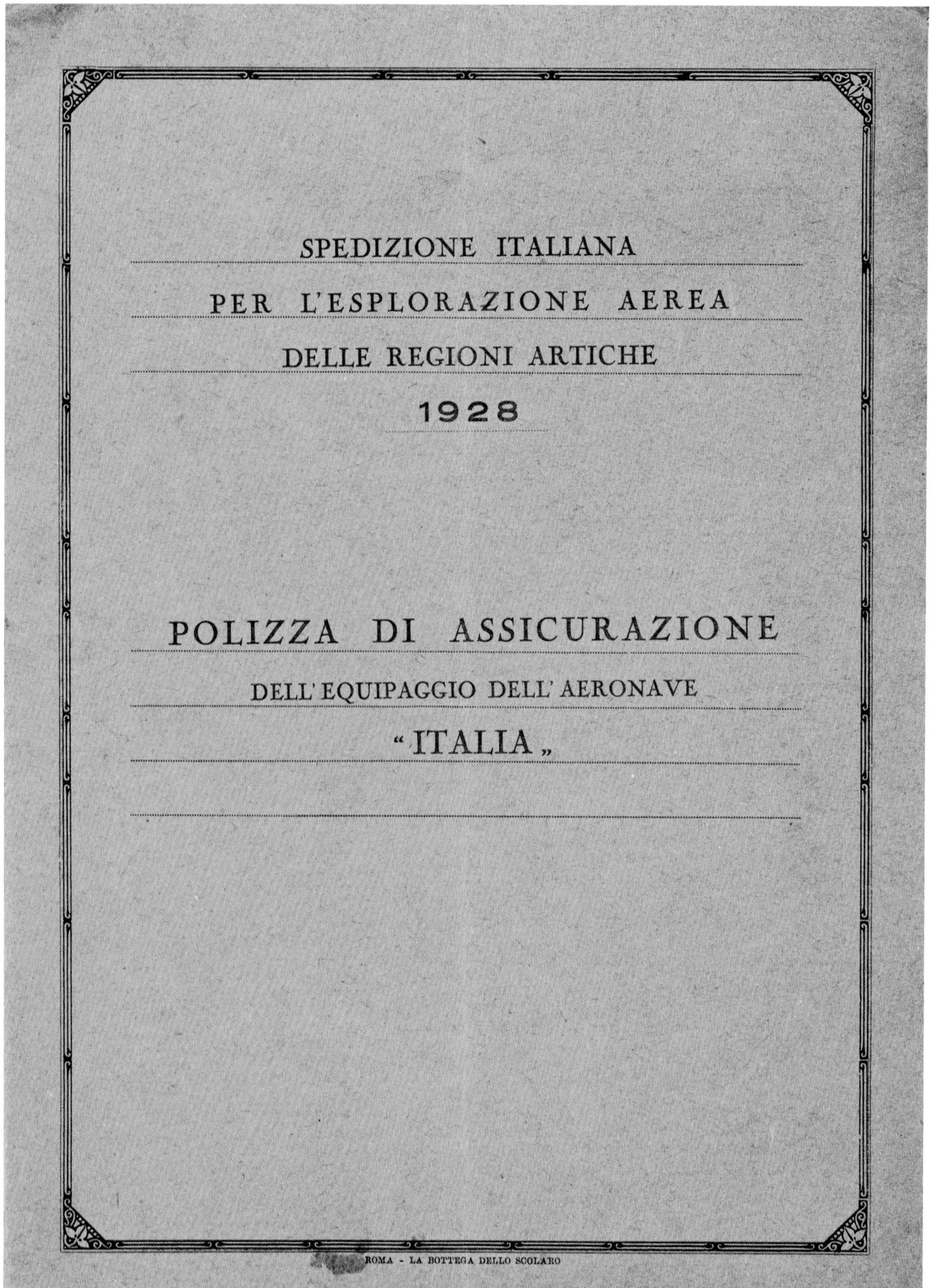

SPEDIZIONE ITALIANA
PER L'ESPLORAZIONE AEREA
DELLE REGIONI ARTICHE
1928

POLIZZA DI ASSICURAZIONE
DELL' EQUIPAGGIO DELL' AERONAVE
"ITALIA"

ROMA - LA BOTTEGA DELLO SCOLARO

gotiations continued, but the last known reference to them is in a letter from Smolensky to Ottolenghi dated May 26, 1926, in which we read "we have had no news about the insurance for the team of the 'Norge'. It might be prudent to ask INA for information."
As is well known, the mission was a success and on May 12, the flags of the three main countries involved (Italy, Norway, and the United States, the latter represented by Lincoln Ellsworth, one of the expedition's primary backers) were dropped from the airship onto the North Pole. However, this important achievement ignited an argument between Amundsen and Nobile over how to divide credit for the feat. In any case, beyond the demonstrative value of the act of flying over the North Pole, the *Norge* expedition in 1926 was not of particular scientific importance. A second mission was therefore planned, organized entirely by the Italians and more focused on exploration and research in a variety of fields (geography, meteorology, physics, etc.). The airship *N-4*, the twin of the *Norge* and renamed *Italia*, left Baggio, Milan on April 15, 1928. The original insurance policy for this expedition's team has been preserved [*fig.* 2]. The text shows the influence of the comments made by Smolensky during the negotiations for the *Norge* policy. As recommended by Smolensky, it was in fact a single policy for all of the companies participating as co-insurers, it was typed on blank paper instead of a pre-printed form, and it indicated the special conditions and each company's share of the risk. The insured party was the Reale Società Geografica Italiana. A table indicated the insurers, the beneficiaries in case of death, and the guaranteed capital, expressed in Italian liras. The largest claim amount was of course for General Umberto Nobile, the expedition's commander, totaling 650,000 liras. Next came Felice Trojani, insured for 300,000 liras and Natale Cecioni, for 200,000; the amounts for the other members of the team were lower. As was to be the case for the policy negotiated in 1926, this policy covered death and permanent disability, including blindness, the loss of two limbs, and a "state of incurable mental insanity that would render the insured permanently incapable of holding any kind of job or occupation." Partial disability was to be compensated with a percentage of the total. Broadly speaking, the list started with the most important parts of the body, continuing down to the individual fingers. An arm was, for example, more valuable than a leg and, and given the period, it is no surprise that left-handedness was not considered, and so a greater percentage was assigned for the loss of the right arm (65%) or hand (60%) than for the left arm (60%) or hand (55%). In the case of multiple injuries, compensation was to be calculated by totaling the percentages assigned to each type of injury, unless the total was equivalent to full disability. As the entity in charge of the Consorzio Italiano di Assicurazioni Aeronautiche, the Unione Italiana di Assicurazione was responsible for managing the contract for the insurers. There were twelve insuring companies, and the highest quota, 26%, was assumed by INA, followed by the Cassa Nazionale Infortuni, Generali, and RAS, with 15% each. The quotas assumed by Assicurazioni d'Italia, Anonima Infortuni, Assicuratrice Italiana, the Compagnia di Assicurazione di Milano, the Fondiaria, and Fiume were much lower. The contract was written up in twelve copies and signed in Rome on April 5, 1928 by the policy holder, all of the insured parties, and the representatives of the insurance companies [*fig.* 3]. Generali was represented by the general agent of Rome, Francesco Berti. From a few handwritten notes we learn that the quotas assumed by Generali were then retroceded to at least twelve companies, all of which were foreign (Banco Vitalicio, Skandinavia, Aachener, Corona, Generala, and La Nationale among them).
The rest of the story of the airship *Italia* is, as many know, sad. The expedition reached the North Pole on May 24, but poor weather prevented the team from landing and they started to go back to the Svalbard islands. However, the terrible weather conditions and

the increased weight of the ice that had formed on the structure of the airship caused it to crash on the ice. It was 10:33 a.m. on May 25, 1928. Ten of the men on the team, including Umberto Nobile, were flung to the ground, while the other six remained on board: their bodies and the wreckage of *Italia* were never found. Various nations took part in the rescue operations, and some of the rescuers, including Amundsen, died. Evidence of these events is also preserved in the life division correspondence for the month of June, relative to the reinsurance for the Savoia-Marchetti *S 55* seaplane, which was piloted by Commander Umberto Maddalena, who was the first to spot the survivors and the "red tent." In this case as well, various reinsurance companies were contacted with an eye towards dividing up the risk, but when the English companies increased their involvement, it was not necessary to further redistribute the burden of coverage. Whereas item no. 13 of the policy transferred by Generali to the Unione Italiana di Riassicurazione on behalf of Anonima Infortuni not only indicated the amounts relative to Nobile's expedition and Maddalena's rescue mission, but also included an entry for "Mechanic Codognotto of the Dornier Wall Marina II Seaplane," in other words, a member of the team of a different plane, one that was piloted by Luigi Penzo and took off from Italy to help the survivors. The *Marina II* also participated in the search for Amundsen, but then crashed on the return back to Italy. On June 23, the Swedish pilot Lundborg managed to land on the ice pack and, following orders, forced Umberto Nobile to accept being rescued first; the general wanted Natale Cecioni to be saved first, as he was suffering from a fractured leg. On July 12, 1928, the Russian icebreaker *Krasin* finally reached the survivors.

The Historical Archive also preserves a few traces of the settlement of various claims towards the end of 1928 and throughout 1929. One document, which was exchanged between the Unione Italiana di Riassicurazione and Generali and dated November 16, 1928, reports the "Pomella claim," referring to the death of Vincenzo Pomella, who died shortly after he hit the ice. A letter from Münchener Rückversicherungs-Gesellschaft to Generali dated October 25, 1929 reports the 75,000-lira settlement of Adalberto Mariano's disability claim following the amputation of one of his legs after he, along with Finn Malmgren and Filippo Zappi, tried to reach to rescuers on foot and lead them to the "red tent." (M.M.)

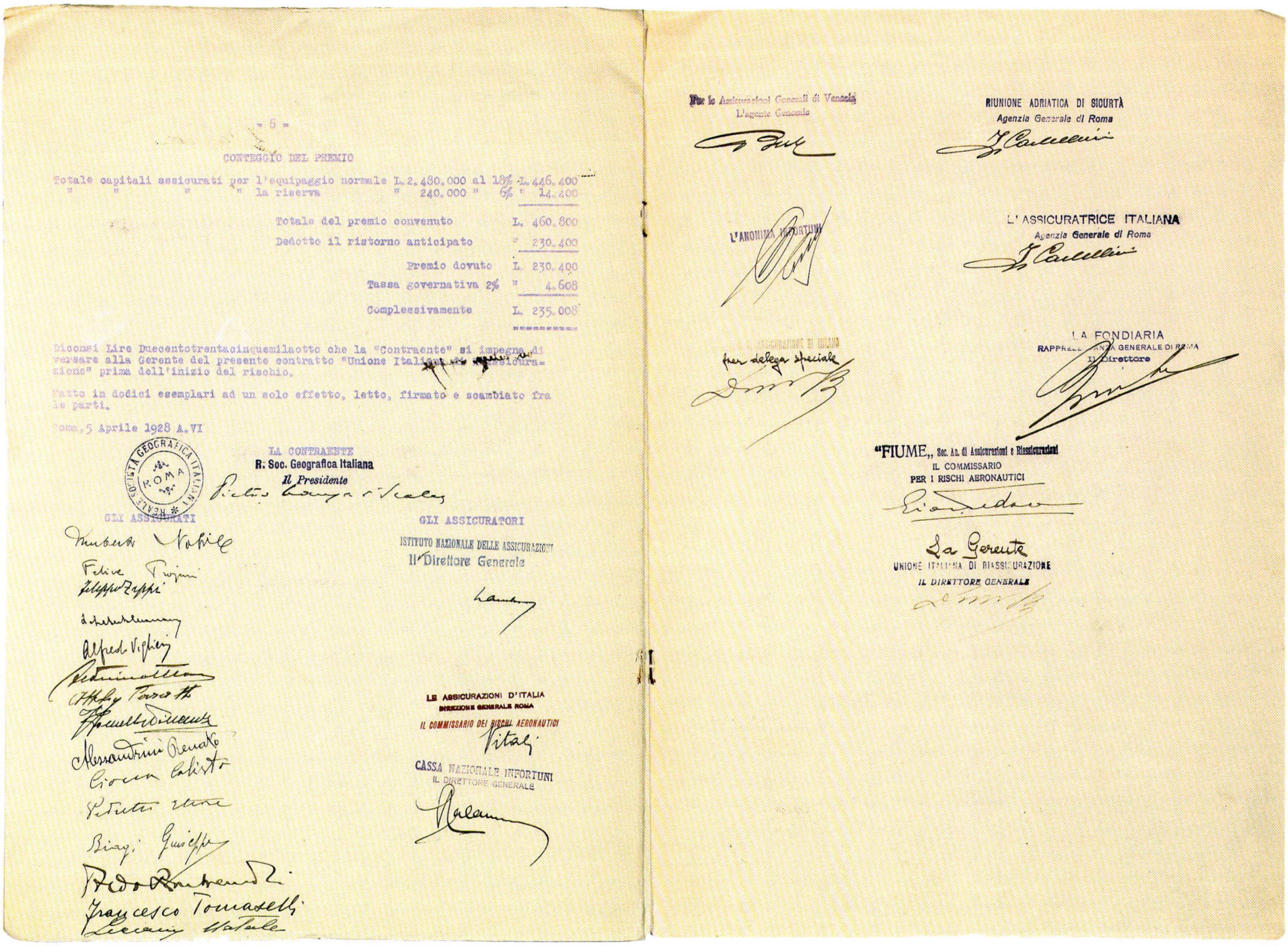

\- 6 -

CONTEGGIO DEL PREMIO

Totale capitali assicurati per l'equipaggio normale L. 2.480.000 al 18% L. 446.400
" " " " la riserva " 240.000 " 6% " 14.400

Totale del premio convenuto L. 460.800
Dedotto il ristorno anticipato " 230.400
Premio dovuto L. 230.400
Tassa governativa 2% " 4.608
Complessivamente L. 235.008

Diconsi Lire Duecentotrentacinquemilaotto che la "Contraente" si impegna di versare alla Gerente del presente contratto "Unione Italiana di Riassicurazione" prima dell'inizio del rischio.

Fatto in dodici esemplari ad un solo effetto, letto, firmato e scambiato fra le parti.

Roma, 5 Aprile 1928 A. VI

LA CONTRAENTE
R. Soc. Geografica Italiana
Il Presidente

GLI ASSICURATI

GLI ASSICURATORI

ISTITUTO NAZIONALE DELLE ASSICURAZIONI
Il Direttore Generale

LE ASSICURAZIONI D'ITALIA
DIREZIONE GENERALE ROMA
IL COMMISSARIO DEI RISCHI AERONAUTICI

CASSA NAZIONALE INFORTUNI
IL DIRETTORE GENERALE

Per le Assicurazioni Generali di Venezia
L'agente Generale

RIUNIONE ADRIATICA DI SICURTÀ
Agenzia Generale di Roma

L'ANONIMA INFORTUNI

L'ASSICURATRICE ITALIANA
Agenzia Generale di Roma

per delega speciale

LA FONDIARIA
Il Direttore

"FIUME" Soc. An. di Assicurazioni e Riassicurazioni
IL COMMISSARIO
PER I RISCHI AERONAUTICI

La Gerente
UNIONE ITALIANA DI RIASSICURAZIONE
IL DIRETTORE GENERALE

3.
Insurance policy for the team of the airship *Italia* (Rome, April 5, 1928), contracting parties' signatures [ASAG, *Versamenti*, scheda 62411]

Bruno de Finetti and Assicurazioni Generali
Lots of Light, and a Little Darkness, on a Long Collaboration

1929
1979

"Professor de Finetti's work, although quiet and so not very eye-catching, is nevertheless fascinating and fruitful, not to mention the luster his collaboration brings us, even on the international sphere, where he becoming increasingly well known." Thus wrote the chief accountant Arturo Scabar in a note dated March 12, 1952 and addressed to the co-manager and staff manager Ottone Zeller, effectively summarizing the role and figure of Bruno de Finetti at Assicurazioni Generali.

The sources on this illustrious mathematician, who started out as a Generali employee and later became a consultant, are not limited to his personnel file [*fig.* 1], a few excerpts from which were shared by Alfeo Zanette at the thirtieth conference of the Associazione per la Matematica Applicata alle Scienze Economiche e Sociali, held in Trieste in 2006, on the one-hundredth anniversary of de Finetti's birth. His work and various aspects of his life also emerge in the life division's technical correspondence and in documentation from the central accounting department.

De Finetti, who began working in Rome at the Istituto Centrale di Statistica (today, ISTAT) on December 1, 1927, applied for work at Generali for the first time in late November 1929. In his *curriculum vitae*, he included his personal data, education, list of publications—which was truly astonishing considering he was only twenty-three at the time—and current employment and duties, as well as his "Civil and Political Activity," from which we learn that he had been a member of the Partito Nazionale Fascista since March 1, 1921. This first attempt did not yield the hoped for results, but de Finetti did not give up, trying again in March 1931, as we read in a reply from the co-manager Pietro Smolensky to de Finetti dated April 7. In this letter, Smolensky explained the main points of the contract: the gross annual salary, work hours, which included what was known as "English Saturday," meaning working only in the morning on Saturdays, and, as a special perk, three weeks of vacation instead of the fifteen days usually provided by contract. The specific start date for the job was left up to de Finetti, presumably due to prior commitments at his previous job, and he began work at Generali on August 1 of that year.

De Finetti began his career at Assicurazioni Generali as an actuary in the life division, but his duties soon extended beyond theoretical research to practical problems, like the start of automating a few operations. He then introduced a system that used what were called Hollerith machines, based on a punch card system invented by the American engineer Herman Hollerith (1860–1929). Using this system, one could insert any kind of information into the machine and rapidly carry out a whole series of calculation, assimilation, and data processing operations, a procedure that would normally require a sizable investment of time and labor. Hollerith was one of the founders of the International Business Machines Corporation, known all over the world by the simpler acronym "IBM." In 1927, IBM opened a branch in Italy (which changed name a number of times), and de Finetti had some contacts there because Assicurazioni Generali was interested in having the most modern work equipment available.

Hollerith machines were first used at Generali in 1932, in the life division, in order to more quickly provide a precise record of the portfolio for the financial statement, automatically calculating the mathematical reserves. The company purchased punching and duplicating, sorting, and tabulating machines [*fig.* 2], which were used, respectively, to punch the information onto the cards; divide them into groups and organize them; and add up and print the data.

A circular stamped by the life division's actuarial office on October 19, 1936, announced: "Since there is a plan to publish a new, revised edition of the Hollerith Code, anyone who has ideas or suggestions concerning this project should contact Bruno de Finetti as soon as possible," affirming de Finetti's central role in the coordination of this activity. The results were positive and in 1937 it was decided to extend the use of

1.
Bruno de Finetti's personnel file (1929–1979)
[ASAG, *Direzione centrale, Servizio del personale, Posizioni personali*, U2GE042999]

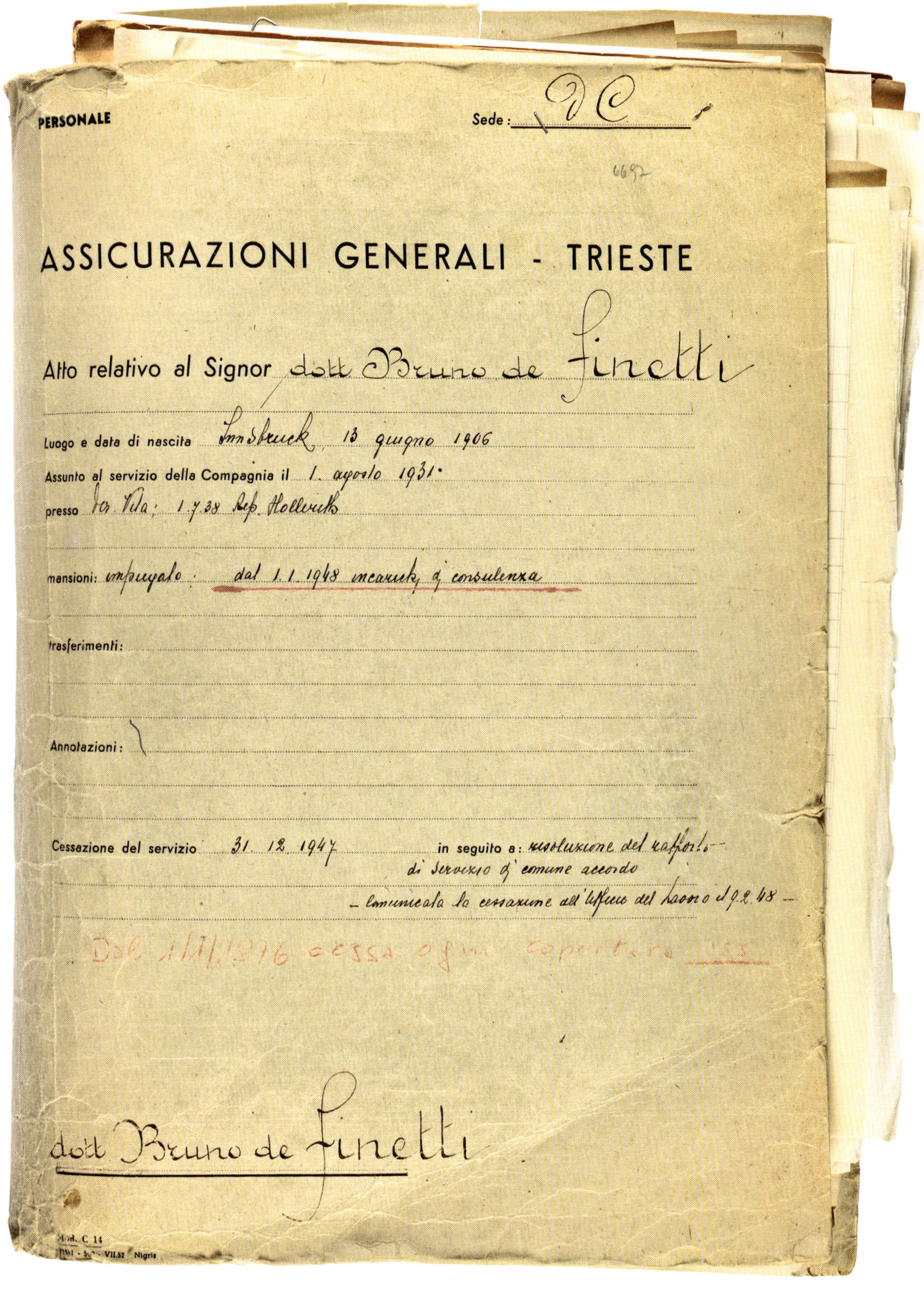
PERSONALE

Sede: VC

6692

ASSICURAZIONI GENERALI - TRIESTE

Atto relativo al Signor dott Bruno de Finetti

Luogo e data di nascita Innsbruck 13 giugno 1906

Assunto al servizio della Compagnia il 1. agosto 1931.

presso Dr. Vita; 1.7.38 Rep. Hollerith

mansioni: impiegato. dal 1.1.1948 incarico di consulenza

trasferimenti:

Annotazioni:

Cessazione del servizio 31.12.1947 in seguito a: risoluzione del rapporto di servizio di comune accordo

– comunicata la cessazione all'Ufficio del Lavoro il 9.2.48 –

Dal 1/1/1976 cessa ogni copertura [illegible]

dott Bruno de Finetti

Mod. C 14

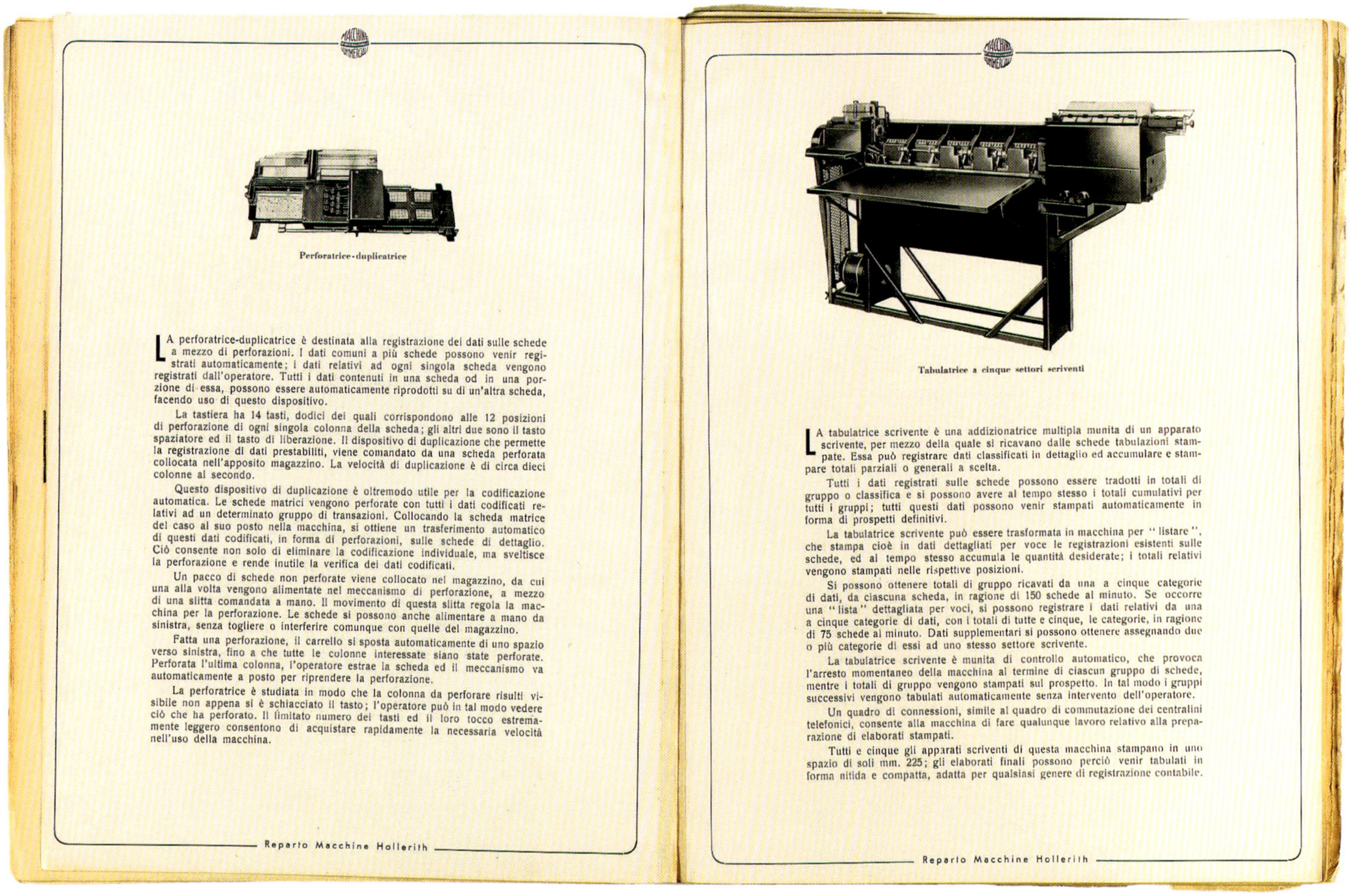

Perforatrice-duplicatrice

La perforatrice-duplicatrice è destinata alla registrazione dei dati sulle schede a mezzo di perforazioni. I dati comuni a più schede possono venir registrati automaticamente; i dati relativi ad ogni singola scheda vengono registrati dall'operatore. Tutti i dati contenuti in una scheda od in una porzione di essa, possono essere automaticamente riprodotti su di un'altra scheda, facendo uso di questo dispositivo.

La tastiera ha 14 tasti, dodici dei quali corrispondono alle 12 posizioni di perforazione di ogni singola colonna della scheda; gli altri due sono il tasto spaziatore ed il tasto di liberazione. Il dispositivo di duplicazione che permette la registrazione di dati prestabiliti, viene comandato da una scheda perforata collocata nell'apposito magazzino. La velocità di duplicazione è di circa dieci colonne al secondo.

Questo dispositivo di duplicazione è oltremodo utile per la codificazione automatica. Le schede matrici vengono perforate con tutti i dati codificati relativi ad un determinato gruppo di transazioni. Collocando la scheda matrice del caso al suo posto nella macchina, si ottiene un trasferimento automatico di questi dati codificati, in forma di perforazioni, sulle schede di dettaglio. Ciò consente non solo di eliminare la codificazione individuale, ma sveltisce la perforazione e rende inutile la verifica dei dati codificati.

Un pacco di schede non perforate viene collocato nel magazzino, da cui una alla volta vengono alimentate nel meccanismo di perforazione, a mezzo di una slitta comandata a mano. Il movimento di questa slitta regola la macchina per la perforazione. Le schede si possono anche alimentare a mano da sinistra, senza togliere o interferire comunque con quelle del magazzino.

Fatta una perforazione, il carrello si sposta automaticamente di uno spazio verso sinistra, fino a che tutte le colonne interessate siano state perforate. Perforata l'ultima colonna, l'operatore estrae la scheda ed il meccanismo va automaticamente a posto per riprendere la perforazione.

La perforatrice è studiata in modo che la colonna da perforare risulti visibile non appena si è schiacciato il tasto; l'operatore può in tal modo vedere ciò che ha perforato. Il limitato numero dei tasti ed il loro tocco estremamente leggero consentono di acquistare rapidamente la necessaria velocità nell'uso della macchina.

Reparto Macchine Hollerith

Tabulatrice a cinque settori scriventi

La tabulatrice scrivente è una addizionatrice multipla munita di un apparato scrivente, per mezzo della quale si ricavano dalle schede tabulazioni stampate. Essa può registrare dati classificati in dettaglio ed accumulare e stampare totali parziali o generali a scelta.

Tutti i dati registrati sulle schede possono essere tradotti in totali di gruppo o classifica e si possono avere al tempo stesso i totali cumulativi per tutti i gruppi; tutti questi dati possono venir stampati automaticamente in forma di prospetti definitivi.

La tabulatrice scrivente può essere trasformata in macchina per "listare", che stampa cioè in dati dettagliati per voce le registrazioni esistenti sulle schede, ed al tempo stesso accumula le quantità desiderate; i totali relativi vengono stampati nelle rispettive posizioni.

Si possono ottenere totali di gruppo ricavati da una a cinque categorie di dati, da ciascuna scheda, in ragione di 150 schede al minuto. Se occorre una "lista" dettagliata per voci, si possono registrare i dati relativi da una a cinque categorie di dati, con i totali di tutte e cinque, le categorie, in ragione di 75 schede al minuto. Dati supplementari si possono ottenere assegnando due o più categorie di essi ad uno stesso settore scrivente.

La tabulatrice scrivente è munita di controllo automatico, che provoca l'arresto momentaneo della macchina al termine di ciascun gruppo di schede, mentre i totali di gruppo vengono stampati sul prospetto. In tal modo i gruppi successivi vengono tabulati automaticamente senza intervento dell'operatore.

Un quadro di connessioni, simile al quadro di commutazione dei centralini telefonici, consente alla macchina di fare qualunque lavoro relativo alla preparazione di elaborati stampati.

Tutti e cinque gli apparati scriventi di questa macchina stampano in uno spazio di soli mm. 225; gli elaborati finali possono perciò venir tabulati in forma nitida e compatta, adatta per qualsiasi genere di registrazione contabile.

Reparto Macchine Hollerith

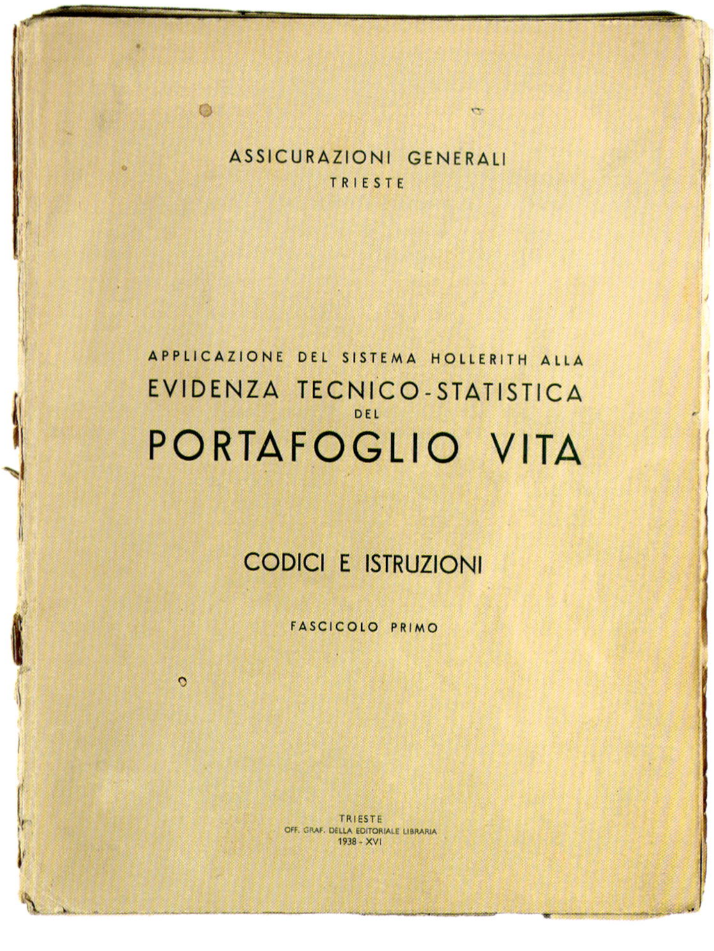

ASSICURAZIONI GENERALI
TRIESTE

APPLICAZIONE DEL SISTEMA HOLLERITH ALLA
EVIDENZA TECNICO-STATISTICA
DEL
PORTAFOGLIO VITA

CODICI E ISTRUZIONI

FASCICOLO PRIMO

TRIESTE
OFF. GRAF. DELLA EDITORIALE LIBRARIA
1938 - XVI

2.
Booklet explaining the application of the Hollerith system, written by Bruno de Finetti (Trieste, 1938), detail of the electronic accounting machines [ASAG, *Direzione centrale*, *Ramo vita*, *Riassicurazione*, *Corrispondenza*, U2GE004855]

3.
Booklet explaining the application of the Hollerith system, written by Bruno de Finetti (Trieste, 1938), cover [ASAG, *Direzione centrale*, *Ramo vita*, *Riassicurazione*, *Corrispondenza*, U2GE004855]

Hollerith machines to the central accounting department, channeling the results produced by all of the divisions, not just life, there, thus automating the calculations needed to draft the financial statement for the non-life divisions. The equipment was updated at the same time, bringing in a variety of new machines (an alphabetical punch, alphabetical tabulator, a summary punch, a reperforator, a calculator). At that point, the facility had grown so much that it needed to be turned into an independent office, named the "Reparto Hollerith", and de Finetti is documented as employed there starting on July 1, 1938. The new office later became the punch card data processing center and still later simply the data processing center.

De Finetti's role as the main contact for such matters is further confirmed in a note that he sent on December 9, 1939 to the accounting liaison office, in which we read a near reprimand for the procedures that had been followed up until then: "The freedom that various offices have enjoyed up until now to create, complete, and change certain codes has led to a range of problems that absolutely must not be allowed to recur. [...] From now on, therefore, all coding will be carried out strictly and exclusively by the Hollerith Office, to which all offices needing to update, complete, or change a code will need to refer. [...] Please also consult the Hollerith Office regarding all coding for non-automated work, since in these cases as well—as we have seen on various occasions—lack of uniformity with the automated portions or failure to observe certain general norms can make later processing more difficult, impractical, and costly."

De Finetti put the experience he gained in Trieste with electronic accounting machines to use developing similar systems elsewhere. In the summer of 1940, he was sent to the Hungary Branch in Budapest to oversee the setting up of the Hollerith system there "and avoid the repetition of the inevitable problems that always crop up when first setting up an automation system," as explained in a note from Scabar. He also traveled on various occasions to Milan for meetings and negotiations at IBM's branch in Italy.

His deep involvement in the organization of the Hollerith system is also reflected in two booklets that he wrote on the application of new machinery to the life insurance portfolio [*fig.* 3]. He also wrote two articles for the *Bollettino*, the company's periodical, one published in 1941 and the other in 1952, in which he explained the various types of electronic accounting machines and how they worked, and provided an objective, if sometimes glowing, report on the limitations and concrete advantages of the new system. While the multiplicity and complexity of the various tasks meant that the actual savings in manual work was relatively low, the "effects of the rationalization and modernization of the systems were felt [...] throughout the company's entire administrative body, protecting it from the dangers of stasis and growing stale" through, for example, the merging of several tasks into a single operation. In the article published in 1952, de Finetti noted that the Hollerith Office set up on the ground floor of the Central Head Office in 1948, and also that, surprisingly, in order to protect the system from aerial bombardments during World War II, the company made a special arrangement with one of its competitors, the Riunione Adriatica di Sicurtà (RAS), with the two companies sharing the use of Assicurazioni Generali's Hollerith machines, which were moved to a collapse-proof building made available by RAS, its own system having been requisitioned, apparently for the war. The documentation relative to this agreement, dated February 2, 1945 and signed by the managers Giulio Cleva and Alberto Melchiori, is preserved in the Historical Archive. The contract details the shifts and expenses, which the two companies split two-thirds Generali and one-third RAS, as well as instructions for using the machines, with a request to inform all employees that there should be no friction in interactions between the two groups and that "no attempts of any kind should be made to acquire the other Company's data, news, or information."

De Finetti also made a fundamental contribution to the company in the area of scientific research, which is reflected in his participation in and collaboration on the organization of prestigious conferences, detailed information about which is found in the life division's technical correspondence. At the Second National Congress of Insurance Sciences, held in Trieste between November 5 and 9, 1932, de Finetti gave three talks. In 1934, an even more prestigious event took place: the Tenth International Congress of Actuaries. Held in Rome between May 4 and 9, under the patronage of Prince Umberto, Edgardo Morpurgo was one of the honorary deputy chairmen and the event was attended by more than 1,500 representatives from forty nations. Interestingly, the first topic for discussion was unemployment insurance, a sign of the times in the terrible aftermath of the Stock Market Crash of 1929. The life division has preserved a mass of correspondence relative to this congress, comprising exchanges between Assicurazioni Generali executives and the most important representatives of the Istituto Italiano degli Attuari, including its chairman, Paolo Medolaghi, and secretary-general, Francesco Paolo Cantelli, both distinguished and internationally renowned mathematicians. The correspondence reveals that Generali was deeply involved in the realization of the event: Cantelli asked Smolensky to send Mosè Jacob and de Finetti, who were joined by Paolo Biró and Gastone Milanese, to work on the organization of the Rome event the week before the start of the congress. When the event was over, Cantelli wrote to Smolensky—and Medolaghi wrote to the Generali chairman, Morpurgo—asking for de Finetti to be allowed to stay in Rome to work on the preparation of the proceedings, together with all of the attendant problems related to printing deadlines, translations, corrections, and reducing the texts to fit within the pre-set maximum number of pages.

Studying the documentation relative to de Finetti's work thus also sheds light on the work of an entire office and the names of some of its main figures: the co-manager Gino Tolentino, Antonio Sereni, Vittorio Longo, and Mario Matteucci for the study and application of the Hollerith system, and the already mentioned Jacob, Biró, and Milanese together with Renato Taucer, Silvio Obry, Federico Zalai, and Guido Marocco for actuarial research.

In contrast, in a way, to his activity at Generali, de Finetti had, in effect, a "second job" as a university professor. In 1930, he qualified for university teaching in the field of mathematical analysis, which allowed him to teach in a private capacity, which is to say without belonging to the faculty. He was already indicated in the documentation as a normal employee, with the title "prof.," and taught courses at the Universities of Padua and Trieste, always trying to impinge as little as possible on his work commitments. He scheduled his lectures for unusual days and times, often Saturdays and either early in the morning or late in the evening, and sometimes even held exam sessions on Sunday. Nevertheless, this "second job," which the company had never opposed, on the contrary granting de Finetti significant freedom of movement, led to occasional conflicts with Gino Baroncini. Various documents bear comments written in pencil by Baroncini, who was general manager at the time and later managing director, such as "it seems to me that the [permission] of going to Padua excludes further special conditions," written on a summary of personal information and conduct report dated December 17, 1937, and "P. de Finetti needs to make up his mind as to whether he wants to be an A. G. executive or a university professor," written on a letter dated October 3, 1938 in which de Finetti communicated to the central secretariat the University of Trieste's request for him to chair an exam committee [*fig.* 4]. Baroncini, who had apparently become impatient, also wrote: "This is fine with me. However, I believe that he should make up the lost work hours" on a letter dated November 6, 1943 in which de Finetti requested for permission to teach for academic year 1943–1944. Relations between de Finetti and Baroncini became particularly tense in July 1942, and at that juncture consideration began to be given to the idea of changing de Finetti's role from that of an employee to that of a consultant, a solution that would meet the needs of both parties. Apparently, as time passed, his academic commitments became more demanding and the restrictions imposed by company life were becoming more and more of a problem (already in 1935, a report was made to the life division Administration that de Finetti and Jacob "systematically abstained from signing" the attendance records). Bruno de Finetti thus handed in his resignation on December 31, 1947, which was described in a note in his personnel file as a "mutually agreed termination of employment." His collaboration with Generali continued, however, uninterrupted, with the stipulation of a consulting contract that went into effect on January 1, 1948 and lasted until 1979. During that period, de Finetti continued his actuarial research, was appointed to make hiring decisions in his field, and investigated the possibility of extending automation to other areas, such as transport reinsurance, real estate, and the life division in Venice. (M.M.)

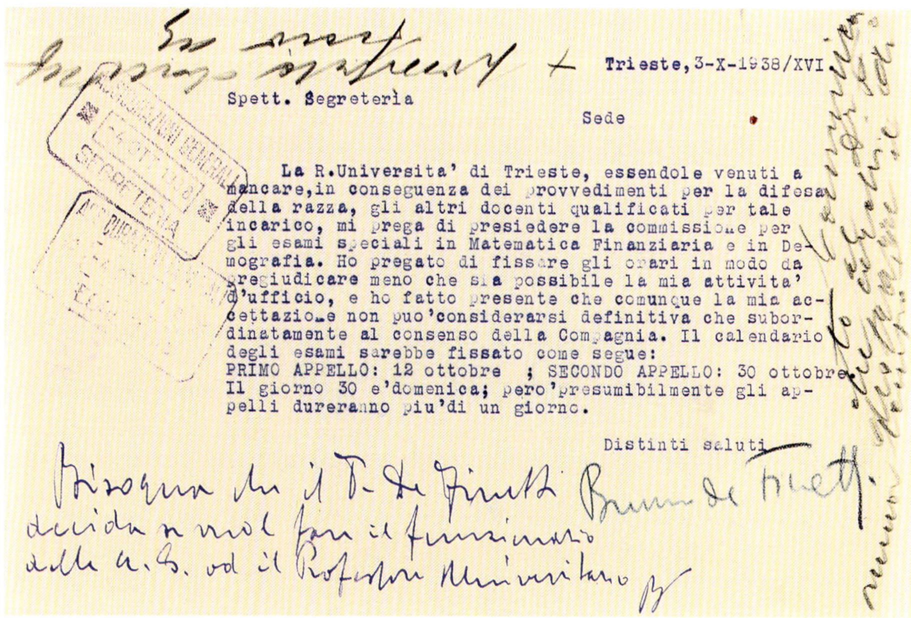

Trieste, 3-X-1938/XVI.

Spett. Segreteria

Sede

La R.Universita' di Trieste, essendole venuti a mancare, in conseguenza dei provvedimenti per la difesa della razza, gli altri docenti qualificati per tale incarico, mi prega di presiedere la commissione per gli esami speciali in Matematica Finanziaria e in Demografia. Ho pregato di fissare gli orari in modo da pregiudicare meno che sia possibile la mia attivita' d'ufficio, e ho fatto presente che comunque la mia accettazione non puo' considerarsi definitiva che subordinatamente al consenso della Compagnia. Il calendario degli esami sarebbe fissato come segue:
PRIMO APPELLO: 12 ottobre ; SECONDO APPELLO: 30 ottobre.
Il giorno 30 e'domenica; pero'presumibilmente gli appelli dureranno piu'di un giorno.

Distinti saluti

Bruno de Finetti

4.
Letter from Bruno de Finetti to the central secretariat, with a handwritten note by the general manager, Gino Baroncini (Trieste, October 3, 1938)
[ASAG, *Direzione centrale*, *Servizio del personale*, *Posizioni personali*, U2GE042999]

Bruno de Finetti

1906
1985

Bruno de Finetti was born in Innsbruck on June 13, 1906 [*fig.* 1]. Both the father, Gualtiero and his mother Elvira Menestrina, belonged to Italian-speaking families of the Trentino bourgeoisie, which comprised several generations in the fields of the liberal professions, higher education and the arts, and who supported the irredentist ideals. In the seventeenth century, the Hapsburg Empire awarded a paternal ancestor with a nobility title in recognition of his military-engineering merits; his father and grandfather were both engineers who specialized in the construction of roads and railways, and the young Bruno was expected to follow in the family tradition. In 1923, after attending high school in Trento, he enrolled at the Politecnico of Milan. While attending his lessons, however, he became acquainted with lecturers such as the economist Ulisse Gobbi, and two of mathematics' most innovative thinkers at that time, Tullio Levi Civita and Giulio Vivanti, who exposed him to new intellectual opportunities. Having noticed his talent for their disciplines, they encouraged him to pursue these kinds of studies. But de Finetti had to work hard to persuade his mother, who was widowed and worried about her son's lack of employment prospects, as the family lived in modest economic conditions. Finally, in 1926, he was able to fulfil his goals and enroll in the fourth year of applied mathematics. The following year he discussed his thesis, based on the same subject, with supervisor Giorgio Vivanti. His first published, scientific paper preceded his degree in 1926. After having read a number of informative articles on biology, of his own volition, de Finetti devised a statistical study on the propagation of Mendelian characters. This earned him Corrado Gini's attention as well as a post, upon completion of his studies, under the distinguished economist and statistician at the Itituto Centrale di Statistica in Rome [*fig.* 2]. There, in 1921 de Finetti worked on the creation of mortality tables, on the comparison between the tables used in previous censuses, and on a study of population growth in Italy.

During his stay in Rome, he developed relationships based on scientific and intellectual exchanges with physicist Enrico Fermi's group, in the famous school located in Via Panisperna, where he became acquainted with the established mathematicians of the previous generation: Federigo Enriques, Guido Castelnuovo and Mauro Picone.

The years from 1926 through 1930 were for de Finetti a period of intense study and scientific research. Some of his preliminary work on probability and the predictive inference on statistics, dates back to this period and, from 1930 through 1931, it would lead him to fully articulate his theory of probability.

In 1930 he became a lecturer in mathematical analysis; however, as the prospects for an academic career remained uncertain, he resolved to pursue hands-on employment, a decision that would not preclude him from pursuing his scientific research. In 1931 he was hired by Assicurazioni Generali, in Trieste, as actuary for the life insurance division where he remained until 1947. Soon after joining the company he was responsible for introducing mechanized work processes based on IBM's punch card system, to the Central Head Office. In his capacity as supervisor-coordinator, over the years that followed he continually improved and revamped the system, keeping abreast of technological advancements. All along, the university remained a constant outlet for de Finetti's appetite for research and teaching, though success did not come easily [*fig.* 3]. He began his career in 1935, spending many years as a simple lecturer, teaching calculus of probabilities at the University in Trieste and later also in Padua. He was eventually nominated professor in 1950 (the title was officially backdated to 1942). In 1936 he won a tenure for the post of professor of financial and actuarial mathematics at the Faculty of Economics and Commerce in Trieste. He never received it; however, because the current legislation did not entitle unmarried men to be awarded. In 1944 he taught mathematics at the Faculty of Economics and Commerce in Trieste. In 1954 he transferred to the Faculty of Economics and Commerce in Rome. In 1961 he made tenure as professor of calculus of probabilities at Sapienza University's Faculty of Science, where he remained until retirement in 1976.

1.
Bruno de Finetti (1928)

2.
Bruno de Finetti with the colleagues
of the Istituto Centrale di Statistica
(Rome, 1931)

In the postwar period, he was equally committed to the world of insurance, in terms of education and collaborated with the Istituto per gli Studi Assicurativi (ISA). This school for basic and further education, was connected to the university and had been founded in 1945, prompted by Trieste's insurance companies, which were intent on fostering a new generation highly-trained experts to fill the staffing shortages inflicted by the war. Between 1945 and 1950, de Finetti wrote extensive essays and manuals on actuarial topics for ISA.

For fifteen years, from 1932 through 1947, de Finetti alternated scientific research and the actuarial profession; activities that were certainly most fruitful for both aspects of his work, although his work commitments must have taken their toll. In 1948 his relationship with Assicurazioni Generali changed into a more flexible consultancy agreement that remained in place until 1979, enabling him to continue to widen his knowledge and skills for the benefit of the company. In 1951 he traveled to Washington to learn about the first electronic computers built in the United States.

Since first joining Assicurazioni Generali, de Finetti devoted his career to solving insurance problems through his actuarial studies, which he had been introduced to through the work on probability. Evidence of this commitment was his participation in the Second National Congress of Insurance Sciences in November 1932 in Trieste, where he presented three papers, and in the International Congress of Actuaries in May 1934, in Rome.

From 1932 his writings mirrored these interests in an exemplary way; in 1940 he began to examine "the problem of retentions," which represented a turning point for the actuarial field and provided a solution to a question that had long racked the brains of mathematicians concerned with reinsurance. He successfully demonstrated what was (the retention problem for proportional reinsurance) the optimum amount to be withheld in relation to the share to be ceded for the purpose of, as he himself wrote: "Minimizing risk within the predetermined margins and with a minimal loss of income." De Finetti elaborated a mathematical model that analyzed the criterion of "mean-variance." Between 1939 and 1942 he was devoted to the theory of risk and "the problem of the gambler's ruin," which concerned the individual and collective frameworks of risk. These topics lead him to formulate a theorem for the collective theory of risk (de Finetti's theorem or asymptotic formula), to determine an insurance company's level of safety; these studies would be further developed until the early 1950s.

The results of his actuarial studies, which he attained well before the Americans economists in the 1950s (who were awarded a Nobel Prize that he would have deserved), comprise nonetheless only a portion of his extensive work. De Finetti's bibliography lists almost four hundred titles over a span of fifty years, covering topics that range from theoretical economics to mathematical economics and epistemology. As the founder of the concept of subjective probability and the "logic of uncertainty," he promoted critical and relativistic thinking and was contrary to any form of rigid, schematization of knowledge, and opposed all forms of determinism and intolerance. For example he argued that: "This criticism does not presume to demonstrate the impossibility of realizing a truth that no longer requires adjusting: such an intention would be contradictory, precisely because it would embody such a truth. Instead, it intends to demonstrate how easily illusions are created and to warn against them; wanting to discourage idle foolishness in embracing a certain concept for all eternity, when tomorrow it may be refuted, and when its success depends on its intrinsic ability to establish itself, and last for a certain period of time, which are attributes that cannot be changed with the stroke of a magic wand, simply by conferring it with the status of 'absolute truth.'" (as quoted in Fulvia de Finetti and Luca Nicotra, *Bruno de Finetti: un matematico scomodo* [Leghorn: Belforte Editore Libraio, 2008], 169).

De Finetti did not regard this research as mere abstraction, but considered his role as a scientist a deeply moral one, which was committed to civic progress.

He obtained much recognition in Italy and abroad including: an invitation in 1935 to hold a round of conferences at the Institut Poicaré in Paris; a study and teaching sojourn in the United States in 1950 and in 1956; further to a nomination by the economist Franco Modigliani in 1961, the appointment as a Fellow of the Econometric Society; member of the International Statistical Institute; honorary member of the Swiss and French actuarial institutes; and honorary member of the Accademia Nazionale dei Lincei. In 1982 the Luiss University in Rome awarded him with an honorary degree in economics, in the presence of the President of the Republic, Sandro Pertini.

Equally high-profile were the enterprises that benefited of his support. In 1952–1953 Mauro Picone invited him to the Istituto Nazionale per l'Applicazione del Calcolo (INAC), which was established at the Consiglio Nazionale delle Ricerche (CNR); in 1956 he was asked to join the working group of the Comité Européen des Assurances (CEA), which concerned itself with the application of electronics in the insurance sector; in 1970 he joined the Centre International de Formation Européenne (CIFE), which disseminated awareness on European unity to new generations of executives.

Between 1965 and 1975 he led the Centro Internazionale Matematico Estivo (CIME), an enterprise that saw the participation of world-renowned scientists and economists give lectures and seminars for the benefit of young Italian economists.

Equally engaged in the reform of teaching mathematics in middle and high schools, he became president of Mathesis, an association that advocated more modern teaching methods and the development of critical thinking.

He died in Rome on July 20, 1985.

Bibliography

De Finetti, Bruno. *Un matematico e l'economia*. Milan: F. Angeli, 1969.

Ricordo di Bruno de Finetti professore dell'Ateneo triestino. Atti del convegno Trieste 30–31 maggio 1986. Trieste: Department of Applied Mathematics Bruno de Finetti, 1987 (with a list of writings by Bruno de Finetti, 1926–1982).

Israel, Giorgio. "De Finetti, Bruno." In *Dizionario Biografico degli Italiani*, vol. XXXIII, 783–86. Rome: Istituto dell'Enciclopedia Italiana, 1987.

Conte, Alberto. "Dagli anni Trenta a oggi." In Kline Morris, *Storia del pensiero matematico*, vol. II, *Dal Settecento a oggi*, italian edition by Alberto Conte, 1415–27. Turin: Einaudi, 1999.

Pitacco, Ermanno. "De Finetti, Bruno." In *Encyclopedia of actuarial science*, edited by Josef L. Teugels and Biørn Sundt, vol. I, *A–D*, 421–23. Chichester: J. Wiley and Sons, 2004.

De Ferra, Claudio. "De Finetti, la rivoluzione della probabilità." *Assicurazioni. Rivista di diritto, economia e finanza delle assicurazioni private* I (2005): 185–99.

De Finetti, Fulvia and Nicotra, Luca. *Bruno de Finetti: un matematico scomodo*, Leghorn: Belforte Editore Libraio, 2008.

Pressacco, Flavio. "Bruno de Finetti, Actuarial Sciences and the Theory of Finance in the 20th Century." In *Vinzenz Bronzin's Option Pricing Models: Exposition and Appraisail,* edited by Wolfgang Hafner and Heinz Zimmermann, 510–33. Heidelberg: Springer, 2009.

Bruno de Finetti: Milano, 8 giugno 2006, edited by Giorgio Lunghini and Adele Robbiati Bianchi. Milan: LED, 2010.

Lucarelli, Stefano and Lunghini, Giorgio. "De Finetti, Bruno." In *Il contributo italiano alla storia del pensiero. Economia*, 604–09. Rome: Istituto dell'Enciclopedia Italiana, 2012.

Bruno de Finetti. Un matematico tra utopia e riformismo, edited by Giuseppe Amari and Fulvia de Finetti. Rome: Ediesse, 2015.

(A.M.)

UNIVERSITÀ DEGLI STUDI
DI TRIESTE

Trieste, 3 ottobre 1945.

scritto al Prof de Finetti 8.10.45

Il Prorettore

Spettabile Direzione centrale
delle ASSICURAZIONI GENERALI
TRIESTE

Il Prof. de Finetti è stato da me incaricato, con altri due colleghi, e con un gruppo di ingegneri e tecnici della città, di provvedere alla organizzazione della Facoltà di ingegneria presso questa Università, di imminente istituzione.

Il lavoro, arduo e delicato, richiede una cura assidua da parte dei delegati: e io mi rivolgo a codesta On.le Direzione, verso la quale il Prof. de Finetti ha degli obblighi, affinchè voglia gentilmente fargli quelle agevolazioni che lo svolgimento del compito stesso richiede.

Di ciò l'Università Vi sarà profondamente grata, come di un segno che codesto Istituto ha a cuore le sue sorti e quelle degli studi.

E con i più sentiti ossequi

IL PRORETTORE
(Prof. Salvatore Satta)

ASSICURAZIONI GENERALI
6 OTT 1945
SEGRETERIA

3.
Letter of the vice chancellor of the University of Trieste, Salvatore Satta, which informs that de Finetti has been entrusted with the organization of the Faculty of Engineering (Trieste, October 3, 1945)
[ASAG, *Direzione centrale*, *Servizio del personale*, *Posizioni personali*, U2GE042999]

Agencies of the "Empire"
Generali and the Italian Colonies

1936
1974

As a result of the Italo-Ethiopian War, the Italian Empire was proclaimed on May 9, 1936 and, on June 1, a unity authority was instituted, called Africa Orientale Italiana, which united the new territories with the country's older colonies, Eritrea and Somalia. The new situation gave a major boost to the development of work throughout the region, and Generali lost no time in getting involved. Two officers—Guido Cavalieri Bianchini in Eritrea and Nicolò Bagatella in Somalia—were already on the scene in May 1936 as observers to explore the possibilities for additional expansion. When Italy occupied Addis Ababa, the company sent its representative Cesare Bellini, who was given signatory power, to further study the situation and organize the start of activity.

Generali had already been long present in the portion of the Horn of Africa under Italian control, although in a more limited way. An early attempt was made in 1886 to open an agency in the port city of Massawa, but the company's presence did not become more solid and clearly defined until the mid-1920s, when it set up main agencies in Asmara and Massawa (Eritrea) and in Mogadishu (Somalia), where there had previously been an average adjustment office for the transport division. Whereas it had been present in the other Italian colony in Africa, Libya, since the end of the nineteenth century, having stipulated an agency agreement with the firm Enrico Labi fu Isach in Tripoli (originally called Tripoli of Barbary to distinguish it from the Tripoli in northern Lebanon). The firm's activity there is documented from at least 1899, and after awhile sub-agencies were set up for the region of Cyrenaica in Benghazi, headed by Elia Fargion, and in Derna, managed by the firm Haggidakis & Pallavicino, both of which became main agencies in early 1923. A report dated March 20, 1930 provides a brief description of the location of the office of the Enrico Labi company in Tripoli: it was in the old town, "on a little street (zenghet) adjacent to the little square where you find the Banco di Roma," and was closed on Saturdays, since the staff was Jewish. The letter also noted that it would be opportune to move the agency to a more central location to improve its visibility and image, although several years passed before this vision was realized.

Inspection reports and excerpts from correspondence describe life in the colonies and the conditions the Generali men found themselves working in, experiencing extreme difficulties and circumstances well beyond normal everyday agency life. An early report on Libya, and Tripoli in particular, from December 1921, provided an overall view of the colony for the purpose of defining possible goals for developing the company's activity, noting the constant change in people and shops due to the immigration of numerous merchants from Italy ("and delusions were high," as the author of the report laconically put it), "the disgraceful conditions of the port, which prevent the timely arrival of goods," the lack of training and entrepreneurial drive among the local representatives, the terrible risk of fire coverage due to the structure of the buildings, the indifference of the Muslim residents to life insurance, the fact that the Italians were for the most part soldiers and employees and therefore had limited economic resources and lived in conditions of high risk, and, finally, the danger posed in Cyrenaica by the still-active trade in contraband ammunition. Although the overall picture was quite negative, the report had a positive view of the future, advising that the company not be caught unprepared when the situation stabilized. The reports on Cyrenaica reveal harsh details about the repression of the region, which was pacified just after 1931. In two memos sent to Vittorio Brovedani, who was a co-manager at the Venice Head Office at the time, we read: "To get to Barce [Al-Marj], you have to take the train, and on the very last train car there are four machine guns set up on a revolving platform. Barce lies near the edge of the Gebel mountain range. Before arriving at Sidi Gibrin station, the road next to the train tracks is filled with the unburied bodies of camels and sheep that died while being transported during the deportations of the Kabyle people from the interior to the coast. Standing in front of the government commissioner's office, I almost always see a Moorish hangman who, in addition to his salary, receives an extra 200 liras for every execution he carries out—two months ago, seventeen people were hung in a single day" (Benghazi, February 26, 1931). And: "The current conditions in Cyrenaica are beyond what one could ever possibly imagine since its livestock economy has been completely destroyed. The locals have been gathered into camps near the coast where they are kept under surveillance. They live on rations of barley provided by the government (from that collected in their areas) and no one knows how the situation will be resolved" (Tripoli, March 2, 1931).

Communication sent from Eastern Africa over the course of 1936 provides details about the conditions of everyday life [*fig.* 1]. Acclimating to the Eritrean climate was extremely challenging. Shortly after he arrived in Massawa, Alessio Cargnelli wrote of atrocious heat, insects, and suffocating dust. In Asmara, located at an altitude of 2,300 meters, the rarefied air caused fatigue and made engines run inefficiently, and there were constant changes in the weather as well as food problems. Business trips [*fig.* 2] often led to experiences well outside the norm. After he became a fiduciary inspector for Eritrea and Somalia, a terrible adventure befell Cavalieri Bianchini. On April 20, 1937, during a flight from Mogadishu to Dire Dawa, in the Harar region of Ethiopia, a powerful storm and a gas leak forced his plane to crash-land in the brush. The area was occupied by hostile groups of locals. Having called for help by radio, ten guns, ammunition, and food were airdropped to the nine men from the plane, and that night, Italian soldiers and colonial troops reached their location. After a two-day march on foot, on the backs of mules, and in trucks, always with a military escort, they arrived in Dire Dawa, from which they were able to depart again for Asmara. Another story is preserved in a letter dated July 30, 1937: Bellini, who was the manager of the Addis Ababa agency, proposed an exploratory

ALA LITTORIA S. A.

ALLEGATO N. 8204

Membro dell'« ASSOCIAZIONE INTERNAZIONALE DEL TRAFFICO AEREO »

Biglietto IM № 356927

Servizio autobus / motoscafo alle ore:

da: Assab

all'aeroporto di: Asmara

(valido, se di ritorno, fino al)

NOME DEL PASSEGGERO Giovannini Guido

Il nome della Compagnia, che effettua il trasporto, è indicato nel testo del biglietto.
Il biglietto è valevole soltanto se presentato con la copertina.

1.
The residence in Asmara that the Società Coloniale Italiana provided for Guido Cavalieri Bianchini, and his Lancia Augusta (Asmara, July 9, 1936)
[ASAG, *Direzione centrale, Segreteria organizzazione*, OGG001131768]

2.
Plane ticket belonging to Guido Giovannini (an average adjuster in Massawa) for a flight from Assab to Asmara on Ala Littoria, the first Italian State airline (Assab, March 26, 1939)
[ASAG, *Direzione centrale, Servizio del personale, Posizioni personali*, U2GE042953]

mission to the Central Head Office. The mission, to be entrusted to staff member Remo Bortolosso, was to be carried out "along the railroad from Addis Ababa to the French Somalia border. It would require traveling using all kinds of means, from riding in freight cars to hopping onto passing trucks, sleeping rough and ready, in tents or even in the open air, using makeshift means in order to be able to stop at any of the tiny train stations along the way, especially where there are military facilities. Completing a mission of this kind requires physical stamina and being accustomed to hardship, and our collaborators in AOI can lay claim to both, having fought in the war."

The road network was extremely precarious more or less everywhere. In Somalia, the roads were described as tracks that became unusable when it rained. The Mogadishu-Harar road, which was open to trucks, was infested with raiders, and it was necessary to travel in a column formation in order to deter raids, although this method had the disadvantage that "if a truck stopped it was tipped off the road and over into the ravine with all of its load." In Asmara, where the distances from one place to another made cars necessary for work, the maximum life expectancy of a car was two years, due to the terrible roads and heavy rainfall. In these conditions, even ordinary events became small adventures, as happened in June 1937 to a truck near Metemma, along the Ethiopia and Sudan border. Its engine having caught fire due to the excessive effort needed to get through the muddy terrain during the rainy season, the truck had to be abandoned. Its driver, Eugenio Pavesi, "on foot in thick brush, in a dangerous area, with a flooded river behind him, making the return to Metemma a challenge, with the terrain and fords becoming impassable, was forced to join up with a group of roadside assistance soldiers who were trying to retreat to Om-Ager. The journey lasted for weeks, and all of the men in the party were struck with fever. Upon reaching Om-Ager, Pavesi was hospitalized and was not able to get to Asmara until

August 30. That is why the accident report is late and rather vague." Moreover, the truck, which was abandoned outdoors for months unguarded, was subjected to theft and damage.

The company's request to operate in the Empire's territories was submitted to the Ministry of Corporations in August 1936, and the authorization arrived on March 1, 1937, receiving further approval from the Ministry of Italian Africa on June 25. Generali's activity in the colonies, including Libya, was also carried out on behalf of the subsidiaries Anonima Infortuni and Anonima Grandine. It initially depended on the Società Coloniale Italiana, which was founded in 1899 and dedicated to a range of business activities in the region and had already represented the company since 1931 in Mogadishu (to take an example, a letter dated December 3, 1931 and addressed to the Venice Head Office reports the excellent results obtained by the recently introduced guarantee for the surgery benefit, called "BOC," which was used to counter competition from the Istituto Nazionale delle Assicurazioni). The agreement was signed on July 15, 1936 by Marco Ara and Vittorio Brovedani, from the Venice Head Office, since at the time the colonies were under the same management as the Italian agencies. The Società Coloniale Italiana acted as a sole agent to run its own offices as Assicurazioni Generali (including the two subsidiaries) offices as well, in exchange for a percentage of their yield.

The agency network grew quickly. Additional employees were sent to strengthen the Asmara office, but the plan from the beginning was always to focus on the capital, Addis Ababa (often abbreviated "Aba" in the documentation), setting up an office that was independent from the Società Coloniale Italiana and stationing a fiduciary inspector on site to oversee operations throughout the whole Empire (the first inspector was Cesare Bellini, who was replaced by Sergio Scimonelli in mid-1939). Offices were opened in Keren, Agordat, Dekemhare, Assab, Gondar, Dessie, Dire Dawa, Harar, Jimma, and Merca. Scimonelli's arrival led to a further painstaking inspection of all of the regions and agencies, the conclusion of which was that rather than new development, it would be better to proceed gradually, without installing an already complete system modeled on the Italian agencies, since work was still limited and unstable. The region with the best organization was Eritrea, and the Asmara agency was considered a prototype to be used in the future for the Empire's other capital cities.

The company was also involved in numerous building initiatives. The June/July 1936 issue of the *Bollettino* reported that the Council of Directors approved Chairman Edgardo Morpurgo's proposal to allocate ten million liras for "Ethiopian development." The Board of Directors and the Executive Committee meeting minutes also mention the acquisition of various properties between 1937 and 1940. The old Addis Ababa office, mentioned by Cesare Bellini in a letter dated June 6, 1937 to deputy general manager Angelo Ara ("I will send you photographs of the interior and exterior of our office soon. It is small and humble in comparison to many others belonging to the Company, but our work is carried out with no less loyalty and effort"), was moved to a more suitable site in 1939 [*fig.* 3]. Providing staff with housing was a major problem that was resolved by building small residences, called "Villa Venezia," with a few common areas for employees: one was built in 1937 in Asmara, and another in Addis Ababa the following year.

The mid-1930s were also a period of growth for the main areas of Libya. In a letter dated May 8, 1936, the Venice Head Office encouraged the local agencies to pick up insurance business from the new tourist facilities, like the ones that sprouted up with the redevelopment of the Tripoli lido ("to welcome the vast numbers of beachgoers—local, Italian, and from other countries in North Africa. Large platforms were set up together with cold buffets, cafés, and restaurants") and the newly opened grand hotel in Benghazi, the Berenice. For the annual Tripoli trade fair in 1937, Generali considered the advantages of setting up its

3.
The new office for the Addis Ababa agency on Via Tripoli, later renamed Via Duca di Genova (Addis Ababa, August 1939)
[ASAG, *Direzione centrale, Segreteria organizzazione*, U2GE025707]

4.
The Nahum building on Corso Vittorio Emanuele 149-173 in Tripoli, showing the damage caused by bombardments a few years after the war had ended (Tripoli, January 11, 1949)
[ASAG, *Direzione centrale, Segreteria organizzazione*, U2GE025728]

own pavilion, in part with the aim of bringing its significant contribution to the development of the colonies to the attention of the authorities visiting the event.

When the racial laws were promulgated at the end of 1938, all of the agents in Libya had to be given notice, and with this came the problem of replacing them. Moreover, on October 1, 1939, the agreement with the Società Coloniale Italiana was canceled, well in advance of its five-year duration. The reasons for this emerge in the letters and reports of Generali staff in Addis Ababa: restricted freedom of movement for the company, high commission expenses, a secondary place on the market, insufficient work spaces, and the subsidiary's inadequate attention to promotional activity.

The outbreak of World War II marked the rapid demise of the Italian colonies. The territories of Eastern Africa suffered the most, their connections with Italy being cut off early on. Valuable information is preserved in the reports prepared by the regional manager, Scimonelli, and by Fernando Fiaschi, head of the Asmara agency. The first problem to arise was that of absences caused by the call to arms, which led to the closure of a number of sub-agencies. The short-lived conquest of British Somalia in August 1940 constituted a brief positive interlude during the conflict and a bright spot in the news sent from the region to the Venice Head Office. Scimonelli immediately investigated the possibilities for work, but as revealed in his report, the situation was still too unstable: the region was underdeveloped, still in the process of occupation and so under total military control, and almost entirely off-limits to civilians and private businesses. The company needed to wait for the situation to settle down before opening sub-agencies under Addis Ababa: the progression of the war did not leave time for starting new projects. In 1941, the situation plummeted and became increasingly dramatic. In the midst of this turmoil, the Generali staff proved itself to be deeply loyal to the company. In a letter dated March 11, the government authorities of Eritrea indicated the precautionary measures to be taken in case of "the retreat of the defense," including the transfer of securities, stocks, and important documents that would otherwise need to be destroyed. Twenty days later, on April 1, Asmara was occupied by the British troops. Fiaschi wrote to Venice and Trieste, summarizing the events as follows: "Keren has fallen, Teclesan has surrendered, countless soldiers have fled to Asmara, where they have changed into civilian clothes. As soon as Eritrea was occupied, the Allies issued an order for all those who had been soldiers, even for just a day, to present themselves at Fort Baldissera and give themselves up as prisoners. Obviously, not all of them showed up." Fiaschi was among those who refused to turn themselves in, but since he ran the risk of being arrested at any given moment, the head of the Asmara agency sent a six-page report to both Head Offices describing the steps that had been taken to put the office in order. To work out how to handle the crisis caused by the occupation, at the end of July 1941 representatives from almost all of the most important national insurance companies met, with Scimonelli representing Assicurazioni Generali and its subsidiaries. Relations with the agency network within the Empire having been interrupted, it was impossible to communicate the assumption of risks to the Head Offices, have regular contact with clients, and carry out the necessary work for claims, and so it was mutually agreed to temporarily stop business, "with the reciprocal obligation to refrain from all operations relative to issuing new policies and collecting premiums in all divisions." On October 23, however, Fiaschi wrote letters to the Venice Head Office and Scimonelli, affirming that work had not been compromised and that "it can in no way whatsoever be interpreted as collaboration with the occupying authorities," adding that "we cannot forget, for that matter, that an open agency breeds trust and tranquility in the

5.
The Asmara agency on Avenue Haile Selassie I 145, formerly Corso Italia [Asmara, second half of the twentieth century]
[ASAG, *Direzione centrale, Segreteria organizzazione*, OGG001041902]

6.
The new office in Mogadishu, moved by Guglielmo Grosso and Gino Capone from Via Principe di Piemonte 16 to Viale Regina Elena 25 (Mogadishu, November 16, 1950)
[ASAG, *Direzione centrale, Segreteria organizzazione*, U2GE025783]

public and the entire staff which, as you yourselves rightly believe, cannot be abandoned." Continuing work also helped to keep the "specter of arrest, internment camps, and prison" at bay, "a specter ever looming over those who could not prove that their work is stable and well defined." In the end, Fiaschi was interned on March 29, 1943 and sent a memo from the camp in Dekemhare to his staff entrusting the employee Marcella Ciccaglioni with the management of the main agency in Asmara, concluding with the following words: "I strongly ask for camaraderie among all of my collaborators, who I thank for everything that they have done and will do, and who I formally guarantee that the companies I represent, with their hundred years of generosity, will suitably reward all who collaborate honestly and intelligently."

During the war, the "Villa Venezia" in Asmara hosted various people, the disabled, and refugees. At first, accommodation was offered free of charge, but then, as the emergency situation dragged on, a modest amount of rent was asked from those who were able to pay. Unfortunately, the building suffered some small-scale theft and a lot of damage during this period, such that in December 1945, when Fiaschi returned to Asmara, renovation work needed to be done to prevent even worse damage during the rainy season. The "Villa Venezia" in Addis Ababa was instead plundered by its English occupants, according to Scimonelli's wife.

At least two of the company's employees in Eastern Africa were among the fallen: Angelo Nolli, an agent in Mogadishu, who died in combat in Jubaland, Somalia, and Remo Bortolosso, who died defending Keren. Scimonelli's personal story also reflects the overall tragedy of the events. Enlisted at the end of March 1941, he was captured in Dessie one month later and brought to Addis Ababa. Taken to a military hospital, he escaped dressed as an Arab, hidden by friends and using fake documents obtained for him by an agent from Riunione Adriatica di Sicurtà. Leaving the Ethiopian capital, Scimonelli went to Asmara, but he was captured and condemned to a year of prison in Massawa. His family also suffered a harsh fate. After living for some time with locals in the brush, they were forced to go to the internment camp in Dire Dawa, where his youngest daughter died of an illness. The others were later put on a boat in Berbera and sent back to Italy. Their sea journey lasted more than forty days, during which many people died.

Conditions in Libya were not much different. The English invasion of Cyrenaica forced the agents in Benghazi and Derna to flee to Tripoli. In Benghazi, one female employee remained, whose name has not been preserved in the documentation but who "saved the archives and office documents and kept the agency running." Considerable damage was caused by air bombing in Benghazi and Tripoli [*fig.* 4]. In a letter dated March 8, 1941, we read "Tripoli is running normally in every sector. Benghazi is being hosted by Tripoli and running normally administratively, although at a slower pace. Derna is no longer running." Finally, on January 23, 1943, when the city was occupied, even the Tripoli agency was forced to stop its activity.

After the war, the process of reorganization was slow and laborious. At first, the British occupiers blocked Italian companies from resuming their work, and Eritrea was the only place where it was possible to continue activity [*fig.* 5] without the difficulties encountered in the other former colonies, although there were still reports of banditry and aggression against Italian residents. In Libya, the company resumed ties with Alberto Fresco and Elia Fargion, the old representatives in Tripoli and Benghazi that the company had been forced to let go due to the racial laws. The agency in the Libyan capital was reestablished in April 1949. In Somalia, which was placed in trust, with Italy appointed as the trustee by the United Nations for the period between 1950 and 1960, the Mogadishu agency was re-opened for business [*fig.* 6]. When Eritrea was annexed to the Empire of Ethiopia in 1952, the company considered the possibility of reactivating its presence in the region. In the minutes of the Board of Directors meeting held on October 2, 1952, we read that "the Ethiopian community is not prejudiced against Italy, but Abyssinian nationalism might make it advisable for our interests in Ethiopia to be handled by a subsidiary."

Between 1969 and 1974, military coups undermined the political order in all of the former colonies. The direct consequences included the revocation of foreign companies' authorization to operate and the creation of national companies. In the span of just a few years, all of the businesses gradually closed, having to sell their properties, transfer their portfolios to local companies, and dismiss a large part of their staff. (M.M.)

Italian Colonialism in Africa and the Presence of Assicurazioni Generali

1882 Purchase of the Bay of Assab

1885 Occupation of Massawa

1886 Agency in Massawa entrusted to Giuseppe Luccardi, in 1895 the agency was entrusted to V. Bienenfeld & Co.

1889 Protectorate on the coast between Warsheik, Mogadishu, Merca, and Barawa

1890 Proclamation of the colony of Eritrea

1899 Assicurazioni Generali represented by the firm Enrico Labi fu Isach in Tripoli

1912 The Treaty of Lausanne formalized the conquest of the regions of Tripolitania, Cyrenaica, and Fezzan, which were definitively unified in 1934 with the proclamation of the general governorship of Libya, becoming a single colony. On November 20, 1912, the office of colonial affairs, a body within the Ministry of Foreign Affairs, became the Ministry of the Colonies

1923 The sub-agencies in Benghazi and Derna become main agencies, respectively, on January 1 and February 1

1924 Agency in Asmara entrusted to the Banca Coloniale di Credito; in 1925 it became an independent main agency

1926 Opening of a main agency in Mogadishu

1927 Massawa becomes a main agency

1935-1936 The Italo-Ethiopian War. In 1936, the Empire is proclaimed (May 9). June 1, 1936, the territories of Eritrea, Somalia, and Ethiopia are unified into a single administrative unit called Africa Orientale Italiana (AOI)

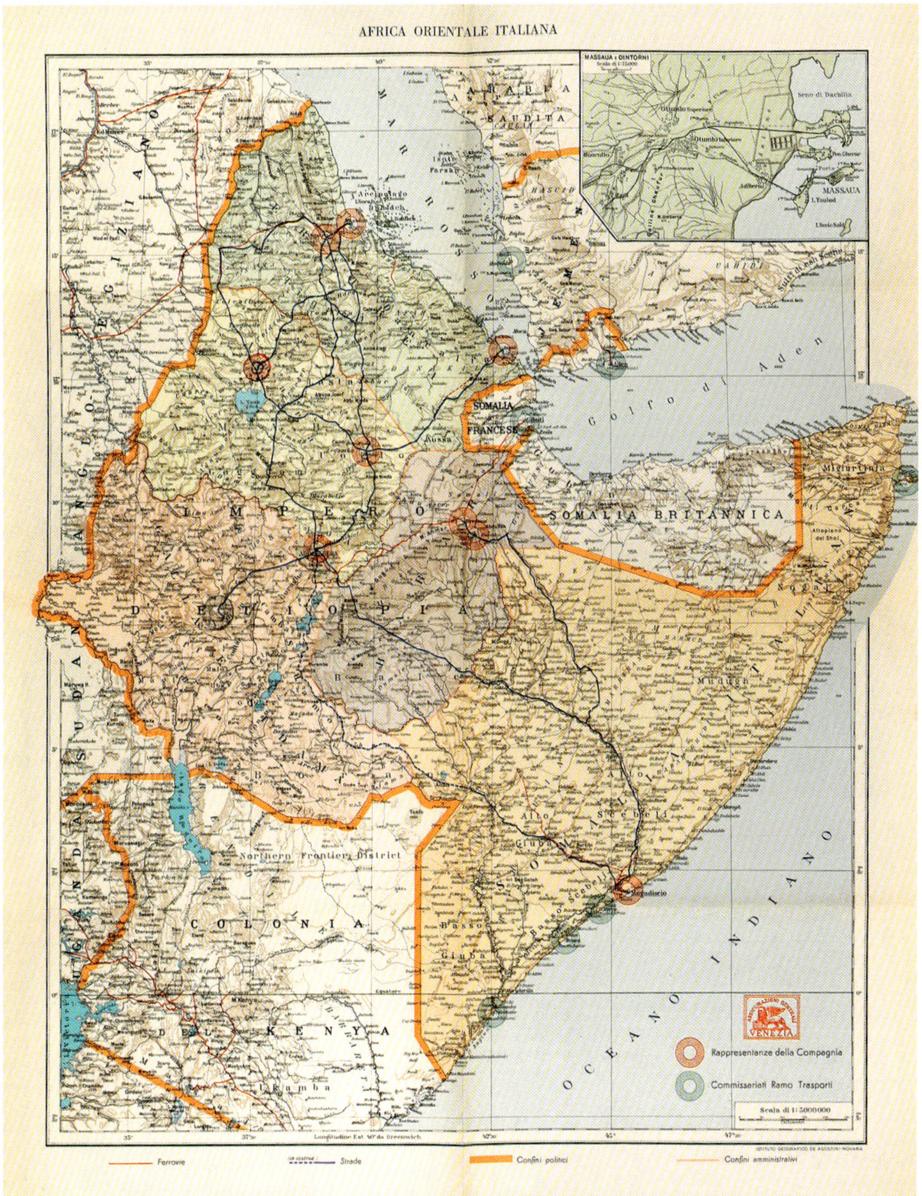

7.
Map of Africa Orientale Italiana enclosed with the Venice Head Office's circular no. 3400 (Venice, July 12, 1937)
[ASAG, *Direzione centrale, Segreteria organizzazione*, U2GE025783]

1937 The institution of the Ministry of Italian Africa (April 8), replacing the Ministry of the Colonies. Division of the AOI into six governorships: Amara, Eritrea, Harar, Galla and Sidama, Scioà, Somalia (November 15)

1937 The Ministry of Italian Africa authorizes operations in AOI territory. Opening of the main agency in Addis Ababa

1937-1938 Development of the agency network in the AOI, with the opening of sub-agencies in Agordat, Keren, Dessie, Mekele, and Merca, and special agencies in Assab, Dekemhare, Dire Dawa, Jimma, Gondar, and Harar [*fig. 7*]

1940 Conquest of British Somaliland (entered Berbera on August 19)

1941 English occupation of Africa Orientale Italiana (February–April)

1943 English occupation of Libya

1947 With the Treaty of Paris, Italy was forced to give up all of its colonies

1947-1952 British protectorate of Eritrea

1951 Libyan independence (United Kingdom of Libya; from 1969, the Libyan Arab Republic)

1952 Eritrea federated with the Empire of Ethiopia (then annexed in 1962 and restored to independence in 1993)

1950-1960 Italian Trusteeship Administration established in Somalia by the United Nations; from 1960, the Federal Republic of Somalia

1971 Plan to close operations in Libya; closure of activity in Ethiopia and transfer of portfolio to national companies

1972 Closure of the agency in Asmara (March 31); closure of activity in Somalia

1974 Military coup in Ethiopia and end of the Empire of Ethiopia

Seven Years of Horror

With World War II and the Beginning of the Atomic Age, the World Plummeted into a Moral Abyss

1939
1945

The violent escalation of warmongering of the preceding years reached its apex in 1939. The cynical games played by the various dictators, frequently placing the tremulous western democracies before a fait accompli, could no longer, or no longer wished to be, strategically concealed.
In March, Hitler violated the Munich Agreement and invaded Czechoslovakia, creating the German Protectorate of Bohemia and Moravia. Meanwhile, in August, the German-Soviet Nonaggression Pact (better known as the Molotov-Ribbentrop Pact after the Foreign Ministers who signed it) gave the green light to the political and military operations that led humanity to World War II. In fact, a secret protocol devised by the two countries involved dividing up Poland between them, which began on September 1 [*fig.* 1] when German troops claimed Danzig and the "Polish corridor," the Soviet troops following suit two weeks later. For more than a year, and so until 1941 when Germany launched "Operation Barbarossa," attacking the URSS, the Nazis and Communists lived in harmony on the spoils of the Slavic State.
During the occupation, Soviet soldiers massacred thousands of Polish officers in the Katyń forest, burying their bodies in mass graves. This bleak example was followed in subsequent years by the Yugoslavians, who used the *foibe*, natural hollows on the eastern Italian border, for their ethnic cleansing of the region. Nazi aggression against even neutral countries forced the reluctant western powers, France and Great Britain, to intervene, but the events of the first year of conflict, marked by an unexpected and almost revolutionary German war tactic (the *Blitzkrieg*, or "lightning war"), brought France to collapse. The French were forced to sign a truce in Compiègne, on the same train car in which the Germans had signed their surrender at the end of World War I, clearly revealing the revanchist motivation behind all of the events that had taken place in Germany in the previous twenty years.
Great Britain was also on the brink of collapse, but was able to hold out thanks to the strong spirit and courage of a people worthy of its imperial tradition as well as the charisma of its leader, Winston Churchill. In this context, Benito Mussolini, bound to Germany by the Pact of Steel and blinded by the momentary apparent triumph of its ally, led Italy, on June 10, 1940 [*fig.* 2], to catastrophe, convinced that with "one thousand dead" he would be able to participate as a winner in the divvying up of Europe.
The conflict instead turned out to be disastrous on all fronts (Africa, Greece, Russia, and Yugoslavia as well as the Mediterranean), and the worst repercussions were suffered by Italians in the eastern regions. In March 1941, Yugoslavia's inclusion in the Tripartite Pact (Germany, Italy, and Japan), which was almost immediately withdrawn due to a coup in Belgrade, led to what the Germans called "Operation Punishment," the invasion of the Balkan country. Once again, Il Duce got involved getting pulled along by Germany, generating a series of harsh reciprocal reprisals that the Slavs understood as absolving the persecutions carried out against the Italians of the region. The reprisals were carried out especially after the truce of September 3, 1943, made public on September 8, after the Anglo-American landing in Sicily and the removal of Mussolini, who was replaced by Pietro Badoglio in July. This was the beginning of one of the most shameful pages in the history of Italy.
The reversal of alliances [*fig.* 3], King Victor Emmanuel III fleeing Rome and leaving the population at the mercy of events, the armed forces, left without orders, collapsing (although various factors set into motion the anti-German and anti-Fascist resistance), and the birth of the Repubblica Sociale Italiana, which was considered a "Puppet State" of Nazi Germany, with all of the violence and reprisals that this entailed, opened up a period of civil war that, in addition to unleashing vendettas and reckonings at the end of the war (and during the early postwar period), sanctioned the start of a season of poison and opposition

1.
A few German soldiers launched the invasion of Poland on September 1, 1939, removing the border barrier

2.
Benito Mussolini announcing that Italy had entered the war from the balcony of the Palazzo Venezia in Rome on June 10, 1940

3.
Marshal Pietro Badoglio, flanked by the American general Maxwell Taylor, reading the declaration of war against Germany on October 13, 1943

4.
Victims of the Holocaust: The deportation of the Jews from the Łódź ghetto to the concentration camp in Auschwitz

5.
An aerial view of Hiroshima shows the complete devastation of the city after the explosion of the atom bomb

among the Italian population that the country is still today finding it difficult to overcome.
While the civil war continued, the resistance forces, comprising the reborn parties united in the Comitato di Liberazione Nazionale (CLN), were already reaching an agreement about how to rebuild the nation: in 1944, in Salerno, where the Communist leader Palmiro Togliatti implemented the celebrated "turn," an agreement to collaborate with the conservative parties, the Badoglio government began to think of appointing a constituent assembly, an issue that was then at the center of Italian political life when the war ended.
The appalling events that led to the gradual victory of the Allies are well known: the turn of the war in the Pacific after the Battle of the Midway (June 1942), with the Americans gaining the upper hand in spite of the fierce determination of the Japanese, seen previously in the conflict with China and then in the 1941 attack on Pearl Harbor, the Soviet resistance after the German and Italian invasion, the decisive moment of which was the Battle of Stalingrad, which was fought from house to house between August 23, 1942 and February 2, 1943, and the decisive landing in Normandy in 1944. The Nazi crimes were harshly punished with the total destruction of Germany and the abominable violence waged on the population when the Soviets reached Berlin, where Hitler killed himself, ending the war in Europe.
Humanity, dumbfounded and desperate, found itself living in a world that had been completely transformed, materially and, most of all, ethically and ideologically.
In fact, beyond the events of those years that were strictly connected to the war, the horrors that emerged as it raged on were devastating, showing the world's plunge into a moral abyss: from the persecution of the Jews (the Shoah)—and of other groups considered inferior or deviant—in the Nazi concentration camps, the definitive symbol of which became Auschwitz [*fig.* 4], to the carpet bombing that razed the cities to the ground, in some cases burning the population with phosphorus bombs that left no escape, like in Dresden, Germany. This madness reached its apex when the United States used the atom bomb against Japan on August 6 and 9, 1945 in Hiroshima and Nagasaki. Both cities were literally dissolved by the explosions [*fig.* 5], and a new period of history opened up, based on the terror of nuclear war perceived as a prelude to the possible self-destruction of the human race.
For Europe, guilty and the victim of its own senselessness, all of this meant the definitive loss of its long-held political, economic, and cultural centrality, in the name of a new bipolar division of the world led by the winning superpowers: the United States and the USSR. The clash between the two reciprocally menacing ideological and economic systems led to the risk of a new conflict the potential consequences of which would have been so catastrophic that, according to the great scientist Albert Einstein, a later World War IV would have been fought with sticks and stones, the only "technological" tools left for the human race. (D.R.)

In Brief

1939
April 1: The leader of the nationalist forces, Francisco Franco, announced the end of the Spanish Civil War following the conquest of Madrid and Valencia, the last republican strongholds.

1939
June 18: Three months after becoming pope, Pius XII proclaimed St. Francis of Assisi and St. Catherine of Siena the patron saints of Italy, citing the "clear splendor of their works and virtues."

1939
July 4: The baseball champion Lou Gehrig, struck by the grave neurological disease that was named after him (now better known as ALS), said goodbye to his fans at Yankee Stadium in New York.

1939
December 15: The blockbuster *Gone with the Wind*, based on the eponymous novel by Margaret Mitchell, premiered in Atlanta. Starring Clark Gable and Vivien Leigh, it won eight Oscars, the record until 1958.

1940
June 9: Fausto Coppi won the Giro d'Italia when he was just twenty years and eight months old (and still holds the record today as the youngest winner in the history of the race). The next day, Italy entered the war.

1940
September 12: In France, a cave complex was discovered by chance, the Caves of Lascaux, an invaluable example of prehistoric art for their painted decoration dated to the Upper Paleolithic period.

1940
November 13: Debut at the Broadway Theatre of Disney's film *Fantasia*, masterwork of the animation film, made of episodes based on classical music directed by Leopold Stokowski.

1940
December 29: London suffered the most violent German air bombardment of the whole war. The photo of St. Paul's Cathedral unharmed surrounded by the smoke of the fires became a symbol of English tenacity.

1941
May 5: After the British advance, Haile Selassie returned triumphant to Addis Ababa, exactly five years after the Italian occupation, and was officially reinstated as emperor of Ethiopia.

1941
June 22: German troops invaded the Soviet Union.
The disastrous outcome of Operation Barbarossa, the code name for the attack, was a decisive turning point in the war.

1941
December 7: Japanese planes bombarded the American fleet in Pearl Harbor, sinking numerous ships and killing more than two thousand people. The United States were thus brought into World War II.

1942
July 6: The thirteen-year-old Anne Frank hid with her family in a secret refuge in Amsterdam, hoping to escape the Shoah. She spent two years there, described in her now world-famous *Diary*, until her family's arrest.

1942
August 4: The New York debut of the movie *Holiday Inn*, in which Bing Crosby sings *White Christmas*. The song, written by Irving Berlin, won an Oscar and hit record sales as a single.

1942
November 4: The British Eighth Army, commanded by General Montgomery, broke through the El-Alamein front, in Egypt, in spite of heroic resistance from the Italian and German forces, particularly the Folgore division.

1942
December 2: The atomic pile built by Enrico Fermi was activated in Chicago, a critical turn in the Manhattan Project that went on to develop the nuclear bombs that were dropped on Japan in 1945.

1943
January 23: The film *Casablanca* was released in the United States, starring Humphrey Bogart and Ingrid Bergman. A moving love story, as well as a vehicle for war propaganda, it won three Oscars.

1943
February 2: Soviet troops won the Battle of Stalingrad, annihilating the German forces. After the dramatic retreat of the Italian Alpine Corps from the Don River, the defeat of the Axis on the eastern front was complete.

1943
April 6: Antoine de Saint-Exupéry, a writer and aviator (he died in 1944 on a reconnaissance flight), published *The Little Prince*, a fable about the meaning of life and friendship.

1944
June 6: Operation Overlord was launched with the landing in Normandy, an Allied plan to liberate France and invade Germany from the west. This date has gone down in history as the D-Day par excellence.

1944
July 1: The Bretton Woods conference began. During the meeting, the World Bank and the International Monetary Fund were instituted and the exchange rate was tied to the convertibility of the dollar into gold.

1944
July 20: A military plot against Hitler failed on this day, and Colonel von Stauffenberg, who carried out the attempt, was shot that night. The other conspirators were put to death after a short trial.

1944
December 26: The play *The Glass Menagerie* was performed at the Civic Theater in Chicago for the first time. The play, filled with autobiographical references, was Tennessee Williams' first big success.

1945
February 4: The Yalta conference began, during which the leaders of Great Britain, the United States, and the Soviet Union, Churchill, Roosevelt, and Stalin, laid the foundations for the division of Europe into two zones.

1945
September 2: Aboard the American battleship *Missouri*, which was anchored in the Bay of Tokyo, the Japanese formally surrendered, putting an end to World War II.

The War Chronicles
World War II Stories about War Risk

1939
1948

Various insurance sectors cover war risk and, as is evident from the directors' minutes, it was part of the contractual terms from the very beginning of Generali's history; specifically, in the transport division and maritime insurance. During the nineteenth century, it was also added to the life insurance division, offering coverage to military personnel.
When the World War I broke out, the Venice Head Office immediately issued a number of circular letters defining the parameters for the life insurance agreements, which had to specify whether the insured were classified as deployed by the army, the health services or the regional militia. The changing times and the rapid progress of the war industry are already captured in a circular of 1915 that reads: "We were committed to offer insurance against damage arising from bombs and all kinds of bullets, whether they be dropped by planes, airships or any other air machine" (circular no. 7/3 dated March 7, 1916).
Nonetheless, the period that is documented in more comprehensive detail is the one that concerns the World War II. As early as 1935, as recorded in the Council of Directors' minutes no. 152 of December 21, Assicurazioni Generali had obtained government approval "for the important role it played in the establishment of the Consorzio Rischi Guerra, for which it has taken on the majority of the commitment, in times that are not trouble-free." In November 1939, when the conflict had just begun, the legislation was further improved with Royal Decree no. 1939 on the war risks for maritime and air transport.
The documents of the life department, the representative office and the circulars, contain some testimonies about the coverage of war risks: a decree by the Ministry of Corporations issued in 1940 ruling that this kind of coverage be included free of charge in the life insurance policies of civilians; the negotiations between various reinsurance companies to agree on the management of said risks; the correspondence with the Spanish and Belgian Branches during the August of 1941 to assess how to manage the volunteers for the Russian front; the discussions in July 1942 on whether to insure an entire troupe of four thousand Flemish soldiers who fought for the German army; and immediately following the end of the war, exchanges with Alleanza Assicurazioni, one of the Group's companies, concerning the insurance of Italian soldiers leaving for Somalia after the mandate issued by the UN in 1949, for the trusteeship of the former colony.
However, the most interesting information is found among the documentation of the transport division, which shines a light on many noteworthy yet tragic events. The papers report on all the "hull damages" in relation to the coverage of large vessels and the claims they submitted. Mostly filed in alphabetical order, according to the ship's name, the documentation is divided into two parts. The first concerns the underwriting of risk and contains the lists of hulls accepted, the policies [*fig.* 1] and the bills of sale to the coinsurance partners (as the value of these insurance covers was very steep, the risk was usually shared between different companies). The second, more voluminous part, concerns the damages incurred and contains: insurance claims; excerpts from the onboard journals; inspection reports (with evidence of the first use of photography in damage assessments); legal actions in cases where the ship owner abandoned ship and the insurance company refuted the abandonment; correspondence between internal departments such as the legal office and central accounting, and other organizations such as the Unione Italiana di Riassicurazione, the Ministry of Communications, and the Consorzio Italiano Assicurazione Rischi Speciali Trasporti (CIARST). As such, the documentation makes it possible to retrace some of the biggest and saddest events that involved Italy during the World War II.
The first claims were reported in the period preceding Italy's entry into the war, mostly in the North Sea, an area that was already heavily mined and subject to incursions by the German aviation. Such was the case of *Fianona*, which was damaged by a mine on

November 21, 1939 while in British waters. A month later the steamship *Comitas*, in transit from Djibouti to Antwerp, suffered an even worse fate; the ship was struck in the middle, splitting in half and getting stranded at Vlissingen, Holland, on the Belgian border. The captain claimed a "total loss" [*fig.* 2]. There is no shortage of non-Italian insured: on January 15, 1940 the *U-Boat 44* on course toward South Africa, sank the Dutch *Arendskerk* off the coast of Brittany; thus sinking a boat from a nation that was still neutral at the time. On May 15, 1940 a convoy of three steamships—the *Antonio Locatelli*, the *Foscolo* and the *Fidelitas*—was attacked by German planes while on the river Scheldt outside the Antwerp harbor. The captain of the first of the three ships, Mario Rivarola, recorded the event in great detail in the onboard journal: "At 9:00 the roar of the engines alerted me to the German airplanes flying towards us. [...] The attacks occurred a total of five times, and on each occasion about ten bombs were dropped [...]. The most violent and desperate and furious attack was the last, which I watched from the bridge. There was a downpour of bombs off the starboard bow; I counted ten, one after the other, trying to block us with the fire; the last thing we heard was the crackle of the machine gun, 9:40 hours." One goes on to read that the most serious damage was inflicted to the *Foscolo*: "At 13:10 near Zeebruge [...] once again we are attacked by a German plane [...] the national steamship 'Foscolo' is hit and we watch the crew abandon ship and getting into the lifeboats." What took place on June 10, 1940 and in the days that followed the declaration of war, is what some refer to as the collective suicide of the Italian merchant marine. The lack of notice and in some cases, the complete failure to order the return to the homeland, resulted in the loss of over two hundred ships of large tonnage, almost a third of the civil fleet. Many of these were seized and reused by the enemy. Some captains opted for scuttling despite the reprisals for sabotage, which they knew they would incur on top of certain imprisonment.

1.
Insurance policy against war risks for the steamship *San Giuseppe* (Milan, April 21, 1941)
[ASAG, *Direzione centrale, Ramo trasporti, Danni corpi, Rischi guerra*, U2GE028285]

RAMO TRASPORTI

DUPLICATO
da valere fino alla sostituzione
con l'originale bollato e registrato

Agenzia Generale per Milano/L.
Polizza N. 41937
Repertorio N.

ASSICURAZIONI GENERALI

SOCIETÀ ANONIMA ISTITUITA NEL 1831
Capitale sociale interamente versato Lire 120.000.000 — Fondi di garanzia oltre Due Miliardi e 786 Milioni
SEDE IN TRIESTE

POLIZZA ITALIANA PER L'ASSICURAZIONE DEI RISCHI
DI GUERRA SU CORPI DI NAVI
(Edizione 20-12-1939-XVIII)

La Compagnia ASSICURAZIONI GENERALI assicura alle condizioni generali qui a tergo stampate ed a quelle particolari che seguono alla spett. NOVA GENUENSIS Soc. An. - Genova
al premio di 0,11 (cent.undici per cento) pagabile per contanti
la somma di L. 6,803,322.= (Seimilioni ottocentotremila trecentoventidue) =========
sopra corpo, attrezzi macchine, spese d'armamento, interessi ed esborsi
della nave a vapore di bandiera italiana nominata:

„SAN GIUSEPPE"

Capitano ... classificata 100 A.I.I. nel Registro Italiano Navale
la cui valutazione ammonta a Lit.6,803,322.= da valere per un mese di giacenza nel porto di NORFOLK (U.S.A.) - a partire dalle ore 12 del giorno 21 Aprile 1941.=
VALUTAZIONE : Resta convenuto che la somma assicurata con la presente polizza non potrà in nessun caso eccedere la valutazione risultante dalla Tabella delle Valutazioni per la sicurtà suCorpi di Navi, approvata dal "COMITATO DI VIGILANZA" per l'assicurazione dei rischi di guerra della navigazione marittima ed aerea, e pertanto la responsabilità degli assicuratori sarà comunque limitata al valore di Tabella.
Qualora la somma assicurata, dovesse risultare inferiore alla valutazione desumibile dalla suaccennata Tabella, l'Assicurata si intenderà scoperta d'assicurazione, per il minimo importo assicurato.

La sicurtà del suddetto piroscafo si intenderà nulla qualora il piroscafo stesso alla data data odierna (21 aprile 1941) risultasse già perduto.

Milano addì 21 Aprile 1941/XIX -X

Premio 0,11 % sulla
Somma assicurata di L. 6,803,322.= L. 7,483,65
Addizionale Gestione
Diritto di Polizza „ 424,20
imp.entrata 23,70
Tassa di Registro e Bollo „ 175,30
Totale L. 8,106,85

Visto:
Reg.to a Milano il 28 Aprile 1941,XIX
N.o 166178 Vol. 1728/1 Esatto L.
L'ISPETTORE IL RICEVITORE

ASSICURAZIONI GENERALI
per copia conforme
"ASSICURAZIONI GENERALI„
(Ramo Trasporti)
AGENZIA GENERALE per MILANO e la LOMBARDIA

La presente polizza non è perfezionata, e non obbliga l'assicuratore, se non è regolarmente firmata dal medesimo o dal suo rappresentante, e se inoltre non sia effettuato l'integrale pagamento del premio pattuito. Perciò in nessun caso il ... del premio prima della firma della polizza, o la firma della polizza ... del pagamento del premio, obbligano o possono obbligare l'assicuratore.

LIT. D&G. - TRIESTE

2.
Inspection of the steamship *Comitas*, accompanying photo (Vlissingen, December 1939)
[ASAG, *Direzione centrale, Ramo trasporti, Danni corpi, Rischi guerra*, U2GE028462]

The initial, painful consequences of the war were felt on three main fronts. First, in the North Sea, where numerous ship owners had chartered their vessels in service of Monopolio Carboni for the supply of coal to the Ministry of Communications, an institution which in the documentation is often abbreviated to Monocarbo. On the evening of March 7, 1940 the *Amelia Lauro* had no chance of going unscathed: the target of an aerial bombing by the Germans, it was rescued by the British and taken to Immingham for repairs; here it was seized at the start of the hostilities. In a letter dated May 27, Achille Lauro's ship owner emphasizes the urgency caused by the looming war and thereby his great concern for the fate of his ship: "We reiterate that all time lost is to the detriment of this ship because it is clear that delaying the ship in England will soon result in what can easily be imagined. Therefore, we would prefer that it is moved as quickly as possible." The steamships *Gioacchino Lauro* and *Marzocco*, which were employed for the supply of coal along Great Britain's eastern coast, were also immediately captured.

Secondly, vessels became the victims of war in the waters of the Indian and Pacific oceans. The greatest losses were incurred by Lloyd Triestino, which had many routes to the East. On June 11, the steamship *Remo* was kidnapped in Fremantle, South-Western Australia; while the *Romolo* scuttled en route between the Solomon and the Caroline islands; a similar fate befell the *Timavo*, which as the liquidation acts describe, was fleeing from South Africa: "While the steamship 'Timavo' was navigating north of Durban [...] war was declared, on 6.11.1940, while chased by enemy seaplanes it sank at lat. 27° 48' south, long. 32° 40' east." The *Jerusalem*, owned by the company Adriatica, was no luckier. It also departed Durban in haste: on June 11, the ship managed to reach the safe harbor of Lourenço Marques [Maputo] in neutral Portuguese Mozambique, but due to the forced pace, "to avoid capture by a British cruiser, its engine was damaged." The ship stayed there until the armistice on September 8, 1943 when by order of the Italian government it was transferred to the British for deployment as a hospital ship.

Thirdly, the losses were felt in the Mediterranean. The motor vessels *Adige* and *Rodi* were seized in Malta, resulting in the disembarkation of the soldiers and part of the crew, who were transferred to the concentration camps. In Gibraltar the steamship *Cellina* was captured despite the attempt to destroy it. Also near Gibraltar, the tanker *Olterra* was successfully scuttled; the ship was later refloated, repaired and kept safe in the nearby Spanish harbor of Algeciras, where it was secretly deployed by a team of the Italian royal navy in raids against the British base.

Such situations did not serve as experience and similar events continued to occur at a later time. Already by the end of March and the beginning of April 1941, a number of ships (*Alberta*, *Belvedere*, *Leme*, *San Giuseppe*…) were seized by the American authorities from the harbors in the Atlantic and the Pacific, indicating that tensions had reached a peak height. At the same time, other steamships suffered the same fate while moored in nations that were politically allied with the United States or in any case not "benevolently neutral" (the *Recca* was seized in Havana, while the *Fella* was burned down by its crew to avoid capture in Puntarenas, Costa Rica). In a note sent by the shipping company Garibaldi to Assicurazioni Generali on April 21, 1941, regarding the steamships *Adamello* and *Ircania* that had been placed "under surveillance," the first in Montevideo and the second in Jacksonville, Florida, one reads that "notoriously, Uruguay obeys orders coming from North America and therefore one might expect the worst." It is also noted that the Ircania's crew was incarcerated and later sentenced for sabotage. Each of these vessels was declared a write-off immediately after December, 11 when Italy declared war on the United States following Japan's attack on Pearl Harbor.

The so-called "convoy battles" in the Mediterranean were fought between the Italian navy and the British to guarantee and counteract each other in the transportation of troops, fuel and supplies, specifically to the Balkans and the African fronts. Among the files on war risks, the one about the *Galilea* recounts the tragedy of the passenger ship that was deployed as a hospital ship and for the transport of troops; which was sunk between March 28 and 29, 1942 while returning to Italy from Greece. Hundreds of soldiers perished, most of them members of the Alpine battalion Gemona. The file is marked "without follow up" as the ship was not insured against war risks. A similar incident, though perhaps less known, occurred to the *Paganini*, which was transporting troops and supplies to Durrës during the first weeks of the conflict. To this day, the cause of the explosion that sank the ship, whether an accident, sabotage or a torpedo, remains unclear. There is evidence that an investigation was undertaken; however, a year after the incident, a note from the insurance company Levant in Genoa informed Generali's transport division that, "The cause for the loss of the steamship *Paganini*—notice 6/28/1940—which burned and sunk approximately 12 miles from Durrës has not yet been ascertained."

The war also imposed all kinds of precautions at sea, blackouts being among them. Consequently, part of the damages relating to war resulted from collisions between vessels of the same nationality. It so happened that on the night between August 28 and 29, 1940 two steamships, *Sacro Cuore* and *Cadamosto*, collided off the coast of Ancona. A memo by the naval inspector Mario Alhaique reads: "The war had already begun: all lights were out, the coast was completely dark, the lighthouses and lamps had been extinguished. The moonless night was dim and the two vessels, like twins in shape and size, cruised quietly in the deepest darkness following opposing routes."

There are numerous reports of the aerial bombings endured by the many Italian harbors in Genoa, Livorno, Civitavecchia, Naples, Crotone [*fig.* 3], Venice and Trieste during the years of the conflict.

Equally well documented are the events on both

3.
Inspection of the steamship *Dea Mazzella*, accompanying photos (Naples, September 25, 1942) [ASAG, *Direzione centrale, Ramo trasporti, Danni corpi, Rischi guerra*, U2GE028284]

Moored in the Crotone harbor, the steamship *Dea Mazzella* endured two bombardments in just a few days. On September 1, 1941 the machine room and the officers' lounge, were hit by incendiary and cluster bombs, which in addition to the damage, caused the death of the cook and wounded several members of the crew. Just three days later, on September 4, in a second air raid the hold of the *Dea Mazzella* was hit, which caused the partial sinking of the ship

Pfo. " DEA MAZZELLA "

APPLICAZIONE DEL TAMPONE SUL FASCIAME ESTERNO A NAVE GALLEGGIANTE TAMPONATO LO SQUARCIO SUL FASCIAME INTERNO

the African fronts. When the war broke out, several vessels including those of Lloyd Triestino, became trapped in the Red Sea and sought refuge in the harbors of Eastern Africa where they remained inactive until the fall of those colonies. Many scuttled just before the British troops arrived (in February in Kismayo, Somalia, and early April in Massawa, Eritrea), or they were captured while breaching the blockade to get to Madagascar, which was under the control of Vichy France. The *Somalia* and the *Duca degli Abruzzi* succeeded in this undertaking, but managed only to postpone the same sad fate as the other runaways; they both scuttled in the Diego Suarez harbor [Antsiranana] in early May 1942, to avoid being captured by the British who had invaded the large African island to prevent the Japanese from occupying it.
The North African routes imposed considerable losses on the Italian merchant marine. The steamship *Manzoni* was hit by British torpedo bombers in early July 1940 while it was moored in Tobruk harbor in Libya. The *Isarco* was sunk in September 1941 by a Dutch submarine on its course from Africa to Naples. The claims for damages submitted to Generali to commence the processes for compensation, inform on the fluctuating situation on the Libyan front. As one can read from the documents, at the beginning of 1941 when the British invaded Cyrenaica, Derna first and Benghazi second, the fleet of vessels owned by Società Coloniale Italiana and deployed for cabotage (barges, pontoons, tugboats…), "were destroyed following superior orders of a military nature." The subsequent return of the axis troops called for a revision of the estimated damages, as well as efforts to recover any equipment. On January 23, 1943 Tripoli's fleet suffered the same fate, reporting a total loss "due to enemy occupation," by then operations in Africa were heading towards their inevitable conclusion.
The proclamation of the armistice on September 8, 1943 brought with it moments of great confusion coupled with heroic events and days of anarchy. In

those days there were tens of cases involving Italian merchant ships. In a great many files one reads that the reason for a claim was that the ship "had been transferred to the German authorities by the military." In other instances, lootings were carried out by the German troops and even the local population. Some crews resorted to scuttling so as not to surrender their ship to the former allies; among them is the peculiar case of the *Conte Verde*, scuttled in Shanghai on September 9, to avoid appropriation by the Japanese. Notable is the report from the first officer of the motor tanker *Ardor*, which was fleeing Istria to seek refuge in Kotor, following the orders from the naval command in Pula. On the afternoon of September 9, it was attacked by German planes and the captain Giovanni Biino, ordered his crew to seek shelter. When the attack was over and the damage was inspected, "we searched for the crew but only 8 people escaped unscathed or with minor injuries, two were severely wounded […]. All who were missing, the crew including the captain, had disappeared and I consider them dead because, as mentioned above, they were in the same spot where the ship was hit and was totally ripped apart." In total the number of missing people was eleven.

During the last days of the war, damages to the civil fleet were still being reported. In the claim pertaining to the liquidation for damages incurred by the steamship *Leneo* during clashes in the Genoa harbor, the events are thus described: "[…] on the morning of April 26, 1945 while moored in this harbor at the Mogadishu pier, damages were incurred to various parts of the hull, aloft, and to the engine, further to an onboard fire caused by the explosion of a weapons store at the Eritrea pier, and which was triggered by a shootout between Germans and partisans at the Silos Occhetti."

Even after 1945 accidents were still being reported; among the remnants of the war that had just ended, were the mined areas that had not yet been cleared [*fig.* 4], and which created new casualties especially for fishing vessels. (M.M.)

4.
Diagram showing the mined areas of Adriatic Sea between the Volano harbor and Fano [1948]
[ASAG, *Direzione centrale*, *Ramo trasporti*, *Danni corpi*, *Rischi guerra*, U2GE028214]

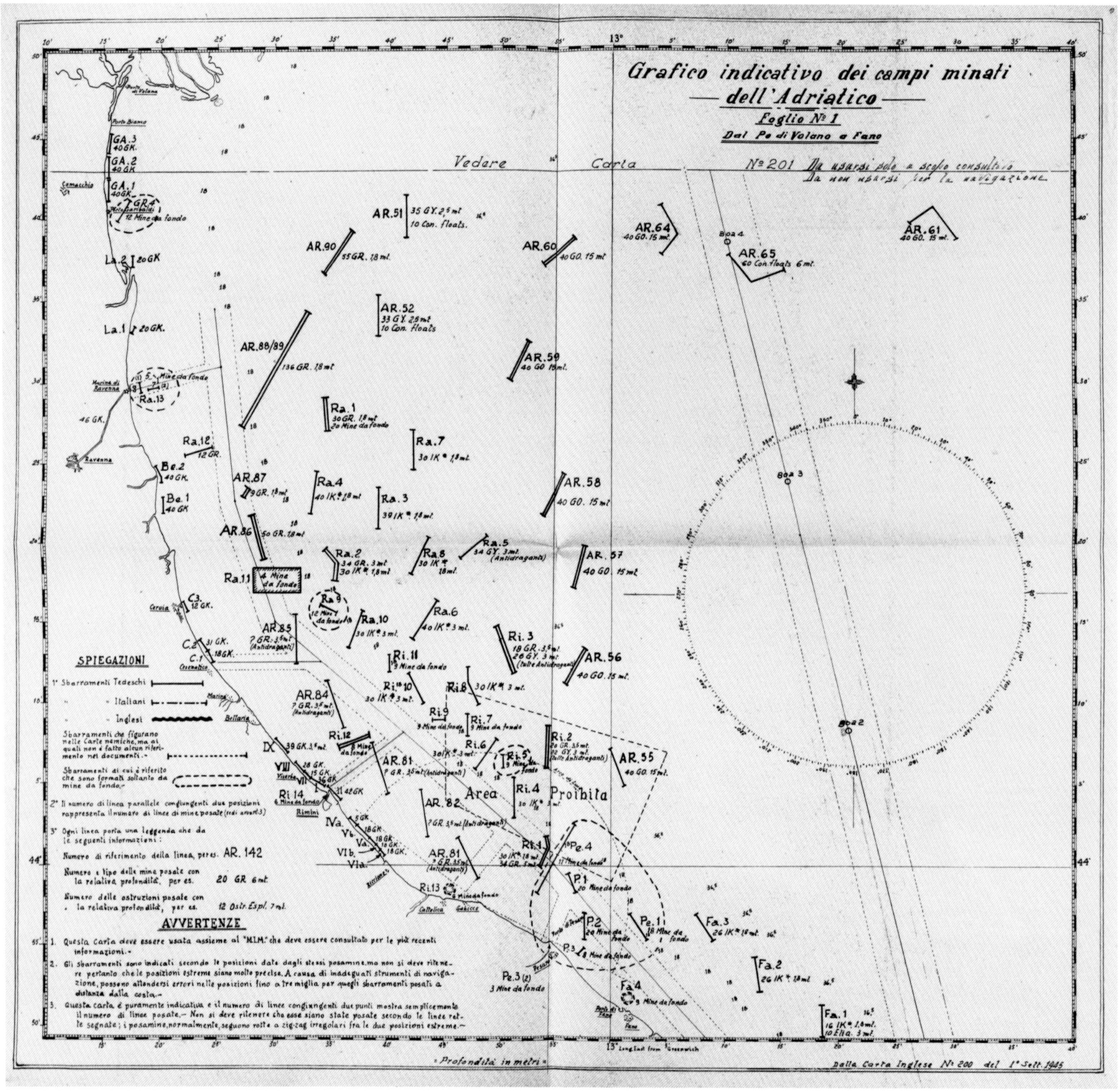

The *Baron Gautsch*

The *Baron Gautsch* was a passenger ship owned by Österreichischer Lloyd, and later Lloyd Triestino, after Trieste became part of Italy. The company was founded in 1833 with the participation of the Assicurazioni Generali Austro-Italiche. Just a few days from the beginning of the World War I, on August 13, 1914 the steamship sank en route to Dalmatia. The shipwreck was caused by a naval mine off the Istrian coast, between Pula and Rovinj, which caused the death of over one hundred people. Once they received the insurance payout, the shipping company announced it would abandon the vessel to the co-insurers, the principal amongst them being Assicurazioni Generali with a 40% share. While the oldest papers appear to be lost, the Historical Archive enables the reconstruction of the final part of the *Baron Gautsch*'s history [*fig.* 5]. The relict was not identified until 1958 when the Compagnia Industriale Mercantile (CIM) in Trieste purchased it to commence the recovery operations. But a legal dispute with the Yugoslav authorities arose over the ownership rights. The dispute lasted many years and ultimately, the ship was never recovered. Today the shipwreck is under the protection of the Croatian Ministry of Culture and is explored by scuba divers.

5.
Articles from *Il Piccolo*, which concern the relict of the steamship *Baron Gautsch* (Trieste, 1958-1972)
[ASAG, *Direzione centrale, Ramo trasporti, Danni corpi*, U2GE028201]

AFFONDATO DA UNA MINA QUARANTAQUATTRO ANNI FA

Sarà risollevato dagli abissi il relitto del «Baron Gautsch»

Le prime osservazioni dei palombari scesi sul fondo a una quarantina di metri - Riportati a galla alcuni strumenti della nave

SI RIPARLA A CAPODISTRIA DI RECUPERARE LA NAVE AFFONDATA NELL'AGOSTO DEL 1914

ESPLORATO DA «SUB» AMERICANI IL RELITTO DEL «BARON GAUTSCH»

IL PICCOLO-Trieste 25 APR.1960

LA NAVE AFFONDATA NEL 1914 AL LARGO DI ROVIGNO

Nel ricupero del «Baron Gautsch» conflitto sulle acque territoriali

Un palombaro triestino che dieci anni fa localizzò il relitto ne rivendica la proprietà in comune con una Compagnia locale

COLO' A PICCO NELLE ACQUE DI ROVIGNO CINQUANTAQUATTRO ANNI FA

Gli jugoslavi sarebbero decisi a ricuperare il «Baron Gautsch»

Cinquantacinque anni or sono: il piroscafo del Lloyd Austriaco «Baron Gautsch» in porto a Lussinpiccolo nell'estate del 1913

Group Stories

The Merger of Anonima Infortuni and Anonima Grandine with Assicurazioni Generali

1940
1948

The first discussions pertaining to the merger date back to autumn 1940, to a meeting between the top managers of the three companies concerned: Generali's general manager, Gino Baroncini; Anonima Infortuni's general manager, Alberto Melchiori; Anonima Grandine's manager, Umberto Baccolini. On this occasion, the possibility of merging the two publicly traded companies into a single entity named, Anonime Generali Riunite, was considered. The new company should provide the solution to Generali's difficulties abroad, specifically in France and Germany, where life and non-life divisions were operated together, while they had to be separate from each other. Backed by chairman Giuseppe Volpi, the matter was put to the Management Committee (meeting of November 26), seeking an official resolution to proceed with the project in collaboration with the Managements and the Boards of Auditors of the other two companies. In spring the following year, the merger was postponed mostly because of the new rules on reserves and capital increases (Royal Law Decree no. 1714 of December 27, 1940 that introduced a special 100% tax on the transfer of reserves and capital), which made it prohibitive to carry out any transactions that involved the increase of capital, such as using the publicly traded companies' reserves to generate share capital. The situation generated much uncertainty, even on the part of Baroncini who, given the circumstances, deferred the matter until the war had ended [*fig.* 1]. In 1942 the project was reexamined further to the new tax concessions for mergers (Royal Law Decree no. 192 of March 5, 1942), but was shelved due to the inadequate implementation time. Other unforeseeable reasons caused the merger to be postponed year after year, until the World War II broke out and the plan was shelved for lack of opportunities [*fig.* 2].

As the war progressed, the political propaganda targeting Generali became increasingly abusive; accused of being a Jewish stronghold, the chairman's position became increasingly critical. In that climate, the company felt vulnerable, and the issue of moving the headquartes from Trieste resurfaced. The option of temporarily relocating the Central Head Office to the town of Grado was considered, but the chairman pushed for a definitive solution such as transferring the registered office to Rome. In a letter dated February 11, 1943 Volpi urges Baroncini to relocate, noting that this should have taken place in 1918, he also mentions coaching tactfully quorum ("indoctrinating our friends") to ensure the motion would pass at the General Meeting. The items for resolution included: the statutory amendments required by the introduction of a new Civil Code; the addition of a managing director; the option of holding General Meetings outside Trieste. The matter concerning the registered office, was a secondary item. In his letter, Volpi mentioned discussing it with Fulvio Suvich, chairman of the Riunione Adriatica di Sicurtà (RAS), whom he described as "rather cold" on the issue. Well aware of the challenges arising from temporarily relocating the offices, Baroncini resolved to delay the topic until the circumstances made it unavoidable. Opting to move the registered office to Venice or Rome was a different matter entirely; a temporary solution would have involved places near the city considered as the permanent location. A number of objections to a "war transfer" arose in informal meetings. The Board's Trieste contingent (Demetrio Economo, Giovanni Scaramangà, Mario Tripcovich and deputy chairman Antonio Cosulich) were mostly unsupportive; though they were in favor of convening the Meetings in a city other than of registered office—as set out in article 16 of the charter (letter from Baroncini to Volpi dated April 3, 1943).

As a precautionary measure, at the end of June 1943 the Board resolved to set up a Head Office in Rome for the duration of the war, in the event of an invasion or in case of a division between northern and southern Italy disrupted the communications between the Head Offices. It would comprise a group of officers already working in various capacities in Rome, who would be given representational powers and become company signatories for the normal running of the company (including Anonima Grandine and Anonima Infortuni). The group was accountable to Arcangelo Paturzo and Francesco Berti, co-manager of the Special Office for

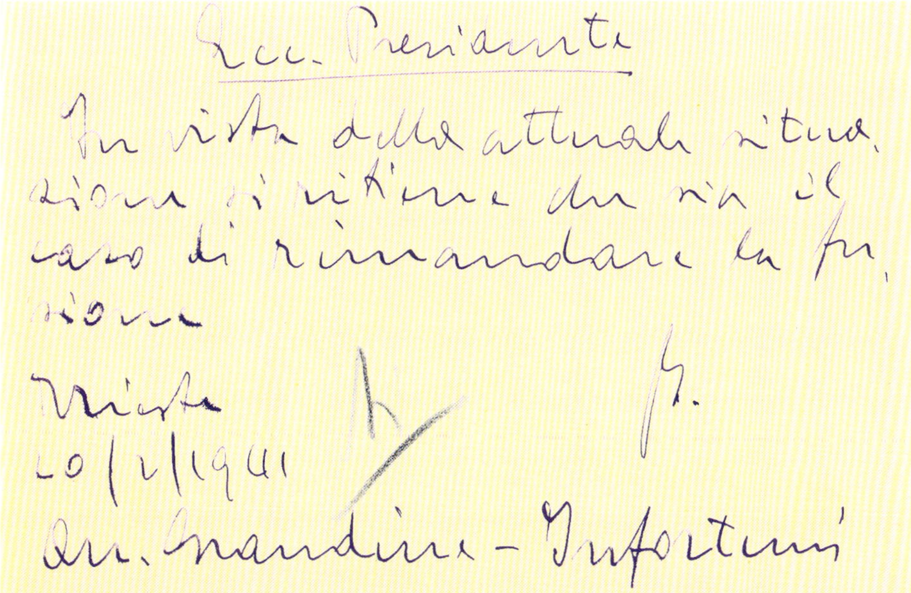

Ecc. Presidente

In vista della attuale situazione si ritiene che sia il caso di rimandare la fusione

Trieste 20/2/1941

An. Grandine - Infortuni

1.
Note by Gino Baroncini to Giuseppe Volpi (Trieste, February 29, 1941) [ASAG, *Presidenza e organi sociali, Presidenti e vicepresidenti, Gino Baroncini*, U2GE024022]

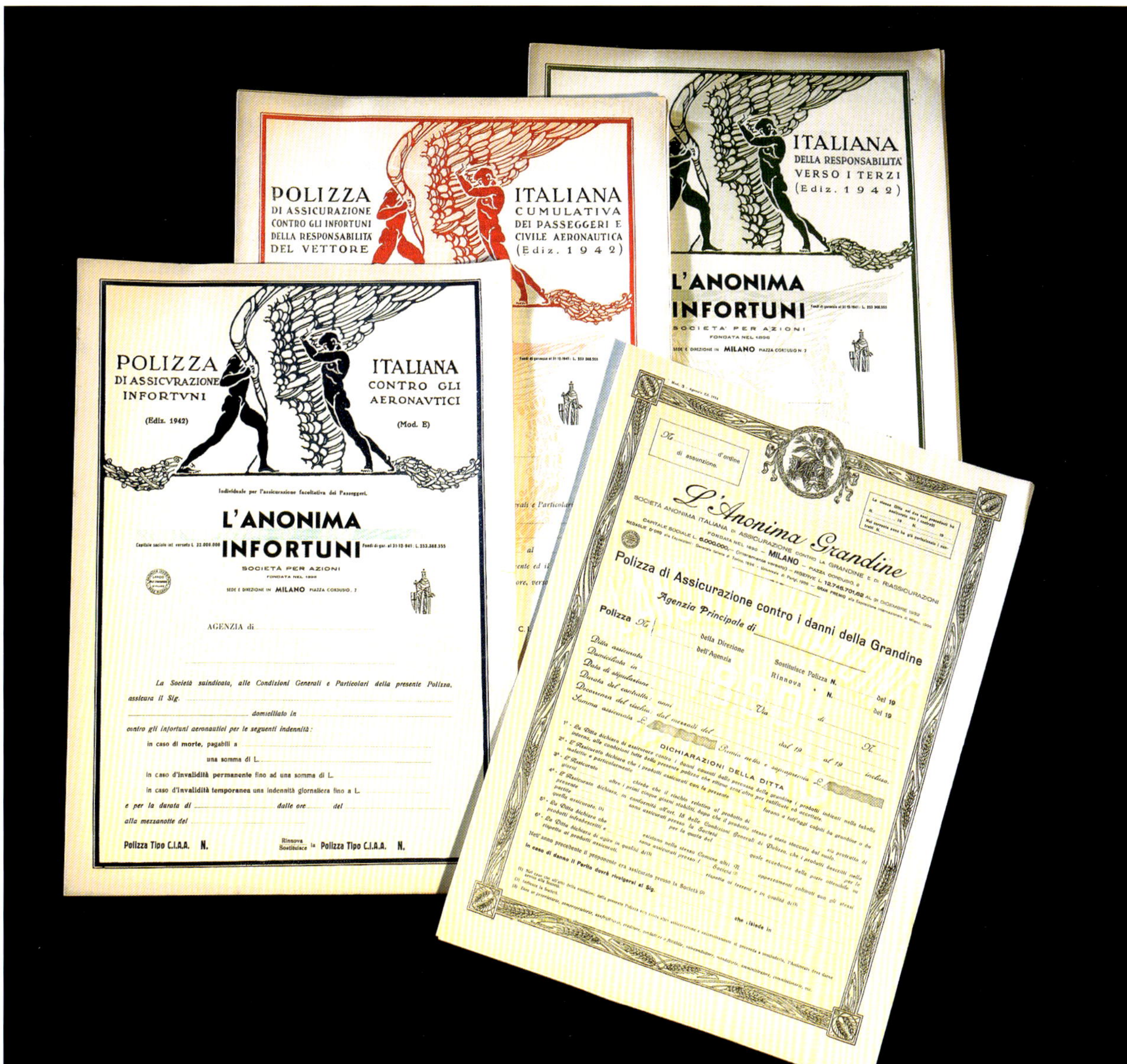

2.
Policies of the Anonima Infortuni and Anonima Grandine companies (twentieth century) [ASAG, *Direzione centrale, Ufficio delegato, Corrispondenza*, OGG001125161 and *Versamenti*, scheda 62440]

the Transport Division, and deputy manager of the general agency in Rome, respectively.
In carrying out their duties, they were accountable to the company's Management in Rome, i.e. to deputy chairman Giorgio Pitacco, to Michele Sulfina (who would officially leave the company at the end of the year to work in the capital in the capacity of "unidentified consultant") and to the legal consultant, Ranieri Babboni.
On September 8, Italy surrendered to the Anglo-American forces and signed the armistice. On September 14, the German troops launched operation *Wolkenbruch* (operation cloudburst) to gain control of Venezia Giulia and the provinces of Ljubljana and Istria that after the Armistice of Cassibile had been occupied by the Yugoslav partisans, and took hold of Trieste.
Despite the times, efforts were made to instill a degree of normalcy and manage complex technical and financial challenges, with many areas being temporarily outside the growth areas, including the southern part of the peninsula. Many of the staff who had been drafted, were dismissed and reinstated, while the casual staff were switched to occupational mobility and given severance bonuses in order to avoid immediate layoffs. As a precaution, the archive for the life division and other departments was relocated to Scodovacca near Cervignano, in the province of Udine; a weekly despatch was set up among the internal staff which included the clerk, Ugo Avian, who were assisted by local workers.
In November, after much thought, Volpi resigned as chairman and was replaced by his deputy, Antonio Cosulich.
In the spring of 1944 Trieste was hit by the first Allied bombing. By then the German military only occupied a few central, key locations, while Josip Broz's troops (also known as Tito) were set to conquer the city. By order of the commissioner of the *Adriatisches Küstenland* (the supreme commissioner of the Adriatic coast, comprising: the provinces of Friuli, Gorizia, Trieste, Istria, Ljubljana and the Kvarner region, together with the embedded territories of Sussak, Buccari, Ciabar, Castua and Veglia [respectively, Sušak, Bakar, Čabar, Kastav and Krk], which were all under German military administration led by Friedrich Rainer), about sixty of Generali's employees were recruited as "volunteers" for the work camp of Praproce in Istria at the foot of Monte Taiano [Slavnik], to construct the fortifications in defense of the eastern front [*fig.* 3].
In May 1945 Tito's supporters occupied Trieste and officially annexed it to Yugoslavia. The citizens of Trieste had to carry a Yugoslavian identity card, while the Italian residents that had arrived post 1918 were expelled. Eventually, the Allied and Yugoslav commands reached a temporary compromise over Trieste's occupation. On June 9, Tito reached an agreement that saw the Yugoslav troops withdraw behind the Morgan Line, a border that divided Venezia Giulia into the territories occupied by the Anglo-Americans and the Yugoslavs. The Allies then took control of the city and its hinterland: and thus the Allied Military Government (AMG) began to operate in this part of the region. For fear that the offices would be requisitioned by the partisans, some of the Central Head Office's rooms were put at the disposal of the British troops.
The 1946–1947 peace agreements established the Free Territory of Trieste (FTT)—its *status quo* was ratified in February 1947 with the Paris Treaty—a region under the aegis of the United Nations, divided in two: zone A comprised Trieste and its province and was under Allied control, zone B comprised the Karst plateau and the northern coast of Istria and was under Yugoslav control. With the Peace Treaty coming into force, the constitution of the FTT, and pursuant to article 3 of the charter, Assicurazioni Generali was legally considered a citizen of the FTT, thereby becoming a foreign company in Italy. In the face of such circumstances, and having duly considered the current situation and its possible political and economic ramifications, the Board resolved to put the matter of the relocation of the registered office to another city, specifically Rome,

Those of Praproce

The German military ruled that the companies conducting business in the city had to supply a number of people, proportionately to the number of their employees, to reinvigorate the Todt Organization (OT). Named after its owner and creator, Fritz Todt, the construction company first operated in Nazi Germany and later in the German-occupied territories, building infrastructure and fortifications by using forced labor.

In this instance, Generali's employees, who were recruited, created a booklet that comically described the vicissitudes in the labor camp.

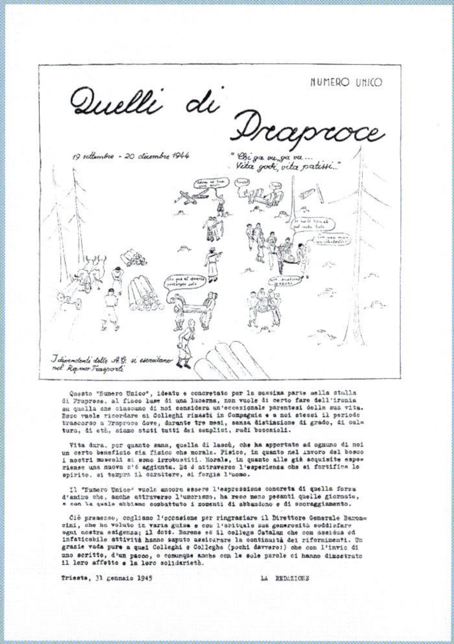

NUMERO UNICO

Quelli di Praproce

19 settembre - 20 dicembre 1944

"Chi ga ve, ga ve...
Vita godi, vita patissi..."

I dipendenti delle A.G. si esercitano nel Ramo Trasporti

Questo "Numero Unico", ideato e concretato per la massima parte nella stalla di Praproce, al fioco lume di una lucerna, non vuole di certo fare dell'ironia su quella che ciascuno di noi considera un'eccezionale parentesi della sua vita. Esso vuole ricordare ai Colleghi rimasti in Compagnia e a noi stessi il periodo trascorso a Praproce dove, durante tre mesi, senza distinzione di grado, di coltura, di età, siamo stati tutti dei semplici, rudi boscaioli.

Vita dura, per quanto sana, quella di lassù, che ha apportato ad ognuno di noi un certo beneficio sia fisico che morale. Fisico, in quanto nel lavoro del bosco i nostri muscoli si sono irrobustiti. Morale, in quanto alle già acquisite esperienze una nuova s'é aggiunta. Ed é attraverso l'esperienza che si fortifica lo spirito, si tempra il carattere, si forgia l'uomo.

Il "Numero Unico" vuole ancora essere l'espressione concreta di quella forza d'animo che, anche attraverso l'umorismo, ha reso meno pesanti quelle giornate, e con la quale abbiamo combattuto i momenti di abbandono e di scoraggiamento.

Ciò premesso, cogliamo l'occasione per ringraziare il Direttore Generale Baroncini, che ha voluto in varia guisa e con l'abituale sua generosità soddisfare ogni nostra esigenza; il dott. Barone ed il collega Catalan che con assidua ed infaticabile attività hanno saputo assicurare la continuità dei rifornimenti. Un grazie vada pure a quei Colleghi e Colleghe (pochi davvero!) che con l'invio di uno scritto, d'un pacco, o comunque anche con le sole parole ci hanno dimostrato il loro affetto e la loro solidarietà.

Trieste, 31 gennaio 1945 LA REDAZIONE

3.
Quelli di Praproce, reproduction
[Leone Veronese, "Una piccola pagina di storia delle Generali," *Bollettino delle Assicurazioni Generali* 8 (1995)]

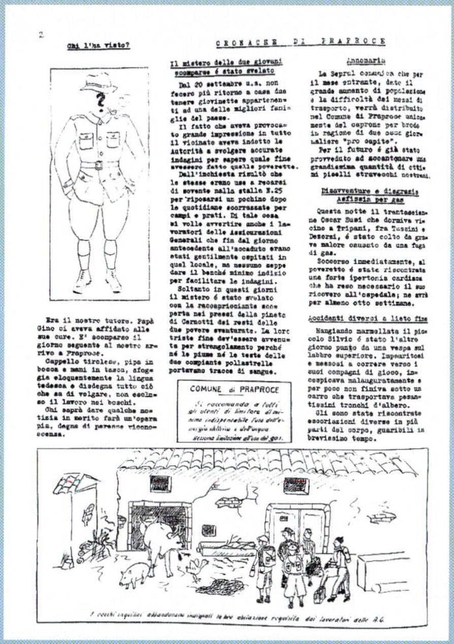

2

Chi l'ha visto?

CRONACHE DI PRAPROCE

Era il nostro tutore. Papà Gino ci aveva affidato alle sue cure. E' scomparso il giorno seguente al nostro arrivo a Praproce.

Cappello tirolese, pipa in bocca e mani in tasca, sfoggia eloquentemente la lingua tedesca e disdegna tutto ciò che sa di volgare, non escluso il lavoro nei boschi.

Chi saprà dare qualche notizia in merito farà un'opera pia, degna di perenne riconoscenza.

Il mistero delle due giovani scomparse é stato svelato

Dal 20 settembre u.s. non fecero più ritorno a casa due tenere giovinette appartenenti ad una delle migliori famiglie del paese.

Il fatto che aveva provocato grande impressione in tutto il vicinato aveva indotto le Autorità a svolgere accurate indagini per sapere quale fine avessero fatto quelle poverette.

Dall'inchiesta risultò che le stesse erano use a recarsi di sovente nella stalla N.25 per riposarsi un pochino dopo le quotidiane scorrazzate per campi e prati. Di tale cosa si volle avvertire anche i lavoratori delle Assicurazioni Generali che fin dal giorno antecedente all'accaduto erano stati gentilmente ospitati in quel locale, ma nessuno seppe dare il benché minimo indizio per facilitare le indagini.

Soltanto in questi giorni il mistero é stato svelato con la raccapricciante scoperta nei pressi della pineta di Cernotti dei resti delle due povere sventurate. La loro triste fine dev'essere avvenuta per strangolamento perché né le piume né le teste delle due compiante pollastrelle portavano tracce di sangue.

COMUNE di PRAPROCE

Si raccomanda a tutti gli utenti di limitare al minimo indispensabile l'uso dell'energia elettrica e dell'acqua. Nessuna limitazione all'uso del gas.

Annonaria

La Sepral comunica che per il mese entrante, dato il grande aumento di popolazione e la difficoltà dei mezzi di trasporto, verrà distribuito nel Comune di Praproce unicamente del caprone per brodo in ragione di due oncie giornaliere "pro capite".

Per il futuro é già stato provveduto ad accantonare una grandissima quantità di ottimi piselli stravecchi nostrani.

Disavventure e disgrazie
Asfissia per gas

Questa notte il trentaseienne Oscar Susi che dormiva vicino a Tripani, fra Tassini e Desorsi, é stato colto da grave malore causato da una fuga di gas.

Soccorso immediatamente, al poveretto é stata riscontrata una forte ipertonia cardiaca che ha reso necessario il suo ricovero all'ospedale; ne avrà per almeno otto settimane.

Accidenti diversi a lieto fine

Mangiando marmellata il piccolo Silvio é stato l'altro giorno punto da una vespa sul labbro superiore. Impauritosi e messosi a correre verso i suoi compagni di gioco, inciampicava malauguratamente e per poco non finiva sotto un carro che trasportava pesantissimi tronchi d'albero.

Gli sono state riscontrate escoriazioni diverse in più parti del corpo, guaribili in brevissimo tempo.

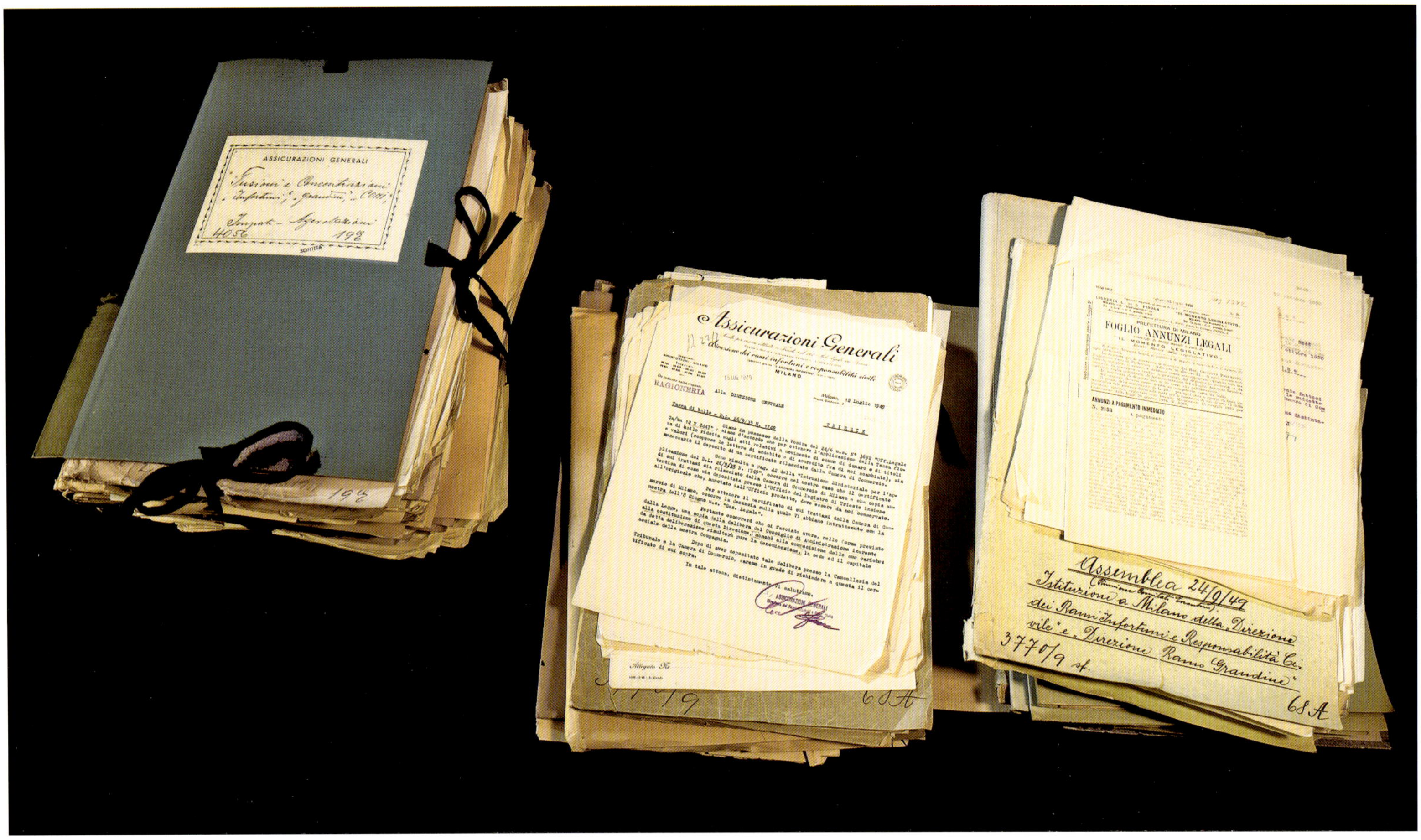

4.
Documents of the merger between the Anonima Infortuni and Anonima Grandine within Assicurazioni Generali (1939–1976)
[ASAG, *Direzione centrale, Consulenza legale, Pratiche esaurite,* U2GE046708 and U2GE046745]

to the Shareholders' Meeting for consideration. In which case, Trieste would remain a merely administrative center. The Shareholders' Meeting convened on January 29, 1947 and approved the motion, but not without some heated complaints from a number of shareholder who raised concerns about the possible repercussions on the city's economy. Nonetheless, the resolution put an end to an ongoing debate that, in the history of Generali, had resurfaced periodically in response to international factors, and that revoked the special powers conferred to the representatives in Rome (in actual fact, the Executive Committee had already approved the decision in May 1946, and the Board ratified it in August that year).

Having resolved the vexed question, the focus was on resuming business as usual and to mend the network in a Group that, over the years, had successfully established itself across the five continents through sheer tenacity and hard work. The merger of the Anonima Grandine and Anonima Infortuni was reexamined. Because in those challenging times, underscored by inflation and the discrepancy between income and expenditure, the prospect of harnessing work and resources into a single unit had become a matter of urgency.

Having the Executive Committee deemed the merger of the two subsidiaries with Assicurazioni Generali, an appropriate plan in view of the considerable savings that would result in staff and general expenditures, and having been assured of both parties' unanimous intent, at its meeting of May 2, 1947, it resolved that the studies on the matter should proceed as quickly as possible in cooperation with the companies' legal representatives. Present at the negotiating table were: the chairman of Anonima Grandine, Mario Abbiate, and the manager Baccolini; the general manager of Anonima Infortuni, Mario Padoa, and the general managers Michele Sulfina, Alberto Melchiori and Marco Ara, together with Chairman Cosulich for Generali. Once an initial framework for the project was agreed, though not without some concerns raised by Ara who failed to see its advantages, the dates for the individual Board meetings were set, at the meeting of May 31, 1947 it was resolved to incorporate the Managements of Anonima Grandine and Anonima Infortuni into Assicurazioni Generali [*fig.* 4]. The driving factor behind the decision was financial. By uniting the three Boards of Directors, Managements and general departments, and by merging the offices in a single location, the management costs would be significantly reduced with the added benefit of saving on tax. Additionally, the setup would be conducive to a unified investment strategy; the coordination and strengthening of the various branches; increased opportunities to develop the business abroad; and improving and updating the services and work procedures, all of which would result in clear savings. It was a well-known fact that the major international companies in Britain, Canada and Argentina, as well as the German company Allianz and the Italian RAS, had merged with their specialized affiliates once they had become successful. For all these reasons the merger between Anonime and Assicurazioni Generali was deemed not only necessary, but also pressing, in light of the time constraints on the exemption from transfer tax. After all, the parent company's urgency to merge into a single organization was not less felt by the subsidiaries. In this new context, the matter of whether the registered office should remain in Rome or be transferred to Milan was carefully considered. The consensus was that it would be prudent to keep the current situation, given that making immediate changes over such a short time might be perceived as hasty. In any event, the transfer of the registered office to Milan could only take place once the actual merger had occurred and the practical aspects for actualizing the transfer had been taken care of. Having all the benefits been considered, the deed for the merger by incorporation into Assicurazioni Generali was signed on February 12, 1948. (S.S.)

Gino Baroncini

1893
1970

Gino Baroncini was born in Imola on March 29, 1893 into a modest, peasant family [*fig.* 1]. The father was a miller and his mother an elementary school teacher; the parents desired a higher social status for their son and encouraged him to study bookkeeping, which he completed in 1913 in Bologna. His qualification was followed by the first employment in the capacity of teacher in a technical school in the province of Ferrara. Due to a slight limp, he was unfit for military service and did not experience the rite of passage for the young people of his generation: the trenches of World War I. Among the political struggles taking place during the first postwar period, the Romagna region was shaken and confused, marked by violence and political passions, filled with conflict not only between opposing Republican and Socialist factions, but also within the same Fascist movement of which Baroncini had been one of the first adherents, distinguishing himself as an exponent of the Fascist squads next to Leandro Arpinati, leader of Romagna's squads. Violence and devastation struck individual militants, party headquarters, labor union centers. In August 1921 Baroncini participated in transforming the Fascist movement into a party, and became a member of Emilia-Romagna's Central Committee. He expressed his radical convictions and opposition to the "pacification pact" with the Socialists and the Confederazione Generale del Lavoro, by writing in *L'Assalto*, a newspaper expressing the values of the unionists, Fascism's most extreme and uncompromising faction. However, his ill-concealed differences of opinion and his desire for autonomy, proved incompatible with the need for compromise of the prevailing movement already in power. Following fierce, also personal, clashes with Dino Grandi—a prominent leader in Bologna's Fascist movement from late 1923 through to early 1924—and feeling marginalized, Baroncini resolved to retire once and for all from politics. Meanwhile, he began his professional career within the local, cooperative world of health insurance, a network fertile in experiences, thanks to the efforts that the Republican and Socialist movements had poured into the sector since the start of the century. In 1919 he became the director of Mutue Agrarie di Assicurazione (hail and accidents) in Bologna; from there, began his interest in studying the challenges of this particular insurance category, and his attempts to revive a sector that had always been marked by great unpredictability. In 1922 he became the president of the Consorzio Cooperative Agricole. In 1932 the Mutue Agrarie di Assicurazione merges with Assicurazioni Generali. At this time, he meets Edgardo Morpurgo who appreciates his technical and organizational talents, so much so that in 1933, Assicurazioni Generali's chairman promotes him to manager of the Anonima Grandine in Milan, one of the company's first Italian subsidiaries. In 1934 Baroncini becomes chairman of the Alleanza Assicurazioni, a small company dealing in life insurance and targeting working class clients, recently acquired by Assicurazioni Generali. By the mid-1930s he had achieved a considerable career, which in addition to the titles mentioned earlier, also included: councilor of the Federazione Nazionale Fascista delle Imprese Assicuratrici; vice president of the Mutua Italiana Assicurazione Bestiame (MIAB); councilor of the Concordato Italiano Grandine. In 1932 he rejoined the Fascist Party with Arpinati's support and reclaimed his membership card, a symbol of loyalty to the regime, and which for a man of commerce and industry represented a valuable asset for negotiating in the State and public spheres. He had therefore achieved the state of expert insurer and was known for being involved in Fascism, both qualities that appealed to Edgardo Morpurgo who, as the racial campaign drew closer, in 1937 resolved to strengthen the company politically without having to make professionally-questionable appointments. Thus Baroncini becomes one of Assicurazioni Generali's three general managers, together with Michele Sulfina and Morpurgo. He would even retain his position under Giuseppe Volpi's new chairmanship (September 1938) providing Michele Sulfina, who should have renounced his post due to the anti-Semitic laws, with an official justification for having to support a newly-appointed manager.

After Italy joined the war, in September 1940 Baroncini and Volpi supported a proposal by the representatives of Germany's major insurance companies, to create a reinsurance company to fill the void that the wrecked operability of Lloyd's of London had left in the European reinsurance market. Thereby constituting what would become one of the largest companies in the private and public sectors in Italy—Assicurazioni Generali, Riunione Adriatica di Sicurtà (RAS), Istituto Italiano delle Assicurazioni (INA), Le Assicurazioni d'Italia (Assitalia)—and in Germany, Münchener Rück; thereby creating a monopoly to the detriment of the English and French enterprises.
Facilitating the inception of the Compagnia di Roma (as the group of reinsurance companies would be named), would turn out to be the worst charge that the Anglo American allies that occupied the Venezia Giulia would accuse him of. In July 1945 the Allied Military Government declared Baroncini "persona non grata" in Trieste, together with Assicurazioni Generali's deputy general manager Giulio Cleva, who during the war had chaired a number of subsidiaries in Central Europe (Prague's Moldavia; Budapest's Providentia; Leipzig's Deutscher Lloyd; Sofia's Vitocha) and was accused of being a collaborationist.
In reality Baroncini's position was complex. Between September 1943 and June 1945 the company experiences a dark period marked by serious danger. When the German troops occupied Trieste isolating it from the Italian territory, Sulfina was forced into hiding, Volpi was arrested in Rome by the Nazis, and the new chairman Cosulich was arrested on two occasions (in September 1944 at the request of the authorities in Salò, and in February 1945 by the Germans); hence it was no coincidence that Gino Baroncini was appointed managing director in Trieste, finding himself invested with the highest level of responsibility that a manager facing those events should bear.
Through the mediations between the German senior insurance executives and the chief administrative officer, Bruno Coceani, who from 1940 would become

1.
Gino Baroncini (1960)
[ASAG, *Presidenza e organi sociali, Presidenti e vicepresidenti, Gino Baroncini*, U2GE023967]

2.
Chairman Gino Baroncini reads the annual report at the Shareholders' General Meeting (1960); from left to right: Francesco Cincotti and Alberto Melchiori, general managers; Carlo Faina, deputy chairman; Baroncini; Giancarlo Frè, deputy chairman; Giuseppe Bufano and Franco Mannozzi, general managers.
[ASAG, *Presidenza e organi sociali, Presidenti e vicepresidenti, Gino Baroncini*, U2GE023967]

a member of the Board of Assicurazioni Generali, he was able to thwart the maneuvers of the invaders, which aimed to put the two companies in Trieste under compulsory administration and appropriate their sizeable wealth of technical provisions.
The laborious compromise was finalized in February 1944 with the appointment of two German administrators to the Board, and a German central manager (Karl Alexander Schaefer, Joseph Joham, Hans Ommert respectively), who were selected among a list of names suggested by the company and which mustn't have displeased the German authorities.
In June 1944, the appointment of a new Board comprised of members residing in Trieste enabled the company to continue its operations and maintain contacts with its Branches in occupied Europe; meanwhile, the government of Salò was also involved in a failed attempt to put the company under compulsory administration. The company also protected itself from the German's attempts to confiscate the dividends of non-Aryan shareholders. According to reports by the executives of the Comitato di Liberazione Nazionale (CLN), at this time Baroncini provided financial assistance to the Resistance. The German retreat was followed on May 1, 1945, with the occupation by the Yugoslav troops, the incarceration of Antonio Cosulich, chairman, Demetrio Economo, member of the Board, Oliviero Tripcovich, brother of member of the Board Mario who had managed to vanish. Baroncini's son, Giuseppe, was also arrested but released further to the payment of a ransom. The Yugoslav authorities declare the company national property and proceed to put it under compulsory administration, a measure that was circumvented with the appointment of a Slovenian official employed by the company. The Anglo-American allies that occupied Venezia Giulia subjected Gino Baroncini to a purging process and confiscation of his belongings; therefore, from 1945 through 1947 Gino Baroncini does not appear among the company's governing bodies. At that time, he also faced two trials in Bologna in connection to his past in the squadrismo and his activities in the

Fascist Party; in both instances he was acquitted in 1946. His offer to resign was rejected by the company.

It is fair to say that overall, his contribution is well regarded, given that he was able to protect the company's interests despite the ill-fate experienced in the city and territory of Trieste under various military occupations, and the company was able to preserve its corporate integrity, and retain a substantial portion of its operations despite the challenges and the destruction brought on by the war. In July 1947, after the purge was revoked following termination of the activity of the Epuration Commission, Baroncini rejoined the company in the capacity of general manager and maintaining positions of power for the following twenty years. Therefore, it can be said that he represented an element of continuity in a corporate history that was, nevertheless, destined to undergo profound renewal in the period following World War II.

As long as Michele Sulfina remained in service, he shared the position of managing director (from 1948), and that of deputy chairman (from 1956). It is likely that the first phase of the postwar reconstruction occurred with both the contributions. In 1953 the company could proudly state that, despite the loss of territories beyond the Iron Curtain, it had finally managed to fully reinstate its business portfolios to match pre-war values.

In 1956 Baroncini becomes deputy chairman, managing director, and general manager. In March 1960 he was appointed chairman while also keeping the positions of managing director and general manager; a concentration of powers that had previously been attained only by Edgardo Morpurgo [*fig.* 2].

In 1965, however, the enormous complexity of managing an international Group whose interests were spread across five continents, and which under Baroncini's chairmanship had been consolidated into subsidiaries and associated companies while at the same time introduced new foundations in African countries that had recently attained independence, it was advised he split his responsibilities and share the role of managing director with another, younger executive, the general manager Franco Mannozzi.

In 1968 Baroncini withdrew from active corporate life for health reasons, and was appointed honorary chairman.

He died in Bologna on October 31, 1970.

Sources

ASAG. *Direzione centrale, Servizio del personale, Posizioni personali.* U2GE050098, personnel file of Gino Baroncini, 1937–1980.

IRSML, b. XXXVIII, n. 8026 (3), Gino Baroncini, *Promemoria per le Assicurazioni Generali*, Trieste, June 8, 1945.

"Baroncini Gino." In *Biografia finanziaria italiana. Guida degli amministratori e dei sindaci delle società anonime per azioni*, edited by G. Casellato, Ezio Lodolini, Alessandro Welczowsky, 70. Rome: Ditta E. Armani, 1935.

"Tre testimonianze significative e un profilo." *Bollettino delle Assicurazioni Generali* 11–12 (1970).

Bibliography

De Felice, Renzo. *Mussolini il fascista, I. La conquista del potere: 1921–1925*. Turin: Einaudi, 1966.

Lyttelton, Adrian. *The Seizure of Power. Fascism in Italy, 1919–1929.* London: Weidenfeld and Nicolson 1973.

Marani, Angela. *Gino Baroncini: un capitano d'industria*, edited by Franco Merlini. Imola: Associazione Giuseppe Scarabelli, 2000.

Millo, Anna. *Trieste, le assicurazioni, l'Europa. Arnoldo Frigessi di Rattalma e la Ras.* Milan: Franco Angeli, 2004.

Simili, Filippo. *Gino Baroncini e il sindacalismo fascista bolognese.* Graduation thesis on Contemporary History. Bologna: University of Bologna, Faculty of Letters and Philosophy, 2004–2005.

Favaretto, Tito. "Lo sviluppo dell'attività internazionale delle Assicurazioni Generali tra il XIX e il XX secolo." In *Assicurare 150 anni di Unità d'Italia. Il contributo delle assicurazioni allo sviluppo del Paese*, edited by Paolo Garonna, 93-151. Rome: ANIA, 2011.

(A.M.)

An Iron Curtain from Stettin to Trieste

Italy is Reborn into a World Divided: The Age of the Superpowers

1946
1967

The World War II fulfilled what many historians and political scholars still today consider a constituent war, i.e. a conflict that because of its size and peculiarities gave way to the kind of upheavals that enacted radical and long lasting change on an international scale. An initial outcome of the postwar period, was the revolutionary practice of legitimately enabling the victors to legally pursue the losers on behalf of the international community, in trials for the crimes they had committed during the conflict. At the well-known Nuremberg trial [*fig.* 1], the surviving Nazi commanders were tried and convicted; some receiving the death penalty. The judgment was read on the night between September 30 and October 1, 1946. However, once they vanquished the Nazi peril, those very victors started to compete over the German intellects, by means of espionage and actual kidnappings, and resorting to a fierce financial and political opposition that culminated in that Winston Churchill described, "From Stettin in the Baltic to Trieste in the Adriatic, an Iron Curtain has descended across the Continent." This Iron Curtain would divide Europe and, metaphorically, the whole world.

Again, as in the World War I, the hotspot in the immediate postwar period was Venezia Giulia. More specifically, after the Yugoslav occupation of the region, the Trieste question resurfaced. At that time Trieste was the only point of debate because Istria, Fiume [Rijeka] and Dalmatia were firmly controlled by Tito's Yugoslavia, as set out by the 1947 Paris Peace Treaty, which triggered the exodus of about 300,000 people (not just Italians, but also numerous Slovene and Croatian collaborationists and anti-communists). People fled to preserve their national identities and to escape a type of communism that was settling behind Trieste, and which was becoming notorious for its massacres and ethnic cleansing. Trieste, still controlled by the Anglo-Americans, was therefore set to enjoy independent status as the Free Territory of Trieste (FTT); but the city found itself at the center of a dispute [*fig.* 2] that was temporarily resolved with the London Memorandum of October 1954, which declared that Trieste should be returned to Italy (zone A), but also that more Istrian territory (zone B) would be lost. In those troubled years, such a situation caused the city's exclusion from the extraordinary changes that manifested for the Italian people. Starting with an electoral process underscored by a universal suffrage that included women; followed by the constitutional referendum of June 2, 1946 that resulted in a victory for the Republic; and the election of a Constituent Assembly that would lay the legal foundations for the new Italian democracy, with the new Constitution coming into effect on January 1, 1948.

The elections that followed in April that same year, resulted in a clear victory for the Democrazia Cristiana led by Alcide De Gasperi, moving the socialist-communist component to the opposition and permanently ending the phase of alliance with the resistance. Thus commenced a long period of catholic power in Italy that would lead to the economic boom of the 1960s and cement Italy's western, pro-American position on the international, political arena. This status was certainly facilitated not only by the victors' decisions over the redistribution following the war, but also through the involvement of the so-called Marshall Plan (officially the European Recovery Program), which replaced the UNRRA (United Nations Relief and Rehabilitation Administration). The Marshall Plan consisted of a financial aid plan, launched by the United States in 1948 to assist the nations that had suffered grave destruction during the war. The program was essential to Italy's recovery, and was also extended to the eastern bloc countries. These however, were forced to decline, subsequent to the URSS's objections, which saw the program as a vehicle for capitalist penetration of its satellite states. Thereby, Europe underwent a complete division that was globally sanctioned by the constitution of supranational military organizations such as NATO (1949) on one side, and the Warsaw Pact (1955) on the other. The division reached its apex with the division of

1.
Some of the defendants at the Nuremberg Trial, who were accused of having committed war crimes and crimes against humanity

2.
1953: the people of Trieste take to the streets to demand the reunification of the city with Italy

3.
The American President John F. Kennedy, during a visit to West Berlin; on June 26, 1963 he gave a famous speech that ended with the statement: "Ich bin ein Berliner"

4.
Marines stationed in Korea in 1953

5.
A United States' airman taken prisoner in Vietnam in 1967

Germany into two parts in 1949: the capitalist system in the West with Bonn as the capital, and the Communist system in the East. The old capital Berlin, was divided into West Berlin (controlled by the United States, Great Britain and France), and East Berlin (the capital of DDR, Deutsche Demokratische Republik, controlled by the USSR). Through events that have become part of the collective imaginary, Berlin came to symbolize the cold war. Such events included the Berlin airlift to carry supplies to the city after the blockade of 1948–1949 imposed by the Soviet Union; the dividing wall built by the Soviet Union in 1961 to stop the eastern population from escaping; and the unforgettable speech by American President J.F. Kennedy on his visit to West Berlin on June 26, 1963 [*fig.* 3], which ended with the declaration: "Ich bin ein Berliner" to acknowledge the complex situation of the people of Berlin, surrounded by the Communist State, and who symbolized the universal struggle for freedom. Those years were underscored by the constant threat of conflict, as was evident from every sphere of human activity, and which fortunately did not eventuate in military conflict. The world was paralyzed by the nuclear threat, the premise of which rested on the doctrine of "mutual assured destruction" from which no one could escape. There were, however, localized conflicts such as the Korean War (1950–1953) and that in Vietnam (which from 1960 went through various stages). These conflicts, which were sparked by the urge to contain the expansion of Communism across the globe, were the most dramatic [*figs.* 4–5], yet they clearly distinguished between conventional warfare and nuclear war.

While some key countries tried to extricate themselves from the superpowers' control—those of the future non-aligned movement that at the Bandung Conference of 1955 would be led by India (which attained independence in 1947), Egypt, Yugoslavia and Communist China, which from 1966 would undergo a dramatic cultural revolution under Mao Zedong—the decolonization movement provided uncertain independence for Africa and Asia's emerging economies, which had recently freed themselves of European colonialism only to find themselves under the supremacy of the United States and the USSR.

Similarly, the European continent found itself yielding to the demands of the two superpowers, and, as a result, its history followed two divergent paths. In the West, the doctrine of Europeanism emerged, which aimed for unity through consensus and readily accepted political rights. These values could be pursued because, after Germany's defeat, there was no politically strong and naturally dominant power left on the continent. In Zurich on September 19, 1946, Churchill suggested the creation of the United States of Europe, which caused quite a stir given that the social and political situation still felt the hatred from the recent conflict. The Frenchman Robert Schuman (inspired by Jean Monnet, commissioner for economic planning), proposed to combine the production and consumption of coal and steel, and to create an institution that was open to all European States, beginning with France and Germany.

This was the first time that the States were asked to delegate part of their sovereignty to a supranational, binding body. In order not to repeat the mistakes of the first postwar period, which unleashed Germany's revanchism, France offered Germany the opportunity for recovery by joining the free and democratic Western Europe. On April 18, 1951 the European Coal and Steel Community (ECSC) was established; marking the first organization by the Inner Six (France, West Germany, Italy, Belgium, Netherlands and Luxembourg). This was followed on March 25, 1957 by the Treaty of Rome, which established the European Economic Community (ECSC) and the European Atomic Energy Community (EAEC); together with the ECSC these two bodies lead the way to the European Community Charter: the starting point for the European unification some decades later.

While Western Europe bravely undertook a challenging journey to provide history with a new course of pacification and integration, the same did not come to pass behind the Iron Curtain where the USSR kept extending its supremacy. A glimmer of change within the totalitarian regime was anticipated in 1953, with Stalin's death and the start of the de-Stalinization process, which shifted the accountability for the atrocities away from the Communist ideology, and attributed them to the Georgian dictator's delusions of grandeur. The denunciation of such crimes on February 1956, at the 20th Congress of the Communist Party by the new leader Nikita Khrushchev, provided a glimmer of hope for the liberalization of Communism. A hope that quickly faded when, a few months later, on November 4, the tanks of the Warsaw Pact [*fig.* 6] rolled into the streets of Budapest to crush any reformist attempts by the Hungarian people. The heroic revolt [*fig.* 7] was left to its own devices by the West, which in those days was engrossed in resolving the issue of the Egyptian nationalization of the Suez Canal. The French and English military's intervention to protect their interests, was swiftly curtailed by the United States, which irrefutably demonstrated the European powers' subjection to the United States. The incident also involved Israel—the Jewish state founded in 1948 to redress the sins of the world for the Shoah, and which was constantly under threat from the Palestinians on whose territory the new state was established—and the surrounding Arab states, which made the Middle East one of the main sources of tension and a threat to world peace.

Meanwhile, on the opposite side of the globe, peace appeared to be shattered when the two superpowers became engaged in a standoff. Between 1961 and 1962 the Soviets installed a number of missile launch facilities in defense of Fidel Castro's [*fig.* 8] Communist Cuba, right in front of the United States. At no other time in history was an escalation into a full-scale nuclear war that close. Fortunately, the Soviets announced that they would not force the United States' military blockade and that they would withdraw the missiles, which concluded the world's fear of the inevitable end. But for this match between enemy and rival systems, the world was not enough and so a new frontier opened up to the competition in military, scientific and technological research; and in this race to conquer space, the USSR was initially in the lead. On October 4, 1957 it launched the first artificial satellite in history, the *Sputnik 1*; the following month it sent the first living creature into orbit, the dog Lajka (despite knowing that, at best, she would not survive reentry into the atmosphere). After a few more years of development in space technology, it was the human's turn: on April 12, 1961 Yuri Gagarin orbited the earth onboard the spacecraft *Vostok 1* [*fig.* 9]. While the Soviets pursued the launch into space of men and women (Valentina Tereshkova being the first on June 16, 1963), which were interspersed by tragedies that were never publicly announced, but witness by radio amateurs who were able to intercept dramatic communications between the spacecrafts and the Bajkonur base; the Americans were experiencing a considerable technological lag. However, the apparent disadvantage gave President Kennedy the opportunity to describe the new frontier to the American people and to set a goal: to reach the moon within the decade. The space age was taking off, and human kind began looking skyward, perceiving it as less distant or unreachable. In this at least, people of all faiths and ideologies were united. (D.R.)

6–7.
Two pictures of the Hungarian revolution of 1956: Soviet tanks rolling into Budapest; insurgents waving the national flag

8.
The Cuban and Soviet Union leaders in a lithograph depicting the political alliance between the two Communist regimes

9.
The launch of the *Vostok 1* spacecraft manned by Yuri Gagarin, the first man in space

In Brief

1946
July 5: French dressmaker Louis Réard invents the modern two-piece bathing suit (a similar garment had been worn in ancient times), which he names "bikini," after the atoll where the atomic bomb tests were carried out.

1947
March 12: American President Harry Truman introduces the Truman Doctrine, a foreign policy aimed at counter acting the expansion of Communism by supporting free countries, and which will set the stage for the Marshall Plan.

1948
May 14: declaration of the establishment of the State of Israel; the following day, the armies of the neighboring Arab States wage an attack and the conflict leads to the exodus of over 700,000 Palestinians.

1948
December 26: Cardinal Mindszenty, Primate of Hungary, is incriminated by the Communist regime, tortured and imprisoned. In 1956 he is released by the revolutionaries and granted asylum by the United States embassy.

1949
February 19: the American Ezra Pound is awarded the prestigious Bollingen Prize for poetry; accused of treason for being a Fascist sympathizer, from 1945 he was incarcerated in a psychiatric hospital.

1953
June 2: coronation of Queen Elizabeth II following a period of mourning; her reign which commenced sixteen months earlier with the death of King George VI, since 2015 has become the longest in British history.

1953
July 26: the revolutionaries' unsuccessful attack of the Moncada Barracks in Santiago de Cuba marks the start of a revolution that in six years brings Fidel Castro and Ernesto Che Guevara's *barbudos* to power.

1954
July 31: an Italian expedition led by Ardito Desio conquers the K2; the summit is reached by Achille Compagnoni and Lino Lacedelli, with the crucial support of Walter Bonatti, who would be acknowledged many years later.

1954
November 4: the 1952 Nobel Peace Prize is awarded to medical missionary Albert Schweitzer, who in 1953 failed to collect the award because he didn't want to leave the hospital he founded in Lambaréné, Gabon.

1957
March 6: with the words "Ghana, your beloved country is free forever," Kwame Nkrumah announces the former Gold Coast's independence; it's the first Sub-Saharan country to decolonize.

1958
October 28: Angelo Giuseppe Roncalli, Patriarch of Venice, is elected pope taking the name John XXIII; in 1962 he brings about a turning point for the Church by convening the Second Vatican Council.

1959
March 10: the people of Lhasa's uprising against the Chinese occupation of Tibet ends in a violent crackdown by the Beijing troops; the Dalai Lama flees to India to avoid incarceration.

1959
October 29: the indomitable Gauls, Asterix and Obelix make their debut in the world of comic magazines; the adventures are drawn by Albert Uderzo and written by René Goscinny, who also authors Lucky Luke.

1960
September 3: Livio Berruti wins the 200-meter dash at the Rome Olympics; the event also awards gold to champion marathoner Abebe Bikila, who runs barefoot, and the boxers Nino Benvenuti and Cassius Clay.

1962
October 5: preview screening of the Bond movie, *Dr. No*, the first film based on the character by Ian Fleming; Sean Connery plays the lead role supported by Bond girl, Ursula Andress.

1963
January 3: the Beatles explode onto the world stage with a tour of Scotland and abroad; in the recently finalized lineup are: John Lennon, Paul McCartney, Ringo Starr and George Harrison.

1963
August 28: about 250,000 people march on Washington demanding civil rights for African Americans; the march culminates in Martin Luther King Jr.'s famous speech remembered for the peroration, "I have a dream."

1963
November 22: America mourns President John F. Kennedy, who was assassinated in Dallas; Lee Harvey Oswald, the man accused of his murder, will in turn be shot dead while being transferred to prison.

1964
May 14: ceremony during the construction of the Aswan High Dam on Nile River basin; to prevent the flooding of the temples of Abu Simbel, the monuments are dismantled and rebuilt on higher ground.

1964
August 27: *Mary Poppins*, Walt Disney's movie based on the children's books by Pamela Lyndon Travers, debuts at Grauman's Chinese Theatre in Hollywood; the magical nanny is played by Julie Andrews.

1966
July 30: England, host of the FIFA World Cup tournament, wins the title. In the first round, North Korea surprisingly defeats Italy and finishes above them; "fatal Korea" becomes synonymous with ludicrous defeat.

1966
September 8: NBC airs the first episode of the new television series, *Star Trek*, which follows the adventures of the Spaceship *Enterprise* and its crew, led by Captain James T. Kirk and Science Officer Spock.

1966
November 4: Italy is ravaged by strong weather; the Arno river floods, causing dozens of casualties and serious damage Florence's artistic heritage; the emergency volunteers are named, "mud angels".

1967
May 28: the 65-year-old Englishman Francis Chichester, who nine months earlier set sail from Plymouth on his yawl, completes the solo circumnavi-gation of the globe, having passed the three great capes.

Mario Abbiate

1872
1954

Born in Genoa on February 14, 1872, Mario Abbiate dedicated the first part of his public life, from the Giolitti era to the advent of Fascism, to his commitment to introduce social security in Italy [*fig.* 1].
Educated in a family that valued the Risorgimento (his father Giuseppe volunteered under Garibaldi), in 1893 he graduated with a degree in literature and law at the Turin University, which in those days was an environment bustling with intellectual activity and dominated by illustrious teachers such as Arturo Graf, in Italian literature, and Salvatore Cognetti De Martiis in political economy and sociology.
Following his graduation, he moved to the province of Vercelli where the family owned agricultural lands, and commenced his political experiences in the local Council, which in liberal Italy, constituted the true center of political life. He became city councilor of Caresana in 1895, councilor for the province of Vercelli in 1902, municipal councilor of Vercelli in 1905. In 1899 he interrupted his electoral experience to become a member of the provincial administrative Council, a supervisory body of the local authorities, which gave him the opportunity to learn all about the administrative apparatus' operations.
In 1900 he joins Vercelli's Associazione Popolare Liberale, an organization that was not unfamiliar with radical democrats, the mission of which was to attain compulsory elementary education, and streamline the State's bureaucratic structure. Also in 1900 he joined the Federazione Italiana delle Società di Mutuo Soccorso, of which he would be the president from 1912 through 1920, while also being nominated councilor of the Lega Nazionale delle Cooperative.
Thus he demonstrated a personal interest in the issues of the civil society that was establishing the means for the underprivileged to manage the uncertainties they faced and join the existing debates between the Democratic and Socialist forces over the need to introduce a comprehensive legislation on social security and pension.
A liberal who embraced progressive reform, he believed in the need to widen the existing social and political rights from the narrow basis of representation on which the liberal State had rested since its constitution. His legal training led him to consider the legal and regulatory aspects of the problems facing the workforce, according to solution-based principles, in which the State's was the moderator and governor of the class struggle.
In 1903, with the support of Filippo Turati and the economist and socialist collaborator Giovanni Montemartini, he appears among the promoters of the Consiglio Superiore del Lavoro, an advisory body to government, of which he was part until it was abolished by the Fascists in 1923.
Elected member of Parliament in the Constituency of Vercelli in 1909, he joined the radical group at the Chamber of Deputies and fought tirelessly to ensure that the compulsory workplace accident insurance, was extended to other covers such as old age, sickness, and work-related disability. He proposed that the State take a more active role in protecting the workforce, and a mixed insurance plan that was complementary to those in the private sector.
The postwar period provided more favorable conditions in support of his ideals. In 1919, having been appointed senator of the Kingdom, further to the proposal by the Prime Minister Francesco Saverio Nitti, he first joins the Unione Democratica Sociale, followed by the more radical group Unione Democratica. In the same year he became the president of the Ufficio Nazionale per il Collocamento, which was established after the compulsory insurance against involuntary unemployment created the same year, and is also nominated as employers' representative and vice president of the Cassa Nazionale per le Assicurazioni Sociali, which can be regarded as a precursor of the Istituto Nazionale della Previdenza Sociale (INPS).
Meanwhile, he resumed the international activities that the conflict had interrupted. From 1906 he was the secretary-general of the Federazione Internazionale della Mutualità, for which he had drafted the charter; after the war he was part of the Bureau In-

ternational du Travail in Geneva, for three years. As a scholar of social issues also pertaining to agricultural work, he was nominated as representative for Italy at the Istituto Internazionale di Agricoltura, an organization that can be considered at the origin of what would become the Food and Agriculture Organization (FAO) after the second world war.

In 1919 he was nominated president of a government commission responsible for drafting a proposal for legislature on compulsory health insurance. Reformulating certain elements of a more radical project he had been working on since 1916, the commission proposed a reform that closely resembled a universal model of welfare, which failed due to the opposition coming from conservative interests.

Between May and June 1920, he was a minister for Nitti's second government, first as Minister for Industry, Trade and Labor; then taking on the newly established Ministry of Labor and Social Security, which should have dedicated itself to these specific issues. Despite the short duration of his charges, he managed to propose the reform of the Consiglio Superiore del Lavoro, in which the joint representation between workers and employers had the powers of a legislative delegation, almost an "agreement between manufacturers" for the development of social citizenship.

But those were the last signs of a political phase that had exhausted its chances of reviving Giolitti's design for mediating the social forces.

Abbiate was aware that since the inception of Mussolini's government, Fascism negated all those principles upon which liberal Italy was built. In 1925, after repeatedly expressing his disapproval in the senate over what had already become a repressive and anti-liberal regime, he retired from public life and moved to Milan. Nonetheless, due to the institutional structure and workings of the senate, which then was a royally appointed body, he would not decline an invitation to take part in a senatorial commission for agriculture between 1939 and August 1943.

1.
Chairman Mario Abbiate giving a speech at a meeting of the General Council of Assicurazioni Generali on June 13, 1953. From the left: deputy chairman Mario Tripcovich, Mario Abbiate, managing directors and general managers Michele Sulfina and Gino Baroncini.
[From *Bollettino delle Assicurazioni Generali* 7 (1953), 16]

2.
Letter signed by Mario Abbiate, in which he accepts the appointment as managing director of Assicurazioni Generali (January 15, 1947)
[ASAG, *Direzione centrale, Servizio del personale, Posizioni personali*, U2GE050074]

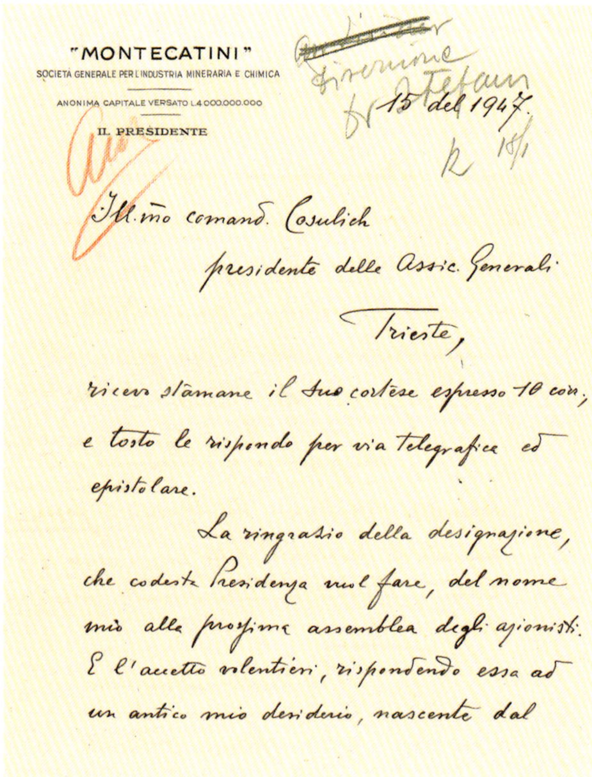

"MONTECATINI"
SOCIETÀ GENERALE PER L'INDUSTRIA MINERARIA E CHIMICA
ANONIMA CAPITALE VERSATO L.4.000.000.000
IL PRESIDENTE

Ill.mo comand. Cosulich
presidente delle Assic. Generali
Trieste,

ricevo stamane il Suo cortese espresso 10 corr., e tosto le rispondo per via telegrafica ed epistolare.

La ringrazio della designazione, che codesta Presidenza vuol fare, del nome mio alla prossima assemblea degli azionisti. E l'accetto volentieri, rispondendo essa ad un antico mio desiderio, nascente dal

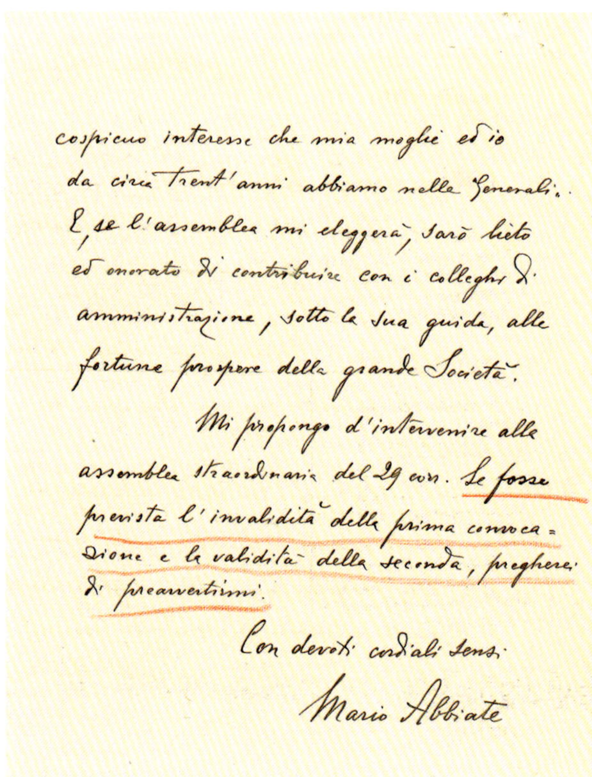

cospicuo interesse che mia moglie ed io da circa trent'anni abbiamo nelle Generali. E, se l'assemblea mi eleggerà, sarò lieto ed onorato di contribuire con i colleghi di amministrazione, sotto la Sua guida, alle fortune prospere della grande Società.

Mi propongo d'intervenire alla assemblea straordinaria del 29 corr. Se fosse prevista l'invalidità della prima convocazione e la validità della seconda, pregherei di preavvertirmi.

Con devoti cordiali sensi.

Mario Abbiate

In fact, during the 1920s and 1930s he devoted himself to farming his lands in Lombardy, introducing land reclamation works and new agricultural and breeding programs.

Following the Liberation, in 1945 Mario Abbiate returned to public life as a member of the Consulta Nazionale and, after a constitutional order confirmed a senatorial seat in the senate's first term of the Republic. Among the Milanese business community, he was well-known and respected also for his managerial skills, which he'd demonstrated when running a small manufacturing plant belonging to his wife's family; but mostly for refusing to compromise with Fascism. This set him apart as a member of a new ruling class that identified with the new democratic institutions. In March 1946 he was invited to chair the first Board of Directors elected after the war for the company Montecatini, a position he held until 1948. Also in 1946 and thanks to his farming experience, he became chairman of the Anonima Grandine, a subsidiary of Assicurazioni Generali; the following year, in May 1947 the subsidiary, together with the Anonima Infortuni, would merge with the company as part of a production restructure strategy.

Thus, Abbiate became part of Assicurazioni Generali's Board at a very sensitive time [*fig.* 2]. The company had recently resolved to relocate its registered office to Rome to keep it on Italian soil, if the Free Territory of Trieste actually were to be realized as was expected (but eventually not implemented, as later would be known), further to the peace treaty signed in February 1947 between Italy and the winning powers.

Additionally, the loss of the central European markets including those behind the Iron Curtain, and the loss of the company's assets in the war then subjected to long compensatory procedures, demanded a comprehensive recapitalization plan in order to ensure recovery, and which could only be pursued by turning to the Italian financial market, and which would in fact be accomplished by increasing the share capital fivefold between 1947 and 1953.

In 1948 Mario Abbiate is promoted to Assicurazioni Generali's highest office. His chairmanship signified the company's intention to maintain its privileged ties to Italy. From his part, in carrying out his mandate Abbiate would recall—as he would note in 1950 in the company's *Bollettino*—the same values that had inspired him throughout his public life, and which had remained relevant: savings, reciprocity, association, understood as the foundations of insurance and the guarantee for prosperity and social cohesion.
Having requested not to be re-elected chairman due to health reasons connected to his advanced age, at the end of his term of office in June 1953, he is co-opted from the Executive Committee.
He died in Milan on June 5, 1954.

Bibliography

"L'augurale saluto del Presidente." *Bollettino delle Assicurazioni Generali* 1 (1950): 1.
"Alla memoria del sen. Abbiate." *Bollettino delle Assicurazioni Generali* 6–7 (1954): 55–56.
Mario Abbiate, 1872–1954. Milan: Officine Grafiche Elli & Pagani, 1956.
Mario Abbiate nel suo tempo e contro il suo tempo: discorsi di mezzo secolo, [edited by] Guido Maria Baldi. Vercelli: Tip. editrice "La Sesia", 1958.
Abbiate Mario, www.senato.it.
Quaranta, Flavio. "Alle origini dello stato sociale in Italia: le proposte di Mario Abbiate per una riforma integrale della previdenza al tempo della grande guerra." *Bollettino storico vercellese* 2 (2005): 131–54.
—. "Le origini dell'assicurazione contro gli infortuni agricoli e il ruolo svolto da Mario Abbiate." *Rivista di storia dell'agricoltura* 2 (2008): 3–36.
—. "Mario Abbiate nel novantesimo anniversario dell'istituzione del Ministero per il lavoro e la previdenza sociale." *Rivista degli infortuni e delle malattie professionali* 1 (2010): 163–82.
—. "I sindaci dell'età giolittiana." In *Vercellesi illustri. I sindaci cittadini tra Otto e Novecento*, edited by Antonino Ruffino, 107–58. Vercelli: Vercelli Viva, 2014.
—. "Mario Abbiate, la grande guerra e la riforma dello Stato sociale in Italia." In *Il Vercellese e la grande guerra*, edited by Giovanni Ferraris, 529–61. Vercelli: Società Storica Vercellese, 2015.
(A.M.)

The Organization Post World War II
Business Resumes Despite a Loss of Assets

1945
1954

The first meeting of the Board after the Liberation, held in Trieste on June 21, 1945, provides insight into the extensive problems that the company faced in order to reinstate normalcy in the insurance business following the World War II. At that time, in Trieste it was not yet possible to transmit or receive any regular news and no one knew anything about Germany, where the company had substantial interests, nor of the countries in the Russian block; in Rome, it was difficult to communicate with the outside world as well. In fact, any exchanges with the Allies were limited to communications with the United States because: "Practically, the Allies' attitude is to keep all trade relations restricted to those between Government and Government."

Only gradually was it possible to piece together a clear overview of the situation in the various regions, to gather the data to ascertain the damages to the life and non-life divisions, the cash losses, the damage to the company property resulting from the bombings and the occupation, and to prepare the 1945 financial report for the Head Office and the numerous foreign subsidiaries.

So began the company's years of intense diplomatic negotiations, which called upon many individuals to help release seized property and resume business activities in those countries in which the business permits had been withdrawn. Evidently, the problem of the frozen assets abroad was a government matter to be addressed within the framework of the peace agreements signed between Italy and the other countries; nonetheless, the company closely followed the negotiations and in some cases was actively engaged through its representatives' work on the committees responsible for the timely assessment of problems relating to insurance. Memos and written requests on behalf of the company, sometimes coupled with those of Riunione Adriatica di Sicurtà (RAS), were submitted formally and informally to Italian and foreign ambassadors, legislative committees, and numerous Italian government offices.

The sources available in the Historical Archive to piece together these years are rich and varied; from the minutes of the Board and the Executive Committee that faithfully record the negotiations taking place in the different countries, to the documents produced by the offices concerned (legal affairs, foreign operations, representative office, special accounts).

The participants in this demanding and pain-staking work were numerous because the political and diplomatic challenges were many and complex. First the chairmen: foremost Antonio Cosulich, and from 1948 Mario Abbiate, then from 1953 Mario Tripcovich, who all travelled to Rome frequently to meet Italian and foreign ambassadors and ministers; and to Paris, to follow the peace agreement negotiations. The liaisons with the new Italian ministries were nurtured by the representative office, specifically by Ranieri Babboni—who was also the first president of the Associazione Nazionale fra le Imprese Assicuratrici (ANIA), which succeeded the Fascist Federation—and Berardo Ruggiero, both were lawyers who worked in Rome during the difficult war years (and Ruggiero for many more decades yet) [*fig.* 1].

In 1944–1945 they were joined by Michele Sulfina and Marco Ara, who worked with them in an unofficial capacity and played a key role in relaunching Assicurazioni Generali's business in the postwar period ("Here we work with great class with Sulfina, M. Ara and the others," letter from Babboni to general manager Giulio Cleva, Rome, June 15, 1945).

In relation to general managers: Sulfina, Ara and Gino Baroncini, it must be noted that after the Liberation, Italy's new political-governmental framework affected the company's internal structure as well. The most notable changes concerned the reintegration of the Jewish staff and the epuration procedures applied to the supporters of the Partito Nazionale Fascista, the Repubblica of Salò and the German occupation—to those who had benefited personally from their political affiliations. Amidst this tangled governance framework addressing the sensitive issue of

1.
Timber and sand bags protect the windows of the Palazzo delle Assicurazioni Generali used as a bomb shelter (Rome, June 18, 1940).

This building in Via Nomentana 231–233 in Rome is the property of Assicurazioni Generali. In the late 1930s numerous government measures were implemented to defend built-up areas from the threat of air raids, among them, new buildings were required to build bomb shelters for the tenants. Such measures were intensified after Italy entered the war on June 10, 1940. The company also built shelters and made arrangements to protect its buildings form air raids in Italy and abroad, usually by strengthening and isolating the basements as in this building in Via Nomentana. The minutes of the governing bodies record that building suffered some damage around July 25, 1943, a date close to the allied forces' first bombing of Rome on July 19

The East Department

2.
Geographical map of the regions of operation under the East department (Trieste, 1912)
[ASAG, *Direzione centrale, Direzione per l'oriente, Corrispondenza*, scheda 63988]

Before the creation of the foreign operations department, the company's operations, administration and accounting divisions abroad were managed by the foreign agencies secretariat. While most European regions were managed directly by the central secretariat, the foreign agencies secretariat looked after Bulgaria and Greece and, more importantly, all those regions beyond Europe. The East department, which was specifically responsible for present-day Greece, Albania, Turkey, Bulgaria, Syria, Lebanon, Egypt and Tunisia, was probably the precursor of the foreign agencies secretariat that eventually absorbed it [*fig.* 2]. The foreign agencies were responsible for managing increasingly complex problems, such as the unique financial and political situation in each country, legislation on insurance, the knowledge of contracts and agreements between agencies and buyers. With the closure of the foreign agencies secretariat in 1939, the management of operations was assigned to the office for organization and development; the responsibilities strictly relating to the production of insurance were given to the respective technical divisions; while accounting was transferred to the industrial accounting department. Since November 1938, the personnel department was already handling the administration of all Italian and foreign staff, pursuant to: "A restructure of administrative services with the inclusion of new officers" (Rossi's letter to the Central Head Office in Trieste, July 4, 1945), following the forced resignations of all Jewish staff members.

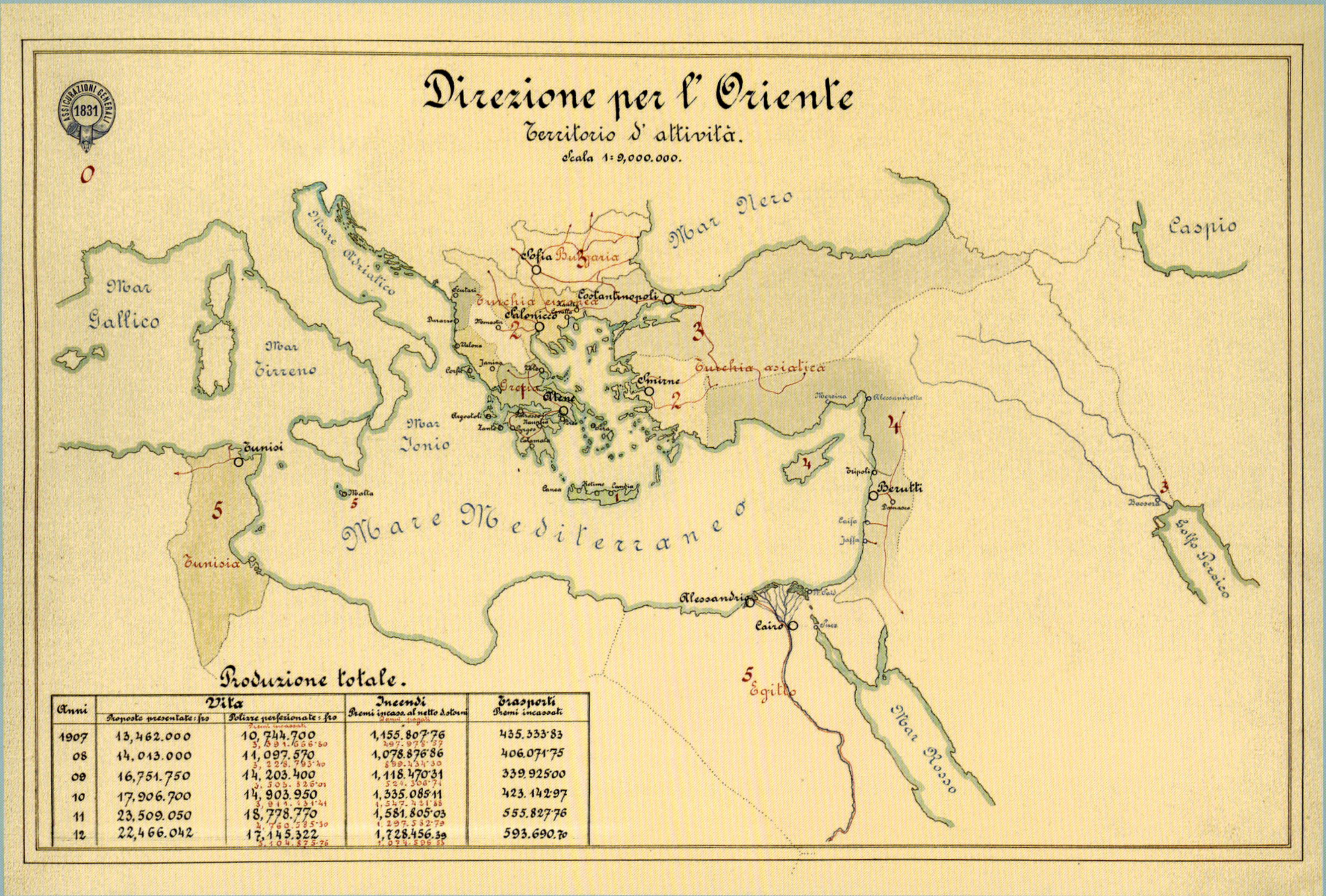

epuration, the situation in Venezia-Giulia was even more complex. There, the legislation of the American military authority was in force in addition to Italian law; a unique situation that imbued the local expulsions with characteristics that were vastly different from the rest of Italy.

The racial laws had been revoked by Royal Decree in January 1944, but in Venezia-Giulia in 1945, with a general order by the Allied Military Government (AMG). Since 1938 the racial laws had determined that Jewish employees could not even work in private insurance companies; the only exception being those "discriminated" Jews who had been exonerated on special merits. Ara resigned in 1938, shortly after Edgardo Morpurgo; Sulfina who was not affected by the racial laws was dismissed in 1943 during the German occupation, though by that time he had already formally stepped back from his managerial responsibilities. Ara and Sulfina worked in Rome until June 1945, when the Board determined they should be reinstated as general managers. Sulfina's journey was more convoluted because soon after, in September 1945, he faced epuration by the AMG and was dismissed from all responsibilities. The archival material does not reveal the official motivation for this decision, but from other sources, it is understood that another such order was issued against the director of RAS, Arnoldo Frigessi, when the Allied Control Commission suspected Frigessi and Sulfina of negotiating agreements between Italian and German companies. In any case, the matter was eventually shelved and Sulfina returned to work on October 14, 1946.

At the time, Generali undertook its own internal epuration process. During the Yugoslav occupation of Trieste in May 1945, the company used an indirect staff ballot to appoint an internal committee to submit to the chairmanship a list of people to be banished from the company. At that level, no specific legislation on epuration had yet been drafted, so this first commission did not undertake any reviews and eventually split up, only to regroup according to the regulations set out by the Allied Governments in October that year. The commission was chaired by Edoardo Buda (president of section IV of the Epuration Commission of First Instance in Trieste, which presided over private enterprises), and an advisory committee comprising eleven of Generali's employees including: Giuseppe Segneri; a staff representative (Bruno Veneziani); and a company representative (Nicolò Linder, replaced by Oreste Lago in March 1946). According to the documentation in the Historical Archive (which contains some of the unofficial minutes of the trials presided by the Commission in January 1946, and the AMG's epuration notices for about fifty-six employees), Generali's Commission compiled first-hand a list of about fifty people to be banished, including Biagio Marin and Bruno de Finetti, and contemplated various measures that ranged from periods of leave without pay, to dismissal in fewer cases. Among the highest-ranking positions on the list was that of general manager Baroncini. Further measures for Assicurazioni Generali's staff came into effect in 1947. It's not easy to retrace Baroncini's journey. Having been absent from company life since May 1945, he appealed the dismissal even though he hadn't been sentenced by the Epuration Commission, which however, did terminate his governance activities on June 30, 1947. The first Executive Committee meeting in which his presence is recorded again is dated July 25, 1947. Baroncini also faced two trials by the ordinary judicial authorities in Bologna in connection to his role in the Partito Nazionale Fascista during the 1920s and for the charge of having organized action squads to carry out acts of violence and vandalism during the period from 1919 through 1925. He was declared not guilty in both instances for not having committed such acts.

Baroncini, Sulfina (both also managing directors from 1948), Ara and Alberto Melchiori, all general managers, were the key players in the company's relaunch in the postwar period. They worked closely with many officers from different departments (legal affairs, industrial accounting, and more), specifical-

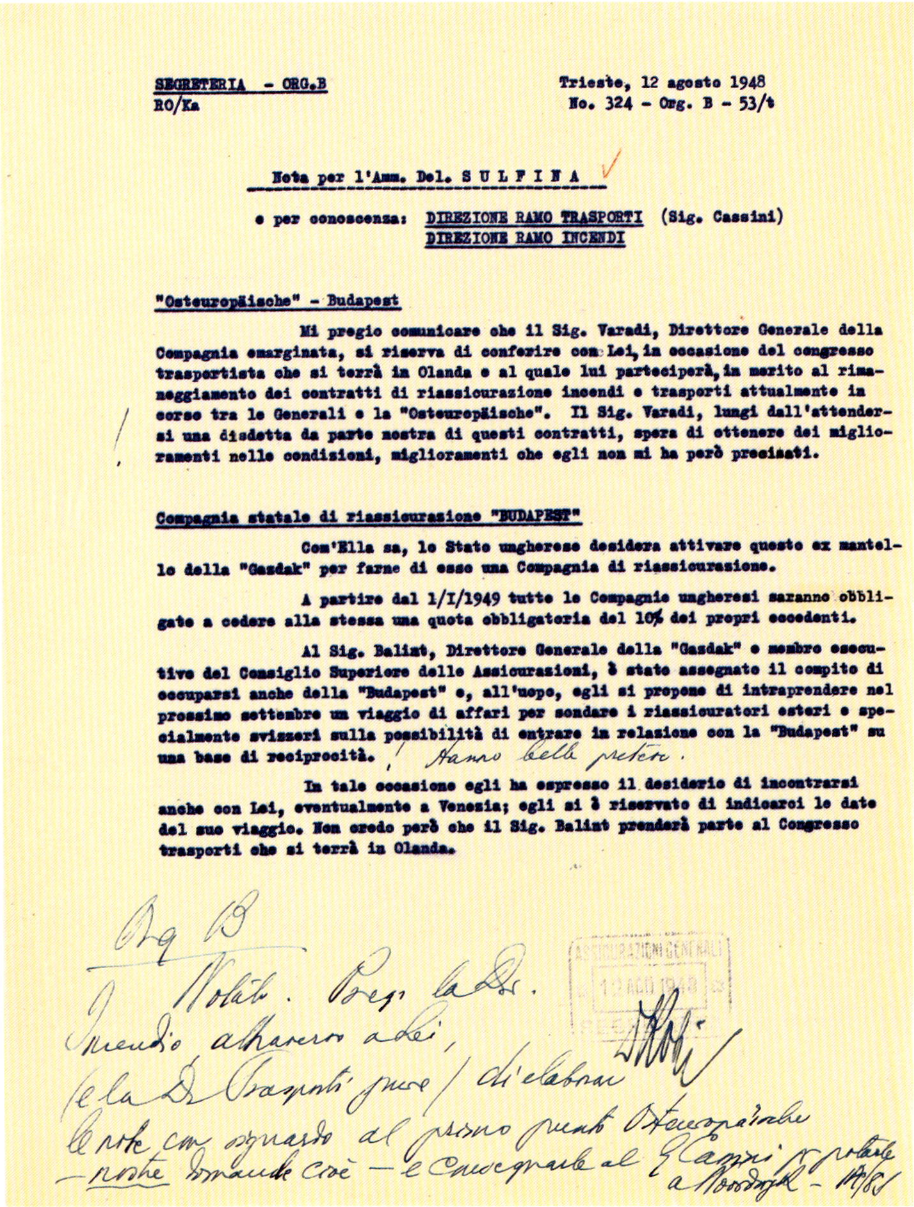

SEGRETERIA - ORG.B
RO/Ka

Trieste, 12 agosto 1948
No. 324 - Org. B - 53/t

Nota per l'Amm. Del. S U L F I N A

e per conoscenza: DIREZIONE RAMO TRASPORTI (Sig. Cassini)
DIREZIONE RAMO INCENDI

"Osteuropäische" - Budapest

Mi pregio comunicare che il Sig. Varadi, Direttore Generale della Compagnia emarginata, si riserva di conferire con Lei, in occasione del congresso trasportista che si terrà in Olanda e al quale lui parteciperà, in merito al rimaneggiamento dei contratti di riassicurazione incendi e trasporti attualmente in corso tra le Generali e la "Osteuropäische". Il Sig. Varadi, lungi dall'attendersi una disdetta da parte nostra di questi contratti, spera di ottenere dei miglioramenti nelle condizioni, miglioramenti che egli non mi ha però precisati.

Compagnia statale di riassicurazione "BUDAPEST"

Com'Ella sa, lo Stato ungherese desidera attivare questo ex mantello della "Gazdak" per farne di esso una Compagnia di riassicurazione.

A partire dal 1/I/1949 tutte le Compagnie ungheresi saranno obbligate a cedere alla stessa una quota obbligatoria del 10% dei propri eccedenti.

Al Sig. Balint, Direttore Generale della "Gazdak" e membro esecutivo del Consiglio Superiore delle Assicurazioni, è stato assegnato il compito di occuparsi anche della "Budapest" e, all'uopo, egli si propone di intraprendere nel prossimo settembre un viaggio di affari per sondare i riassicuratori esteri e specialmente svizzeri sulla possibilità di entrare in relazione con la "Budapest" su una base di reciprocità.

In tale occasione egli ha espresso il desiderio di incontrarsi anche con Lei, eventualmente a Venezia; egli si è riservato di indicarci le date del suo viaggio. Non credo però che il Sig. Balint prenderà parte al Congresso trasporti che si terrà in Olanda.

3.
Letter from Alberto Rossi to Michele Sulfina regarding the Hungarian subsidiary, Osteuropäische, which includes Sulfina's handwritten notes (Trieste, 12 August 1948)
[ASAG, *Direzione centrale, Segreteria organizzazione, Corrispondenza*, U2GE059869]

ly with the central secretariat, which over time had specialized in coordinating the operational channels in foreign countries up to the point where it generated a separate and highly-relevant service: the foreign operations department. After the foreign agencies secretariat was closed in 1939, it was decided to establish an independent office to organize and develop the services pertaining to different nations, and to include them in those already present in Europe, to be handled directly by the central secretariat. There worked Gottardo Artico, Alberto Rossi, and Giuseppe Segneri, deputy manager who was in charge when the manager Giuseppe Stefani was away. In 1942 a new division of labor was introduced subsequent to the division of the territories into two groups: organization A, led by Renato Sambri, was responsible for Central Europe; organization B, led by Giuseppe Segneri, was responsible for the countries already managed by the foreign agencies. The division into organizations A and B was refined in 1947 (under managers Renato Sambri and Alberto Rossi) and remained in force until 1949 [*fig.* 3].
These are but some of the men who managed the many problems of the second postwar period. In 1945 in Austria, Germany, France, Belgium, Holland, Great Britain, Brazil, Spain, the United States, Greece, Egypt, Syria and Israel, the company's assets were either seized, or its business permits had been revoked (and often the first situation affected operations). In some cases, such as France, the assets remained frozen for many years; and due to the troubles connected to the issue of Italian assets in Tunisia, the Italian government was unable to bring into effect the Italian-French agreements and thereby release Italian assets in France, including those of Generali. The release of assets in Lebanon and Switzerland was arranged mid-1947; in Egypt and in the Philippines in 1948; in Cyprus in 1949; in Iraq, Greece, France and Tunisia in 1951; in Brazil also in 1951, after very long diplomatic negotiations due to the release of assets being tangled in Italian-Brazilian

diplomatic relations; and finally, in Belgium in 1952. Although in 1946 the company was already witnessing satisfactory results in some countries, in some cases a return to normal insurance work took years. It must be noted that in Germany, following the *Anschluss*, Generali's and Erste Allgemeine's Head Offices in Vienna had taken on a central role for the German area, incorporating the portfolios for Poland and the Sudeten region. The company had been running through Erste Allgemeine for over a century and after the war ended, the challenge was to reorganize German operations efficiently and independently, even if not in a prime position; Generali's priority was the reinsurance business and to gain the majority control over German companies Deutscher Lloyd Leben and Deutscher Lloyd Sach. Direct contacts with Reginald Fritsch, who ran the company's Berlin office, took place only in October 1947 and led to the selection of Johann Friedrich Schippmann, manager of Deutscher Lloyd Leben, as the ideal candidate to coordinate and control the work in Hamburg, Frankfurt, Munich and Berlin. In 1948 Carl Rieck was appointed general representative for Germany, with the permit to operate in the three western areas having been renewed. Nonetheless, a number of issues remained unresolved until the next decade: first, the loss of the eastern area; the relocation of the headquarters from Berlin subsequent to the communication challenges faced with West Germany; and the integration of the organizational networks into subsidiaries. Deutscher Lloyd Leben relocated its headquarters from Leipzig to Munich in 1949, and Deutscher Lloyd Sach from Berlin between 1955 and 1956 in view of unifying the activities of the two subsidiaries into a single office in Munich in 1956. In managing the German operations, the central office in Frankfurt became increasingly more important and in April 1957, it became the Branch for Germany, responsible for the fire, theft, transport and life divisions (until then life insurance had been managed by Deutscher Lloyd Leben) [*fig.* 4]. In 1952 the meetings of the International Committee took take place in London to settle the debits and credits with Germany up to 1945 (whereby Generali boasted considerable credits, both with the reinsurance market and the nation).

Although in Austria the initial postwar period was favorable for Generali, initially the company operated exclusively through the Erste Allgemeine. The subsidiary's commissioned management ended in 1947, after Fritz Hummel the new *Vorstand*, who also represented the headquarters in Vienna, was elected and approved by the Austrian government. Following the restoration of the buildings devastated by the war, the company focused on Erste Allgemeine's internal organization, and on improving the coordination between the parent company and the subsidiary. In the 1950s, the company's legal procedures to recover the shares sold to the German companies during the *Anschluss*, ted to a majority shareholding in Wiener Allianz.

Beyond Europe, the Americas signified a key region for the company. Compared to Canada and the South American countries, the recovery process proved more challenging in the United States, where it only came to fruition in the 1950s. Before the end of the war, the company had been able to rely on several American contacts, which had been secured by officers such as Arturo Coen, Ignazio Hornik, and Siegfried Berliner, who had left Europe due to the racial persecutions. However, the key man in the United States was Ottocaro Weiss, who almost immediately and for a very long time pursued the lengthy procedures for the release of Assicurazioni Generali's assets that eventuated in 1949. Thanks to his reports on the American marketplace, a long-standing decision was reached to commence operations through a majority shareholding of Buffalo, an established American company. The acquisition of the majority shareholding took place in 1950, with a partially guaranteed investment by the Banca Commerciale Italiana. The permit to trade in

the United States under the name of The General Insurance Company of Trieste and Venice – United States Branch, was obtained later, in 1953.
As early as 1945 Generali's officers and the Ministry of Foreign Affairs began to divulge news of temporary receiverships and measures for taking control of the private insurance business in the countries in the Russian block. But Italy's diplomatic situation posed further challenges. The Treaty of Paris signed by Italy in February 1947, granted the allied nations the right to nullify all existing bilateral agreements with Italy, giving them the option to confiscate all Italian assets abroad as a means of reparation for the war. Thus Russia was entitled to confiscate all Italian property in Romania, Hungary and Bulgaria.
In Hungary, Rossi was able to travel to Budapest only in 1946 and ascertain that despite the destruction of the local Branch, business showed signs of recovery, and that Assicurazioni Generali and its subsidiary Providentia, were in the lead. In November, the assets of Italian companies and those with Italian financial interests were frozen by the Russian government leading to cash flow problems; in Hungary the company operated the longest, until 1950, whereas Generali was no longer able to pursue its activities in Poland from 1945. By September 1947 the situation in the whole region was seriously compromised and divided into countries where it was no longer possible to work (Poland, Yugoslavia and Czechoslovakia, with negotiations taking place in the latter over possible compensation for nationalization), and countries in which the situation was less drastic (Romania, Hungary and Bulgaria, a country where it was possible to work in reinsurance). A year later, the State took control of insurance in Romania and Bulgaria as well, and the insurance business dwindled with the exception of Hungary, where it remained stable. As the insurance business in the Russian block took on increasingly legal connotations, it was entrusted to Nicolò Benedetti, head of the company's legal affairs department. Benedetti worked on the negotiations for the La Malfa agreement that was signed on December 11, 1948 in Moscow. The agreement regulated the transfer of Italian property to Russia in the three eastern European countries set out in art. 74 of the Peace Treaty (Bulgaria, Romania, Hungary). It also covered Generali's claim for compensation for losses incurred from appropriations and nationalizations in Czechoslovakia, Poland and Yugoslavia. The negotiations for reaching consensus for the assessment of Italian propriety, pursuant to the La Malfa agreement, were complex, with three committees comprising Italian and Soviet representatives working eight months in Hungary, Bulgaria and Romania in 1949. Beside the diplomats, the Italian party included some of Assicurazioni Generali's officers: Osvaldo Botta, lawyer in Sofia; Renato Sambri in Bucharest; and Alberto Rossi in Budapest; all of whom participated in the meetings of the commission and the subcommittee for insurance, coordinated by Botta and with financial advice provided by Raimondo Levi. The work of the Italian and Russian committees did not end in agreement, however, and their disagreements were recorded in the minutes. Similarly, the negotiations for Yugoslavia, Czechoslovakia and Poland in 1950 failed to reap tangible results.
Assicurazioni Generali's legal claims for compensation for war damages and losses incurred abroad from nationalization, remained open for a long time and, in some cases, are part of recent history. Although many countries lacked an intergovernmental agreement for the shared assessment of confiscated property, the Italian Law no. 1050, of October 29, 1954, determined the government's compensation to owners of Italian property abroad that was lost as a result of the Peace Treaty (such appropriations were taken in lieu of Italy's reparation to the allied countries); subsequently Law no. 1066, of December 6, 1971, resulted in additional compensation by the Ministry of Finance, according to various re-evaluation criteria. (R.S.)

4.
Advertising postcards from
the German Branch
[mid-twentieth century]
[ASAG, *Miscellanea*, scheda 6808]

Michele Sulfina

1883
1957

Born in Brăila Romania, on July 29, 1883, into a Jewish family thought to have originated in Galicia (Poland). Originally, Michele Sulfina's surname was Schwefelberg (until the law required it be changed into Italian in 1930). At seventeen he commenced his career at Generala, the company's Romanian subsidiary, which during a phase of expansion in 1900 moved from the first office in the grain port at the mouth of the Danube, to the capital Bucharest [*fig.* 1]. In the hope of improving his career prospects, and perhaps induced by the alarming growth of anti-Semitism in his country, a few years later Sulfina emigrated to Paris. He found employment in a French commercial bank, Louis Dreyfus & Co. that specialized in the trade of grain; there he acquired considerable experience in the sector of sea and land transport insurance, as well as a broad understanding of international trade.

When the war broke out, Edgardo Morpurgo had immediately understood that the crisis that was about to befall the European insurance business, would have direct repercussions on the transport sector. France and Great Britain had imposed an embargo that prohibited any ongoing contractual relationships between companies of enemy countries, and which resulted in shortages within the reinsurance sector. In Michele Sulfina, who had developed his technical abilities outside the company, possessed a university degree and was fluent in six languages, Morpurgo identified the required skills to handle that unique situation.

His employment negotiations began in December 1914 and due to the laborious conditions imposed by the war, they only came to fruition in August 1915. Sulfina settled in Rome, which after the embargo against the Central Empires—also adopted by Italy—had become the center of the Italian insurance industry.

The conditions created by the war meant that the Istituto Nazionale delle Assicurazioni (INA) was able to provide essential support through widening its network. The public institution had been created in 1912 for the purpose of giving the State monopoly over the life insurance sector, a measure that was expected to come into effect in 1923.

Meanwhile, in August 1914 INA had added maritime reinsurance to its suite of products, later adding war risk, under the navigation sector, and including reinsurance for all other sectors by 1918. After the war ended, in January 1920, it had managed to directly reinsure all elementary risks.

While the conflict persisted, it was to the private insurance industry's benefit to support the Italian reinsurance sector, as institutions such as INA took on a growing number of risks while providing the opportunities to withstand the adverse effects of inflation. Nonetheless, as soon as the conflict ceased, it was no longer advantageous to remain in competition with what was a potentially hostile competitor. Having recently become an incorporated company under Italian law, the office in the capital fulfilled a sensitive role for Assicurazioni Generali apropos public power. Sulfina, having been first appointed special manager of the transport division in 1920, then deputy general manager in Rome in 1922, strove to protect the company's interests. In April 1923, a new law regulated the practice of the Italian insurance sector and abolished the State's monopoly over life insurance, and ensuring harmony between the public and the private sectors. This heralded a transition in which the State's role in the economy was destined to become ever more pervasive at a time when internationally, the economy and financial systems based on free trade and unrestricted capital as they were in the prewar era, were well and truly over. The postwar reconstruction clashed with the proliferation of money multipliers, the instability of foreign exchange rates, economic nationalism, quantitative restrictions on goods and currency, and clearing agreements. The 1920s were characterized by an atmosphere of precariousness, oscillating between apparent growth and success and sudden decline, until the international markets precipitated like never before due to the stock market crash of October 1929, followed by the devaluation of the pound sterling in April 1931, and the German bank collapse in 1931. Among the central European banks affected by the crisis, and that were important to Assicurazioni Generali, was Vienna's Creditanstalt. What followed was a financial recession that spread globally, followed by the depreciation of currencies, a drop in value for goods and securities, and the default on bank loans. In 1926—the year in which Italy announced the revaluation of the lira at "Quota 90"—Michele Sulfina was called to Trieste and promoted to general manager of the company so that he could devote himself to its financial management. As he expressed at a public event in 1933, at the height of the great depression, he was aware that the international instability was so disruptive that it threatened to jeopardize the viability of the insurance industry, which was grappling with a drastic reduction of income from its investments. He postulated new compensatory tools such as special reserves for life insurance to be funded by insurer and the insured. Though it was just an idea, it was intended to inspire further investigation about opportunities for reinsurance, and pointed to the severity of the crisis, which had to be dealt with on a daily basis in a concrete and pragmatic way.

In response to these financial woes, in 1925, the Italian State took control of the currencies and exchange rates, and prescribed strict guidelines for commercial interactions with foreign countries, intervening in the organization of currencies and exchange rates; measures that after 1931 became ever more restrictive. For a large international company such as Assicurazioni Generali, it was crucial to convince the policymakers (a number of ministries and public bodies) that reinsurance played a key role in the balance of payments; thus the company successfully negotiated the maximum allowed reserve in foreign assets for its foreign operations, limits that

1.
Michele Sulfina (1930s)
[ASAG, *Versamenti*, scheda 28264]

were increased in 1936 further to the devaluation of the lira. The prominence of Sulfina's role in this area was confirmed at the end of the war, when in February 1946 the Constituent Assembly requested to interview him—despite at the same time being accused of collaborationism by the Anglo-Americans—in the capacity of expert advisor on foreign currency and foreign trade. Although the area of direct international business was fraught with all sorts of challenges (securities, high taxation, monetary problems, and control over the exchange), in those years Sulfina and the company's executive management did not forgo a cornerstone of insurance, namely the geographical balancing of portfolios, i.e. the pursuit of expansion strategies across international markets, specifically beyond Europe (Latin America, Canada, South Africa, Dutch East Indies). In this respect, the company depended on the collaboration with its traditional banking partner, the Banca Commerciale Italiana (COMIT), which had remained the most active Italian bank in the foreign market, even after the State bailout orchestrated by the Istituto per la Ricostruzione Industriale (IRI) in 1933.

But the situation in Europe was about to get worse. In Germany, Nazism's rise to power advocated a foreign policy designed to inhibit free trade relations, leaving Assicurazioni Generali to compete with the German insurance industry's aggressive plans to dominate the central European market, which from the company's inception, had constituted its core interests. By taking advantage of the 1936 bankruptcy of Phönix, a major Austrian company, the German giants Allianz and Münchener Rück. were successful in their unscrupulous maneuver to drive out (at least temporarily) the two competitors from Trieste, Assicurazioni Generali and Riunione Adriatica di Sicurtà (RAS), and thus gain control over the Austrian market. In March 1938, together with Chairman Morpurgo and the central manager Camillo Gentilli, Sulfina participated in negotiations with the German executives in Venice. Their contractual positions however, in the eyes of the Germans, were destined to become increasingly more tenuous while in Italy, the propaganda foreshadowing the anti-Semitic measures was gaining momentum. As a result of complex negotiations between the leaders of the two corporate companies of Trieste Mussolini in person—which for reasons of space we cannot delve into here—in November 1938 Michele Sulfina, together with Arnoldo Frigessi of Rattalma of RAS, succeeded in keeping his position as general manager of Assicurazioni Generali by means of a special regulation that allowed those officials whom the governing bodies of the two companies deemed to be irreplaceable, to remain in service. The goal was to secure a degree of stability within the two insurance companies, without the loss of valuable human resources at a time when they were facing unprecedented attacks in Europe.

Initially, about twenty officials were able to keep their positions in both companies; nonetheless, as the ethnic measures intensified during the course of the war, eventually they would all have to resign. So it can be said that the cases of Michele Sulfina and Arnoldo Frigessi are two remarkable exceptions in the history of the Italian anti-Semitic persecutions.

It is unclear whether Sulfina was able to stay in a position that was demoted to a basic technical rank, given that in order to conform with the new anti-Semitic legislation, from December 1938 he was officially unable to participate in the governing bodies. The new chairman Giuseppe Volpi promised him assistance, including a passport to seek refuge abroad should the need arise; indeed, having been an Italian citizen since 1928, the anti-Semitic legislation now denied him a passport. When the events deteriorated, though, he did not possess it. The truth remains that Volpi played a more significant role in his negotiations with the German insurance industry than that of which Sulfina would be accused of after the war. On the other hand, in terms of reinsurance, Sulfina claimed to have backed a plan for the internal distribution of reinsurance to nurture the two companies in Trieste (known as the Centro Temporaneo di Compensazione Riassicurativa), which during the war were no longer able to use reinsurers in allied countries.

On September 8, 1943, as the German troops occupied Trieste, Sulfina feared for his life. Escaping far from the city, forced into hiding and losing all contacts with the executive bodies, he was dismissed from the company. He sought refuge in Rome. In June 1945 his position as Assicurazioni Generali's general manager was confirmed; but while he was intent on reorganizing Assicurazioni Generali's offices in the freed territories, in September, the Allied Military Government of the Venezia Giulia removed him and Frigessi from office as part of the epuration measures that targeted the heads of private companies. Despite the Italian government's intervention, which was motivated by concerns over its economic recovery being compromised, a year later in October 1946, Sulfina and Frigessi were both acquitted by the Anglo-American authorities. Reinstated to the post of Assicurazioni Generali's general manager in October 1946, Sulfina participated in the company's second restoration. In 1948 he was promoted to managing director and focused on reorganizing the foreign business, which as a result of the cold war had lost the markets in Central and Eastern Europe. He became a member of the Board in western subsidiaries such as Concorde in Paris, Covadonga in Madrid, Banco Vitalicio de España in Barcelona, Société d'Assurances Générales in Istanbul, and the Buffalo Insurance Co. Ltd in the United States. In 1953, on the occasion of his retirement, he was honored with the title of deputy chairman. He died in Rome on October 25, 1957.

Sources

ASAG. *Direzione centrale, Servizio del personale, Posizioni personali.* U2GE042578, personnel file of Michele Sulfina, 1914–1964.

"Interrogatorio del dott. Michele Sulfina (27 febbraio 1946)." In Ministero per la Costituente, *Rapporto della commissione economica presentato all'Assemblea Costituente*, vol. II, *Problemi monetari e commercio estero, II, Appendice alla relazione (Interrogatori, questionari, monografie)*, 62–70. Rome: Istituto Poligrafico dello Stato, 1946.

"Michele Sulfina." *Bollettino delle Assicurazioni Generali* 10–11 (1957): 1–6.

Works

Sulfina, Michele. "I rischi di impiego dei capitali e le variazioni del valore della moneta nelle assicurazioni vita." In *Atti del secondo congresso nazionale di scienza delle assicurazioni. Trieste, 5–8 novembre 1932*, 127–32. Rome: G. Randi, 1933–1934.

Bibliography

Il centenario delle Assicurazioni Generali, 1831–1931, [edited by Giuseppe Stefani]. Trieste: Editrice la Compagnia, 1931: 203.

Feldman, Gerald D. "Concorrenza e collaborazione tra le compagnie d'assicurazione dell'Asse: Munich Re, Generali e Ras (1933–1943)." *Imprese e storia* 24 (2001): 249–71.

Millo, Anna. *Trieste, le assicurazioni, l'Europa. Arnoldo Frigessi di Rattalma e la Ras*. Milan: Franco Angeli, 2004.

Favaretto, Tito. "Lo sviluppo dell'attività internazionale delle Assicurazioni Generali tra il XIX e il XX secolo." In *Assicurare 150 anni di Unità d'Italia. Il contributo delle assicurazioni allo sviluppo del Paese*, edited by Paolo Garonna, 93–151. Rome: ANIA, 2011.

(A.M.)

Mogliano Veneto: Halfway between Venice and Milan

Creating a Head Office for Italy

1948
1991

The 1948 merger between Anonime Infortuni e Grandine and Assicurazioni Generali, brought to the fore an issue that had long been overdue, namely that of the organization's operational management, both at a central and peripheral level. First, the company faced specific administrative challenges that arose from the unusual presence of five general managers (three in Trieste, one in Venice and one in Milan). Such a structure weakened the leadership's authority, causing the erroneous assignment of responsibilities both in relation to the Central Head Office and between the managers themselves, whereby unity would have been assured with a single authority represented by one or two people at the helm of the company. Secondly, following the death of the general manager, Marco Ara, there was a need to reorganize the Venice Head Office to focus its activities on more sales-oriented purposes, specifically, in the sector of life insurance. It was therefore necessary to revive and strengthen the relationships between Venice and its outskirts, to undertake administrative restructures, simplify the operational processes, and eliminate any double-handling by shifting some of the work to the Central Head Office while developing the organization's regional inspectorate and agencies. Finally, the matter of the registered office's location needed to be reviewed. In 1947 the choice fell on Rome, a decision dictated by political necessity as Rome made it possible to overcome any localized misgivings. However, as a result of the merger and the establishment of two new divisions, namely accident insurance and public liability and hail insurance; the office in Milan, which had established itself as one of the company's most prominent, beckoned the registered office and the Central Head Office. After lengthy discussions by the Board and the Executive Committee, no solution was finalized until the mid-1950s [*fig.* 1]. Once the chairman's role was finalized (representational powers, oversight of all governing bodies, and company business), the accountabilities for the key figures to manage the company's business were clearly identified, subject to the powers of the governing bodies and pursuant to the charter. One or two managing directors, who had been promoted among the company's technical staff and who embodied the organization's living labor, were invested with the highest responsibilities by the governing bodies responsible for general matters. They were supported in the day-to-day running of the business by the general managers, to whom the various divisions and departments heads reported. The general managers and the managing directors, who were also general managers, introduced a Management Committee to act as a conduit between the Executive Committee and the general managers, and for the purpose of coordinating technical and administrative operations across the different managements. The charter of 1951 reintroduced the General Council that had been suppressed in 1939. This was a collaborative body that provided high-level advice on matters of insurance and finance, and which comprised the members elected at the General Meeting by the Board and the general managers. Its purpose was to bank on its members' influence and expertise to drive the company's growth in the Americas, Asia and Africa, and to utilize their suite of relevant competencies to establish Assicurazioni Generali's power on the international insurance market [*fig.* 2]. As a result, the number of members on the Board was reduced, streamlining the Board and making it more effective in carrying out its legal mandate. The management of the accident insurance division was replaced by a general manager, Mario Padoa, who was assisted by central manager Francesco Cincotti in addition to a co-manager and two deputy managers. The management of the hail insurance division was led by central manager, Umberto Baccolini, and a deputy manager, subject to the Central Head Office's wider powers, which were based on the seniority of the above-mentioned representatives to corresponding degrees. Given the Venice Head Office's predominantly commercial activities, it was resolved to introduce a central manager, Francesco Ommassini, and to support him with an official whose title was no higher

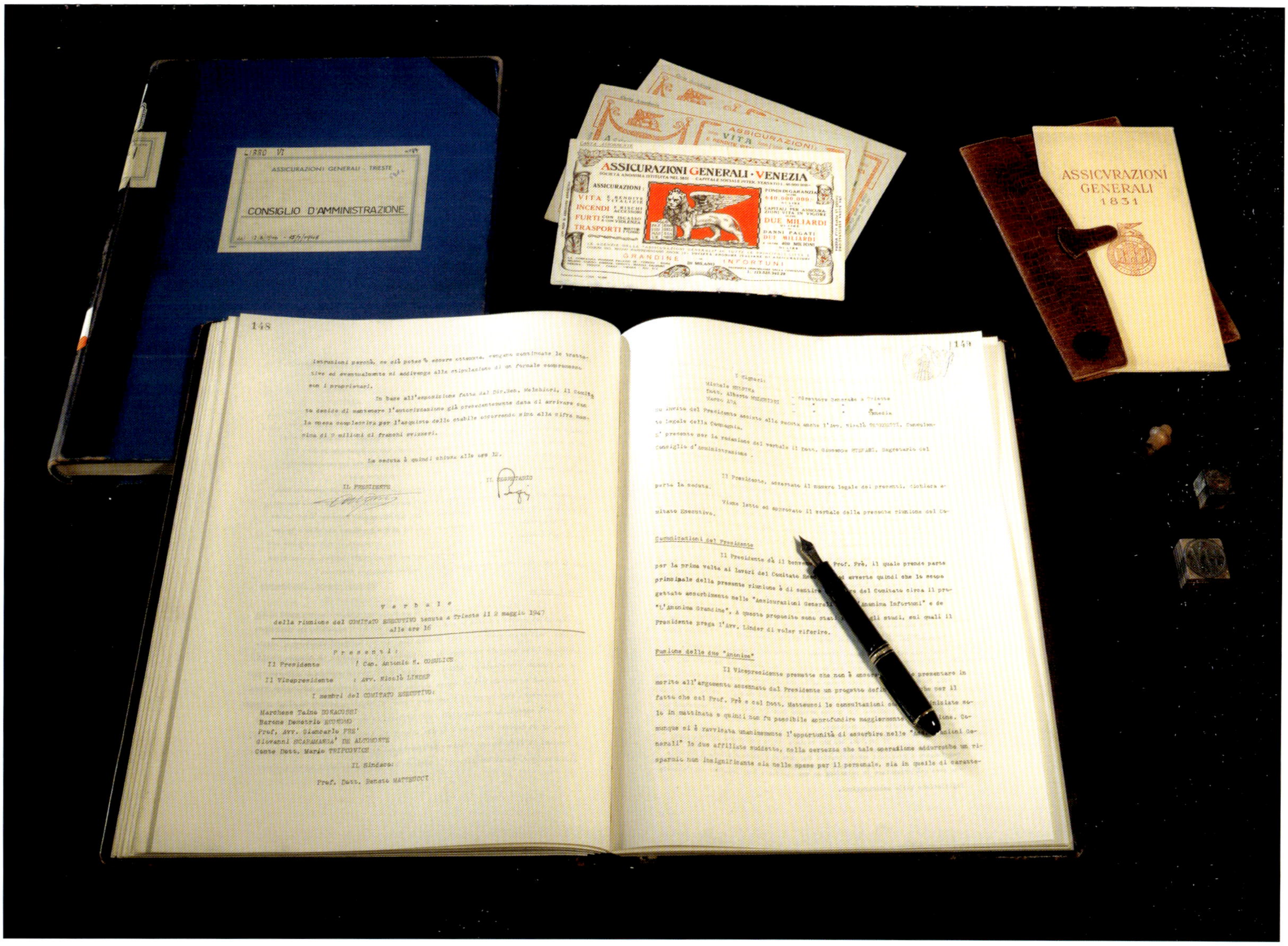

1.
The volumes containing the minutes of the Board and the Executive Committee (twentieth century) [ASAG, *Presidenza e organi sociali, Verbali, Consiglio di amministrazione*, vol. 1270 and *Comitato esecutivo*, vol. 1310]

than manager, responsible for overseeing the commercial operations. The position was given to an agent from Ferrara, Franco Mannozzi. The Central Head Office comprised no more than four general managers, which at the time were: Alberto Melchiori, Michele Sulfina (who after resigning in 1953, was replaced by Giuseppe Bufano) and Baroncini, the latter were also managing directors. The Head Offices in Venice and Milan, which had enjoyed great autonomy, were placed under the authority of the the Central Head Office, together with all their various departments. From the outset it was clear that the ideal solution would have been to create a single, central management to unite the three legal offices not only administratively, but also physically; however, due to technical-political and mostly financial reasons, that option proved unfeasible at the time. The idea of moving the registered office in Rome to Milan, was also dismissed. In 1955 Baroncini resolved for practical and structural reasons, to unite the two managements, and nominate Baccolini and Cincotti, central managers at the time, to lead this new division. Meanwhile, chairman Mario Tripcovich proposed to call the new organization resulting from such merger: Milan Head Office. Thereby, in Italy, the organization consisted of a multi-level structure: Trieste was the Central Head Office for the entire Group and specifically for business abroad, with competencies in life, transport, aviation, fire and reinsurance sectors. Milan became the Head Office for Italy in relation to car liability insurance, and other public liability and non-life types of policies (accident and health, hail, livestock); it reached across the entire network of agencies, though limited to these sectors of activity. Venice became accountable for all other sectors, which were not covered by the Milan Head Office (fire, theft, credits and securities, crystal), as well as the network of agencies and general agencies in Turin, Milan, Genoa, Venice, Florence, Rome and Naples that depended on it. With the signing of the London Memorandum in 1954, Trieste and its hinterland were once and for all returned to Italy. Subsequently, a process of restitution was undertaken with regard to the premises of the Central Head Office, which since 1945 had been occupied by the Anglo-American Command. Three years later, the matter of the registered office was again put to the Board of Directors following Trieste's mayor, Gianni Bartoli's request for a transfer, but at the time the matter was not received favorably (meeting of May 27, 1957). In June 1960 the chairmanship was offered to Gino Baroncini, who also kept the positions of managing director and general manager; after Edgardo Morpurgo, this appointment signaled the reinstatement of the top position by a company man. His work focused on consolidating the company internally, by reorganizing the upper management, as well as externally. He promoted policies that advanced the interests of major bodies and national organizations, he reassembled real estate investments, revitalized farmsteads, and set the foundations for a plan of re-entry and expansion in Western Europe. He was supported by Bufano and Melchiori, two general managers in Trieste; Mannozzi, who was in charge of Venice Head Office; and Cincotti, from the Head Office in Milan, which was thus considered equal to Venice [*fig.* 3]. Over time Enrico Randone recognized that Baroncini had fought "tooth and nail to maintain Assicurazioni Generali's identity tied to Trieste." While acknowledging the disadvantages posed by the geographical position, Randone also recognized "a great advantage: we are far from Rome and politics and this fact compensates for all the disadvantages. We have the luxury of being free of policymakers" (Angela Marani, *Gino Baroncini: un capitano d'industria*, edited by Franco Merlini [Imola: Associazione Giuseppe Scarabelli, 2000]).

During the first postwar period, the company focused on establishing itself abroad; however, from the late 1960s it directed its attention to the consolidation of the Group. This included the company's image, which led to shortening its name to "Generali," but foremost, the company's policy for Italy was addressed: the three-pronged management was wasting financial and

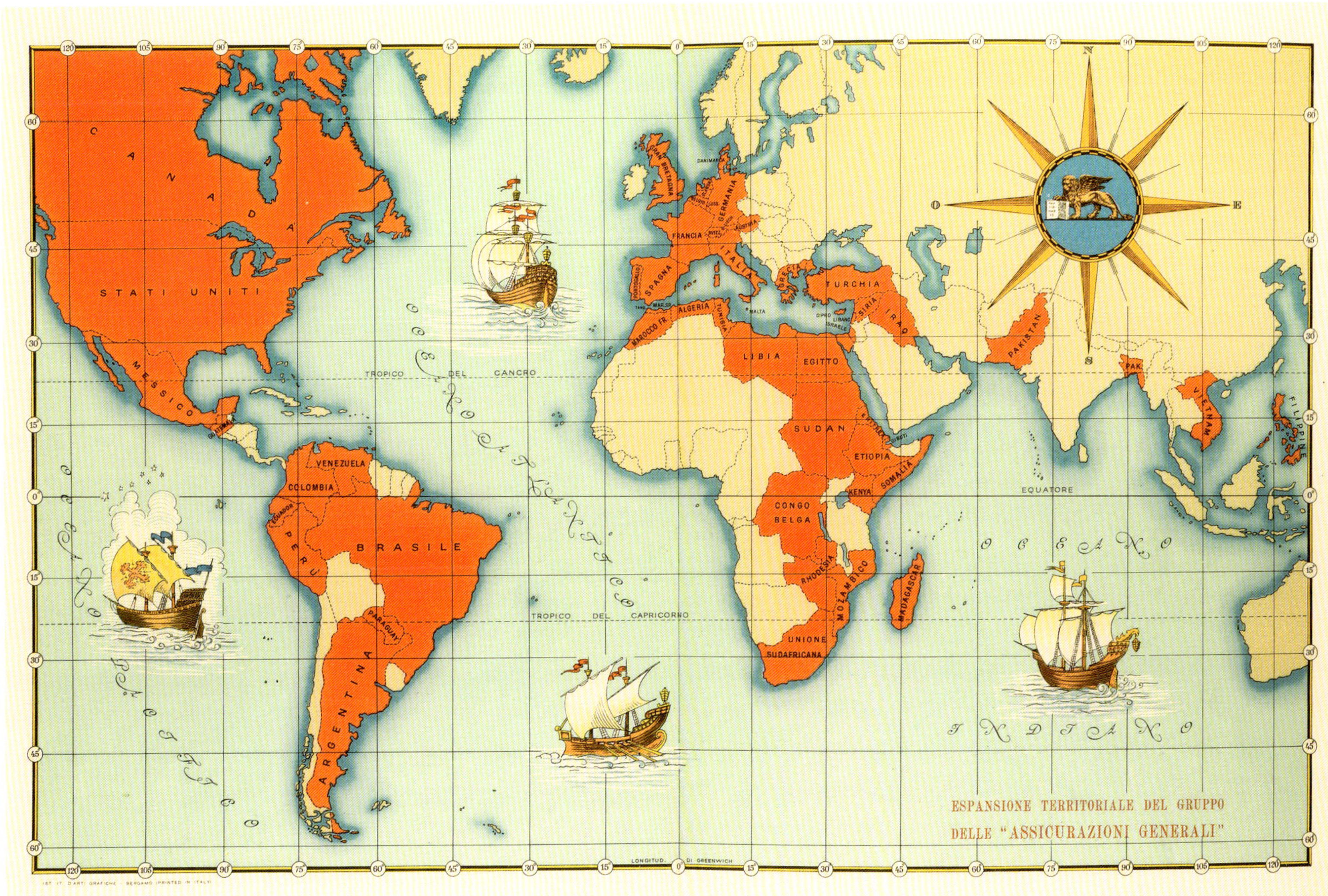

2.
The national expansion of the Assicurazioni Generali Group (1953) [ASAG, *Direzione centrale*, *Ragioneria centrale*, *Bilanci*, OGG001114934]

3.
Gino Baroncini and Franco Mannozzi. Photo taken at the conference of the Istituto per gli Studi Assicurativi at the University of Trieste (June 3, 1960) [ASAG, *Versamenti*, scheda 28265]

staffing resources. As a result, chairman Cesare Merzagora's main objective was to modernize the company's administrative and technical operations. Starting at the helm, he undertook a review of the governing bodies and restructured the highest levels of management: first, he appointed more than two deputy chairmen, two of which were managing directors. In Merzagora's view, such nominations would relieve the chairmanship of a number of responsibilities and strengthen the leadership, while remaining true to a principle he held dear, that is to assign the highest authority to those individuals that had "devoted decades of work or even their entire working lives" to the company (Executive Committee minutes of April 28, 1970). The company could thus depend on the contribution of four general managers (two in Trieste, one in Venice and one in Milan), in addition to the work of the central managers.

The Head Offices in Venice and Milan, which hitherto had remained unconnected, each reporting back to the Central Head Office via their individual divisions, commenced in those years, to share resources and know-how, which began with the restructure of the data processing centers. The central data processing service (known as SCED in Italian) was established in 1970; it was accountable to then co-manager, Umberto Della Casa who oversaw the three data processing centers in the three Head Offices. The following year, as a result of the merger of Venice and Milan's centers, a new data processing center (CED) was opened in Mestre. The increased workload pertaining to compulsory public liability car insurance (as of January 1971) had boosted the automation processes, specifically in the Milan Head Office, leading to a review of the Group's entire system. As a result of the severe operating challenges affecting the Head Office in the Venetian lagoon and the operations in other countries, the reviews already under way were coupled to those specific to the corporate restructure, in order to improve the organization and to coordinate operations across the peninsula. To this end, at the chairman's request, a special committee for Italy (COSIT in Italian) was established in the spring of 1975, with the mandate to review the company's technical, commercial and administrative structure and to implement necessary measures to improve the company's outcomes. These measures and their corresponding deadlines, were set out in a document entitled, "Plan for Italy": the management of this plan was incorporated in the procedures of the foreign operations department in the Central Head Office. To carry out its work, COSIT relied on working groups and inter-managerial panels to implement new operational processes with the aim of increasing accountability for the commercial aspects at all levels. To do this it availed itself of the specialized knowledge and expertise in the insurance market of three foreign insurers: Antoine Bernheim, Fritz Hummel and André Rosa; as well as the work of the managing directors, which was coordinated by general manager Emilio Dusi, under the supervision of deputy chairman and managing director, Fabio Padoa.

In order to lighten the workloads of Eugenio Coppola di Canzano and Dusi, the two general managers under managing director Randone, a division of responsibilities was called for at that time; this was accomplished by assigning each central manager (Alvaro Costa, Giovanni Del Pesco and Della Casa) with specific areas of responsibility and making each accountable to their relevant general manager. As well, a personnel managers meeting was introduced, to ensure the policies were consistent across the entire sector. Furthermore, significant technical improvements were made, after the reform of the non-life and life divisions portfolios. Another of COSIT's projects was to merge the three Head Offices' accounting departments, introducing automation to the non-life divisions and to the issuance of policies. The company's entire peripheral organization was then streamlined with the inception of the sales department in Venice in 1975. COSIT's work also addressed the restructure of the agencies by creating the agents council to act as conduits between the agencies and the Head Office. A restructure of the company's administrative organization in 1976, lead to the Central Head Office's use of SISM (inter-managerial secretarial structures and methods); the purpose of which was to coordinate the numerous divisions, departments and local offices, and to ascertain the compliance of these departments with the need for efficiency and economy by improving the work tools and conditions. Eventually, the plan for Italy was extended to the subsidiaries such as Agricoltura, Navale, Carnica, Trieste e Venezia, and La Venezia. Work began to improve their premises and internal structures, and to determine a unique identity for each.

In the early 1980s the Group headed by Assicurazioni Generali, comprised thirty-five insurance companies and sixty-seven financial, real estate and agricultural companies. These were organized according to three Head Offices (Trieste, Venice, Milan), eight local offices, and over five hundred agencies distributed across the entire national territory. The increasing workload, which was a result of the massive development in automated internal processes, required the setting of long-term strategies to improve the productivity of administrative and technical procedures. The SCED was structured into three CED (Mestre, Milan, Trieste), of which the one in Mestre—being the center with the greater processing power and centralized data management system—required additional resources of staff and technology, in addition to larger premises to accommodate its growing size.

For some time, the company had identified the most suitable site to set up the department on land it owned in Mogliano Veneto, which was centrally-located in relation to the three Italian Head Offices. Through this project, the company set out to resolve other managerial challenges that were both financial and organizational. Specifically, the merger of the accounting departments required streamlined systems and methods such as uniting the archives and warehouses; then there was the organization of the Group's professional school to provide technical, administrative and sales training to production and administrative staff. On March 20, 1982 the Board received a plan for the entire project in Mogliano and architect Pierluigi Spadolini was hired to design the architectural and urban plan. The first part of the works commenced in 1984. These were intended to house the CED, the school, and the Venice Head Office's departments such as the accounting offices and the general archives, which would most benefit from the proximity to the data center.

In view of the EEC's liberalization of the market, more effective strategies were called for; in this regard the company's decision of where to establish the headquarters for all of Italy's operations was crucial. Thus, the issue of creating a single Head Office emerged mostly, through chairman Enrico Randone. As a result, the completion of a management complex in Mogliano Veneto gained immediate support. Yet the long-standing decision to unite the two Head Offices meant that Procuratie Vecchie's historical address would be vacated, and required the transfer of staff from Venice and also Milan. The merger was motivated by financial reasons and by the need to modernize and update the criteria and philosophies of portfolio management in a coherent way, and which until then, had been handled according to selection criteria between insurance branches, with the division of insurance offers according to two great categories: "business customers" handled mostly in Milan, and "individual customers" handled in Venice. Upon this plan's completion, it became necessary to undertake a reorganization of the managerial services starting November 1, 1985 pursuant to the marketing plan: "companies and people."

Once part of the offices were moved to the new premises in Mogliano Veneto, at the meeting on December 6, 1988, the chairman informed the Executive Committee that the unification plan for the company's operational and managerial departments in Italy had come to fruition, with the appointment of general manager Luigi Molinari for the combined Head Office of Venice and Milan, and which henceforth, would operate under the name "Head Office for Venice and Milan." All technical-commercial activities for the Italian operations were articulated to ensure a correlation with the market for companies, and that for people, giving rise to two distinct sectors within the organization: the "Companies Division" and the "People's Division," which were entrusted to central managers Giampaolo Brugnoli and Fabio Cerchiai respectively.

At this point in time it was timely to address the matter of the registered office: it was resolved that the company's registered office and Central Head Office would reside in Trieste, while the managerial offices would be unified under the "Head Office for Italy," which comprised the offices of Milan and Venice-Mogliano Veneto. Taking a cue from the small committees for personnel and operations that were already active in the areas of information technology, the Management Committee was created in the new organization. It comprised the managing directors, the general managers and the deputy general managers; the body was empowered to provide direction and make decisions of an operational nature, for the purpose of providing coherent advice to managerial issues. In the light of these constitutional changes, determined at the Extraordinary Shareholders' Meeting on June 30, 1990, and which combined the specific competencies of two Head Offices by making the accountabilities of each interdependent and complementary, and in the light of all the related instrumental changes; the exclusive accountabilities of the Central Head Office as well as those of the Head Office for Italy were also evaluated at the meeting on September 20. The powers conferred on the Central Head Office included all the typical activities of a parent company such as the management and coordination of activities of the company and the Group in Italy and abroad. Specifically, activities such as the management of corporate, legal and financial affairs; any activity connected to the real estate sector and reinsurance, whether inward or outward reinsurance, except facultative; the supervision of the international insurance business; staff policies and so on. The activities delegated to the Head Office for Italy concerned the technical, administrative and commercial organization of insurance activities in Italy, with the exclusion of the transport and aviation divisions, the activities of which remained within the framework of the Head Office in Trieste. The central headquarters in Mogliano Veneto, was completed in 1991, thus affording the proximity of all activities pertaining to Italian operations. (S.S.)

Work, Produce and Conserve: The Importance of Documents

Rich and varied is the twentieth century's collection of documents kept in the fonds of the Historical Archive, and which is useful in reconstructing the history of the central headquarters in Mogliano Veneto [*fig.* 4]. First, the suite of minutes from the governing bodies such as the Board, the Executive Committee, the Council and the General Meetings, are interesting sources to understand the dynamics of corporate policy-making that underpinned the project, the challenges and the consequent constitutional changes, and to identify the key players. Equally important is the technical, or work-related, documentation pertaining to the "Plan for Italy" such as the documents and reports prepared for the Executive Committee meetings and the subsequent minutes, all preserved in the foreign operations departments fonds and that concerning the activities of COSIT. The latter are co-mingled with the documentation that was produced by the the direct stakeholders such as Emilio Dusi and Fabio Padoa in fulfilling their duties, and is reorganized in the managing directors' fonds. With regard to the design side, from a structural, technological, and reorganization of personnel level, some information can be gleaned from general manager Umberto Della Casa's papers, as he was responsible for SCED, SISM and personnel department. A wealth of information is provided by the fonds relating to this department, both for the company history of those who personally contributed to creating the Head Office for Italy (e.g. their personnel files), as well as in reconstructing the company's evolving organizational structure (opening new departments or offices, career advancements, distribution of competencies and so on) through the internal memoranda. The ledgers of the Head Office in Venice and Milan have also been preserved, albeit only a portion and only for certain years. The documents identified have not been reordered, but are equipped with search tools to aid the researcher, such as synthesized guides (which maintain the consistency, the chronological parameters, the producer's brief history and so on), computerized census cards, which are helpful to quickly identify a single folder, and scans of a portion of the ledgers and the minutes of the governing bodies.

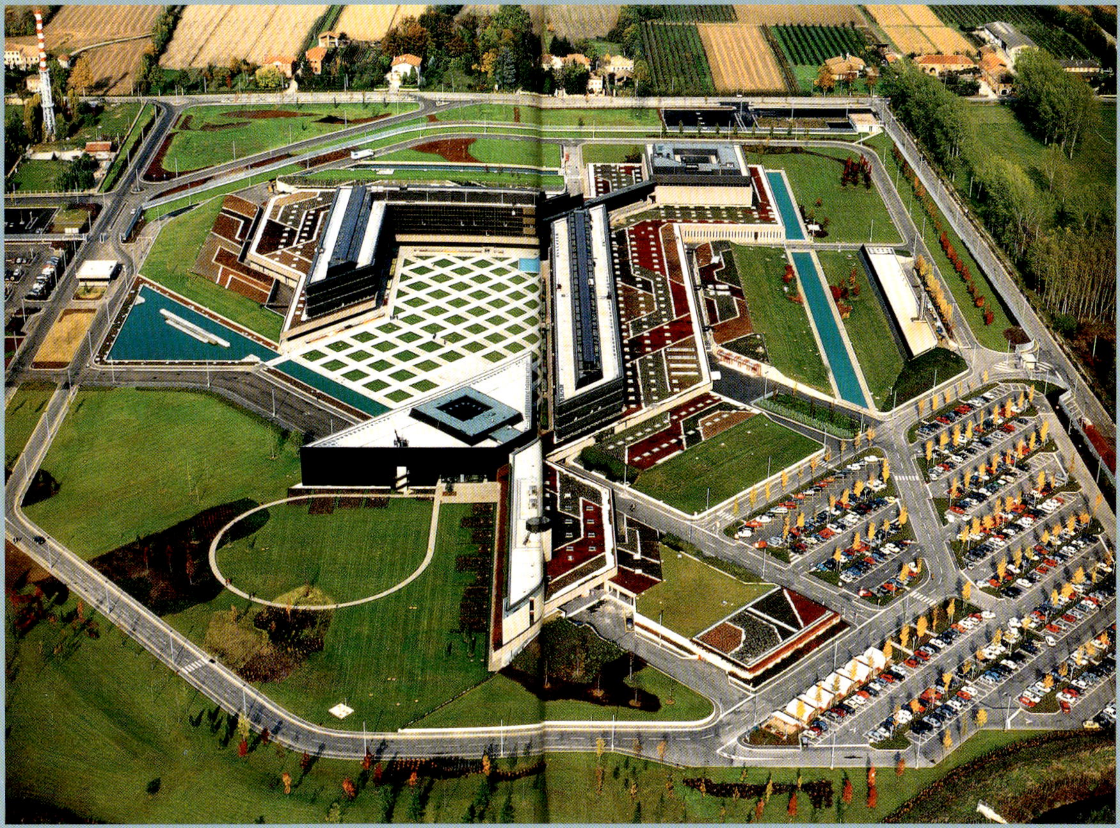

4.
The headquarters in Mogliano Veneto (1992)
[Servizi generali delle Assicurazioni Generali (ed.), *Centro Direzionale (di) Mogliano Veneto*, (s.a.)]

Cesare Merzagora

1898
1991

Born on November 9, 1898 in Milan, Cesare Merzagora's family was part of the white-collar bourgeoisie [*fig.* 1]. However, his father's sudden death prevented him from completing his accountancy qualification. In 1917 he enlisted as volunteer in the army and, in the capacity of second lieutenant, fought in the battles of the Karst Plateau, the Piave river, and the battle of Caporetto. He remained in uniform until January 1920, when he resolved to undertake a banking career and was employed in the head office of the Banca Commerciale Italiana (COMIT) in Milan.

A year later he was transferred to the Sofia branch in Bulgaria, which was part of COMIT's extensive network of subsidiaries abroad, and where he remained eight years. In 1923 he was promoted to head of the secretarial office, and in 1927 he took on the role of consular agent for Italy, in Plovdiv. He returned to Milan in March 1929 in the capacity of co-manager. Thanks to his proven ability to develop the bank's business interests and his understanding of local business and finance, he was given the responsibility of special inspector for the French-speaking regions and the Balkan, specifically Yugoslavia, Hungary, Turkey and Greece. There he successfully nurtured relationships with the press, political and diplomatic circles, which also exposed him to detailed information that he dutifully included in its reports.

The international economic crisis of the 1930s had a great impact on the Italian banking sector and on COMIT, which was burdened by capital expenditures and needed to be bailed out by public funds; thus it transitioned from a mixed bank into one of ordinary credit. Relegated to the foreign service, accountable to a central manager, and also possibly dissatisfied with COMIT's new role since it was under State control, Merzagora's career aspirations, which he had demonstrated since his time in Bulgaria, became frustrated. After devoting eighteen years to banking, in 1938 a new opportunity arose in the industry sector when the racial laws forced Pirelli's CEO to resign. In November 1938 Merzagora replaced him and in just a few years, inside this company with a high international profile, he rose to positions that were increasingly more prominent among the Italian industry sector. With the outbreak of the war, Merzagora extended his responsibilities to the group's foreign business, where he implemented significant financial and administrative cutbacks. He also successfully sold significant shareholdings of Pirelli in Basel to Swiss holders, thus preventing the company from incurring seizures in the Allied Countries and Latin America.

During the German occupation he became part of the company's Executive Committee, which oversaw operations in Northern Italy, and in his capacity as managing director, he steered the governance of the company.

Meanwhile, he joined the underground anti-fascist movement and, as a representative of the Liberal Party, he openly entered the Comitato di Liberazione Nazionale Alta Italia, on behalf of which he chaired the Commissione Centrale Economica which was mandated to facilitate manufacturing's transition back to a normal economy after the war. In April 1945 while Pirelli's proprietors, the brothers Alberto and Piero were banished, he took on the role of superintendent, steering the company towards economic recovery in the challenging postwar period. In March 1946 when the Pirellis were reinstated and the new board was appointed, Merzagora was given the mere role of member on the Board, as a consultant, despite having actively campaigned in their support. Although the outcome was disappointing, the position gave him access to many of Pirelli's associated companies' Boards such as Bastogi, Credito Italiano, and Alfa Romeo. Of particular interest are his attitudes toward the Istituto per la Ricostruzione Industriale (IRI), which he would have liked to see relegated to a mere financial institution solely to prevent any political meddling; and toward the Ente Finanziamenti Industriali (EFI), which Merzagora had been a part of since its inception in 1939, when it was conceived to sell loans to shareholder industries against the State. Having taken on the latter's presidency in 1949, his vision was to transform it into a credit bank of medium and long term loans; thereby reviving the mixed bank model in force prior to the 1936 Banking Act, which prevented commingling between banks and industry. Banca d'Italia's (and perhaps also Mediobanca's) opposition, meant that the project failed and Merzagora watched his support base, which comprised a strong entrepreneurial contingent, dissolve. Following a new law that set out the incompatibilities with a parliamentary office, he left EFI in 1951, resolving to pursue a political life that had commenced within the Consulta Nazionale in 1945, with renewed determination. In May 1947 De Gasperi offered him a post as an independent Minister for Foreign Trade, a position that was endorsed until March 1949, when Merzagora resigned over disputes on economic policy, and over which the government had been unable to reach consensus. Striving for a revival in international trade and the stabilization of the lira, Merzagora strongly supported manufacturers' interests, especially Lombardy's, the industrialists being suspicious of any kind of State interference into the economy. As a committed liberal, Merzagora supported the Schuman Declaration against any kind of protectionism in the steel industry, and for opening the borders to trade in order to improve the Italian products' competitiveness.

In the election of April 18, 1948 he accepted De Gasperi's offer to run as an independent candidate for the Senate on the list of the Democrazia Cristiana; the seat was confirmed with the elections of 1953 and 1958. In March 1963 he was appointed senator for life. In June 1953 he was elected chairman of the Senate; a nomination that followed a period of

1.
Cesare Merzagora during his trip to the Netherlands (November 1970) [ASAG, *Presidenza e organi sociali, Presidenti e vicepresidenti, Fabio Padoa*, U2GE027355]

heated criticism in Parliament over the electoral reforms, which had introduced a majority bonus system, referred to as the 'fraudulent law'; he presided by enforcing governance and reviving the political life in the central trenches of Parliament. In 1955 he was nominated to become the president of the Republic; however, tensions within the Democrazia Cristiana party resulted in a lack of backing for him, and after the third ballot his nomination had to be withdrawn. Over the following years he attained increasingly significant positions while the center-left parties' plans slowly came into focus, plans that were designed to introduce financial planning tools in order to manage the economy more closely.

During the summer of 1964, which coincided with the leadership crisis that lead to the resignation of Prime Minister Aldo Moro, he advocated for a technical government, for the reformation of the public sector, capable to preside in opposition to the socialist agenda. Moro's re-nomination persuaded him to resign; however. But when the President of the Republic, Antonio Segni, suddenly took ill and his incapacitation became protracted, Merzagora stepped in as the deputy head of State from August through December 1964; a role which he carried out with an exemplary sense of duty.

Nonetheless, the ongoing disagreements that isolated him from the government's political sphere, were destined to deepen. He found an outlet for his criticisms in November 1967 when, in a public speech, Merzagora denounced the decay of political morality and the parties' involvement in the institutions. The fallout was so severe, that he was forced to resign, and thus end his political career.

In June 1968 he became the chairman of Assicurazioni Generali, having been nominated by the outgoing chairman Gino Baroncini, who was leaving due to health issues. Deputy chairman Carlo Faina, who was a close personal friend of many years, as well as manager, and later on chairman of Montecatini from 1946 through 1965, and who was on the governing bodies of Assicurazioni Generali since 1950, also nominated him.

The recent (1966) merger between Montecatini and Edison, afforded the Montedison group, which at the time was in the middle of murky maneuvers, a significant overall participation in Generali. Merzagora, who in 1970 became Montedison's chairman by virtue of this shares, after coming across the chemical company's slush funds, resigned in order to avoid signing the financial reports.

While not exceeding 5 percent, Montedison—which at the time was led by controversial entrepreneur, Eugenio Cefis—positioned itself among Generali's top three shareholders with Mediobanca (4.34%), and Banca d'Italia (2.48%); while the remaining share capital was spread among small shareholders. Merzagora devoted much effort in keeping the company's independence, inevitably turning to Mediobanca, the most influential shareholder set to become a pivotal mediator in maintaining the fragile balance of power. In 1973–1974 the sale of Montedison's shareholdings in Generali through Fingest, turned Euralux in Luxembourg into a treasure-chest that comprised shares from Mediobanca, Lazard Frères and Assicurazioni Generali, enabling it to close shareholders' agreements that Merzagora might have avoided, had he had a choice in the matter. These were factors that motivated Merzagora to recognize the importance of the small shareholders' role: from the early days of his presidency he strived to improve the dissemination of information through valuable communication tools such as consolidated financial statements that provided details about the Group's activities abroad, as well as six-monthly newsletters to shareholders to provide detailed and timely updates on company business.

Merzagora left Assicurazioni Generali in 1979 with a nomination as honorary chairman. He remained in touch with the political and financial debate through his intense editorial activities in Italy's

premier newspapers, alternating his collaborations between *La Repubblica* and the *Corriere della Sera* [*fig.* 2].
He was a complex personality who from a young age had exhibited a keen interest in the arts and humanities. In his later years he demonstrated an aptitude for sculpture and design and mintage of medals.
He died in Rome on May 1, 1991.

Bibliography

"Il saluto del Presidente Merzagora." *Bollettino delle Assicurazioni Generali* 5–6 (1968): 2–4.
"Il commiato del Presidente Merzagora all'assemblea dei soci della Compagnia." *Bollettino delle Assicurazioni Generali* 40 (1979), special edition: 2–4.
Cesare Merzagora. Il ricordo del suo impegno istituzionale, e civile, delle sue capacità imprenditoriali, della sua produzione artistica, Senato della Repubblica, Palazzo Giustiniani, 12 novembre 1999. S.l., s.a. [1999–2000].
Cesare Merzagora, un artista da scoprire. Trieste: Editoriale Generali, 1999.
Merzagora, Cesare. *Lo strano paese. Scritti giornalistici 1944–1986,* edited by Nicola De Ianni. Naples: Prismi, 2001.
De Ianni, Nicola. "I mutamenti del lavoro nelle assicurazioni: le Generali da Baroncini a Merzagora (1968–1979)." In *Il lavoro come fattore produttivo e come risorsa nella storia economica italiana*, edited by Sergio Zaninelli and Mario Taccolini, 445–65. Milan: Vita e Pensiero, 2002.
Cesare Merzagora. Il presidente scomodo, edited by Nicola De Ianni e Paolo Varvaro. Naples: Prismi, 2004 (with contributions by Nicola De Ianni, Franco Bonelli, Donato Barbone, Elisa Boccia, Giandomenico Piluso, Gianpaolo Mastroianni, Paolo Varvaro). University of Naples "Federico II."
Cesare Merzagora. Il presidente scomodo di uno strano paese. Atti del convegno "Cesare Merzagora. Bilancio storiografico, testimonianze, eredità." Napoli, 8 ottobre 2004, edited by Nicola De Ianni and Paolo Varvaro. Naples: Prismi, 2005.
De Ianni, Nicola. "Merzagora, Cesare." In *Dizionario Biografico degli Italiani,* vol. LXXIII, 757-62. Rome: Istituto dell'Enciclopedia Italiana, 2009.
(A.M.)

2.
A caricature of Merzagora by Giorgio Forattini (1979)
[ASAG, *Direzione centrale, Segreteria centrale, Relazioni pubbliche e pubblicità, Corrispondenza,* U2GE047960]

Between Europe and America: Life Insurance in Trieste
From the Reconstruction to the Aetna Agreement

1951
1966

Life insurance was always a key sector in the activities of the company, particularly during the course of the twentieth century. The volumes of documents generated by the various offices reporting to the life insurance management in Trieste, recount the integrated development of the life insurance sector in Italy and abroad, from the 1930s through the 1970s.
To begin with, the division of responsibilities, including those over life insurance, between Trieste and Venice must be noted. Further to a Board resolution, it was long established that the Venice Head Office took care of the technical and administrative organization of the work in Italy, while Trieste was responsible for the reinsurance contracts and for the organization abroad. In any case, liaisons with the Central Head Office were necessary for adjusting the life insurance rates across the nation, which were subject to approval by the Ministry of Industry, and to apply any amendments to the policies' general conditions.
Overall, in Italy the 1920s were pivotal in determining the laws governing life insurance, which saw the establishment of fixed rules intended to stay in place for many decades, even after the Republic was established. Royal Decree no. 966 of April 29, 1923, which came into force with regulation no. 63 on January 4, 1925, repealed the State's monopoly over life insurance (Law no. 305 of April 4, 1912) and rescinded the dues of private companies to the Istituto Nazionale delle Assicurazioni (INA); thus encouraging private insurers to re-enter the sector. The 1925 provisions that were updated with the new Civil Code of 1942, were articulated only in 1959, in a comprehensive regulation no. 449, dated February 13. Under the Fascist regime the government had resolved to integrate the insurance business by merging small insurance companies into large groups, and stipulating agreements among insurers, one of them being the Consorzio Italiano per l'Assicurazione Vita Rischi Tarati (CIRT), established in 1927 and of which Generali was a member.
The company's life insurance management needed to keep constantly up-to-date on the guidelines pertaining to its activities; not only because it was a legal requirement, but also to partake, when appropriate, in the development of surveys and recommendations that the industry associations submitted to the lawmakers. Key to this process was the participation of representatives from both life insurance divisions in Trieste and Venice, as well as bodies such as the Technical Life Committee (including its more restricted departments and the various specialized committees), which was established within the Associazione Nazionale fra le Imprese Assicuratrici (ANIA), the Istituto Italiano degli Attuari, later joined by the Ordine Nazionale degli Attuari. Within these organizations, complex relationships with other insurance companies took place; among the most notable competitors were Riunione Adriatica di Sicurtà (RAS), the other large Italian private insurer, and INA.
Probably because of the specialized skills it required, the life insurance management in Trieste, which in the 1960s comprised about seventy people, has always been defined by the enduring career paths of its managers across various offices, both within the division and the Central Head Office (often the managers in life insurance were also deputy managers or central managers). Most notable among many are: Vittorio Longo (joining Generali in 1925 he led the life insurance division from the Post-World War II to 1969); Silvio Obry; Mario Frilli; Fabio Ara (following Longo as manager until 1977); Lucio Agacci (co-manager with Ara); Paolo Iona (succeeding Ara as manager); Guido Caristi; Lucio Bruno; Giorgio Balzer; Giorgio Fanin; Guido du Ban; Renato Taucer; Giuseppe Beisone; Giorgio Liveris and Elio Moccia. For some, retirement constitutes a fairly recent event. The majority of the managers were actuaries with the exception of Ettore Chersi, administrative manager from 1938 through 1946, and Fabio Ara who was responsible for reinsurance in the life insurance division, both of whom had studied law; while Raffaele Invrea, who was responsible for the actuarial office from 1939 through 1940, was an engineer.

The First Years of the Twentieth Century

After the nineteenth-century innovations introduced by director Vitale Laudi in 1907, the life insurance division was reorganized into two subsections. One section was technical and was headed by actuary and executive, Julius Graf. The other section was administrative and was headed by deputy executive Massimiliano Engel, who worked in life insurance for fifty years until 1933. This division of labor, which according to the minutes was intended to be discontinued in 1911 when Graf left the company, instead appears to have lasted a long time, at least until the 1940s. The actuary office group insurance, reinsurance and portfolios all reported to the technical section, while the administrative section took care of issuing policies, risk selection, variations and the claim settlement. In 1919 the administration of life reinsurance was simplified through the adoption of a single bordereau report. In 1932, an automated system was introduced with the use of Hollerith's punch cards (the company's first trials were in the life insurance division). After a coordinated process of implementation, the automation of actuarial work was completed with the participation, as is known, of Bruno de Finetti and the division staff (until 1938 Gino Tolentino was the conduit for Hollerith).

1.
The life insurance employees photographed on the occasion of manager Massimiliano Engel's fiftieth anniversary in service (Trieste, [1933])
[ASAG, *Versamenti*, scheda 28264]

Visible behind them, is a portrait of Vitale Laudi. Massimiliano Engel at the center; to his right is Sante D'Alvise, deputy general manager; to his left is Pietro Smolensky; second from the left is Vittorio Longo; fourth from the left in the second row is Gastone Milanese, actuary in the life insurance until 1937, then transferred to Paris where he became manager in 1949

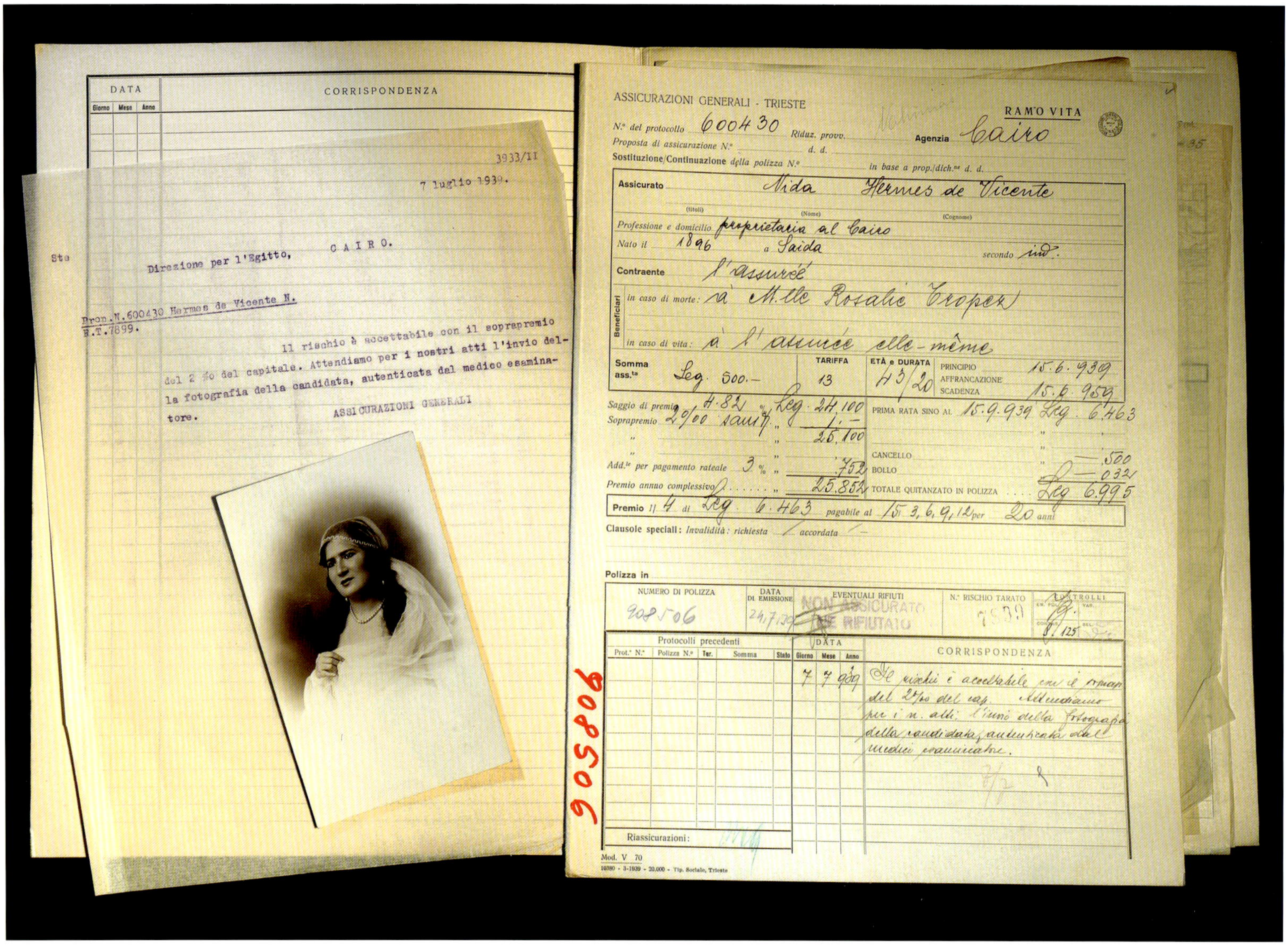

2.
A private insurance file from the Egyptian Branch (Trieste-Cairo, 1939)
[ASAG, *Direzione centrale*, *Ramo vita*, *Attuariato*, *Protocolli*, U2GE002003]

The fonds of Trieste's life insurance division does not currently contain many files of the insured, even though there had to have been many, given that Trieste kept proof of all the policies that were issued. For each individual deal, the acquisitions office drew up a contract for common and ascertained risks (and stamped it "GERITA," an acronym for *gestione rischi tarati* [management of ascertained risks]). Supposedly, Trieste's administrative work must have been massive and on repeated occasions there were attempts to streamline the workload; in 1949, for instance, it was resolved to allow France, Austria, Hungary, Spain and Belgium to be accountable for the management of their portfolios. The files that remain, relate to Egypt, Israel and Albania; they contain proposals, correspondence between the foreign branch offices and Trieste, reports from the medical auditor and sometimes, as in this case, a photograph of the insured

Noteworthy among the key figures in this half a century of history, is Pietro Smolensky. Graduating in mathematics in Vienna, he started out as a Hapsburg citizen and became an Italian one in 1922. He was hired by Generali in 1907 where he worked with great success until the racial laws came into effect. In his capacity as actuary, he headed the technical department from 1920; in June 1937 he was promoted to manager of the entire division and responsible for: liaising with the other departments; advertising; and international coordination of life insurance activities (it was his idea to insure surgery risk, as later done by other companies nationally and internationally). He was very involved with the Istituto Italiano degli Attuari—a scientific association of insurance engineers the inception of which Smolensky had personally supported and of which he became the deputy chairman in 1934—publishing numerous articles in the institute's newspaper and participating in the annual congress.

His personal history is closely linked to that of the division, but in 1938 it was suddenly interrupted. Together, the life insurance management and the Hollerith department had ninety employees, as well as three executives (Smolensky, Chersi and Gino Tolentino) and four officers (Renato Ascoli, Federico Zalai, Ettore Gentilli and Guido Marocco), with a Jewish constituency of 9% among the clerical staff and over 70% in management. When the racial laws forced the company to dismiss its Jewish staff, the consequences were detrimental, not just for those who were made redundant, but also for the company itself, which had been deprived of valuable collaborators. To compensate, Generali began recruiting new staff and making new appointments; it hired Francesco Paolo Cantelli, who was the secretary of the Istituto Italiano degli Attuari, as the technical consultant for the life insurance division in the Central Head Office. Smolensky, who was recorded as having resigned on November 1, 1938, departed for Argentina in March 1939, where he settled and worked for Continental. His daughter Eleonora Maria, a historian, describes her family—in the book written with Vera Vigevani Jarach *Tante voci, una storia: italiani ebrei in Argentina, 1938–1948* (Bologna: il Mulino, 1998)—noting that when her father's dismissal became public knowledge, he became inundated with job offers.

The 1938 *Anschluss* and the events that followed, which in a short time led to the outbreak of the World War II and to Italy also entering the conflict, had direct consequences for the insurance market and the company's organizational structure, including that of life insurance. The company strategy needed to come to terms with Italy's political position during the conflict, specifically where its German ally was concerned, and the formidable competition posed by the German companies, in addition to that of the INA, which was facilitated by government interventionism. The Branch in Vienna became the center of activity for the *Deutsches Reich*, and because the German insurance laws prohibited the combined practice of damage and life insurances, the Vienna Office was assigned life insurance (while the subsidiary Erste Allgemeine in Vienna, managed the non-life types of policies). During these years, the balance of power between Italy and Germany determined Trieste's playing field, even in countries where its presence was already established, such as in Eastern Europe. The copies of the outgoing correspondence from the life insurance division (which the company referred to as "green copies" based on the color of the carbon copies in the 1960s and 1970s), the office for general business, and the actuarial office in particular, bear witness to the complexities of the historical context and the multiple fronts on which it was necessary to operate. With the political context constantly shifting, the company and division managers frequently found themselves negotiating for opportunities to insure and reinsure in various countries. Nonetheless, the business maintained a semblance of normalcy: with all the division offices carrying out their usual functions.

Besides the actuarial office and that for general business that acted as the division secretariat, the other offices included the portfolio office, which computed the reserves; the reinsurance office, for inward and outward reinsurance operations; the risk options office and the issuance (or adoption) office, for the examination of medical and financial issues of the insured [*fig.* 2]; the correspondence office; the claim settlement office; the variation office and the statistics office. The work was organized according to a structure defined in the 1930s, and which as we'll see, remained in place for a long time despite the fact that the specific administrative activities would vary.

The end of the war concluded these dramatic years; and so began the laborious process of reconstruction and the coming to terms with the fundamental changes in political balance. For the life insurance division this meant having to contend with the liquidation of portfolios in countries under the Iron Curtain.

Perhaps the documentation that most clearly allows the reconstruction of the activities in Trieste's life insurance management during the 1950s and 1960s, is the correspondence of the actuarial office, because that is where manager Longo wrote from. Despite it all, those were years of consistent growth in the life insurance division, both in terms of the amount of policies issued and the capital insured, which reaped remarkable profits and enhanced the company budgets thanks to considerable output in Italy and abroad. As well, in those years, Alleanza stood out among the foreign and national subsidiaries.

The outgoing correspondence of the 1950s was organized by country, giving an overview of the activities in the life insurance division. The issues grappled with in those years concerned the new national laws on compulsory social security, which saw the inception of institutions for the relevant industry sectors such as, for insurance, the Istituto Nazionale della Previdenza Sociale, which dealt with profit sharing for life insurance policyholders; the revaluation of life insurance; nuclear risks; and group insurance. The relationship with the governmental body INA, which played a prominent role in the industry, was essential in defining the company's policy and that of all private insurers.

The agreement signed on January 31, 1966 in Milan, between Generali and the American companies Aetna Life and Casualty (with headquarters in Hartford, Connecticut), led to comprehensive changes to the organizational structure in life insurance. The basis for the agreement was the intention of the two large groups to provide reciprocal insurance cover to clients outside their respective areas of operation (*i.e.* insuring Aetna's American clients outside of Canada and America by leaning on Generali, while using Aetna for the clients of the Generali Group in the United States). The organization of these new activities, which included reinsurance transfers between Aetna and Generali, was complex. The arrangement resulted in four trade agreements on life insurance: two concerned inward and outward reinsurance for Group Health in the United States and Canada, and all other regions; the other two concerned Group Life. The preliminary phase of the trade agreements proved demanding, though not as much as their actual implementation, which involved numerous subsidiaries from both groups, and also lead to new trade agreements such as those with Australia.

The documentation of the life insurance division is invaluable in reconstructing the complexities of the behind-the-scenes operations. To begin with, it is noted that as early as 1964 the division submitted a number of studies to the Central Head Office on the characteristics of group insurance in individual European countries. A significant shift in balance in the relationship with the foreign branches had manifested in the early 1960s after reports to the Frankfurt Branch had become less frequent—and after having asserted its autonomy—and more players emerged, like Alessandro Cordero di Montezemolo, head of Generali's representative office in New York. At management level the conduits for the trade agreement, especially in the initial stages, were Montezemolo

3.
Photo taken on the occasion of the signing of the Aetna agreement (Milan, January 13, 1966)
[ASAG, *Presidenza e organi sociali, Presidenti e vicepresidenti, Gino Baroncini*, U2GE023998]

From left to right: Olcott D. Smith, Fabio Padoa and Gino Baroncini before the prints gifted to Smith, Aetna's president

who remained in New York until the end of 1972, and Fabio Padoa who had a brilliant career as superintendent of foreign affairs [*fig.* 3]. In 1965, when Baroncini had already considered retiring, a significant change at the helm took place: Alberto Melchiori and Giuseppe Bufano retired; Franco Mannozzi was promoted to managing director; while Arturo Scabar and Padoa were appointed general managers. Padoa was also appointed managing director in 1968, and deputy chairman in 1970.

Before concluding the agreement, in October 1965 Aetna's management undertook a visit to Trieste and to Generali's main Branch Offices in Europe. The briefing, to examine the opportunities for collaboration with the life insurance division, took place on October 12, and focused on group insurance both in case of death and in case of life, in case the contracts contemplated pension plans. Thus, Generali launched the employee benefits scheme (benefits such as pension funds, health care and policies that are offered by the employer to the employees), a sector that was already well established in the United States, and which would become one of Generali's core businesses globally. Relying on Generali's ability to operate directly and indirectly in most of Europe, Aetna would point out profitable American companies with representation in various European countries, and receive a share of the new business by way of reinsurance. However, unlike group insurance, which the company already handled, according to the new trade agreement a contract stipulated between a company in the United States and local representatives in various countries, would result in a single deal the total profit of which exceeded that of several nations. As well, such a transaction would include health and accident insurance, which were handled by Generali's Head Office in Milan. While the first requests for tenders arrived and the important meetings with the Hartford representatives, the division managers of branches and of subsidiaries for life insurance were under way, the challenges gradually came into focus. What was needed was to quickly devise international and local procedures to bridge the American social security models with the consolidated, competitive ones in different countries; to equally consider the center and the periphery; to bring the staff up to date on group insurance; and to make it possible to issue timely, centralized and consistent tenders for international clients. It was also necessary to devise new procedures to streamline the interactions between the Head Offices in Trieste, Venice, and Milan and the Branch in New York, the latter redirecting all the American proposals and managing the communications with Aetna [*fig.* 4].

After the mission to Hartford with Central Manager Eugenio Coppola di Canzano from the Central Head Office, Giorgio Balzer from the life insurance division and Mariano De Martino from Milan, between late 1966 and 1967 the procedure for the Group Life sector was finalized. This lead to Generali's Worldwide Group Plan (GWG), which contemplated the mutual exchange of premiums and scores for a client shared by Aetna and Generali (Twentieth Century Fox among their first clients).

These years marked the start of a boom in life insurance, as testified by the burst of documentation. In 1966 the life division alone generated eight hundred outgoing letters signed by Longo, Ara and Agacci; the following year the amount almost tripled. The requests for tenders for group insurance and pensions, which in 1966 were just forty, by 1967 had grown to about eight hundred. In 1970 a new group insurance service was introduced into the actuary office, which had initially managed all of Aetna's work—with the exception of reinsurance, which was handled by Ara. This new service was headed by Agacci (in the capacity of co-manager), and included two tender offices that would later be joined by one for international liaisons in 1973. The activities for issuing, risk selection and claim settlement, were cut back to mere risk selection, which in those years had become part of actuarial services. The other part of the division was responsible for portfolios and reinsurance, and was headed by manager Ara.

Compared to the casualty and property divisions, life insurance was a groundbreaker in more ways than one. Over time, as the most crucial aspects of the agreement were resolved, products and procedures were refined and advertising campaigns organized. The Aetna agreement was the launch pad for many young officers in the division who, over the years, were transferred abroad to strengthen the organization's employee benefits in Brussels, New York, London, and Frankfurt. Most notably in 1972, Brussels became the venue for the General European Marketing Office (GEMO), Generali and Aetna's common European headquarters and long since Generali's point of reference for this branch of insurance. (R.S.)

4.
Commemorative medal of the Aetna agreement (1966) [CGG]

Insurance without Frontiers

Assicurazioni Generali in the European Community

1957
1990

Historically, Assicurazioni Generali's international profile, specifically in Europe, has been characterized by its numerous branches, agencies and subsidiaries across the world, and for its dealings in reinsurance [*fig.* 1].

In his article, "L'assicurazione come attività internazionale", which appeared in the *Bollettino* of 1964, the longstanding company executive Fabio Padoa (who was central manager, general manager, managing director and deputy chairman), wrote: "In a world such as ours [...], in which despite much discussion of international collaboration, where foreign exchange restrictions and financial frameworks of different kinds persist between countries, insurance is an example of a free business that would not exist if it weren't for the collaboration across borders."

After the World War II the company worked at a top level with the new supranational bodies, and among them were the first institutions of the European Community such as the European Coal and Steel Community (ECSC) and, mostly after the 1957 Rome Treaty, the European Economic Community (EEC), as well as the European Atomic Energy Community (EURATOM). The company also worked with the first regional organization set up in the postwar period: the Organization for European Economic Cooperation (OEEC), which became the Organization for Economic Cooperation and Development (OECD).

The birth of the EEC, and the long evolution leading to a single European market place in 1992 (and in 1990 to the freedom to provide insurance services in the non-life sector), which vanquished the once the bureaucratic constraints and the fee schedules which hindered the circulation of goods and services, had direct repercussions on the company's industrial policy and its representational activities.

Established in 1953, the Comité Européen des Assurances (CEA) was and still is the conduit for dealing with the bodies of the EEC, bringing together and permanently uniting the national associations of many European countries, including Italy, one of its first members. The committee undertakes to examine the common problems in insurance and to formulate ideas and proposals for the international bodies; at the forefront: EEC and OECD (since 2012 Insurance Europe).

The company's representatives were immediately active on CEA's various temporary committees and working groups, and still are today; the project of a common market offered important changes in insurance that were fundamental in defining Generali's international strategy and because it was elaborated at Group level [*fig.* 2], the strategy would have been very differed according to whether it was applied to closed markets and individual nations, or to a single market.

The company was always first in line in shaping, anticipating and adapting to the EEC's market peculiarities. From the moment Generali's Head Office in Milan became responsible for motor vehicle insurance and accident insurance, the CEA working group for motor insurance, was often presided by Generali's Milanese executives. Francesco Cincotti, who was the central manager and later the general manager for Milan—as well as deputy chairman of the health working group for some years—was the president of the motor insurance group from 1956, a defining time for the sector. The evolution of massive international road transit posed new challenges that required unified European policies. In those years the green paper system was introduced, an international insurance document that permitted motorist to transit in countries with a compulsory insurance scheme. The green paper was based on a system of national bureaux; in Italy, it was the Ufficio Centrale Italiano (UCI), which combined all the providers of car public liability insurance, and which in the early years was led by Cincotti himself. Today the green card is no longer needed to transit through the EU countries, although it is still recognized in some countries outside the EU. If one considers how different the framework for the legislation was a few decades ago, compared to the current-day one (in Italy the legal obligation for motor insurance was enforced in 1969, and seatbelts and helmets became compulso-

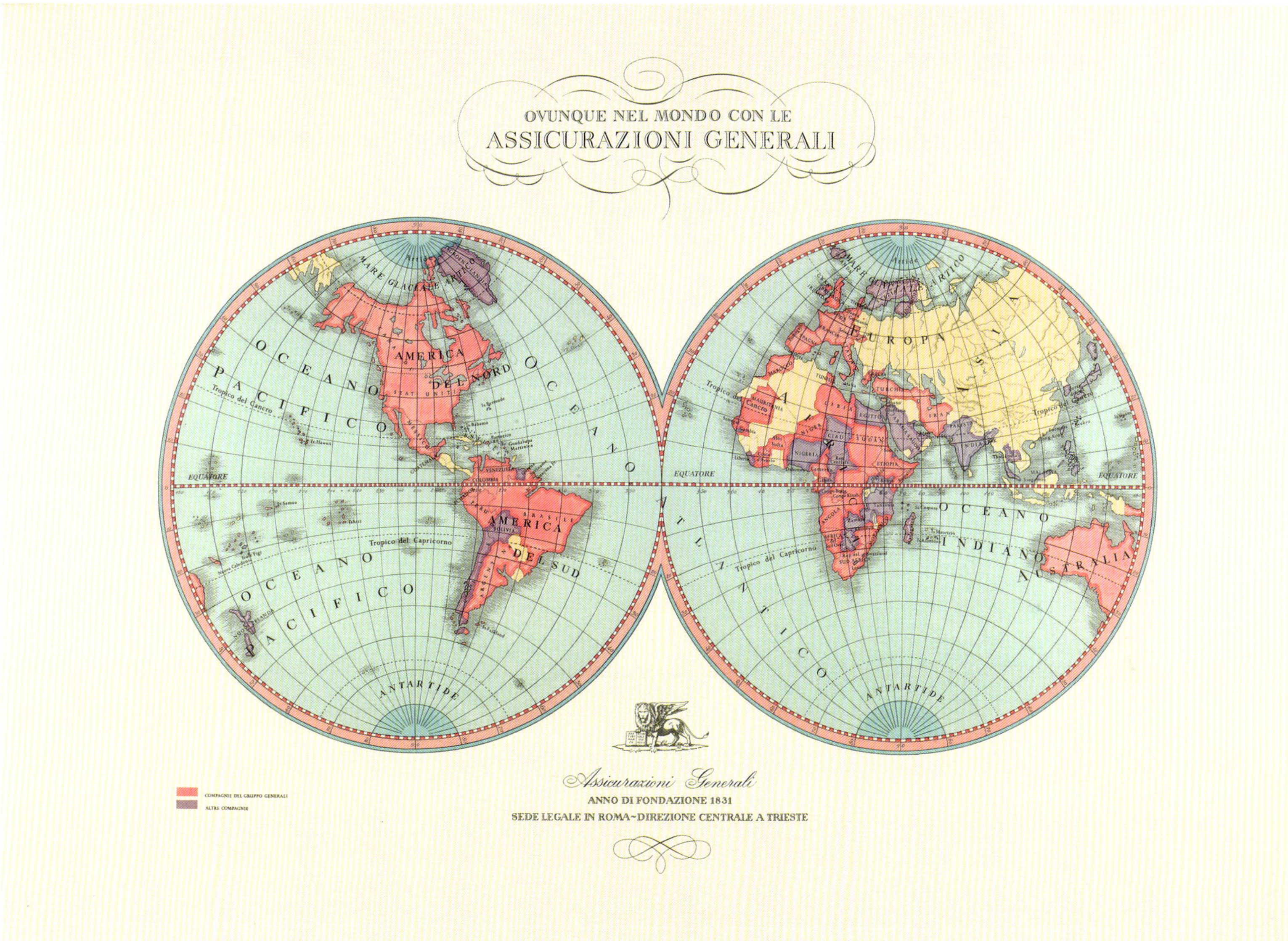

1.
Map depicting the world of Generali
[1967]
[BCAG]

2.
Advertising foldout for the European insurance policy (1960)
[ASAG, *Miscellanea*, scheda 6808]

ry in the 1980s), the importance of the green paper is even more remarkable.

After Cincotti, it was Enrico Randone who as the conduit for car insurance took on increasingly important projects in this area—this in addition to the work he did inside the company where, in the decade 1969–1979 from central manager he was promoted to chairman and managing director—in CEA (from 1973 through 1977 he was the chairman and then deputy chairman of the car working group, and in 1976 he headed a commission of experts that submitted a proposal for a European motor insurance policy in Brussels); the Associazione Nazionale fra le Imprese Assicuratrici (ANIA); and the UCI. As chairman of Generali he was no longer directly involved with CEA, but remained its conduit, helping define the company's international policy for the sector.

During the 1970s another Milanese company executive, Mariano De Martino, joined him at CEA and his work in the sector lead to the establishment of a dedicated office, what is currently known as the service named Group EU & International Affairs of the Head Office.

Within the detailed framework of international company associations, one worthy of mention is the important role played by the research department, which since the 1970s has promoted numerous conferences and studies with a focus on the relationship between the insurance industry and the EEC.

For a long period of time, spanning from the 1950s through the 1980s, Fabio Padoa was the conduit for the company's international relations. Padoa was a contact of note because he was an outstanding insurer (in fact, responsible for Generali's foreign markets) and because he valued training and insurance studies. His contributions in this area are numerous and significant: he promoted the foundation Geneva Association, a.k.a. International Association for the Study of Insurance Economics of which he was the president; the Istituto Nazionale per la Formazione Professionale Assicurativa (IFA nowadays is in-

3.
Published articles by Fabio Padoa (1956–1976)
[ASAG, *Presidenza e organi sociali, Presidenti e vicepresidenti, Fabio Padoa*, U2GE027330]

corporated in ANIA); and the Consorzio Universitario per l'Ingegneria nelle Assicurazioni (CINEAS).
His representational duties on behalf of Generali were prestigious: president of ANIA's commission for international relations, from 1964; president of the EEC working group "5b," which united private experts and members of public supervisory bodies on insurance; and longstanding vice president and president of CEA in the 1970s and 1980s.
He was very active on various CEA committees, in some cases even prompting their creation, and dedicated himself to issues he considered crucial for the development of the EEC, such as productivity; the relationship between countries in the EEC and those outside it; and insurance training. These are recurring themes throughout his personal history. Very early in 1959, for example, he proposed the collection of European statistical data on productivity, entrusting a CEA working group with reports on issues pertaining to insurance, and which had been constituted at the Economic Commission for Europe—a body that worked under the aegis of the United Nations and was tasked with managing the relationship with Eastern Europe. Member of the working group for the problems of the Common European Market (CEM) in the 1960s, in the 1970s he presided over the Commission for *Information et Liaison*, which developed ties between the insurers in members of the Common European Market, those outside it, and the OECD, acting as an EEC agent in disseminating information to the insurers of non-CEM countries on various projects with a CEM mandate (freedom to provide services, the liberalization of co-insurance). In 1982 he became the president of a new training working group that he had created, and which became permanent.
In his numerous and popular published writings, and in his files [*fig.* 3], these two drives materialize in a complementary manner; it's an organic vision that is not just technical about the issues that the Treaty of Rome raised on the insurance business.
His knowledge of the foreign market, thanks to Generali's international scope, afforded him a complete understanding of the European framework, which combined with an aptitude for diplomatic relations proved useful to the CEA and the EEC, in addition to his role as company manager.
Given the European market's importance for Generali, the company's entire industrial policy was articulated in response to the EEC's developments, striking an ever-changing balance between centralization, which was fostered by the parent company and prominent local autonomy. A great example of this is the "Aetna" deal. The 1966 agreement between Generali and the American group Aetna Life and Casualty, which provided reciprocal insurance covers to the customers outside their respective areas of operation, led Generali to review its organizational model and to centralize the employee benefits sector (pension funds and/or health care policies offered by the employer to the employees) through the establishment of the Generali Worldwide Group Plan (GWG) and the Generali European Marketing Office (GEMO) in Brussels. On the other hand, it must not be forgotten that it was the specialization of the individual national branches that guaranteed the company's international success.
Among the specific commercial projects relating to the EEC, in 1960 there was the launch of the European insurance policy; this was a life insurance policy that followed the insured through changes of residence within the CEM, adjusting the currency for each new country. In the 1980s a turning point in the life insurance sector was the introduction of with-profits policies—in 1978 Generali first introduced policies with profit sharing, perfecting them gradually up to the special management of life insurance (GESAV), which combined mixed policies with pensions—which had been promoted by the managing director Alfonso Desiata and Paolo Iona, manager of life insurance in Trieste. The European insurance policy became a mixed policy and a with-profits policy. The premiums and benefits were calculated in the European Currency Unit (ECU), the currency in use before the introduction of the Euro,

and which protected the underwriters from the devaluation of the Lira in comparison to the other European currencies. The first insurance policies in ECU were introduced in 1982. They comprised a single premium with a cover guaranteed by an EURATOM debenture loan. Subsequently the European policies had both single and annual premiums, with special investment management in the ECU. At that time, the non-life insurance introduced the Ecuhotel policy, a product that provided cover for the hospitality sector.

Equally interesting is taking a brief look at the company's international advertising strategy, which was increasingly characterized by a need for cohesion.

Almost simultaneously to the European insurance policy, in 1961 the company press office published the booklet *Insurance in the Common Market*, which was widely distributed in Italy and abroad. It described the insurances on offer in each country of the EEC (initially these were six: Italy, Germany, France, Belgium, Luxembourg and The Netherlands) to investors and foreign brokers, specifically American ones, and noted Generali's agencies, branches and subsidiaries in each state. Both the pamphlet and the European insurance policy were characterized by a special logo, with an "E" for Europe at the center, intertwined with the Lion of Saint Mark, against the background, the CEM borders.

In subsequent years, the company developed its internal structure to cater for its promotional needs and, in 1975, it introduced an advertising department. Like the press office that was within the sphere of the central secretariat, it eventually developed into the public relations and publicity office. A global campaign to divulge a strong Group identity, was developed for the first time in 1970, hand-in-hand with the decision to standardize the company name by using the name "Generali" globally ("Da oggi chiamateci Generali" read the motto in the print campaign). A style manual was issued to ensure all offices and agencies complied with the use of the logo of the lion.

In 1984 an organic advertising campaign was launched ("Generali: un libro aperto") and, under many aspects, 1990 was a crucial year. As mentioned before, it marked the opening up of the EU common market for the non-life insurance sector. It was also the launch of the company's first international advertising campaign across eight European countries ("Generali, the insurer without frontiers") [*fig.* 4], and the simultaneous launch of the Group's single new logo. Not surprisingly, as a result of the 1992 merger of the public relations, internal relations, publicity and publishing offices, a new business unit came into being: communication department, which was led by Armando Zimolo. Its purpose was to coordinate and enhance the flow of information of the company and the Group. (R.S.)

4.
Poster of the advertising campaign "Generali, the insurer without frontiers" (1991)
[CGG]

Fabio Padoa

1911
2012

For almost two decades, Fabio Padoa lead Assicurazioni Generali's foreign department from 1957 to 1976, after succeeding Michele Sulfina [*figs.* 1–3]. As Sulfina's 'heir' he managed the company's operations and, through his work, he carried on a corporate tradition that was over one hundred years old. This tradition was shaped by a cosmopolitan culture, informed by experiences within a closely-knit network of relationships, and personal contacts that included leaders of international insurance and finance. A tradition that was nevertheless capable of innovation; Padoa was well aware that although specialist industry knowledge was a prerequisite for all management, it was no longer sufficient to successfully lead an enterprise. In a society that was becoming increasingly more complex, compared to that which followed the World War II, and which questioned social hierarchies based exclusively on authority, rather than leadership and consensus, Padoa saw the business as a living organism, comprised of the people who worked there. He felt that the company needed to encompass a broader dimension: "It must be enriched—he argued—by a spiritual component. It must resemble a chosen family, express emotional values beyond its financial purposes, represent style and values and it cannot endure without active participation."

Born in Naples on January 7, 1911, Fabio Padoa was educated in an environment that was closely connected to Assicurazioni Generali's management. The father, Mario Padoa, was Jewish. Born in 1879 in the province of Bologna, he relocated to Trieste a few years later (where in 1883 his sister Albertina was born and who would later marry Marco Ara). He began his career in the Romanian subsidiary after which he divided his responsibilities between Concorde in Paris, where he had moved to in 1907 and became its general manager in 1920; and Anonima Infortuni in Milan, becoming its general manager in 1923. In 1928 this position allowed him to become part of Generali's Board of Directors and eventually member of its General Council from 1930 through 1937. The following year, he was appointed to the Council of Directors. After the war, in 1947 Anonima Infortuni merged with its parent company and Mario Padoa headed Assicurazioni Generali's Milan Head Office. In 1950 he became once again, part of the Board of Directors and later the General Council. Thanks to his international competencies and having successfully dealt with the challenging and recurring currency and financial crises of the 1920s and 1930s, he was regarded as one of the most knowledgeable insurers of his time. In March 1946, at a time when Italy's nascent economic reconstruction was still exposed to the risks of inflation, the Constituent Assembly requested to interview him on the issues faced by the insurance industry in relation to the foreign market—an invitation that, as an insurance manager, he shared exclusively with Michele Sulfina.

His son, Fabio, decided to undertake the same career. Graduating in law in 1933 in Milan and following a four-month stint volunteering for Erste Allgemeine Unfall in Vienna, in 1931 he began an apprenticeship that was deliberately chosen in Central Europe at a time when it was still the company's pulsating business center and comprised countries with the most established and productive markets. It also enjoyed the sector's most close-knit relationships in direct, indirect, and reinsurance work. After an initial period at Erste Allgemeine Unfall, from 1934 through 1935, Padoa transferred to the company's Branch in Vienna where he managed a group of companies in Poland, Romania and Yugoslavia, acquiring skills in the claims, liability, accident, accounting, budget and reinsurance sectors.

Following the *Anschluss* in March 1938 and the implementation of the racial Nuremberg laws in Austria, the risks that the German companies' aggressive policies posed to the two prominent companies of Trieste became more acute and, in all probability, were decisive in returning him to the homeland without delay. He was reassigned to the main agency in Genoa in April 1938. There, he was able to build on his expe-

1.
Fabio Padoa, at the center, and Cesare Merzagora, second from the right, are welcomed by the deputy chairman of the Banco Vitalicio Manuel Garí-Arana in Barcelona (Barcelona, May 1970)
[ASAG, *Presidenza e organi sociali, Presidenti e vicepresidenti, Fabio Padoa*, U2GE027327]

2.
Fabio Padoa and Cesare Merzagora in Germany (Munich, April 1970) [ASAG, *Presidenza e organi sociali, Presidenti e vicepresidenti, Fabio Padoa*, U2GE027355]

rience by learning about the transport sector in anticipation of a transfer to London, a plan that would never eventuate.
Between September and November 1938, Italy had adopted the anti-Semitic laws, the effects of which greatly aggrieved the Padoa family. His father, Mario, was deposed from all his responsibilities whereas Fabio, according to the law, was from a "mixed" marriage (his mother Elena Schioppa was a catholic with no Jewish ancestry), which enabled Fabio Padoa to keep his employment, albeit as the manager of Alleanza Vita's agency in Florence. In October 1940 he was recruited as an army reserve officer in North Africa and Sicily, where in July 1943, he became prisoner of the Anglo-American forces. After the war and having returned to civilian life, in 1946 he attained a second degree, in philosophy, at the University of Florence where he obtained tenure. Until 1949, he taught history and philosophy in a lyceum in the province of Genoa. Though not a momentous experience, it would shape his values and personality. Many years later, in consideration of a manager's prerequisites he noted that the profession demanded unique educational skills in relation to its employees, and the ability to motivate and lead staff in their daily tasks.
Like many Italians of his generation, for over a decade his life had been subjected to unpredictable changes between 1938 and 1949, as a result of which he was forced to readjust his goals. Eventually, in 1949, the conditions were such that Fabio Padoa was able to resume his youthful career goals; at the end of that same year he returns to Alleanza Vita in Milan in the capacity of deputy manager, where he remained until April 1953; after which he was offered the same post in Assicurazioni Generali's Head Office in Trieste. During the 1950s, he climbed the internal career ladder: being promoted from manager to central manager in 1959. During the first years that followed his return, he directed Italy's internal market place, which was experiencing a significant

3.
Fabio Padoa in Brazil (April 1973) [ASAG, *Presidenza e organi sociali, Presidenti e vicepresidenti, Fabio Padoa*, U2GE027355]

recovery hand in hand with the country's economic growth and even demonstrated potential for expansion, specifically in the life insurance sector, which was underdeveloped campared to its potential for growth. His work was not limited to operations, and also included staff development for the agencies that operated across Italy; in this area, he emphasized the importance of psychology and communication when dealing with clients. These values were also evident in a series of conferences and articles he published in the corporate magazine, in which he expressed his educational aims in a lively writing style.
During a long visit to the Americas in 1957, Padoa began a series of activities aimed at those international markets that would play a key role in Assicurazioni Generali's future. From the start of the decade, following the loss of the eastern European market, the strategy was to consolidate and grow the company by focusing on the markets in France, Germany, Austria and Spain, while seeking opportunities abroad, in the United States and Latin America. Padoa traveled back in 1963, a trip that was as productive as the first. In 1969 he undertook the first mission as company manager in Australia; to expand the existing operations in the vast continent. In 1965—the same year in which he became Assicurazioni Generali's general manager—Padoa stipulated an agreement with the American company Aetna Life and Casualty, thus widening the company's business reach in a market that had traditionally been difficult for Italian companies to penetrate. He thought of applying the unique model adopted by the North American company, which was based on mutual cooperation and assistance across all multinational operations, and thereby modernizing insurance's international characteristics.
Another matter that concerned Padoa was the process of European economic and monetary integration as sanctioned by the Treaty of Rome in 1957, and modeled after the European Payments Union (EPU) in 1950, and endorsed by the European Monetary Agreement (EMA) in 1958.
The liberalization of the insurance sector as part of an expected and more extensive suite of liberalization of goods and services, lead him to view European integration as a turning point for the insurance business, which would lead to the removal of borders and the introduction of a communal legislation; thus becoming an integral part of the wider international community [*fig.* 4]. Chairman Merzagora rewarded his commitment by promoting him to managing director responsible for the foreign sectors and the budget in 1968, and to deputy chairman in 1970. However, in a landscape affected by growing economic instability and troubled by inflation, their collaboration became strained by opposing strategic goals: while Padoa valued the managerial aspect of insurance, Merzagora focused on the company's financial assets and real estate investments.
In February 1976, upon turning 65 and having reached the prescribed age limit for managing directors, Padoa resigned, and in June 1977, also resigned from the deputy chairmanship. He continued to participate on the Group's many Boards (in Holland, Belgium, Spain and Austria) throughout the 1980s; until 1992 he was a member of the Board in the parent company. Though removed from corporate responsibilities in Italy, his professional life remained productive for many more years. He pursued his interest for Europe's integration of the insurance market through the Comité Européen des Assurances (CEA), an organization established in 1953 to represent the national associations of nineteen European countries and of which he became the president in 1976. He was also a spokesman of the European Economic Community (EEC) and the Organization for Economic Cooperation and Development (OECD). The international prestige that he achieved in the global insurance market, led him to become president of the Geneva Association from 1976 through 1983, a think-tank for the insurance industry that he had founded in Paris in 1973 together with the former French Prime Minister, Raymond Barre, and Orio Giarini, and with the par-

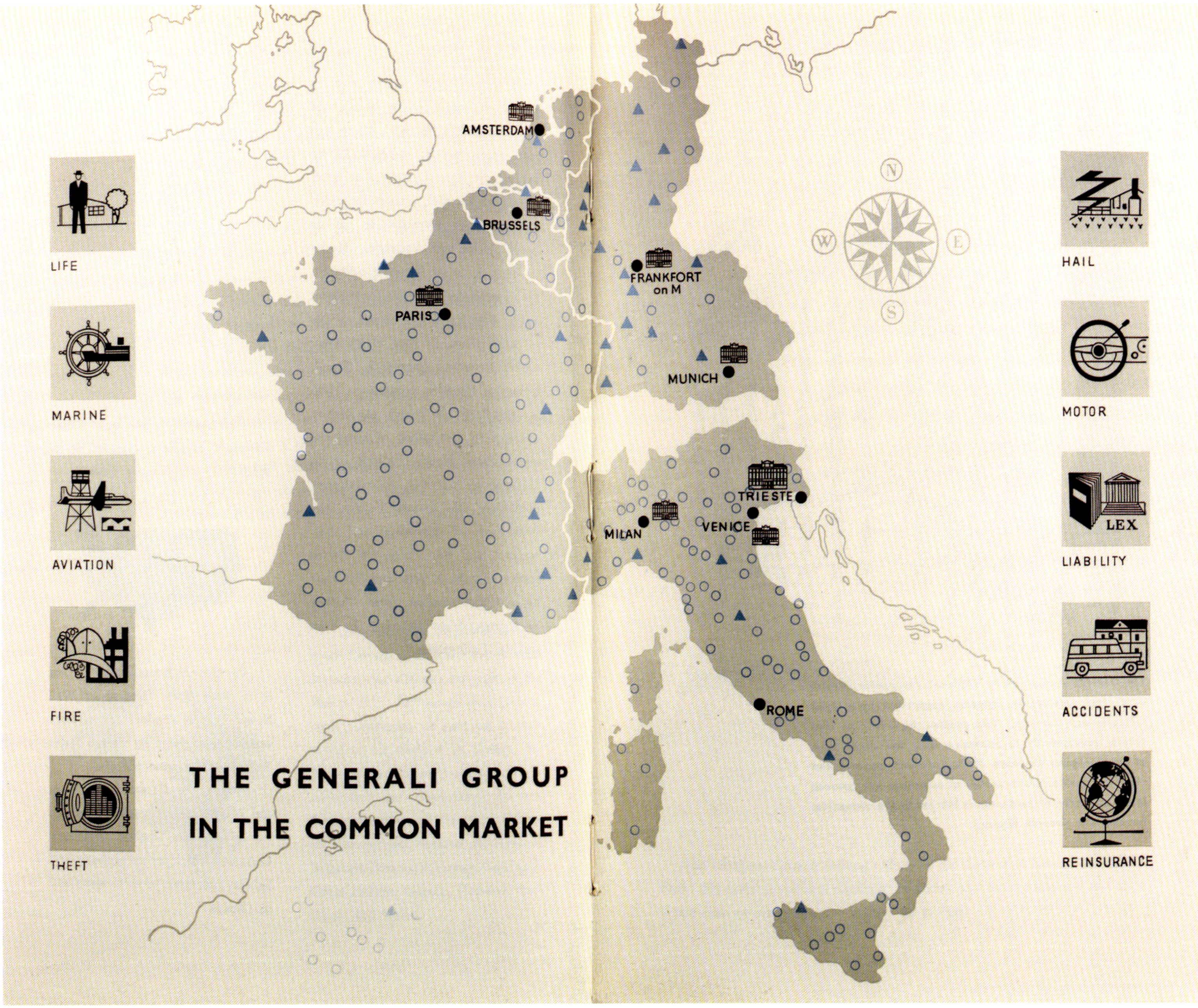

4.
Map of the Generali Group in the CEM from *Insurance in the Common Market* (1961)
[ASAG, *Miscellanea*, scheda 6808]

ticipation of Europe's largest insurance companies. In 1976 he became counselor of the Consiglio Nazionale dell'Economia e del Lavoro (CNEL) as a representative of the insurance industry.

His most significant contribution is articulated in a long 1992 proposal for the reform of the Italian pension system, the goals of which aimed to fix the existing anomalies, restore the public accounts, and lessen the conflictual social climate; all objectives that Italy needed to achieve in order to fulfil Europe's Maastricht Treaty. Fiercely Europeanist, he believed that integration with Europe was an opportunity to improve the Italian social and political systems. Up to his last years of activity, he devoted a modest but essential effort to education and training. As the president of the Istituto Nazionale per la Formazione Assicurativa (IFA), he supported a school-to-work approach, a training project for the young generations on the subject of insurance and, specifically, a greater knowledge of insurance.

He died in Milan on August 17, 2012.

Sources

ASAG. *Direzione centrale, Servizio del personale, Posizioni personali.* U2GE042662, personnel file of Fabio Padoa, 1935–1978; U2GE042661, personnel file of Mario Padoa, 1914–1968.

"Interrogatorio del dott. Mario Padoa, direttore generale dell'Anonima Infortuni (11 marzo 1946)," in Ministero per la costituente, *Rapporto della commissione economica presentato all'Assemblea Costituente*, vol. III, *Problemi monetari e commercio estero*, II, *Appendice alla relazione (Interrogatori, questionari, monografie)*, 151–54. Rome: Istituto Poligrafico dello Stato, 1946.

"La scomparsa del consigliere generale gr. uff. Mario Padoa." *Bollettino delle Assicurazioni Generali* 3–4 (1968), p. 77.

Works

Padoa, Fabio. "L'assicurazione italiana: panorama 1951." *Bollettino delle Assicurazioni Generali* 5–6 (1953): 1–3.

—. "C'è una tecnica della fiducia." *Bollettino delle Assicurazioni Generali* 12 (1953): 16–17.

—. "Vendere sicurezza: la funzione degli assicuratori." *Bollettino delle Assicurazioni Generali* 1 (1955): 3–6.

—. "Il mercato italiano: luci e ombre." *Bollettino delle Assicurazioni Generali* 2–3 (1955): 7–9.

—. "Uomini-sì e uomini-no." *Bollettino delle Assicurazioni Generali* 6–7 (1955): 12–13.

—. *Vendere sicurezza*. Milan: Alleanza Assicurazioni, 1955.

—. "Assicurazione privata e mercato commune." *Bollettino delle Assicurazioni Generali* 5–6 (1958): 9–12.

—. "L'assicurazione di persone nel Mercato Comune." *Bollettino delle Assicurazioni Generali* 10–11 (1960): 7–11.

—. "L'assicurazione come attività internazionale." *Bollettino delle Assicurazioni Generali* 6–7 (1964): 15–20.

—. "L'avvenire della vendita assicurativa." *Bollettino delle Assicurazioni Generali* 8 (1973): 1–4.

—. "Siamo ricchi e poveri." *Bollettino delle Assicurazioni Generali* 22 (1975): 1–3.

—. "Le assicurazioni private e il mercato comune europeo." In *Problemi attuali delle assicurazioni private e della previdenza sociale*, edited by the Faculty of Statistical, Demographic and Actuarial Sciences at the University of Rome. Milan: Giuffrè, 1960: 20–25.

—. "Le assicurazioni di persone nella Comunità Europea." *Assicurazioni. Rivista di diritto, economia e finanza delle assicurazioni private* 4–5 (1960): 3–20.

—. "È l'ora dell'assicurazione multinazionale." *Diritto e pratica dell'assicurazione* 4 (1968): 674–77.

—. "Assicurazione e distribuzione." *Assicurazioni. Rivista di diritto, economia e finanza delle assicurazioni private* 4–5 (1972): 368–77.

—, and Passanisi, Emilio. "Impiego e controllo delle riserve tecniche delle imprese assicuratrici: legislazione italiana, legislazioni europee e direttive comunitarie." *Assicurazioni. Rivista di diritto, economia e finanza delle assicurazioni private* 6 (1972): 713–69.

—. “La normativa comunitaria nel settore assicurativo: il ruolo delle compagnie triestine.” In *Seminario su: “Il processo di integrazione europea ed i suoi riflessi sull’economia di Trieste e della Regione Friuli-Venezia Giulia”*, duplicated copy. S.l., s.a. [1976?].
—. “Profili internazionali del controllo sulle imprese assicuratrici.” *Assicurazioni. Rivista di diritto, economia e finanza delle assicurazioni private* 6 (1978): 628–39.
—. “La conduzione dell’impresa.” In *L’assicurazione internazionale*, 79-87. Milan: Hoepli, 1983 (quote on 79–80).
—. *La sicurezza sociale e il ruolo delle Compagnie di assicurazione*, edited by Assicurazioni Generali S.p.A. Trieste, Assicurazioni Generali, 1983: 29–32.
—. *La riforma della previdenza: un’Italia diversa è a portata di mano*. Bologna: il Mulino, 1992.
Bruschi, Luciano and Cova, Marina. *I giovani e le assicurazioni. Modelli formativi per un’integrazione scuola-lavoro*, preface by Fabio Padoa. Milan: Guerini & Associati, 1996.

Bibliography

De Felice, Renzo. *Storia degli ebrei italiani sotto il fascismo*, new expanded edition. Turin: Einaudi, 1993: 349–51.
De Ianni, Nicola. “Tra industria e finanza. Alle Assicurazioni Generali (1968–1979).” In *Cesare Merzagora. Il presidente scomodo*, edited by Nicola De Ianni and Paolo Varvaro, 120–47, 161, 177. Naples: Prismi, 2004.
Fauri, Francesca. *L’integrazione economica europea 1947–2006*. Bologna: il Mulino, 2006.
Favaretto, Tito. “Lo sviluppo dell’attività internazionale delle Assicurazioni Generali tra il XIX e il XX secolo.” In *Assicurare 150 anni di Unità d’Italia. Il contributo delle assicurazioni allo sviluppo del Paese*, edited by Paolo Garonna, 93–151. Rome: Ania, 2011.
(A.M.)

Glimpses in Black and White

The Real Estate Business in Pictures: Palazzo Geiringer's Renovation

1966

Over the years, Generali acquired office spaces that were specifically designed for and by them in all main European cities and elsewhere, by selecting the most strategic and desirable locations. These buildings were not intended as mere work spaces, or simply for show, they were residential real estate investments that upgraded, developed and enhanced various urban areas.
Worthy of note are the company's great works that were undertaken in Italy's major city centers, among which a stand out was the restoration of Palazzo delle Procuratie Vecchie in Venice. It was executed by architect Giulio Fano (the first renovation dates back to 1909–1914, when the company became the majority owner; the second took place in 1941–1943, during the acquisition of the remaining lots). Another standout is the construction of the building in Piazza Venezia, in Rome (1902–1907). The latter was designed by architect Giuseppe Sacconi, who was also responsible for planning the square that showcased the Vittoriano building. The alterations were carried out by Eugenio Geiringer, who was the technical consultant on all Milanese projects. Other works of note include the excavation around Piazza Cordusio in Milan, which became the site of the building designed by Luca Beltrami (1897–1900); a new project by the engineer Pietro Fenoglio (1909–1911), in the area of Piazza Solferino in Turin; an old block in Via Roma, expropriated by the city of Palermo, which became the site of an elegant building by architect Ernesto Basile (1912); and several minor works across the peninsula's other cities.
Equally extensive were the works that in term of real estate, over the years, were carried out in Trieste, which was Generali's historic home and, as such, significant contributions to the city's revitalization were made. The site of the headquarters, in Piazza Luigi Amedeo Duca degli Abruzzi, was constructed by Geiringer between 1884 and 1886. He had been working as an independent building renovations consultant for the company, at least since 1871 [*fig.* 1]. Various projects were considered such as the acquisition of the Hotel de la Ville (built on the waterfront during the first half of the nineteenth century and based on a project by Giovanni Degasperi); the Hierschel building in Corso Italia (constructed in 1833 and designed by Antonio Buttazzoni for Mosè Hierschel, a rich merchant in Trieste); and a plot of land owned by Stefano Paximadi, in Via della Stazione—today's Corso Cavour (formerly della Posta Vecchia then Riva delle Poste, due to the post office being located on the ground floor of the Paximadi building from 1798)—between Via Machiavelli, formerly dei Forni, and Via Torrebianca, formerly Contrada Carinzia. Finally, the choice fell on the latter, which allowed for the construction of a new building that would be equipped with comfortable spaces, a modern electrical system (the city's first), a hydronic heating system for the transit zones, and gas heating in the rooms, and which had the option of future extensions towards the boundary areas.
Simultaneously to the new construction projects, Generali put in place an ongoing property repair and maintenance schedule for their buildings, which included the renovation of buildings of particular artistic and historic value, the purchase of which dated back to the beginning of the company's real estate investments. At times it was necessary to undertake renovations that, without altering the outer appearance of the buildings, allowed for the reorganization of the internal space, and the update of equipment to keep up with modern-day requirements. This is why a major renovation to the Central Head Office took place in the second half of the 1960s: to provide a new access point to the main agency's hall, from Via Machiavelli, and to open up the public space and widen the offices behind the cashier's desk on the mezzanine.
The most comprehensive works consisted of the lobby and the grand staircase in Piazza Duca degli Abruzzi. To create a new assembly hall on the first floor, and to build the required space for the main agency on the mezzanine below, the staircase was removed and a slab

1.
Assicurazioni Generali's building,
Palazzo Geiringer, headquarters
of the Central Head Office, Trieste
[1925–1928]
[ASAG, *Versamenti*, scheda 27520]

was created. The empty stairwell, behind the two rear columns in the lobby, was closed off. The bronze relief by Gigi Supino, commemorating the fallen World War I Italian soldiers, which in 1926 had been placed on the landing, below the sculptural group *Previdenza* (1886) by Ivan Rendić , was repositioned at the floor below opposite the main entrance [*figs.* 2–3].
Another plan, in Via Machiavelli, consisted of covering the courtyard adjacent to the stairwell next to the entrance, to house a lab and an archive. The plan increased the usable area inside the building and provided for an assembly hall, agency offices, and a public space. By sacrificing the square footage occupied by the offices of the agricultural firms, which were relocated, a flight of stairs was installed to gain access from Via Machiavelli. On the second and third floors, in the rooms for building attendants, the transport division and life archives, a service freight elevator was installed. The renovations included updating the wall coverings, the furniture and light fittings in the relevant rooms, and refurbishing the waste management, the electrical and the air conditioning systems. At the start of March 1966, the renovation to the grand staircase in the lobby of the cashier's desk, the mezzanine and the first floor (construction works) were completed, the second part of the renovation (masonry work) were completed in June.
Simultaneously, a complete restoration of the ancient Palazzo Stratti in Piazza dell'Unità d'Italia was underway. Lucio Arneri and Paolo Scarpa had been specifically requested to lead the project due to the precarious structural condition. Originally, the building housed the historic Caffé degli Specchi, which was designed by Antonio Buttazzoni in 1839 and opened the same year. Generali purchased the building in 1846 and, among other structural upgrades, carried out a comprehensive renovation of the facade (1865–1872), according to a project by Eugenio Geiringer and Domenico Righetti. Significant improvements to the café's interior design had already been made in 1933 when, on the occasion of the café's 1950s anniversary celebration, the furnishings were upgraded by the café keepers Cesareo and Carmeli. The building became location of the general agency in Trieste, and that of other high-profile offices including the executive guestrooms, housed in the attic.
Meanwhile, opposite Palazzo Stratti, another restoration of a historic building was underway. The venue, the Grand Hotel Duchi d'Aosta (originally named Hotel Garni, then Vanoli), was built in 1873 by Geiringer and Giovanni Righetti, and was once the venue of the eighteenth-century Locanda Grande, where the illustrious archaeologist and art historian, Johann Joachim Winckelmann [*figs.* 4–5] was murdered.
As for the Head Office headquarters, the first upgrades were scheduled just a few years after the build was completed, and date back to the early twentieth century. Engineer Giorgio Polli, who took over in 1904 following Geiringer's death, supervised the works.
Born in Trieste in 1862, he was employed in the shipyard of Pola, and worked for the company on a two-year trial basis, from 1886 through 1888; after which he was hired by the city and commenced working independently. In this guise, as technical and artistic consultant, he offered his services together with his son Carlo, and managed Generali's buildings. According to the documents that are kept in his personnel file, he was first contracted by Generali in 1914, with the agreement being renewed in 1924. He was granted the ability to freely exercise his profession along with fulfilling his obligations towards Generali. He was given an office in the Central Head Office (because he was also part of the technical section, which had been in operation since 1910, he was tasked with monitoring and administering the company buildings), however, he was exempted from abiding to the regulations in place for the other employees. The relationship was governed by two important commissions for the revitalization of two urban areas: one in Budapest, the other in Trieste's center, in the Isola di Chiozza, a traditional meeting place for Italians. He was also engaged as a consultant on several construction

2.
Assicurazioni Generali's building, Palazzo Geiringer, grand staircase [post 1926] and former stairwell with scaffolding, Trieste (1966)
[ASAG, *Versamenti*, scheda 27520]

3.
Assicurazioni Generali's building, Palazzo Geiringer, assembly hall, Trieste (1966)
[ASAG, *Versamenti*, scheda 27520]

works in Warsaw, Vienna, Budapest and Lviv. Beside the maintenance work on some of Trieste's buildings, in the late 1920s he setup the offices for the Central Head Office, on the first floor in Via Cavour, and on the first and second floors in Via Trento.

In view of a huge construction plan across Italy's main city squares, Assicurazioni Generali resolved to enhance their real estate department and to recruit a senior professional with the required qualifications to take on the tasks that the company would entrust to him. After considering the most suitable candidates, the company selected Riccardo Gairinger, Eugenio Geiringer's son (whose surname had meanwhile been Italianized), who was chosen based on the talent and expertise he had demonstrated through his previous work, and also for the company itself. Gairinger had graduated in civil engineering at the University of Graz and began his activity in a foreign, high-profile construction company; later he founded his own eponymous company, which in the period between the two world wars, carried out many highly-regarded construction projects, specifically in Trieste. A noteworthy example is the renovation of the stock exchange building in addition to the numerous buildings constructed for Generali, among them the one named Volti di Chiozza, and one along Corso Italia (formerly Corso Vittorio Emanuele III). The latter was built on a plot that bordered with the shore of Largo Riborgo, Corso Italia, and Via Tor Bandena, which had become available following the city's demolition of the old town. The work was carried out between 1936 and 1937, based on a project by Marcello Piacentini and featured a gallery named after the gold medalist Arrigo Protti. The gallery, which spanned the length of the entire block, was embellished with frescoes by Carlo Sbisà [*fig.* 6].

Thus Gairinger was hired by the Central Head Office in Trieste on April 1, 1930 and was immediately responsible for all technical, administrative and financial business pertaining to the property management office. He was in charge of the buildings situated in Italy and abroad, in cooperation with the general manager, Gino Cavaglieri, who from 1926 had been responsible for the administration of all the buildings across all states. The collaboration with Gairinger was particularly valuable to the company in connection to the intensive real estate program it had undertaken from before the World War II and which had picked up during the postwar years. The design and project management of many high-profile buildings across numerous Italian cities are attributed to him; with these projects, the company made a valuable contribution to the postwar reconstruction policy and in a larger sense, helped to strenghten the country's economy. As a result, in 1960 Gairinger was awarded the gold medal for labor. When the contract terminated in 1938 (the year the collaboration with Polli expired), due to the racial laws, he was reinstated in the Roman offices in 1944, and in Trieste the following year in the capacity of manager from 1949 through 1961—the year he retired.

The minutes of the Management, the Executive Committee and the Council of Directors' meetings are precious sources for piecing together the events pertaining to the company's real estate business, providing information about the balance sheets, the acquisitions, the appointment of contractors, the updates on work in progress, etc. The paperwork produced by the legal office concerns the requests for permits and licenses, disputes, lease contracts, etc. The real estate documents concern the technical, administrative and financial aspects of managing the buildings. The collection of the financial statements provides an annual update on the property value, with schedules divided by countries and cities from the 1950s up to 1970; these include an insert depicting the projects undertaken in the building and agricultural sectors in Italy and abroad. Of particular interest are the personnel files of the professionals who, in various capacities, have provided their expertise to the company and thereby contributed to the property development in all of Europe. (S.S.)

4.
Assicurazioni Generali's building, Palazzo Stratti, Trieste (1971)
[ASAG, *Direzione centrale, Ragioneria centrale, Bilanci*, OGG001114935]

5.
Assicurazioni Generali's building, Grand Hotel Duchi d'Aosta, Trieste (1971)
[ASAG, *Direzione centrale, Ragioneria centrale, Bilanci*, OGG001114935]

6.
Assicurazioni Generali's building, Palazzo di Corso Italia (Galleria Protti), Trieste (1936), original photograph by Foto Circoli-Pozzar
[ASAG, *Versamenti*, scheda 29805]

The Isola di Chiozza

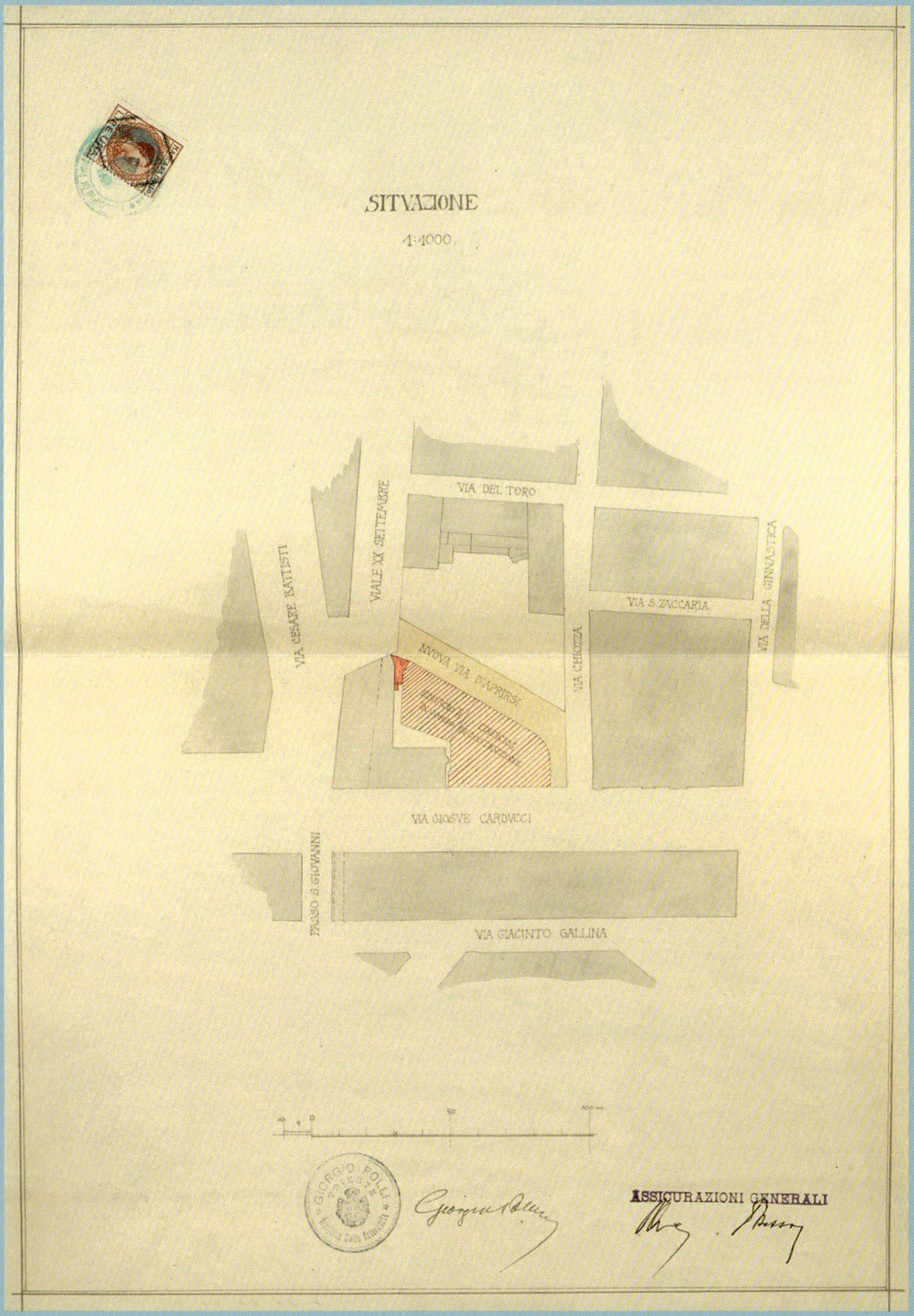

In 1910 the company purchased the so-called Isola di Chiozza, a cluster of buildings located between Via Carducci, Via Crispi—formerly Via Chiozza—Via del Toro, and Viale XX Settembre—formerly Via dell'Acquedotto [*fig.* 7]. The property of Pietro Giorgio Chiozza, it was a large real estate complex in the city's topographical center, in one of Trieste's most classic nineteenth century areas. That great delta of land, known as Borgo Chiozza, became the residents' meeting place in the early twentieth century, after the districts of Guardiella, Rozzol and Scorcola were developed on the city outskirts, where the two streams flowed together: one named dello Scoglio, which flowed along Via Battisti (formerly Corsia Stadion after Count Franz Seraph Stadion, governor of Küstenland, who in 1846 had it filled in for sanitary reasons), the other flowing from Via della Tesa to Via Carducci (formerly Via del Torrente). It got its name from the original owner Carlo Luigi Chiozza, who moved to Trieste in 1779 from Loano, near Genoa and built a soap factory in Piazza del Ponterosso. Over time the enterprise became a financial powerhouse and expanded into other business areas such as trading in colonial goods and becoming a point of reference among Trieste's bourgeoisie. A clause in Carlo Luigi Chiozza's bequest ensured that the factory would remain in business, thus ensuring the revenue from the ancestral capital would continue to benefit his legitimate heirs. And so, after the surrounding

7.
Isola di Chiozza, Trieste: a new project bearing Giorgio Polli's signature (1923)
[ASAG, *Direzione centrale, Consulenza legale, Pratiche esaurite,* U2GE046807]

buildings were demolished, in the 1920s the tiny soap factory still existed, having been relocated to the Guardiella district. In 1913, when the old houses were demolished to make room for a new road, today's Via Muratti, the city acquired the property and divided it into two sections, each with two buildings. The first, on the side of Via Carducci and Via Crispi, the second toward Via del Toro and Viale XX Settembre. The demolition was carried out by the company Buttoraz & Ziffer; the construction by Union Bau-Gesellschaft. In January 1915 the works for the first building block commenced, but were interrupted at the end of that year because of the war, and never resumed. On several occasions the municipal authorities contacted Assicurazioni Generali asking they recommence the reconstruction work in the area, both to revive the local economy and to remedy the unfortunate state of abandonment in which the area had been left. Work resumed in May 1923 and concluded in August 1924, when work began on the second group of buildings, namely those along Viale XX Settembre, Via Crispi and the Excelsior Theater in Via Muratti, which were completed in September 1925. The work was given to the firms Buttoraz & Ziffer and Gairinger, under the supervision of architect Giorgio Polli.

Still standing on the corner of Via Carducci and Via Battisti, was an old manor house known as Volti di Chiozza. Built in 1801, in a neoclassic style, by architect Antonio Mollari, who also built the stock exchange, the house was fully restored in 1850 by architect Francesco Catolla, from Trieste, who added a third floor and various disparate decorative elements. Under the porticos was an ancient café named Ai Volti, which under the Hapsburg rule became the meeting place of Trieste's youth and the stage of some heated patriotic demonstrations. On May 23, 1915 the café was set on fire and pillaged, resulting in the loss of the antique furniture and a number of paintings by Domenico Fabris, from Udine. The company Dreher took over the venue's management in 1919. Immediately after the war, the building was declared of historical interest; however, the bad state of disrepair called for its demolition and subsequent reconstruction. The project submitted by Polli was approved by royal fine arts authorities, on the proviso that the new design replicated the neoclassical elements of the old facades in the new ones [*figs.* 8-9]. Unlike the original, the new building with the additional level, is characterized by seven large arches, a lateral courtyard and a terrace with a balustrade and an attic that is crowned by statues symbolizing the *Law*, the *Earth*, *Fertility*, the *Strength of Weapons*, *Labor*, and *Thought*. There is also a frieze adorned with allegories of the glorious Risorgimento battles: 1831, 1848, 1858, 1866, 1870, 1918, all works by the Genoese artist Gigi Supino. The works commenced in December 1925 and concluded in September 1927.

8.
Isola di Chiozza, Trieste (1914)

9.
Demolition of Casa Chiozza, Trieste (1925)

From Jan Palach's Blaze to the Implosion of Communism

The Events of 1968 Shook up the West and the Soviet Era Seemed Eternal, but in Just a Few Short Years, the Fate of the World Changed

1968
1989

"A small step for man, a giant leap for mankind:" with those words, the American astronaut Neil Armstrong (followed by Edwin Aldrin; the pilot, Michael Collins, remained in orbit) made the first-ever human footprint on the moon [*fig.* 1]. The romantic dream that had spanned the centuries thanks to timeless works of art and literature finally came true on that magical night between July 20 and 21, 1969. At that moment, it seemed as though humanity had no further limits before it and would soon be able to realize even its most audacious plans for future space travel. A space age had arrived that had been until then the stuff of science fiction books, but over time, unfortunately, a great many hopes had to be downsized: the everyday needs of our planet turned out to be too numerous and too dramatic. In fact, after five further missions to the Moon, including the failed launch of the spacecraft *Apollo 13*, NASA ended the moon program early and since then (December 1972), no human being has set foot off the Earth.

Other projects were launched, however, like the space labs, which involved, among other things, collaboration between the United States and the Soviet Union, a sign that the Cold War was thawing, and, starting in 1981, the Space Shuttle program, which aimed toward increasingly frequent trips with large crews between Earth and the space labs. The complexity and excessive costs of the project, together with safety problems and the tragic loss of human life in a few incidents, forced NASA to gradually cut back this space program, partly in light of having learned from experience that, at least with the technology of the twentieth century, the human body was not able to handle more daring trips.

The new space frontier did, however, develop in one particular area: that of the strategic military use of telecommunications satellites. The use of spy satellites and the space shield (a defense system against possible nuclear attacks) in fact made it possible for United States President Ronald Reagan to persuade the Soviet Union, which was aware of its technological inferiority, to see reason. The space age thus remained, for the moment, a utopia in the face of an ever-dramatic earthly reality.

During the years of lunar conquest, humanity was in fact in a state of turmoil all over the planet. It was the age of the overly-mythicized 1968, with its widespread revolts against an overall social system that was considered authoritarian, and older generations that were seen as behind the times and incapable of thinking creatively about the future. It was a worldwide rebellion that started at the University of California, Berkeley, where the destructive thought of Herbert Marcuse was promoted, and then spread to Europe, with the "French May" [*fig.* 2]. Subversive ideology in Italy, but also in Germany, gave rise to a period of terrorism. In Italy, these were the infamous Years of Lead, a long period of violence that stained the peninsula with blood, starting on December 12, 1969, a tragic day on which bombs were detonated in Piazza Fontana and Piazza della Scala in Milan, and three other attacks were carried out in Rome. These events triggered the series of attacks known as the "Strategy of Tension." There were acts of terrorism carried out by the left (the Brigate Rosse and others) and the right (first and foremost, the Nuclei Armati Proletari), and State massacres (the main ones were those in Brescia and Bologna and the Italicus Express bombing), strategies of opposite extremes—phenomena that still leave us fumbling in the dark today—the symbolic culmination of which was an attack on the heart of the State by the Brigate Rosse, who kidnapped and murdered the former Italian Prime Minister Aldo Moro and his bodyguards in 1978 [*fig.* 3].

The world was on the constant brink of uncontrollably grave international crisis. Governments were taken over by coups in Greece, Chile, and Argentina and the Middle East question was becoming increasingly embittered, with a progression of conflicts and terrorist violence that even touched Trieste, when on August 4, 1972, the Palestinian group Black September attacked an oil refinery there. In September of

1.
Astronauts Neil Armstrong and Edwin "Buzz" Aldrin, the first men to set foot on the moon, on July 20, 1969

2.
The occupation of the Sorbonne, the historic Paris university, was one of culminating moments of the student protest movement that erupted in 1968

JAN PALACH
* 11.8.1948 † 19.1.1969
JAN ZAJÍC
* 3.7.1950 † 25.2.1969

that year, the same terrorist organization carried out an attack at the Olympic Village in Munich, resulting in the deaths of eleven Israeli athletes, a German police officer, and five of the terrorists. The next year, tensions in Arab-Israeli countries culminated in the Yom Kippur War, generating an "oil shock" that forced the West to acknowledge its dependency on the OPEC countries for oil. The minute that supplies were blocked, austerity measures were passed that changed daily life for people and society for a couple of years and, most of all, sent the price of barrels of crude oil through the roof.

The most glaring events played out, however, in the arena of superpower politics. In the United States, the problems were mostly related to the racial question and the abysmal management of the Vietnam War, which ended with disengagement, in reality defeat, forcing thousands of South Vietnamese into exile; Saigon was in fact conquered by the Viet Cong on April 30, 1975. The real competition was between the United States and Communism, and what was at stake was supremacy over the world stage. Throughout that entire period, the Soviet Union expressed its endless aggression through the use of tanks, an index of its strategic/military backwardness, which would become clear in the mid-1980s.

There were countless main players during this historic period, which, in the span of just a few years, saw the destiny of the world undergo radical change. The Prague Spring, which began in Czechoslovakia in 1968, demonstrated above all the impossibility of making Communism more liberal. The dream of Alexander Dubček and his people of launching a "national path to socialism" was cut short that August, when the troops of the Warsaw Pact invaded the country. "Limited sovereignty" was forcefully imposed, a concept that Leonid Brezhnev used to stress that the western borders of the satellite countries were considered Soviet Union borders to all intents and purposes: no attempt at emancipation from the USSR's rigid control was tolerated. The Czechoslovakian resistance gave the world a modern symbol for the struggle for freedom: a young man, twenty-year-old Jan Palach, who set fire to himself on January 16, 1969 in Václavské náměstí, Prague, to claim his country's right to independence [*fig.* 4]. "Torch number 1," as Palach called himself in his farewell message, died three days later, and other young men (including Jan Zajíc and Evžen Plocek) followed his example.

The Soviet Union thought that its political repression had quashed the push for change, but at the Vatican, Communism's most spiritually authoritative adversary, plans were underway for a historic event: the election in 1978 of the archbishop of Cracow, Karol Wojtiła, to the papacy, with the name John Paul II [*fig.* 5]. The Polish pope was the true author of the havoc that struck the Communist system, succeeding in uniting the working and Catholic masses of Poland and thus making the country, with the rise of the Solidarność trade union (1980) led by Lech Wałęsa, a true nightmare for both the national authorities and those of the Soviet Union. Support from other major international political leaders, in particular Margaret Thatcher in the United Kingdom and Ronald Reagan in the United States, raised the level of the conflict, especially after the Soviet invasion of Afghanistan in 1979. For the USSR, the attack represented the failure of its own military power, bogged down in the Asian country, but also raised awareness of the backwardness of the Soviet system. In 1985, it was therefore decided to bring a new man, an extremely skillful communicator, to the head of the party and the government: Mikhail Gorbachev, who two years later launched a broad program of reforms called *perestrojka* (reconstruction), based on *glasnost'* (transparency) and with which he tried to save whatever could be salvaged of a system that was by that point destined for collapse.

The end of the epoch, which it had seemed would stretch on for eternity, was sealed by the sudden and unexpected (at least in the eyes of public opinion worldwide) implosion of Communism, highlight-

3.
On March 16, 1978, on Via Fani in Rome, the terrorists of the Brigate Rosse kidnapped Aldo Moro, the leader of the Democrazia Cristiana, after killing his five bodyguards

4.
The monument in Václavské Náměstí in Prague in memory of Jan Palach and Jan Zajíc, the two young patriots who set themselves on fire, killing themselves, in 1969 to protest the Soviet occupation of Czechoslovakia

5.
Pope John Paul II looks out from the loggia of St. Peter's Basilica in Rome after his election to the papacy, on October 16, 1978

ed by a total paradox in Czechoslovakia during the "year of miracles," as some defined 1989. In January, in Prague, the writer and exponent of the civil rights movement (formerly Charta 77) Václav Havel was arrested as he was about to commemorate the martyrdom of Jan Palach. While in prison, Havel was held up as the foremost enemy of the State and its ideology, but due to the acceleration of events, on December 29 of that same year, as a result of the peaceful "Velvet Revolution" that had begun after the fall of the Berlin Wall, he was elected president of the republic—as would also happen the following year in Poland to Lech Wałęsa, the leader of Solidarność—and received in Parliament by an applauding crowd that included even those who had always been against him.

What took place during those fitful days in Czechoslovakia was an extraordinarily peaceful transition (to be replicated three years later when Slovakia broke off) within a political and social dynamic that was running through all of Eastern Europe. The revolution's most dramatic episode (one, however, marked by a great deal of ambiguity that is still today far from being clear) was the execution by firing squad of the Romanian dictator Nicolae Ceausescu and his wife after a farcical trial and a hunt for agents of the mythicized local secret police, the Securitate, in what appeared to be no more than a reckoning among members of the same political "family."

The driver of the movement, which not even the nomenklatura of the eastern countries could control any longer, was the opening up of the Berlin Wall, which had uncompromisingly divided the city since 1961, symbolizing the global struggle between free Capitalism and Communism. What went down in history as "the fall of the wall" took place on the night of November 9, when thousands of East Germans raced from the other side as soon as they heard on the radio that they could travel freely abroad [*fig.* 6]. This event created a domino effect that upset the entire Communist system. It is to Gorbachev's great merit that, at that critical juncture, he ordered the border guards that night to let the people crossing over go and to refrain from any kind of violent reaction, even though he knew that this would mean that start of rapid, uncontrollable motion towards the reunification of Germany and the dissolution of the USSR [*fig.* 7].

The world was heading towards an epoch-making change, one that was in appearance characterized by the triumph of freedom, but instead turned out to be directionless, after the collapse of the Soviet giant, which, although it had made use of ideological oppression and nuclear threat, had been one of the two pillars of the "balance of terror." Insecurity, disorder, and the reappearance of (ethno)nationalism and pseudo-religious conflicts are the defining features of the contemporary world, marked by dramatic developments that make it increasingly bleak and unpredictable. (D.R.)

6.
An emblematic image of the collapse of the Communist regimes in Eastern Europe: the fall of the Berlin Wall

7.
Barricades set up in Vilnius by demonstrators fighting for Lithuania's independence from the Soviet Union

In Brief

1968
October 16: After having won gold and bronze medals in the 200-meter race at the Olympic Games in Mexico City, Tommie Smith and John Carlos, both African American, protested racism by each raising a black-gloved fist.

1969
August 18: After "three days of peace, love, and music," marking the apex of "hippie culture," the festival held near the town of Woodstock, in the State of New York, closed with a concert of Jimi Hendrix.

1969
December 12: The massacre in Piazza Fontana, Milan started off a series of bomb attacks (the most serious in Bologna in 1980) known as the "strategy of tension," the details of which remain obscure today.

1970
April 17: After a malfunction on board signaled with the famous phrase "Okay, Houston, we've had a problem here," the space mission *Apollo 13* ended with a successful sea landing in the Pacific Ocean.

1970
June 17: Italy, led by its top scorer Gigi Riva, beat West Germany 4 to 3 in an emotional FIFA World Cup semi-final at the Azteca Stadium in Mexico City, but the tournament was won by Brazil, with Pelé.

1972
February 21: United States President Richard Nixon arrived in China for an official, weeklong visit. The trip was the prelude to the re-establishment of diplomatic relations between the two countries.

1973
September 11: In Chile, General Augusto Pinochet, the commander of the army, took power, overturning the leftist government. President Salvador Allende died during the coup, possibly a suicide.

1973
December 10: Konrad Lorenz, the founder of ethology, won the Nobel Prize for his research on the innate components of behavior, and in particular the phenomenon of "imprinting" in wild geese.

1975
April 30: Two years after the United States withdrew, the Vietnam War ended when Saigon was taken by North Vietnamese forces, and the country was reunited under the Communist leadership based in Hanoi.

1976
May 6: A disastrous earthquake 6.4 in magnitude hit Friuli, killing nearly 1,000. Over 100,000 people were evacuated from forty-five towns razed to the ground and others seriously damaged.

1976
July 18: In Montreal, the fourteen-year-old Romanian gymnast Nadia Comaneci won the gold medal for uneven parallel bars, becoming the first in the history of the Olympics to receive a perfect ten.

1977
January 31: The Georges Pompidou National Art and Cultural Centre opened in Paris, commissioned by the French president it was named after and designed by architects Renzo Piano and Richard Rogers.

1977
May 25: The film *Star Wars* opened, starring Alec Guinness and Harrison Ford, among others. It was the first in the movie saga created by George Lucas, the heroes of which became part of the collective imagination.

1979
February 1: Just a few days after the flight of Shah Reza Pahlavi, the Ayatollah Khomeini returned to Iran from France and became the country's spiritual leader, establishing an Islamic republic.

1979
May 4: In the United Kingdom, the overwhelming victory of the Conservative Party brought party leader Margaret Thatcher to the head of government. She was the first female prime minister in Europe.

1979
December 27: The troops of the Soviet Red Army invaded Afghanistan with the aim of installing Babrak Karmal as president, but, unable to defeat the mujahideen, they were forced to retreat in 1989.

1981
May 5: Bobby Sands was the first to die among the imprisoned IRA militants carrying out a hunger strike to the death in protest against prison conditions. 100,000 people attended his funeral.

1982
June 8: During the war for control of the Falkland Islands, the Argentine air force destroyed two Royal Navy landing craft, but a few days later, British forces reconquered the contested islands.

1983
March 27: The TV miniseries *The Thorn Birds*, from the eponymous novel by Colleen McCullough about the tormented love between Father Ralph and Meggie, premiered with huge success in the United States.

1986
April 26: A cloud of radioactive material was released by a reactor in the nuclear power station in Chernobyl, Ukraine. More than 300,000 people were forced to evacuate by the environmental contamination.

1987
December 8: Mikhail Gorbachev and Ronald Reagan signed an agreement to destroy all of the intermediate-range nuclear missiles installed by the Soviet Union and the United States on European territory.

1988
December 2: Benazir Bhutto became the first female leader of a Muslim country, winning the election held in Pakistan after the death of General Zia-ul-Haq and the end of his regime.

1989
June 2: The movie *Dead Poets Society* debuted on American screens, starring Robin Williams as a professor who teaches his students to look at things from different perspectives.

1989
June 4: The student protests in Tiananmen Square, Beijing, demanding political reform and greater freedom of speech and press, were violently brought to an end with tanks.

Generali in Space
Pioneers in a Frontier Market, with Feet Firmly on the Ground

1978
2001

The space insurance division started out as an internal office within the aviation division, which in turn originated in the transport division (Board minutes no. 136 of July 19, 1932, mention an aviation division had been in operation for some years; it should be noted that early 1924 saw the inception of the Consorzio Italiano di Assicurazione Aeronautica, which Generali readily joined). The space risks technical office was officially established in mid 1978; however, on December 19, 1977 in reporting to the Board, the general manager Eugenio Coppola di Canzano noted: "Aerospace is a new market that offers interesting opportunities not only in Italy but also abroad," and he urged for, "an adequate strengthening of operations in the division's management." The following year on February 28, he reported: "Our process to strengthen the operations in the [aviation] division is underway to develop the space insurance business. We are expanding our technical knowledge in this challenging field with the support of a new consultant. We plan to create a new office that will operate internationally, thanks to an organic framework that will embrace the other Companies in the Group."
Actually, Generali had already entered the sector in the early 1960s, though its contacts with the aerospace industry were limited. An early article entitled "Aspetti economici dei voli spaziali," appeared in the August-September 1960 edition of the *Bollettino* and discussed a conference on the topic, which was presided by Epicarmo Corbino, professor of economic politics at the University of Naples Federico II. The introductory remarks of the article are visionary: "The topic is highly relevant and concerns the insurance industry, albeit indirectly— for now." In the years that followed, more articles appeared at the hands of "Arcus," the pseudonym of the *Bollettino*'s future director Carlo Ulcigrai, with catchy titles designed to arouse interest for an industry undergoing feverish development: "Fra terra ed astri. Un tema che appassionerà gli assicuratori futuri"—*Bollettino delle Assicurazioni Generali* 2 (1961)—and "Rischi del futuro e compiti degli assicuratori"—*Bollettino delle Assicurazioni Generali* 1 (1962).
Before long, these predictions materialized. The first contact with the space exploration industry took place in 1963, when an accident policy for the employees of the European commission in charge of the sector, was evaluated. In April of the following year, the European Space Research Organization (ESRO), the body created by the commission that in 1975 established the European Space Agency (ESA), applied for insurance cover for the launch of the *Skylark* and *Centaure* sounding rockets from the sites of Salto di Quirra in Sardinia; Ile du Levant in France; and Kiruna in Sweden. In 1964 an insurance cover for the San Marco project was granted. The program, invented by Luigi Broglio who is considered the father of Italian astronautics, was developed in collaboration with the United States and would lead Italy to become one of the first nations beside the United States and the Soviet Union, to launch its own satellite into orbit. The Consiglio Nazionale delle Ricerche (CNR) entrusted Generali with the provision of insurance for the project, through it agencies in Rome and Ferrara: from transporting the Santa Rita, ENI's oil rig converted into a launch pad, from the port of Taranto in the waters off the East African coast, between Somalia and Kenya; to the operations for launching the satellite into orbit; to accident insurance for the technical staff.
Following this first step, the space insurance sector experienced a considerable impetus from 1977, the year in which Generali won the tender for *Sirio*, the Italian telecommunication satellite that experimented the transmission of very high frequency bands [*fig.* 1]. The event was recorded in several minutes. Specifically, in reporting on the matter at the Executive Committee meeting of May 24, 1977, Coppola di Canzano noted that, "the insurance problems pertaining to the launch—and in fact the entire operation—are extremely complex, not least because it is the first insurance cover of its kind in Italy, and one of the very

1.
Informative brochure of the space risks technical office, with an image of the *Sirio* satellite launch (1983) [ASAG, *Direzione centrale, Ramo spazio*, U2GE045501]

few in existence globally." He then described the four kinds of cover provided. The first three concerned the different stages in the satellite's lifespan. The pre-launch included the transportation of the materials from Italy to the launch pad, and assembling, testing, fueling, and integrating the satellite to the rocket launcher, which was also ensured. The launch cover ranged from the possibility of minimum damage to the equipment, to the failure to launch into orbit, or a total loss, for a period of forty-five days, which was the time required to execute all the functional checks. The life cover concerned the operational life of the satellite, what later would be referred to as "in orbit." The fourth and final cover was public liability toward third parties, and concerned the staff of CNR, Compagnia Industriale Aerospaziale, and NASA, for a duration of time equal to the sum of the first three stages. When the *Sirio* was launched on August 26, 1977 from the Cape Canaveral launch site, deputy manager Benito Pagnanelli was there to assist in the capacity of technical insurance manager of the aviation division. Years later, Pagnanelli recalled his experience in an interview: "Because Italy had no other such programs underway, we turned to the global market and created a specialized unit, a technical office with full time staff, supported by a large number of external consultants."

Initially, Paolo Albanese was in charge of the space risks technical office; from 1981 it was entrusted to Giovanni Gobbo, who prior to joining Generali had acquired considerable experience working both on the San Marco project with CNR, and the *Sirio* launch for the satellite services company Telespazio. After 1978 the sector grew swiftly and decisively, becoming increasingly more specialized and relying on administrative offices, technical services, and contract management and by the mid-1990s, a secretariat and a laboratory. In 1987, after a restructure to some internal services, the divisions for aviation, fire, miscellaneous risk, and passive reinsurance were combined into a single section reporting to Pagnanelli.

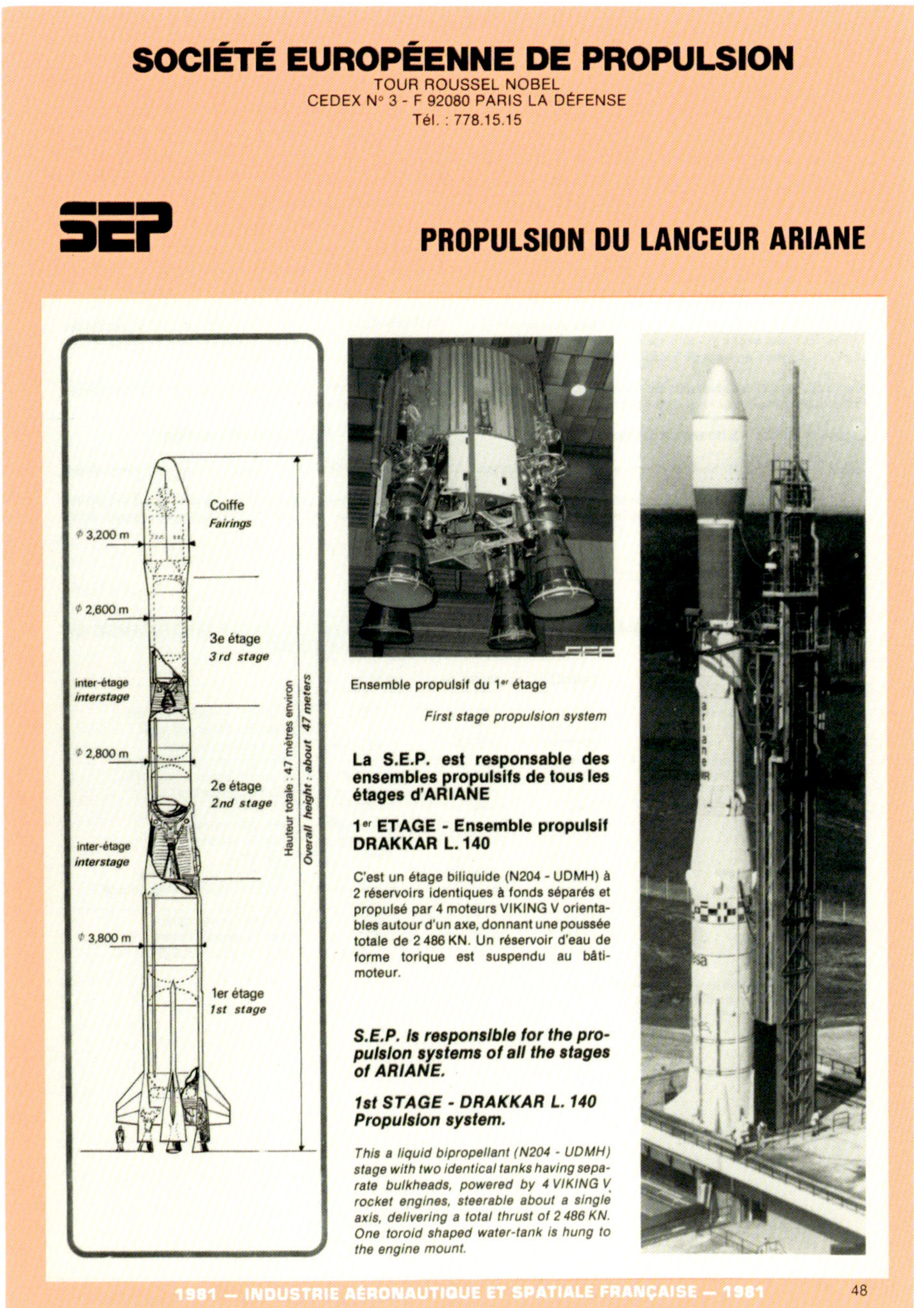

2.
The *Ariane* rocket (Paris, 1981)
[ASAG, *Direzione centrale, Ramo spazio*, U2GE043996]

3.
Space Log, *Space News* and *Esa Bulletin* (1983-1994)
[ASAG, *Direzione centrale*, *Ramo spazio*, U2GE043939 e U2GE043820]

Although underwriting the cover for the *Sirio* satellite constituted an exceptional deal, from the outset space insurance proved to be a highly mercurial market that offered high revenues, but also implicated extremely high risks. A few weeks after *Sirio*'s success, on September 13, 1977 ESA's *OTS* (Orbital Test Satellite) was made explode just 54 seconds into its flight, because of a malfunction to the rocket launcher, causing a 29 million-dollar loss. This event, coupled with a Japanese accident valued at 15 million dollars, led to the almost complete depletion of the global amount of premiums collected in over ten years of activity. In December 1979, four days after its launch, the American satellite *Satcom 3* was lost; resulting in what the Board minutes of May 27, 1980 declared to be: "The most significant claim for hull damages that has ever occurred," totaling a damage of 77 million dollars. Despite these disasters, the confidence in progress remained steadfast, and the first half of the 1980s brought some excellent results. First, with the launch of the Space Transportation System (STS) program, in which the *Space Shuttle* was deployed to transport multiple satellites in a single trip, and to capture and return them from orbit. Secondly, with the start of Europe's competition with NASA, using the *Ariane* rockets [*fig.* 2], which were launched from the Kourou base in French Guiana.

Within a short time Generali became one of the leaders in the sector. There was a focus on the staff's high level of technical training to ensure that, as Pagnanelli would remark: "The insurer, in addition to being the underwriter of risk, can also act as an effective consultant on preventive measures" [*fig.* 3]. Given that until then, no statistical rationale for claims had been devised yet, a database was created for the purpose of facilitating accurate risk assumption. Its status allowed the company to work closely with many major players, witnessing constant and fast-paced technological advancements as well as the big catastrophes taking place within the aerospace sector. The year 1986 was especially tough due to the *Space Shuttle Challenger* disaster on January 28, which exploded on takeoff on the 25th mission of the STS program. Meanwhile, a number of failures in the *Ariane* rocket resulted in a temporary suspension of its launches. With the space programs put on hold, especially those with a commercial objective, *i.e.* those closely linked to the insurance sector, the immediate repercussions on the industry were inevitable. However, an unexpected outcome from the setbacks and the consequent suspension of the space launch market's missions in the West, was that China put forward its launch pads and the *Long March 3* rocket. The collaboration with the Chinese was followed a few years later by the political and economic opening up of the Soviet Union, which invested resources and skills into the space market. This signaled a swift recovery for space insurance, and by 1987, it once again registered positive results. In 1991 the business turnover and the high level of expertise attained in this area, lead to unbundling the space risks technical office from the aviation division. The newly established space division remained under Gobbo's leadership and was supervised by Pagnanelli, who by then, supervised the entire non-life sector.

The leading position attained within the aerospace insurance sector, translated into the increased capacity to take on value at risk in a constantly expanding global insurance market. The contribution exceeded 12% throughout the 1990s (in 1995 the maximum underwriting capacity for the space insurance sector was about 80 million dollars compared to a global total of 550 million dollars, which in a few years grew to 850 million globally). On several occasions the company found itself in the lead when stipulating contractual agreements; therefore, having the honor and duty to set out the conditions for the contracts on offer. The four types of cover articulated for the satellite *Sirio* became the templates for all subsequent insurance policies that were stipulated in the following decades. Later improvements contemplated the addition of the design and experimentation phases, which in-

4–5.
The ESA space center in Kourou, main entrance and launch pad (May 1991)
[ASAG, *Direzione centrale, Ramo incendi*, U2GE041741]

volved several external bodies (governments, space agencies, satellite launch companies, satellite builders and owners, and insurers). The launch phase was further refined through the commissioning phase, *i.e.* the satellite's transition from the launch phase to the operative phase, which involved opening the antennas and the solar panels, and the comprehensive testing of all operational systems (electrical power, trim, telemetry, remote control, thermal control, and propulsion). Furthermore, the timeline to carry out these check was extended from the forty-five days previously prescribed for the *Sirio*, to one hundred and eighty days. Overall, the processes that carried the highest degree of risk were always associated with loading the propellant during the pre-launch phase and the takeoff, during the launch phase. The insurance cover was extended to: individual transponders, *i.e.* the satellite units for the reception and transmission of signals; launch delays such as the one that occurred in January 1989 during the space industry's first strike by the staff of the Kourou space center [*figs.* 4–5], which delayed the launch of the Japanese satellite *Jc-Sat 1* by several days; and interruptions to major televised events, typically sports, which were broadcast by satellite.

Over time, the claims were prompted by new factors such as space debris, i.e. fragments of defunct equipment adrift, which posed two kinds of risk. First, the impact with operational equipment in orbit (in 1991 an incident of this kind is thought to have caused the loss of power to the *Aurora 2* satellite, reducing its life expectancy by two years and resulting in a financial loss of over 6 million dollars). Secondly, the falling back to Earth of the debris itself, thanks to the use of ever-improving materials that are resistant to the friction caused by the atmosphere, which constitutes a public liability risk. A further challenge for insurers has emerged more recently, caused by the formation of bacteria inside orbiting space stations, some of which have been known to corrode the equipment.

There were numerous contacts and exchanges with representatives of other insurance companies, governmental agencies and technicians of space industry from around the world. In addition to the trips to the United States, specifically in 1977 on the occasion of the launch of the *Sirio* satellite, in May 1985 the Japanese insurers Tokio Marine and Dowa, who worked in the space sector, the local space agency NASDA (National Space Development Agency) and NHK, the national broadcasting organisation, extended an invitation to visit to the Tanegashima space center. The documentation speaks to meetings in Trieste, during the second half of the 1980s, with officials from Swedish, Belgian, and Indian companies. But two of Pagnanelli's trips in 1988 were particularly noteworthy. The first, which took place in May, was to the state-controlled insurance company People's Insurance Company of China (PICC), in Beijing, that operated on a monopoly basis. A note of May 17 reads: "Once again, there was great interest in our space insurance business. [...] They are very keen for us to provide their specialized staff with internships in our Trieste Office." The second trip took place in July, at the Soviet launch site of Bajkonur (now in Kazakhstan), where the *Sputnik* was launched in 1957 and, in 1961, Yuri Gagarin became the first man in space. The occasion of that visit, which was shared with delegates from USA, Britain and Germany, represented the first time a western insurance company entered a cosmodrome in the USSR. The meeting set the foundations for an intensive cooperation with the Russian space agency Glavkosmos; to the extent that for the launch of September 5, 1989, the *Soyuz* shuttle was given the opportunity to apply the logo with the winged lion. This event would be repeated in 1992, on a *Proton* rocket, a spacecraft that immediately aroused considerable interest for the degree of reliability demonstrated over time.

The company also played a key role in supporting important scientific projects, knowledge sharing and cooperating with the different stakeholders in the space sector. Following an initial round of meetings in December 1978, with a focus on space activities, on April 5 and 6, 1979 the first conference entitled "Evoluzione tecnologica e attività spaziali negli anni '80. Impegni economici e implicazioni assicurative," was held in Trieste. The event was organized entirely by Generali. There were thirteen keynote speakers who gave presentations on technical, commercial and insurance topics. Among others: a RAI [Italian radio-television company] spokesperson discussed the financial aspects of direct-broadcast satellite television; Telespazio representatives explained the Earth observation satellite programs; two NASA technicians presented the STS program two years before the *Space Shuttle* missions officially began. By the second conference, which took place in Rome in March 1983 and which from then on became a regular biennial event, the number of keynote presentations doubled and the participants also grew steadily over the years. In 2001, on the occasion of the eleventh conference, the numbers had swelled from just over two hundred people up to five hundred delegates from over thirty different countries. In addition to the representatives from the major space agencies, the manufacturing industry, the telecommunications companies, the insurance companies and the brokerage firms, legal experts were also invited, specifically those specializing in civil liability, who would otherwise not necessarily keep up with the developments in scientific research. The various conferences always shed a light on the most topical issues and presented the most innovative projects and discoveries, making an important contribution in pushing the boundaries of a frontier that, as the company leaders had often noted, could be traced back to the underwriting of Umberto Nobile's expedition in the airship *Italia*. This genuine pioneering spirit was epitomized in Enrico Randone's welcome speech at the first space conference in Trieste. The then deputy chairman and managing director noted "the need to contribute knowledge to a field that is becoming preeminent in the process of economic development," and concluding: "Generali's interest in space insurance is not fleeting nor inspired by marketing concerns, but responds to clear operational goals, consistent with the philosophy of a company that wants to be of its time."

In Trieste the space insurance experience came to a close at the end of the 1990s when the business was transferred to the London Branch, together with the other non-life divisions. (M.M.)

Enrico Randone

1911
1998

Enrico Randone was born in Naples on January 2, 1911. His father Vincenzo, had married Daria Senni and was employed as a ministry official. He spent the first part of his childhood in Lazio, then in Rome [*fig.* 1]. Being a precocious student, Randone attained his senior high school leaving qualification in 1926, at the age of fifteen. That same year, his father's sudden death forced him to seek employment in order to continue his studies, which he concluded in 1931 with a degree in law. Until 1932 he worked for the same company that had employed him as a boy, the Società Italiana di Servizi Marittimi (SITMAR), initially, as a simple clerk and after graduation, as a legal and administrative officer. In 1932 SITMAR merged with Lloyd Triestino further to a general rationalization of the principal navigation companies. At that time, he resolved to become self-employed and, as a young lawyer, took on the liquidations of some of the minor companies in which SITMAR had a financial interest, thus gaining prominence among the capital's commercial and financial sphere.
In 1937 he was hired by Assicurazioni Generali's legal department in Trieste [*fig.* 2]. In 1942 he was promoted to officer, thus kicking off his career inside the company in which he would attain the highest level of leadership. Interrupted by the draft, from 1940 through September 1943, and again from November 1943 through April 1945 when he served as lieutenant for the Repubblica Sociale Italiana army, he would spend a decade working in litigation.
Having resumed civilian life, he continued his work in Rome (where he took on a temporary assignment in 1943 that became permanent in 1946); he was promoted to deputy secretary in the representative office in 1949. In 1956 he was transferred to Trieste in the capacity of deputy manager of the research office. During that time, he delved into the risks associated with the industrial exploitation of nuclear power and its civil liabilities, both new fields (in 1957 the European Community signed the European Atomic Energy Community– EURATOM Treaty) that signaled the growing complexity of insurance and its international relevance.
Soon after, he agreed to transfer from administrative and legal work, which until then had been the exclusive focus of his career, to a more operational role. He undertook a period of training at the subsidiary Concorde in Paris, which controlled Assicurazioni Generali's French interests; the company's Branch in Barcelona; the agency in Bologna; and in September 1957, he arrived in Milan in the capacity of co-manager. In 1955 the Milan Head Office was restructured according to a corporate de-centralization plan to share competencies with Venice and Trieste, making Milan responsible for the whole Italian business for: motor vehicle insurance, liability for different branches, non-life insurance (accident, sickness, hail and livestock), as well as the network of agencies in these sectors of activity. Although the work was limited to specific and limited sectors, it offered great managerial autonomy, which Randone sometimes claimed even when dealing with the highest corporate authorities. Promoted to manager in 1961, and central manager in 1967, in 1970 he became general manager as a result of an internal change of management driven by the chairman, Cesare Merzagora, who had recently taken leadership of the company.
During the Milanese period that lasted eighteen years, until 1975, Randone developed the Italian insurance market in those sectors for which he was accountable; a market in which Assicurazioni Generali was a clear leader, attracting about thirty percent of the business compared to other companies, and dominating the European and foreign markets. Nevertheless, more opportunity for growth remained, particularly during Randone's time, when the average per capita income was on the increase and the country experienced the advent of mass motorization. Thus motor vehicle insurance was destined to collect a great many premiums, which Assicurazioni Generali tripled in just a decade, from 1960 through 1970; although the simultaneous increase in claims and the

1.
Enrico Randone (1979)
[ASAG, *Presidenza e organi sociali, Presidenti e vicepresidenti, Enrico Randone*, U2GE023746]

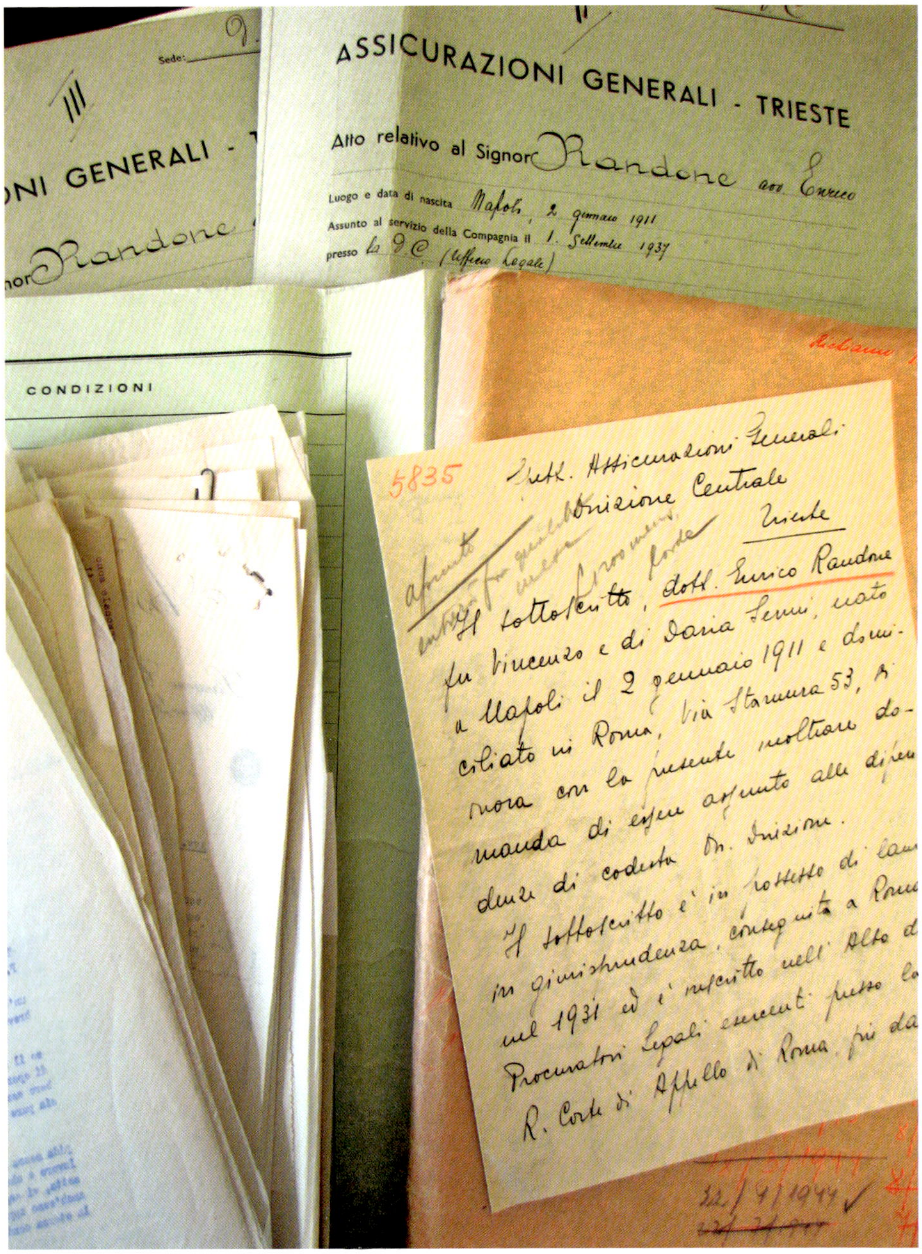

2.
Personnel file with *curriculum vitae* signed by Enrico Randone (1937) [ASAG, *Direzione centrale, Servizio del personale, Posizioni personali*, U2GE042629]

competition's slashed rates in Italy and abroad became a thorn in the company's side, which was often lamented in the annual reports. Despite doubling its business turnover, the company was unable to compensate for the increasing managerial costs due to external, cyclical factors such as the slackening of financial growth and the resurgence of inflation and, in 1974, this resulted in a heavy deficit which would affect the industry's bottom line.

Beside the financial situation mentioned above, political uncertainty over the introduction of mandatory motor vehicle insurance, which Italy introduced in 1969, and the rumors surrounding its nationalization, further affected the precarious situation despite Randone's efforts to extend the agencies' networks and provide the agents with vocational training. The Implementation Decree, not approved until 1971, followed the lively discussions within the Associazione Nazionale fra le Imprese Assicuratrici (ANIA), a group of insurance companies that did not unanimously support the introduction of fixed tariffs and premiums pursuant to a decree. According to Randone's own account, together with other company leaders and with his legal expertise, he lobbied for a legislation to be drafted that would include some of the insurers' proposals, thus mitigating the general conditions set out in the policy.

Randone's commitment was not limited to the Italian context. From 1970, after he became general manager in Milan, he represented the company in his dealings with international organizations. Despite the setbacks caused by the worsening financial situation and the monetary destabilization, during the early 1970s, particularly in Europe insurance companies nevertheless accepted the supranational integration process as an unavoidable reality. From 1973 through 1977 Randone chaired the working group on motor vehicle insurance for the Comité Européen des Assurances (CEA), which was founded in 1953, and which, from the beginnings of Europe's unification had been studying the common issues of the insurance sector with a view to market integration. In 1976 Randone lead a commission of experts to advise the European Commission on public liability as it pertained to car insurance. Within ANIA, on whose Board he sat, he concerned himself with motor vehicle insurance. In 1971 he was nominated president of the Associazione Internazionale tra gli Assicuratori Grandine (AIAG), which at the time comprised one hundred and seventy-one companies globally, proving that its relevance was not limited to the sector but extended to a qualified, international circle of insurers. In June 1975 he returned to Trieste following a request by Chairman Merzagora to fill the position of managing director responsible for the Italian market and human resources. The two men shared a vision for the company's financial renewal (with the exception of the technical reserves), and focused their attention on those shareholders who had become the most influential such as Mediobanca and Lazard Frères in Paris, as a means of staving off any unwelcome external interference. In 1976 he added the role of deputy chairman to that of managing director, a responsibility that preempted him as Merzagora's chosen successor, once the latter would vacate the chairmanship [*fig.* 3]. In June 1979 Randone was appointed chairman, a post he kept for twelve years until 1991. He was always perceived as an insider; someone who ensured the company's continuity, after Merzagora's charmanship had given rise to a number of conflicts amongst the management. Through the support of the two managing directors, Eugenio Coppola di Canzano (1980–1995) and Alfonso Desiata (1978–1990), in 1981 Randone acquired the position of third managing director and immediately asserted his authority by promoting autonomy for the company and in the decision-making process; which quickly resulted in conflict with the aging honorary chairman, who might have expected to continue to exert his influence. Randone—as he himself admitted—maintained the established consultative process with Enrico Cuccia and Antoine Bernheim, who during the Merzagora era had been influential shareholders, thus striking a fine balance with the need for independence, which might have at times been mistaken for defensiveness, but which in time proved to be consistent with the company's consolidation and growth.

Randone's chaimanship mirrors his professional expertise in a unique way. Assicurazioni Generali was an international Group with a worldwide network of affiliates and subsidiaries; nonetheless, Italy and Europe where Randone had learned the trade, received his special attention. During the central phase of his chairmanship (1980–1990) the net growth in Italy—based on the gross reinsurance premiums collected—registered an increase that went from 25.2% (a decrease compared to the 1970s when it was around 30%) to 38%, greatly exceeding any previous figures thanks also to the results of the life insurance sector. Randone paid particular attention to the Italian insurance market (where he was also chairman of the subsidiary Anonima Assicurazioni and of the affiliated Unione Italiana di Riassicurazione–UNIORAS), a market which in that period attracted entrepreneurs with dubious interests (such as Raul Gardini, Carlo De Benedetti, Cesare Romiti) compared to those who considered insurance as the non-speculative management of private savings. Thus Randone was party to the heated debates and internal conflicts in the Italian capitalist world, albeit from a very specific perspective, and of which Assicurazioni Generali were a part by virtue of Randone's previous associations on the boards of external companies such as Mediobanca, Banco Ambrosiano Veneto, Ferruzzi Finanziaria, Italjolly and Gemina. Even after the Single European Act (SEA) actualized the economic and financial liberalization in 1986, Assicurazioni Generali's strategy in Europe remained conservative. The acquisition of small-to-medium-sized companies in Great Britain, Switzerland, France and Austria became more prevalent during the second half of the decade, after the international market demonstrated greater monetary and economic stability.

Of the most prominent European subsidiaries, Ran-

3.
The president of Fiat, Giovanni Agnelli, visits the farms of the Generali Group. The guests of the Poggiobello farm in Udine (1978), at the center from the left: Agnelli; deputy chairman and managing director Enrico Randone; public relations manager Carlo Ulcigrai [ASAG, *Presidenza e organi sociali, Presidenti e vicepresidenti, Enrico Randone*, U2GE023746]

done was the chairman of Generali France, and deputy chairman of the Erste Allgemeine in Vienna. During the course of his chairmanship he endowed the company with a global vision and opened a general agency in Tokyo. Alas the coveted plan to add to its presence in the closed United States' market, remained unfulfilled. Limited success—compared to more ambitious European objectives that awaited 1992 with the liberalization of services—was obtained in 1988 in France with a proposal to control the Compagnie du Midi, a small share of the capital of which, Assicurazioni Generali already owned. Despite the backing of Mediobanca and Lazard, Assicurazioni Generali was faced with the French company's opposition, who chose to unite with the powerful AXA. Meanwhile the company from Trieste had to be satisfied with reaching an agreement; thus still increasing its minority shareholding. On the other hand, great success was achieved by reentering the Hungarian market, in which the company had existed since its inception in the 1830s, and which was then under a Communist regime that, nonetheless, was not averse to granting the West limited openings. After eight years of patient negotiations, in 1989 a joint venture agreement was signed, by virtue of which Assicurazioni Generali were the first in Europe to access that traditional market and, in 1991, becoming major shareholders of the company that was created for that purpose.

Retiring from the chairmanship in July 1991, Enrico Randone was nominated honorary chairman. He died in Milan on March 10, 1998.

Sources

ASAG. *Direzione Centrale*, *Servizio del Personale*, *Posizioni personali*. U2GE042629, personnel file of Enrico Randone, 1938–1975.

Assicurazioni Generali S.p.A. *Bilancio e relazioni del 144° esercizio-1975 – Bilancio 1991 160° anno di attività.*

Gruppo Assicurazioni Generali. *Bilancio consolidato 1975 – Bilancio consolidato del gruppo Generali, esercizio 1991.*

Assicurazioni Generali S.p.A. *Bilanci delle società controllate e collegate*, 1980–1991.

"Ricordo del Presidente d'onore Enrico Randone." *Bollettino delle Assicurazioni Generali* 17–18 (1998): 9–11.

Works

Randone, Enrico. "Verso la copertura dei rischi atomici." *Bollettino delle Assicurazioni Generali* 8–9 (1956): 5–10.

—. "I problemi della responsabilità civile nucleare e della sua regolamentazione." *Bollettino delle Assicurazioni Generali* 3 (1960): 31–37.

—. "Il disegno di legge italiano sull'energia nucleare." *Bollettino delle Assicurazioni Generali* 3 (1960): 39–42.

—. "La disciplina legale della responsabilità civile dell'esercente nucleare nella nuova legge italiana." *Bollettino delle Assicurazioni Generali* 3 (1963): 1–6.

—. "Assicurazione europea e integrazione economica." *Bollettino delle Assicurazioni Generali* 9 (1963): 1–7.

Bibliography

Di Martino, Anna. *Il leone delle Generali*. Milan: Elio Sellino Editore, 1992.

Favaretto, Tito. "Lo sviluppo dell'attività internazionale delle Assicurazioni Generali tra il XIX e il XX secolo." In *Assicurare 150 anni di Unità d'Italia. Il contributo delle assicurazioni allo sviluppo del Paese*, edited by Paolo Garonna, 93-151. Rome: Ania, 2011.

Millo, Anna. "Randone, Enrico." In *Dizionario Biografico degli Italiani*. Rome: Istituto dell'Enciclopedia Italiana, to be published.

(A.M.)

INDEXES

The tables of the components of the company's corporate representation comprise the names of the members, elected or appointed, of its statutory bodies from 1901 to 1982, and are arranged both chronologically and alphabetically: the first table presents the members of the company leadership over time; the second outlines the *cursus honorum* of each individual. In the interest of completion, the latter list also includes the names of a few individuals already listed in the alphabetical table of the nineteenth century, as they held posts spanning the nineteenth and twentieth centuries.

The two lists are to be understood as neither biographical summaries of the individuals' lives nor a historical summary of the development of the company bodies over time, but rather as a useful tool for facilitating the work of archival researchers and a clear primary reference for the more general reader. In-depth knowledge of the charters remains the indispensable foundation for the complete understanding of the development of the corporate representation.

The sources consulted for the compilation of the lists include the minutes of the leadership bodies, the corporate charters, the *specimina firmae* that accompanied the circular letters, the printed financial statements and, where possible, personnel files.

The names of the posts and the composition of the company bodies changed due to modifications, sometimes profound ones, in corporate structure over time. The changes considered to have been most important are elaborated upon in the notes at the bottom of the page.

The duration of each post has been indicated in terms of the start year and the end year, with the year understood as the period between two consecutive General Meetings. While elections and appointments were always recorded, information about when posts ended is sometimes imprecise. In the alphabetical table, this is indicated by the symbol ">," meaning that the year given as the end of the post is simply that of the last available documentary attestation. The end year of posts continuing after 1982 has been indicated with "…" The chronological table also indicates "new appointments," which is to say posts that went into effect at a General Meeting (or at a later time, in the case of replacements or posts begun before the end of the solar year; resignations and retirements were, instead, never recorded and can only be deduced through comparison with the minutes for the successive General Meeting).

Beyond the different logics underpinning the composition of each table, the alphabetical list also includes the names of various deputy members of the Board of Directors, meaning individuals who carried out functions analogous to those of their principals when absent. These names were not, however, indicated in the chronological table to avoid complicating its consultation.

A final observation concerns the standardization of names, with respect to language, spelling and the presence of prefixes, compound last names, noble titles and predicates: in the case of different versions of the same name, the most frequently used and/or most complete one was preferred. Sometimes it was not possible to work out the full version of an abbreviated form, while, in cases of homonymy, the patronymic was indicated in order to remove ambiguity.

Chronological Table of Corporate Representation

1901
Directors
Besso Giuseppe, Besso Marco, Bozza Camillo, Romanin-Jacur Emanuele
Deputy Directors
Costì Giovanni, Fano Giacomo, Levi Giacomo, Papadopoli Aldobrandini Nicolò, Vivante de Villabella Fortunato
Auditors
Da Zara Giuseppe, Eisner de Eisenhof Giacomo, Levy Carlo J.
Board of Directors
Berchet Guglielmo, Brunner Leopoldo, Brunner Rodolfo, Brusomini Eugenio, Burgstaller de Bidischini Giuseppe, Chimirri Bruno, Dreyfus-Louis Louis, Florio Ignazio di Ignazio, Franchetti Augusto, Gentilomo Oscar, Jachia Gino, de Jókai Maurus, Mekler de Traunwies Lodovico, Miller de Aichholz Vincenzo, Morpurgo Pietro Luigi, Mosconi Guglielmo, Pullè Leopoldo, Rava Enrico, Ricchetti Ettore, Salem Marco, Segrè Salvatore B., Tiepolo Lorenzo, Treves dei Bonfili Alberto, Treves dei Bonfili Camillo, Weinberg Leopoldo, Xydias Typaldo Dionisio
Secretary-General
Richetti de Terralba Edmondo
Deputy Secretary-General
Luzzati Gioberti
Secretary (Venice)
Kellner Arturo
Deputy Secretary (Venice)
Ara Carlo
Censors
Burgstaller de Bidischini Giuseppe, Morpurgo Pietro Luigi, Treves dei Bonfili Alberto

1902
Directors
Besso Marco, Bozza Camillo, Romanin-Jacur Emanuele, Vivante de Villabella Fortunato
Deputy Directors
Costì Giovanni, Da Zara Giuseppe, Fano Giacomo, Levi Giacomo, Papadopoli Aldobrandini Nicolò
Auditors
Burgstaller de Bidischini Giuseppe, Morpurgo Pietro Luigi, Treves dei Bonfili Alberto
Deputy Auditors
Brunner Leopoldo, Brusomini Eugenio, Xydias Typaldo Dionisio
Board of Directors
Artelli Filippo, Berchet Guglielmo, Besso Michelangelo, Brunner Rodolfo, Chimirri Bruno, Currò Rosario, Dreyfus-Louis Louis, Florio Ignazio di Ignazio, Franchetti Augusto, Gentilomo Oscar, Jachia Gino, de Jókai Maurus, Mekler de Traunwies Lodovico, Mosconi Guglielmo, Pullè Leopoldo, Rava Enrico, Ricchetti Ettore, Salem Marco, Scaramangà de Altomonte Giovanni, Segrè Salvatore B., Tiepolo Lorenzo, Treves dei Bonfili Camillo, Weinberg Leopoldo
Secretary-General
Richetti de Terralba Edmondo
Deputy Secretary-General
Luzzati Gioberti
Secretary (Venice)
Kellner Arturo
Deputy Secretary (Venice)
Ara Carlo
Censors
Brunner Leopoldo, Treves dei Bonfili Alberto, Xydias Typaldo Dionisio

1903
Directors
Besso Marco, Bozza Camillo, Romanin-Jacur Emanuele, Vivante de Villabella Fortunato
Deputy Directors
Costì Giovanni, Da Zara Giuseppe, Fano Giacomo, Levi Giacomo, Papadopoli Aldobrandini Nicolò
Auditors
Burgstaller de Bidischini Giuseppe, Morpurgo Pietro Luigi, Treves dei Bonfili Alberto
Deputy Auditors
Brunner Leopoldo, Brusomini Eugenio, Xydias Typaldo Dionisio
Board of Directors
Artelli Filippo, Berchet Guglielmo, Besso Michelangelo, Brunner Rodolfo, Chimirri Bruno, Currò Rosario, Dreyfus-Louis Louis, Florio Ignazio di Ignazio, Franchetti Augusto, Gentilomo Oscar, Jachia Gino, de Jókai Maurus, Mekler de Traunwies Lodovico, Mosconi Guglielmo, Pullè Leopoldo, Rava Enrico, Ricchetti Ettore, Salem Marco, Scaramangà de Altomonte Giovanni, Segrè Salvatore B., Tiepolo Lorenzo, Treves dei Bonfili Camillo, Weinberg Leopoldo
Secretary-General
Richetti de Terralba Edmondo
Deputy Secretary-General
Luzzati Gioberti
Secretary (Venice)
Kellner Arturo
Deputy Secretary (Venice)
Ara Carlo
Censors
Artelli Filippo, Scaramangà de Altomonte Giovanni, Tiepolo Lorenzo

1904
Directors
Besso Marco, Bozza Camillo, Romanin-Jacur Emanuele, Vivante de Villabella Fortunato
Deputy Directors
Costì Giovanni, Da Zara Giuseppe, Fano Giacomo, Levi Giacomo, Papadopoli Aldobrandini Nicolò
Auditors
Burgstaller de Bidischini Giuseppe, Morpurgo Pietro Luigi, Treves dei Bonfili Alberto
Deputy Auditors
Brunner Leopoldo, Brusomini Eugenio, Xydias Typaldo Dionisio
Board of Directors
Artelli Filippo, Berchet Guglielmo, Besso Michelangelo, Brunner Rodolfo, Currò Rosario, Dreyfus-Louis Louis, Florio Ignazio di Ignazio, Franchetti Augusto, Gentilomo Oscar, Jachia Gino, de Jókai Maurus, Mekler de Traunwies Lodovico, Mosconi Guglielmo, Pullè Leopoldo, Rava Enrico, Ricchetti Ettore, Salem Marco, Scaramangà de Altomonte Giovanni, Segrè Salvatore B., Tiepolo Lorenzo, Treves dei Bonfili Camillo, Weinberg Leopoldo
Secretary-General
Richetti de Terralba Edmondo
Deputy Secretary-General
Luzzati Gioberti
Secretary (Venice)
Kellner Arturo
Deputy Secretary (Venice)
Ara Carlo
Censors
Artelli Filippo, Scaramangà de Altomonte Giovanni, Tiepolo Lorenzo

1905
Directors
Besso Marco, Bozza Camillo, Romanin-Jacur Emanuele, Vivante de Villabella Fortunato
Deputy Directors
Costì Giovanni, Da Zara Giuseppe, Fano Giacomo, Levi Giacomo, Papadopoli Aldobrandini Nicolò
Auditors
Burgstaller de Bidischini Giuseppe, Morpurgo Pietro Luigi, Treves dei Bonfili Alberto
Deputy Auditors
Brunner Leopoldo, Brusomini Eugenio, Xydias Typaldo Dionisio
Board of Directors
Artelli Filippo, Berchet Guglielmo, Besso Michelangelo, Brunner Rodolfo, Currò Rosario, Dreyfus-Louis Louis, Florio Ignazio di Ignazio, Gentilomo Oscar, Jachia Gino, Luzzatto Angelo, Mekler de Traunwies Lodovico, Mosconi Guglielmo, Pullè Leopoldo, Rava Enrico, Ricchetti Ettore, Salem Marco, Scaramangà de Altomonte Giovanni, Segrè Salvatore B., Tiepolo Lorenzo, Treves dei Bonfili Camillo, Weinberg Leopoldo
Secretary-General
Richetti de Terralba Edmondo
Deputy Secretary-General
Luzzati Gioberti
Secretary (Venice)
Kellner Arturo
Deputy Secretary (Venice)
Ara Carlo
Censors
Artelli Filippo, Scaramangà de Altomonte Giovanni, Tiepolo Lorenzo

1906
Directors
Besso Marco, Bozza Camillo, Romanin-Jacur Emanuele, Vivante de Villabella Fortunato
Deputy Directors
Costì Giovanni, Da Zara Giuseppe, Fano Giacomo, Levi Giacomo, Papadopoli Aldobrandini Nicolò
Auditors
Burgstaller de Bidischini Giuseppe, Morpurgo Pietro Luigi, Treves dei Bonfili Alberto
Deputy Auditors
Brunner Leopoldo, Brusomini Eugenio, Xydias Typaldo Dionisio
Board of Directors
Artelli Filippo, Berchet Guglielmo, Besso Michelangelo, Brunner Rodolfo, Currò Rosario, Deutsch Giulio, Finali Gaspare, Florio Ignazio di Ignazio, Gentilomo Oscar, Jachia Gino, Luzzatto Angelo, Mekler de Traunwies Lodovico, Mosconi Guglielmo, Pullè Leopoldo, Rattazzi Urbano, Rava Enrico, Ricchetti Ettore, Salem Marco, Scaramangà de Altomonte Giovanni, Segrè Salvatore B., Tiepolo Lorenzo, Treves dei Bonfili Camillo, Weinberg Leopoldo
Secretary-General
Richetti de Terralba Edmondo
Deputy Secretary-General
Luzzati Gioberti
Secretary (Venice)
Kellner Arturo
Deputy Secretary (Venice)
Ara Carlo
Censors
Artelli Filippo, Scaramangà de Altomonte Giovanni, Tiepolo Lorenzo

1907
Directors
Besso Marco, Bozza Camillo, Romanin-Jacur Emanuele, Vivante de Villabella Fortunato
Deputy Directors
Artelli Filippo (from November 20), Costì Giovanni, Da Zara Giuseppe, Fano Giacomo, Kellner Arturo (from November 20), Levi Giacomo, Papadopoli Aldobrandini Nicolò
Auditors
Burgstaller de Bidischini Giuseppe, Morpurgo Pietro Luigi, Treves dei Bonfili Alberto
Deputy Auditors
Brunner Leopoldo, Brusomini Eugenio, Xydias Typaldo Dionisio
Board of Directors
Artelli Filippo (until November 20), Berchet Guglielmo, Besso Michelangelo, Bois de Chesne Carlo, Brunner Rodolfo, Currò Rosario, Deutsch Giulio, Finali Gaspare, Florio Ignazio di Ignazio, Frankfurter Alberto, Gentilomo

Oscar, Jachia Gino, Joel Otto, Luzzatto Angelo, Mekler de Traunwies Lodovico, Mosconi Guglielmo, Pullè Leopoldo, Rattazzi Urbano, Rava Enrico, Ricchetti Ettore, Salem Marco, Scaramangà de Altomonte Giovanni, Schütz Gustavo, Segrè Salvatore B., Tiepolo Lorenzo, Treves dei Bonfili Camillo, Weinberg Leopoldo

Secretary-General
Richetti de Terralba Edmondo

Deputy Secretary-General
Luzzati Gioberti

Secretary (Venice)
Kellner Arturo (until November 20), Morpurgo Edgardo (from November 20)

Deputy Secretary (Venice)
Ara Carlo (until June 1), Errera Adolfo (from June 1)

Censors
Artelli Filippo, Scaramangà de Altomonte Giovanni, Tiepolo Lorenzo

1908

Directors
Besso Marco, Bozza Camillo, Romanin-Jacur Emanuele, Vivante de Villabella Fortunato

Deputy Directors
Artelli Filippo, Costì Giovanni, Da Zara Giuseppe, Fano Giacomo, Kellner Arturo, Levi Giacomo, Papadopoli Aldobrandini Nicolò

Auditors
Burgstaller de Bidischini Giuseppe, Morpurgo Pietro Luigi, Treves dei Bonfili Alberto

Deputy Auditors
Brunner Leopoldo, Brusomini Eugenio, Xydias Typaldo Dionisio

Board of Directors
Berchet Guglielmo, Besso Michelangelo, Bois de Chesne Carlo, Brunner Rodolfo, Currò Rosario, Deutsch Giulio, Finali Gaspare, Florio Ignazio di Ignazio, Frankfurter Alberto, Gentilomo Oscar, Jachia Gino, Joel Otto, Luzzatto Angelo, Mekler de Traunwies Lodovico, Mosconi Guglielmo, Pullè Leopoldo, Rattazzi Urbano, Rava Enrico, Ricchetti Ettore, Salem Marco, Scaramangà de Altomonte Giovanni, Schütz Gustavo, Segrè Salvatore B., Tiepolo Lorenzo, Treves dei Bonfili Camillo, Weinberg Leopoldo

Secretary-General
Richetti de Terralba Edmondo

Deputy Secretary-General
Luzzati Gioberti

Secretary (Venice)
Morpurgo Edgardo

Deputy Secretary (Venice)
Errera Adolfo

Censors
Luzzatto Angelo, Scaramangà de Altomonte Giovanni, Tiepolo Lorenzo

1909

Chairman
Besso Marco

Directors
Besso Marco, Bozza Camillo, Romanin-Jacur Emanuele, Treves dei Bonfili Alberto (from May 19), Vivante de Villabella Fortunato

Deputy Directors
Artelli Filippo, Costì Giovanni, Da Zara Giuseppe, Fano Giacomo, Levi Giacomo, Papadopoli Aldobrandini Nicolò

Auditors
Brusomini Eugenio (from May 19), Burgstaller de Bidischini Giuseppe, Morpurgo Pietro Luigi, Treves dei Bonfili Alberto (until May 19)

Deputy Auditors
Brunner Leopoldo, Brusomini Eugenio (until May 19), Tiepolo Lorenzo (from May 19), Xydias Typaldo Dionisio

Board of Directors
Berchet Guglielmo, Besso Michelangelo, Bois de Chesne Carlo, Brunner Rodolfo, Currò Rosario, Deutsch Giulio, Finali Gaspare, Frankfurter Alberto, Gentilomo Oscar, Jachia Gino, Joel Otto, Luzzatto Angelo, Mekler de Traunwies Lodovico, Mosconi Guglielmo, Pullè Leopoldo, Rattazzi Urbano, Rava Enrico, Ricchetti Ettore, Salem Marco, Scaramangà de Altomonte Giovanni, Schütz Gustavo, Segrè Salvatore B., Tiepolo Lorenzo (until May 19), Treves dei Bonfili Camillo, Weinberg Leopoldo

Secretary-General / Director-in-Charge (from November 30)
Richetti de Terralba Edmondo

Deputy Secretary-General / Deputy Director-in-Charge (from November 30)
Luzzati Gioberti

Secretary (Venice) / Secretary Director (from November 30)
Morpurgo Edgardo

Deputy Secretary (Venice) / Deputy Secretary Director (from November 30)
Errera Adolfo

Censors
Luzzatto Angelo, Scaramangà de Altomonte Giovanni, Tiepolo Lorenzo

1910

Chairman
Besso Marco

Directors
Artelli Filippo (until September 3), Besso Marco, Bozza Camillo, Brunner Rodolfo (from July 7), Costì Giovanni, Da Zara Giuseppe, Fano Giacomo (until May 24), Levi Giacomo, Luzzati Gioberti (from December 3), Papadopoli Aldobrandini Nicolò, Romanin-Jacur Emanuele, Treves dei Bonfili Alberto, Vivante de Villabella Fortunato

Auditors
Brusomini Eugenio, Burgstaller de Bidischini Giuseppe, Morpurgo Pietro Luigi

Deputy Auditors
Brunner Leopoldo, Tiepolo Lorenzo, Xydias Typaldo Dionisio

Board of Directors
Berchet Guglielmo, Besso Michelangelo, Bodio Luigi, Bois de Chesne Carlo, Brunner Rodolfo (until July 7), Currò Rosario, Deutsch Giulio, Economo Demetrio, Finali Gaspare, Frankfurter Alberto, Gentilli Ermanno, Gentilomo Oscar, Jachia Gino, Joel Otto, de Kniep Giulio, Luzzatto Angelo, Mekler de Traunwies Lodovico, Mosconi Guglielmo, Pullè Leopoldo, Rattazzi Urbano, Rava Enrico, Ricchetti Ettore, Sacerdoti Giulio, Salem Marco, Salom Ettore, Scaramangà de Altomonte Giovanni, Schütz Gustavo, Segrè Salvatore B., Treves dei Bonfili Camillo, Weinberg Leopoldo

Director-in-Charge
Richetti de Terralba Edmondo

Deputy Directors-in-Charge
Luzzati Gioberti (until December 3), Luzzatto Giuseppe (from December 3), Schütz Carlo (from December 3)

Secretary Director (Venice)
Morpurgo Edgardo

Deputy Secretary Director (Venice)
Errera Adolfo

Censors
Berchet Guglielmo, Luzzatto Angelo, Scaramangà de Altomonte Giovanni

1911

Chairman
Besso Marco

Directors
Besso Marco, Bozza Camillo, Brunner Rodolfo, Costì Giovanni, Da Zara Giuseppe, Levi Giacomo, Luzzati Gioberti, Papadopoli Aldobrandini Nicolò, Romanin-Jacur Emanuele, Treves dei Bonfili Alberto, Vivante de Villabella Fortunato

Auditors
Brusomini Eugenio, Burgstaller de Bidischini Giuseppe, Morpurgo Pietro Luigi

Deputy Auditors
Brunner Leopoldo, Tiepolo Lorenzo, Xydias Typaldo Dionisio

Board of Directors
Berchet Guglielmo, Besso Michelangelo, Bodio Luigi, Bois de Chesne Carlo, Bylandt-Rheidt Arturo, Currò Rosario, Economo Demetrio, Ehrentheil Emanuele, Finali Gaspare, Frankfurter Alberto, Gentilli Ermanno, Gentilomo Oscar, Jachia Gino, Joel Otto, de Kniep Giulio, Luzzatto Angelo, Pullè Leopoldo, Rattazzi Urbano, Rava Enrico, Ricchetti Ettore, Sacerdoti Giulio, Salem Marco, Salom Ettore, Scaramangà de Altomonte Giovanni, Schütz Gustavo, Segrè Salvatore B., Treves dei Bonfili Camillo, Weinberg Leopoldo

Director-in-Charge
Richetti de Terralba Edmondo

Deputy Directors-in-Charge
Luzzatto Giuseppe, Schütz Carlo

Secretary Director (Venice)
Morpurgo Edgardo

Deputy Secretary Director (Venice)
Errera Adolfo

Censors
Berchet Guglielmo, Luzzatto Angelo, Scaramangà de Altomonte Giovanni

1912

Chairman
Besso Marco

Directors
Besso Marco, Bozza Camillo, Brunner Rodolfo, Costì Giovanni, Da Zara Giuseppe, Levi Giacomo, Luzzati Gioberti, Papadopoli Aldobrandini Nicolò, Romanin-Jacur Emanuele, Treves dei Bonfili Alberto, Vivante de Villabella Fortunato

Auditors
Brusomini Eugenio, Burgstaller de Bidischini Giuseppe, Morpurgo Pietro Luigi

Deputy Auditors
Brunner Leopoldo, Tiepolo Lorenzo, Xydias Typaldo Dionisio

Board of Directors
Artom Vittorio (from December 16), Berchet Guglielmo, Besso Michelangelo, Bodio Luigi, Bois de Chesne Carlo, Brunner Alfredo, Bylandt-Rheidt Arturo, Cavalieri Vittorio Lionello (from December 16), Currò Rosario, Derschatta de Standhalt Giulio, Economo Demetrio, Ehrentheil Emanuele, Finali Gaspare, Frankfurter Alberto, Gentilli Ermanno (until September), Gentilomo Oscar, Hardegg Francesco (from December 16), Jachia Gino, Joel Otto, de Kniep Giulio, Luzzatto Angelo, Pullè Leopoldo, Rava Enrico, Ricchetti Ettore, Sacerdoti Giulio, Salem Marco, Salom Ettore, Scaramangà de Altomonte Giovanni, Schütz Gustavo, Segrè Salvatore B., Treves dei Bonfili Camillo, Weinberg Leopoldo

Director-in-Charge
Richetti de Terralba Edmondo

Deputy Directors-in-Charge
Luzzatto Giuseppe, Schütz Carlo

Secretary Director (Venice)
Morpurgo Edgardo

Deputy Secretary Director (Venice)
Errera Adolfo

Censors
Berchet Guglielmo, Luzzatto

Angelo, Scaramangà de Altomonte Giovanni

1913
Chairman
Besso Marco
Directors
Besso Marco, Bozza Camillo, Brunner Rodolfo, Costì Giovanni, Da Zara Giuseppe, Levi Giacomo, Luzzati Gioberti, Papadopoli Aldobrandini Nicolò, Richetti de Terralba Edmondo (from March 21), Romanin-Jacur Emanuele, Treves dei Bonfili Alberto, Vivante de Villabella Fortunato
Auditors
Brusomini Eugenio, Burgstaller de Bidischini Giuseppe, Morpurgo Pietro Luigi
Deputy Auditors
Brunner Leopoldo, Tiepolo Lorenzo, Xydias Typaldo Dionisio
Board of Directors
Artom Vittorio, Berchet Guglielmo, Besso Michelangelo, Bodio Luigi, Bois de Chesne Carlo, Brunner Alfredo, Bylandt-Rheidt Arturo, Cavalieri Vittorio Lionello, Currò Rosario, Derschatta de Standhalt Giulio, Economo Demetrio, Finali Gaspare, Frankfurter Alberto, Gentilomo Oscar, Hardegg Francesco, Jachia Gino, Joel Otto, de Kniep Giulio, Luzzatto Angelo, Pullè Leopoldo, Rava Enrico, Ricchetti Ettore, Sacerdoti Giulio, Salem Marco, Salom Ettore, Scaramangà de Altomonte Giovanni, Schütz Gustavo, Segrè Salvatore B., Treves dei Bonfili Camillo, Weinberg Leopoldo
Director-in-Charge
Richetti de Terralba Edmondo (until March 20), Morpurgo Edgardo (from June 20)
Deputy Directors-in-Charge
Ehrentheil Emanuele (from June 20), Luzzatto Giuseppe (until June 19), Schütz Carlo
Secretary Director (Venice)
Morpurgo Edgardo (until June 19), Luzzatto Giuseppe (from June 20)
Deputy Secretary Director (Venice)
Errera Adolfo
Censors
Berchet Guglielmo, Luzzatto Angelo, Scaramangà de Altomonte Giovanni

1914
Chairman
Besso Marco
Directors
Besso Marco, Bozza Camillo, Brunner Rodolfo, Costì Giovanni, Da Zara Giuseppe, Levi Giacomo, Luzzati Gioberti, Papadopoli Aldobrandini Nicolò, Richetti de Terralba Edmondo, Romanin-Jacur Emanuele, Treves dei Bonfili Alberto, Vivante de Villabella Fortunato
Auditors
Brusomini Eugenio, Burgstaller de Bidischini Giuseppe, Morpurgo Pietro Luigi
Deputy Auditors
Brunner Leopoldo, Sacerdoti Giulio, Xydias Typaldo Dionisio
Board of Directors
Artom Vittorio, Besso Michelangelo, Bodio Luigi, Bois de Chesne Carlo, Brunner Alfredo, Bylandt-Rheidt Arturo, Cavalieri Vittorio Lionello, Currò Rosario, Derschatta de Standhalt Giulio, Economo Demetrio, Finali Gaspare, Frankfurter Alberto, Hardegg Francesco, Jachia Gino, Joel Otto, Kahanè Giuseppe (from June 10), de Kniep Giulio, Levi Della Vida Ettore (from June 10), Luzzatto-Fegiz Giuseppe, Molmenti Pompeo Gherardo, Pullè Leopoldo, Rava Enrico (until March 28), Ricchetti Ettore, Salem Marco, Salom Ettore, Scaramangà de Altomonte Giovanni, Schütz Gustavo, Segrè Salvatore B., Treves dei Bonfili Camillo, Weinberg Leopoldo
Director-in-Charge
Morpurgo Edgardo
Deputy Directors-in-Charge
Ehrentheil Emanuele, Schütz Carlo
Secretary Director (Venice)
Luzzatto Giuseppe
Deputy Secretary Director (Venice)
Errera Adolfo
Censors
Artom Vittorio, Bois de Chesne Carlo, Scaramangà de Altomonte Giovanni
Deputy Censor
Besso Michelangelo

1915
Chairman
Besso Marco
Directors
Besso Marco, Brunner Rodolfo, Brusomini Eugenio, Costì Giovanni, Da Zara Giuseppe, Economo Demetrio, Luzzati Gioberti, Papadopoli Aldobrandini Nicolò, Ricchetti Ettore, Romanin-Jacur Emanuele, Treves dei Bonfili Alberto, Vivante de Villabella Fortunato
Auditors
Morpurgo Pietro Luigi, Sacerdoti Giulio, Xydias Typaldo Dionisio
Deputy Auditors
Artom Vittorio, Brunner Leopoldo, Frankfurter Alberto
Board of Directors
de Albori Riccardo, Besso Michelangelo, Bodio Luigi, Bois de Chesne Carlo, Brunner Alfredo, Bylandt-Rheidt Arturo, Cavalieri Vittorio Lionello, Currò Rosario, Derschatta de Standhalt Giulio, Grimani Filippo, Hardegg Francesco, Jachia Gino, Joel Otto, Kahanè Giuseppe, Levi Della Vida Ettore, Luzzatto-Fegiz Giuseppe, Molmenti Pompeo Gherardo, Pullè Leopoldo, Salem Marco, Salom Ettore, Scaramangà de Altomonte Giovanni, Schütz Gustavo, Segrè Salvatore B., Treves dei Bonfili Camillo, Tripcovich Diodato, Valerio Alfonso, Volpi di Misurata Giuseppe, Weinberg Leopoldo, Weiner Alessandro
Director-in-Charge
Morpurgo Edgardo
Deputy Directors-in-Charge
Ehrentheil Emanuele, Schütz Carlo
Secretary Director (Venice)
Luzzatto Giuseppe
Deputy Secretary Director (Venice)
Errera Adolfo
Censors
Artom Vittorio, Bois de Chesne Carlo, Scaramangà de Altomonte Giovanni
Deputy Censor
Besso Michelangelo

1916[1]
Chairman
Besso Marco
Directors
Besso Marco, Brunner Rodolfo, Brusomini Eugenio (until February), Costì Giovanni, Da Zara Giuseppe, Economo Demetrio, Luzzati Gioberti, Papadopoli Aldobrandini Nicolò, Ricchetti Ettore, Romanin-Jacur Emanuele (until April 27), Treves dei Bonfili Alberto, Vivante de Villabella Fortunato
Auditors
Morpurgo Pietro Luigi, Sacerdoti Giulio, Xydias Typaldo Dionisio
Deputy Auditors
Artom Vittorio, Brunner Leopoldo, Frankfurter Alberto
Board of Directors
de Albori Riccardo, Besso Michelangelo, Bodio Luigi, Bois de Chesne Carlo, Brunner Alfredo, Cavalieri Vittorio Lionello, Currò Rosario, Derschatta de Standhalt Giulio, Grimani Filippo, Hardegg Francesco, Jachia Gino, Joel Otto (until April 27), Kahanè Giuseppe, Levi Della Vida Ettore, Luzzatto-Fegiz Giuseppe, Molmenti Pompeo Gherardo, Pullè Leopoldo, Salem Marco, Salom Ettore, Scaramangà de Altomonte Giovanni, Schütz Gustavo, Segrè Salvatore B., Treves dei Bonfili Camillo (until September 05), Tripcovich Diodato, Valerio Alfonso, Volpi di Misurata Giuseppe, Weinberg Leopoldo, Weiner Alessandro
Director-in-Charge
Morpurgo Edgardo
Deputy Directors-in-Charge
Ehrentheil Emanuele, Schütz Carlo
Secretary Director (Venice)
Luzzatto Giuseppe
Deputy Secretary Director (Venice)
Errera Adolfo

1917
Chairman
Besso Marco
Directors
Besso Marco, Brunner Rodolfo, Costì Giovanni, Da Zara Giuseppe, Economo Demetrio, Luzzati Gioberti, Papadopoli Aldobrandini Nicolò, Ricchetti Ettore (until August), Treves dei Bonfili Alberto, Vivante de Villabella Fortunato
Auditors
Morpurgo Pietro Luigi, Sacerdoti Giulio, Xydias Typaldo Dionisio
Deputy Auditors
Artom Vittorio, Brunner Leopoldo, Frankfurter Alberto
Board of Directors
de Albori Riccardo, Besso Michelangelo, Bodio Luigi, Bois de Chesne Carlo, Brunner Alfredo, Cavalieri Vittorio Lionello, Currò Rosario, Derschatta de Standhalt Giulio, Grimani Filippo, Hardegg Francesco, Jachia Gino, Kahanè Giuseppe, Levi Della Vida Ettore, Luzzatto-Fegiz Giuseppe, Molmenti Pompeo Gherardo, Pullè Leopoldo (until May), Salem Marco, Salom Ettore, Scaramangà de Altomonte Giovanni, Schütz Gustavo, Segrè Salvatore B., Tripcovich Diodato, Valerio Alfonso, Volpi di Misurata Giuseppe, Weinberg Leopoldo, Weiner Alessandro
Director-in-Charge
Morpurgo Edgardo
Deputy Directors-in-Charge
Ehrentheil Emanuele, Schütz Carlo
Secretary Director (Venice)
Luzzatto Giuseppe
Deputy Secretary Director (Venice)
Errera Adolfo

1918
Chairman
Besso Marco
Directors
Besso Marco, Brunner Rodolfo, Costì Giovanni, Da Zara Giuseppe, Economo Demetrio, Luzzati Gioberti (until August), Papadopoli Aldobrandini Nicolò, Treves dei Bonfili Alberto, Vivante de Villabella Fortunato
Auditors
Morpurgo Pietro Luigi, Sacerdoti Giulio, Xydias Typaldo Dionisio (until August)
Deputy Auditors
Artom Vittorio, Brunner Leopoldo, Frankfurter Alberto
Board of Directors
de Albori Riccardo, Besso Michelangelo, Bodio Luigi, Bois de Chesne Carlo, Brunner Alfredo, Cavalieri Vittorio Lionello, Currò Rosario, Derschatta de Standhalt Giulio, Grimani Filippo, Hardegg Francesco, Jachia Gino, Kahanè

Giuseppe, Levi Della Vida Ettore, Luzzatto-Fegiz Giuseppe, Molmenti Pompeo Gherardo, Salem Marco, Salom Ettore, Scaramangà de Altomonte Giovanni, Schütz Gustavo, Segrè Salvatore B., Tripcovich Diodato, Valerio Alfonso, Volpi di Misurata Giuseppe, Weinberg Leopoldo, Weiner Alessandro

Director-in-Charge
Morpurgo Edgardo

Deputy Directors-in-Charge
Ehrentheil Emanuele, Schütz Carlo

Secretary Director (Venice)
Luzzatto Giuseppe

Deputy Secretary Director (Venice)
Errera Adolfo

1919

Chairman
Besso Marco

Directors
Besso Marco, Brunner Rodolfo, Costì Giovanni, Da Zara Giuseppe, Economo Demetrio, Grimani Filippo, Papadopoli Aldobrandini Nicolò, Treves dei Bonfili Alberto, Valerio Alfonso, Vivante de Villabella Fortunato

Auditors
Morpurgo Pietro Luigi, Sacerdoti Giulio

Deputy Auditors
Artom Vittorio, Brunner Leopoldo, Frankfurter Alberto

Board of Directors
de Albori Riccardo, Besso Michelangelo, Bodio Luigi, Bois de Chesne Carlo, Brunner Alfredo, Cavalieri Vittorio Lionello, Currò Rosario, Derschatta de Standhalt Giulio, Hardegg Francesco, Jachia Gino, Kahanè Giuseppe, Levi Della Vida Ettore, Luzzatto-Fegiz Giuseppe, Molmenti Pompeo Gherardo, Salem Marco, Salom Ettore, Scaramangà de Altomonte Giovanni, Schütz Gustavo, Tripcovich Diodato, Volpi di Misurata Giuseppe, Weinberg Leopoldo, Weiner Alessandro

Director-in-Charge
Morpurgo Edgardo

Deputy Directors-in-Charge
Ehrentheil Emanuele, Schütz Carlo

Secretary Director (Venice)
Luzzatto Giuseppe

Deputy Secretary Director (Venice)
Errera Adolfo

1920

Chairman
Besso Marco (until October 7), Morpurgo Edgardo (from October 28)

Directors
Besso Marco (until October 7), Brunner Rodolfo, Costì Giovanni, Da Zara Giuseppe, Economo Demetrio, Grimani Filippo, Papadopoli Aldobrandini Nicolò, Treves dei Bonfili Alberto, Valerio Alfonso, Vivante de Villabella Fortunato

Auditors
Morpurgo Pietro Luigi, Sacerdoti Giulio

Deputy Auditors
Artom Vittorio, Brunner Leopoldo, Frankfurter Alberto

Board of Directors
de Albori Riccardo, Besso Michelangelo, Bodio Luigi, Bois de Chesne Carlo, Brunner Alfredo, Cavalieri Vittorio Lionello, Currò Rosario, Derschatta de Standhalt Giulio, Hardegg Francesco, Jachia Gino, Kahanè Giuseppe, Levi Della Vida Ettore, Luzzatto-Fegiz Giuseppe, Molmenti Pompeo Gherardo, Salem Marco, Salom Ettore, Scaramangà de Altomonte Giovanni, Schütz Gustavo, Tripcovich Diodato, Volpi di Misurata Giuseppe, Weinberg Leopoldo, Weiner Alessandro

Director-in-Charge
Morpurgo Edgardo

Deputy Directors-in-Charge
Ehrentheil Emanuele, Schütz Carlo

Secretary Director (Venice)
Luzzatto Giuseppe

Deputy Secretary Director (Venice)
Errera Adolfo

1921

Chairman
Morpurgo Edgardo

Directors
Brunner Rodolfo, Da Zara Giuseppe, Economo Demetrio, Grimani Filippo, Papadopoli Aldobrandini Nicolò, Treves dei Bonfili Alberto, Valerio Alfonso, Vivante de Villabella Fortunato

Auditors
Brunner Leopoldo, Morpurgo Pietro Luigi, Sacerdoti Giulio

Deputy Auditors
Artom Vittorio, Bois de Chesne Carlo (from January 31), Frankfurter Alberto

Board of Directors
Besso Michelangelo, Brunner Alfredo, Cavalieri Vittorio Lionello, Costì Giovanni, Cosulich Antonio Nicolò, Currò Rosario, Hardegg Francesco, Jachia Gino, Kahanè Giuseppe, Levi Della Vida Ettore, Luzzatto-Fegiz Giuseppe, Molmenti Pompeo Gherardo, Pogliani Angelo, Pollich Ettore, Salom Ettore, Scaramangà de Altomonte Giovanni, Schütz Gustavo, Toeplitz Giuseppe, Tripcovich Diodato, Venezian Vittorio, Volpi di Misurata Giuseppe, Weiner Alessandro

Director-in-Charge
Morpurgo Edgardo

Deputy Directors-in-Charge
Ehrentheil Emanuele, Schütz Carlo

Secretary Director (Venice)
Luzzatto Giuseppe

Deputy Secretary Director (Venice)
Errera Adolfo

Censors
Besso Michelangelo, Bois de Chesne Carlo (until January 31), Scaramangà de Altomonte Giovanni, Venezian Vittorio (from June 30)

1922[2]

Chairman
Morpurgo Edgardo

Council of Directors
Ara Camillo, Bois de Chesne Carlo, Brunner Arminio, Brunner Rodolfo, Da Zara Giuseppe, Economo Demetrio, Errera Adolfo, Mayer Teodoro, Molmenti Pompeo Gherardo, Sacerdoti Giulio, Scaramangà de Altomonte Giovanni, Valerio Alfonso, Venezian Vittorio, Vivante de Villabella Fortunato

Executive Committee
Ara Camillo, Brunner Rodolfo, Scaramangà de Altomonte Giovanni

Auditors
Artom Vittorio, Brunner Leopoldo, Morpurgo Pietro Luigi

Deputy Auditors
Besso Michelangelo, Currò Rosario, Frankfurter Alberto

Board of Directors
Borghese Scipione, Brunner Alfredo, Brusoni Giacomo, Cavalieri Vittorio Lionello, Chiggiato Giovanni, Cini Vittorio, Cornaggia Medici Castiglioni Carlo Ottavio, Cosulich Antonio Nicolò, Georgiadis Giorgio, Hardegg Francesco, Jachia Gino, Levi Della Vida Ettore, Luzzatto-Fegiz Giuseppe, Marchesano Giuseppe, Oberti Zaccaria, Pollich Ettore, Preiss Jaroslav, Salom Ettore, Schütz Carlo, Schütz Gustavo, Toeplitz Giuseppe, Tripcovich Diodato, Volpi di Misurata Giuseppe, Weiner Alessandro, Wollemborg Maurizio

General Manager
Morpurgo Edgardo

Deputy General Managers
Besso Vittorio (from November 28), Ehrentheil Emanuele, Sulfina Michele (from May 15)

General Manager (Venice)
Luzzatto Giuseppe

Managers (Venice)
Ara Marco, Cavaglieri Gino

1923

Chairman
Morpurgo Edgardo

Council of Directors
Ara Camillo, Bois de Chesne Carlo, Brunner Arminio, Brunner Rodolfo, Da Zara Giuseppe (until July 28), Economo Demetrio, Errera Adolfo, Mayer Teodoro, Molmenti Pompeo Gherardo, Sacerdoti Giulio, Scaramangà de Altomonte Giovanni, Valerio Alfonso, Venezian Vittorio, Vivante de Villabella Fortunato

Executive Committee
Ara Camillo, Brunner Rodolfo, Scaramangà de Altomonte Giovanni

Auditors
Artom Vittorio, Brunner Leopoldo, Morpurgo Pietro Luigi

Deputy Auditors
Besso Michelangelo, Currò Rosario, Frankfurter Alberto

Board of Directors
Broglia Giuseppe, Brunner Alfredo, Brusoni Giacomo, Cini Vittorio, Cornaggia Medici Castiglioni Carlo Ottavio, Cosulich Antonio Nicolò, Cremonesi Filippo, Dentice di Frasso Alfredo, Georgiadis Giorgio, Hardegg Francesco, Jachia Gino, Luzzatto-Fegiz Giuseppe, Marchesano Giuseppe, Morpurgo Elio, Oberti Zaccaria (until October 5), Pollich Ettore, Preiss Jaroslav, Salom Ettore, Schütz Carlo, Schütz Gustavo, Segre Guido, Terni Girolamo (until September 16), Toeplitz Giuseppe, Tripcovich Diodato, Volpi di Misurata Giuseppe, Weiner Alessandro, Wollemborg Maurizio

General Manager
Morpurgo Edgardo

Deputy General Managers
Besso Vittorio (until October 3), Ehrentheil Emanuele, Sulfina Michele

General Manager (Venice)
Luzzatto Giuseppe

Managers (Venice)
Ara Marco, Cavaglieri Gino

1924

Chairman
Morpurgo Edgardo

Council of Directors
Ara Camillo, Bois de Chesne Carlo, Brunner Arminio, Brunner Rodolfo, Economo Demetrio, Errera Adolfo, Mayer Teodoro, Molmenti Pompeo Gherardo, Sacerdoti Giulio, Scaramangà de Altomonte Giovanni, Valerio Alfonso, Venezian Vittorio, Vivante de Villabella Fortunato

Executive Committee
Ara Camillo, Brunner Rodolfo, Scaramangà de Altomonte Giovanni

Auditors
Artom Vittorio, Brunner Leopoldo, Morpurgo Pietro Luigi

Deputy Auditors
Besso Michelangelo, Currò Rosario, Frankfurter Alberto

Board of Directors
Broglia Giuseppe, Brunner Alfredo, Brusoni Giacomo, Cini Vittorio, Cornaggia Medici Castiglioni Carlo Ottavio, Cosulich

Antonio Nicolò, Cremonesi Filippo, Dentice di Frasso Alfredo, Gattegno Benveniste D., Georgiadis Giorgio, Hardegg Francesco, Jachia Gino, Luzzatto-Fegiz Giuseppe, Marchesano Giuseppe, Mercurio Alfonso, Morpurgo Elio, Parodi Emanuele Vittorio, Pollich Ettore, Preiss Jaroslav, Salom Ettore, Schütz Carlo, Schütz Gustavo, Segre Guido, Steiner Rodolfo, Toeplitz Giuseppe, Toja Guido, Tripcovich Diodato, Ucelli Giulio, Volpi di Misurata Giuseppe, Wollemborg Maurizio, Zino Dionisio

General Manager
Morpurgo Edgardo

Deputy General Managers
Ehrentheil Emanuele, Sulfina Michele

General Manager (Venice)
Luzzatto Giuseppe

Managers (Venice)
Ara Marco, Cavaglieri Gino

1925

Chairman
Morpurgo Edgardo

Council of Directors
Ara Camillo, Bois de Chesne Carlo, Brunner Arminio, Brunner Rodolfo, Economo Demetrio, Errera Adolfo, Mayer Teodoro, Molmenti Pompeo Gherardo, Sacerdoti Giulio, Scaramangà de Altomonte Giovanni, Valerio Alfonso, Venezian Vittorio, Vivante de Villabella Fortunato

Executive Committee
Ara Camillo, Brunner Rodolfo, Mayer Teodoro, Scaramangà de Altomonte Giovanni

Auditors
Artom Vittorio, Brunner Leopoldo, Morpurgo Pietro Luigi

Deputy Auditors
Besso Michelangelo, Currò Rosario, Frankfurter Alberto

Board of Directors
Bonacossi Taino, Broglia Giuseppe, Brunner Alfredo, Brusoni Giacomo, Cini Vittorio, Cornaggia Medici Castiglioni Carlo Ottavio, Cosulich Antonio Nicolò, Cremonesi Filippo, Dentice di Frasso Alfredo, Gattegno Benveniste D., Georgiadis Giorgio, Hardegg Francesco, Jachia Gino, Luzzatto-Fegiz Giuseppe, Marchesano Giuseppe, Mercurio Alfonso, Morpurgo Elio, Parodi Emanuele Vittorio, Pollich Ettore, Preiss Jaroslav, Revedin Antonio, Salom Ettore, Schütz Carlo, Segre Guido, Steiner Rodolfo, Toeplitz Giuseppe, Toja Guido, Tripcovich Diodato, Ucelli Giulio, Volpi di Misurata Giuseppe, Wollemborg Maurizio, Zino Dionisio

General Manager
Morpurgo Edgardo

Deputy General Managers
Ehrentheil Emanuele, Sulfina Michele

General Manager (Venice)
Luzzatto Giuseppe

Managers (Venice)
Ara Marco, Cavaglieri Gino

1926

Chairman
Morpurgo Edgardo

Managing Director
Morpurgo Edgardo (from November 23)

Council of Directors
Ara Camillo, Bois de Chesne Carlo, Brunner Arminio, Brunner Rodolfo, Cremonesi Filippo (from November 23), Economo Demetrio, Ehrentheil Emanuele (from November 23), Errera Adolfo, Luzzatto Giuseppe, Mayer Teodoro, Molmenti Pompeo Gherardo, Sacerdoti Giulio, Scaramangà de Altomonte Giovanni, Toeplitz Giuseppe, Valerio Alfonso, Vivante de Villabella Fortunato (until October 12)

Executive Committee
Ara Camillo, Brunner Rodolfo, Mayer Teodoro, Scaramangà de Altomonte Giovanni

Auditors
Artom Vittorio, Brunner Leopoldo, Morpurgo Pietro Luigi

Deputy Auditors
Besso Michelangelo, Cini Vittorio, Currò Rosario

Board of Directors
Banelli Giovanni, Boggio Oscar (from November 23), Bonacossi Taino, Broglia Giuseppe, Brunner Alfredo, Brusoni Giacomo, Cornaggia Medici Castiglioni Carlo Ottavio, Cosulich Antonio Nicolò, Cremonesi Filippo (until November 23), Dentice di Frasso Alfredo, Gattegno Benveniste D., Georgiadis Giorgio, Horváth Leopoldo, Jachia Gino, Lubomirski Stanislaw, Luzzatto-Fegiz Giuseppe, Marchesano Giuseppe, Mercurio Alfonso, Morpurgo Elio, Parodi Emanuele Vittorio, Pollich Ettore, Preiss Jaroslav, Revedin Antonio, Salom Ettore, Schütz Carlo, Segre Guido, Solza Mario, Steiner Rodolfo, Tripcovich Mario, Ucelli Giulio, Vitali Vittorio Carlo, Wollemborg Maurizio, Zino Dionisio

General Managers
Cavaglieri Gino (from November 23), Morpurgo Edgardo, Sulfina Michele (from November 23)

Deputy General Managers
Ehrentheil Emanuele (until November 23), Sulfina Michele (until November 23), Ara Angelo (from November 23), Cleva Giulio (from November 23), D'Alvise Sante (from November 23)

General Manager (Venice)
Ara Marco (from November 23)

Managers (Venice)
Ara Marco (until November 23), Cavaglieri Gino (until November 23), Corti Giulio (from November 23), Vivante Giorgio (from November 23)

1927

Chairman
Morpurgo Edgardo

Managing Director
Morpurgo Edgardo

Council of Directors
Ara Camillo, Bois de Chesne Carlo, Brunner Arminio, Brunner Rodolfo, Cremonesi Filippo, Economo Demetrio, Ehrentheil Emanuele, Errera Adolfo, Luzzatto Giuseppe, Mayer Teodoro, Molmenti Pompeo Gherardo, Sacerdoti Giulio, Scaramangà de Altomonte Giovanni, Toeplitz Giuseppe, Valerio Alfonso

Executive Committee
Ara Camillo, Brunner Rodolfo, Mayer Teodoro, Scaramangà de Altomonte Giovanni

Auditors
Artom Vittorio, Brunner Leopoldo, Morpurgo Pietro Luigi

Deputy Auditors
Besso Michelangelo, Cini Vittorio, Currò Rosario

Board of Directors
Banelli Giovanni, Boggio Oscar, Bonacossi Taino, Broglia Giuseppe, Brunner Alfredo, Brusoni Giacomo, Cornaggia Medici Castiglioni Carlo Ottavio, Cosulich Antonio Nicolò, Dentice di Frasso Alfredo, Gattegno Benveniste D., Georgiadis Giorgio, Horváth Leopoldo, Jachia Gino, Lubomirski Stanislaw, Luzzatto-Fegiz Giuseppe, Marchesano Giuseppe, Mercurio Alfonso, Morpurgo Elio, Parodi Emanuele Vittorio, Pollich Ettore, Preiss Jaroslav, Revedin Antonio, Salom Ettore, Schütz Carlo, Segre Guido, Solza Mario, Steiner Rodolfo, Tripcovich Mario, Ucelli Giulio, Vitali Vittorio Carlo, Wollemborg Maurizio, Zino Dionisio

General Managers
Cavaglieri Gino, Morpurgo Edgardo, Sulfina Michele

Deputy General Managers
Ara Angelo, Cleva Giulio, D'Alvise Sante

General Manager (Venice)
Ara Marco

Managers (Venice)
Corti Giulio, Vivante Giorgio

1928

Chairman
Morpurgo Edgardo

Managing Director
Morpurgo Edgardo

Council of Directors
Ara Camillo, Bois de Chesne Carlo, Brunner Arminio, Brunner Rodolfo, Cremonesi Filippo, Economo Demetrio, Ehrentheil Emanuele, Errera Adolfo, Luzzatto Giuseppe, Mayer Teodoro, Sacerdoti Giulio, Scaramangà de Altomonte Giovanni, Toeplitz Giuseppe, Valerio Alfonso

Executive Committee
Ara Camillo, Bois de Chesne Carlo, Brunner Rodolfo, Scaramangà de Altomonte Giovanni

Auditors
Artom Vittorio, Brunner Leopoldo, Morpurgo Pietro Luigi

Deputy Auditors
Besso Michelangelo, Currò Rosario, Luzzatto-Fegiz Giuseppe

Board of Directors
Banelli Giovanni, Boggio Oscar, Bonacossi Taino, Broglia Giuseppe, Brunner Alfredo, Cini Vittorio, Cornaggia Medici Castiglioni Carlo Ottavio, Cosulich Antonio Nicolò, Dentice di Frasso Alfredo, Gattegno Benveniste D., Georgiadis Giorgio, Horváth Leopoldo, Jachia Giacomo, Jachia Gino, Lubomirski Stanislaw, Marchesano Giuseppe, Mercurio Alfonso, Morpurgo Elio, Niccolini Pietro (from December 18), Olivetti Gino (from December 18), Padoa Mario (from December 18), Parodi Emanuele Vittorio, Petschek Walter (from December 18), Preiss Jaroslav, Revedin Antonio, Salom Ettore, Segre Guido, Solza Mario, Steiner Rodolfo, Stirbey Barbu (from December 18), Tripcovich Mario, Vitali Vittorio Carlo, Volpi di Misurata Giuseppe (from December 18), Wollemborg Maurizio, Zino Dionisio

General Managers
Cavaglieri Gino, Morpurgo Edgardo, Sulfina Michele

Deputy General Managers
Ara Angelo, Cleva Giulio, D'Alvise Sante

General Manager (Venice)
Ara Marco

Managers (Venice)
Corti Giulio, Vivante Giorgio

1929

Chairman
Morpurgo Edgardo

Managing Director
Morpurgo Edgardo

Council of Directors
Ara Camillo, Bois de Chesne Carlo, Brunner Arminio, Brunner Rodolfo, Cremonesi Filippo, Economo Demetrio, Ehrentheil Emanuele, Errera Adolfo, Luzzatto Giuseppe, Mayer Teodoro, Sacerdoti Giulio, Scaramangà de Altomonte Giovanni, Toeplitz Giuseppe, Valerio Alfonso

Executive Committee
Ara Camillo, Bois de Chesne Carlo, Brunner Rodolfo, Scaramangà de Altomonte Giovanni

Auditors
Artom Vittorio, Brunner Leopoldo, Morpurgo Pietro Luigi
Deputy Auditors
Besso Michelangelo, Currò Rosario, Luzzatto-Fegiz Giuseppe
Board of Directors
Banelli Giovanni, Boggio Oscar, Bonacossi Taino, Broglia Giuseppe, Brunner Alfredo, Cini Vittorio, Cornaggia Medici Castiglioni Carlo Ottavio, Cosulich Antonio Nicolò, Dentice di Frasso Alfredo, Gattegno Benveniste D., Georgiadis Giorgio, Horváth Leopoldo, Jachia Giacomo, Lubomirski Stanislaw, Marchesano Giuseppe, Mercurio Alfonso, Morpurgo Elio, Niccolini Pietro, Olivetti Gino, Padoa Mario, Parodi Emanuele Vittorio, Petschek Walter, Preiss Jaroslav, Revedin Antonio, Salom Ettore, Segre Guido, Solza Mario, Steiner Rodolfo, Stirbey Barbu, Tripcovich Mario, Vitali Vittorio Carlo, Volpi di Misurata Giuseppe, Wollemborg Maurizio, Zino Dionisio
General Managers
Cavaglieri Gino, Morpurgo Edgardo, Sulfina Michele
Deputy General Managers
Ara Angelo, Cleva Giulio, D'Alvise Sante
General Manager (Venice)
Ara Marco
Managers (Venice)
Corti Giulio, Vivante Giorgio

1930
Chairman
Morpurgo Edgardo
Managing Director
Morpurgo Edgardo
Council of Directors
Ara Camillo, Bois de Chesne Carlo, Brunner Rodolfo, Cremonesi Filippo, Economo Demetrio, Ehrentheil Emanuele, Errera Adolfo, Luzzatto Giuseppe, Mayer Teodoro, Sacerdoti Giulio, Scaramangà de Altomonte Giovanni, Toeplitz Giuseppe, Valerio Alfonso
Executive Committee
Ara Camillo, Bois de Chesne Carlo, Economo Demetrio, Scaramangà de Altomonte Giovanni

Statutory Auditors
Marchesano Enrico, Matteucci Renato, Morpurgo Pietro Luigi
Deputy Auditors
Besso Michelangelo, Dall'Armi Antonio
General Council
Artom Vittorio, Banelli Giovanni, Bonacossi Taino, Broglia Giuseppe, Brunner Alfredo, Brunner Leopoldo, Cini Vittorio, Cornaggia Medici Castiglioni Carlo Ottavio, Cosulich Antonio Nicolò, Dentice di Frasso Alfredo, Deutsch Otto, Gattegno Benveniste D., Horváth Leopoldo, Jachia Giacomo, Lubomirski Stanislaw, Marchesano Giuseppe, Mercurio Alfonso, Morpurgo Elio, Niccolini Pietro, Olivetti Gino, Padoa Mario, Parodi Emanuele Vittorio, Petschek Walter, Preiss Jaroslav, Revedin Antonio, Salom Ettore, Segre Guido, Solza Mario, Stirbey Barbu, Tripcovich Mario, Vitali Vittorio Carlo, Volpi di Misurata Giuseppe, Wollemborg Maurizio, Zino Dionisio
General Managers
Cavaglieri Gino, Morpurgo Edgardo, Sulfina Michele
Deputy General Managers
Ara Angelo, Cleva Giulio, D'Alvise Sante
General Manager (Venice)
Ara Marco
Managers (Venice)
Corti Giulio, Vivante Giorgio

1931
Chairman
Morpurgo Edgardo
Managing Director
Morpurgo Edgardo
Council of Directors
Ara Camillo, Bois de Chesne Carlo, Brunner Rodolfo, Cremonesi Filippo, Economo Demetrio, Ehrentheil Emanuele, Errera Adolfo, Luzzatto Giuseppe, Mayer Teodoro, Sacerdoti Giulio, Scaramangà de Altomonte Giovanni, Segre Guido, Toeplitz Giuseppe
Executive Committee
Ara Camillo, Bois de Chesne Carlo, Economo Demetrio, Scaramangà de Altomonte Giovanni

Statutory Auditors
Marchesano Enrico, Matteucci Renato, Morpurgo Pietro Luigi
Deputy Auditors
Besso Michelangelo, Dall'Armi Antonio
General Council
Alberti Giovanni, Banelli Giovanni, Bonacossi Taino, Broglia Giuseppe, Brunner Alfredo, Brunner Leopoldo, Cini Vittorio, Cornaggia Medici Castiglioni Carlo Ottavio, Cosulich Antonio Nicolò, Dentice di Frasso Alfredo, Deutsch Otto, Frignani Giuseppe, Gattegno Benveniste D., Horváth Leopoldo, Jachia Giacomo, Kraemer Hans, Lubomirski Stanislaw, Manaut René Victor, Marchesano Giuseppe, Morpurgo Elio, Niccolini Pietro, Olivetti Gino, Padoa Mario, Parodi Emanuele Vittorio, Petschek Walter, Pitacco Giorgio, Preiss Jaroslav, Revedin Antonio, Salom Ettore, Solza Mario, Tripcovich Mario, Valerio Alfonso, Vitali Vittorio Carlo, Volpi di Misurata Giuseppe, Wollemborg Maurizio
General Managers
Cavaglieri Gino, Morpurgo Edgardo, Sulfina Michele
Deputy General Managers
Ara Angelo, Cleva Giulio, D'Alvise Sante
General Manager (Venice)
Ara Marco
Managers (Venice)
Corti Giulio, Vivante Giorgio

1932
Chairman
Morpurgo Edgardo
Managing Director
Morpurgo Edgardo
Council of Directors
Ara Camillo, Bois de Chesne Carlo, Brunner Rodolfo, Cremonesi Filippo, Economo Demetrio, Ehrentheil Emanuele, Errera Adolfo, Luzzatto Giuseppe, Mayer Teodoro, Sacerdoti Giulio, Scaramangà de Altomonte Giovanni, Segre Guido, Toeplitz Giuseppe
Executive Committee
Ara Camillo, Bois de Chesne Carlo, Economo Demetrio, Scaramangà de Altomonte Giovanni

Statutory Auditors
Marchesano Enrico, Matteucci Renato, Morpurgo Pietro Luigi
Deputy Auditors
Besso Michelangelo, Dall'Armi Antonio
General Council
Alberti Giovanni, Banelli Giovanni, Biancardi Dionigi, Bonacossi Taino, Broglia Giuseppe, Brunner Alfredo, Brunner Leopoldo, Cini Vittorio, Cornaggia Medici Castiglioni Carlo Ottavio, Cosulich Antonio Nicolò, Dentice di Frasso Alfredo, Frignani Giuseppe, Gattegno Benveniste D., Horváth Leopoldo, Jachia Giacomo, Kraemer Hans, Lubomirski Stanislaw, Manaut René Victor, Marchesano Giuseppe, Morpurgo Elio, Niccolini Pietro, Olivetti Gino, Padoa Mario, Parodi Emanuele Vittorio, Petschek Walter, Pitacco Giorgio, Preiss Jaroslav, Quaglia Giuseppe, Revedin Antonio, Salom Ettore, Solza Mario, Tripcovich Mario, Valerio Alfonso, Vitali Vittorio Carlo, Volpi di Misurata Giuseppe, Wollemborg Maurizio
General Managers
Cavaglieri Gino, Morpurgo Edgardo, Sulfina Michele
Deputy General Managers
Ara Angelo, Cleva Giulio, D'Alvise Sante
General Manager (Venice)
Ara Marco
Managers (Venice)
Corti Giulio, Vivante Giorgio

1933
Chairman
Morpurgo Edgardo
Managing Director
Morpurgo Edgardo
Council of Directors
Ara Camillo, Bois de Chesne Carlo, Brunner Rodolfo, Cremonesi Filippo, Economo Demetrio, Ehrentheil Emanuele, Errera Adolfo, Luzzatto Giuseppe, Mayer Teodoro, Sacerdoti Giulio, Scaramangà de Altomonte Giovanni, Segre Guido, Toeplitz Giuseppe
Executive Committee
Ara Camillo, Bois de Chesne Carlo, Economo Demetrio, Scaramangà de Altomonte Giovanni

Statutory Auditors
Marchesano Enrico, Matteucci Renato, Morpurgo Pietro Luigi
Deputy Auditors
Besso Michelangelo, Dall'Armi Antonio
General Council
Alberti Giovanni, Banelli Giovanni, Biancardi Dionigi, Bonacossi Taino, Broglia Giuseppe, Brunner Alfredo, Brunner Leopoldo, Cini Vittorio, Cornaggia Medici Castiglioni Carlo Ottavio, Cosulich Antonio Nicolò, Dentice di Frasso Alfredo, Frignani Giuseppe, Gattegno Benveniste D., Horváth Leopoldo, Jachia Giacomo, Kraemer Hans, Manaut René Victor, Marchesano Giuseppe, Morpurgo Elio, Niccolini Pietro, Olivetti Gino, Padoa Mario, Parodi Emanuele Vittorio, Petschek Walter, Pitacco Giorgio, Preiss Jaroslav, Revedin Antonio, Salom Ettore, Solza Mario, Tripcovich Mario, Valerio Alfonso, Vitali Vittorio Carlo, Volpi di Misurata Giuseppe, Wollemborg Maurizio
General Managers
Cavaglieri Gino, Morpurgo Edgardo, Sulfina Michele
Deputy General Managers
Ara Angelo, Cleva Giulio, D'Alvise Sante
General Manager (Venice)
Ara Marco
Managers (Venice)
Corti Giulio, Vivante Giorgio

1934
Chairman
Morpurgo Edgardo
Managing Director
Morpurgo Edgardo
Council of Directors
Ara Camillo, Bois de Chesne Carlo, Brunner Rodolfo, Cini Vittorio, Cosulich Antonio Nicolò, Cremonesi Filippo, Economo Demetrio, Ehrentheil Emanuele, Mayer Teodoro, Scaramangà de Altomonte Giovanni, Segre Guido, Tripcovich Mario
Executive Committee
Ara Camillo, Bois de Chesne Carlo, Economo Demetrio, Scaramangà de Altomonte Giovanni

Statutory Auditors
Balella Giovanni, Coceani Bruno, Matteucci Renato
Deputy Auditors
Besso Michelangelo, Dall'Armi Antonio
General Council
Banelli Giovanni, Bocciardo Arturo, Bonacossi Taino, Broglia Giuseppe, Brunner Alfredo, Cornaggia Medici Castiglioni Carlo Ottavio, De Michelis Giuseppe, Dentice di Frasso Alfredo, Frassati Alfredo, Frignani Giuseppe, Gattegno Benveniste D., Giunta Francesco, Horváth Leopoldo, Jachia Giacomo, Kraemer Hans, Manaut René Victor, Marchesano Giuseppe, Morpurgo Elio, Niccolini Pietro, Olivetti Gino, Padoa Mario, Perrone Compagni Dino, Petschek Walter, Pitacco Giorgio, Preiss Jaroslav, Revedin Antonio, Rossini di Valgrande Aldo, Salom Ettore, Solza Mario, Talaat Harb Mohamed Pacha, Valerio Alfonso, Veroi Giuseppe Pietro, Volpi di Misurata Giuseppe, Wollemborg Maurizio
General Managers
Morpurgo Edgardo, Sulfina Michele
Deputy General Managers
Ara Angelo, Cleva Giulio, D'Alvise Sante
General Manager (Venice)
Ara Marco
Managers (Venice)
Corti Giulio, Vivante Giorgio

1935
Chairman
Morpurgo Edgardo
Managing Director
Morpurgo Edgardo
Council of Directors
Ara Camillo, Bois de Chesne Carlo, Brunner Rodolfo, Cini Vittorio, Cosulich Antonio Nicolò, Cremonesi Filippo, Economo Demetrio, Mayer Teodoro, Scaramangà de Altomonte Giovanni, Segre Guido, Tripcovich Mario
Executive Committee
Ara Camillo, Bois de Chesne Carlo, Economo Demetrio, Scaramangà de Altomonte Giovanni
Statutory Auditors
Balella Giovanni, Coceani Bruno, Matteucci Renato
Deputy Auditors
Besso Michelangelo, Dall'Armi Antonio
General Council
Banelli Giovanni, Bocciardo Arturo, Bonacossi Taino, Broglia Giuseppe, Brunner Alfredo, De Michelis Giuseppe, Dentice di Frasso Alfredo, Frassati Alfredo, Frignani Giuseppe, Gattegno Benveniste D., Giunta Francesco, Horváth Leopoldo, Jachia Giacomo, Kraemer Hans, Manaut René Victor, Marchesano Giuseppe, Morpurgo Elio, Niccolini Pietro, Olivetti Gino, Padoa Mario, Perrone Compagni Dino, Petschek Walter, Pitacco Giorgio, Preiss Jaroslav, Revedin Antonio, Rossini di Valgrande Aldo, Salom Ettore, Solza Mario, Talaat Harb Mohamed Pacha, Valerio Alfonso, Veroi Giuseppe Pietro, Volpi di Misurata Giuseppe, Wollemborg Maurizio
General Managers
Morpurgo Edgardo, Sulfina Michele
Deputy General Managers
Ara Angelo, Cleva Giulio, D'Alvise Sante
General Manager (Venice)
Ara Marco
Managers (Venice)
Corti Giulio, Vivante Giorgio

1936
Chairman
Morpurgo Edgardo
Managing Director
Morpurgo Edgardo
Council of Directors
Ara Camillo, Bois de Chesne Carlo, Brunner Rodolfo, Cini Vittorio, Cosulich Antonio Nicolò, Cremonesi Filippo, Economo Demetrio, Mayer Teodoro, Scaramangà de Altomonte Giovanni, Segre Guido, Tripcovich Mario
Executive Committee
Ara Camillo, Bois de Chesne Carlo, Economo Demetrio, Scaramangà de Altomonte Giovanni
Statutory Auditors
Balella Giovanni, Coceani Bruno, Matteucci Renato
Deputy Auditors
Besso Michelangelo, Dall'Armi Antonio
General Council
Banelli Giovanni, Battistella Giacomo, Bocciardo Arturo, Bonacossi Taino, Broglia Giuseppe, Brunner Alfredo, Castelli Leone, De Michelis Giuseppe, Dentice di Frasso Alfredo, Frassati Alfredo, Frignani Giuseppe, Gattegno Benveniste D., Giunta Francesco, Horváth Leopoldo, Jachia Giacomo, Joham Giuseppe, Kraemer Hans, Manaut René Victor, Marchesano Giuseppe, Morpurgo Elio, Niccolini Pietro, Olivetti Gino, Padoa Mario, Perrone Compagni Dino, Petschek Walter, Pitacco Giorgio, Preiss Jaroslav, Rossini di Valgrande Aldo, Salom Ettore, Solza Mario, Talaat Harb Mohamed Pacha, Valerio Alfonso, Veroi Giuseppe Pietro, Volpi di Misurata Giuseppe, Wollemborg Maurizio
General Managers
Morpurgo Edgardo, Sulfina Michele
Deputy General Managers
Ara Angelo, Cleva Giulio
General Manager (Venice)
Ara Marco
Managers (Venice)
Corti Giulio, Vivante Giorgio

1937
Chairman
Morpurgo Edgardo
Managing Director
Morpurgo Edgardo
Council of Directors
Ara Camillo, Balella Giovanni, Brunner Rodolfo, Cini Vittorio, Cosulich Antonio Nicolò, Cremonesi Filippo, Economo Demetrio, Mayer Teodoro, Padoa Mario, Scaramangà de Altomonte Giovanni, Segre Guido, Tripcovich Mario
Executive Committee
Ara Camillo, Economo Demetrio, Scaramangà de Altomonte Giovanni
Board of Auditors
Cingolani Mario (Statutory Auditor), Coceani Bruno (Statutory Auditor), Dall'Armi Antonio (Deputy Auditor), Frè Giancarlo (Deputy Auditor), Matteucci Renato (Chief Auditor)
General Council
Banelli Giovanni, Battistella Giacomo, Bocciardo Arturo, Bonacossi Taino, Broglia Giuseppe, Castelli Leone, De Michelis Giuseppe, Dentice di Frasso Alfredo, Frassati Alfredo, Frignani Giuseppe, Gattegno Benveniste D., Giunta Francesco, Horváth Leopoldo, Jachia Giacomo, Joham Giuseppe, Kraemer Hans, Manaut René Victor, Marchesano Giuseppe, Montesi Ilario, Morpurgo Elio, Niccolini Pietro, Olivetti Gino, Perrone Compagni Dino, Perusino Carlo (from November 29), Petschek Walter, Pitacco Giorgio, Preiss Jaroslav, Rossini di Valgrande Aldo, Salom Ettore, Sanguinetti Giorgio, Solza Mario, Talaat Harb Mohamed Pacha, Valerio Alfonso, Veroi Giuseppe Pietro, Volpi di Misurata Giuseppe, Wollemborg Maurizio
General Managers
Baroncini Gino, Morpurgo Edgardo, Sulfina Michele
Deputy General Managers
Ara Angelo, Cleva Giulio
Central Manager
Gentilli Camillo
General Manager (Venice)
Ara Marco
Managers (Venice)
Brovedani Vittorio, Corti Giulio, Vivante Giorgio

1938 (until December 20)
Chairman
Morpurgo Edgardo (until September 12), Volpi di Misurata Giuseppe (from September 12)
Deputy Chairmen
Cosulich Antonio Nicolò (from September 12), Pitacco Giorgio (from September 12)
Managing Director
Morpurgo Edgardo (until September 12)
Council of Directors
Ara Camillo, Balella Giovanni, Brunner Rodolfo, Cini Vittorio, Cosulich Antonio Nicolò (until September 12), Cremonesi Filippo, Economo Demetrio, Mayer Teodoro, Padoa Mario, Rossini di Valgrande Aldo, Scaramangà de Altomonte Giovanni, Segre Guido, Tripcovich Mario
Executive Committee
Ara Camillo, Cremonesi Filippo, Economo Demetrio, Rossini di Valgrande Aldo, Scaramangà de Altomonte Giovanni
Board of Auditors
Cingolani Mario (Statutory Auditor), Coceani Bruno (Statutory Auditor), Dall'Armi Antonio (Deputy Auditor), Frè Giancarlo (Deputy Auditor), Matteucci Renato (Chief Auditor)
General Council
Banelli Giovanni, Barzini Luigi, Battistella Giacomo, Bocciardo Arturo, Bonacossi Taino, Broglia Giuseppe, Castelli Leone, Dentice di Frasso Alfredo, Frassati Alfredo, Frignani Giuseppe, Giunta Francesco, Jachia Giacomo, Joham Giuseppe, Manaut René Victor, Marchesano Giuseppe, Montesi Ilario, Morpurgo Elio, Niccolini Pietro, Olivetti Gino, Perrone Compagni Dino, Perusino Carlo, Petschek Walter, Pitacco Giorgio (until September 12), Preiss Jaroslav, Salom Ettore, Sanguinetti Giorgio, Solza Mario, Talaat Harb Mohamed Pacha, Valerio Alfonso, Veroi Giuseppe Pietro, Volpi di Misurata Giuseppe (until September 12), Wollemborg Maurizio
General Managers
Baroncini Gino, Morpurgo Edgardo, Sulfina Michele
Deputy General Manager
Cleva Giulio
Central Manager
Gentilli Camillo
General Manager (Venice)
Ara Marco (until November 8)
Managers (Venice)[3]
Baroffio Luigi (from November 8), Brovedani Vittorio, Corti Giulio (until October 31), Ommassini Francesco (from November 8), Vivante Giorgio (until October 31)

1938 (from December 20)
Chairman
Volpi di Misurata Giuseppe
Deputy Chairmen
Cosulich Antonio Nicolò, Pitacco Giorgio

Board of Directors
Artelli Filippo[4], Balella Giovanni, Banelli Giovanni, Battistella Giacomo, Bocciardo Arturo, Bonacossi Taino, de Capitani d'Arzago Giuseppe, Cerruti Vittorio, Cini Vittorio, Cremonesi Filippo, Della Gherardesca Giuseppe, Dentice di Frasso Alfredo, Economo Demetrio, Frassati Alfredo, Frignani Giuseppe, Galli Carlo, Giunta Francesco, Grandi Dino, Montesi Ilario, Niccolini Pietro, Oberti di Valnera Edmondo, Perrone Compagni Dino, Rossini di Valgrande Aldo, Scaramangà de Altomonte Giovanni, Tahon di Revel Ignazio, Tripcovich Mario, Veroi Giuseppe Pietro

Management Committee
Balella Giovanni, Cini Vittorio, Cremonesi Filippo, Economo Demetrio, Rossini di Valgrande Aldo, Scaramangà de Altomonte Giovanni, Tripcovich Mario

Board of Auditors
Benedetti Nicolò (Statutory Auditor), Coceani Bruno (Statutory Auditor), Dall'Armi Antonio (Deputy Auditor), Frè Giancarlo (Deputy Auditor), Matteucci Renato (Chief Auditor)

General Managers
Baroncini Gino, Sulfina Michele

Deputy General Manager
Cleva Giulio

Central Manager
Gentilli Camillo

Managers (Venice)
Baroffio Luigi, Brovedani Vittorio, Ommassini Francesco

1939

Chairman
Volpi di Misurata Giuseppe

Deputy Chairmen
Cosulich Antonio Nicolò, Pitacco Giorgio

Board of Directors
Artelli Filippo, Balella Giovanni, Banelli Giovanni, Battistella Giacomo, Bocciardo Arturo, Bonacossi Taino, de Capitani d'Arzago Giuseppe, Cerruti Vittorio, Cini Vittorio, Cremonesi Filippo, Della Gherardesca Giuseppe, Dentice di Frasso Alfredo, Economo Demetrio, Frassati Alfredo, Frignani Giuseppe, Galli Carlo, Giunta Francesco, Grandi Dino, Montesi Ilario, Niccolini Pietro, Oberti di Valnera Edmondo, Perrone Compagni Dino, Rossini di Valgrande Aldo, Scaramangà de Altomonte Giovanni, Tahon di Revel Ignazio, Tripcovich Mario, Veroi Giuseppe Pietro

Management Committee
Balella Giovanni, Cini Vittorio, Cremonesi Filippo, Economo Demetrio, Rossini di Valgrande Aldo, Scaramangà de Altomonte Giovanni, Tripcovich Mario

Board of Auditors
Benedetti Nicolò (Statutory Auditor), Coceani Bruno (Statutory Auditor), Dall'Armi Antonio (Deputy Auditor), Frè Giancarlo (Deputy Auditor), Matteucci Renato (Chief Auditor)

General Managers
Baroncini Gino, Sulfina Michele

Deputy General Manager
Cleva Giulio

Managers (Venice)
Baroffio Luigi, Brovedani Vittorio, Ommassini Francesco

Secretary[5]
Stefani Giuseppe

1940

Chairman
Volpi di Misurata Giuseppe

Deputy Chairmen
Cosulich Antonio Nicolò, Pitacco Giorgio

Board of Directors Artelli Filippo, Balella Giovanni, Banelli Giovanni, Battistella Giacomo, Bocciardo Arturo, Bonacossi Taino, de Capitani d'Arzago Giuseppe, Cerruti Vittorio, Cini Vittorio, Coceani Bruno, Cremonesi Filippo, Della Gherardesca Giuseppe, Economo Demetrio, Frassati Alfredo, Frignani Giuseppe, Galli Carlo, Giunta Francesco, Grandi Dino, Montesi Ilario, Oberti di Valnera Edmondo, Orsi Pietro, Perrone Compagni Dino, Rossini di Valgrande Aldo, Scaramangà de Altomonte Giovanni, Tahon di Revel Ignazio, Tripcovich Mario, Veroi Giuseppe Pietro

Management Committee
Balella Giovanni, Cini Vittorio, Cremonesi Filippo, Economo Demetrio, Rossini di Valgrande Aldo, Scaramangà de Altomonte Giovanni, Tripcovich Mario

Board of Auditors
Benedetti Nicolò (Statutory Auditor), Cappelletti Ugo (Deputy Auditor), Dall'Armi Antonio (Deputy Auditor), Frè Giancarlo (Statutory Auditor), Matteucci Renato (Chief Auditor)

General Managers
Baroncini Gino, Sulfina Michele

Deputy General Manager
Cleva Giulio

Managers (Venice)
Brovedani Vittorio, Ommassini Francesco, Scolari Francesco

Secretary
Stefani Giuseppe

1941

Chairman
Volpi di Misurata Giuseppe

Deputy Chairmen
Cosulich Antonio Nicolò, Pitacco Giorgio

Board of Directors Artelli Filippo, Balella Giovanni, Banelli Giovanni, Battistella Giacomo, Bocciardo Arturo, Bonacossi Taino, de Capitani d'Arzago Giuseppe, Cerruti Vittorio, Cini Vittorio, Coceani Bruno, Cremonesi Filippo, Della Gherardesca Giuseppe, Economo Demetrio, Frassati Alfredo, Frignani Giuseppe, Galli Carlo, Giunta Francesco, Grandi Dino, Montesi Ilario, Oberti di Valnera Edmondo, Orsi Pietro, Perrone Compagni Dino, Rossini di Valgrande Aldo, Scaramangà de Altomonte Giovanni, Tahon di Revel Ignazio, Tripcovich Mario, Veroi Giuseppe Pietro

Management Committee
Balella Giovanni, Cini Vittorio, Cremonesi Filippo, Economo Demetrio, Rossini di Valgrande Aldo, Scaramangà de Altomonte Giovanni, Tripcovich Mario

Board of Auditors
Benedetti Nicolò (Statutory Auditor), Cappelletti Ugo (Deputy Auditor), Dall'Armi Antonio (Deputy Auditor), Frè Giancarlo (Statutory Auditor), Matteucci Renato (Chief Auditor)

General Managers
Baroncini Gino, Sulfina Michele

Deputy General Manager
Cleva Giulio

Central Manager
Melchiori Alberto (from December 18)

Managers (Venice)
Brovedani Vittorio, Ommassini Francesco, Scolari Francesco

Secretary
Stefani Giuseppe

1942

Chairman
Volpi di Misurata Giuseppe

Deputy Chairmen
Cosulich Antonio Nicolò, Pitacco Giorgio

Board of Directors
Artelli Filippo, Balella Giovanni, Banelli Giovanni, Battistella Giacomo, Bocciardo Arturo, Bonacossi Taino, de Capitani d'Arzago Giuseppe, Cerruti Vittorio, Cini Vittorio, Coceani Bruno, Della Gherardesca Giuseppe, Economo Demetrio, Frassati Alfredo, Frignani Giuseppe, Galli Carlo, Giunta Francesco, Grandi Dino, Montesi Ilario, Oberti di Valnera Edmondo, Orsi Pietro, Perrone Compagni Dino, Rossini di Valgrande Aldo, Scaramangà de Altomonte Giovanni, Spada Veralli Potenziani Ludovico, Tahon di Revel Ignazio, Tripcovich Mario, Veroi Giuseppe Pietro

Management Committee
Balella Giovanni, Cini Vittorio, Economo Demetrio, Galli Carlo, Rossini di Valgrande Aldo, Scaramangà de Altomonte Giovanni, Tripcovich Mario

Board of Auditors
Cappelletti Ugo (Statutory Auditor), Dall'Armi Antonio (Deputy Auditor), Flegar Ruggero (Deputy Auditor), Frè Giancarlo (Statutory Auditor), Matteucci Renato (Chief Auditor)

General Managers
Baroncini Gino, Sulfina Michele

Deputy General Manager
Cleva Giulio

Central Manager
Melchiori Alberto

Managers (Venice)
Brovedani Vittorio, Ommassini Francesco

Secretary
Stefani Giuseppe

1943

Chairman
Volpi di Misurata Giuseppe (until November 8), Cosulich Antonio Nicolò (from November 8)

Deputy Chairmen
Cosulich Antonio Nicolò (until November 8), Pitacco Giorgio

Managing Director
Baroncini Gino

Board of Directors
Artelli Filippo, Balella Giovanni, Banelli Giovanni, Battistella Giacomo, Bonacossi Taino, de Capitani d'Arzago Giuseppe, Cerruti Vittorio, Coceani Bruno, Della Gherardesca Giuseppe, Economo Demetrio, Frassati Alfredo, Galli Carlo, Giunta Francesco, Grandi Dino, Montesi Ilario, Oberti di Valnera Edmondo, Perrone Compagni Dino, Rossini di Valgrande Aldo, Scaramangà de Altomonte Giovanni, Spada Veralli Potenziani Ludovico, Tahon di Revel Ignazio, Tripcovich Mario, Veroi Giuseppe Pietro

Executive Committee
Balella Giovanni, Cerruti Vittorio, Economo Demetrio, Galli Carlo, Rossini di Valgrande Aldo, Scaramangà de Altomonte Giovanni, Tripcovich Mario

Board of Auditors
Cappelletti Ugo (Statutory Auditor), Dall'Armi Antonio (Deputy Auditor), Flegar Ruggero (Deputy Auditor), Frè Giancarlo (Statutory Auditor), Matteucci Renato (Chief Auditor)

General Managers
Baroncini Gino, Sulfina Michele

Deputy General Manager
Cleva Giulio

Central Manager
Melchiori Alberto

Central Manager (Venice)
Brovedani Vittorio

Manager (Venice)
Ommassini Francesco

Secretary
Stefani Giuseppe

1944

Chairman
Cosulich Antonio Nicolò

Deputy Chairman
Conti di Verampio Ettore
Board of Directors Artelli Filippo, Banelli Giovanni, Bocciardo Arturo, Bonacossi Taino, Borletti Senatore, Dall'Armi Giobatta, Economo Demetrio, Gavazzi Giuseppe, Joham Giuseppe, Montesi Ilario, Muratti Giusto, Oberti di Valnera Edmondo, Scaramangà de Altomonte Giovanni, Schaefer Carlo Alessandro, Stavro Santarosa Michele, Tornani Emanuele, Tripcovich Mario
Executive Committee
Bonacossi Taino, Economo Demetrio, Scaramangà de Altomonte Giovanni, Schaefer Carlo Alessandro, Tripcovich Mario
Board of Auditors
Cappelletti Ugo (Statutory Auditor), Dall'Armi Antonio (Deputy Auditor), Flegar Ruggero (Deputy Auditor), Frè Giancarlo (Statutory Auditor), Matteucci Renato (Chief Auditor)
General Manager
Baroncini Gino
Deputy General Manager
Cleva Giulio
Central Manager
Melchiori Alberto
Central Manager (Venice)
Brovedani Vittorio
Manager (Venice)
Ommassini Francesco
Secretary
Stefani Giuseppe

1945
Chairman
Cosulich Antonio Nicolò
Deputy Chairman
Conti di Verampio Ettore
Board of Directors Baldissera Giacomo, Bonacossi Taino, Borletti Senatore, Cappelletti Ugo (from June 21), Cerruti Vittorio, Cingolani Mario, Dall'Armi Antonio (from June 21), Economo Demetrio, Frassati Alfredo, Gavazzi Giuseppe, Joham Giuseppe, Langheim Paolo Giovanni, Linder Nicolò, Muratti Giusto, Pitacco Giorgio (from August 7 to August 25), Scaramangà de Altomonte Giovanni, Stavro Santarosa Michele, Tornani Emanuele, Tripcovich Mario
Executive Committee
Bonacossi Taino, Economo Demetrio, Frassati Alfredo, Pitacco Giorgio (from August 7 to August 25), Scaramangà de Altomonte Giovanni, Tripcovich Mario
Board of Auditors
Cappelletti Ugo (Statutory Auditor, until June 21), Dall'Armi Antonio (Deputy Auditor, until June 21), Flegar Ruggero (Deputy Auditor), Frè Giancarlo (Statutory Auditor), Matteucci Renato (Chief Auditor)
General Managers
Baroncini Gino (until April 17), Sulfina Michele (from June 21 to September 11)
Deputy General Manager
Cleva Giulio
Central Manager
Melchiori Alberto
General Manager (Venice)
Ara Marco (from August 20)
Central Manager (Venice)
Brovedani Vittorio (until April 16)
Manager (Venice)
Ommassini Francesco
Secretary
Stefani Giuseppe

1946
Chairman
Cosulich Antonio Nicolò
Deputy Chairmen
Conti di Verampio Ettore (until March 20), Linder Nicolò
Board of Directors Baldissera Giacomo, Bonacossi Taino, Borletti Senatore, Brunner Rodolfo, Cappelletti Ugo, Cerruti Vittorio, Cingolani Mario (until August 6), Cleva Giulio, Dall'Armi Antonio (until June 10), Economo Demetrio, Frassati Alfredo, Gavazzi Giuseppe, Iachia Giacomo, Joham Giuseppe, Langheim Paolo Giovanni, Muratti Giusto, Scaramangà de Altomonte Giovanni, Stavro Santarosa Michele, Tornani Emanuele, Tripcovich Mario
Executive Committee
Bonacossi Taino, Brunner Rodolfo, Economo Demetrio, Frassati Alfredo (until August 12), Scaramangà de Altomonte Giovanni, Tripcovich Mario
Board of Auditors
Coranda Francesco (Deputy Auditor), Flegar Ruggero (Statutory Auditor), Frè Giancarlo (Statutory Auditor), Hermet Guido (Deputy Auditor, until September 16), Matteucci Renato (Chief Auditor)
General Managers
Melchiori Alberto (from August 12), Sulfina Michele (from October 14)
Deputy General Manager
Cleva Giulio (until August 12)
Central Manager
Melchiori Alberto (until August 12)
General Manager (Venice)
Ara Marco
Manager (Venice)
Ommassini Francesco
Secretary
Stefani Giuseppe

1947
Chairman
Cosulich Antonio Nicolò
Deputy Chairmen
Linder Nicolò (until October 10), Abbiate Mario (from October 10)
Board of Directors
Abbiate Mario (until October 10), d'Agostino Alberto (from May 31), Baldissera Giacomo, Bonacossi Taino, Bonomi Ivanoe, Borletti Senatore, Cappelletti Ugo, Cerruti Vittorio, Cingolani Mario (from December 29), Cleva Giulio, Conti di Verampio Ettore (from May 31), Cornaggia Medici Giovanni Maria (from May 31), Economo Demetrio, Frassati Alfredo, Frè Giancarlo, Galli Carlo (from December 29), Gavazzi Giuseppe, Giussani Camillo (from December 29), Iachia Giacomo, Joham Giuseppe, Langheim Paolo Giovanni, Marzotto di Valdagno-Castelvecchio Gaetano (from December 29), Muratti Giusto, Nogara Bernardino (from May 31), Rossini di Valgrande Aldo (from December 29), Scaramangà de Altomonte Giovanni (until October 10), Stavro Santarosa Michele, Tornani Emanuele, Tripcovich Mario
Executive Committee
Bonacossi Taino, Economo Demetrio, Frè Giancarlo, Scaramangà de Altomonte Giovanni (until October 10), Tripcovich Mario
Board of Auditors
Baldin Paolo (Deputy Auditor), Coranda Francesco (Deputy Auditor), Flegar Ruggero (Statutory Auditor), Greco Eugenio (Statutory Auditor), Matteucci Renato (Chief Auditor)
General Managers
Baroncini Gino, Melchiori Alberto, Sulfina Michele
General Manager (Venice)
Ara Marco
Managers (Venice)
Ciarlini Renato (from May 31), Ommassini Francesco
Secretary
Stefani Giuseppe

1948[6]
Chairman
Abbiate Mario
Deputy Chairman
Tripcovich Mario
Managing Directors
Baroncini Gino, Sulfina Michele
Board of Directors d'Agostino Alberto, Baldissera Giacomo, Borletti Senatore, Cappelletti Ugo, Cerruti Vittorio, Cingolani Mario, Cleva Giulio, Conti di Verampio Ettore, Cornaggia Medici Giovanni Maria, Cosulich Antonio Nicolò, Da Zara di Serra Marco, Economo Demetrio, Frassati Alfredo, Frè Giancarlo, Galli Carlo, Giussani Camillo, Iachia Giacomo, Joham Giuseppe, Langheim Paolo Giovanni, Marzotto di Valdagno-Castelvecchio Gaetano, Muratti Giusto, Nogara Bernardino, Rossini di Valgrande Aldo, Stavro Santarosa Michele, Tornani Emanuele
Executive Committee
d'Agostino Alberto, Baldissera Giacomo, Borletti Senatore, Cosulich Antonio Nicolò, Economo Demetrio, Frè Giancarlo
Board of Auditors
Baldin Paolo (Deputy Auditor), Coranda Francesco (Deputy Auditor), Flegar Ruggero (Statutory Auditor), Greco Eugenio (Statutory Auditor), Matteucci Renato (Chief Auditor)
General Managers
Ara Marco (Venice Head Office), Baroncini Gino (Central Head Office), Melchiori Alberto (Central Head Office), Padoa Mario (Milan Head Office)[7], Sulfina Michele (Central Head Office)
Managers (Venice)
Ciarlini Renato, Ommassini Francesco
Secretary
Stefani Giuseppe

1949
Chairman
Abbiate Mario
Deputy Chairman
Tripcovich Mario
Managing Directors
Baroncini Gino, Sulfina Michele
Board of Directors d'Agostino Alberto, Baldissera Giacomo, Borletti Senatore, Cappelletti Ugo, Cerruti Vittorio, Cingolani Mario, Cleva Giulio, Conti di Verampio Ettore, Cornaggia Medici Giovanni Maria, Cosulich Antonio Nicolò, Da Zara di Serra Marco, Economo Demetrio, Frassati Alfredo, Frè Giancarlo, Fusco Stanislao, Galli Carlo, Giussani Camillo, Iachia Giacomo, Joham Giuseppe, Langheim Paolo Giovanni, Marzotto di Valdagno-Castelvecchio Gaetano, Muratti Giusto, Nogara Bernardino, Rossini di Valgrande Aldo, Salom Ettore, Stavro Santarosa Michele, Tornani Emanuele
Executive Committee
d'Agostino Alberto, Baldissera Giacomo, Borletti Senatore, Cosulich Antonio Nicolò, Economo Demetrio, Frè Giancarlo
Board of Auditors
Baldin Paolo (Deputy Auditor), Coranda Francesco (Deputy Auditor), Flegar Ruggero (Statutory Auditor), Greco Eugenio (Statutory Auditor), Matteucci Renato (Chief Auditor)
General Managers
Ara Marco (Venice Head Office), Baroncini Gino (Central Head Office), Melchiori Alberto (Central Head Office), Padoa Mario (Milan Head Office), Sulfina Michele (Central Head Office)

Central Managers
Baccolini Umberto (Milan Head Office), Bidoli Marino (Central Head Office), Ommassini Francesco (Venice Head Office), Scolari Francesco (Central Head Office)
Manager (Venice)
Ciarlini Renato
Secretary
Stefani Giuseppe

1950
Chairman
Abbiate Mario
Deputy Chairman
Tripcovich Mario
Managing Directors
Baroncini Gino, Sulfina Michele
Board of Directors d'Agostino Alberto, Baldissera Giacomo, Borletti Senatore, Cappelletti Ugo, Cerruti Vittorio, Cingolani Mario, Cleva Giulio, Conti di Verampio Ettore, Cornaggia Medici Giovanni Maria, Cosulich Antonio Nicolò, Da Zara di Serra Marco, Economo Demetrio, Frassati Alfredo, Frè Giancarlo, Fusco Stanislao, Galli Carlo, Giussani Camillo, Iachia Giacomo, Joham Giuseppe, Langheim Paolo Giovanni, Marzotto di Valdagno-Castelvecchio Gaetano, Muratti Giusto, Nogara Bernardino, Padoa Mario, Rossini di Valgrande Aldo, Salom Ettore, Stavro Santarosa Michele, Tornani Emanuele
Executive Committee
d'Agostino Alberto, Baldissera Giacomo, Borletti Senatore, Cosulich Antonio Nicolò, Economo Demetrio, Frè Giancarlo
Board of Auditors
Baldin Paolo (Deputy Auditor), Coranda Francesco (Deputy Auditor), Flegar Ruggero (Statutory Auditor), Greco Eugenio (Statutory Auditor), Matteucci Renato (Chief Auditor)
General Managers
Baroncini Gino (Central Head Office), Melchiori Alberto (Central Head Office), Sulfina Michele (Central Head Office)
Central Managers
Baccolini Umberto (Milan Head Office), Bidoli Marino (Central Head Office), Ommassini Francesco (Venice Head Office), Scolari Francesco (Central Head Office)
Managers (Venice)
Ciarlini Renato, Mannozzi Franco
Secretary
Stefani Giuseppe

1951
Chairman
Abbiate Mario
Deputy Chairman
Tripcovich Mario
Managing Directors
Baroncini Gino, Sulfina Michele
General Council
Adler Roberto, Agnelli Giovanni, Arrivabene Valenti Gonzaga Leonardo, Artelli Filippo, Balella Giovanni, Bruno Luigi, Cappelletti Ugo, Cingolani Mario, Cleva Giulio, Corbino Epicarmo, Corinaldi Adolfo, Cornaggia Medici Giovanni Maria, Economo Giovanni, Faina Carlo, Gaggia Achille, de Gamazo y Abarca Juan Antonio, Joham Giuseppe, Mahmoud Nedim Oyar, Manaut René Victor, Marinotti Franco, Marzotto di Valdagno-Castelvecchio Gaetano, Matarazzo Francisco, Orsi Mangelli Paolo, Pacelli Marcantonio, Padoa Mario, Pierson Allard, Roi Antonio, Salom Ettore, Stavro Santarosa Michele, Tornani Emanuele
Board of Directors
d'Agostino Alberto, Baldissera Giacomo, Borletti Senatore, Cerruti Vittorio, Conti di Verampio Ettore, Cosulich Antonio Nicolò, Da Zara di Serra Marco, Economo Demetrio, Frassati Alfredo, Frè Giancarlo, Fusco Stanislao, Galli Carlo, Giussani Camillo, Iachia Giacomo, Muratti Giusto, Nogara Bernardino, Rossini di Valgrande Aldo
Executive Committee
d'Agostino Alberto, Baldissera Giacomo, Borletti Senatore, Cosulich Antonio Nicolò, Economo Demetrio, Frè Giancarlo
Board of Auditors
Baldin Paolo (Deputy Auditor), Coranda Francesco (Deputy Auditor), Flegar Ruggero (Statutory Auditor), Greco Eugenio (Statutory Auditor), Matteucci Renato (Chief Auditor)
General Managers
Baroncini Gino (Central Head Office), Melchiori Alberto (Central Head Office), Sulfina Michele (Central Head Office)
Central Managers
Baccolini Umberto (Milan Head Office), Bidoli Marino (Central Head Office), Ommassini Francesco (Venice Head Office), Scolari Francesco (Central Head Office)
Managers (Venice)
Ciarlini Renato, Mannozzi Franco
Secretary
Stefani Giuseppe

1952
Chairman
Abbiate Mario
Deputy Chairman
Tripcovich Mario
Managing Directors
Baroncini Gino, Sulfina Michele
General Council
Adler Roberto, Agnelli Giovanni, Arrivabene Valenti Gonzaga Leonardo, Artelli Filippo, Balella Giovanni, Bruno Luigi, Burnier Henry, Cappelletti Ugo, Cingolani Mario, Cleva Giulio, Corinaldi Adolfo, Cornaggia Medici Giovanni Maria, Dagna Egidio, Economo Giovanni, Faina Carlo, Gaggia Achille, de Gamazo y Abarca Juan Antonio, Joham Giuseppe, Mahmoud Nedim Oyar, Manaut René Victor, Marinotti Franco, Marzotto di Valdagno-Castelvecchio Gaetano, Matarazzo Francisco, Orsi Mangelli Paolo, Pacelli Marcantonio, Padoa Mario, Pierson Allard, Pilotti Massimo, Roi Antonio, Romanin Jacur Michelangelo, Salom Ettore, Stavro Santarosa Michele, Tornani Emanuele
Board of Directors
d'Agostino Alberto, Baldissera Giacomo, Borletti Senatore, Cerruti Vittorio, Conti di Verampio Ettore, Cosulich Antonio Nicolò, Da Zara di Serra Marco, Frè Giancarlo, Fusco Stanislao, Galli Carlo, Giussani Camillo, Iachia Giacomo, Muratti Giusto, Nogara Bernardino, Rossini di Valgrande Aldo
Executive Committee
d'Agostino Alberto, Baldissera Giacomo, Borletti Senatore, Cosulich Antonio Nicolò, Frè Giancarlo
Board of Auditors
Baldin Paolo (Deputy Auditor), Coranda Francesco (Deputy Auditor), Flegar Ruggero (Statutory Auditor), Greco Eugenio (Statutory Auditor), Matteucci Renato (Chief Auditor)
General Managers
Baroncini Gino (Central Head Office), Melchiori Alberto (Central Head Office), Sulfina Michele (Central Head Office)
Central Managers
Baccolini Umberto (Milan Head Office), Bidoli Marino (Central Head Office), Ommassini Francesco (Venice Head Office)
Managers (Venice)
Ciarlini Renato, Mannozzi Franco
Secretary
Stefani Giuseppe

1953
Chairman
Tripcovich Mario
Deputy Chairmen
Giussani Camillo, Sulfina Michele
Managing Director
Baroncini Gino
General Council
Adler Roberto, Agnelli Giovanni, Arrivabene Valenti Gonzaga Leonardo, Artelli Filippo, Balella Giovanni, Bruno Luigi, Burnier Henry, Cappelletti Ugo, Cingolani Mario, Cleva Giulio, Corinaldi Adolfo, Cornaggia Medici Giovanni Maria, Dagna Egidio, Faina Carlo, de Gamazo y Abarca Juan Antonio, Joham Giuseppe, Mahmoud Nedim Oyar, Manaut René Victor, Marinotti Franco, Marzotto di Valdagno-Castelvecchio Gaetano, Matarazzo Francisco, Orsi Mangelli Paolo, Pacelli Marcantonio, Padoa Mario, Pierson Allard, Pilotti Massimo, Roi Antonio, Romanin Jacur Michelangelo, Salom Ettore, Stavro Santarosa Michele, Tornani Emanuele
Board of Directors
Abbiate Mario, d'Agostino Alberto, Baldissera Giacomo, Borletti Senatore, Cerruti Vittorio, Conti di Verampio Ettore, Cosulich Antonio Nicolò, Da Zara di Serra Marco, Frè Giancarlo, Fusco Stanislao, Galli Carlo, Iachia Giacomo, Muratti Giusto, Nogara Bernardino, Rossini di Valgrande Aldo
Executive Committee
Abbiate Mario, d'Agostino Alberto, Baldissera Giacomo, Borletti Senatore, Cosulich Antonio Nicolò, Frè Giancarlo
Board of Auditors
Baldin Paolo (Deputy Auditor), Coranda Francesco (Deputy Auditor), Flegar Ruggero (Statutory Auditor), Greco Eugenio (Statutory Auditor), Matteucci Renato (Chief Auditor)
General Managers
Baroncini Gino (Central Head Office), Bufano Giuseppe (Central Head Office), Melchiori Alberto (Central Head Office)
Central Managers
Baccolini Umberto (Milan Head Office), Bidoli Marino (Central Head Office), Cincotti Francesco (Milan Head Office), Ommassini Francesco (Venice Head Office)
Managers (Venice)
Ciarlini Renato, Mannozzi Franco
Secretary
Stefani Giuseppe

1954
Chairman
Tripcovich Mario
Deputy Chairmen
Giussani Camillo, Sulfina Michele
Managing Director
Baroncini Gino
General Council
Adler Roberto, Agnelli Giovanni, Arrivabene Valenti Gonzaga Leonardo, Artelli Filippo, Balella Giovanni, Bruno Luigi, Burnier Henry, Cappelletti Ugo, Cingolani Mario, Corinaldi Adolfo, Cornaggia Medici Giovanni Maria, Dagna Egidio, Faina Carlo, de Gamazo y Abarca Juan Antonio, Joham Giuseppe, Manaut René Victor, Marinotti Franco, Matarazzo Francisco, Orsi Mangelli Paolo, Pacelli Marcantonio, Padoa Mario, Pierson Allard, Pilotti Massimo,

Quaglia Giuseppe (from November 9), Roi Antonio, Romanin Jacur Michelangelo, de Rothschild Elie (from November 9), Salom Ettore, Stavro Santarosa Michele, Taliani de Marchio Francesco Maria (from November 9), Tornani Emanuele, Tridente Nicola (from November 9), Volpi Leopoldo Giuseppe (from November 9)

Board of Directors
d'Agostino Alberto, Baldissera Giacomo, Borletti Senatore, Cerruti Vittorio, Conti di Verampio Ettore, Cosulich Antonio Nicolò, Da Zara di Serra Marco, Frè Giancarlo, Fusco Stanislao, Galli Carlo, Iachia Giacomo, Muratti Giusto, Nogara Bernardino, Rossini di Valgrande Aldo

Executive Committee
d'Agostino Alberto, Baldissera Giacomo, Borletti Senatore, Cosulich Antonio Nicolò, Frè Giancarlo

Board of Auditors
Baldin Paolo (Deputy Auditor), Coranda Francesco (Deputy Auditor), Flegar Ruggero (Statutory Auditor), Greco Eugenio (Statutory Auditor), Matteucci Renato (Chief Auditor)

General Managers
Baroncini Gino (Central Head Office), Bufano Giuseppe (Central Head Office), Melchiori Alberto (Central Head Office)

Central Managers
Baccolini Umberto (Milan Head Office), Bidoli Marino (Central Head Office), Cincotti Francesco (Milan Head Office), Ommassini Francesco (Venice Head Office)

Managers (Venice)
Ciarlini Renato, Mannozzi Franco

Secretary
Stefani Giuseppe

1955

Chairman
Tripcovich Mario

Deputy Chairmen
Giussani Camillo, Sulfina Michele

Managing Director
Baroncini Gino

General Council
Adler Roberto, Agnelli Giovanni, Arrivabene Valenti Gonzaga Leonardo, Artelli Filippo, Balella Giovanni, Bruno Luigi, Burnier Henry, Cappelletti Ugo, Cingolani Mario, Corinaldi Adolfo, Cornaggia Medici Giovanni Maria, Dagna Egidio, Faina Carlo, de Gamazo y Abarca Juan Antonio, Joham Giuseppe, Manaut René Victor, Marinotti Franco, Matarazzo Francisco, Orsi Mangelli Paolo, Pacelli Marcantonio, Padoa Mario, Pierson Allard, Pilotti Massimo, Quaglia Giuseppe, Roi Antonio, Romanin Jacur Michelangelo, de Rothschild Elie, Salom Ettore, Taliani de Marchio Francesco Maria, Tornani Emanuele, Tridente Nicola, Villalonga Villalba Ignacio, Volpi Leopoldo Giuseppe

Board of Directors
d'Agostino Alberto, Baldissera Giacomo, Borletti Senatore, Cerruti Vittorio, Conti di Verampio Ettore, Cosulich Antonio Nicolò, Da Zara di Serra Marco, Frè Giancarlo, Fusco Stanislao, Galli Carlo, Iachia Giacomo, Muratti Giusto, Nogara Bernardino, Rossini di Valgrande Aldo

Executive Committee
d'Agostino Alberto, Baldissera Giacomo, Borletti Senatore, Cosulich Antonio Nicolò, Frè Giancarlo

Board of Auditors
Baldin Paolo (Deputy Auditor), Flegar Ruggero (Statutory Auditor), Greco Eugenio (Statutory Auditor), Matteucci Renato (Chief Auditor)

General Managers
Baroncini Gino (Central Head Office), Bufano Giuseppe (Central Head Office), Melchiori Alberto (Central Head Office)

Central Managers
Baccolini Umberto (Milan Head Office), Bidoli Marino (Central Head Office), Cincotti Francesco (Milan Head Office), Mannozzi Franco (Venice Head Office)

Manager (Venice)
Ciarlini Renato

Secretary
Stefani Giuseppe

1956

Chairman
Giussani Camillo

Deputy Chairmen
Baroncini Gino, Sulfina Michele

Managing Director
Baroncini Gino

General Council
Adler Roberto, Agnelli Giovanni, Arrivabene Valenti Gonzaga Leonardo, Artelli Filippo, Bruno Luigi, Burnier Henry, Cappelletti Ugo, Cingolani Mario, Corinaldi Adolfo, Cornaggia Medici Giovanni Maria, Dagna Egidio, Faina Carlo, de Gamazo y Abarca Juan Antonio, Joham Giuseppe, Manaut René Victor, Marinotti Franco, Matarazzo Francisco, Orsi Mangelli Paolo, Pacelli Marcantonio, Padoa Mario, Pilotti Massimo, Quaglia Giuseppe, Roi Antonio, Romanin Jacur Michelangelo, de Rothschild Elie, Salom Ettore, Taliani de Marchio Francesco Maria, Tridente Nicola, Villalonga Villalba Ignacio, Volpi Leopoldo Giuseppe

Board of Directors d'Agostino Alberto, Baldissera Giacomo, Balella Giovanni, Borletti Senatore, Cerruti Vittorio, Conti di Verampio Ettore, Cosulich Antonio Nicolò, Da Zara di Serra Marco, Frè Giancarlo, Fusco Stanislao, Galli Carlo, Iachia Giacomo, Muratti Giusto, Nogara Bernardino, Rossini di Valgrande Aldo, Tripcovich Mario

Executive Committee
d'Agostino Alberto, Baldissera Giacomo, Borletti Senatore, Cosulich Antonio Nicolò, Frè Giancarlo, Tripcovich Mario

Board of Auditors
Baldin Paolo (Deputy Auditor), Flegar Ruggero (Statutory Auditor), Greco Eugenio (Statutory Auditor), Matteucci Renato (Chief Auditor), Pesle Silvio (Deputy Auditor)

General Managers
Baroncini Gino (Central Head Office), Bufano Giuseppe (Central Head Office), Melchiori Alberto (Central Head Office)

Central Managers
Baccolini Umberto (Milan Head Office), Cincotti Francesco (Milan Head Office), Mannozzi Franco (Venice Head Office)

Managers (Venice)
Ciarlini Renato, Ducros Gastone

Secretary
Stefani Giuseppe

1957

Chairman
Giussani Camillo

Deputy Chairmen
Baroncini Gino, Sulfina Michele

Managing Director
Baroncini Gino

General Council
Adler Roberto, Agnelli Giovanni, Arrivabene Valenti Gonzaga Leonardo, Artelli Filippo, Bruno Luigi, Burnier Henry, Cappelletti Ugo, Cingolani Mario, Corinaldi Adolfo, Cornaggia Medici Giovanni Maria, de Courten Raffaele, Dagna Egidio, de Gamazo y Abarca Juan Antonio, Joham Giuseppe, Luzzatto Fegiz Pierpaolo, Manaut René Victor, Marinotti Franco, Matarazzo Francisco, Orsi Mangelli Paolo, Pacelli Marcantonio, Padoa Mario, Pilotti Massimo, Quaglia Giuseppe, Roi Antonio, Romanin Jacur Michelangelo, de Rothschild Elie, Salom Ettore, Taliani de Marchio Francesco Maria, Tridente Nicola, Villalonga Villalba Ignacio, Volpi Leopoldo Giuseppe

Board of Directors d'Agostino Alberto, Baldissera Giacomo, Balella Giovanni, Borletti Senatore, Cerruti Vittorio, Conti di Verampio Ettore, Cosulich Antonio Nicolò, Da Zara di Serra Marco, Faina Carlo, Frè Giancarlo, Fusco Stanislao, Galli Carlo, Iachia Giacomo, Muratti Giusto, Nogara Bernardino, Rossini di Valgrande Aldo, Tripcovich Mario

Executive Committee
d'Agostino Alberto, Baldissera Giacomo, Borletti Senatore, Cosulich Antonio Nicolò, Frè Giancarlo, Tripcovich Mario

Board of Auditors
Baldin Paolo (Deputy Auditor), Flegar Ruggero (Statutory Auditor), Greco Eugenio (Statutory Auditor), Matteucci Renato (Chief Auditor), Pesle Silvio (Deputy Auditor)

General Managers
Baroncini Gino (Central Head Office), Bufano Giuseppe (Central Head Office), Melchiori Alberto (Central Head Office)

Central Managers
Cincotti Francesco (Milan Head Office), Mannozzi Franco (Venice Head Office)

Managers (Venice)
Ciarlini Renato, Ducros Gastone

Secretary
Stefani Giuseppe

1958

Chairman
Giussani Camillo

Deputy Chairman
Baroncini Gino

Managing Director
Baroncini Gino

General Council
Adler Roberto, Agnelli Giovanni, Arrivabene Valenti Gonzaga Leonardo, Bruno Luigi, Burnier Henry, Cingolani Mario, Corinaldi Adolfo, Cornaggia Medici Giovanni Maria, de Courten Raffaele, Dagna Egidio, von Finck Augusto, de Gamazo y Abarca Juan Antonio, Joham Giuseppe, Luzzatto Fegiz Pierpaolo, Manaut René Victor, Marinotti Franco, Matarazzo Francisco, Orsi Mangelli Paolo, Pacelli Marcantonio, Padoa Mario, Pilotti Massimo, Quaglia Giuseppe, Ravano Alberto, Roi Antonio, Romanin Jacur Michelangelo, de Rothschild Elie, Salom Ettore, Serventi Giovanni, Taliani de Marchio Francesco Maria, Tridente Nicola, Villalonga Villalba Ignacio, Volpi Leopoldo Giuseppe

Board of Directors
d'Agostino Alberto, Artelli Filippo, Baldissera Giacomo, Balella Giovanni, Borletti Senatore, Cappelletti Ugo, Cerruti Vittorio, Conti di Verampio Ettore, Da Zara di Serra Marco, Faina Carlo, Frè Giancarlo, Fusco Stanislao, Galli Carlo, Iachia Giacomo, Muratti Giusto, Nogara Bernardino, Rossini di Valgrande Aldo, Tripcovich Mario

Executive Committee
d'Agostino Alberto, Baldissera Giacomo, Borletti Senatore, Frè Giancarlo, Fusco Stanislao, Tripcovich Mario

Board of Auditors
Baldin Paolo (Deputy Auditor), Flegar Ruggero (Statutory Auditor), Greco Eugenio (Statutory Auditor), Matteucci Renato (Chief Auditor), Pesle Silvio (Deputy Auditor)

General Managers
Baroncini Gino (Central Head Office), Bufano Giuseppe (Central Head Office), Melchiori Alberto (Central Head Office)
Central Managers
Cincotti Francesco (Milan Head Office), Mannozzi Franco (Venice Head Office)
Managers (Venice)
Ciarlini Renato, Ducros Gastone
Secretary
Stefani Giuseppe

1959
Chairman
Giussani Camillo
Deputy Chairman
Baroncini Gino
Managing Director
Baroncini Gino
General Council
Adler Roberto, Agnelli Giovanni, Arrivabene Valenti Gonzaga Leonardo, Bruno Luigi, Burnier Henry, Cingolani Mario, Corinaldi Adolfo, Cornaggia Medici Giovanni Maria, de Courten Raffaele, Dagna Egidio, von Finck Augusto, de Gamazo y Abarca Juan Antonio, Luzzatto Fegiz Pierpaolo, Manaut René Victor, Marinotti Franco, Matarazzo Francisco, Orsi Mangelli Paolo, Padoa Mario, Pilotti Massimo, Quaglia Giuseppe, Ravano Alberto, Roi Antonio, Romanin Jacur Michelangelo, de Rothschild Elie, Salom Ettore, Serventi Giovanni, Taliani de Marchio Francesco Maria, Tridente Nicola, Villalonga Villalba Ignacio, Volpi Leopoldo Giuseppe
Board of Directors
d'Agostino Alberto, Artelli Filippo, Baldissera Giacomo, Balella Giovanni, Borletti Senatore, Cappelletti Ugo, Cerruti Vittorio, Conti di Verampio Ettore, Da Zara di Serra Marco, Faina Carlo, Frè Giancarlo, Fusco Stanislao, Galli Carlo, Iachia Giacomo, Muratti Giusto, Pacelli Marcantonio, Rossini di Valgrande Aldo, Tripcovich Mario
Executive Committee
d'Agostino Alberto, Baldissera Giacomo, Borletti Senatore, Frè Giancarlo, Fusco Stanislao, Tripcovich Mario
Board of Auditors
Baldin Paolo (Deputy Auditor), Flegar Ruggero (Statutory Auditor), Greco Eugenio (Statutory Auditor), Matteucci Renato (Chief Auditor), Pesle Silvio (Deputy Auditor)
General Managers
Baroncini Gino (Central Head Office), Bufano Giuseppe (Central Head Office), Cincotti Francesco (Central Head Office), Mannozzi Franco (Central Head Office), Melchiori Alberto (Central Head Office)
Central Managers
Padoa Fabio (Central Head Office), Scabar Arturo (Central Head Office)
Managers (Venice)
Ciarlini Renato, Ducros Gastone
Secretary
Stefani Giuseppe

1960
Chairman
Baroncini Gino
Deputy Chairmen
Faina Carlo, Frè Giancarlo
Managing Director
Baroncini Gino
General Council
Adler Roberto, Agnelli Giovanni, Arrivabene Valenti Gonzaga Leonardo, Bruno Luigi, Burnier Henry, Cingolani Mario, Corinaldi Adolfo, Cornaggia Medici Giovanni Maria, de Courten Raffaele, Dagna Egidio, von Finck Augusto, de Gamazo y Abarca Juan Antonio, Luzzatto Fegiz Pierpaolo, Manaut René Victor, Marinotti Franco, Matarazzo Francisco, Orsi Mangelli Paolo, Padoa Mario, Pilotti Massimo, Quaglia Giuseppe, Ravano Alberto, Roi Antonio, Romanin Jacur Michelangelo, de Rothschild Elie, Salom Ettore, Serventi Giovanni, Taliani de Marchio Francesco Maria, Tridente Nicola, Villalonga Villalba Ignacio, Volpi Leopoldo Giuseppe
Board of Directors
d'Agostino Alberto, Artelli Filippo, Baldissera Giacomo, Balella Giovanni, Borletti Senatore, Cappelletti Ugo, Cerruti Vittorio, Conti di Verampio Ettore, Da Zara di Serra Marco, Fusco Stanislao, Galli Carlo, Muratti Giusto, Pacelli Marcantonio, Rossini di Valgrande Aldo, Tripcovich Mario
Executive Committee
d'Agostino Alberto, Baldissera Giacomo, Borletti Senatore, Fusco Stanislao, Tripcovich Mario
Board of Auditors
Baldin Paolo (Deputy Auditor), Caresano Pietro (Deputy Auditor), Flegar Ruggero (Statutory Auditor), Matteucci Renato (Chief Auditor), Pesle Silvio (Statutory Auditor)
General Managers
Baroncini Gino (Central Head Office), Bufano Giuseppe (Central Head Office), Cincotti Francesco (Central Head Office), Mannozzi Franco (Central Head Office), Melchiori Alberto (Central Head Office)
Central Managers
Padoa Fabio (Central Head Office), Scabar Arturo (Central Head Office)
Manager (Venice)
Ducros Gastone
Secretary
Stefani Giuseppe

1961
Chairman
Baroncini Gino
Deputy Chairmen
Faina Carlo, Frè Giancarlo
Managing Director
Baroncini Gino
General Council
Adler Roberto, Agnelli Giovanni, Bruno Luigi, Burnier Henry, Chiodi Cesare, Cingolani Mario, Corinaldi Adolfo, Cornaggia Medici Giovanni Maria, Dagna Egidio, von Finck Augusto, de Gamazo y Abarca Juan Antonio, Lambert Léon, Luzzatto Fegiz Pierpaolo, Manaut René Victor, Marinotti Franco, Matarazzo Francisco, Orsi Mangelli Paolo, Padoa Mario, Pierson Jan Lodewijk, Pilotti Massimo, Ravano Alberto, Romanin Jacur Emanuele, de Rothschild Elie, Serventi Giovanni, Taliani de Marchio Francesco Maria, Tridente Nicola, Villalonga Villalba Ignacio, Volpi Leopoldo Giuseppe
Board of Directors
d'Agostino Alberto, Artelli Filippo, Baldissera Giacomo, Balella Giovanni, Borletti Senatore, Cappelletti Ugo, Conti di Verampio Ettore, Da Zara di Serra Marco, Fusco Stanislao, Galli Carlo, Muratti Giusto, Pacelli Marcantonio, Rossini di Valgrande Aldo, Tripcovich Mario
Executive Committee
d'Agostino Alberto, Baldissera Giacomo, Borletti Senatore, Fusco Stanislao, Tripcovich Mario
Board of Auditors
Baldin Paolo (Deputy Auditor), Caresano Pietro (Deputy Auditor), Flegar Ruggero (Statutory Auditor), Matteucci Renato (Chief Auditor), Pesle Silvio (Statutory Auditor)
General Managers
Baroncini Gino (Central Head Office), Bufano Giuseppe (Central Head Office), Cincotti Francesco (Central Head Office), Mannozzi Franco (Central Head Office), Melchiori Alberto (Central Head Office)
Central Managers
Padoa Fabio (Central Head Office), Scabar Arturo (Central Head Office)
Manager (Venice)
Ducros Gastone
Secretary
Stefani Giuseppe

1962
Chairman
Baroncini Gino
Deputy Chairmen
Faina Carlo, Frè Giancarlo
Managing Director
Baroncini Gino
General Council
Adler Roberto, Agnelli Giovanni, Bruno Luigi, Burnier Henry, Chiodi Cesare, Cingolani Mario, Corinaldi Adolfo, Cornaggia Medici Giovanni Maria, Dagna Egidio, von Finck Augusto, de Gamazo y Abarca Juan Antonio, Lambert Léon, Luzzatto Fegiz Pierpaolo, Manaut René Victor, Marinotti Franco, Matarazzo Francisco, Mattioli Raffaele, Orsi Mangelli Paolo, Padoa Mario, Pierson Jan Lodewijk, Ravano Alberto, Romanin Jacur Emanuele, de Rothschild Elie, Serventi Giovanni, Taliani de Marchio Francesco Maria, Tridente Nicola, Villalonga Villalba Ignacio
Board of Directors
d'Agostino Alberto, Artelli Filippo, Baldissera Giacomo, Balella Giovanni, Borletti Senatore, Cappelletti Ugo, Conti di Verampio Ettore, Da Zara di Serra Marco, Fusco Stanislao, Galli Carlo, Ghigi Pellegrino, Muratti Giusto, Pacelli Marcantonio, Rossini di Valgrande Aldo, Tripcovich Mario
Executive Committee
d'Agostino Alberto, Baldissera Giacomo, Borletti Senatore, Fusco Stanislao, Tripcovich Mario
Board of Auditors
Baldin Paolo (Deputy Auditor), Caresano Pietro (Deputy Auditor), Flegar Ruggero (Statutory Auditor), Matteucci Renato (Chief Auditor), Pesle Silvio (Statutory Auditor)
General Managers
Baroncini Gino (Central Head Office), Bufano Giuseppe (Central Head Office), Cincotti Francesco (Central Head Office), Mannozzi Franco (Central Head Office), Melchiori Alberto (Central Head Office)
Central Managers
Padoa Fabio (Central Head Office), Scabar Arturo (Central Head Office)
Managers (Venice)
Citteri Umberto, Ducros Gastone, Dusi Emilio
Secretary
Stefani Giuseppe

1963
Chairman
Baroncini Gino
Deputy Chairmen
Faina Carlo, Frè Giancarlo
Managing Director
Baroncini Gino
General Council
Adler Roberto, Agnelli Giovanni, Bruno Luigi, Burnier Henry, Chiodi Cesare, Cingolani Mario, Corinaldi Adolfo, Cornaggia Medici Giovanni Maria, Dagna Egidio, von Finck Augusto, de Gamazo y Abarca Juan Antonio, Lambert Léon, Laure Pierre, Luzzatto Fegiz

Pierpaolo, Manaut René Victor, Marinotti Franco, Martinez de Irujo y Artazcoz Luis, Matarazzo Francisco, Mattioli Raffaele, Orsi Mangelli Paolo, Padoa Mario, Pierson Jan Lodewijk, Ravano Alberto, Romanin Jacur Emanuele, de Rothschild Elie, Serventi Giovanni, Taliani de Marchio Francesco Maria, Villalonga Villalba Ignacio

Board of Directors d'Agostino Alberto, Artelli Filippo, Baldissera Giacomo, Balella Giovanni, Borletti Senatore, Cappelletti Ugo, Conti di Verampio Ettore, Da Zara di Serra Marco, Fusco Stanislao, Galli Carlo, Ghigi Pellegrino, Muratti Giusto, Pacelli Marcantonio, Rossini di Valgrande Aldo, Tripcovich Mario

Executive Committee
d'Agostino Alberto, Baldissera Giacomo, Borletti Senatore, Fusco Stanislao, Tripcovich Mario

Board of Auditors
Baldin Paolo (Deputy Auditor), Caresano Pietro (Deputy Auditor), Flegar Ruggero (Statutory Auditor), Matteucci Renato (Chief Auditor), Pesle Silvio (Statutory Auditor)

General Managers
Baroncini Gino (Central Head Office), Bufano Giuseppe (Central Head Office), Cincotti Francesco (Central Head Office), Mannozzi Franco (Central Head Office), Melchiori Alberto (Central Head Office)

Central Managers
Padoa Fabio (Central Head Office), Scabar Arturo (Central Head Office)

Managers (Venice)
Citteri Umberto, Ducros Gastone, Dusi Emilio

Secretary
Stefani Giuseppe

1964

Chairman
Baroncini Gino

Deputy Chairmen
Faina Carlo, Frè Giancarlo

Managing Director
Baroncini Gino

General Council
Adler Roberto, Agnelli Giovanni, Bruno Luigi, Burnier Henry, Chiodi Cesare, Cingolani Mario, Clarke Ashley, Cornaggia Medici Giovanni Maria, Dagna Egidio, De Benedetti Camillo, von Finck Augusto, Iachia Gino Giuseppe, Lambert Léon, Laure Pierre, Luzzatto Fegiz Pierpaolo, Manaut René Victor, Marinotti Franco, Martinez de Irujo y Artazcoz Luis, Matarazzo Francisco, Mattioli Raffaele, Padoa Mario, Pierson Jan Lodewijk, Ravano Alberto, Romanin Jacur Emanuele, de Rothschild Elie, Serventi Giovanni, Taliani de Marchio Francesco Maria, Villalonga Villalba Ignacio

Board of Directors
d'Agostino Alberto, Artelli Filippo, Baldissera Giacomo, Balella Giovanni, Borletti Senatore, Cappelletti Ugo, Conti di Verampio Ettore, Da Zara di Serra Marco, Fusco Stanislao, Galli Carlo, Ghigi Pellegrino, Muratti Giusto, Orsi Mangelli Orsino, Pacelli Marcantonio, Rossini di Valgrande Aldo

Executive Committee
d'Agostino Alberto, Baldissera Giacomo, Borletti Senatore, Fusco Stanislao

Board of Auditors
Baldin Paolo (Deputy Auditor), Caresano Pietro (Deputy Auditor), Flegar Ruggero (Statutory Auditor), Matteucci Renato (Chief Auditor), Pesle Silvio (Statutory Auditor)

General Managers
Baroncini Gino (Central Head Office), Bufano Giuseppe (Central Head Office), Cincotti Francesco (Central Head Office), Mannozzi Franco (Central Head Office), Melchiori Alberto (Central Head Office)

Central Managers
Padoa Fabio (Central Head Office), Scabar Arturo (Central Head Office)

Managers (Venice)
Citteri Umberto, Dusi Emilio

Secretary
Stefani Giuseppe

1965

Chairman
Baroncini Gino

Deputy Chairmen
Faina Carlo, Frè Giancarlo

Managing Directors
Baroncini Gino, Mannozzi Franco

General Council
Adler Roberto, Agnelli Giovanni, Bruno Luigi, Burnier Henry, Chiodi Cesare, Cingolani Mario, Clarke Ashley, Cornaggia Medici Giovanni Maria, Dagna Egidio, De Benedetti Camillo, von Finck Augusto, Iachia Gino Giuseppe, Lambert Léon, Laure Pierre, Luzzatto Fegiz Pierpaolo, Manaut René Victor, Marinotti Franco, Martinez de Irujo y Artazcoz Luis, Matarazzo Francisco, Mattioli Raffaele, Padoa Mario, Pierson Jan Lodewijk, Ravano Alberto, Romanin Jacur Emanuele, de Rothschild Elie, Serventi Giovanni, Taliani de Marchio Francesco Maria, Villalonga Villalba Ignacio

Board of Directors
Artelli Filippo, Baldissera Giacomo, Balella Giovanni, Borletti Senatore, Bufano Giuseppe, Cappelletti Ugo, Conti di Verampio Ettore, Da Zara di Serra Marco, Fusco Stanislao, Galli Carlo, Ghigi Pellegrino, Melchiori Alberto, Muratti Giusto, Orsi Mangelli Orsino, Pacelli Marcantonio, Rossini di Valgrande Aldo

Executive Committee
Baldissera Giacomo, Borletti Senatore, Fusco Stanislao, Ghigi Pellegrino

Board of Auditors
Baldin Paolo (Deputy Auditor), Caresano Pietro (Deputy Auditor), Flegar Ruggero (Statutory Auditor), Matteucci Renato (Chief Auditor), Pesle Silvio (Statutory Auditor)

General Managers
Baroncini Gino (Central Head Office), Cincotti Francesco (Central Head Office), Mannozzi Franco (Central Head Office), Padoa Fabio (Central Head Office), Scabar Arturo (Central Head Office)

Central Manager
Polacco Carlo (Venice Head Office, from June 28)

Manager (Venice)
Citteri Umberto

Secretary
Stefani Giuseppe

1966

Chairman
Baroncini Gino

Deputy Chairmen
Faina Carlo, Frè Giancarlo

Managing Directors
Baroncini Gino, Mannozzi Franco

General Council
Adler Roberto, Agnelli Giovanni, Bruno Luigi, Burnier Henry, Chiodi Cesare, Cingolani Mario, Clarke Ashley, Cornaggia Medici Giovanni Maria, Costa Giacomo, Dagna Egidio, De Benedetti Camillo, von Finck Augusto, Iachia Gino Giuseppe, Lambert Léon, Laure Pierre, Luzzatto Fegiz Pierpaolo, Manaut René Victor, Marinotti Franco, Martinez de Irujo y Artazcoz Luis, Matarazzo Francisco, Mattioli Raffaele, Padoa Mario, Pierson Jan Lodewijk, Ravano Alberto, de Rothschild Elie, Serventi Giovanni, Taliani de Marchio Francesco Maria, Villalonga Villalba Ignacio

Board of Directors
Artelli Filippo, Baldissera Giacomo, Balella Giovanni, Borletti Senatore, Bufano Giuseppe, Cappelletti Ugo, Conti di Verampio Ettore, Da Zara di Serra Marco, Fusco Stanislao, Ghigi Pellegrino, Melchiori Alberto, Muratti Giusto, Orsi Mangelli Orsino, Pacelli Marcantonio, Romanin Jacur Emanuele, Rossini di Valgrande Aldo

Executive Committee
Baldissera Giacomo, Borletti Senatore, Fusco Stanislao, Ghigi Pellegrino

Board of Auditors
Baldin Paolo (Statutory Auditor), Caresano Pietro (Statutory Auditor), Davanzo Luciano (Deputy Auditor), Pesle Silvio (Chief Auditor), Sarpellon Mario (Deputy Auditor)

General Managers
Baroncini Gino (Central Head Office), Cincotti Francesco (Central Head Office), Mannozzi Franco (Central Head Office), Padoa Fabio (Central Head Office), Scabar Arturo (Central Head Office)

Central Manager
Polacco Carlo (Venice Head Office)

Managers (Venice)
Citteri Umberto, Leardini Urbano

Secretary
Dusi Emilio

1967

Chairman
Baroncini Gino

Deputy Chairmen
Faina Carlo, Frè Giancarlo

Managing Directors
Baroncini Gino, Mannozzi Franco

General Council
Adler Roberto, Agnelli Giovanni, Bruno Luigi, Burnier Henry, Chiodi Cesare, Cingolani Mario, Clarke Ashley, Cornaggia Medici Giovanni Maria, Costa Giacomo, Dagna Egidio, De Benedetti Camillo, von Finck Augusto, Hummel Fritz, Iachia Gino Giuseppe, Lambert Léon, Laure Pierre, Luzzatto Fegiz Pierpaolo, Martinez de Irujo y Artazcoz Luis, Matarazzo Francisco, Matteucci Renato, Mattioli Raffaele, Padoa Mario, Pierson Jan Lodewijk, Ravano Alberto, Rosa André, de Rothschild Elie, Serventi Giovanni, Taliani de Marchio Francesco Maria, Villalonga Villalba Ignacio

Board of Directors
Artelli Filippo, Baldissera Alberto (from October 4), Baldissera Giacomo (until October 3), Balella Giovanni, Borletti Senatore, Bufano Giuseppe, Cappelletti Ugo, Conti di Verampio Ettore, Fusco Stanislao, Ghigi Pellegrino, Melchiori Alberto, Merzagora Cesare (from October 4), Muratti Giusto, Orsi Mangelli Orsino, Pacelli Marcantonio, Romanin Jacur Emanuele, Rossini di Valgrande Aldo

Executive Committee
Baldissera Giacomo (until October 3), Borletti Senatore, Fusco Stanislao, Ghigi Pellegrino, Orsi Mangelli Orsino (from October 4)

Board of Auditors
Baldin Paolo (Statutory Auditor), Caresano Pietro (Statutory Auditor), Davanzo Luciano (Deputy Auditor), Pesle Silvio (Chief Auditor), Sarpellon Mario (Deputy Auditor)

General Managers
Cincotti Francesco (Central Head

Office), Mannozzi Franco (Central Head Office), Padoa Fabio (Central Head Office), Polacco Carlo (Central Head Office), Scabar Arturo (Central Head Office)

Central Managers
Coppola di Canzano Eugenio (Central Head Office), Dusi Emilio (Central Head Office), Randone Enrico (Milan Head Office)

Managers (Venice)
Acutis Franco, Citteri Umberto, Leardini Urbano

Secretary
Dusi Emilio

1968

Honorary Chairman
Baroncini Gino

Chairman
Merzagora Cesare

Deputy Chairmen
Faina Carlo, Frè Giancarlo

Managing Directors
Mannozzi Franco, Padoa Fabio

General Council
Adler Roberto, Bruno Luigi, Burnier Henry, Chiodi Cesare, Cingolani Mario, Clarke Ashley, Conti di Verampio Ettore, Cornaggia Medici Giovanni Maria, Costa Giacomo, Dagna Egidio, von Finck Augusto, Hummel Fritz, Iachia Gino Giuseppe, Lambert Léon, Laure Pierre, Luzzatto Fegiz Pierpaolo, Martinez de Irujo y Artazcoz Luis, Matarazzo Francisco, Mattioli Raffaele, Pierson Jan Lodewijk, Ravano Alberto, Rosa André, de Rothschild Elie, Serventi Giovanni, Villalonga Villalba Ignacio

Board of Directors
Artelli Filippo, Baldissera Alberto, Balella Giovanni, Baroncini Gino, Borletti Senatore, Bufano Giuseppe, Cappelletti Ugo, De Benedetti Camillo, Fusco Stanislao, Ghigi Pellegrino, Melchiori Alberto, Muratti Giusto, Orsi Mangelli Orsino, Pacelli Marcantonio, Romanin Jacur Emanuele, Rossini di Valgrande Aldo

Executive Committee
Borletti Senatore, Fusco Stanislao, Ghigi Pellegrino, Orsi Mangelli Orsino

Board of Auditors
Baldin Paolo (Statutory Auditor), Caresano Pietro (Statutory Auditor), Davanzo Luciano (Deputy Auditor), Pesle Silvio (Chief Auditor), Sarpellon Mario (Deputy Auditor)

General Managers
Cincotti Francesco (Central Head Office), Mannozzi Franco (Central Head Office), Padoa Fabio (Central Head Office), Polacco Carlo (Central Head Office)

Central Managers
Acutis Franco (Venice Head Office), Coppola di Canzano Eugenio (Central Head Office), Dusi Emilio (Central Head Office), Randone Enrico (Milan Head Office)

Managers (Venice)
Citteri Umberto, Leardini Urbano

Secretary
Dusi Emilio

1969

Honorary Chairman
Baroncini Gino

Chairman
Merzagora Cesare

Deputy Chairman
Faina Carlo

Managing Directors
Mannozzi Franco, Padoa Fabio

General Council
Adler Roberto, Agusta Domenico, Bruno Luigi, Burnier Henry, Chiodi Cesare, Cingolani Mario, Clarke Ashley, Conti di Verampio Ettore, Cornaggia Medici Giovanni Maria, Costa Giacomo, Dagna Egidio, von Finck Augusto, Hummel Fritz, Iachia Gino Giuseppe, Lambert Léon, Laure Pierre, Luzzatto Fegiz Pierpaolo, Martinez de Irujo y Artazcoz Luis, Matarazzo Francisco, Mattioli Raffaele, Pierson Jan Lodewijk, Ravano Alberto, Rosa André, de Rothschild Elie, Serventi Giovanni, Smith Olcott, Villalonga Villalba Ignacio

Board of Directors
Artelli Filippo, Baldissera Alberto, Balella Giovanni, Baroncini Gino, Borletti Senatore, Bufano Giuseppe, Cappelletti Ugo, De Benedetti Camillo, Fusco Stanislao, Ghigi Pellegrino, Melchiori Alberto, Muratti Giusto, Orsi Mangelli Orsino, Pacelli Marcantonio, Romanin Jacur Emanuele, Rossini di Valgrande Aldo

Executive Committee
Borletti Senatore, Fusco Stanislao, Ghigi Pellegrino, Orsi Mangelli Orsino

Board of Auditors
Baldin Paolo (Statutory Auditor), Caresano Pietro (Statutory Auditor), Davanzo Luciano (Deputy Auditor), Pesle Silvio (Chief Auditor), Sarpellon Mario (Deputy Auditor)

General Managers
Cincotti Francesco (Central Head Office), Mannozzi Franco (Central Head Office), Padoa Fabio (Central Head Office), Polacco Carlo (Central Head Office)

Central Managers
Citteri Umberto (Venice Head Office), Coppola di Canzano Eugenio (Central Head Office), Dusi Emilio (Central Head Office), Randone Enrico (Milan Head Office)

Managers (Venice)
Boccato Silvio, Leardini Urbano, Prosperini Roberto

Secretary
Dusi Emilio

1970

Honorary Chairman
Baroncini Gino

Chairman
Merzagora Cesare

Deputy Chairmen
Faina Carlo, Mannozzi Franco, Padoa Fabio

Managing Directors
Mannozzi Franco, Padoa Fabio

General Council
Adler Teodoro, Agusta Domenico, Bruno Luigi, Burnier Henry, Cameli Filippo, Cingolani Mario, Clarke Ashley, Conti di Verampio Ettore, Cornaggia Medici Giovanni Maria, Costa Giacomo, Dagna Egidio, von Finck Augusto, Gasbarri Mario, de Gennaro Gino, Hummel Fritz, Iachia Gino Giuseppe, Lambert Léon, Luzzatto Fegiz Pierpaolo, Martinez de Irujo y Artazcoz Luis, Matarazzo Francisco, Mattioli Raffaele, Pierson Jan Lodewijk, Polacco Carlo, Rosa André, de Rothschild Elie, Serventi Giovanni, Smith Olcott, Spender Percy C., Taittinger Guy, Villalonga Villalba Ignacio

Board of Directors
Artelli Filippo, Baldissera Alberto, Balella Giovanni, Baroncini Gino, Borletti Senatore, Bufano Giuseppe, Cappelletti Ugo, Cincotti Francesco, De Benedetti Camillo, Fusco Stanislao, Ghigi Pellegrino, Melchiori Alberto, Muratti Giusto, Orsi Mangelli Orsino, Pacelli Marcantonio, Romanin Jacur Emanuele, Rossini di Valgrande Aldo

Executive Committee
Borletti Senatore, De Benedetti Camillo, Fusco Stanislao, Ghigi Pellegrino, Orsi Mangelli Orsino

Board of Auditors
Baldin Paolo (Statutory Auditor), Caresano Pietro (Statutory Auditor), Davanzo Luciano (Deputy Auditor), Pesle Silvio (Chief Auditor), Sarpellon Mario (Deputy Auditor)

General Managers
Coppola di Canzano Eugenio (Central Head Office), Dusi Emilio (Central Head Office), Polacco Carlo (Central Head Office), Randone Enrico (Milan Head Office)

Central Managers
Citteri Umberto (Venice Head Office), Colnaghi Angelo (Milan Head Office), Rossi Alberto (Central Head Office)

Managers (Venice)
Boccato Silvio, Leardini Urbano, Prosperini Roberto

Secretary
Dusi Emilio

1971

Chairman
Merzagora Cesare

Deputy Chairmen
Faina Carlo, Mannozzi Franco, Padoa Fabio

Managing Directors
Mannozzi Franco, Padoa Fabio

General Council
Adler Teodoro, Agusta Corrado, Cameli Filippo, Clarke Ashley, Conti di Verampio Ettore, Cornaggia Medici Giovanni Maria, Costa Giacomo, Dagna Egidio, von Finck Augusto, Gasbarri Mario, de Gennaro Gino, Hummel Fritz, Iachia Gino Giuseppe, Lambert Léon, Leone Giovanni, Luzzatto Fegiz Pierpaolo, Martinez de Irujo y Artazcoz Luis, Matarazzo Francisco, Mattioli Raffaele, Pierson Jan Lodewijk, Polacco Carlo, Rosa André, de Rothschild Elie, Serventi Giovanni, Smith Olcott, Spender Percy C., Taittinger Guy, Villalonga Villalba Ignacio

Board of Directors
Artelli Filippo, Baldissera Alberto, Balella Giovanni, Borletti Senatore, Bufano Giuseppe, Cappelletti Ugo, Cincotti Francesco, De Benedetti Camillo, Fusco Stanislao, Ghigi Pellegrino, Muratti Giusto, Orsi Mangelli Orsino, Pacelli Marcantonio, Romanin Jacur Emanuele, Rossini di Valgrande Aldo

Executive Committee
Borletti Senatore, De Benedetti Camillo, Fusco Stanislao, Ghigi Pellegrino, Orsi Mangelli Orsino

Board of Auditors
Baldin Paolo (Statutory Auditor), Caresano Pietro (Statutory Auditor), Davanzo Luciano (Deputy Auditor), Pesle Silvio (Chief Auditor), Sarpellon Mario (Deputy Auditor)

General Managers
Coppola di Canzano Eugenio (Central Head Office), Dusi Emilio (Central Head Office), Polacco Carlo (Central Head Office), Randone Enrico (Milan Head Office)

Central Managers
Citteri Umberto (Venice Head Office), Colnaghi Angelo (Milan Head Office), Rossi Alberto (Central Head Office)

Managers (Venice)
Boccato Silvio, Leardini Urbano, Prosperini Roberto

Secretary
Dusi Emilio

1972

Chairman
Merzagora Cesare

Deputy Chairmen
Faina Carlo, Mannozzi Franco, Padoa Fabio

Managing Directors
Mannozzi Franco, Padoa Fabio

General Council
Adler Teodoro, Agusta Corrado,

Cameli Filippo, Clarke Ashley, Conti di Verampio Ettore, Cornaggia Medici Giovanni Maria, Costa Giacomo, Dagna Egidio, von Finck Augusto, Gasbarri Mario, de Gennaro Gino, Hambro Jocelyn O., Hummel Fritz, Iachia Gino Giuseppe, Lambert Léon, Luzzatto Fegiz Pierpaolo, Martinez de Irujo y Artazcoz Luis, Matarazzo Francisco, Mattioli Raffaele, Pierson Jan Lodewijk, Polacco Carlo, Rosa André, de Rothschild Elie, Serventi Giovanni, Smith Olcott, Spender Percy C., Taittinger Guy, Villalonga Villalba Ignacio

Board of Directors
Artelli Filippo, Baldissera Alberto, Balella Giovanni, Borletti Senatore, Bufano Giuseppe, Cappelletti Ugo, Cincotti Francesco, De Benedetti Camillo, Fusco Stanislao, Ghigi Pellegrino, Muratti Giusto, Orsi Mangelli Orsino, Pacelli Marcantonio, Romanin Jacur Emanuele, Rossini di Valgrande Aldo

Executive Committee
Borletti Senatore, De Benedetti Camillo, Fusco Stanislao, Ghigi Pellegrino, Orsi Mangelli Orsino

Board of Auditors
Baldin Paolo (Statutory Auditor), Caresano Pietro (Statutory Auditor), Davanzo Luciano (Deputy Auditor), Pesle Silvio (Chief Auditor), Sarpellon Mario (Deputy Auditor)

General Managers[8]
Coppola di Canzano Eugenio, Dusi Emilio, Randone Enrico, Zanardi Giorgio

Central Managers
Citteri Umberto (Venice Head Office), Colnaghi Angelo (Milan Head Office)

Secretary
Dusi Emilio

1973

Chairman
Merzagora Cesare

Deputy Chairmen
Faina Carlo, Mannozzi Franco, Padoa Fabio

Managing Directors
Mannozzi Franco, Padoa Fabio

General Council
Adler Teodoro, Agusta Corrado, Artelli Filippo, Bonacossi Orsini Franca, Bufano Giuseppe, Bustos Javier, Cameli Filippo, Cappelletti Ugo, Cincotti Francesco, Clarke Ashley, Cornaggia Medici Giovanni Maria, Costa Giacomo, Crociani Camillo, von Finck August, Gasbarri Mario, de Gennaro Gino, Hambro Jocelyn O., Iachia Gino Giuseppe, Johnson Donald M., Lambert Léon, Luzzatto Fegiz Pierpaolo, Matarazzo Francisco, Mattioli Raffaele, Milanese Gastone, Pierson Jan Lodewijk, Polacco Carlo, de Rothschild Elie, Serventi Giovanni, Spender Percy C., Taittinger Guy, Villalonga Villalba Ignacio

Board of Directors Baldissera Alberto, Balella Giovanni, Bernheim Antoine, De Benedetti Camillo, Fusco Stanislao, Ghigi Pellegrino, Hummel Fritz, Muratti Giusto, Orsi Mangelli Orsino, Pacelli Marcantonio, Romanin Jacur Emanuele, Rosa André, Rossini di Valgrande Aldo, Vignuzzi Guido

Executive Committee
Bernheim Antoine, De Benedetti Camillo, Fusco Stanislao, Ghigi Pellegrino, Hummel Fritz, Orsi Mangelli Orsino, Rosa André

Board of Auditors
Baldin Paolo (Statutory Auditor), Caresano Pietro (Statutory Auditor), Davanzo Luciano (Deputy Auditor), Pesle Silvio (Chief Auditor), Sarpellon Mario (Deputy Auditor)

General Managers
Coppola di Canzano Eugenio, Dusi Emilio, Randone Enrico, Zanardi Giorgio

Central Managers
Citteri Umberto (Venice Head Office), Colnaghi Angelo (Milan Head Office)

Secretary
Dusi Emilio

1974

Chairman
Merzagora Cesare

Deputy Chairmen
Faina Carlo, Mannozzi Franco, Padoa Fabio

Managing Directors
Mannozzi Franco, Padoa Fabio

General Council
Adler Teodoro, Agusta Corrado, Artelli Filippo, Bonacossi Orsini Franca, Bufano Giuseppe, Bustos Javier, Cameli Filippo, Cappelletti Ugo, Cincotti Francesco, Clarke Ashley, Cornaggia Medici Giovanni Maria, Costa Giacomo, Crociani Camillo, Egeland Leif, von Finck August, Gasbarri Mario, de Gennaro Gino, Hambro Jocelyn O., Iachia Gino Giuseppe, Johnson Donald M., Lambert Léon, Luzzatto Fegiz Pierpaolo, Matarazzo Francisco, Milanese Gastone, Pierson Jan Lodewijk, Polacco Carlo, de Rothschild Elie, Serventi Giovanni, Spender Percy C., Taittinger Guy

Board of Directors
Baldissera Alberto, Bernheim Antoine, De Benedetti Camillo, Fusco Stanislao, Ghigi Pellegrino, Hummel Fritz, Muratti Giusto, Orsi Mangelli Orsino, Pacelli Marcantonio, Romanin Jacur Emanuele, Rosa André, Vignuzzi Guido

Executive Committee
Bernheim Antoine, De Benedetti Camillo, Fusco Stanislao, Ghigi Pellegrino, Hummel Fritz, Orsi Mangelli Orsino, Rosa André

Board of Auditors
Baldin Paolo (Statutory Auditor), Caresano Pietro (Statutory Auditor), Davanzo Luciano (Deputy Auditor), Pesle Silvio (Chief Auditor), Sarpellon Mario (Deputy Auditor)

General Managers
Coppola di Canzano Eugenio, Dusi Emilio, Randone Enrico, Zanardi Giorgio

Central Managers
Colnaghi Angelo (Milan Head Office), de Privitellio Pietro (Central Head Office)

Secretary
Dusi Emilio

1975

Chairman
Merzagora Cesare

Deputy Chairmen
Mannozzi Franco, Padoa Fabio

Managing Directors
Padoa Fabio, Randone Enrico

General Council
Adler Teodoro, Agusta Corrado, Artelli Filippo, Bonacossi Orsini Franca, Bufano Giuseppe, Bustos Javier, Cameli Filippo, Cappelletti Ugo, Cincotti Francesco, Clarke Ashley, Cornaggia Medici Giovanni Maria, Costa Giacomo, Crociani Camillo, Egeland Leif, von Finck August, Gasbarri Mario, de Gennaro Gino, Hambro Jocelyn O., Iachia Gino Giuseppe, Johnson Donald M., Lambert Léon, Luzzatto Fegiz Pierpaolo, Matarazzo Francisco, Milanese Gastone, Pierson Jan Lodewijk, Polacco Carlo, de Rothschild Elie, Serventi Giovanni, Spender Percy C., Taittinger Guy

Board of Directors Baldissera Alberto, Bernheim Antoine, De Benedetti Camillo, Ghigi Pellegrino, Hummel Fritz, Muratti Giusto, Orsi Mangelli Orsino, Ortona Egidio, Pacelli Marcantonio, Romanin Jacur Emanuele, Rosa André, Rossi Alberto, Vignuzzi Guido

Executive Committee
Bernheim Antoine, De Benedetti Camillo, Ghigi Pellegrino, Hummel Fritz, Orsi Mangelli Orsino, Rosa André

Board of Auditors
Baldin Paolo (Statutory Auditor), Bruno Paolo (Deputy Auditor), Caresano Pietro (Statutory Auditor), Davanzo Luciano (Chief Auditor), Sarpellon Mario (Deputy Auditor)

General Managers
Coppola di Canzano Eugenio, Dusi Emilio, Zanardi Giorgio

Central Managers
Colnaghi Angelo (Milan Head Office), de Privitellio Pietro (Central Head Office)

Secretary
Dusi Emilio

1976

Chairman
Merzagora Cesare

Deputy Chairmen
Mannozzi Franco, Padoa Fabio, Randone Enrico

Managing Director
Randone Enrico

General Council
Adler Teodoro, Agusta Corrado, Artelli Filippo, Barbosa da Silva Edmundo P., Bonacossi Orsini Franca, Bustos Javier, Cameli Filippo, Cincotti Francesco, Clarke Ashley, Costa Giacomo, Egeland Leif, Einaudi Mario, Filer John H., von Finck August, Fock Cornelis L. W., Gasbarri Mario, de Gennaro Gino, Hambro Jocelyn O., Iachia Gino Giuseppe, Lambert Léon, Luzzatto Fegiz Pierpaolo, Matarazzo Francisco, Polacco Carlo, de Rothschild Elie, Spender Percy C., Taittinger Guy, Zanardi Giorgio

Board of Directors Baldissera Alberto, Bernheim Antoine, De Benedetti Camillo, Ghigi Pellegrino, Hummel Fritz, Muratti Giusto, Nicolò Rosario, Orsi Mangelli Orsino, Ortona Egidio, Pacelli Marcantonio, Pagliazzi Paolo, Romanin Jacur Emanuele, Rosa André

Executive Committee
Bernheim Antoine, De Benedetti Camillo, Ghigi Pellegrino, Hummel Fritz, Nicolò Rosario, Orsi Mangelli Orsino, Rosa André

Board of Auditors
Baldin Paolo (Statutory Auditor), Bonel Paolo (Deputy Auditor), Bruno Paolo (Deputy Auditor), Caresano Pietro (Statutory Auditor), Davanzo Luciano (Chief Auditor)

General Managers
Coppola di Canzano Eugenio, Dusi Emilio

Central Managers
Bonsi Maurizio (Venice Head Office), Costa Alvaro (Central Head Office, from September 28), Del Pesco Giovanni (Central Head Office, from September 28), Della Casa Umberto (Central Head Office, from September 28), Desiata Alfonso (Central Head Office), Sironi Franco (Milan Head Office)

Secretary
Desiata Alfonso

1977

Chairman
Merzagora Cesare

Deputy Chairmen
De Benedetti Camillo, Luzzatto Mario, Randone Enrico

Managing Director
Randone Enrico

General Council
Adler Teodoro, Agusta Corrado,

Artelli Filippo, Barbosa da Silva Edmundo P., Bonacossi Orsini Franca, Bustos Javier, Cameli Filippo, Cincotti Francesco, Clarke Ashley, Costa Giacomo, Egeland Leif, Einaudi Mario, Escámez López Alfonso, Filer John H., von Finck August, Fock Cornelis L. W., Gasbarri Mario, de Gennaro Gino, Hambro Jocelyn O., Iachia Gino Giuseppe, Lambert Léon, Luzzatto Fegiz Pierpaolo, Muntadas-Prim Salvadó Antonio, Polacco Carlo, de Rothschild Elie, Spender Percy C., Taittinger Guy, Zanardi Giorgio

Board of Directors
Baldissera Alberto, de Banfield-Tripcovich Raffaello (from December 19), Bernheim Antoine, Dusi Emilio, Ghigi Pellegrino, Hummel Fritz, Mannozzi Franco, Muratti Giusto, Nicolò Rosario, Orsi Mangelli Orsino, Ortona Egidio, Pacelli Marcantonio, Padoa Fabio, Pagliazzi Paolo, Romanin Jacur Emanuele, Rosa André

Executive Committee
Bernheim Antoine, Ghigi Pellegrino, Hummel Fritz, Nicolò Rosario, Orsi Mangelli Orsino, Rosa André

Board of Auditors
Baldin Paolo (Statutory Auditor), Bonel Paolo (Deputy Auditor), Bruno Paolo (Deputy Auditor), Caresano Pietro (Statutory Auditor), Davanzo Luciano (Chief Auditor)

General Managers
Coppola di Canzano Eugenio, Desiata Alfonso, Dusi Emilio

Central Managers
Bonsi Maurizio (Venice Head Office), Costa Alvaro (Central Head Office), Del Pesco Giovanni (Central Head Office), Della Casa Umberto (Central Head Office), Sironi Franco (Milan Head Office)

Secretary
Desiata Alfonso

1978

Chairman
Merzagora Cesare

Deputy Chairmen
De Benedetti Camillo, Luzzatto Mario, Randone Enrico

Managing Directors
Desiata Alfonso, Dusi Emilio, Randone Enrico

General Council
Adler Teodoro, Agusta Corrado, Barbosa da Silva Edmundo P., Bonacossi Orsini Franca, Boon Hendrik N., Bustos Javier, Cameli Filippo, Cincotti Francesco, Cingano Francesco, Clarke Ashley, Costa Giacomo, Egeland Leif, Einaudi Mario, Escámez López Alfonso, Filer John H., von Finck August, Fock Cornelis L. W., Gasbarri Mario, de Gennaro Gino, Griffin David, Hambro Jocelyn O., Lambert Léon, Luzzatto Fegiz Pierpaolo, Muntadas-Prim Salvadó Antonio, Polacco Carlo, de Rothschild Elie, Spender Percy C., Taittinger Guy, Zanardi Giorgio

Board of Directors Baldissera Alberto, de Banfield-Tripcovich Raffaello, Bernheim Antoine, Ghigi Pellegrino, Hummel Fritz, Mannozzi Franco, Nicolò Rosario, Ortona Egidio, Pacelli Marcantonio, Padoa Fabio, Pagliazzi Paolo, Romanin Jacur Emanuele, Rosa André

Executive Committee
Bernheim Antoine, Ghigi Pellegrino, Hummel Fritz, Nicolò Rosario, Rosa André

Board of Auditors
Baldin Paolo (Statutory Auditor), Bonel Paolo (Deputy Auditor), Bruno Paolo (Deputy Auditor), Davanzo Luciano (Chief Auditor), Gimpel Bruno (Statutory Auditor)

General Managers
Bonsi Maurizio, Coppola di Canzano Eugenio, Sironi Franco

Central Managers
Costa Alvaro (Central Head Office), Del Pesco Giovanni (Central Head Office), Della Casa Umberto (Central Head Office), Fegitz Fabio (Central Head Office), Molinari Amato Luigi (Milan Head Office), Prosperini Roberto (Venice Head Office)

Secretary
Desiata Alfonso

1979

Honorary Chairman
Merzagora Cesare

Chairman
Randone Enrico

Deputy Chairmen
De Benedetti Camillo, Luzzatto Mario, Rosa André

Managing Directors
Desiata Alfonso, Dusi Emilio

General Council
Adler Teodoro, Agusta Corrado, Barbosa da Silva Edmundo P., Bonacossi Orsini Franca, Boon Hendrik N., Bustos Javier, Cameli Filippo, Cincotti Francesco, Cingano Francesco, Clarke Ashley, Costa Giacomo, Egeland Leif, Einaudi Mario, Escámez López Alfonso, Filer John H., von Finck August, Fock Cornelis L. W., Gasbarri Mario, de Gennaro Gino, Griffin David, Hambro Jocelyn O., Lambert Léon, Luzzatto Fegiz Pierpaolo, Muntadas-Prim Salvadó Antonio, Polacco Carlo, de Rothschild Elie, Spender Percy C., Treichl Heinrich, Zanardi Giorgio

Board of Directors
Baldissera Alberto, de Banfield-Tripcovich Raffaello, Bernheim Antoine, Ghigi Pellegrino, Hummel Fritz, Mannozzi Franco, Merzagora Cesare, Nicolò Rosario, Ortona Egidio, Pacelli Marcantonio, Padoa Fabio, Pagliazzi Paolo, Romanin Jacur Emanuele

Executive Committee
Bernheim Antoine, Ghigi Pellegrino, Hummel Fritz, Nicolò Rosario

Board of Auditors
Baldin Paolo (Statutory Auditor), Bonel Paolo (Deputy Auditor), Bruno Paolo (Deputy Auditor), Davanzo Luciano (Chief Auditor), Gimpel Bruno (Statutory Auditor)

General Managers
Bonsi Maurizio, Coppola di Canzano Eugenio, Sironi Franco

Central Managers
Costa Alvaro (Central Head Office), Del Pesco Giovanni (Central Head Office), Della Casa Umberto (Central Head Office), Fegitz Fabio (Central Head Office), Molinari Amato Luigi (Milan Head Office), Prosperini Roberto (Venice Head Office)

Secretary
Pastori Guido

1980

Honorary Chairman
Merzagora Cesare

Chairman
Randone Enrico

Deputy Chairmen
De Benedetti Camillo, Luzzatto Mario, Rosa André

Managing Directors
Coppola di Canzano Eugenio, Desiata Alfonso

General Council
Adler Teodoro, Agusta Corrado, Barbosa da Silva Edmundo P., Bonacossi Orsini Franca, Boon Hendrik N., Bustos Javier, Cameli Filippo, Cincotti Francesco, Clarke Ashley, Costa Giacomo, Egeland Leif, Einaudi Mario, Escámez López Alfonso, Filer John H., Fock Cornelis L. W., Gasbarri Mario, de Gennaro Gino, Griffin David, Hambro Jocelyn O., Lambert Léon, Legorreta Augustin F., Luzzatto Fegiz Pierpaolo, Muntadas-Prim Salvadó Antonio, Polacco Carlo, de Rothschild Elie, Spender Percy C., Treichl Heinrich, Zanardi Giorgio

Board of Directors Baldissera Alberto, de Banfield-Tripcovich Raffaello, Bernheim Antoine, Cingano Francesco, Dusi Emilio, Hummel Fritz, Mannozzi Franco, Nicolò Rosario, Ortona Egidio, Ossola Rinaldo, Pacelli Marcantonio, Padoa Fabio, Romanin Jacur Emanuele

Executive Committee
Bernheim Antoine, Cingano Francesco, Dusi Emilio, Hummel Fritz, Nicolò Rosario

Board of Auditors
Baldin Paolo (Statutory Auditor), Bonel Paolo (Deputy Auditor), Bruno Paolo (Deputy Auditor), Davanzo Luciano (Chief Auditor), Gimpel Bruno (Statutory Auditor)

General Managers
Bonsi Maurizio, Della Casa Umberto, Giussani Camillo, Sironi Franco

Central Managers
Costa Alvaro (Central Head Office), Del Pesco Giovanni (Central Head Office), Fegitz Fabio (Central Head Office), Molinari Amato Luigi (Milan Head Office), Prosperini Roberto (Venice Head Office)

Secretary
Pastori Guido

1981

Honorary Chairman
Merzagora Cesare

Chairman
Randone Enrico

Deputy Chairmen
De Benedetti Camillo, Luzzatto Mario, Rosa André

Managing Directors
Coppola di Canzano Eugenio, Desiata Alfonso, Randone Enrico

General Council
Adler Teodoro, Agusta Corrado, Barbosa da Silva Edmundo P., Bonacossi Orsini Franca, Boon Hendrik N., Bustos Javier, Cincotti Francesco, Clarke Ashley, Costa Giacomo, Egeland Leif, Einaudi Mario, Escámez López Alfonso, Filer John H., Fock Cornelis L. W., Gasbarri Mario, de Gennaro Gino, Griffin David, Hambro Jocelyn O., Lambert Léon, Legorreta Augustin F., Luzzatto Fegiz Pierpaolo, Muntadas-Prim Salvadó Antonio, Polacco Carlo, de Rothschild Elie, Spender Percy C., Treichl Heinrich, Zanardi Giorgio

Board of Directors
Baldissera Alberto, de Banfield-Tripcovich Raffaello, Bernheim Antoine, Cingano Francesco, Dusi Emilio, Hummel Fritz, Mannozzi Franco, Nicolò Rosario, Ortona Egidio, Ossola Rinaldo, Pacelli Marcantonio, Padoa Fabio, Romanin Jacur Emanuele

Executive Committee
Bernheim Antoine, Cingano Francesco, Dusi Emilio, Hummel Fritz, Nicolò Rosario

Board of Auditors
Baldin Paolo (Statutory Auditor), Bonel Paolo (Deputy Auditor), Braggiotti Gerardo (Statutory Auditor), Bruno Paolo (Deputy Auditor), Davanzo Luciano (Chief Auditor)

General Managers
Bonsi Maurizio, Della Casa Umberto, Giussani Camillo, Sironi Franco

Central Managers
Costa Alvaro (Central Head Office), Del Pesco Giovanni (Central Head Office), Fegitz Fabio (Central Head Office), Molinari Amato Luigi (Milan Head Office), Prosperini Roberto (Venice Head Office)

Secretary
Pastori Guido

1982

Honorary Chairman
Merzagora Cesare

Chairman
Randone Enrico

Deputy Chairmen
De Benedetti Camillo, Luzzatto Mario, Rosa André

Managing Directors
Coppola di Canzano Eugenio, Desiata Alfonso, Randone Enrico

General Council
Adler Teodoro, Agusta Corrado, Bailey William O., Barbosa da Silva Edmundo P., Bonacossi Orsini Franca, Boon Hendrik N., Bustos Javier, Clarke Ashley, Costa Giacomo, Egeland Leif, Einaudi Mario, Escámez López Alfonso, Fock Cornelis L. W., Gasbarri Mario, de Gennaro Gino, Griffin David, Hambro Jocelyn O., Lambert Léon, Legorreta Augustin F., Lenti Libero, Luzzatto Fegiz Pierpaolo, Muntadas-Prim Salvadó Antonio, Polacco Carlo, de Rothschild Elie, Samuels Nathaniel, Treichl Heinrich, Winterstein Wilhelm, Zanardi Giorgio

Board of Directors
Baldissera Alberto, de Banfield-Tripcovich Raffaello, Bernheim Antoine, Cingano Francesco, Dusi Emilio, Fanelli Giuseppe, Hummel Fritz, Nicolò Rosario, Ortona Egidio, Ossola Rinaldo, Pacelli Marcantonio, Padoa Fabio, Romanin Jacur Emanuele

Executive Committee
Bernheim Antoine, Cingano Francesco, Dusi Emilio, Hummel Fritz, Nicolò Rosario

Board of Auditors
Baldin Paolo (Statutory Auditor), Bonel Paolo (Deputy Auditor), Braggiotti Gerardo (Statutory Auditor), Bruno Paolo (Deputy Auditor), Davanzo Luciano (Chief Auditor)

General Managers
Bonsi Maurizio, Della Casa Umberto, Giussani Camillo, Sironi Franco

Central Managers
Fegitz Fabio (Central Head Office), Gutty Gianfranco (Central Head Office), Molinari Amato Luigi (Milan Head Office), Prosperini Roberto (Venice Head Office), Vergna Remo (Central Head Office)

Secretary
Pastori Guido

[1] Shareholder Meetings were not held during World War I, which meant that the company posts were not renewed during that period. As concerned the censors, since the financial statements for the years 1915–1919 were not presented, they are not indicated in the tables for the years 1916–1920. In 1921, the year in which the summary financial statement for 1915–1919 needed to be checked, the censors appointed in 1915 were still operative. Whereas the members of the Board of Directors and the auditors (the latter also members of the Board of Directors) were indicated even though they had not been operative. Their presence in the company organization between 1916 and 1920 was reconstructed through comparison of the summary view of the corporate representation attached to the financial statement published in 1915 and the contents of the minutes of the General Meeting held on January 31, 1921.

[2] On approval of the new charter, the figures of general manager and deputy general manager were introduced, along with other changes. From then on, between one and three managers were appointed at the Venice Head Office to assist the general manager or the deputy general manager or to manage the office itself, if necessary. They were not strictly speaking part of the top management bodies (Council of Directors or, later, Board of Directors), but were specially appointed by them, rather than being elected at the General Meeting.

[3] On the role of the managers in Venice, see note 2. From this time until 1943, the post of general manager or central manager, the latter having been introduced in 1937, remained vacant.

[4] Namesake of Artelli Filippo elected to the Board of Directors in 1902.

[5] Although it had been provided for in the charter since 1930, the role of secretary was now stably assigned to a single person. From this time on, the post would concern the Board of Directors, the Management Committee, the Executive Committee, and the General Council.

[6] Although at the statutory level there had always been a distinction between the Central Head Office in Trieste and the Venice Head Office, and this distinction remained in force until 2012, it stopped being expressed in the printed financial statements in 1948, the summary view of the corporate representation limiting itself to indicating the general managers without listing which office they worked in, almost in emphasis of the transversality of the role and duties with respect to geographical location. To facilitate consultation, this indication has been maintained in parentheses.

[7] The Milan Head Office was in fact constituted by the incorporation of Anonima Infortuni and Anonima Grandine into Assicurazioni Generali in 1948. The name "Milan Head Office" was officially approved by the Executive Committee in 1955 but not confirmed at the statutory level until 1972.

[8] In the new charter, the assignment of general managers to individual head offices was no longer provided for, only the specification of duties. For central managers and managers on the other hand, it remained necessary to establish both their assignment to a head office and their duties. From this point forward, the Venice manager was no longer indicated on the chronological table, since the new charter did not specify the composition of the individual head offices and a specific role for this post was no longer established.

Alphabetical Table of Corporate Representation

Abbiate Mario
Member of the Board of Directors
1947
Deputy Chairman
1947–1948
Chairman
1948–1953
Member of the Board of Directors
1953–1954
Member of the Executive Committee
1953–1954

Acutis Franco
Manager (Venice)
1967–1968
Central Manager (Venice)
1968–1969

Adler Roberto
Member of the General Council
1951–1970

Adler Teodoro
Member of the General Council
1970–…

Agnelli Giovanni
Member of the General Council
1951–1967

Agostino Alberto d'
Member of the Board of Directors
1947–1965
Member of the Executive Committee
1948–1965

Agusta Corrado
Member of the General Council
1971–…

Agusta Domenico
Member of the General Council
1969–1971

Alberti Giovanni
Member of the General Council
1931–1934

Albori Riccardo de
Member of the Board of Directors
1915–1920

Ara Angelo
Deputy General Manager
1926–1937

Ara Camillo
Member of the Council of Directors
1922–1938
Member of the Executive Committee
1922–1938

Ara Carlo
Deputy Secretary (Venice)
1896–1907

Ara Marco
Manager (Venice)
1922–1926
General Manager (Venice)
1926–1938
General Manager (Venice)
1945–1950

Arrivabene Valenti Gonzaga Leonardo
Member of the General Council
1951–1961

Artelli Filippo
Member of the Board of Directors
1902–1907
Censor
1903–1907
Deputy Director
1907–1910
Director
1910

Artelli Filippo
Member of the Board of Directors
1938–1945
Member of the General Council
1951–1958
Member of the Board of Directors
1958–1973
Member of the General Council
1973–1977

Artom Vittorio
Member of the Board of Directors
1912–1915
Censor
1914–1915
Deputy Auditor
1915–1922
Auditor
1922–1930
Member of the General Council
1930–1931

Baccolini Umberto
Central Manager (Milan)
1949–1957

Bailey William O.
Member of the General Council
1982– …

Baldin Paolo
Deputy Auditor
1947–1966
Statutory Auditor
1966–…

Baldissera Alberto
Member of the Board of Directors
1967–…

Baldissera Giacomo
Member of the Board of Directors
1945–1967
Member of the Executive Committee
1948–1967

Balella Giovanni
Statutory Auditor
1934–1937
Member of the Council of Directors
1937–1938
Member of the Board of Directors
1938–1944
Member of the Management Committee
1938–1944
Member of the General Council
1951–1956
Member of the Board of Directors
1956–1974

Banelli Giovanni
Member of the Board of Directors
1926–1930
Member of the General Council
1930–1938
Member of the Board of Directors
1938–1945

Banfield–Tripcovich Raffaello de
Member of the Board of Directors
1977–…

Barbosa da Silva Edmundo P.
Member of the General Council
1976–…

Baroffio Luigi
Manager (Venice)
1938–1940

Baroncini Gino
General Manager
1937–1945
Managing Director
1943–1944
General Manager
1947–1966
Managing Director
1948–1968
Deputy Chairman
1956–1960
Chairman
1960–1968
Honorary Chairman
1968–1970
Member of the Board of Directors
1968–1970

Barzini Luigi
Member of the General Council
1938

Battistella Giacomo
Member of the General Council
1936–1938
Member of the Board of Directors
1938–1944

Benedetti Nicolò
Statutory Auditor
1938–1942

Berchet Guglielmo
Member of the Board of Directors
1897–1913
Censor
1910–1913

Bernheim Antoine
Member of the Board of Directors
1973–…
Member of the Executive Committee
1973–…

Besso Giuseppe
Deputy Secretary-General
1879–1885
Secretary-General
1885–1895
Director
1895–1901

Besso Marco
Secretary-General
1877–1885
Deputy Director
1885–1886
Director
1886–1891
Manager (Venice)
1891–1920
Chairman
1909–1920

Besso Michelangelo
Deputy Member of the Board of Directors
1902
Member of the Board of Directors
1902–1922
Deputy Censor
1914–1915
Censor
1921
Deputy Auditor
1922–1930
Deputy Auditor
1930–1937

Besso Vittorio
Deputy General Manager
1922–1923

Biancardi Dionigi
Member of the General Council
1932–1934

Bidoli Marino
Central Manager
1949–1956

Boccato Silvio
Manager (Venice)
1969–1973

Bocciardo Arturo
Member of the General Council
1934–1938
Member of the Board of Directors
1938–1943
Member of the Board of Directors
1944–1945

Bodio Luigi
Member of the Board of Directors
1910–1920

Boggio Oscar
Member of the Board of Directors
1926–1930

Bois de Chesne Carlo
Member of the Board of Directors
1907–1921
Censor
1914–1915
Censor
1921
Deputy Auditor
1921–1922
Member of the Council of Directors
1922–1937
Member of the Executive Committee
1928–1937

Economo Giovanni
Member of the General Council
1951–1953

Egeland Leif
Member of the General Council
1974–…

Ehrentheil Emanuele
Member of the Board of Directors
1911–1913
Deputy Director-in-Charge
1913–1922
Deputy General Manager
1922–1926
Member of the Council of Directors
1926–1934

Einaudi Mario
Member of the General Council
1976–…

Eisner de Eisenhof Giacomo
Deputy Member of the Board of Directors
1875–1881
Member of the Board of Directors
1881–1886
Censor
1881–1886
Auditor
1886–1901

Eisner Giulio
Deputy Member of the Board of Directors
1901

Errera Adolfo
Deputy Secretary (Venice)
1907–1909
Deputy Secretary Director (Venice)
1909–1922
Member of the Council of Directors
1922–1934

Escámez López Alfonso
Member of the General Council
1977–…

Faina Carlo
Member of the General Council
1951–1957
Member of the Board of Directors
1957–1960
Deputy Chairman
1960–1975

Fanelli Giuseppe
Member of the Board of Directors
1982–…

Fano Giacomo
Deputy Member of the Board of Directors
1881–1890
Member of the Board of Directors
1890–1897
Censor
1896–1897
Auditor
1897–1900
Deputy Director
1900–1910
Director
1910

Fegitz Fabio
Central Manager
1978–…

Filer John H.
Member of the General Council
1976–1982

Finali Gaspare
Member of the Board of Directors
1906–1914

Finck August von
Member of the General Council
1958–1980

Flegar Ruggero
Deputy Auditor
1942–1946
Statutory Auditor
1946–1966

Florio Ignazio di Ignazio
Member of the Board of Directors
1892–1908

Fock Cornelis L. W.
Member of the General Council
1976–…

Franchetti Augusto
Member of the Board of Directors
1884–1905

Frankfurter Alberto
Member of the Board of Directors
1907–1915
Deputy Auditor
1915–1926

Frassati Alfredo
Member of the General Council
1934–1938
Member of the Board of Directors
1938–1944
Member of the Board of Directors
1945–1951
Member of the Executive Committee
1945–1946

Frè Giancarlo
Deputy Auditor
1937–1940
Statutory Auditor
1940–1947
Member of the Board of Directors
1947–1960
Member of the Executive Committee
1947–1960
Deputy Chairman
1960–1968

Frignani Giuseppe
Member of the General Council
1931–1938
Member of the Board of Directors
1938–1943

Fusco Stanislao
Member of the Board of Directors
1949–1975
Member of the Executive Committee
1958–1975

Gaggia Achille
Member of the General Council
1951–1953

Galli Carlo
Member of the Board of Directors
1938–1944
Member of the Management Committee
1942–1943
Member of the Executive Committee
1943–1944
Member of the Board of Directors
1947–1966

Gamazo y Abarca Juan Antonio de
Member of the General Council
1951–1964

Gasbarri Mario
Member of the General Council
1970–…

Gattegno Benveniste D.
Member of the Board of Directors
1924–1930
Member of the General Council
1930–1937

Gavazzi Giuseppe
Member of the Board of Directors
1944–1947

Gennaro Gino de
Member of the General Council
1970–…

Gentilli Camillo
Central Manager
1937–1939

Gentilli Ermanno
Member of the Board of Directors
1910–1912

Gentilomo Oscar
Deputy Member of the Board of Directors
1885
Member of the Board of Directors
1886–1913

Georgiadis Giorgio
Member of the Board of Directors
1922–1929

Ghigi Pellegrino
Member of the General Council
1962
Member of the Board of Directors
1962–1980
Member of the Executive Committee
1965–1980

Gimpel Bruno
Statutory Auditor
1978–1981

Giunta Francesco
Member of the General Council
1934–1938
Member of the Board of Directors
1938–1944

Giussani Camillo
Member of the Board of Directors
1947–1953
Deputy Chairman
1953–1956
Chairman
1956–1960

Giussani Camillo
General Manager
1980–…

Grandi Dino
Member of the Board of Directors
1938–1944

Greco Eugenio
Statutory Auditor
1947–1959

Griffin David
Member of the General Council
1978–…

Grimani Filippo
Member of the Board of Directors
1915–1919
Director (Venice)
1919–1921

Gutty Gianfranco
Central Manager
1982–…

Hambro Jocelyn O.
Member of the General Council
1972–…

Hardegg Francesco
Member of the Board of Directors
1912–1926

Hermet Guido
Deputy Auditor
1946

Horváth Leopoldo
Member of the Board of Directors
1926–1930
Member of the General Council
1930–1938

Hummel Fritz
Member of the General Council
1967–1973
Member of the Board of Directors
1973–…
Member of the Executive Committee
1973–…

Iachia Giacomo
Member of the Board of Directors
1946–1960

Iachia Gino Giuseppe
Member of the General Council
1964–1977

Deputy Auditor
1909–1913

Tivoli Federico
Member of the Board of Directors
1896–1901

Toeplitz Giuseppe
Member of the Board of Directors
1921–1926
Member of the Council of Directors
1926–1934

Toja Guido
Member of the Board of Directors
1924–1925

Tornani Emanuele
Member of the Board of Directors
1944–1951
Member of the General Council
1951–1956

Treichl Heinrich
Member of the General Council
1979–...

Treves dei Bonfili Alberto
Member of the Board of Directors
1888–1902
Censor
1891–1902
Auditor
1902–1909
Maneger (Venice)
1909–1921

Treves dei Bonfili Camillo
Member of the Board of Directors
1879–1916

Tridente Nicola
Member of the General Council
1954–1962

Tripcovich Diodato
Member of the Board of Directors
1915–1925

Tripcovich Mario
Member of the Board of Directors
1926–1930
Member of the General Council
1930–1934
Member of the Council of Directors
1934–1938
Member of the Board of Directors
1938–1948

Member of the Management Committee
1938–1943
Member of the Executive Committee
1943–1948
Deputy Chairman
1948–1953
Chairman
1953–1956
Member of the Board of Directors
1956–1963
Member of the Executive Committee
1956–1963

Ucelli Giulio
Member of the Board of Directors
1924–1928

Valerio Alfonso
Member of the Board of Directors
1915–1919
Director
1919–1922
Member of the Council of Directors
1922–1931
Member of the General Council
1931–1938

Venezian Vittorio
Member of the Board of Directors
1921–1922
Censor
1921
Member of the Council of Directors
1922–1925

Vergna Remo
Central Manager
1982–...

Veroi Giuseppe Pietro
Member of the General Council
1934–1938
Member of the Board of Directors
1938–1944

Vignuzzi Guido
Member of the Board of Directors
1973–1976

Villalonga Villalba Ignacio
Member of the General Council
1955–1973

Vitali Vittorio Carlo
Member of the Board of Directors
1926–1930

Member of the General Council
1930–1934

Vivante Giorgio
Manager (Venice)
1926–1938

Vivante de Villabella Fortunato
Deputy Member of the Board of Directors
1885–1886
Member of the Board of Directors
1886–1898
Deputy Director
1898–1902
Director
1902–1922
Member of the Council of Directors
1922–1926

Volpi di Misurata Giuseppe
Member of the Board of Directors
1915–1925
Member of the Board of Directors
1928–1930
Member of the General Council
1930–1938
Chairman
1938–1943

Volpi Leopoldo Giuseppe
Member of the General Council
1954–1961

Weinberg Leopoldo
Member of the Board of Directors
1898–1921

Weiner Alessandro
Member of the Board of Directors
1915–1924

Winterstein Wilhelm
Member of the General Council
1982–...

Wollemborg Maurizio
Member of the Board of Directors
1922–1930
Member of the General Council
1930–1938

Xydias Typaldo Dionisio
Member of the Board of Directors
1898–1902
Censor
1902
Deputy Auditor
1902–1915

Auditor
1915–1918

Zanardi Giorgio
General Manager
1972–1976
Member of the General Council
1976–...

Zino Dionisio
Member of the Board of Directors
1924–1930
Member of the General Council
1930–1931

Index of Illustrations that Are not Part of the Generali Group's Archives or Collections

1920. *The Death of Joan of Arc*, Rouen, Bibliothèque Municipale de Rouen Cabinet d'Estampes (DeAPL)

1921. *Charlie Chaplin and Jackie Coogan in Chaplin's film* The Kid (GraNYC)

1921. Liu Chun-hua, *The Young Mao Zedong going to the Mines of Anyuan to lead the Miners' Strike, 1967*, detail (GraNYC)

1921. *Ceremony at the Altare della Patria in Rome, for the burial of the Unknown Soldier, 1921*, detail (IL)

1921. *The signers of the treaty to establish the Irish Free State. From left to right: Arthur Griffith, Eamonn Duggan, Michael Collins, and Robert Barton, December 6, 1921*, in Walter Hutchinson, *Story of the British Nation*, Vol. IV, London, s.a. (PC)

p. 133
fig. 1
Adolf Hitler at a brownshirts parade in Nuremberg in 1927 (Intf)

fig. 2
Giacomo Balla, *Mussolini and the quadrumvirate in October 1922*, private collection (DeAPL)

fig. 3
Achille Beltrame, *The Signing of the Lateran Treaty, 1929*, in *La Domenica del Corriere* (DeAPL)

p. 134
fig. 4
Unemployed men in line at a soup kitchen during the Great Depression, *c.* 1930 (UIG)

fig. 5
Leni Riefenstahl (UB)

fig. 6
Achille Beltrame, *Marshal Badoglio leading his victorious troops into Addis Ababa*, in *La Domenica del Corriere*, May 17, 1936 (DeAPL)

fig. 7
Vittorio Pisani, *The Spanish national infantry and the Italian legionnaires in Madrid during the Spanish Civil War*, in *La Tribuna Illustrata*, April 9, 1939, detail (ME)

In Brief pp. 136–137
1922. *Tutankhamun's stone sarcophagus and gilded interior sarcophagus* (GraNYC)

1925. *Scene from the Broadway musical* No, no, Nanette, *with music by Vincent Youmans* (GraNYC)

1925. *"When Shall We Three Meet Again?"*, cartoon from an American newspaper, 1925, detail (GraNYC)

1926. *Poster for the film* Battleship Potemkin *directed by Sergej M. Ejzenštejn, 1925* (Intf)

1927. *Charles Lindbergh and the* Spirit of St. Louis *just before take-off from Roosevelt Airfield, New York, in the direction of Paris, May 20, 1927* (GraNYC)

1927. *Funeral of Sacco and Vanzetti* (TF)

1928. *Portrait of Alexander Fleming, the discoverer of penicillin, in his laboratory*, private collection (Ib)

1928. *Chiang Kai-shek, Chinese general and politician, c.* 1930. (GraNYC)

1928. *Mickey Mouse's debut on the big screen in* Steamboat Willie (TF2)

1929. *A car race on the Circuit de Montecarlo, c.* 1930, Florence, Raccolte Museali Fratelli Alinari (AA)

1930. *Marlene Dietrich as Lola with Rosa Valetti in* The Blue Angel, *directed by Josef von Sternberg* (UB)

1931. *The ocean liner* Rex *arrives in New York. In the background, a panoramic view of the city*, Florence, Raccolte Museali Fratelli Alinari (AA)

1932. *The Yellow Cruise coming down Toksun Pass, in China*, 1931 (RV)

1933. *The outlaw Bonnie Parker pretending to rob her partner Clyde Barrow*, detail (GraNYC)

1933. *Primo Carnera knocks out Jack Sharkey, becoming the heavyweight champion*, detail (RV)

1934. *The character Poirot (from the novels by Agatha Christie) in front of one of the cars of the Orient Express* (TF)

1934. *Vittorio Pozzo, the coach for the Italian national team, giving instructions to his players during the break before extra time during the 1934 World Cup match against Czechoslovakia* (GraNYC)

1934. Vittorio Pisani, *The Assassination of Alexander I of Yugoslavia and a French minister in Marseilles by Croatian separatists, October 9, 1934*, in *La Tribuna Illustrata*, 1934 (DeAPL)

1934. *Luigi Pirandello, winner of the Nobel Prize in Literature, in his office on Via Antonio Bosio in Rome* (AB)

1935. *Mao Zedong in Yan'an (Shaanxi) at the end of the Long March* (RV)

1936. *Jesse Owens at the 1936 Olympic Games in Berlin, where he won the gold medal for the long jump, setting a new world record* (UB)

1937. *The German airship* Hindenburg *on fire at the air station in Lakehurst, New Jersey, May 6, 1937* (GraNYC)

1938. *Orson Welles, director, producer, screenwriter, actor, photographed during a radio program* (GraNYC)

1938. *Germans walking by the broken glass of shops owned by Jews after the "Night of Broken Glass" on November 9-10, 1938* (UIG)

p. 163
fig. 2
The Ara brothers, from left, Marco, Giuseppe, Angelo, and Camillo, Udine, 1915-1918, Trieste, Fototeca dei Civici Musei di Storia ed Arte di Trieste (Fondo Fototeca dei Civici Musei di Storia ed Arte, photo Giornalfoto)

p. 177
fig. 1
Bruno de Finetti, 1928 (Courtesy of Fulvia de Finetti)

p. 178
fig. 2
Bruno de Finetti with his colleagues at the Istituto Centrale di Statistica, 1931 (Courtesy of Fulvia de Finetti)

p. 191
fig. 1
The Polish Campaign: German soldiers removing the barrier at the German-Polish border, on the road to Sopot, Gdynia, and Gdansk, beginning the invasion of Poland, September 1, 1939 (UB)

fig. 2
Il Duce, Benito Mussolini, announcing that Italy had joined the war, from the Palazzo Venezia in Rome, June 10, 1940 (IL)

fig. 3
Marshal Pietro Badoglio reading the declaration of war on Germany, standing beside the American general Maxwell Taylor, October 13, 1943 (DeAPL)

p. 192
fig. 4
The deportation of the Jews from the Łódź ghetto to the concentration camp in Auschwitz, Poland, July 1944 (RV)

fig. 5
Aerial photo of Hiroshima, Japan, completely destroyed by the atomic bomb, March 1946 (GraNYC)

In Brief pp. 194-195
1939. *General Francisco Franco salutes his victorious troops from the balcony during the Spanish Civil War*, Istituto Luce, 1939 (IL)

1939. Munollo, *Pope Pius XII (Eugenio Pacelli) just after his election*, in *La Domenica del Corriere*, March 5, 1939, detail (ME)

1939. *American baseball player Lou Gehrig at the ceremony for Lou Gehrig Appreciation Day, held at Yankee Stadium in New York on the day he retired due to his diagnosis of amyotrophic lateral sclerosis*, July 4, 1939, detail (GraNYC)

1939. *Clark Gable and Vivian Leigh in* Gone with the Wind *(WHA)*

1940. *Fausto Coppi, Italian cyclist* (RV)

1940. *A paleolithic wall painting in the caves of Lascaux/Dordogne, discovered in 1940* (GraNYC)

1940. *Mickey Mouse as the Sorcerer's Apprentice in the animated film* Fantasia *by James Algar* (TF3)

1940. *St. Paul's Cathedral surrounded by smoke and flames, during the World War II bombardments* (ME)

1941. *Haile Selassie, the emperor of Ethiopia, working in his office in the palace in Addis Ababa, c.* 1942 (GraNYC)

1941. *German tanks passing through a Soviet town during the invasion of Russia in fall 1941* (GraNYC)

1941. *Clouds of smoke surrounding the USS* Arizona *in Pearl Harbor on December 7, 1941, during World War II* (GraNYC)

1942. *The twelve-year-old Anna Frank, doing her homework*, 1941 (GraNYC)

1942. *Poster for the film* Holiday Inn *starring Bing Crosby, Marjorie Reynolds, Fred Astaire, and Virginia Dale*, detail (PP)

1942. *General Bernard Montgomery watching his armored vehicles in north Africa during World War II* (RV)

1942. *Scientists observing the first controlled chain reaction at the University of Chicago* (TF)

1943. *Humphrey Bogart and Ingrid Bergman in* Casablanca, 1942 (GraNYC)

1943. Hans Sontheimer, *Stalingrad, 1944* (LC)

1943. *The cover of* The Little Prince *by Antoine de Saint-Exupéry, 1942*, detail (TF)

1944. *D-Day: American soldiers landing on Utah Beach during the invasion of Normandy, June 6, 1944* (GraNYC)

1944. *John Maynard Keynes speaking at the Bretton Woods Conference about postwar reconstruction and the economic order* (UIG)

1944. *Trial of the July 20, 1944 conspirators in Rastenburg: Judge Roland Freisler reading the verdict* (UB)

1944. *Tennessee Williams*, 1950 (UB)

1945. *The Allied leaders at the Yalta Conference, February 4–11, 1945. Seated from left to right: Churchill, Roosevelt, and Stalin* (TF)

1945. *General Douglas MacArthur watching the Japanese representatives, on board the USS* Missouri, *before the signing of the Japanese surrender that brought World War II to a close, September 2, 1945* (UIG)

p. 215
fig. 1
The Nuremberg Trials. In the first row, from left: Hermann Göring, Rudolf Hess, Joachim von Ribbentrop, and Wilhelm Keitel; in the back row, from left: Karl Dönitz, Erich Raeder, Baldur von Schirach, Fritz Sauckel, and Alfred Jodl, 1945 (Leo)

fig. 2
Fedele Toscano, *Protesters in Trieste on the Rive*, October 1953 (AT)

p. 216
fig. 3
John F. Kennedy and the mayor of West Berlin, Willy Brandt, looking over the Berlin Wall, June 26, 1963 (TF)

fig. 4
American Marines headed towards helicopters to be brought to the front during the Korean War, March 1953 (GraNYC)

Fig. 5
A captured US Air Force major guarded by a woman with a gun in a rice field, during the Vietnam War, 1967 (CW)

p. 219
fig. 6
Soviet armored vehicles in the streets of Budapest during the Hungarian Revolution, 1956, detail (TF)

fig. 7
People on a tank outside Parliament in Budapest, 1956 (TF)

fig. 8
Jurij Vladimirovich Kershin, *Eternal, indestructible friendship between Cuba and the Soviet Union*, poster, 1963, Moscow, Russian State Library, detail (FAI)

fig. 9
Take-off of the Vostok *space capsule with cosmonaut Yuri Gagarin on board*, 1961 (RN)

In Brief pp. 220-221
1946. *Sunbathing, model in a bikini* (RV)

1947. *Harry Truman, the 33rd president of the United State, at his desk at the White House, c.* 1945 (GraNYC)

1948. *An Israeli flag being raised at a military camp*, June 1948 (UB)

1948. Walter Molino, *Cardinal Mindszenty accused of treason and espionage*, in *La Domenica del Corriere*, February 6, 1949, detail (ME)

1949. *The American poet Ezra Pound returning to the United States to face charges of treason*, 1945 (GraNYC)

1953. *Queen Elizabeth II with her family on the balcony of Buckingham Palace after her coronation, June 2, 1953* (GraNYC)

1953. *Fidel Castro, Cuban revolutionary and head of state, with Ernesto "Che" Guevara in the Sierra Maestra, Cuba, c.* 1957, detail (UB)

1954. *The expedition of Ardito Desio, Achille Compagnoni, and Lino Lacedelli conquers K2*, July 31, 1954 (DeAPL)

1954. *Albert Schweitzer, French theologian, physician, and musicologist, at the hospital in Lambaréné, French Equatorial Africa (today, Gabon)* (GraNYC)

1957. *Prime Minister Kwame Nkrumah greets the crowd from the balcony at midnight on the day on which the Gold Coast became the independent State of Ghana*, March 6, 1957 (TF)

1958. *Portrait of Pope John XXIII (Angelo Giuseppe Roncalli), c.* 1960, detail (UB)

1959. *The Tibetan rebels surrendering and giving up their weapons*, March 21, 1959 (UB)

1959. *René Goscinny, French writer, c.* 1970 (RV)

1960. *Livio Berruti winning the 200-meter race at the Rome Olympics*, September 1960 (TF)

1962. *Ursula Andress and Sean Connery in* Dr. No *(Eon)*

1963. *The Beatles: John Lennon, Paul McCartney, Ringo Starr, and George Harrison, c.* 1960 (UB)

1963. Warren K. Leffler, *Protestors with signs demanding equal rights, integrated schools, and decent housing during the March on Washington, August 28, 1963* (GraNYC)

1963. *The coffin of President John Fitzgerald Kennedy, wrapped in the American flag, in the United States Capitol rotunda*, November 1963, detail (GraNYC)

1964. *Preparations for moving the temple of Abu Simbel, Egypt*, 1960 (TF)

1964. *Julie Andrews in the film* Mary Poppins *by Robert Stevenson* (Intf)

1966. *Bobby Moore, carried in triumph by his teammates, holds up the Jules Rimet cup after England won against West Germany*, July 30, 1966 (TF)

1966. *Leonard Nimoy (Mr. Spock) and William Shatner (Captain James T. Kirk) in* Star Trek (RG)

1966. *The "mud angels" who saved the volumes in the Biblioteca Nazionale in Florence after the flood of 1966* (RCS)

1967. *Francis Chichester on board the* Gipsy Moth IV *in Greenwich, before his solo trip around the world* (PA)

p. 227
fig. 1
Wood and sacks of sand used for protection in front of the windows of the Assicurazioni Generali building, used as an anti-aircraft refuge, June 18, 1940, Istituto Luce (IL1)

p. 279
fig. 8
Isola di Chiozza, Trieste, May 5, 1914, Trieste, Fototeca dei Civici Musei di Storia ed Arte di Trieste (Fondo Fototeca dei civici musei di storia ed arte, photo Pietro Opiglia)

fig. 9
Demolition of the Chiozza house, Trieste, 1925, Trieste, Fototeca dei Civici Musei di Storia ed Arte di Trieste (Fondo Fototeca dei civici musei di storia ed arte, photo Pietro Opiglia)

p. 281
fig. 1
The astronauts of Apollo 11, *Neil Armstrong and Edwin "Buzz" Aldrin, planting the American flag on the Moon*, July 20, 1969 (UB)

fig. 2
The French May at the Sorbonne in Paris, May 1968 (RV1)

p. 282
fig. 3
View of Via Fani after the kidnapping of Aldo Moro and assassination of his bodyguards, March 16, 1978 (TE)

fig. 4
Inscription on the memorial plaque to Jan Palach and Jan Zajíc in Saint Wenceslas Square in Prague (TF1)

fig. 5
Election of Pope John Paul II (Karol Józef Wojtyła): the pope looking out from the loggia of Saint Peter's Basilica in Vatican City, October 16, 1978, detail (TE)

p. 285
fig. 6
The crowd standing on the Berlin Wall after its fall, November 10, 1989 (Intf)

fig. 7
The events of January 1991 in the historic center of Vilnius, 1991 (TF)

In Brief pp. 286-287
1968. *The 1968 Olympic Games in Mexico City, medal ceremony: Tommie Smith and John Carlos raise closed fists in a sign of protest; at left, Peter Norman*, October 16, 1968 (TF)

1969. *Jimi Hendrix's concert at Woodstock*, August 18, 1969 (IW)

1969. *The Piazza Fontana massacre in Milan: interior of the Banca Nazionale dell'Agricoltura*, December 12, 1969 (TE)

1970. *Recovery of the* Apollo 13 *spacecraft on board the USS* Iwo Jima *in the southern Pacific Ocean* (GraNYC)

1970. *World Cup semifinal in Mexico in 1970, the Federal Republic of Germany against Italy*, June 17, 1970 (UB)

1972. *Zhou Enlai, the Chinese prime minister, at a state dinner with United States President Richard Nixon in Beijing* (TF)

1973. *The military coup in Chile overturned the government of Salvador Allende* (WHA)

1973. *Konrad Lorenz, Austrian zoologist, biologist, and Nobel Prize winner, known for his studies of the behavior of animals in their natural habitat*, May 1966 (TF)

1975. *The fall of Saigon and occupation of the presidential palace*, April 30, 1975 (RV)

1976. *Friuli earthquake: working to save survivors under the rubble* (RCS)

1976. *Nadia Comaneci performing her routine on the uneven bars at the Montreal Olympics* (RCS)

1977. *The exterior of Centre Georges Pompidou in Paris, inaugurated in 1977* (TF)

1977. *Peter Mayhew (C3PO), Mark Hamill (Luke Skywalker), Alec Guinness (Obi-Wan Kenobi), and Harrison Ford (Han Solo) in* Star Wars (RG)

1979. *The Ayatollah Khomeini in Tehran after his return from exile in January 1979* (TF)

1979. *Prime Minister Margaret Thatcher on a visit to the British Hovercraft Corporation in East Cowes, during her election campaign*, June 8, 1983 (PA)

1979. *Armed Afghan mujahideen fighters* (Ib)

1981. *Three masked members of the IRA fire blanks in front of the coffin of Bobby Sands, who died on hunger strike*, May 1981 (PA)

1982. *The Falklands War (or Malvinas War): the British Royal Navy ship* Sir Galahad *ablaze in Bluff Cove, near the Fitzroy base in the western part of the Falklands, after the Argentine air attack*, June 8, 1982 (TF)

1983. *Richard Chamberlain and Rachel Ward in* The Thorn Birds, *an American televised miniseries* (RG)

1986. *Barbed wire with a radioactive danger zone sign, in the area of the nuclear power plant in Chernobyl*, 2006 (RN)

1987. *United States President Ronald Reagan and Soviet General Secretary Mikhail Gorbachev after exchanging INF Treaty documents at the White House* (UB)

1988. *Benazir Bhutto, a Pakistani politician, at her wedding in Karachi*, December 1987 (RV2)

1989. *Robin Williams in* Dead Poets Society (RG)

1989. *A group of Chinese students protesting in Tienanmen Square in Beijing* (RN)

Abbreviations

AA: Archivio Alinari, Florence
AB: Archivio Bruni / Mananged by Alinari
ANSA: ANSA licensed by Archivi Fratelli ALINARI/ Tofano heirs
ART: ARTOTHEK / Alinari
AT: Archivio Toscani / Managed by Archivi Alinari, Florence
CW: Ullstein Bild – Thomas Billhardt – Camera Work - Alinari
DeAPL: DeA Picture Library, licensed to Alinari
Eon: EON PRODUCTIONS – TopFoto / Alinari
FAI: Fine Art Images / Alinari
GraNYC: Granger, NYC / Archivi Alinari
Ib: Iberfoto / Alinari
IL: Istituto Luce /Managed by Alinari
IL1: Istituto Luce
Im: Imagno / Alinari
Im1: Imagno / Barbara Pflaum
Intf: Interfoto / Alinari
IW: The Image Works / Alinari
LC: Mary Evans / Library of Congress
Leo: Ullstein Bild – LEONE – Alinari
ME: Mary Evans / Alinari Archives
ME1: ©David Cohen Fine Art / Mary Evans Picture Library
PA: ©PA Photos / TopFoto / Alinari
PC: The Print Collector / HIP / TopFoto / Alinari
PP: PARAMOUNT PICTURES / Ronald Grant Archive / Mary Evans / Alinari
RCS: RCS / Managed by the Archivi Alinari
RG: ©Ronald Grant Archive / TopFoto / Alinari
RN: Ria Novosti / Alinari
RV: Roger-Viollet/ Alinari
RV1: Janine Niepce /Roger-Viollet / Alinari
RV2: ©Françoise Demulder / Roger-Viollet / Alinari
TE: Team / Alinari
TF: TopFoto / Alinari
TF1: ©TopFoto / Mel Longhurst / Alinari
TF2: ©1928 Disney. TopFoto / Alinari
TF3: ©1940 Disney. TopFoto / Alinari
UB: Ullstein Bild / Alinari
UIG: Universal Images Group / Alinari
WHA: World History Archives / Alinari

Index of Names*

* The index does not include the mention of names in the "In Brief" timelines or in image captions.

The editors of the volume would like to thank the following
for their kind collaboration:

Cristina Bragaglia (Fondazione Palazzo Coronini Cronberg, Gorizia)
Eleonora Bressa (Biblioteca Rosminiana, Rovereto)
Marina Bressan
Aldo Castellani
Claudia Colecchia, Cristina Klarer and Claudia Morgan (Fototeca dei Civici Musei di Storia ed Arte di Trieste)
Antonietta Colombatti (Archivio di Stato di Trieste)
Pierpaolo Dorsi and Paolo Santoboni (Soprintendenza Archivistica del Friuli Venezia Giulia, Trieste)
Giorgio Fanin
Paola Maria Filippi (Università degli studi di Bologna)
Fulvia de Finetti
Franco Finocchiaro (Biblioteca Comunale Centrale Sormani, Milano)
Lodovico Galli
Stefania Glori and Maria Lia Orsa Lumbroso (Fondazione Marco Besso, Roma)
Roberto Gruden
Marzio Lipari
Claudio Luglio (Archivio Luglio Editore, Trieste)
Francesca Malvezzi and Simona Stecchini (Unicredit Group Historical Archives, Milano)
Annamaria Miot
Umberto Nadalut
Guido Ongaro (Archivio Museo Piccola Caprera, Ponti sul Mincio, Mantova)
Alessandro Paglia
Flavio Quaranta
Gerhard and Renate Schreiber
Eleonora Maria Smolensky
Dieter Strasser (†)
Rosanna Supino
Mauro Tabor and Livio Vasieri (Comunità Ebraica di Trieste)
Raffaella Zanola

and the following colleagues for their valuable contributions:

Rossana Flegar (Group Employee Communication)
Monica Micci (Archivio storico INA Assitalia)
Marco Molino (Group Media & Web Communications)
Alberto Paletta (Editorial Office)
Maurizio Salich and Roberto Sciuca (Group Reinsurance, Life Reinsurance)
Sergio Sirianni (Generali Real Estate)
and the staff of the Group Head Office: Historical Archive of Assicurazioni Generali, Centro Stampa Trieste, Corporate Heritage, Group External Communications & Corporate Identity, Representative Office and Ufficio Posta Trieste.

First edition December 2016
ISBN 978-88-317-2383-1
www.marsilioeditori.it

Translations
Contextus srl, Pavia
(Sarah Elizabeth Cree, Christine Guthry)

Repro
Linotipia Saccuman, Vicenza

Printed by
Papergraf s.r.l., Piazzola sul Brenta (Padova)
for Marsilio Editori® s.p.a., Venice

EDITION	YEAR
10 9 8 7 6 5 4 3 2 1	2016 2017 2018 2019 2020